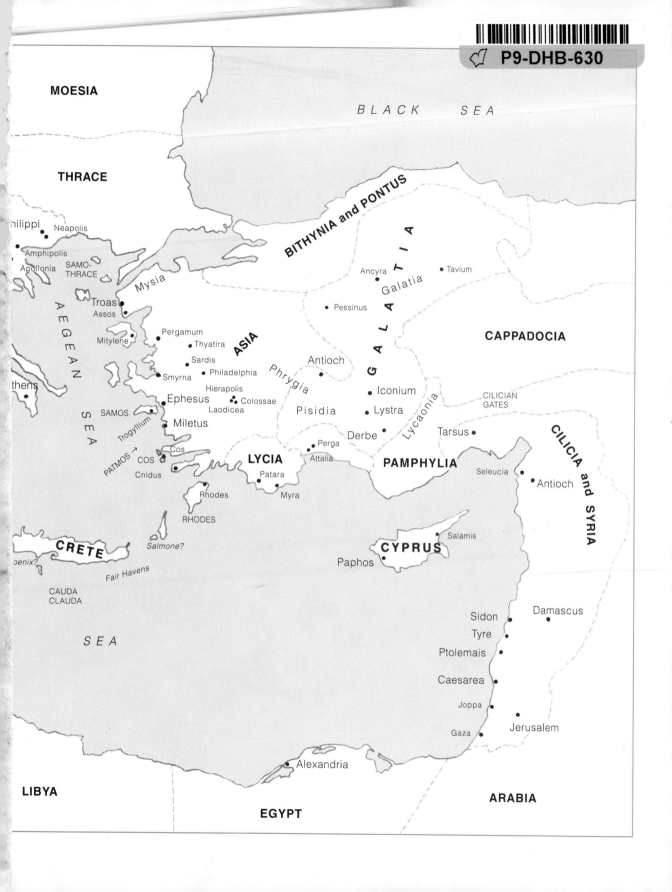

MOESIA

BLACK SEA

THRACE

BITHYNIA and PONTUS

GALATIA

hilippi
Neapolis

Amphipolis
Apollonia

SAMO-
THRACE

Ancyra
Galatia
Tavium

Mysia

Pessinus

CAPPADOCIA

Troas
Assos

AEGEAN

Pergamum
Thyatira
ASIA

Antioch

CILICIAN
GATES

Mitylene

Sardis
Smyrna
Philadelphia

Phrygia

Iconium

Lycaonia

thens

Hierapolis
Ephesus
Colossae
Laodicea

Lystra

CILICIA and SYRIA

SAMOS

SEA

Pisidia

Derbe

Tarsus

Miletus

Trogyllium

Antioch

PATMOS
COS
Cos

LYCIA

Perga
Attalia

PAMPHYLIA

Seleucia

Cnidus

Patara

Myra

Rhodes

RHODES

CRETE

Salmone?

CYPRUS

Salamis

oenix?

Fair Havens

Paphos

CAUDA
CLAUDA

Sidon
Damascus

SEA

Tyre

Ptolemais

Caesarea

Joppa

Jerusalem

Gaza

LIBYA

Alexandria

ARABIA

EGYPT

NEW TESTAMENT STORY

An Introduction

FOURTH EDITION

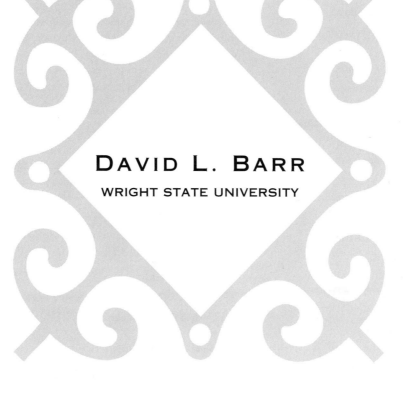

DAVID L. BARR

WRIGHT STATE UNIVERSITY

WADSWORTH
CENGAGE Learning™

Australia • Brazil • Japan • Korea • Mexico • Singapore • Spain • United Kingdom • United States

To all my students,
but especially for
Elizabeth and Nathaniel

WADSWORTH
CENGAGE Learning™

New Testament Story: An Introduction,
Fourth Edition
David L. Barr

Religion Editor: Worth Hawes

Editorial Assistant: Kamilah Lee

Technology Project Manager: Julie Aguilar

Marketing Manager: Christina Shea

Marketing Assistant: Mary Anne Payumo

Marketing Communications Manager: Darlene Amidon-Brent

Project Manager, Editorial Production: Jerilyn Emori

Creative Director: Rob Hugel

Art Director: Maria Epes

Print Buyer: Barbara Britton

Permissions Editor: Mardell Glinski Schultz

Production Service: Anne Draus, Scratchgravel Publishing Services

Text Designer: Lisa Berman

Photo Researcher: John Hill

Copy Editor: Ann Delgehausen

Cover Designer: Yvo Riezebos

Cover Image: David Barr

Compositor: Newgen

For product information and technology assistance, contact us at
Cengage Learning Customer & Sales Support, 1-800-354-9706

For permission to use material from this text or product, submit all requests online at **www.cengage.com/permissions**. Further permissions questions can be e-mailed to **permissionrequest@cengage.com**.

Library of Congress Control Number: 2007938835

ISBN-13: 978-0-534-62748-5

ISBN-10: 0-534-62748-X

Wadsworth Cengage Learning
10 Davis Drive
Belmont, CA 94002-3098
USA

Cengage Learning products are represented in Canada by Nelson Education, Ltd.

For your course and learning solutions, visit **academic.cengage.com**.

Purchase any of our products at your local college store or at our preferred online store **www.ichapters.com**.

Printed in the United States of America
1 2 3 4 5 6 7 12 11 10 09 08

Contents

4 PAUL'S LETTERS TO HIS FOLLOWERS   103

Philemon, Philippians, Galatians, Corinthians

5 PAUL'S ADDRESS TO THOSE OUTSIDE HIS CIRCLE   150

Romans

6 PAUL FOR A NEW DAY   184

Colossians, Ephesians, Timothy, Titus

7 ECHOES OF OTHER STORIES   216

James, Jude, Hebrews, Peter

13 THE DAWN OF A NEW DAY   429

The Apocalypse of John

14 THE STORY AFTER THE WRITINGS   471

One Story from Many

PREFACE

Just because we lack imagination is no reason to think that the ancients did.
Amos Wilder (1976:53)

Those who talk of reading the Bible "as literature" sometimes mean, I think,
reading it without attending to the main thing it is about; like reading Burke
with no interest in politics, or reading the Aeneid with no interest in Rome.
That seems to me to be nonsense. But there is a saner sense in which the Bible,
since it is after all literature, cannot properly be read except as literature; and
the different parts of it as the different sorts of literature they are.
C. S. Lewis (1958:2–3)

The degree to which we moderns are shaped by books is difficult to overemphasize. Our rooms are littered with them; at least my study is as I finish writing this. It is hard to remember that books are a relatively recent invention, only five centuries old. Before Gutenberg printed the Bible from moveable type in 1456, most of our forebears worked with handwritten manuscripts, a far different medium. Even with printing, books did not become widely available until the invention of a machine to manufacture paper, early in the nineteenth century.

A whole new way of studying the Bible developed in conjunction with this new technology. The first printed Greek edition of the New Testament was published by Erasmus of Rotterdam in 1516, under the title *Novum Instrumentum*, a new instrument. Other study books soon followed: dictionaries, concordances, lexicons, atlases, commentaries. These new instruments made it possible to analyze the biblical writings in ways never before possible. They have allowed us to move closer to their original contexts and meanings than any generation has since the third century. We now know more about what Corinth was like in Paul's day than has been known for a thousand years—a momentous gain indeed.

But there has also been a significant loss, for with the emergence of this new print technology the Bible became an object of silent study. When copies were scarce, people studied the Bible by reading it aloud, discussing it, telling its stories. It was a living book carried by the living voice. This is certainly how all the New Testament writings were originally presented and how they were most often experienced until modern times. This silencing of the Bible, brought about by the widespread availability of books, has made it a distant work for many people today.

Another, more subtle change resulted from producing the whole Bible as one book. When we encounter the various writings bound together in one volume, we easily fail to distinguish between the kinds of writing contained in the Bible. We have forgotten how to listen to a gospel, a letter, a farewell speech, a revelation. Nor does it help much that our schools have largely abandoned the study of classical antiquity, so that ancient forms of rhetoric and religion are foreign to students today.

GOALS

In a small way this book will (I fondly hope) compensate for some of these losses while capitalizing on the great gains of the past two centuries of biblical studies. Pursuing this goal has called attention to four issues: orality, rhetoric, context, and literary technique. This book explores the *oral nature* of the New Testament world and especially the extent to which good stories were told and retold. It surveys the stories in, and behind, the New Testament writings and analyzes those writings as a set of interacting stories, not just as discrete documents.

The dominance of oral media in that world mandates serious attention to the art of rhetoric, the stylized means of persuasion so highly developed by the ancients. Hence, this book emphasizes *rhetoric*. The Introduction identifies the various kinds of rhetoric practiced in the ancient world, and the chapters that follow show how the various authors employed them.

Attention to rhetoric demands that we also be concerned about the *historical setting* and *social context* of these writings. Ancient rhetoric entailed more than the use of certain stylistic devices; rhetoric addressed all three elements of communication: speaker, speech, and audience. All three are implicit in the rhetorical product, and we must explore all three when we study each of the New Testament documents. We begin to address this need in Chapter 1, titled "Preparing to Hear the Stories: The Cultural Contexts of the First Audience." This chapter provides a brief historical orientation, surveys the major cultural institutions (politics, family, education, work), and gives an orientation to religion in that world. Additional historical information is given in the chapters where it is most relevant. There are also numerous quotations from other ancient writings included in each chapter to help illuminate the documents studied. We will deal explicitly with the social context of these writings, helping readers come to terms with the values and concerns of ancient Mediterranean societies. From the most basic notion of what it means to be a person to broad social values such as honor and shame, it is important to see that these documents stem from a world very different from our own.

EMPHASES

This fourth edition also attempts to deal more carefully with historical terminology, trying to use words that are appropriate for the first-century context. Many words commonly used (like *Christians, Jews, churches, salvation, Christology*) are inappropriate for the first century because of the specialized meanings they later developed. I have tried to use reasonable substitutes (*Jesus followers, Judeans* (particularly in Chapter 1), *assemblies, health, rescue, characterization of Jesus*, and such). It has not always been easy, and I am sure my attempt has not always been successful. I have become convinced that such shifts in terminology are necessary if we hope to hear these texts in their original context.

This book also emphasizes the *literary nature* of all the New Testament documents, whether they are letters, narratives, essays, or more specialized genres. Insofar as it is possible, these writings are compared with others of a similar kind to show what the ancients may have expected to hear from such writings. Each is also examined for its overall structure, its use of particular literary devices, and its "story."

The idea of story works in a number of ways: some writings tell a story (the narratives); all writings imply a story (about the writer and the audience); and each of these writings existed within, and attempted to proclaim, the charter stories of the faith of these early believers. The men and women who listened to these writings explained their world by telling stories—of how the world came to be, how it has fallen and may be redeemed, and how it will eventually end. For those who wrote and heard these works, that charter story was the story of Jesus. We endeavor to hear their stories.

Thus, Chapter 2 explores what may be known about the stories of Jesus *before* the documents were written, and Chapter 14 reflects on the meanings that Christians found in these documents *after* they were collected into a canon. In the intervening chapters, each New Testament writing is studied in its approximate chronological order and in conjunction with other writings of a similar type. Because of space restrictions all are not discussed in equal depth. With Paul, for example, two letters (1 Thessalonians and Romans) are studied in detail, and the others are treated in sufficient depth to enable the interested reader to proceed to independent study. In each case, our study provides a sense of the overall work and its historical and social context, focusing on important sections. A reading guide and study questions are provided for each writing.

ORGANIZATION

The New Testament writings are treated in two groups: the story in letters and the story in narratives. In each section the writings are studied in the general order in which they were written. Thus, we begin with the earliest letters of Paul, consider the main body of his writings, examine writings connected to the Pauline tradition, and finally look at other letters connected with other traditions (for example, those of James and Peter). We then study the works that are written as narratives, the four Gospels, Acts, and the Apocalypse, again in the likely order of their composition.

A major goal of this book is to enable students to do their own research on the New Testament. Each chapter provides directed readings of the writings themselves, and each ends with resources for "Learning on Your Own." That section begins with important terms and review questions and continues with lists of the important research topics deriving from the chapter and the resources with which to pursue independent research. This fourth edition not only updates these resources but also provides a major reorganization to enable students to pursue their interests more easily. A few select items are noted after the heading "Taking the Next Step," followed by a list of "Topics for Special Studies" with several bibliographic suggestions for each topic (these would be suitable for term projects). A general discussion on "Doing Your Own Research" in Appendix A has been updated to explain the major research tools in the field and to provide direction for tapping the vast resources of the World Wide Web.

My goal in providing these resources is to offer beginning students guideposts for reading the biblical literature with a sense of direction. It is my firm conviction that one person cannot tell another what a work of literature means. Although we can learn from others' readings (thus, each chapter lists a range of traditional and modern, including feminist, readings), such summaries are no substitute for reading the actual texts. Meaning emerges only in the reading of the literature itself. The goal of each chapter is to enable the student to read the New Testament document for herself or himself. To try to understand a work of literature by reading *about* it is—to take a phrase from David Ben-Gurion—like kissing one's bride through the veil. If this book should serve to remove some of the veils that too readily obscure the beauty and power of these writings, it will have been worth the labor of its making.

ALTERNATIVES: A NOTE FOR INSTRUCTORS

Readers who would prefer to study the narrative works first might begin with the methodological discussions in the Introduction, follow with the discussion of the story contexts in Chapters 1 and 2, and then move to Chapter 8, which introduces the study of the Gospels. After studying the individual Gospels (Chapters 9 through 12), one might move to the discussion of "Canon, Story, and History" in Chapter 14, which discusses the complicated issues connected with deriving historical information about Jesus from various sources. From there it would be an easy matter to move back to Chapter 3 and take up the study of Paul's Letters. I have tried to arrange the vocabulary to minimize the difficulty of doing this.

Those who want a deeper understanding of the issues of translation, textual transmission, and canon before engaging individual writings could move from the preliminary remarks on these issues in the Introduction to the more substantial discussion of them in Chapter 14 ("The Making of the Canon"). For a case study in textual criticism, see the discussion of the alternative endings of Mark's Gospel in Chapter 9 ("The Sense of an Ending").

ACKNOWLEDGMENTS

The labor of making this book has not been entirely mine, of course. And genres being what they are, this is the place to thank those without whose assistance this book would not be. Numerous people have provided suggestions for revision. That so many would take time to suggest improvements is eloquent testimony to the vitality of introductory studies in New Testament. I have greatly benefited from the many suggestions from colleagues, such as Sheila E. McGinn (John Carroll University), Perry V. Kea (University of Indianapolis), Michael Willett Newheart (Howard University School of Divinity), and Joseph Morris, CM (St. John's University), all of whom have used the book with students in the classroom.

I continue to be most grateful to Edward C. Hobbs (Wellesley College), who coupled extensive suggestions for improvement with sufficient praise for the earlier edition to inspire me to persevere in the task of revision. Mikeal C. Parsons (Baylor University) provided many helpful suggestions and much encouragement. John E. Brown (Harford Community College) suggested revisions and provided extensive examples of learning objectives based on the text that helped me think about what readers were learning. Several people used the earlier edition and took time to write me with lists of errors and suggestions for improvement, including M. Eugene Boring (Texas Christian University), Douglas Oakman (Pacific Lutheran University),

Irvin W. Batdorf (United Theological Seminary, emeritus), and Robert A. Kraft (University of Pennsylvania).

I owe a great debt to the many readers who commented on specific chapters, especially to those students in several classes who patiently read (and criticized) various sections, thereby saving their fellow students from many unintended obscurities. Then there are my colleagues who shared their particular expertise and offered many helpful suggestions (and even a few I did not find helpful). I am deeply grateful to R. Alan Culpepper (Mercer University), Janice Capel Anderson (University of Idaho), John Darr (Boston College), Beverly Gaventa (Princeton Theological Seminary), Dennis Ronald MacDonald (Iliff School of Theology), Robert Wall (Seattle Pacific University), and John R. Donahue (Jesuit School of Theology at Berkeley).

Finally, let me reiterate my appreciation to those who were with me at the beginning and helped improve the first edition of this book: Dennis Smith, Catherine Albanese, John Carey, James Carse, Charles Thomas Davis, Arthur Dewey, Robert Fowler, Gene Gallagher, Robert Hann, Judith Kovacs, Shirley Lund, Elizabeth Struthers Malbon, Grant Osborn, Edmund Perry, Vernon Robbins, Robert Straukamp, and Charles Talbert.

Thanks are also due to people at Wright State University who graciously provided many small services that enabled this project to move forward, especially my former chair and now dean, Charles Taylor, who has been consistently supportive of my scholarly work; a library staff who supplied me with many books and articles; and our administrative assistant, Siobhan Semmett, who diligently handled many details of department operations while I was busy writing.

Finally, this fourth edition would not have been possible without the constant encouragement and enthusiasm of my editors, Worth Hawes and Patrick Stockstill, and the able support of Kamilah Lee, editorial assistant. In addition to updating the discussion, the goals for this edition included producing a more readable, more attractive, and more user-friendly work. To the degree that this has been accomplished, it is due to the labors of two able colleagues. I am very grateful to Anne Draus (Scratchgravel Publishing Services), who oversaw a very tight production schedule and is responsible for the look of the final product. And I am especially indebted to Ann Delgehausen (Trio Bookworks), whose careful reading and many suggestions always found ways to help me say more clearly what I intended—an author's highest hope for an editor.

I welcome suggestions from all who use this book. You can write me at the Department of Religion, Wright State University, Dayton, OH 45435, or by e-mail at david.barr@wright.edu.

David L. Barr

BASIC CHRONOLOGY OF THE NEW TESTAMENT ERA

For a detailed chronology of the New Testament era, see Appendix B (page 506).

Date	Major Events in Empire	Major Events in Palestine	Writers/Writings
323	Death of Alexander	Beginning of Hellenistic Age	Torah translated into Greek (about 300–150?)
200	Beginnings of Roman expansion		
170	Seleucid invasion of Egypt	Persecution of Antiochus	Daniel
150	Jews Expelled from Rome Qumran founded (150 BCE–CE 70)	Pharisees and Sadducees appear	Dead Sea Scrolls (150 BCE–CE 70)
63		Roman control (Pompey)	
44	Assassination of Julius Caesar		
37		Herod the Great, King of Judea	
27	Augustus rules (age 36)		Virgil (P/L) (70–19)
CE			Strabo (G/G) (64 BCE–CE 21)
6		Direct Roman Rule of Palestine Hillel and Shammai	
14	Augustus dies; Tiberias rules (age 56)	Pilate rules (26–36) Death of Jesus (30)	Philo of Alexandria (30 BCE–CE 45)
37	Tiberius dies; Caligula rules (age 25)		
41	Caligula assassinated; Claudius rules (age 51)	Herod Agrippa made king	
50		Felix rules (51–59)	Seneca (1–65)
54	Claudius dies; Nero rules (age 17)		Paul (?–64)
62		Death of James	Pliny the Elder (E/L) (23–79)
64	Fire at Rome—persecution Death of Paul, Peter?		Colossians ?
66		First Judean War begins	
68	Suicide of Nero; civil chaos; Vespasian rules (age 60)		
70		Temple destroyed Yohanan ben Zakkai	Mark Josephus (H/G) (37–95)
79	Death of Vespasian; Titus rules (age 40)		Ephesians ?
81	Titus dies; Domitian rules (age 30)		Matthew 1 Peter ? Luke-Acts; Quintilian (R/L) fl.
90		Gamaliel II Council of Yavneh ?	Josephus, *Jewish Antiquities* John

Date	Major Events in Empire	Major Events in Palestine	Writers/Writings
			Apocalypse
96	Domitian dies; Nerva rules (age 66)		1 Clement
98	Death of Nerva; Trajan rules (age 45)		Pastorals ?
			Pliny the Younger
117	Death of Trajan; Hadrian rules (age 41)		Gospel of Peter ?
			2 Peter ?
			Didache
		Rabbi Akiba (d. 132)	Basilides
135		Second Judean Revolt, by Bar Kochba	Polycarp's To the Philippians
138	Hadrian dies; Antoninus Pius rules (age 51)		
140		Jerusalem made a Gentile City: Jupiter Capitolinus	Apocalypse of Peter ?
150	Martyrdom of Polycarp		Justin Martyr (G) (100–165)
			Marcion Valentinus
			Acts of Paul
160	Pius dies; Marcus Aurelius rules (age 40)		Diatessaron of Tatian
	Martyrdom of Justin at Rome		Irenaeus (130–202)
170	Martyrdoms at Lyons		Apuleius (P/L) (123–185)
	Martyrdoms at Scillium		The Golden Ass
180	Aurelius dies; Commodus rules (age 19)		Celsus (Ph/G) fl.
190	Commodus dies; Septimius Severus rules (age 48)		Galen (D/G) (129–199)
			Acts of Peter ?
			Clement (150–215)
			Tertullian (E/L) (160–240)
200			Mishnah (Hebrew)

Note: Dates are often approximate.
Abbreviations:
G = Greek author; L = Latin author
O = Orator; H = Historian; P = Poet; R = Rhetorician; Ph = Philosopher; G = Geographer; E = Essayist; B = Biographer
BCE = Before Common Era (numbers same as BC); CE = Common Era (numbers same as AD)
fl. = flourished; ? = uncertain date or chronological placement

INTRODUCTION

THE THREE WORLDS OF THE TEXT

Reading the New Testament as Story

The World within the Text: Literature

The World behind the Text: History

The World in front of the Text: Our Culture

Maps for the World: Using Methods

Traveling in the Worlds of the Text

Learning on Your Own

   The contents of this story are not 100% clear.
Everybody's on their own.

Andy Sipowitz, *NYPD Blue*
(suggesting a warning label for some stories,
like the song "Pop Goes the Weasel")

Stories are wonderful things and, like our friends, come in all different sizes, shapes, and colors. Some stories are small and trivial, designed only to make us laugh; other stories are grand and exhilarating, designed to make us willing to give up even our lives for the reality they represent; most are middle-range stories, designed to entertain us while they shape and enforce the sense of the world we each possess. Some stories are obvious and explicit; others are implicit and need to be drawn out. We all, for example, have implicit stories of our lives, though few of us ever have or ever will make that story explicit by writing an autobiography. Nevertheless, we tell our lives as stories. We even say, when we hear about someone doing something that seems odd to us, that we wonder what the story behind that is.

This book attempts to explore the stories in and behind the writings in the collection we now call the New Testament. This is a rather complicated task, requiring both rigor and imagination. But before we go further, let me explain why I have written this book by telling you a bit of my own story. I grew up attending a small church in rural Michigan, a church that delighted in the Bible. We had a community of people who really liked one another: adults, young people, kids, old people. We studied the Bible diligently and understood it to be our story.

I am afraid we often confused the biblical story with our rural American assumptions about life. We naively applied the Bible directly to ourselves with a devotional and wholly uncritical reading. Our doctrinal sieve carefully sifted out any ideas that did not agree with our own notions. Yet I learned to delight in the Bible and found in it a new and fascinating world. I devoted my life to its study.

The longer I studied the biblical writings, the more complex they appeared. As I learned to ask disciplined questions, I found unexpected and exciting answers. As I learned more about the biblical world, I discovered meanings I never imagined. Eventually I became convinced that we who claimed to regard the Bible so highly were really not listening to it. Though we accused others of neglecting the Bible, we insisted that it always say what we had predetermined it would. We were so concerned to fit the Bible into our world that we neglected their world.

There are of course many points of contact between these two worlds; the task of being human today shares much with the concerns and struggles of our ancestors. But there is also much that has changed. We need to think about some of these changes, but that will be easier if we take a specific story. Please do the following exercise before you continue your reading.

READING AND REFLECTION

Read the story of Jesus' birth in Luke 2:1–22 and 39.

1. What do the shepherds do in this story?
2. Where did the shepherds find the newborn Jesus?
3. What parts of the Christmas story are not found in Luke's story?

THE WORLD WITHIN THE TEXT: LITERATURE

The first, and also the final, thing we must grasp about a text is the world it creates, or what in this book I am calling its **story**. This is both a simple and a very complicated idea. Sometimes the story is on the surface as it is in the story from Luke you have just read; other times the story is below the surface, implied by what the text tells us, as it is in Paul's letters. I'll return to the letters below, but first let's look at the more obvious case of the Gospels.

Luke's story of Jesus' birth is easy enough to understand that even a small child can grasp it. It has drama, spectacle, and a very simple story about how Jesus was born. But is it so simple? When we look more closely at the actual telling of the story, numerous questions arise. It starts "in those days," but just which days are these? Why is it placed in the reigns of Caesar Augustus and Quirinius of Syria? What is the purpose of including the census? Why is Bethlehem called a city when it was usually called a village? And why is it linked to David? What is added to the story by setting it in the animal quarters? What is the role of the shepherds in the story? These and other questions need to be explored to get at the world within the text.

For our current purposes, however, it will do to just consider the shepherds. One way to characterize their role in the story is to say that they are completely unexpected witnesses to momentous events. They do all the things a good witness must do: hear, obey, see, tell. And they find a receptive audience (2:18). Now these are exactly the major themes of Luke's whole work, which includes both the Gospel and the book of Acts (as we will discuss in the chapter on Luke). Luke began his story by saying he would tell of things "handed on to us by those who from the beginning were eyewitnesses and servants of the word" (1:2). And when he told the story of the replacement of Judas, the apostle who betrayed Jesus and then died, he says the person must be someone who had "accompanied us during all the time that the Lord Jesus went in and out among us, beginning from the baptism of John until the day when he was taken up from us—one of these must become a witness with us to his resurrection" (Acts 1:21–22). In fact, we could characterize the Gospel of Luke as a witness *of* Jesus' great deeds and the book of Acts as a witness *to* Jesus' great deeds. Thus the appearance of the shepherds is exactly right for the story Luke intends to tell (but would be wholly out of place in Matthew's story and so does not appear there).

While the world of the text, its story, is our primary concern in this book, two other worlds must be examined, for they both reveal and obscure that world. These are usually called the world behind the text and the world in front of the text. Or, if you prefer, you could think of them as the world prior to the writing of the text and the world after the writing of the text.

THE WORLD BEHIND THE TEXT: HISTORY

You have probably already wondered about aspects of the birth story and their relation to history. When did this occur? Who was the emperor Augustus? What is the significance of this census? What was Bethlehem like in those days? What about Nazareth? Who was David? What is important about a firstborn son? What did it mean to be engaged? Should an engaged couple be expecting a child? Why did they

Hirmer Verlag, Munich

Roman Coin from about 70 CE   This seated figure represents Judea (as the inscription says), seated in a pose of mourning. It marks a very significant event for the study of early Judaism and Christianity: the destruction of Jerusalem by the Romans in the year 70. Before that destruction, Jerusalem was the center of the Jesus movement, which thus maintained strong ties with Jewish people. After 70, Jesus' followers looked to other centers and became less and less Jewish. Knowing which writings came before this event, and which came after, will be important.

wrap the baby in cloths? What were inns like? Was it common for people to be with the animals? And so on. None of these questions is answered in the story, but all would have been answerable by the audience for whom it was written because they are part of the world behind the text.

To take just one example, the original audience of this story would most likely have understood that Jesus was born in a private home (not a stable), a home crowded with other guests, so that the only place left for them was that part of the house normally used to quarter the animals. The usual word for an inn in Greek is *pandokeion*, which Luke uses in the story of the good Samaritan in Luke 10:34. Literally it means a place that welcomes all. The word in the birth story is *kataluma*, meaning living quarters. So the contrast in the world behind the story is not between a room in an inn versus a room in a stable, but between being welcomed as a guest into proper guest quarters and being lodged in that part of the house normally used for the animals. The animals have likely been turned out and the whole house now filled with people. Knowing such historical detail helps us better imagine the story being told. But knowing some historical details can complicate a story.

Sometimes the things we learn about that world raise serious questions about the meaning of the story. For example, there is no evidence of the kind of *universal* census that Luke uses as the setting for this story, and Quirinius was governor of Syria beginning in 6 CE, years after the likely date of Jesus' birth (perhaps in 7 BCE). The Romans did take a limited census of Judea in 6 CE when they assumed direct administrative control after the death of Herod the Great and the failure of his son to control the region, but again this would have been years after the birth of Jesus.

Either Luke knew about a census that has been completely omitted from the historical record or else he chose this census as the setting for his story for nonhistorical reasons. A census, and the accompanying taxation, was the most blatant example of Roman domination; perhaps Luke wanted to set the story of this new savior born in David's city in the context of Roman oppression. We must remember that this story was not written at the time of Jesus' birth, but decades later in quite a different setting.

So we must learn to think of two worlds behind texts: the world at the time of the story and the world at the time of the writing of the story. Each text reflects not only the historical background of the story it tells but also the historical context of the author. Luke has chosen to tell this story in this way because it seemed appropriate to do so at that particular time in history. We must also investigate the world behind the text at the point of its composition, asking when and why it was written.

Knowing about the world behind the text will bring these works to life as the real experiences of real people. It will also highlight the differences between their world and ours. In our world animals are housed in stables and so we tend to imagine that in this story. We need to be aware of how later readings influence our understanding.

THE WORLD IN FRONT OF THE TEXT: OUR CULTURE

We can begin to see how our culture controls our understanding if we ask what elements of the Christmas story are missing in Luke. Most readers today have some expectation of what ought to be in the story of Jesus' birth; they have heard that story many times. Because so many others have read these stories and because their interpretations have entered into our cultural heritage, we cannot approach them with the immediacy of their first audience. There is a world in front of the text, sometimes clarifying the text, sometimes obscuring it, that we have to be conscious of in our reading.

It takes effort to read about the Last Supper and not imagine Jesus and his disciples sitting around a table after the manner of Leonardo da Vinci's famous painting. In fact, they were lying on their sides on couches, with two or three people to a couch (see John 13:23). So too, when we read that Paul was "in prison," we might picture something like a medieval dungeon, but this would be entirely inappropriate. As we will see, no such prisons existed in the ancient world. In fact imprisonment was not even a form of punishment permitted under Roman law. To be imprisoned in that world simply meant to be detained (perhaps even in a private home—as Paul was at Rome in Acts 28:30) until your case came up for trial or until punishment could be exacted.

Paul never refers to himself as a Christian, but it is very difficult for us not to think of him as a Christian (and to understand that term in accord with our own experience). We think of churches as buildings, and when we hear about being saved we most likely think of something like a Billy Graham rally. But all of this is from the world in front of the text. In fact nearly all the terms of the New Testament that we hear as religious terms (*salvation, redemption, sin, repentance, belief,* and so on) were part of ordinary speech with standard secular meanings. While we cannot escape the meanings that have been attached to these terms, we can become aware of their ancient meanings.

The simple truth is that we will never be able to read these texts in the same way the first-century audience did. Even if we read against the grain and try to subvert earlier readings, we are reacting to them. The best we can hope is to be aware of how earlier interpretations shape our own perceptions of the text.

We should be aware, for example, that beginning already in the second century and culminating in the monumental work of Augustine (345–430 CE), the North African bishop, people began to read the New Testament writings as if they were philosophical treatises, drawing out their implied theology. Since Augustine it has been nearly impossible to read these documents without considering their supposed theology. This theological reading evolved throughout the Middle Ages into a very elaborate system that envisioned four levels of meaning in every text: the literal, the symbolic, the ethical, and the spiritual. A little Latin verse, here freely translated, plays on these levels of meaning:

> *The literal shows us what was done;*
> *The symbol shows how faith is won;*
> *The moral gives us rules for life;*
> *The spiritual shows where we end our strife.*
> *(Grant, 1963:119)*

All four levels of meaning were bound up into a comprehensive philosophical-theological system, coming to magnificent expression in the works of Thomas Aquinas (1225–1274).

Then in the sixteenth century another radical shift occurred with the new readings proposed by the Protestant reformers. These reformers sought to strip away many of the institutionalized interpretations that had grown up in the previous centuries, reading instead for an understanding of personal salvation. Still a theological reading, this new approach made the Bible personally relevant to the reader and so stimulated an enormous increase in translations, study aids, and individual study.

This Protestant, personalized reading has come to be the dominant reading, whether the subsequent direction has been toward revivalism, rationalism, or fundamentalism. It would take us too far afield to explore the influence of each of these on American culture. I will only note how much of our reading is still influenced by the great clash of rationalist and fundamentalist interpreters in the late nineteenth and early twentieth centuries. The curious result of that struggle was that the rationalists won the academic debate, but the fundamentalists won the popular mind. Most of my students come to the university with little experience of any reading other than the literal, personal, theological interpretation.

My point here is not that this reading is wrong (I find some persuasive readings in all approaches, mixed with unpersuasive ones). My point is that this is a reading of the text shaped by the way our culture has developed since the text was written: the world in front of the text. If we have any hope of entering into a dialogue with the text, rather than just projecting our meanings back into it, we must learn to account for this world.

The chapters that follow will continually draw attention to the differences between our world and the world of the New Testament, but let me suggest the pervasiveness of the problem by two brief examples. First, consider Table I.1, which is based on a series of comparisons between our culture and cultures of the Mediterranean world set forth by Bruce Malina.

Second, consider the significance of the fact that nearly all the official interpreters of the Bible from antiquity to the twentieth century have been male. But since the 1980s women have joined the ranks of professional scholars in increasing numbers. These women have propounded exciting new readings of these texts, readings that men never saw. These **feminist readings** (I use the term in the broad sense to mean any reading grounded on women's life experiences) help us see these ancient texts more clearly. They create a new kind of foreground that lets us see how opaque has been the foreground of male life experience to certain aspects of these texts—especially the places of women in them. In addition, they create new possibilities for seeing the lives of real women and men for whom these texts were written. Once again we become aware of the world in front of the texts.

TABLE I.1	A COMPARISON OF MODERN AND ANCIENT CULTURAL VALUES	
Value or Activity	*Modern*	*Ancient*
What is most important about you?	Doing: what you've done	Being: who you are
Who is most important?	Individuals: self (self-determination)	Associates: family, peers (public esteem)
Which time orientation guides one's behavior?	Act for the future; live in the present; ignore the past	Act for the present; be aware of the past; ignore the future
What is our relation to nature?	Mastery over nature	Subordinate to nature
What is human nature like?	Neutral	Mixture of good and evil
How much money, food, and other goods exist?	Infinite supply; more is created all the time	Limited supply; fixed amount
Why do things happen?	Caused by impersonal forces	Caused by other personal beings (natural and supernatural)
What motivates people to do things?	Money or success	Honor
What controls people's behavior?	Guilt (sin)	Shame (purity)
How does one obtain the available goods?	Rights, law: all are equal before the law	Patronage; who you know

Based on Bruce Malina's work, especially *The New Testament World: Insights from Cultural Anthropology* (John Knox, 1981) and *The Social World of Luke-Acts* (edited by Jerome H. Neyrey, Hendrickson, 1991). We will see later that these very broad generalizations apply somewhat differently to men and women.

We will never obliterate our culture and get back to an original reading of these texts, but we can become aware of our culture and the ways it influences our reading. And we can adopt critical ways of reading that help us distinguish what is in the world in front of the text from the text itself. These ways of reading are called *methods*, a word derived from two Greek words, *meta* (with) and *hodos* (road), for these methods let us travel down the same road together. Carefully followed they can help us enter with our imaginations into the world that was the original context of these writings.

MAPS FOR THE WORLD: USING METHODS

While more than a dozen specific methods can be identified in the study of the New Testament writings, they can be broadly categorized into three major approaches: historical, social, and literary. Taken together these methods produce reasonably precise pictures of the situations of most of the New Testament writers and allow us to hear the individual voices of Matthew, Mark, Luke, Paul, and the rest. This is exciting work, but work nonetheless.

THE ROLE OF HISTORICAL STUDIES

A historical understanding of a text is one that is appropriate and likely for the historical situation in which the text was composed. We make the basic assumption that an author was trying to communicate something meaningful to the audience for which he or she wrote. This approach attempts to discover who wrote the text, when it was written, and what issues it was intended to address in its own time. Only when we grasp the historical situation of both author and audience can we hope to understand the message communicated. This approach, often called the **historical-critical method**, is the distinguishing mark of the modern study of the Bible.

History attempts to reconstruct a version of the past, based on certain rules and procedures—much as a detective attempts to solve a crime following specific rules of evidence. In the case of history, the rules include collecting and correlating all the available data from the time and place being investigated, giving preference to data that can be validated in some way, and recognizing that all sources have their biases. On the one hand the historian attempts to be objective and let the past speak for itself; on the other hand the historian aims to understand the past by analogy to the present. The tension between these two goals is never completely resolved.

The great strength of the historical method in all areas of study has been to free us from the tyranny of our present situation by showing us the past. In studies of literature, the historical method creates distance, and thus a measure of objectivity, between the reader and the text. Such disciplined objectivity will allow us to hear more truly what the biblical writers intended to say without insisting that they say only what we believe.

But this distance can also become a problem. Historical study can create such a chasm between us and the text that we forget that those human beings were very like us and wrestled with problems we encounter today. The other two methods help bridge this gap.

THE ROLE OF SOCIAL ANALYSIS

Many contemporary scholars are finding ways to overcome the limitations of historical analysis. One such approach investigates the social world of these texts, attempting to place each in its specific social context, concerned not merely with "who" and "when" but also with "how" and "in what kind of society." Social analysis sees these texts as part of the cultural practices of ancient societies. It is common to speak of two approaches to social analysis: one that focuses on specific data, such as occupation, housing patterns, diet (sometimes called social history) and one that focuses on cross-cultural models, such as honor, patronage, social organization (sometimes called social science). I think the two approaches are mutually enhancing. We will try to explain these texts both by attempting to find models that illustrate their power and meaning (such as patrons and clients, honor and shame, or peasants and elites) and by seeking to discover the actual social settings of specific texts (utilizing such things as archaeology, history, and economic data).

The major advantages of social analysis methods are the way they help us overcome our cultural biases and the way they bring to life the real world of social interaction in which the early believers experienced these texts. They focus our attention on the practical, political, and social questions these texts involved. Such analysis reveals that the texts do not deal with ideas alone; the ideas relate to actual lives of real people.

Yet this very concern with the real world can be misleading if it ignores the literary and imaginative character of these writings. Social scientific analysis can become so concerned with the social background that it ignores the great beauty, artistry, and intellectual daring of these writings.

Both historical and social analyses are indispensable to the goals of this book, and both will be used in the discussions that follow. But the primary purpose of this study is to bring these ancient texts to life as works of literature. This book is written for all who wish to hear afresh the stories of the New Testament writers.

THE ROLE OF LITERARY CRITICISM

Before the historical and social study of the Bible developed, about two centuries ago, people naively lived in the stories of the biblical text. They delighted in them. Today we need to recapture some of their delight without their naïveté. In fact, a major current movement in biblical studies is attempting this by means of literary studies of these texts, with strong emphasis on narrative analysis.

The elements of a narrative include plot, setting, character, point of view, imagery, theme, effect on the reader, and related ideas. Narrative analysis attempts to discern how these multiple elements work together to produce certain meanings. The application of narrative criticism to the four Gospels, Acts, and Revelation is easy to imagine, for these are narrative works that consciously tell a story. We will discuss the details in Chapter 7 when we consider how stories are told. But quite a few of the New Testament writings are not narratives; they are letters and essays in the form of letters. Our literary analysis of the letters will be twofold, analyzing their stories and analyzing their persuasive techniques.

Letters as Literature: Their Structure and Their Stories

When Paul wrote his letters (between 50 and 60 CE), letters were already a recognized literary form; much of the enduring fame of Cicero (106–43 BCE) was based on the more than nine hundred letters he published. Seneca (who was Paul's contemporary) and Pliny (in the generation after Paul) saw the value of publishing their letters. Literary theorists even developed rules for letter writing, and the composition of suitable letters was a routine exercise in the schools. Not only were students expected to be able to write an appropriate letter on a specific subject, but they were also expected to be able to write in the styles of the great masters. Topics ranged from the personal to the political to the philosophical, and included an enormous business correspondence.

But whether the letter was a common business or personal note or whether it was a formal writing meant for publication, ancient letters shared many traits. We will survey these traits by examining the letters first as words written on a page (documents) and then as words spoken aloud by someone reading the letter (an oral performance).

As written documents, letters can be interpreted using the same techniques of literary criticism that we apply to other writings. Two aspects of the letters will especially concern us: their structures and their stories, both of which are implicit in the writings.

In Paul's time the structure of a letter was relatively fixed, and it will pay for us to give careful attention to how Paul followed that pattern and how he deviated from it. In addition, the letters contain an arrangement of words and images, allusions and quotations, logical argument, and liturgical design. Each letter must be studied for its overall shape and pattern, and for the way that pattern reflects the writer's approach to life. We will begin developing the tools to analyze these structures in Chapter 3.

While looking for implicit structures in these letters is relatively common—usually under the rubric of an outline—rarely have interpreters consciously asked for the stories implicit in the letters. Even so, nearly every commentary on Paul's letters has imagined some context for each letter: where Paul was, what had already happened between Paul and the recipients, why Paul was writing, what was going to happen next. It is this imagined context that provides at least the first level of story implicit in every letter. Additional levels of story we will explore include the life-story of the writer and the writer's understanding of the story of what God had done in Jesus.

We face, of course, the dilemma that these stories are not actually told in the letters, only implied. But an implied story is still a story, an ambiguity found in the definition of the word *story*: a "series of events that are or may be narrated" (*Oxford English Dictionary*). Thus, while a story actually told becomes a narrative with a plot, the same story could be told in a variety of narratives with different plots. The story of a love affair between two young people from rival groups could be narrated as *Romeo and Juliet* or as *West Side Story*. In addition, the same story could be told in different ways. One could tell a story from the beginning in chronological order, or begin in the middle or even at the end, filling in the earlier incidents with flashbacks or reports. But the important point is that the story is separate from the narrative that relates the story. In the letters we have evidence for the story of the writer even though we lack an actual narrative.

This larger sense of story provides the dominant metaphor for this book, which is asking you to think in terms more natural to the ancient world. Our age is accustomed to analyzing human behavior in a variety of modes, a tendency greatly enhanced by the division of our universities into various disciplines. But the ancients had no universities and no academic disciplines. An educated person studied all available knowledge, from philosophy to astronomy to medicine. Today we tend to explain things in terms of disciplinary perspectives: history, literature, sociology, theology, psychology, anthropology, and so on. Of these, only the first two had been invented in antiquity, and they in a very elementary sense.

This is not because the ancients did not think and speak about the same things we do (social groups, ideas, self-understanding, for example), nor were their theories necessarily inferior to our own. There is much psychological insight in the Greek tragedies, for example, but in the form of stories told. Nearly all ancient literature and history, and a good deal of philosophy and religion, involved the telling of stories. Consider, for example, how the ancient Jews confessed their faith. They did not formulate theological doctrines or even write logical creeds. Listen:

> *A wandering Aramean was my ancestor, who went down into Egypt and lived there as an alien, few in number, and there became a great nation, mighty and populous. When the Egyptians treated us harshly and afflicted us, by imposing hard labor on us, we cried to the LORD, the God of our ancestors; the LORD saw our affliction, our toil, and our oppression. The LORD brought us out of Egypt with a mighty hand . . . and brought us into this place and gave us this land, a land flowing with milk and honey. (Deut. 26:5–9)*

This is not theology but a summary of a story, the kind anthropologists call a **charter story** because it provides the warrant for Jewish life. In a similar way, the story of Jesus, especially the story of his death and resurrection, was a charter story for his followers, for these foundation events provided meaning for their lives—their charter. Each group seems to have had somewhat differing versions of this story. We can see plainly that each Gospel, for example, presents its own account of this charter story, but some version of it was assumed by both the writers and the audiences of the New Testament letters. This sacred story was the ultimate source of all the ideas, arguments, and actions found in the letters.

We will probe the individual variations on this story as we examine each writing, but it will be useful first to have some sense of the basic story before beginning our study of the individual letters. Chapter 1 sketches the basic shape and content of the Jesus story.

We must listen for the stories even if what we read seems to be about ethics or ideas. Too often, interpreters of the letters have gotten caught up in the argument and forgotten to hear the story. They have debated Paul's attitude toward women based on the following kind of passage:

> *Any woman who prays or prophesies with her head unveiled disgraces her head—it is one and the same thing as having her head shaved. . . . For this reason a woman ought to have a symbol of authority on her head, because of the angels. (1 Cor. 11:5, 10)*

How often have interpreters debated Paul's ideas without noticing those angels standing over in the corner! In what sort of story did Paul and these early Christian women live that they had to be aware of such heavenly guests? And what was going on at Corinth that made people concerned about head coverings? To what extent is Paul trying to control women who are claiming new freedoms? We can answer such questions only if we can discover the story behind them. Indeed, it is impossible to talk about Paul's letters without telling stories: He had been forced to leave Thessalonica, was worried about his followers there, and so wrote to them. He was in jail and met a runaway slave and needed to write to his master, Philemon. Challenged in Galatia by opponents who discounted his authority, he needed to defend himself.

These letters, then, will reveal three stories—or rather three levels of one story. At the most obvious level they reveal the story of the interaction between Paul and his followers. Probed further, they imply Paul's story of himself—not an autobiography, to be sure, but a movement of action within which his life made sense. Finally, they also contain Paul's story of Jesus, the ground of his most basic convictions. In this sense, the letters contain a story of Jesus, and of Paul, and of his followers even though they do not contain narratives.

We may illustrate this meaning from our own experiences. Each of us has a story, in the sense that we understand our lives in a connected fashion and relate them to some larger meaning. In fact, each of us lives in several stories—the story of our nation, our school, our family, our circle of friends, our sense of the real purpose of life. These larger stories provide the framework for our personal stories. Remembering our stories enables us to appreciate how the ancients understood their lives. In the following pages I have chosen not to speak of the theology of Paul, or of his psychology or sociology, though elements that correspond to these modern concerns will be discussed. Instead, I will speak of Paul's stories concerning himself and his communities, and his larger story of Jesus, which I think are more appropriate categories for this introductory approach. As your own study advances, you may wish to ask more modern questions, but begin by listening for the stories.

Our notion of story is thus a broad one: it includes the stories told in narratives, the charter story implied in the letters as well as the narratives, the community stories that the letters and narratives reveal, and the personal stories of the individual writers. There are strong correlations between charter, life, and personal stories: each level of a story implies and reflects the others. We will understand the letters only if we understand their story contexts.

Obviously, this will be easiest to do when we come to the Gospels, which are not only stories but also narratives. The book of Revelation, too, is largely narrative. If story is so basic, should we perhaps begin with these narratives and work backward to the earlier nonnarrative literature? This is a possibility, and it would have the advantage of examining all that we can know about Jesus before considering the letters that certainly assume much about Jesus. But it has the disadvantage of interpreting an earlier age by a later one. We must not assume that Paul's story of Jesus was simply equivalent to one of the later Gospels. We must not use the Gospels as a standard by which we judge the other writings. It is not that the narrative literature controls the earlier letters, but that both the letters and the narratives rest on their own basic stories of Jesus and on the histories of the communities from which and to which they were written. We must endeavor to hear these stories.

Letters as Oral Performance: Understanding Rhetoric

Hearing is the proper verb in regard to the ancients, since nearly their whole experience of literature was aural. Whether public or private, reading was done out loud. Even much later, in the fifth century, Augustine tells us he was bewildered that Ambrose was reading without pronouncing the words (*Confessions* 6.3). People simply did not ordinarily read silently. If we pay attention to the wording, we will seldom find reference to readers in ancient texts; they speak of the hearer of the message (for example, Rev. 1:3 and Heb. 5:11). When they do speak of a reader they generally mean the person who read it aloud for others. Publication consisted of reading the work aloud at a public gathering. No doubt this was also the way in which Paul's letters were encountered by their earliest audience. In fact, it is likely that all the literature in the New Testament was first presented orally.

This orality of the documents means that we must strive to hear them and not simply to read them. Read them out loud. Even in translation they make a different impression when encountered as a spoken word. This orality also implies that we should not be overly subtle with the meaning we find. Examining carefully and at leisure the fine points of a written text is quite different from hearing it read without having a text in front of you. Interpretations that depend on nuances of text or on minor changes in wording should be approached with caution.

Because the letters were originally presented orally, our analysis of them must include as a central component a study of how the ancients were trained to speak and listen, the study of *rhetoric*. Training in **rhetoric** was a basic part of the educational process, and since the time of Aristotle (384–322 BCE) students were taught that an oral presentation involved three distinct elements: speaker, audience, and discourse. As a speaker, one had to demonstrate one's own character (*ethos*), stir the emotions of the audience (*pathos*), and present a logically convincing case (*logos*). How these three effects were achieved depended on the situation in which one spoke. Ancient rhetoric was always situational.

The rhetoric of conflict. Ancient rhetoric was developed in three primary situations. First, there were the speeches in the courts of law, where male citizens could sue each other for a great variety of alleged offenses from the trivial to the capital. This *defense rhetoric* (usually called *judicial rhetoric*) sought to influence the audience to make a judgment about something that had happened in the *past*. In ancient law courts, the jury consisted of all interested citizens and was usually very large. (For example, a jury of over five hundred convicted Socrates and sentenced him to death.) Verdict was by majority vote. Because citizens originally represented themselves, they needed to know how to speak well. If a plaintiff failed to gain a conviction, he was liable for the amount for which he had sued. Consequently, judicial rhetoric was the most highly organized form of ancient rhetoric; prosecution and defense represented its positive and negative forms.

Both forms followed a common pattern. You would begin with an introduction designed to elicit the sympathy of the audience and then proceed to tell the story of what had happened (as seen by your side, of course). Then you would enunciate the point of contention and set forth your case, followed by various kinds of proofs. Finally, you would attempt to refute the other side and move to a conclusion that both summarizes your case and stirs the emotions of the audience. Although this basic pattern was susceptible to great variation and elaboration, speakers were trained to organize their presentations this way and listeners expected it. So should we.

The rhetoric of decision making. Another kind of rhetoric developed in the popular assembly, what we would call the legislature. Again the audience could include all male citizens, so the speaker needed to influence a large body of people, but now the wisdom of some *future* action was under debate. Grounded in these public deliberations, this form of rhetoric is often called *deliberative rhetoric*. Again, there were two possibilities: the exhortation (we ought to do this) and the dissuasion (we ought not).

The basic techniques of deliberative rhetoric involved setting forth propositions and advancing proofs for them, but great variation and elaboration were possible. Indeed, deliberative rhetoric could follow the same basic pattern as judicial rhetoric: introduction, narrative, case, proof, rebuttal, conclusion.

The rhetoric of exhortation. A third kind of speech, found in a variety of contexts (such as political gatherings, philosophical lectures, religious ceremonies, and social occasions), sought to demonstrate a certain truth: democracy is a dangerous form of government; honor is the highest virtue; one ought to be chaste; a certain person is noble. The funeral oration, for example, sought to demonstrate the virtue and excellence of the departed in a eulogy or encomium. This *demonstrative rhetoric* sought to persuade the hearers to hold some view toward a certain person or action in the *present*. Again there were two forms: positive and negative. As the encomium sought to praise, the invective sought to denounce some person or vice.

Demonstrative rhetoric specialized in sweeping generalizations, lists of virtues and vices, appeals to maxims and tradition. It could be very loosely organized, or it could follow the more formal organization of judicial rhetoric. In its way the funeral oration sought to prove the "innocence" of the subject in a way not unlike the courtroom defense, but not in regard to a specific crime. Rather the speaker sought to move the audience to a general admiration (just as invective sought a wholesale denunciation).

The basic distinctions between the three kinds of rhetoric are summarized in Table I.2, and their typical structural elements are presented in Table I.3.

We will explore examples of each of these kinds of rhetoric in the New Testament writings, but a word of caution is in order here. While the ancients had a passion for clear and logical distinctions in theory, in practice these three forms of rhetoric often overlapped, and any given presentation might use more than one. Learn to listen for stirring introductions and conclusions, for narrative backgrounds and logical proofs and rebuttals. Try to determine if a given writing seems more interested in defense, deliberation, or demonstration, and you will be better able to determine its structure and will begin to experience the stories behind it.

TRAVELING IN THE WORLDS OF THE TEXT

With these general maps to guide us, we will now explore the writings of the New Testament. We will emphasize the world of the text, concentrating on literary analysis. But it would be folly to neglect the worlds behind and in front of the text.

TABLE I.2   TYPES OF RHETORIC

Type	Setting	Circum-stance	Time Concern	Technique	Degree of Complexity	Purpose
Rhetoric of defense	Courts	Conflict	Past	Narrative Case Proof Rebuttal	High	To persuade to the speaker's viewpoint, proving innocence or guilt
Rhetoric of deliberation	Assembly Legislature	Decision making	Future	Proposition Proof	Moderate	To decide an issue or course of action
Rhetoric of demonstration	Public meetings (schools, funerals, holidays, etc.)	Practice of virtue Ceremony	Present	Maxims Lists	Low	To demon-strate that something is so

Because the New Testament writings are documents from a history and a culture far different from ours, any comprehensive attempt to understand them must be also a study of history and of society—both theirs and ours.

ATTENDING TO THE EARLIEST MEANINGS

Though I have assumed that the original meaning of these texts is somehow the most important or most interesting understanding of them, not all literary critics would agree. Early in the twentieth century a new school of literary criticism developed in reaction to the overwhelming concern of previous critics for historical and biographical interpretations of the literary texts. The older criticism argued that one could understand Shakespeare only if one related his plays to incidents in his life. The New Critics, as they called themselves, argued that works of literature are autonomous and independent: once an author sends a poem out into the world the author loses all control over it. The whole meaning of the poem is found in the poem, according to these critics.

In one sense this is true. What an author intended to say does not have priority over what he or she actually said. Sometimes the work says less than the author intended—sometimes more. And many a writer has discovered that they said more than they consciously understood at the time, but things they also intended! Only close analysis of the writing will reveal its meaning. Ultimately, justification for any interpretation of a text must be the actual content of the text, not some supposed original meaning.

TABLE I.3 AN OVERVIEW OF THE STRUCTURE OF RHETORICAL COMPOSITIONS

General Element	Defense/Prosecution	Deliberation	Demonstration
Introduction (*Exordium*) Always designed to introduce main ideas and gain the audience's sympathy	Important to establish the speaker's character; could be elaborate	Useful to establish the speaker's credentials to speak on the issue	Useful to identify the speaker with the cause and to establish virtuous character
Narrative (*Narratio*) Optional in all but defense; designed to set a context favorable to one's case	To tell one's version of the disputed incident or to establish the general character of the defendant	To give the background of the action being debated or to show why some action needs to be taken	To relate incidents of praise or blame for a person, virtue, or vice
Case (*Partitio*) A clear, concise statement of the point(s) at issue	Person is innocent or guilty, did or did not do a certain thing	Audience should or should not determine to do a certain thing	Perhaps a summary statement to make a transition into the next section
Proof (*Probatio*) Reasons for the audience to adopt your point of view	Crucial and probably longest section of the presentation, consisting of carefully reasoned arguments	Crucial, often making an argument from cause to effect (do X so Y may result)	Crucial, but often more a list of virtues or appeals to maxims and common experience than an argument
Rebuttal Reasons why the opposite point of view is wrong	Necessary to react to the arguments of the opposing side, since there is always prosecution and defense	Optional unless the issue is actively contested	Optional, perhaps more a vilification of those who would follow another path
Appeal (*Exhortatio*) Statements, petitions, stories, appeals designed to move the audience to take action on the case	Crucial	Important	Optional
Conclusion (*Peroratio*) Summarize and reiterate one's basic point(s) in a way that gains the audience's sympathy; strong emotional element	Crucial to gain the audience's sympathy (and vote!)	Important to move the audience to the proper decision	Important to make a strong final appeal

In another sense, this concentration on the text alone is false, because it is impossible. It appeared possible to the New Critics only because they dealt with nearly contemporary texts written in English. Paul wrote to the Galatians: "*Christo sunestauromai; zo de ouketi ego.*" No one can interpret this text by itself; we cannot even translate it into English without a historical consideration of what these words meant in Paul's time. Even when translated ("I was crucified with Christ; I no longer live"), they make no sense unless we understand both the general historical practice of Roman crucifixion and the specific historical event of the crucifixion of Jesus. Yet even with that knowledge the meaning of the sentence is not obvious. Clearly, Paul was not crucified with Christ; clearly he still lived. We need to know more about Paul, his general view of the world, his religious practices, his relation to the Galatians, and the specific problem he was addressing in Galatia when he formulated these words. Such historical investigation is indispensable for an understanding of these texts. Without it we will continue to read our own ideas into the text—a far less interesting enterprise.

Our goal, then, is to hear these documents in something like their original key: to try to understand what they may have meant to the people who first heard them. This implies two further considerations. First, it implies that our concern is with the ancient world. Though it may be important to discover what the New Testament means for us today, this study is about something overheard; it seeks to unravel other people's meanings. This approach allows us to achieve some distance and a critical perspective on issues and ideas.

This does not mean that what we read will be irrelevant for our time. Reading about other people's problems can prove useful for the insight it provides about our wholly different problems (which is why, I suspect, so many people read newspaper advice columns). In addition, we stand a better chance of making a convincing interpretation for our time if we first understand how the texts were interpreted in their time. The foundation on which all later interpretations must be built consists of deciphering and ultimately understanding the meaning of the work in relation to the time when it was written.

Second, our goal implies that we can listen to these writings in somewhat the same way as the original hearers. But three obstacles stand in our way: we speak a different language (these writings were all in Greek); we live nearly two millennia later (the intellectual and historical changes present even greater differences than those between Greek and English); we bring different expectations to the texts.

Language and Translations

A moment's reflection will show how great the gulf is that separates our age and experience from those of the ancients. Even when we share the same words, the meanings often differ. For example the Greek verb *pisteuein* is usually translated into English as *to believe* and the cognate noun *pistis* comes into English as *faith*. But in English, "to have faith" and "to believe" imply two quite different kinds of activities. To have faith implies a religious stance toward the world; to believe refers to holding ideas to be true—with the implication that one cannot prove them so. In Greek the two words share the same root, meaning to trust, and we will often misconstrue the meaning if we think in terms of a set of beliefs. This language problem is great. Words like *Lord, Savior, law,* and *love* must be interpreted according to their first-century context, where they meant things quite different from what these English words mean to us today.

One pervasive difference stems from the fact that many of the key words used by these writers have come to be used almost exclusively in a religious context, whereas they were originally secular words used in everyday life. The word *church* for example (*ekklesia* in Greek) referred to the assembly of citizens in a city. *Salvation* meant health and wholeness. *Redemption* was a term from the slave trade. A *savior* was anyone who provided rescue, perhaps the patron of a city and especially the emperor. As a general rule, do not assume that these basic words had special religious meaning to the original audience.

Some modern translators have attempted to lessen this problem by translating not the words but the ideas behind the words. They ask, What would the typical Greek-speaking person have understood by these words? How can we say that in English? This theory of translation is called *dynamic equivalence* because it seeks a living English equivalent to the Greek. These translations produce varied results, from rather strict paraphrases (Today's English Version) to very loose paraphrases (the Living Bible), with others forming a middle ground (Phillips's translation, *The New Testament in Modern English*; the Jerusalem Bible; the New English Bible, now the Revised English Bible). These are very useful translations, but one major problem with a translation based on the theory of dynamic equivalence is that there is no check on a translator who misjudges the original meaning, then radically alters the text by inserting his or her own views (as happens frequently in the Living Bible). Nonetheless, I strongly urge you to consult such translations frequently.

Other modern translators use what is called a theory of *word equivalence*, attempting to find English words that correspond to each of the Greek words in the original. This technique produces a translation that is fairly literal but not always easily understood. The translators of the King James Version (1611) used this approach, as did the translators of the modern descendant of that version, the Revised Standard Version. Other modern translations (the New International Version, the New American Bible) are based on the same philosophy. The latest edition of the Revised Standard Version, the New Revised Standard Version, has moved somewhat away from this literal practice, especially in the use of gender language. I strongly urge that a modern literal version be your constant companion in the study you have undertaken. In this book I will regularly cite the New Revised Standard Version but will sometimes use other translations, or make my own, when I want to highlight some aspect of the text.

But because the strengths and weaknesses of these two kinds of translations complement each other, an even better strategy would be to read from a variety of translations, some literal, some paraphrased. When serious differences emerge, consult a good commentary that discusses the reasons for such differences. A good study Bible, with scholarly footnotes, will be invaluable. (See the suggestions at the end of the chapter).

Of course this discussion of translations presumes we have a single text to translate, but that is false. No original manuscripts of any ancient writings have survived, only copies. The best copies of the works now in the New Testament are from the period between 200 and 400, that is, one to three hundred years after they were written. There are partial manuscripts and quotations surviving from the second century. The problem is the copies do not agree. If you would look at any given page of a Greek New Testament you would see literally dozens of textual variants, mostly minor. The scholarly study of these variant texts is called *textual criticism*, which attempts not only to provide the most likely original reading but also to account for the variants. It does this by categorizing and tracing the family history of various manuscripts and also by carefully examining each variant, looking for typical scribal errors, marginal notations, characteristic vocabulary, and some reason for the variant (perhaps the original was obscure and some copyist "clarified" it or perhaps made one version agree with another version in a different Gospel). Again, a good study Bible will be useful.

Social Setting

More than language stands in the way of our understanding the ancient world. Think about all the inventions, conveniences, and ideas that have so shaped our modern consciousness: computers and telephones, printing and universities, sociology and critical historiography, psychology and democracy. None of these existed in the New Testament world. (A few free cities with democratic systems existed in the ancient world, but the right to vote was limited—usually to the wealthy, always to the men.) All these changes and much else that we now take for granted were unknown in antiquity. We must be careful not to leap too easily from our experience to that of the ancients.

As a modern person you probably believe that it is good for you to develop your own personality, to become independent of your parents, to take responsibility for yourself. You seek an education in part because you believe in the value of knowledge and in part because you know you can improve your economic standing. You seek to accumulate wealth. You believe in the rule of law, under which all should be treated alike. You accept scientific explanations for things like the weather, your car breaking down, or you getting sick. None of these ideas would have made any sense to the people who first heard the New Testament writings.

Had you lived in first-century Antioch, you would understand that your primary identity is in the solidarity of your family and anyone who would forsake his family and seek personal fulfillment is a "prodigal son" (see Luke 15:11–32). Education can never compensate for innate social class; an educated slave is still a slave. Anyone who would increase wealth is greedy and an enemy of society, for such a person is taking what belongs to others (see Luke 16:13). Most people have no standing before the law, only free citizen men; the rest depend on patrons to protect them. And things don't just happen; personal forces, both natural and supernatural, cause them. The weather, illness, and even the weeds in your garden are the work of other persons (see Matt. 13:24–30). We must give constant attention to the different social outlook presumed in these writings. (Some of these differences are presented in chart form in Table I.1, page 7.)

Expectations of the Text

A third, equally important, obstacle to understanding these texts is one we might miss because it lies within ourselves: we experience these texts in a way impossible to their first hearers. We experience them as a collection, but their original audience encountered them as individual writings. Modern people view the New Testament in various ways (some regard it as Scripture; others consider it infallible; still others view it as just another book). But for its first hearers, the New Testament was not a book at all. Even so basic a concept as *New Testament* did not exist when these works were produced.

The New Testament as a canon. A **canon** is a fixed list of works that belong to a certain category. Eventually early Christians determined such a list of authoritative works, but it took about three centuries to establish the twenty-seven works we know as the New Testament. The earliest audience heard these works one at a time, not as part of a collection. When Paul wrote his second letter to the Corinthians, he could not assume they had the rest of his letters with which to compare it—he was not even sure they had understood his first letter to them (1 Cor. 5:9–12). We, too, will encounter these writings one at a time. Only later (Chapter 14) will we consider the collection as a whole and discuss in more detail how the canon was formed through a process of political and religious inclusion and exclusion.

When these writings were written they were simply placed alongside all the other Christian writings produced in this period, scores of them. You can read some of these other writings in collections of New Testament Apocrypha (for example, Elliott, 1993) and we will discuss some of them as we proceed. Many other writings were lost entirely. The ones that eventually made their way into the canon gained authority over the others. We would miss a great deal if we failed to hear the conversation between these various writing and that between these writings and the others that were excluded from the canon. (For a discussion of what, how, and why writings were included or excluded from the canon, see pages 473–78.)

Today we regard the forms of these writings as unusual. People no longer write gospels. Even our letters are different. If someone were to address a letter to us in the manner of Paul, we would be quite surprised and, perhaps, a little amused. But Paul employed the letter-writing techniques common in his day. We will understand what Paul's correspondents may have understood only when we can imagine what this type of writing meant to people then.

Kinds of writings. Clearly we approach different kinds of writing differently. A letter from a friend you dated in high school will be read with an expectation different from the one you bring to the reading of this book. And the way you read both of these will differ from the way you read a comic book. Various kinds of literature (what critics refer to as **genres**) demand different kinds of reading. We have been programmed by our general experience of life and literature to expect different things from various genres: science fiction is different from history, and both differ from romance.

With what expectations did the earliest hearers of a gospel approach that text? How did their expectations differ when they heard a letter? Did their expectations vary if they knew the author of the letter? These are not easy questions to answer; yet it is useful to raise them so that we may realize some of the difficulties we face in reading these documents as they were originally read. Our discussion of each document will include a discussion of its genre. We can then begin the process of developing a sympathetic imagination on which all successful interpretation is built. The first step is to be aware of the great river of language, history, and literary expectations that separates us from those original hearers. Only then can we begin to build the bridges necessary to carry us across to their side.

APPROACH OF THIS BOOK

The tools used to construct these bridges will consist of a thorough historical investigation of the context of each writing, an examination of the social situation from and to which it spoke, and a careful literary analysis of the text of the documents themselves.

Most of the historical and social information will be introduced when it is relevant to the study of a particular text. Although this has the disadvantage of not allowing a systematic treatment of every topic, it has the advantage of always being useful information. To compensate somewhat for this decentralized approach, there is a preliminary chapter on the everyday lives of early Christians, an attempt to place these people in the real worlds of culture and history.

Then we will consider more precisely how the stories about Jesus developed in this world between the time of Jesus and the earliest writings we possess. Following this we will study these earliest writings: the letters of Paul. Then we consider other letters, first those related to Paul and then those related to other leaders. We will then turn our attention to the narrative writings: the Gospels, the Acts, and the Apocalypse. This arrangement is both generic and roughly chronological. Those who wish to study the stories of Jesus before attempting Paul could jump directly from Chapter 2 to Chapter 8 (the narratives) and then return to a study of the letters.

As we study the specific documents, we will always begin with the text of the biblical writing. Reading that text will lead us to consider the historical and social circumstances of both writer and audience, and understanding those circumstances will return us to a further reading of the text. It is a circle, but I hope not a vicious one.

YOUR ROLE IN ALL THIS

While reading the following pages, you will often find it necessary to put this book down and turn to the biblical writings themselves. This is as it should be, for a work of literature can never adequately be summarized. The most we can do is to point to things we have found useful and say, "Consider this." This book is filled with such pointing, combined with the rich insights of other scholars and my own musings on the text. It will never be my intention to tell you what it *really* means. I pursue the more ambitious goal of providing you with the resources necessary to arrive at your own interpretation.

As you learn, do not be surprised if some of your previous ideas about the New Testament are challenged. That is an inevitable part of the learning process. But, as one of my professors admonished, don't understand too quickly. Do not immediately assume that your earlier idea is completely false just because some new insight seems to call it into question. Do not presume that the new way of reading the writings examined here must be wrong because it is at odds with your earlier understanding. To do either would abort the learning process.

Once, when planning a trip through northern Pennsylvania, I did some reading about the Moravians and planned to visit one of their settlements near Bethlehem. I learned that the Moravians are an egalitarian community, according everyone equal status in life and in death. Thus, they do not permit grave markers of different sizes. Imagine my bewilderment on visiting a cemetery and finding many different sizes of gravestones. Fortunately, while wandering around the cemetery, I met the old caretaker who explained to me that while Moravians recognize no social distinctions, they do recognize innate status differences based on the age that a person had attained at death. Babies, children, adults, and the old all had different-sized memorials. My earlier understanding was not wrong; it was only partial.

This is the process of learning: First we are ignorant; then we learn something and understand something; then we learn more, and what we understood previously is challenged. We may feel ignorant again, but it is a higher-level ignorance. When we learn more, we may be able to reconcile our earlier understanding and our new knowledge or to choose between them. This process never stops as long as we keep learning. Running into an old caretaker every now and then doesn't hurt either.

The following study aids are introduced to help you consolidate the things you are learning. They are very general and represent the sorts of things I would want my students to learn. Your professor may have other ideas, more tailored to your situation. Your professor may also want to help you distinguish the questions and terms that are more important for your particular class. The following provides a starting point.

LEARNING ON YOUR OWN

REVIEWING THE CHAPTER

Names and Terms

Begin to build a vocabulary of the terms, concepts, and methods used in biblical studies. Each of these terms is defined in the reading and is listed in the index. It is important both to have a short definition and to see the contexts in which they are used.

canon	historical-critical method
charter story	rhetoric
feminist reading	story
genre	

Issues and Questions

While there is a nearly endless list of questions one could ask about this material, I have tried to select issues that will help you review the major ideas of each chapter. Again, your professor may help you focus on particular topics or suggest additional ones that would be helpful in your situation.

1. Describe the purpose of each of the three basic methods of New Testament scholarship: historical, social, and literary.
2. Describe the setting, purpose, and basic techniques of the three kinds of rhetoric.
3. What basic problems hinder our attempt to hear the New Testament writings as their original audience might have heard them?

TAKING THE NEXT STEP

If I were beginning serious study of the Bible, my first priority would be to obtain a scholarly study edition. Among the best, listed in the order of my preference, are:

The Access Bible: New Revised Standard Version with the Apocryphal/Deuterocanonical Books. Edited by Gail R. O'Day and David Peterson. Oxford University Press, 1999.

The New Oxford Annotated Bible with Apocrypha. Edited by Michael D. Coogan. Augmented 3rd edition (New Revised Standard Version). Oxford University Press, 2007.

HarperCollins Study Bible: New Revised Standard Version, Including the Apocryphal/ Deuterocanonical Books with Concordance. Edited by Harold W. Attridge. Harper-One, 2006.

The Oxford Study Bible: Revised English Bible, with the Apocrypha. Edited by M. Jack Suggs, Katharine Doob Sakenfeld, and James R. Mueller. Oxford University Press, 2003.

The Catholic Study Bible: New American Bible. Edited by Donald Senior. Oxford University Press, 1990.

Many students prefer to read from the New International Version, a translation produced by a team of conservative scholars. However, I have been unable to locate a good study edition with notes that would be comparable to those in the editions listed above. Perhaps the closest is published by Zondervan (2006), but its orientation is more devotional than academic. It also lacks the Apocrypha.

Perhaps the best starting point to understand scholarly methods is Aageson, 2000, though the work of McKenzie and Haynes, 1993, is also excellent. See also Green, 1995, and Powell, 1998. Also highly recommended are the introductory works on individual methods: On historical criticism see Krentz, 1975, and Achtemeier, 1970. On rhetorical criticism see Kennedy, 1984, and Mack, 1990. On literary criticism see Petersen, 1978b. On narrative criticism see Powell, 1991. On social analysis see Elliott, 1993; Kee, 1980; and Malina, 1981. For a critique see Osiek, 1992b. Malina, 1989b, is a short discussion of the differences between contemporary and first-century understandings of people.

Topics for Special Studies

For general strategies and research tools useful for New Testament study, see Appendix A, "Doing Your Own Research." Also, each chapter will conclude with a selection of topics and resources that will enable you to advance your study as far as your interest takes you.

Origin and Development of the Critical Study of the New Testament

See Baird, 2003; Riches, 1993; Henry, 1979; MacRae and Epp, 1987; Tuckett, 1987; Harvey, 1985; Morgan and Barton, 1988. For a Catholic viewpoint, see Brown, 1981; for a conservative Protestant view, see Harrison et al., 1978, and McKim, 1998.

Methodological Issues in New Testament Studies Today

Longman, 1987, provides an excellent description and evaluation of the history and values of literary method. For a critique of rhetoric, see Malina, 1996, and Schüssler Fiorenza, 1996. Schüssler Fiorenza, 1988, makes a major feminist challenge to the supposed objectivity of the historical method. Wink, 1980, challenges an exclusive reliance on the historical paradigm. For a serious discussion of the methodological issues in studying one of Paul's letters, see Donfried and Beutler, 2000.

The Feminist Approach to New Testament Studies

Anderson, 1991, provides an overview of recent scholarship; Cheney, 1996, discusses feminist reading strategies. See also A. Y. Collins, 1985 (especially the introduction on methods); Martin, 1991; Russell, 1985; Sakenfeld, 1988; Schneiders, 1989; Schüssler Fiorenza, 1983, 1984, 1992; Tolbert, 1983. See also the commentary by Newsom and Ringe, 1992, and the general reflections of Foley, 1982.

Cultural Interpretation

A significant new movement in interpretation is to take conscious account of one's cultural location as an important aspect of interpretation. See the influential work of

Segovia and Tolbert, 1994, 1995. For an excellent example of application to the book of Revelation, see Rhoads, 2005. For an African-American perspective, see Felder, 1991, 2002; Wimbush, 2000, 2003; Bailey, 2003. For a gay perspective see Guest et al., 2006.

Orality versus Literacy in the Origins of Early Christianity

For an introduction see Achtemeier, 1988; for debate about the issues see Dewey, 1995. A more detailed bibliography is given at the end of Chapter 2.

The Relationship of the New Testament Writings to Other Ancient Literature

On the literary forms and contexts of New Testament writings the place to begin is Aune, 1988. For a guide to ancient literature see Rose, 1951. The ancient critics are discussed by Grube, 1965, and Russell, 1981. English translations of excerpts from important ancient literary critics include Gilbert, 1962; Russell and Winterbottem, 1972; and Smith, 1951.

How We Establish the Proper Reading: Textual Criticism

Elliott and Moir, 1995, provide a clear introduction. The current state of affairs is assessed in Ehrman and Holmes, 1995. See also Ehrman, 2006. For different views compare Metzger, 1992b, with Aland and Aland, 1987. On various manuscripts see Elliot and Moir, 1995.

Ehrman, 1993, and Ehrman and Holmes, 2006, discuss the ways theological debates corrupted the texts. Epp, 2005, is an excellent study of how gender ideology influenced texts.

Which Translation Is Best? Overview of Modern Translations

Recent translations are discussed by Metzger, 1992, 2001; Worth, 1992; Lewis, 1991 (NIV); and Bailey, 1990 (NRSV). Nida, 1964, discusses general issues in translating. For the story of English translation see Bobrick, 2001; for a fine history of treating the Bible as literature, see Norton, 2004.

On the move toward more gender-inclusive language, see Mercer, 1990. For ideas about translating the Bible in media other than print, see Soukup and Hodgson, 1997.

Detailed Study of a Particular Method

Start with one of the introductory works listed below and pursue the footnotes.

More advanced works on literary theory: For overviews see McKnight, 1985, and Powell, 1992 (with a nearly exhaustive bibliography, arranged by topic and by biblical writing). Booth, 1983; Chatman, 1978; and Iser, 1974, have been three of the most influential for biblical studies. Other important critics include Scholes and Kellogg, 1966, and Wellek and Warren, 1956. Broader issues of validity and interpretation are addressed well by Armstrong, 1990; see a range of views in Frei, 1974; Hirsch, 1967; and Abrams, 1953.

On rhetoric, see Kennedy, 1972; Anderson, 1996; Clarke, 1963b; and Lausbert, 1998. For a summary handbook, see Porter, 1997. Petersen, 1985, is a wonderful example of the application of literary criticism to Paul (Philemon). See also the seminal work of Wilder, 1990. On theology and rhetoric, see Smit, 1996. For the relation of rhetoric to other methods for studying 1 Thessalonians, see Donfried and Beutler, 2000.

More advanced works on social scientific analysis: Blasi et al., 2002, collects a variety of social science approaches. Examples of the approach include: Malina, 1981, 1986, 1991; Pilch and Malina, 1993; Elliott, 1986, 1993; Fiensy 1991; White, 1991b;

Kee, 1989; Meeks, 1983, 1986; Tidball, 1984. See also Goldmann, 1980; Judge, 1980. Malina, 1996, contrasts social and rhetorical criticisms. For a critique of Malina see Downing, 2000.

More advanced works on the historical method: Harvey, 1966; Collingwood, 1969; Carr, 1973; Handlin, 1979; Bloch, 1967; and especially Finley, 1986, and Cameron, 1990. Carpenter, 1995, and Appleby, Hunt, and Jacob, 1994, pose questions about the purposes of writing history. J. Collins, 1999, both discusses and reconstructs Jewish history. Novak, 2001, discusses the historical method and uses primary sources to reconstruct Christian history.

Additional Books and Articles

Grant and Tracey, 1984, trace the ways the Bible has been interpreted over the centuries.

On the need for understanding the story quality of the New Testament, see Wilder, 1983.

Complete editions of the ancient literary, critical, and philosophical works can be found in the Loeb Classical Library series from Harvard University Press; the format of this series provides English translations with the original language on facing pages. The series includes nearly the whole corpus of Greek and Latin literature.

1

PREPARING TO HEAR THE STORIES

 Money may be regarded as a conventional means of representing a claim or a right to goods or services.

OXFORD CLASSICAL DICTIONARY

I was trying to find the ancient ruins of Philadelphia but was having little luck. People tried to give me directions, but they were too complicated for the language barrier. I just kept going in the direction they pointed and asking again. The people of Turkey had been exceptionally friendly and helpful, so I was a little surprised when the last man I asked for directions waved for me to go away. Then I remembered something I had read in the guidebook: Turks signal "follow me" by waving, palm down toward the ground. And follow him I did; he led me more than a mile, further and further up the hill, till we came to the sparse ancient ruins near the top. He spent more than two hours with me, finally leading me back to the bus station, and would accept no money for his services. He even insisted on buying me çay (a strong, specially brewed tea). We did finally come upon someone in the teashop who spoke enough German that I could express something of how thankful I was. I was thankful, too, for the guidebook, because my first impulse had been to turn away and not bother this fellow more.

My goal in this chapter is to provide something of a guidebook or, more especially, an introduction to the people who continue to live in the stories of the New Testament and to those who were its first audience. It should not surprise us if texts written two thousand years ago—in a different language, to people living in a different part of the world who had different political and economic systems and vastly different family organizations—seem strange to us. It is far more surprising that we understand them at all. And we do understand them, partly, for these people are as like us in some ways as they are different in others. Often they will be both alike and different at the same time. (See the photo on page 28.)

WHO DO PEOPLE SAY THAT I AM?

One day when Jesus was walking with his disciples, he turned to them and said, "Who do people say that I am?" (Mark 8:27). This is exactly how a person in his world would have asked the question of identity, for identity in the ancient world derived from what others thought of you, not from some inner awareness of your true self. Identity was built on a complex of factors—primarily class, status, wealth, and gender—and it included your place in the family and your friendship with others. And there were larger issues, like ethnicity and geography, that shaped people's opinions.

The Greeks, for example, considered people to be either Greeks or barbarians (literally, babblers, that is, those who did not speak Greek!). In a similar way Jews divided the world into Jews and Gentiles. For both groups nothing else could quite compensate for the lack of this basic ethnic identity, at least in theory. In practice, of course, a wealthy, aristocratic Jew would have more in common and more social contact with wealthy aristocratic Romans than with ordinary Jews. The situation was even more complex than that.

The book of Acts presents us with a scene dramatizing the origins of Christianity accompanied by a miracle of communications. Each group hears the new message in its own language. Notice the groups:

PUBLIC LATRINE   There can be no doubt about the function of this public building at Ephesus, for it strongly resembles our modern counterpart. Yet even here the quantity and closeness of the seats imply a different view of the body and its functions. The channel near one's feet, which would have contained water for washing, compensates for the lack of toilet paper.

> *And how is it that we hear, each of us, in our own native language? Parthians, Medes, Elamites, and residents of Mesopotamia, Judea and Cappadocia, Pontus and Asia, Phrygia and Pamphylia, Egypt and the parts of Libya belonging to Cyrene, and visitors from Rome, both Jews and proselytes, Cretans and Arabs—in our own languages we hear them speaking about God's deeds of power. (2:8–11)*

That such a variety of people representing such a range of linguistic groups should all be gathered in one place reveals the cosmopolitan nature of that world. To understand how this came about, and to get a better grasp of how people saw themselves, we need some historical perspective. Using Israel as our focus, we will jump back about six centuries before the beginning of Christianity.

HISTORY

The watershed in Israel's history occurred in 587 BCE, when Jerusalem was conquered by the Babylonians, an event known as the **exile**. Although Israel's fortunes would ebb and flow in the succeeding generations, a basic change had occurred. Before the exile, Israel was an independent nation, often with considerable military and political power. After the exile, Israel was a dependent state living at the mercy of some larger empire. Jews before the exile were simply Judeans (identifying where they lived); Jews after the exile were a people living in someone else's empire, often and increasingly outside Judea.

A succession of empires controlled the Mediterranean region: Babylon, Media, Persia, Greece, and finally Rome. Each of these made important contributions to Jewish culture. The early stories of Genesis are shared with the Babylonians; the idea of the Devil developed through Persian influence. But the contributions of the Greeks are the most significant for the period of the New Testament. The story of their rise to power is interesting.

When the Persians took over the Median empire, they sought to expand their kingdom westward, with good success. They conquered the Greek settlements along the coast of Asia Minor (modern-day Turkey), then in 490 BCE crossed the Aegean Sea and invaded Greece. (See map, Figure 1.1.) It was a grand fight whose major battles have left their names in our textbooks: the Battle of Marathon, the Battle of Thermopylae, and the sea victory at Salamis. The invasion failed, and the Persians eventually withdrew.

The danger caused the Greeks to form a defensive alliance under the leadership of Athens and, with Athenian control of the common treasury, led to a time of unsurpassed economic and cultural flowering: the classical age of Greece. Still, one Greek city often opposed another, especially Athens and Sparta, so they were no threat to anyone else. No threat, that is, until a leader arose from an unlikely source—not Athens or Sparta or even Corinth, but Macedon in the far north.

Philip of Macedon united all Greece under his control, using whatever means necessary: diplomacy, bribery, intrigue, or military force. He amassed a great army under the call to exact revenge on Persia, developed new battle techniques, and even improved weapons. But Philip died before the campaign could be launched, and the army elected his young son, Alexander, to lead them. Only twenty at the time, Alexander not only defeated Persia but kept marching east till he came to India, conquering all in his path (including Israel and even Egypt). (See the animated map, with year markers, at http://www.ac.wwu.edu/~stephan/Animation/alexander.html.) Having reached the Indus River, the army turned to head home,

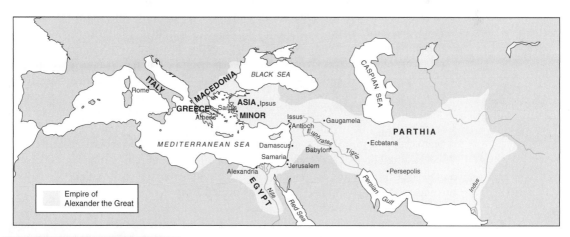

FIGURE 1.1   **EXPANSION OF GREECE**   After fighting off the Persian invasion in the fifth century, the Greeks moved from the defensive posture of the classical age to active offense. They went on the attack under Alexander in the fourth century and conquered not only Persia but Egypt, Babylon, and everything else between Greece and India. By 300 BCE, the whole of the ancient world was ruled by Greeks.

but Alexander died on the way, probably of malaria. He was not quite thirty-three, but he would ever after be known as Alexander the Great.

No one proved powerful enough or clever enough to control this vast empire after Alexander's death. It was soon divided among four of his generals, based in Babylon in the east, Egypt in the south, Syria in the north, and Macedonia in the west, each carving out his own kingdom. These kingdoms would continue to fight among themselves for generations. There would be no common Greek empire, but that hides the more basic fact that the whole of the Mediterranean world was ruled by Greeks.

This brought about tremendous military, political, and economic changes, which we will largely ignore, except to note that Israel lay right between the powerful kingdoms in Syria and in Egypt. The conflicts between these two kingdoms had a profound impact on Israel, a subject I will return to below. For our purposes the crucial changes are cultural. With their particular view of the world ("Greeks and barbarians"), it did not occur to the Greeks to adapt to the ways of their subjects. Instead they transported their culture with them. The Greek language became the common tongue of commerce and politics. Greek customs, dress, arts, sports, religion, temples, and institutions were spread across the whole region. But Greek culture did not obliterate native traditions; it combined with them to produce a dynamic culture, really a variety of Greek-dominated cultures from Italy to Palestine, which we call **Hellenistic** culture. (*Hellenistic* derives from *Hellas*, the Greeks' name for their country, and the suffix *-istic*, meaning "like." Hellenistic culture is not Greek but Greek-like, for it contains many elements from other cultures.) The situation was analogous to what happens today, when American music, dress, and popular culture have spread around the world.

Eventually the Hellenistic kingdoms succumbed to the growing power of Rome, which had for centuries controlled a vast empire to the west. Turning eastward about 200 BCE, Rome eventually controlled most of the territory conquered by Alexander. Administering such distant and disparate areas created enormous strains on Rome's own political system, a republic ruled by an aristocracy. Strong central leadership was needed, and, again, the generals struggled for control. The triumvirate (triple leadership) of Caesar, Pompey, and Crassus soon devolved into a struggle between the western general, Caesar, and the eastern general, Pompey. Caesar's troops prevailed; Pompey fled and was eventually killed. Caesar's triumph was short-lived, for he was assassinated by those who resisted centralized power. Only the names of the players changed. Octavian, Caesar's heir, took control of the west, and Antony, Caesar's trusted lieutenant, ruled the east. Their struggle culminated in Octavian's defeat of Antony in 31 BCE, after which the Roman senate recognized him as the "first among equals" (Princeps) and the "one most honored" (Augustus). He soon added the title supreme commander (emperor) and was in fact the ruler of the Mediterranean world. Rome had been transformed from a republic into an empire that would last another four hundred years.

Rome ruled the world, but it remained a Greek world. Greek culture, language, customs, and religious traditions spread everywhere. Thus the world of the New Testament embodies three overlapping culture categories: Greek, Roman, and other—admittedly a somewhat biased way to phrase it. But it was a biased world. Greece represented to everyone the pinnacle of cultural attainment. Roman artists, for example, were considered great when they could successfully copy a Greek original. And where the Greeks made one statue, the Romans made hundreds of copies of it. But Rome ruled the world; military, political, and economic dominance was theirs. Thus a wealthy Roman with a Greek education was near the top of the social hierarchy.

The others were various: Egyptian, Jewish, North African, Thracian, and many more. The status of people from these cultures rose with a Greek education too, but they would always be provincials to the Romans and Greeks. Thus what we call Hellenistic culture was really a great variety of cultures, as each of these other cultures adopted and adapted Greek culture to its native tradition. You would encounter Artemis, the Greek Goddess and protector of women, wherever you traveled, but she would be assimilated to some local deity. Artemis looked vastly different in Ephesus than in Athens. (See photos on pages 460–61.)

Among these others we are particularly interested in the Jews, for all the writers of the New Testament documents were Jews or deeply influenced by Jews. Jews in this world were a very diverse group, so diverse that many scholars speak of "Judaisms," not "Judaism," for this period. Their diversity stemmed from many factors: geography, language, social class, acculturation, education. In fact the words we translate as "Jew," "Jewish," and "Judaism" all stem from the Greek word for the homeland, Judea. So they might better be translated as "Judean," "those like Judeans," and "those who follow the traditions of Judeans." But the Judeans themselves followed many different paths. We know the names of a dozen or so factions, the most prominent being Sadducees, Pharisees, Essenes, Baptists, and Zealots. They differed in how they regarded the sacred writings, the rituals they followed, how they regarded the Temple, their comfort with Greek culture and language, and in many other ways. (See Chapter 10, pages 330–38, for fuller explanations.)

There were two central Jewish institutions, the Temple and the synagogue. Within Israel the focus of Jewish identity was the Temple, where animal sacrifices and various liturgical rites were performed by priests. In theory there was only one Temple for Jews, and all male Jews were supposed to go there for the three great annual festivals. While it is doubtful that even Jews living in the land could make such regular pilgrimages, certainly Jews living abroad throughout the Roman Empire could not.

The vast majority of Jews in this period did live abroad (they are called the Diaspora), and the focus of their practice was the synagogue, a place of prayer and scripture study dominated by lay leaders, not priests. While useful, the distinction between Jews of the homeland and of the Diaspora can be overdrawn. Diaspora Jews sometimes returned to Jerusalem for festivals (as the Passover scene recounted on pages 27–28 shows), and Jews of the homeland attended their own synagogues. Both were deeply influenced by Hellenization.

Jews who lived among Gentiles adapted more or less to Gentile ways—in language, dress, names, customs. But there were certain points of friction. Many Jews observed the Sabbath day as a day of rest and study, a practice that seemed wasteful and lazy to their Gentile neighbors. Many Jews observed dietary restrictions (especially avoiding pork), which seemed at least odd. Many, probably most, Jews circumcised their male infants, a practice that seemed barbaric to many Greeks. We will see these issues often in our study of the early Christian writings.

CULTURE

In the discussion that follows I will be separately examining aspects of life such as family, friends, status, work, education, leisure, and religion, for that is the way we think about life. I do not want to give the false impression that this is the way the ancients would have thought. Greek does not, for example, have any word that corresponds to our word *religion*. If you could have stopped people on the street in Corinth in Paul's time and asked them what their religion was, they would have had no idea what you were talking about. Religion (as well as most of these other activities) did not exist as an independent social reality. The two major independent social institutions were the family and the city; all other institutions were embedded within these. The ancients would have seen what we call *religion* as an element of their city life (the public aspect) and of their family life (the private aspect). And the same could be said for their status, education, occupation, and much else. With this caveat, let us examine some important aspects of culture.

Status, Class, and Economics

At the most general level of analysis, Greco-Roman society consisted of two groups: the wealthy, ruling elite (perhaps 2 percent of the population) and the great masses of people who were largely peasants and laborers, often existing at subsistence levels. There were, of course, many people living between the extremes of wealth and poverty, but there was no middle class in the modern sense. This was a deeply divided society.

But this general analysis hides at least as much as it reveals, for in that world one's standing rested on a variety of interacting factors; so it could happen that a person from the lowest social class might exercise significant power and influence. Let us look first at the class system. We will use the system in place at Rome, but an analogous system existed in every major city. In descending order, the classes were senators, equestrians (knights), citizens, residents, freedpersons, and slaves. These class identities depended on two primary factors: birth status and wealth. A senator, for example, whose wealth fell below a set amount would lose class status, but an increase in wealth by an ordinary citizen or freedperson, however great, would not allow that person to rise to the higher classes. Women could move up in social class through marriage; men could not, at least in theory.

The senators and knights made up the ruling class, the main difference between them being the size of their fortunes. There were only six hundred senatorial families and little movement into or out of this class. A knight could be raised to the senatorial class for some exceptional public service (assuming he met the criterion of wealth). Typically a young man of the senatorial class would finish his education and achieve a minor administrative position by the time he was twenty. Then he would be eligible for military service as one of the six tribunes of a legion. The best would then rise to some financial office and a seat in the senate. This could be followed by a tour of duty as the governor of a province. A few then moved into judicial work or legionary commands; a career might culminate in a consulship or the governorship of a major province.

Knights could be as wealthy as senators, though they did not need to be. They were the rest of the nobility, those not belonging to the most elite families. (There were perhaps ten or twelve thousand such families in the first century.) Men in

ROMAN DRESS   The toga was the formal dress of the Roman and also the garment in which one would be buried. It seems to have been a large semicircular cloth (perhaps 18 feet along the straight edge and up to 7 feet deep). It was a dignified, but not very convenient, dress, and several emperors had to enforce its use on public occasions by law. The third figure from the left, showing his side, reveals his tunic—worn under the toga outdoors or by itself indoors. It was a short, shirtlike garment falling perhaps to the knees. Women added a skirtlike tunic that reached to the feet. Senators and knights were allowed to add colored stripes to their togas.

this class could aspire to be legionary tribunes or commanders of auxiliary troops or of fleets. They could move on to careers as managers of imperial mines or other state property, midlevel managers of the fire or police brigades, financial officers in provincial administrations, and so on. Many of this class engaged in business and trade (considered beneath the dignity of senators), though never actually working with their hands. Together these two classes ruled the Roman world.

Citizens had numerous rights, both legal and financial. They had access to the courts and various kinds of public support. Many were comfortable and even well off, but many more were poor, living in large apartment buildings in cramped and dirty quarters. In many cities citizens had some power because they voted in elections and in assemblies. Rome's policy of subsidized idleness (the dole) pacified them. In addition, there was a class of resident noncitizens (aliens), who were free but lacked the rights of citizens.

Freedpersons were a transition class: no longer slaves but not yet citizens. Former slaves, they continued to have specific obligations to their former owners, from whom they continued to receive benefits. If their owners were citizens, their children would be citizens. Slaves existed in great numbers and in several categories. Household slaves had a decent life, though they had the legal status of a possession, not a person. They were used as domestic help, child raisers, tutors, medical personnel, scribes, administrators, leather workers, wood carvers, weavers, and so on. Some were slaves by birth, but the vast majority had fallen into slavery either through debt or disaster (a lost war, piracy). Few would be slaves for life, either earning or purchasing their freedom. They came from every ethnic group and attained every educational level. There were no distinguishing marks of slaves, either in ethnicity or manner of dress. Some had businesses of their own and employed their own slaves. Many of these slaves were better off than many citizens, who competed for the same jobs. The lot of field slaves was worse. Used in large numbers on the vast estates of the wealthy, they worked the land. Finally there were the state slaves who worked the mines in grim conditions with no prospect of freedom. Gladiators, athletes, and actors were often slaves. It seems that nearly everyone of substance had slaves, from the emperor to the farmer to the relatively poor citizen—even other slaves. They served in schools, temples, shops, factories, and public works.

Status thus rested on both class and wealth, but these interacted in surprising ways. For example, the emperor's slaves and freedpersons ran most of the bureaucracy of the Roman government and were men of great wealth and power. In part this was because of the resources they controlled, but in part it was also because they were slaves of the emperor. This brings us to a third factor in the status equation: honor.

Honor is easier to define than it is to understand. **Honor** is the public acknowledgment of the power and prestige due to one by one's class, wealth, station, group identity, and accomplishment. That is, it consists of two aspects: a claim to honor and the public recognition that supports that claim. Honor was the most important possession of any Greco-Roman man (it was a male thing, as we will see). The basic claim to honor stemmed from the group, but the individual could gain or lose honor depending on what he (or those for whom he was responsible) did. A man lost honor by any exhibition of weakness, cowardice, foolishness, ignorance, or failure to live up to expectations. Stated another way, when a man failed to receive the public recognition of his rightful honor, he experienced shame. To be shamed was one of the worst fates one could experience.

All social interaction held the potential to increase or decrease one's honor; every public encounter was also an honor contest. Anytime two men entered the same social space, it was necessary to establish their relative degrees of honor; in the exchange one could easily gain and the other lose. There were obvious negative challenges to honor: an insult, a threat, a physical affront. But there were also positive challenges: giving a gift, offering help, inviting to a party, giving praise. In each case the receiver admits the implicit superiority of the giver. Thus each receiver must in turn become a giver, preferably of a bigger party, more extravagant praise, a more valuable gift. Every social interaction required a man to know his own worth and the worth of those with whom he interacted, as well as the likely response of those who witnessed the interaction. Honor was a constant public performance.

Of course, inferiors could accept gifts from superiors. The superior enhanced his honor by such giving, and such honor was far more valuable than the gift. A wealthy and generous man could find a line of people at his front door in the morning, each soliciting some favor or gift, which he would freely grant if he could. And the longer the line the more obvious to all was his honor.

Greco-Roman society was a vast collection of social hierarchies, with the emperor at the top and each class arranged in order below. Within each class, every family and ultimately every male had a specific status based on both group identity and individual accomplishment. This status was marked not only by reputation and titles but even by specific modes of dress. For example, only members of the upper classes could wear a purple stripe on their togas, and the stripe of a senator was broader than the stripe of a knight. Gold rings were likewise limited to the nobility. When you encountered someone on the street, you knew their social location by looking at them. In such a society a network of family and friends was very important.

Family and Friends

Some of the implications of this status consciousness for family and gender roles are obvious. With the stakes so high, we must expect that men would exercise strong control over their families, lest they be shamed by some action of those for whom they were responsible. This led to strong discipline over children and severe limitations on the public activities of women. One of the most shameful things for a man was for his wife to have an affair. Thus women were inculcated with a sense of shame from their earliest years, that is, shame as a positive feeling of protecting honor. One pointed way to put this is to say that in Greco-Roman society men had honor whereas women had shame.

A second implication was for the solidarity of the family unit, which commanded a strong sense of loyalty and trust combined with a distrust of all outsiders. Family secrets would never be shared with those outside, even if it meant lying to them. In fact, lying to outsiders might have been considered a virtue. The family was a unit, and the fortunes of all its members rose and fell together; more specifically, they rose and fell with those of the father. Thus we begin to see how the various roles in the Greco-Roman family functioned.

The parents were not equal partners, but they did have some mutuality. The father was the ruler of the family and its disciplinarian. His authority was absolute, even over adult children. The father was also the primary contact between the family and the outside world. The mother was the obverse of all this. Her place was within the home (where she had great authority); she was to be submissive to her husband and was the primary caregiver in the family. She would have total responsibility for the children until they were about ten, when the father would assume the role of training his sons. But the mother's role in the family was a peculiar one, for she also belonged to another family. In fact, increasingly in this time period Roman women married and remained under the authority of their fathers. This severely limited the husband's authority, at least in theory, and resulted in the woman becoming legally independent upon her father's death. It also created the odd situation that she might inherit from her father but not from her husband.

Parents were responsible for all aspects of their children's lives, including arranging their marriages (usually with their consent). Marriages were not based on romantic love (though there is abundant testimony that real affection developed within marriages) but on social and economic benefit. Girls usually married in their mid- to late teens, boys in their late twenties. Childbirth was very dangerous, and rates of childbearing varied widely by class. Upper-class Roman women had to be encouraged by law to have multiple children. Thus family legislation under Augustus (d. 14 CE) offered increased civil liberties to any citizen woman who bore three children. As negative inducement, a childless couple lost the right to control their legacy, for it passed to relatives who did have children. Many women died in childbirth, resulting in the need for second marriages, often with an even greater age discrepancy than in the first marriage. Many teenage girls wound up marrying men in their forties.

One reason for the need for multiple children was the high rates of infant death, with perhaps half the children dying before their tenth birthday. On average it took perhaps five live births to result in the survival of two children to an age when they might marry and reproduce. See Table 1.1 for various estimates on life expectancy.

Of course you could also have too many children. In rural areas, no doubt, children were an economic benefit, for they soon became additional laborers. But in the cities children were more of an economic drain. This was especially so for girls, because they would have to be provided with a substantial dowry in order to marry appropriately. This is probably the reasoning behind the advice of a businessman traveling at the time of an expected birth:

If you are delivered of child [before I get home], if it is a boy keep it, if a girl discard [abandon] it. (Lewis, 1994:54)

TABLE 1.1   SURVIVAL RATES ESTIMATES

	Carney, 1975	Lewis, 1994	Kretzer and Saller, 1994	USA, 1997 CDC, 1999
Live births	100		100	100
Age 1			72	
Age 6	65			
Age 10			50	
Age 16	40	40		
Age 20				
Age 26	25	20		
Age 46	10	5		94
Age 65	3	2		82
Age 80				50

NOTE: Various scholars have tried to estimate survival rates in antiquity, based largely on inscriptions and epitaphs. Their numbers roughly correspond. People in antiquity *did* live to old age, but far fewer of them did so compared with survival rates today in the United States.

Unwanted children would be abandoned in some public place (doorways, crossroads, temples), probably with the expectation that they would be found and raised by others. They would seldom be raised free, for such abandoned infants could be assumed to have slave status and were usually raised to be sold, with girls often winding up in brothels. The existence of a significant number of slaves with names like Kopreus (meaning "from the dunghill") suggests that many times abandonment was simply disposal.

This practice illustrates the absolute authority of the father, whose word was final on such matters. Even the faintest suspicion that the child was not his would be enough to reject it, as would any physical defect.

Not all marriages were of this standard type. Only citizens could contract legal marriages, and these only between social equals. Those lacking these qualifications often entered into relationships that lacked the legal standing of marriage. Also, divorce and remarriage were common and relatively easy to accomplish. Since the minor children belonged to the father's family, they went with him.

Although this ideal of the nuclear family prevailed and most people lived in such a family, few would live solely in such a family. First, for the common people, housing was too expensive for each family to have its own place. In this case a collection of nuclear and extended families might live in a common space. Second, for the wealthy who did own great homes, a variety of other people would also live there. Anyone who owned a home would also own slaves; in fact a homeowner with only one or two slaves would have been thought of as miserly. The great homes would have dozens and the country estates hundreds. These slaves were part of the family and remained so even after gaining their freedom when they would live elsewhere. At any given time the household might also have guests, live-in tutors, or apprentices learning a trade from the father. Finally, a wealthy household might also include a series of partners, business associates who might have shops along the outer wall of the house or who may have joined with the father in some business venture or land purchase.

A typically affordable home would be built in a large square or rectangle around a central courtyard (see Figure 1.2). The courtyard would be covered but have a central opening through which the rainwater would be channeled from the roof to a central pool. Larger homes might also have an open courtyard or garden area. You entered through a long passageway, coming into the courtyard. At the far end of the courtyard, on a raised platform, was the father's office, where he would receive guests, transact business, keep records, and dispense favors. Around this central area would be a series of more private rooms for sleeping, eating, cooking, storage, entertaining guests, a bathroom (the Romans had indoor plumbing and central heating). The dining room would contain three couches on which the diners would recline (two to five on each), though there might also be chairs on which to sit and eat. There would also be one or more rooms that opened directly to the outside, which would have been used as shops and work places. Each room would be decorated with colorful wall paintings (with mythological, everyday, and erotic scenes) and mosaic tile floors (mostly geometric designs but some pictorial). The central living space was the courtyard, where the women would work at spinning and weaving, children would play, and men would socialize. It would also contain the family shrine commemorating its ancestors, human and divine. Various sacrifices, mostly of food, would be made here to the guardian spirits of the household, including the

Stylized Diagram of a Roman House

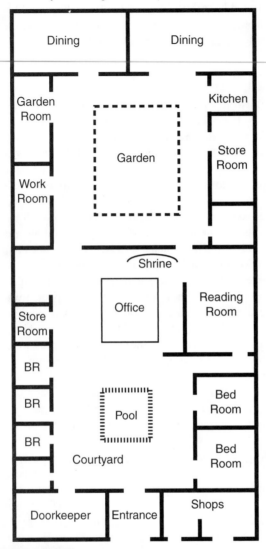

FIGURE 1.2 **TYPICAL ROMAN HOUSE** This stylized diagram shows the different rooms around an inner courtyard of a typical Roman home.

"genius" of the father (his spirit and generative powers). Other rituals carried out here included coming-of-age rites for both boys and girls, weddings, births (including the ritual in which the newborn was laid on the ground and then picked up by the father, signifying inclusion in the family), and funerals.

The father received guests and dispensed favors on a regular (perhaps daily) basis to another group of people connected to the household: clients. Clients were people attached to a household in a system of long-term, mutual obligations. These obligations were more social than legal and were seldom written down. They were nevertheless real. Because many goods and services were not available to ordinary citizens, those with access to them could use that access to help those whom they wished to help. In return they got status, honor, and social influence. (The opening scene of the movie *The Godfather* provides a good modern example of a patron-client relationship.)

For example, one of the duties of a client was the morning greeting to the patron; clients would line up at the door of the patron's house. The longer the line, the more prestigious the patron. The patron would be seated in his office; each client would come in to express his greeting and inquire whether there was anything he might do for his patron. Usually the patron would grant him a small token—a gift or coin or perhaps a favor. Some might even be invited to join the family for dinner. Such open access to the house reminds us just how public was life in that world. This also highlights the need for members of the family to act with discretion and secrecy, for prying eyes were always around.

Patronage is a kind of fictional extension of the family wherein the patron acts as a kind of father (or godfather) to the clients, who in turn give him the honor and obedience of children. It was a relationship between unequals, but it was often couched in the language of friendship. And every patron was likely to be someone else's client, not on this daily basis, but when need arose. The patron of all patrons was the emperor. Wealthy women too served as patrons, both to other women and to men.

In summary, we can see that identity in the ancient world was, unlike the modern ideal of individuality and inner awareness, founded on the realities of the social group. Ethnicity, social status (involving class, wealth, and honor), family status and role within the family, and the network of friends and patrons determined who you were and what others (and you yourself) thought of you. Once we understand this sense of external identity and motivation, much of what we read in the New Testament writings will take on new meaning. Now let us look a bit more at how these people actually lived.

Education, Work, and Leisure

The Greeks had an idealized typology, or model, of the life cycle, divided into periods of seven years, based, of course, on the male experience. *Infancy* ended at age seven and was marked by getting teeth; *childhood* ended at fourteen with the onset of puberty; and what we might call the *teen years* ended at twenty-one with the growth of the beard. The period of *youth* ended at twenty-eight; thereafter one was a *man*. The stages from twenty-eight to thirty-five and from thirty-six to forty-nine seem quite artificial, but after fifty one would be referred to as an *elder*, and after sixty-five as an *old man*. This idealized system corresponds only roughly to real experience.

It is very difficult to estimate the extent of formal schooling. We know that various cities established schools and that many tutors circulated through the empire. These would be informal affairs, lacking a formal building. Much schooling probably occurred in public spaces, such as the portico of a temple. Children of citizens and freedpersons, and occasionally of slaves, might have a few years of basic schooling, depending in part on whether their families could afford the tuition.

Children of the well-to-do, sometimes including girls, began their primary education at about age seven, learning first to read and then to write, both involving a great deal of memorization. Depending on the degree of Greek influence, up to half the school day would be devoted to physical education, primarily the sports associated with the Olympics: running, jumping, discus and javelin throwing, boxing, and wrestling. Girls as well as boys were often educated, though they would have had less emphasis on sports and would have worn some clothing (boys and men participated in sports in the nude). There were even women's athletic games, primarily racing.

Around the age of twelve many students moved on to study content areas, such as mathematics (including geometry), music, astronomy, and especially rhetoric and philosophy. The school day remained divided between physical and academic education, for most boys could look forward to some time in the military. Schooling usually ended around the age of sixteen or seventeen, when they were considered adults (and upper-class males got to don an adult's distinctive toga). Still considered youths, these young adults were expected to show deference to their elders. A few went on for advanced training in rhetoric or philosophy, usually with a tutor. That this relationship with a tutor often involved a sexual aspect traces to the Greek origins of the institution in which it was common for adult men and teenage boys to form sexual pairs. Jews and, to a large extent, Romans rejected the practice.

Most girls were now ready for marriage; most boys began an apprenticeship, usually working with their fathers but sometimes with another relative or friend of the family. After an apprenticeship of perhaps three years, working sunup to sundown, the boy was ready to practice his trade. By their midtwenties most men were ready to establish their own homes. Upper-class men began their military careers around the age of twenty and then moved on to other military or civic administrative positions.

Leisure activities varied enormously by class and location, but some things were common. If we use public buildings as a rough guide, the most popular activities were, in this order, sporting events, the theater, and musical performances. Various kinds of buildings were devoted to sports. Most major cities would have a stadium for track and field sports; running was the premier event, but the stadium might also be used for boxing, wrestling, and riding. Built in an oval with seating all around, the track was typically about 200 yards long (see the photo in Chapter 4, page 114). Major cities might also have a circus, a facility for chariot racing, with between four and twelve teams of horses competing, each horse and rider dressed in a distinctive color. Major cities might also have an arena, which was a multipurpose sports complex associated with games, mostly armed combat between gladiators or with animals. These blood sports, frequently involving death, were very popular and very expensive. Gladiators were often condemned criminals who saw the arena sports as a chance to live, though slaves were also employed. Free citizens sometimes became gladiators because of the hero status a successful gladiator attained. There were even professional female gladiators. Various kinds of ball games were also played, though we are not too sure of the rules. One game seems to involve putting a ball in a net, and another seems to involve moving the ball on the ground by running and throwing (somewhat like modern rugby).

In addition, four great athletic festivals attracted participation from all over the Greek world: the Olympic, Nemean, Isthmian, and Pythian Games. Numerous local festivals were also very popular, such as the Panathenea at Athens. In addition to athletics, these festivals would have included contests in music and poetry. Held every two or four years, these events attracted thousands of visitors.

If a city's stadium held from thirty to fifty thousand people, the next major building was the theater, typically holding from fifteen to twenty thousand. Seating was in a semicircular construction around a raised stage. In front of the stage was a large flat area in which the chorus and dancers performed. Behind the stage was a structure that functioned both as backdrop to the play and as changing and storage rooms for the actors. In the Hellenistic age, comedies seem to predominate over tragedies.

A second type of public building devoted to performance was the music hall (odeum). Smaller than the theater but designed in much the same way, the music hall was used for concerts and competitions, seating perhaps five thousand. Musical performance was a central part of almost every aspect of Greek and Roman culture, especially festivities. (See the photo on page 382.)

The other major public building used for leisure was the bath. Whereas we treat the bath as a private and perfunctory activity, for the Romans it was a major, public, and extended activity. Every city would have at least one bathhouse, often an elaborate building with a dozen or more rooms. Minimally, a bathhouse would have a reception room for socializing, a changing room, a cold room for a bracing dip, a hot room for a plunge bath, and a warm room with a large pool for numerous bathers (both male and female in the first century). Bathers were anointed with oil and scraped with a curved scraper (a strigil) as well as washed and massaged. A typical bath could take two to three hours, often on a daily basis. Wall paintings often portrayed erotic scenes, and the bath was notorious for various kinds of sexual encounters.

Photo by author

ENTRANCE TO THE BATHS OF SCHOLASTICA   These baths were originally built in the first century but were remodeled around 400 by a Christian woman named Scholastica.

Finally, we note a type of public building whose main purpose was not recreational but that nevertheless provided numerous leisure opportunities: the temples. Every city would maintain several large temples, and each temple would imply at least one major public holiday, often more. These would be occasions of parades, performances, and feasts deriving from the sacrifices to the deity. Probably in a large city you could expect five or six such festivals in any given month. Greco-Roman culture had no notion of a Sabbath (only the Jews had a day of rest each week), let alone the idea of a weekend devoted to leisure, but the people had plenty of occasions for celebration. In addition, the temples functioned as community centers, halls for trade guild meetings, lodgings for travelers, and places for family celebrations (see photo on page 366).

READING AND REFLECTION

Read the story of Cornelius in Acts 10, noting indications of social status, household arrangements, and behaviors that might earn honor. Write a short paragraph imagining what you would answer if Cornelius were to ask you, "Who do people say that I am?"

WHAT MUST I DO TO BE SAVED?

There's a story in which Paul and Silas were imprisoned in Philippi when an earthquake opened the doors and freed all the captives. The jailer awoke to the chaos and was ready to kill himself in disgrace that he had allowed the prisoners to escape. But Paul had not left and called to him not to harm himself. The man's response was both relief and fear, and he knelt before Paul and asked him, "What must I do to be saved?" (Acts 16:19–34). Now the questions I want to raise are: Why does the jailer phrase the question this way? From what (or for what) did he think he needed to be rescued (the root meaning of *being saved*)? What would it have meant to be saved? To answer these questions we need to look a bit more closely at aspects of culture that we would call *religious*.

RELIGION

We can begin to get some sense of the religious spirit of the Greco-Roman world from a story about Paul visiting Athens. He gives a speech that begins thus:

> *Athenians, I see how extremely religious you are in every way. For as I went through the city and looked carefully at the objects of your worship, I found among them an altar with the inscription, "To an unknown god." . . . Indeed he is not far from each one of us. For "In him we live and move and have our being"; as even some of your own poets have said, "For we too are his offspring." Since we are God's offspring, we ought not to think that the deity is like gold, or silver, or stone, an image formed by the art and imagination of mortals. (Acts 17:22–29)*

The Greek word here translated "religious" is *deisidaimon*, meaning "to fear the divine." It is an ambiguous word, for such fear can be either craven or pious. In the negative sense Greco-Roman writers identified it with superstition, and Paul is surely playing with the negative potential of the word when he points to an altar dedicated to some God unknown. But Paul also plays with the positive sense, for he wants to proclaim the God of Jesus as just the God unknown to them. In the positive sense, Greek writers spoke of *eusebes* (giving respect, worship) and Roman writers of *pietas* (piety, proper respect). So words associated with religion include *fear*, *respect*, and *honor*; this is the domain of honor discussed above.

In its most basic sense Greco-Roman piety was just the extension of the honor and patronage systems into the realm of the divine. **Piety** is simply showing people the respect they are due, recognizing their honor. This is an ascending scale: a pious son honors his father; a pious citizen honors the emperor; a pious human honors the Gods. And each God has her or his special honor, and like all honor, the honor of the Gods is based on who they are and what they have done.

The ancients pictured the divine world as a hierarchy much like the human world in which they lived. At the top was the supreme God, perhaps identified with Zeus (or Jupiter) or perhaps thought of more abstractly. Next came the great Gods, the Olympian deities and their counterparts in other cultures. Next came a vast array of lesser deities, some very specialized (there was a God of laughter and a Goddess of sleep) and some more universal in their scope (Isis and Asclepius being two of the most popular). These lesser deities were sometimes referred to as *daimon*, which Christians eventually identified as demons. But the *daimon* were not evil in Greco-Roman understanding (though any God could become your enemy). There was also a class of Gods who were originally humans but who had through some heroic deed ascended to the divine, Herakles (or Hercules) being the most famous.

This last category of humans ascended to the divine provides the model for understanding the status of the emperor. Several Roman emperors had done such grand deeds that they were soon understood to have crossed over and become Gods. The grand deed of Julius and Augustus was to bring peace to the world. They had saved the world. The senate officially recognized their divine status, and every emperor thereafter would be known as *son of the divine Julius*. This was not exactly a claim that they were divine, but it suggested that they could become so.

It is perhaps not too much to say that at some basic level all the Gods are saviors, each in his or her own way providing rescue to humans. If we look at the things prayed for we find concerns not far different from modern prayers: health, wealth, happy marriage, safe childbirth, success in one's career, skill in one's craft, strong family relationships, safe journeys, emancipation from slavery, and similar desires. What is different, perhaps, is the sense that each of these concerns comes as a direct gift of the God, and that life is so tenuous that rescue (being saved) is necessary in each area.

We can catch something of the essence of ancient piety in a scene at the end of a second-century novel by Apuleius, known in English by the title *The Golden Ass*. Most of the story consists of the comic exploits of a young man named Lucius, who has inadvertently been transformed into the shape of an ass and in this donkey-form forced to wander through the darker sides of the Roman Empire. Having reached the end of his rope, Lucius prays for deliverance.

After addressing Isis as Queen of Heaven and invoking the names of Ceres, Venus, Artemis, and Proserpine, his prayer continues:

> *Or by whatever name, and by whatever rites, and in whatever form, it is permitted to invoke you, come now and succour me in the hour of my calamity.*

STATUE OF ISIS Combining Oriental mystery and Greek beauty, Isis captured the imaginations of many. She was portrayed in a great variety of forms, but this lovely statue shows her in typical Greek guise, far from her Egyptian origins. Her worship was widespread, established even in Rome despite Romans' hostility to foreign cults. She was commonly portrayed on jewelry and grave monuments and was worshiped in the Roman world into the sixth century.

Support my broken life, and give me rest and peace after the tribulation of my lot. Let there be an end to the toils that weary me, and an end to the snares that beset me. Remove from me the hateful shape of a beast, and restore me to the sight of those that love me. Restore me to Lucius, my lost self. But if an offended God pursues me implacably, then grant me death at least since life is denied me. (Lindsay, 1962:236)

Isis grants Lucius a nighttime visitation. She says, "Behold, Lucius, moved by your prayer I come to you—I, the natural mother of all life." She goes on to identify herself with various Gods, Greek, Phrygian, Roman, Ethiopian, and Egyptian, but claims her "true name, Queen Isis." She adds:

> Behold I am come to you in your calamity. I am come with solace and aid. Away then with tears. Cease to moan. Send sorrow packing. Soon through my providence shall the sun of your salvation arise. (Lindsay, 1962:238)

There is much more, including the obligation on Lucius "that all the remaining days of your life must be dedicated to me and that nothing can release you from this service but death." There is also the promise that, should he prove worthy, through his obedience, devotion, and chastity, he will find that "it is within my power to prolong your life beyond the limits set to it by Fate."

Then after various religious rites and an initiation into the mysteries of Isis, Lucius gives thanks:

> Most holy and everlasting Redeemer of the human race, you munificently cherish our lives and bestow the consoling smiles of a Mother upon our tribulations. There is no day or night, not so much as the minutest fraction of time, that is not stuffed with the eternity of your mercy. You protect men on land and sea. You chase the storms of life and stretch out the hand of succour [rescue] to the dejected. You can untwine the hopelessly tangled threads of the Fates. You can mitigate the tempests of Fortune and check the stars in the courses of their malice. (Lindsay, 1962:250–51)

And the prayer continues with much more extravagant praise, finally ending:

> Howbeit, poor as I am, I shall do all that a truly religious man may do. I shall conjure up your divine countenance within my breast, and there in the secret depths I shall keep divinity for ever guarded. (Lindsay, 1962:251)

With this as background, we can more easily see that the jailer at Philippi was expressing the common feeling of his time: life had left him in the lurch, and he needed rescue. How might he get free of the tangled web of fate that had ensnared him? Paul offered him Jesus as his savior. Now we need to explore this more general sense of being ensnared by life, by looking at the general spirit of the age, what Germans call the *Zeitgeist* and what we will call the worldview.

WORLDVIEWS

In the praise of Isis cited above, Lucius contrasts her mercy with three harsher realities: fate, fortune, and the stars. Understanding these will reveal much about the general feelings about life in that age. He refers first to "the hopelessly tangled threads of the Fates." Fate, in the singular, is one's allotted portion, the natural order of things, and its most obvious reference is to death. Fates, in the plural, were Goddesses who saw to it that justice was done; they pursued any offender till recompense was rendered. There were various Goddesses of fate: Moira, Tyche, Nemesis, the Furies—or perhaps we should say various ways of personifying fate. Fate controls all that happens from birth to death. According to a well-known oracle from Delphi, not even the Gods can escape their fate. All this is good as long as one can see the logic of life. But now fate's clear designs have become hopelessly tangled, according to Lucius. Life seems a maze from which there is no clear path.

This leads to the second expression, "the tempests of Fortune." Fortune too was a Goddess, Lady Luck. Fortuna could win battles, bring the troops home safely, bring children, increase wealth, and much more; temples dedicated to her in each of these guises dotted the Roman world. But Lucius does not experience good luck, only bad. Like fate, fortune seemed to leave one with little control over life. And this leads to the third element, the stars. One of the standard means of gaining control was through astrology, the supposed science of studying the stars and learning how to take advantage of auspicious times and avoid dangers.

But Lucius expresses the need to overcome the "stars in the courses of their malice." Again there is both the sense that things are predetermined, or at least determined by powers beyond one's reach, and that this determination is not in our best interest. The feeling of being at the mercy of faraway, impersonal powers seems to have been widespread in the first century, and it corresponds rather exactly to the changes in political systems over the previous centuries.

In earlier times people lived in independent cities where, even if they had no vote, they knew the people who did. A male citizen of a free city controlled his own environment, or at least had a voice in controlling it and in influencing others. He knew who made decisions and why, and he had recourse to the citizens' assembly and the courts to try to change things. Women would likely have shared this same sense of well-being as part of the patriarchal family. All this changed under the empire. Basic decisions were now made by unknown people, living in faraway Rome. There was no appeal and little hope of influencing such decisions. You were at the mercy of the powers that be. On the political and social level your salvation depended on the quality of your patrons; so too on the broader level we call religion.

The Gods who might serve as your patrons were first of all those of your family. Each Roman family would have its hearth, with its shrine to the special deities and ancestors, located in the courtyard of its house. Next, the Gods of your city might be expected to take a special interest, followed by a deity who might have reason to look out for you (perhaps you had offered sacrifice or special prayers at a temple). And just like in your social life, you would cultivate as many patrons as possible.

This brings us to a consideration of basic differences in worldview between those who believed in many Gods and those who believed in only one. Actually, it is not quite that simple; we need to look at three typical worldviews—monotheism, polytheism, and dualism. Most simply, a **monotheist** is someone who believes there is only one God. One can arrive at this belief by a process of either exclusion or inclusion. The Jews had chosen exclusion; hundreds of years earlier a prophet had proclaimed:

> *You are my witnesses, says Yahweh, and my servant whom I have chosen; that you may know and believe me, and understand that I am he: before me there was no God formed, neither shall there be after me. I, even I, am Yahweh; and besides me there is no savior. (Isa. 43:10–11; New Jerusalem Bible)*

All other Gods were false; only Israel's God, Yahweh, was the true and living God. Thus the worship of any other God was wrong. But many Greeks and Romans arrived at monotheism by a process of inclusion: all Gods and Goddesses are merely reflections of the one true God. Thus the sincere worship of any God is the worship of the one true God. This is the idea behind the prayer of Lucius when he identifies Isis with various other deities, and it undergirds Paul's strategy in the story in Acts when he attempts to identify the unknown God with the God of Jesus. So some Greeks and Romans were monotheists, though of a different sort than the Jews.

However different, all forms of monotheism imagine there is one final force, one ultimate will, behind all that happens. This allows for a very optimistic view of life, provided only that one knows how to reach this God. In their different ways, that is what Lucius, Cornelius, and the Philippian jailer are seeking.

Polytheism, by contrast, accepts the reality of differing Gods, with differing wills, differing powers, and differing allegiances. Lucius's first prayer, where he wonders if perhaps some God has become his implacable foe so that death is to be preferred to his ongoing trials, represents such thinking. Polytheists can be either optimistic or pessimistic, depending on how sure they might be of the power and ability of their Gods. Still there is always a degree of uncertainty, for there are so many spiritual forces out there to be concerned about. The pervasiveness of a polytheistic worldview can be seen in the degree to which additional spiritual forces (angels and demons) come to be recognized even in Jewish writings of the Hellenistic era (both are absent from Jewish writings before the Hellenistic era). Many Jews, while remaining formally monotheists, believed in a plurality of spiritual powers.

The third worldview is **dualism**, which as the name implies imagines only two spiritual forces, with the added idea that they are opposites: good versus evil. Centuries before the New Testament, a Persian religious reformer named Zarathustra, known more commonly by the Greek form of his name, Zoroaster, had rejected the ancient polytheism of his people for the worship of one God, Ahura Mazda. The father of all, Ahura Mazda was said to have begotten twin spirits: one wholly good, the other wholly evil. These spirits struggle for control of the world and of humans; the one to whom we give our allegiance will prevail, according to this intensely ethical reformer. By the time of Israel's exposure to Zoroastrianism, the situation seems to have shifted; Ahura Mazda himself became identified with the good spirit, and his opposite was known as Anra Mainyu, the evil one. Because it proposes two ultimate powers, this system of thought is called *dualism*.

The Jews encountered this dualism during their exile in the sixth century BCE and eventually found it a useful way to explain their own world. They did not adopt it wholesale, for they could not imagine any force equal to their God. Their idea of the absolute power and authority of their God, Yahweh, left no room for equal and opposite forces. This emphasis on the absoluteness of Yahweh is evident in a remarkable story in 1 Kings (22:1–23), in which God is portrayed as the real source of even the lies told by the false prophets: the lying spirit is an underling in the heavenly court of Yahweh.

Although their exalted notion of God did not permit the existence of a second God, the Jews did begin to imagine another spiritual force in rebellion against God: the Devil. Most Christians are surprised to learn there is no mention of the Devil in the part of the Bible they call the Old Testament, and only three references to Satan (Job 1; 1 Chron. 21:1; and Zech. 3:1). Now *Satan* in Hebrew simply means "Accuser," and it is at least arguable that the Satan in these three references accuses but does not deceive or try to destroy. And while later tradition will identify the snake in the Garden of Eden story as the Devil, the text of Genesis never makes this connection.

This developing idea of an evil spiritual force seems to come to sharp focus in relation to historical events that occurred about 180 BCE. As we saw above, Alexander's kingdom had been divided between his generals, and two of their dynasties especially contested for dominance in the eastern Mediterranean: the Ptolemies in Egypt and the Seleucids in Syria. In 175 BCE the Seleucid king named Antiochus IV came to the throne and seemed to have the power to conquer Egypt. The campaign was well begun, but before Antiochus could finish the job, Egypt made an alliance with Rome, which was just beginning to exercise power in the East. Antiochus knew he did not have the power to stand against Rome and withdrew his forces. Perhaps in an effort to unify his kingdom, perhaps to gain some divine advantage, he rigorously reintroduced the worship of the Greek Gods and insisted that all his subjects make appropriate sacrifices to them. Cooperating with certain elements in Jewish society who were extremely open to Greek culture, Antiochus sought to eliminate the most distinctive religious characteristics of the Jewish people: circumcision, dietary restrictions, Sabbath observance, and exclusive worship of one God. He made laws forbidding these practices, executing those who persisted. The Temple in Jerusalem was rededicated to Zeus, and a pig, a common Greek sacrifice (but considered an unclean animal by the Jews), was sacrificed on the high altar. To the faithful it seemed like the end of the world. They had been overtaken by a greater evil than they had ever known. Some Jews resisted, refused, and when they did, a terrible persecution followed. Many were killed, including women and children. It was a time of great suffering, leading to the wars of the Maccabees (recounted in 1 and 2 Maccabees).

Yet the real problem of suffering is never the suffering itself, but rather how to explain it. The deepest anguish, even death itself, can be borne if one knows why one suffers. The traditional answer to the question of suffering was that Israel suffered because of sin: God was punishing and purifying the people. This had been a useful explanation, allowing the people of Israel to recover from the devastation of the exile in 587 BCE when in one swoop they lost the kingship, the temple, the land, and the prophets. This explanation was still given during the new suffering under Antiochus almost four hundred years later, and it was still effective, since few humans can claim to be without sin. Yet the explanation had one serious flaw: it did not explain why this suffering affected only certain people in Israel. Sin might cause suffering, but would that explain who was suffering? It was precisely not the "sinners" who suffered, because those willing to forsake their ancestral faith and go along with these foreign ways were rewarded. Only the faithful suffered. How could one explain that? The Devil.

Jews began to see history as a cosmic power struggle between God and the Devil, and for mysterious reasons the Devil was prevailing. It would not always be so, they concluded; this evil age would (soon) be brought to an end, and a new age of righteousness would dawn. The age to come would be the opposite of this age.

Traditionally Jews had thought of God as the creator and supreme ruler of the world who had given Israel clear rules to be followed. Those who followed these rules could expect to prosper, and it was even thought that one could tell how righteous people were by how blessed they were (with material goods, children, health, reputation). Any future judgment would only confirm what was already obvious.

But in this new view things were seen differently. Although God was the supreme ruler, Satan was in control of this age; and although the rules were clear, there was a sense that they were not adequate. People could keep the rules and still be corrupted by this age. Things were not clear, and those who appeared righteous might not be; and those who appeared unrighteous might have a hidden righteousness. The new age might well bring about the complete reversal of present status, for "the first shall be last and the last first."

Modern scholars have labeled this dualistic worldview **apocalyptic** or *apocalypticism*, but different scholars use these terms with different meanings. The root meaning of both terms is an uncovering of hidden things, a revelation. For some comparisons between this and traditional Jewish views, see Table 1.2. At its most general level, apocalyptic thinking anticipates the near end of the present age and the dawning of a new age, all under the direction of divine forces. This dualistic thinking influenced many in the first century, including even Greek and Roman authors, and we will return to it when we discuss Paul (Chapter 3) and particularly the Book of Revelation (Chapter 14).

The goal of this chapter has been to provide a general introduction to the kinds of people who formed the first audience for the New Testament. They had many of the same concerns that we do, but they experienced those concerns in a different cultural setting, with a different worldview and a different sense of who they were. Who they were depended on their status, deriving from their class, wealth, honor,

---

TABLE 1.2   CONTRASTS BETWEEN TRADITIONAL JEWISH VIEWS OF THE WORLD AND APOCALYPTIC VIEWS

Traditional Jewish Views	*Apocalyptic Views*
God is seen as the creator and lawgiver, completely in control of the world.	God is seen as remote from the world, with evil foes controlling everyday life.
The world is good, though humans do not always live rightly.	Something has gone radically wrong; the world is evil and needs renewal.
The difference between good and evil people is clear, and rewards and punishment are meted out. Things are as they appear.	Truth is hidden; the wicked prosper while the good suffer. Things are the opposite of what they appear. One cannot judge by outward appearances.
People are judged by their deeds, and future judgment will only confirm present experience.	People are judged by their intentions, and future judgment will reverse present experience: the first shall be last.
The future will be like the past, a restoration of a former ideal.	The future will be radically new, and the old world will be completely destroyed, probably by a war between the forces of good and evil.
These ideas are prominent in the works of the prophets, as well as Proverbs and Deuteronomy.	These ideas are prominent in the book of Revelation, the Gospels, and Paul.

and group identity. They identified themselves by outward markers, not by inward conviction. Thus family and a network of friends were of utmost importance. Many children, especially boys and especially in the cities, would receive at least a basic education and apprentice in a career. Marriage and children were expected to follow at the appropriate time. The theater, sports, music, the bath, and festivals provided entertainment. What we call *religion* was everywhere and affected every activity. Giving the proper honor to all, human and divine, was a central virtue. And as one could hope for assistance from human patrons, so too one looked to the divine for rescue from life's trials. But just as your friends could sometimes become your adversaries, so too the Gods could sometimes become opponents. With many Gods, this was easy to imagine. But the Jews had only one God, and they imagined something quite different: the Devil. And with the Devil, a whole new worldview emerged, a dualism of good and evil and a dualism of this age and the age to come. Many felt they lived at the dawning of the new age.

LEARNING ON YOUR OWN

REVIEWING THE CHAPTER

Names and Terms

apocalyptic	honor
dualism	monotheistic
exile	piety
Hellenistic	polytheism

Issues and Questions

1. Why are all the New Testament documents written in Greek rather than in Hebrew?
2. Describe the Roman social order.
3. What were the three major factors that determined a person's status?
4. What were the rights and responsibilities of parents in a Roman family?
5. Describe a typical Roman home.
6. What did city residents do for leisure and recreation?
7. How did the Greco-Roman picture of the divine world reflect the social and political world in which they lived?
8. Why did people in the ancient world feel a need to be "saved"?
9. What two forms of monotheism existed in the Greco-Roman world?
10. How does the Devil fit into a monotheistic system?

TAKING THE NEXT STEP

The best treatment of Roman life is Casson, 1998. Also excellent, but a little uneven, is Bell, 2000. The former is a series of short essays done as case studies; the latter is more encyclopedic. Next, the more specialized work of Osiek and Balch, 1997, is an invaluable study of family dynamics. The best treatment of Palestinian society is Hanson and

Oakman, 1998. For the broader Hellenistic world, and especially urban culture, see Stambaugh and Balch, 1986, which provides an excellent overview of history, travel, economy, social organization, and city life. For an advanced treatment of the social order see Stegemann and Stegemann, 1999.

For dictionary-type definitions of various ancient **cultural values**, see Pilch and Malina, 1993.

Topics for Special Studies

For general strategies and research tools useful for New Testament study see Appendix A, "Doing Your Own Research." Each chapter will conclude with a selection of topics and resources that will enable you to advance your study as far as your interest takes you.

The Origin and Development of Hellenistic Culture

One of the most readable treatments of the ancient world and its bearing on the New Testament is that of Freyne, 1980. A good introduction to the history is Leaney, 1984. See also Bruce, 1969; Lohse, 1976; and Reicke, 1968.

The standard reference is the *Cambridge Ancient History*. For primary sources on the period, see Austin, 1981. A finely nuanced treatment of the period is Sandmel, 1969; see also Sandmel, 1978b, and Rhoads, 1976. For an Israeli perspective see Schürer, 1973–1987. For the effects of Hellenism on the Jews, see Hengel, 1974. Pomeroy, 1991b, explores women's history in antiquity. For a substantial treatment of the economy, see Rostovtzeff, 1986, and Finley, 1973; Applebaum, 1976, considers Jewish economic issues. For the Maccabean struggle against Antiochus IV, see Harrington, 1988.

Life in a Greco-Roman City

For a study of a **specific city**, good resources are available. For **Corinth** see Murphy-O'Connor, 1983; Cadbury, 1931; Engels, 1990; and Witherington, 1995. For **Ephesus** see Koester, 1995; Friesen, 1993; Tilborg, 1996; and Strelan, 1996; see also the bibliography in Oster, 1987. For **Antioch** see Brown and Meier, 1983; Downey, 1961; Haddad, 1949; Liebeschutetz, 1973; Bennett, 1975; Meeks and Wilken, 1978; and Wallace-Hadrill, 1982. **General** works that treat these and other cities include Finegan, 1981; Bean, 1966; Harrison, 1985; and Yamauchi, 1987.

Social Organization and Class Structure

Good treatments of the ancient **social order** include Osborne, 1987; Garland, 1989 (Greek); MacMullen, 1974 (Roman); and Gardner, 1993 (Roman, advanced). Blok and Mason, 1987, treat gender issues. White and Yarbrough, 1995, explore the social world of the first Christians. For an exemplary study of life among the elite, see Jones, 1984.

Honor and Shame

The basic work on Mediterranean societies is Gilmore, 1987. See also Pitt-Rivers, 1963; Peristiany, 1965; and Schneider, 1971 (on women and resources). The best work on the New Testament has been done by Malina; you might start with his work on Jesus and the Gospels (1996, 1993); also see his preliminary work (1981) and the handbook coauthored by Pilch and Malina (1993). Also important are Horrell, 1999, and Matthews, Benjamin, and Camp, 1996. For a critique of this approach see Downing, 2000.

For specific application to New Testament writings see Hendrix, 1984 (Thessalonians); deSilva, 1998 (Corinthians), 1995, and 2000 (Hebrews); MacDonald, 1996 (Pastoral Letters); and Neyrey, 1998 (Matthew).

Patronage

Standard treatments include Gellner and Waterbury, 1977; Wallace-Hadrill, 1989; and Eisenstadt and Roniger, 1984. Both Malina, 1996, and Moxnes, 1988, treat patronage in relation to the Gospels. Crook, 2004, treats it in relation to Paul's conversion. There are also useful discussions in Davis, 1977, and Jones, 1984; also see the reading guide by J. H. Elliott, 1987.

Everyday Life: Family, Work, and Leisure

The best treatment of **family** structures in early Christianity is Osiek and Balch, 1997; but also see Moxnes, 1997. On the Roman family see Rawson, 1986, 1991 (marriage and divorce); Dixon, 1992; Kretzer and Saller, 1991; Hallett, 1984 (fathers and daughters); Bakker, 1994 (religion and family); MacIver, 1971 (family as government); Lewis, 1994 (Egypt); Jenkins, 1986 (Greek and Roman life); Garnsey, 1991 (child rearing); Saller, 1994 (patriarchy); Laiou, 1993 (consent); Walker, 1993 (women and housing); Veyne, 1987 (private life); K. C. Hanson, 1989 (kinship structures); Cohen, 1993 (Jewish family); and the bibliographic essay of K. C. Hanson, 1994.

On the nature and practice of **slavery** see Bradley, 1994, 1987, 1989; Finley, 1980; Tucker, 1982 (women); Kyrtatas, 1987 (Christian); and Osiek's bibliographic essay, 1992.

On the place of **children** in the family and the practice of child abandonment see Dixon, 1992, and Rawson, 1986; see also Lefkowitz and Fant, 1992:87, 100.

Works on aspects of **everyday life and customs** include Jeremias, 1969; Carcopino, 1940; Veyne, 1987; and Clarke, 1963 (higher education). On **travel** see Casson, 1974, and McCasland, 1962. For an excellent discussion of **housing** with abundant illustrations see Clarke, 1991; other good sources include Rawson and Weaver, 1997; Zanker, 1998; and Wallace-Hadrill, 1988.

On vocational training and **working** conditions see Jenkins, 1986 (an overview); Hoch, 1980 (on Paul); Lewis, 1994 (Egypt); Grant, 1977 (early Christianity); Cohen, 1993 (Jews); Lefkowitz and Fant, 1977 (women); and G. R. Watson, 1969 (Roman soldiers).

For **sports** in the ancient world see Harris, 1985; Olivovba, 1985; and Polaikoff, 1987; for Greece see Miller, 1991; Sweet, 1987; and Kyle, 1987 (advanced); for Rome see Balsdon, 1969.

Aspects of Greco-Roman Religion

Probably the best introduction today is Martin, 1987. See also Grant, 1953. The best comprehensive treatment is Beard and others, 1998. Good **sourcebooks** are MacMullen and Lane, 1992; Rice and Stambaugh, 1979; and Ferguson, 1980; and on the **mysteries**, Meyer, 1987. On **popular religion** generally see Teixidor, 1977; MacMullen, 1981; and Beard, 1989. On **magic and astrology** see Faraone and Obbink, 1991; Graf, 1997; and Cumont, 1960. On **mystery** religions see Finegan, 1989, and Ulansey, 1989. Other useful general works include Seltzer, 1989; Ferguson, 1970; Attridge and Oden, 1984; and Nilsson, 1925. For religion in the Roman **army** see Helgeland, 1978, and Birley, 1978. Malina, 1986b, offers a social science perspective on religion in Paul's world. Kraemer, 1979, considers ecstatic religions; Goodman, 1994, looks at conversion and proselytizing. Crook, 2004, provides a new anthropological perspective on conversion. Lieu, North, and Rajak, 1992, examine Jewish life amid paganism. On the **emperor** and religion, see Price, 1984; see also Schowalter, 1993; Botha, 1988; and Kraybill, 1996. On the diversity in these see Cohn-Sherbok and Court, 2001.

See further bibliographies at the end of Chapters 4 and 13.

Additional Books and Articles

The major **primary sources** for the study of this era include:

Apostolic Fathers
Apuleius, *The Golden Ass*
Cicero, *Letters*
Diogenes Laertius, *Lives of Eminent Philosophers*
Eusebius, *History of the Church*
Josephus, *The Antiquities of the Jews; Autobiography; Jewish War*
Philo of Alexandria, *Collected Works*
Plutarch, *Lives*
Suetonius, *The Lives of the Caesars*
Tacitus, *Annals; Histories*
Vitruvius, *On Architecture*

All are available in convenient English translations in the Loeb Classical Library (Harvard University Press). Both the works of Josephus and Philo have now been issued in one-volume format by Hendrickson Publishers; although those are based on dated translations, the editors have endeavored to update them. The convenience (and affordability) of this format more than offsets these limitations. Relevant extracts from these and other documents are conveniently available in Robbins, 1989; Barrett, 1971; Kee, 1984; and Horsley, 1981.

More specialized collections of **primary sources** include the following. On **history**: Austin, 1981; Novak, 2001; Bagnall and Derow, 1981; and Sherk, 1988. On **daily living**: Shelton, 1987; Wiedemann, 1981 (slavery); DeLaine and Johnston, 1999; Kraemer, 1988 (women's religion); and Snyder, 1989 (women writers).

On the **Jewish sources**: See the section on Jewish literature in Appendix A, "Doing Your Own Research." A good collection is Baron and Blau, 1954. Stone, 1984, introduces the variety of apocrypha, pseudepigrapha, and sectarian writings. See also Glatzer, 1969, and Montefiore and Loewe, 1974. For a brief description of the many, often obscure Jewish sources from this era, see the appendix to Stone, 1980. Whittaker, 1984, has collected references to Jews and Christians in Greco-Roman writings.

Major **collections** include the following. On Dead Sea Scrolls: Dupont-Sommer, 1962; Vermes, 1968; and Gaster, 1976. On the Essenes: Vermes and Goodman, 1989. On New Testament Apocrypha: J. K. Elliott, 1994; Hennecke and Schneemelcher, 1992 (1963); and James, 1924. On the pseudepigrapha: Charlesworth, 1983, 1985; and Charles, 1913.

2

THE STORY BEFORE
THE WRITINGS

Storytelling in Earliest Christianity

A STORYTELLING CULTURE

HOW THE STORIES OF JESUS WERE TOLD

THE ORAL STORIES OF JESUS

LEARNING ON YOUR OWN

 Any serious person, when dealing with serious matters, will be reluctant to expose them to envy and misunderstanding by committing them to writing. In a word, then, we can know that when we see a person's written works . . . these are not that person's most serious concerns, that is, if the person is a serious person.
PLATO, *SEVENTH LETTER*

Perhaps the most shocking fact about Jesus, given his enormous influence on later generations, is that he left nothing in writing. Only one story preserved about him shows him reading (in a synagogue, Luke 4:16), though several stories show him asking others whether they have not read something in the Law or Prophets (for example, Matt. 12:5; 19:4; 21:42; Mark 12:26). Thus it is plausible that he could read, but he apparently saw no need to write. All of his teaching and leading was done by word of mouth. Jesus was an oral communicator.

Oral communication was common in an age when the vast majority of people were illiterate. We do not have hard data, but a high estimate of literacy would be 20 percent of the males in a large city. Rates would decline sharply for towns and villages. Female literacy might be half that of males. Thus anyone wishing to address the masses needed to do so orally. An overall estimate might be 5–10 percent (Harris, 1999:272).

There are several reasons for the high rates of illiteracy (no system of public education, little social mobility, no economic advantage), but the bottom line is that reading was unnecessary for most people for most activities. On the rare occasions when something needed to be read or written, individuals could hire scribes. In an oral culture, the ability to speak well and to tell good stories was far more important than literacy.

There was even a *preference* for the oral word over the written. A later writer tells us a story about an early second-century Christian who, although he had copies of the Gospels, gave more credence to the oral stories being told by people who had heard them from the original disciples:

> *For I did not suppose that information from books would help me so much as the word of a living and surviving voice. (Eusebius* Ecclesiastical History *3.39.4)*

There is also a small detail preserved in the New Testament. At the end of the letter known as Second John, the writer adds:

> *Though I have much to write to you, I would rather not use paper and ink, but I hope to come to see you and talk with you face to face, so that our joy may be complete. (2 John 12)*

We get a better feel for the writer's mind with a more literal translation: "I do not wish to do it with black marks on a papyrus sheet; but I hope to be with you and to sound things out mouth to mouth, that our joy may be full." Mouth to mouth communication by the living voice was always the ideal.

The central role of stories in such a culture is easy to imagine. Centuries before Jesus, the Greek philosopher Plato had tried to imagine how we might build an ideal city, and he set forth his vision in dialogue form in *The Republic*. He recognized the way stories control the way we construe the world and our place in it, and he proposed strict control over storytelling:

> We must begin, then, it seems, by a censorship over our storymakers, and what they do well we must pass and what not, reject. And these stories on the accepted list we will induce nurses and mothers to tell to the children and so shape their souls by these stories far rather than their bodies by their hands. But most of the stories they now tell we must reject. (1.177)

Plato understood that nurses and mothers did far more to shape their charges than the physical shaping (of heads, noses, and penises, which they regularly molded by hand massage); they shaped by their stories. Fortunately no one ever achieved the degree of censorship Plato advocated, and a vast profusion of stories were told.

Some were popular stories. When the emperor Claudius died, people told how his death had been forecast by omens: the lightning that struck his father's tomb, the comet that clearly foretold the death of the leader. Things did not just happen, they were part of a larger plot: all of life was a story.

A STORYTELLING CULTURE

Numerous tales were told to entertain; many have survived in various collections. Often they were about faraway places, daring exploits, or grotesque events. One such tale concerned the steward of a large estate who was entrusted with all of his master's property. His wife discovered that he was having an affair with another woman. Enraged, she first destroyed all his account books and everything she could collect from the storeroom. Finally, she killed herself and her infant son. The master was so upset with his erring servant that he ordered him arrested, then had him stripped and smeared with honey and tied to an old fig tree in which a large colony of ants made their home. There he hung until those murderous creatures picked him quite clean. The dry white bones may be seen hanging there to this day, they say.

Such storytelling ran the gamut of human activities from education, where the stories of Homer's *Iliad* were the basic text, to politics, religion, travel, and entertainment. Professional storytellers would be hired to entertain after dinner parties and other special events. Thus, storytelling was an integral part of all aspects of life. One important function of stories was to teach basic lessons about life and the world we live in, such as the error of speaking too freely.

Once there was a philosopher named Secundus, who was called Secundus the Silent because he never spoke. The reason for his silence was a very grave mistake he made as a young man. Having studied philosophy abroad, he adopted the Cynic philosophy and became a vagabond. (**Cynics** believed that society was repressive and sought liberty in the violation of social conventions.) He let his hair and beard grow, and when he returned home neither the servants nor his mother recognized him. His Cynic teachers had taught him that all women were corrupt; the ones considered chaste were only those who had not yet been discovered. He decided to test this idea by trying to arrange a tryst with his mother. When he succeeded, he shamed her by revealing his identity. Unable to bear the disgrace, she hanged herself. Then

Secundus decided that too many evils resulted from free speech and took a lifelong vow of silence.

This silence was his way of attaining the goal of freedom that lay at the heart of most of the religious movements and philosophies of the world, each propounding some special way to achieve it. The Cynic pursued freedom from the cares of life by seeking only what was available in nature. To be natural was everything. This goal was epitomized in a story about Diogenes, the first to call himself a Cynic (literally, a dog). The story goes that the great king Alexander came upon Diogenes basking in the sun and offered to grant him anything he desired. "Then stand aside," replied the philosopher, "so I can see the sun."

As Cynics aimed at freedom through being natural, the **Stoics** took the opposite approach: total self-control. They believed that the universe was rational and orderly (as seen in the order of nature) and that humans possessed this same rationality and could order their lives or their death by it. When Seneca, who had been tutor to the emperor Nero, fell out of favor, he withdrew completely from public life and offered to turn over his large fortune to Nero. But soon he was suspected of participating in a plot to unseat the emperor. Told of his death sentence, Seneca took matters into his own hands. Using a sharp dagger, he cut various veins on his arms and legs and, while bleeding to death, called in his scribe and dictated eloquent discourses. Then, frustrated by the slowness of death, he prevailed upon his physician for a poison, such as had been used on Socrates. But the bleeding had apparently so slowed his circulation that the poison had no effect. He then instructed his slaves to carry him into the hot bath, where he revived enough to die. His last act was to splash some water on a slave near him and exclaim, "I offer this liquid as a libation to Jupiter the Deliverer." (See the complete story in Tacitus *Annals* 15.62–69.)

Such a story shows the Stoic ideal of being absolute master of one's emotions. Perhaps your fate could not be changed, but you could approach it rationally and with inner peace. This too is freedom. Stoics chose the active life, accepting all that comes with it, and welcoming all whether it seems good or bad, grounded in the conviction that reason undergirds all. The other way to peace was to try as much as possible to avoid the complications of the active life. This was the path of the Epicureans.

Epicureans sought freedom by withdrawal from the uncertainties of life, though they would have stated it more positively. Epicurus was a materialist (he believed only in the reality of material things) and a hedonist (he believed that the greatest good was to seek pleasure). The only goal of life was to seek the greatest pleasure, defined as the elimination of bodily and mental suffering. Now some things that seem to bring pleasure are only short-lived or lead quickly to suffering. Drinking wine, for example, is a pleasure, but indulgence leads to pain. Marriage may seem pleasant but inevitably brings much suffering. Even speaking in the public assembly causes more pain than pleasure. The wise man avoids all these and much else. The wise man will not fall in love, seek public recognition, worry about death or funeral rites, punish his slaves, engage in sexual indulgence, marry or raise a family, engage in politics, become a wanderer, or worry about the future. Epicurus taught that death was nothing but cessation of feeling, and therefore not to be feared. He met his own death calmly.

In his seventy-second year he developed a painful blockage of his urinary tract, leading to an infection. After a couple of weeks, he prepared to die. He finalized his will, wrote a letter to a friend, then climbed into his bronze bathtub filled with warm water, drank strong wine, and talked with his friends, encouraging them to remember what he taught, till he died. Here is the letter:

On this blissful day, which is also the last of my life, I write this to you. My continual sufferings . . . are so great that nothing could increase them; but I set above them all the gladness of mind at the memory of our past conversations. But I would have you, as becomes your lifelong attitude to me and to philosophy, watch over the children of Metrodorus.

Such is the story they tell of Epicurus.

The philosopher-mathematician Pythagoras had died centuries before, but his ideas experienced something of a revival in the first century—a kind of new-age blend of philosophy, magic, and mysticism. We label this movement **Neo-Pythagoreanism**, for it was a revival of ancient Pythagoreanism. Pythagoras had discovered the mathematical basis of the musical chords, calculated the movement of the stars, and invented geometry. What all these have in common is the idea of proportionality, of harmony. Harmony was the secret to life. Numbers took on a mystical aura. Within each living being was a fragment of the divine, and each sought harmony with the other—with like seeking like. The main hindrance to this harmony was the body with its appetites and passions. These must be overcome. All disharmony with nature, with the universe, and with the spirit within must be eliminated. Thus Pythagoreans avoided eating animals or even wearing leather or wool. They studied the stars to learn their harmony. They developed music and practiced disciplines of prayer and ecstasy.

The Pythagorean reverence for all life is reflected in one of the several stories told about the death of Pythagoras. According to Diogenes Laertius's *Lives of Eminent Philosophers* (VIII:44), it seems Pythagoras was being pursued by armed men and the only escape route would involve running across a field of beans. Rather than destroy the beans, he halted, was caught, and killed. The story seems to have been regarded as fictitious even in antiquity, but it emphasizes one aspect of the Pythagorean quest for harmony.

Stories like these were told in all sorts of settings: in schools, at parties, over dinner, at an inn, or simply while walking down the road. We easily forget how time-consuming travel was in the ancient world—and how boring. A good traveling companion who knew many stories was valued highly.

The earliest Christian stories were heard in such an environment. I tell you these stories about philosophers not because Jesus propounded a philosophy but because people were accustomed to hearing about the lives and teachings of such folk. Before we begin the study of the writings of these early believers, we need to understand something of the stories behind them. In this chapter we will sketch in broad outline the development of early Christianity and consider some of the evidence of how the stories of Jesus were preserved and used. Then we must probe these stories to learn why they constituted good news (which is what *gospel* means). We will see that the basic shape of the Jesus story as a narrative of Jesus' words and deeds, culminating in his death and resurrection, reflects the oral proclamation of the church.

To tell these stories and to interpret Jesus to their audiences, these believers made use of certain models, or ideal figures drawn from earlier Jewish tradition—models such as Messiah and Son of God. We will examine five such models and see how they helped interpret Jesus. Finally, we will try to reconstruct the elements of the basic story of Jesus in the various ways it was probably told in the years immediately after his death. This is a tentative enterprise because no written sources are available from this period. But that the story was *told* is certain, so we can know, or at least guess, something about that story and its tellers.

STORYTELLING AMONG THE FOLLOWERS OF JESUS

Jesus and his disciples had taken dinner at the house of a friend. As they reclined at the table, a woman unexpectedly anointed Jesus with a large amount of very costly oil—in the manner of anointing a king. The disciples were shocked at her extravagance. But Jesus came to her defense:

> *She has done a beautiful thing to me. . . . Wherever this gospel is preached in the whole world, what she has done will be told in memory of her. (Matt. 26:6–13, RSV)*

And so for more than nineteen hundred years her story has been told (but ironically omitting the name of the woman whose memory it celebrates). The story itself holds the clue to its own preservation. Notice the two verbs: *preached* and *told*. A fundamental aspect of early preaching was telling stories, and these stories were part of the earliest proclamation of the gospel.

This is not surprising. Such storytelling was an integral part of Jewish culture long before, and long after, the first century. Nearly a thousand years before Jesus, for example, a prophet in the royal court, a man named Nathan, had to confront King David on critical charges: adultery and murder. Avoiding a direct approach, Nathan told a story about two men and a pet lamb (see 2 Samuel 11–12). The king was taken in by the story and condemned himself. This power of a story to take one in makes it an effective tool for those who would persuade others.

THE EARLY STORIES OF JESUS DEVELOP

That Jesus himself told stories of a most remarkable kind seems certain. These stories are called **parables**. No one before had ever told stories quite like them, and they provide some of our most authentic information about Jesus. In the parables we find an intense expectation of the coming of God's kingdom and a challenge to see that kingdom in the little things of life: the little seed, the woman making bread, the farmer hiring day laborers. Most importantly, the parables see God's rule as already present, albeit hidden:

> *The kingdom of heaven is like yeast that a woman took and mixed in with three measures of flour until all of it was leavened. (Matt. 13:33)*

Jesus himself seems to have been an enigmatic figure, little understood by his contemporaries. Even his closest followers admit that they did not understand him till after his death and after their further experiences (see John 14:26; 16:12–13; Mark 9:9–10). This discrepancy between the understanding of Jesus before his death and the understanding afterward is at the heart of the problem of discovering what scholars call *the historical Jesus*, because all our sources embody the later understanding. This problem will be easier to address after we have studied the Gospels, so we will reserve discussion of the issues for Chapter 14. What follows here is a brief summary that can be defended on the basis of historical arguments.

One clear thing about Jesus is that he did not fit neatly into expected categories. He showed great religious zeal yet associated with some of the least religious elements in his society. He had been baptized by John but went off on his own, apparently not making baptism a part of his own activity. He gathered an enormous crowd of followers, taking twelve—symbolizing the number of the original tribes of Israel—into an inner circle. Abandoning his own family, he encouraged his followers to do the same, forming an itinerant band that moved about Galilee (mostly) and Judea (a bit). Many sorts of people traveled with him—including some wealthy women who provided financial support.

His most characteristic activities seem to have been healing the sick—including the expelling of demons—and teaching about the reign of God. In fact, a critical part of his approach was the claim that it was the presence of God's reign that allowed for the healings. How could demons be expelled unless the power of their ruler had already been overcome? (see Mark 3:22–27). He does not seem to have addressed, except under pressure from others, what was considered the major issue of the day: how to respond to pagan Rome, which was the new ruler of Palestine, the sacred land.

Jesus did not live long. He probably died in his thirties after a career of only a few years—perhaps even as short as one year. According to the most likely version of the story, he challenged the power elites (both religious and political) by attacking the procedures of the Temple in Jerusalem at the highly charged festival of the Passover (the feast that celebrated Israel's freedom from foreign oppression). He was arrested by the religious authorities but died, ironically, at the hands of the Romans under a charge of insurrection. But that was not the end.

His followers burst forth with an extraordinary energy, telling all who would listen about this Jesus. They believed he was still alive (1 Cor. 15:4–5) and had overcome death (Acts 2:24); some claimed he was still with them (Matt. 18:20) while others said he had ascended into heaven and sat at God's right hand (Luke 24:51; Acts 2:32–33; 1 Pet. 3:21–22). They saw his words and deeds in a radically new way, believing that all the promises in their Bible had come true in him. We know little about those early days; not a single written source has come down to us from the first two decades after Jesus. This was, however, a period of development of a profuse oral tradition (for a chart of these developments see Figure 8.3, page 264).

The first written sources appear around 50 CE: the letters of Paul. Though Paul has left us more records than any other early Jesus follower, we know surprisingly little about him. He seems to have been born in Tarsus, a Greek city in what is today eastern Turkey. He was Jewish, perhaps the son of a Jewish slave who had been taken in war and carried off to Tarsus. If so, his father was an industrious person, probably a leather craftsman, who gained his freedom and, with it, a claim to Roman citizenship for his children. This is not certain, however.

Paul received a good education, in both the Greek and the Jewish traditions. Some say that as a young man he went to Jerusalem, where his father's sister may have lived, to complete his Jewish studies. In any case, this young Paul bitterly opposed those followers of Jesus who were proclaiming Jesus to be a new way to God. But in the process of this opposition Paul himself was transformed—called, he believed, to carry the news of this Jesus to the Gentiles. He began to travel and to proclaim Jesus.

There must have been dozens of people like Paul, though we know little about them. They left little documentary evidence, because they operated primarily in an oral medium, telling stories. Even Paul—who never actually tells stories in his letters—seems to have been familiar with such stories. For example, when he had a problem at Corinth with how to celebrate the Lord's Supper (Communion), he responded to it as follows:

> *The Lord Jesus on the night when he was betrayed took a loaf of bread, and when he had given thanks, he broke it and said, "This is my body that is for you. Do this in remembrance of me." (1 Cor. 11:23–24)*

He added more details, but this sample is sufficient to see that he was familiar with a story about Jesus' last meal and used it to meet a problem. Further, he expected his hearers at Corinth also to know the story. This is not surprising, for it seems very likely that stories of Jesus' Last Supper with his disciples were told repeatedly whenever his followers gathered to celebrate that meal in Communion. Most of what Paul did is hidden from us because he too operated primarily as an oral teacher. Fortunately for us, he sometimes had to resort to writing.

There would have been hundreds of stories like this about what Jesus did, and many more stories retelling those he told; a great number were later written down in various collections. When and where they began to be written is not easy to discover. The ones we possess (the four Gospels) all date from the last third of the first century, but there is reason to suspect earlier sources, many of which were quite different from the four Gospels. (See the discussion in Chapter 8.)

Yet the quest for written sources overlooks the most important fact about these earliest believers: they lived in an oral culture. Stories about Jesus existed long before there were any written Gospels. Before trying to reconstruct some elements of these oral stories, we will consider the more basic question: Who were these storytellers in the decades between Jesus' time and the writing of the Gospels?

THE EARLY STORYTELLERS

Let us reconstruct the situation. Jesus lived in Palestine and probably spoke Aramaic, a language related to Hebrew. In his time, Aramaic was the native tongue for the people of Palestine, Syria, and Babylon. Many of these people (and possibly Jesus) also spoke Greek, and many Jews could at least read Hebrew (which Jesus probably did). Most of the Jesus traditions would have developed in this setting—primarily Aramaic, with some Greek and Hebrew—and many of the sayings seem to have an Aramaic background.

Nevertheless, all four New Testament Gospels were written in Greek, for by the time they were written the story of Jesus had spread to all the major cities of the Roman Empire, and many, perhaps most, of his followers were Gentiles.

The years between the time of Jesus and the writing of the Gospels were a time of tremendous change, when the stories about Jesus crossed profound barriers of language, geography, and culture. This translation was very complex: not only did the storytellers have to find Greek words with which to express the ideas, they also had to make the stories relevant to their Gentile hearers. This may be seen in minor and major details. People in Palestine, for example, understood the special significance of the fig tree, but when the saying was translated for other regions the teller simply said "every tree" (compare Mark 13:28 with Luke 21:21). It made sense in Palestine, where dirt-roofed houses were common, to speak of digging through the roof (Mark 2:4), but Greco-Roman houses had tiled roofs, and the story was translated accordingly (Luke 5:19). At the other end of the scale, certain Jewish categories such as *Messiah* and *Prophet* would not make sense to Gentiles, so new categories, such as *Lord* and *Savior*, had to be developed. Trying to trace such transformations is a fascinating, though inconclusive, endeavor. We will consider more details when we study the Gospels. But who were the people responsible for this monumental work? Who were the tellers of these stories?

On the one hand, the answer is everybody. Earlier, we saw how common storytelling was in this ancient culture. Surely people told the stories of Jesus as they walked on the road (Acts 8:39), sat at dinner (2:46), stood in the marketplace (17:17), and worked at their trades (18:3), among many other activities. Though Paul's letters preserve the names of some of these people, we know little else about them.

Although individuals remain obscure, we do know something about the kind of people they were. When Paul was having some difficulty maintaining order in one of his churches, he chided:

Now you are the body of Christ and individually members of it. And God has appointed in the church first apostles, second prophets, third teachers; then deeds of power, then gifts of healing, forms of assistance, forms of leadership, various kinds of tongues. (1 Cor. 12:27–28)

The ranking that Paul gives here was probably widely accepted (for a somewhat different list, see Eph. 4:11). Though we can no longer be sure of the precise function of each office, the first three, which are explicitly numbered, are reasonably clear.

Apostles were those "sent," the root meaning of the term. In this case they are sent by Jesus as his representatives. Though tradition gives this title especially to the twelve disciples, Paul clearly counted himself among those commissioned and sent by the risen Christ—and thus an apostle (Rom. 1:1; 1 Cor. 9:1–2). And Paul cited other apostles (1 Cor. 15:7), including a woman (Rom. 16:7). as well as some who claimed the office but whom Paul regarded as undeserving of it (2 Cor. 11:13; 12:11). Understood to be Christ's emissary, the apostle possessed a very powerful authority, an authority Paul exercised continually (1 Cor. 4:9; 9:1–2; Philem. 8; 1 Thess. 2:6). When we read Paul's letters, we must understand that they were the letters of an apostle (as he asserts in every letter but Philippians).

Prophets also had a special relation to Christ; through them the risen Christ spoke to the community. Our clearest example of a New Testament prophet is the scene in Revelation 1 in which the risen Jesus appears to, and speaks with, the prophet John. Some of the early prophets are known by name (such as Agabus, Judas, and Silas— Acts 11:27; 15:32), others by some special designation (such as the four daughters of Philip—Acts 21:9), and many more only by allusion (Acts 13:1).

Because they were understood to be inspired by the same Spirit as the ancient prophets, they had the special task of studying the writings of these earlier prophets for their testimony to Christ (1 Pet. 1:10). Unlike the apostles, prophets continued to be active well into the second century, as works like the *Shepherd of Hermas* and the *Didache* (pronounced DID-uh-kay) show. A major issue in late first-century and early second-century works is to distinguish between true and false prophets.

The office of **teacher** seems more prosaic than those of apostle and prophet since it depended less on inspiration and more on hard work. It involved high authority and great responsibility (James 3:1). The model for this office was twofold. Jesus was the model teacher; in fact, half the New Testament references to the word *teacher* concern Jesus. There were also teachers in the synagogues. Though the exact work of the teachers is hard to determine, they were probably responsible for instructing new converts and gathering groups of disciples whom they trained to carry on their work. Teachers were probably the most sedentary of the three groups. Apostles and prophets seem to have imitated the nomadic lifestyle of Jesus.

Apostles, prophets, and especially teachers would have told stories about Jesus as they went about their tasks: preaching, leading worship, teaching new believers, debating with those who disagreed, celebrating events, justifying their behavior, and so on. In these typical life situations the individual stories were told and retold until someone wove them into a connected narrative—a gospel. Though the process by which the Gospels were put together remains obscure, one interesting theory has emerged from a careful study of the sermons in the book of Acts.

HOW THE STORIES OF JESUS WERE TOLD

Out of the myriad of stories of and about Jesus that no doubt once circulated, only the few preserved in the Gospels remain. Written in the last third of the first century, thirty-five to sixty years after Jesus, they represent the culmination of years of telling and retelling, of forgetting and inventing, of condensing and elaborating. The Gospels are a veritable patchwork of such stories, woven together in beautiful and daring ways to produce a larger story. Yet these patches, the individual units of tradition, existed long before the Gospels were written. Like the story of the woman with the oil, they were told while proclaiming the gospel. The Gospel writers shaped this material, developing it into a larger story.

GIVING SHAPE TO THE STORY

On the day of Pentecost, the story goes, Peter was inspired by the Spirit and stood up to proclaim publicly his faith in Jesus, who had been executed some two months earlier.

> *Jesus of Nazareth, a man attested to you by God with deeds of power, wonders, and signs that God did through him among you, as you yourselves know—this man, handed over to you according to the definite plan and foreknowledge of God, you crucified and killed by the hands of those outside the law. But God raised him up, having freed him from death, because it was impossible for him to be held in its power. For David says concerning him, . . . you will not abandon my soul to Hades, or let your Holy One experience corruption. (Acts 2:22–28)*

This short synopsis of the first public proclamation about Jesus may or may not represent what Peter actually said that day, but it surely characterizes the preaching typical of that first generation.

Four characteristics of that proclamation are worth noting: first, it is wholly devoted to telling about the person Jesus; second, it focuses on his death and resurrection, which form the core of the proclamation; third, the death and resurrection are set within the context of what Jesus had done (especially the "mighty works"); and fourth, the whole is enhanced and confirmed by appealing to the Hebrew Scriptures, which are said to refer to Jesus. By this appeal to Scripture the story of Jesus was extended backward to the time of beginnings. Later we will see that by connecting the resurrection with the new age, the storytellers also extended the story forward to the end of the age. Ultimately, the story of Jesus encompasses all human history.

Now let us fill in the outline that Peter's sermon provides us: we must not imagine that ancient speakers would be content with a general allusion to Jesus' mighty deeds. They would tell the stories. A sermon of that period might last for an hour or two, so there was ample time to elaborate (see Acts 20:7). So too, the stories of Jesus' betrayal, trial, and death would be told. It seems likely that these stories formed a connected sequence well before the present Gospels were written, for the sequence is remarkably alike in all four. Many scholars believe that the general shape of the Jesus story as it came to be recorded in the Gospels was developed by the generation of preachers whose pattern is evident in this excerpt from Acts. We must be careful not to assume that this earliest preaching was identical with the present content of the Gospels. As we will see, the present Gospels are products of the late first century, and each transformed the story of Jesus to fit the situation it addressed. Yet some basic story of Jesus' life, death, and resurrection is presupposed in the earliest Christian literature we possess. It seems likely that the shape of the earliest Jesus stories is reflected in the summaries of apostolic preaching found in Acts (namely, mighty deeds + suffering + death + resurrection). We see then that the first generation left its mark on the shape of the story of Jesus; they also provided much of the specific content of that story. Although we have no writings from this earliest period, we can find traces of them in later writings. We will now try to reconstruct some of the meaning they found in Jesus' words and actions.

FINDING MEANING IN THE STORY

For his earliest followers, the problem of understanding Jesus was twofold. How could they make sense of all the different aspects of his life? And how did understanding Jesus help with understanding life? These were not easy questions, and many different answers emerged.

To understand Jesus his earliest followers made use of three sources: memories of what Jesus had said and done, insights from living prophets who claimed ongoing contact with Jesus through the Spirit, and ideas and patterns drawn from the sacred Jewish witings that are now part of the Bible and were then called the Law and the Prophets. These three interacted in dynamic and surprising ways.

For example, Jesus' words and deeds emphasized the coming of God's reign, indeed, actualized that coming. For when a demon was overcome, God's rule actually triumphed. According to the Scriptures, the agent for God's coming kingdom was the Messiah. Therefore, Jesus must be the Messiah. But Jesus had not established a kingdom; he had not expelled the foreign oppressor; he had not become king. This confusion is illustrated in a story set in the time immediately after Jesus' death.

Two of Jesus' followers are traveling in the days after the crucifixion. As they walk along, they are joined by a third person who gets them to tell him stories about Jesus. They conclude their stories by saying, "We had hoped that he was the one to redeem Israel." His death seems to have destroyed that hope. The stranger, whom the reader knows to be Jesus, replies:

> "Oh, how foolish you are, and how slow of heart to believe all that the prophets have declared! Was it not necessary that the Messiah should suffer these things and then enter into his glory?" Then beginning with Moses and all the prophets, he interpreted to them the things about himself in all the scriptures. (Luke 24:25–27)

Notice how their experience of Jesus causes them to read the Scriptures in a new way and how their reading of the Scriptures causes them to understand Jesus in a new way. Try to imagine how this worked.

READING AND REFLECTION

Imagine you were a follower of Jesus and were confused and disappointed at his death. Now read Isa. 52:13–53:12. Imagine having seen the crucifixion, then read Psalm 22. What ideas in these passages seem to describe Jesus and make sense of his death?

Understanding Jesus was a two-way process: what they read in the Scriptures helped them interpret what Jesus said and did; and the words and deeds of Jesus reshaped the meaning formerly attached to the Scriptures. Thus Psalm 22 helped interpret the desolation of Jesus, making even his nakedness meaningful (Ps. 22:18). At the same time, their experience of Jesus gave new meaning to the psalmist's telling God's praises to "the ends of the earth" (Ps. 22:27; see Matt. 28:18–20).

We can see this same two-way process at work in one of our earliest statements about Jesus, probably a fragment from a traditional story that Paul quoted in the opening of his letter to the Romans, where he claims to be a servant of

> the gospel of God, which he promised beforehand through his prophets in the holy scriptures, the gospel concerning his Son, who was descended from David according to the flesh and was declared to be Son of God with power according to the spirit of holiness by resurrection from the dead, Jesus Christ our Lord. (Rom. 1:1–4)

In addition to the conscious use of Scripture and the appeal to the Jesus tradition (the resurrection), we see here an appeal to certain paradigms or models (Son of God; descendant of David) to make sense of Jesus. We can gain a good sense of how some of Jesus' earliest followers understood him by examining the paradigms they applied to him. In each case we will explore the origin and meaning of the paradigm and then ask what it means to understand Jesus this way.

The Messiah

This is one of the earliest and most pervasive of the models used to interpret Jesus. The Greek word for messiah is *Christos*, which in time came to be treated as Jesus' second name: Jesus Christ. **Messiah**, meaning "the anointed," was originally applied to the high priest (Lev. 4:3) and then to the king (1 Sam. 9:16). It soon became a synonym for the king (Ps. 2:1–2), who was understood to have an eternal covenant with God: there was always to be a son of David to sit on the throne of Israel (2 Sam. 7:12–14; Ps. 89:3–4). But it did not happen that way.

When the Babylonians conquered Israel, they obliterated the monarchy. Centuries passed. Israel lived in subjection to the Gentiles, with no king (except for that usurper Herod, who was not even a full-blooded Jew, let alone a Davidite). Expectations grew that God would act, send the anointed, overthrow Gentile domination, establish the kingdom. This hope is vividly expressed in a pious work of the century before Jesus, *The Psalms of Solomon*:

> Lord, you chose David to be king over Israel,
>   and swore to him about his descendants forever,
>   that his kingdom should not fail before you.
> But, because of our sins, sinners rose up against us. . . .
> See, Lord, and raise up for them their king,
>   the son of David, to rule over your servant Israel
>   in the time known to you, O God.
> Undergird him with the strength to destroy the unrighteous rulers,
>   to purge Jerusalem from the Gentiles
>   who trample her to destruction. . . .
> There will be no unrighteousness among them in his days,
>   for all shall be holy,
>   and their king shall be the Lord Messiah.

> (Psalms of Solomon 17:4–5, 21–22, 32; quoted from Charlesworth, 1985)

The overthrow of evil and the establishment of divine rule is *what* the Messiah was expected to accomplish, but *how* he was expected to do this was never agreed upon. Some saw a divine warrior; at least two leaders of rebellions against Rome (Judas the Galilean in 6 CE and Simon bar Kochba in 135 CE) were each acclaimed as the awaited Messiah. Others viewed the coming Messiah as an essentially religious figure, as did the Jews who wrote the Dead Sea Scrolls. Some expected a heavenly figure; others a mortal man. We will examine this great diversity of opinion in more detail when we study Matthew's Gospel.

What, then, did it mean to associate Jesus with this paradigm of the Messiah? The implied story is one of the coming of God's rule, or kingdom, and the associated overthrow of evil. If there were early political versions of the story, suggesting the overthrow of Roman rule, there is little evidence of them in the sources that survive. Probably the paradigm was itself reevaluated based on what Jesus actually did and said. For just as the understanding of Jesus was shaped by this paradigm, the meaning of the paradigm was transformed by the experience of Jesus. What had been conceived of as a political transformation was now understood as a spiritual transformation. Israel might not be free from Roman power, but Jews could be free from the power of "the evil one" (see Matt. 6:9–13). Stories of Jesus healing people or casting out demons would serve as visible demonstrations of this conquest.

Difficulties arose in associating this model with Jesus. Even though Christians redefined the meaning of the Messiah, people continued to expect a new David (or son of David), an earthly king. But instead of destroying the wicked, Jesus himself had suffered and died—a fate never associated with the Messiah before the development of Christianity. Further, the political implications of the Messiah's victory over evil had subversive connotations, for Messiahs tended to be rebels fighting against the power of Rome. In addition, this messianic idea was unique to Jews; Gentiles were not expecting a messiah. As this new movement spread among Gentiles, the Messiah concept had limited power to explain Jesus, because the concept itself had first to be explained to those outside Israel. Although the paradigm of the Messiah explained much about Jesus, it left other things obscure. Other paradigms were needed, especially to explain his suffering.

The Suffering Servant

This enigmatic figure arises out of the complex prophecies of Isaiah. Four songs celebrate the fate of the servant of Yahweh: he would bring justice to the nations; bring light to the nations; bring healing and forgiveness; and, most of all, he would suffer (see Isa. 42:1–4; 49:1–7; 50:4–11; 52:13–53:12). But the servant's suffering would be redemptive: for "with his stripes we are healed" (Isa. 53:5).

In their original context these songs seem to have been an attempt to explain the harsh suffering of Israel's exile: it was not for sins but for the healing of the nations. One song explicitly identifies the servant and Israel:

> And he said to me, "You are my servant, Israel, in whom I will be glorified." (Isa. 49:3)

But in the long history of this tradition, the servant became an ideal type—God's perfect servant. And in the experience of these early believers, Isaiah seemed to describe exactly the fate of Jesus:

> He was despised and rejected by others; a man of suffering and acquainted with infirmity. . . . Therefore I will allot him a portion with the great, and he shall divide the spoil with the strong; because he poured out himself to death, and was numbered with the transgressors; yet he bore the sin of many, and made intercession for the transgressors. (Isa. 53:3, 12. Read the whole song.)

This paradigm made sense of the most difficult aspect of the Jesus tradition—his suffering—and transcended the Messiah title in another way: it pointed to the Gentiles, the nations, as the object of healing and forgiveness. It is no accident that the first story in Acts to portray an outreach to Gentiles uses this paradigm: Philip uses the passage about the **suffering servant** to tell an Ethiopian eunuch "the good news of Jesus" (Acts 8:26–35; see also 1 Cor. 15:3; Phil. 2:7; Matt. 12:18–21; Mark 1:11).

On the positive side, this model showed Jesus' suffering to be part of the divine plan, purposeful and redemptive. Yet the suffering servant ideal focused almost exclusively on the death of Jesus and tended to limit his significance to the past. It lacked a way to deal with his life and teachings; other paradigms were needed.

Wisdom

When we encounter a particularly insightful teacher, we tend to comment on how intelligent or brilliant that person is. Not so for the ancient Jews. They were more apt to comment on how fully the person embodied wisdom or how effective the teacher was at bringing wisdom into the world. The task of teachers was the discovery and explanation of true wisdom. Teachers did not invent wisdom; wisdom existed independently and eternally. Although this eternal wisdom could be thought of as a thing, some went further and pictured **Wisdom** as a person, someone who calls out to humans and offers them understanding. Wisdom could even be pictured as a divine companion:

> *Does not wisdom call,*
> *   and does not understanding raise her voice? . . .*
> *I, wisdom, live with prudence,*
> *   and I attain knowledge and discretion. . . .*
> *By me kings reign,*
> *   and rulers decree what is just;*
> *   by me rulers rule,*
> *   and nobles, all who govern rightly.*
> *I love those who love me,*
> *   and those who seek me diligently find me.*
> *The* LORD *created me at the beginning of his work, . . .*
> *When he established the heavens, I was there, . . .*
> *   then I was beside him, like a master worker;*
> *   and I was daily his delight, rejoicing before him always,*
> *   rejoicing in his inhabited world and delighting in the human race.*
> (Proverbs 8)

This wisdom is not merely an object that one might attain; Wisdom is a subject, a person, who might come to you. In fact, Wisdom has repeatedly come into the world but has seldom been recognized and accepted. Only the wise have responded.

For some this seemed an apt paradigm to describe their experience of Jesus. Jesus was seen as not only having a special wisdom (for example, Matt. 13:54); Jesus was seen as *being* Wisdom:

> *To those who are the called, both Jews and Greeks, Christ the power of God and the wisdom of God. . . . He is the source of your life in Christ Jesus, who became for us wisdom from God, and righteousness and sanctification and redemption. (1 Cor. 1:24, 30)*

This paradigm had the great advantage of emphasizing the words and deeds of Jesus and of portraying Jesus as a revelation of the divine. That Jesus was not accepted and that he was taken up to God's side are also accounted for in this paradigm (see, for example, 1 Enoch 42:1–2, quoted in Chapter 12, page 403). Such a paradigm would also make sense to many others besides Jews, for similar wisdom traditions were known in Egypt, Syria, Babylonia, and other places.

You may have already noticed one possible difficulty with this paradigm: Wisdom is always portrayed as female, for both the Greek and Hebrew words for wisdom are feminine. Of course, for some early storytellers, this may have been a strength. Some women may have developed these ideas as a way to talk about Jesus that included the feminine, as some contemporary women do. But in the dominant tradition, ideas associated with wisdom migrated toward more male-centered models. (See the discussion of the introduction to John's Gospel in Chapter 12.)

The Final Prophet

Although a few individuals in Israel continued to claim prophetic inspiration, the great age of prophecy ended hundreds of years before the time of Jesus. But there were traditions that included the idea that prophecy would once again flourish in the last days (see Joel 2:28–32, used explicitly by early interpreters in Acts 2:14–21). More especially, there were traditions based on the saying in Deut. 18:15 that God would send another prophet like Moses, in fact, a second Moses. This new prophet would renew the revelation from God and restore God's people to holiness. As Moses marked the beginning of Israel's life, so the new Moses would mark a new beginning. He would inaugurate the reign of God.

A related notion was based on the tradition that another prophet, Elijah, did not die but was instead carried off by God (2 Kings 2). Some thought he would return in the last days to witness and to restore God's people (see Mal. 4:5–6; 3:1). We should not imagine that these traditions were firmly fixed. There was great variety. Matthew apparently knew a tradition that included the return of Jeremiah (Matt. 16:14), and John saw two prophets returning before the end (Rev. 11:3–13). Some stories tell of Jesus talking to Moses and Elijah (Mark 9:2–13 and the parallel accounts in Matthew and Luke).

Some Christians identified Jesus as the new Moses (Acts 3:23; 7:37) or used extensive symbols associated with Moses to present Jesus (Matthew 1–7). The image of Jesus as the **final prophet** was widely used in later writings by Jewish followers of Jesus (for example, the *Preaching of Peter*, see pages 209–11). It had the advantage of emphasizing the message of Jesus but failed to explain adequately his suffering and death. Nor did it address his ongoing relation to the community; for that, another paradigm proved useful.

The Son of God

It is not clear just how and with what meaning this title was applied to Jesus. One of the earliest occurrences is the statement quoted by Paul and cited above: "designated Son of God . . . by his resurrection from the dead" (Rom. 1:3). Does this mean that Jesus was revealed to be the Son of God by his resurrection or that he was appointed to that status by virtue of the resurrection? Did he always hold that status, or was it a new position he achieved? The original Greek wording is capable of both meanings.

The affirmation **Son of God** had different meanings for different people in the first century. Generally speaking, the Greeks were more concerned with the category of *being* (and thus were likely to understand the quotation from Paul's letter to the Romans above in the first sense of "revealed"), whereas the Jews thought more in terms of *doing* (and were therefore apt to understand these words in the second sense of "appointed"). To people of the Gentile world, influenced by Greek traditions, the title *Son of God* implied someone of divine descent, usually known through his teaching and wonder-working powers—a sort of divine man whose divinity was evident in his words and works of power.

To Jews, the title *Son of God* meant something quite different. Often it was used as a designation for Israel as God's son (Exod. 4:22–23; Hos. 11:1; notice Matt. 2:15), or for the king as the representative of the people (2 Sam. 7:14; Ps. 2:7). It was also used more broadly for the pious or righteous person (Sir. 4:10). In this regard we note that the expression *servant of God* (Greek *pais*) could also mean "son of God" (Acts 3:13, 26). For Jews the expression *son of* often carried the basic meaning of "having a resemblance to." Just as the "sons of thunder" are those with a thunderlike quality (Mark 3:17, with Luke 9:54), so *son of God* may describe someone with a godlike quality—a pious person.

The difficulty with such a title would be the different interpretations various communities would give it. Outside a Jewish milieu it could easily lose its connection with Jesus' life and come into conflict with Jewish monotheism.

No paradigm was perfect. None matched precisely what Jesus had actually done. Still such models were useful, for each explained something about Jesus. Although a particular community may have emphasized one over the others or may have used one exclusively, most used them together, piling one on another:

> God foretold by the mouth of all the prophets, that his Christ should suffer. . . . Moses said, "The Lord God will raise up for you a prophet from your brethren as he raised me up. . . ." God having raised up his servant [pais], sent him to you first, to bless you. (Acts 3:17, 22, 26, emphasis added; the Greek word pais can be understood as either servant or son.)

The dynamic interaction of these various paradigms, along with other scriptural models, the remembered words and deeds of Jesus, and the revelations of community prophets, constituted the vast body of oral Jesus tradition that would have been known to the hearers of the documents we are about to study. These traditions would be shaped into stories that assisted the hearers in making sense of Jesus and of the world they lived in.

THE ORAL STORIES OF JESUS

We simply do not know the many ways these early believers told Jesus stories. We have only the hints of the speeches in Acts, the implications of Paul's practice drawn from his letters (which are not stories but do presuppose stories), and the later development of gospels of various kinds. Thus, we cannot trace the precise stories of Jesus as they were told in this earliest period. Still we can do something more elemental: we can draw out the implications of how stories are told and apply them to what we know of the oral Jesus tradition. All stories, whether profound or trite, religious or secular, have certain basic elements in common.

What, then, are the elements of a story? Think about the story of Little Red Riding Hood. It starts with the straightforward task of our heroine trying to deliver lunch to her grandmother, but she is opposed by the wolf, who nearly subverts her mission. But victory is snatched from near defeat with the aid of the noble woodsman. We see here three central aspects of a story:

A purpose: a task is ordained to be done.
A commitment: someone rises to the task.
A conflict: adversaries and helpers intervene.

All stories revolve around these three elements. Think about the story of the Exodus from Egypt (Exodus 3–14). The purpose involves the freedom of the Hebrews from Egypt; the commitment is made by Moses; the conflict involves Pharaoh and his magicians on the one side and the assistance of Aaron and the plagues on the other. Notice that the conflict involves things (the plagues) as well as persons. We can see these as three stages in the development of a story: the stage of need, the stage of commitment, and the stage of conflict.

Conflict is central to every story, and this simple outline helps us to see that conflict exists on two levels: there is the primary conflict of the hero attempting to perform the task ordained and the secondary conflict between the hero and those (people and forces) in the story that would prevent the task being done. At this secondary level there are also secondary heroes, helpers who provide the hero with the assistance needed to overcome the forces of opposition. A fourth stage, resolution, is implied in every story but is not always dramatized.

We have then a simple model for how stories are constructed, which we can set forth visually:

	Basic Story Elements
Task/Lack	
Agent	
Conflict	
Opponents	
Proponents	
Resolution	

It will not always be as easy to identify these story elements as this chart suggests, but it is a useful exercise to try to see how individual stories work.

READING AND REFLECTION

Read, analyze, and chart the story of the good Samaritan in Luke 10:29–37 according to this model. Who needs to receive something? Who delivers it? With what assistance or resistance?

Unlike many stories, the story of the good Samaritan dramatizes the thing lacking: a traveler is beaten and left for dead. Who will rise to the challenge of helping him? Two characters fail to accept the challenge, implying that there must be danger in the situation. A new and unlikely character, a foreigner, accepts the challenge but must then perform the task, which leads to the next stage, the struggle (here, loading the man on the donkey, carrying him to the inn, providing for his keep). The stage of resolution or success (in this case, healing) is only implied in the story in Luke.

Once we see how these stories work, we can begin to notice other things about them. When we chart the story of Little Red Riding Hood and the story of the good Samaritan we can observe a basic difference between them. In the fairy tale, good overcomes evil by superior power, and evil is destroyed; in the parable, good overcomes evil by self-sacrifice. We may refer to the former as a story of justice, in which people get what they deserve, and to the latter as a story of mercy. This tension between justice and mercy pervades the New Testament stories.

If we chart the version of the Jesus story, which we discern in the proclamation of Peter (Acts 2), we find that it is basically a story of mercy. Thus:

	Peter's Story of Jesus
Task/Lack	The people need forgiveness
Agent	Jesus
Conflict	
Opponents	The people, who oppose and kill him
Proponents	His mighty works and resurrection
Resolution	Forgiveness is available

Although we do not know what was actually said, we can make some inferences about the incidents used to tell this story. Given the task, we can conjecture that the actual telling of the Jesus story implied in this brief synopsis would have contained incidents that demonstrated God's intention to redeem Israel. It seems that citing Scripture was the primary means of showing this purpose, and we would expect incidents to be developed that show how Jesus' deeds corresponded to scriptural foretelling. We might also expect incidents that show Jesus accepting the challenge, though he might be tempted to turn aside. Finally, the conflict implies many stories of Jesus' confrontation with the people and a strong emphasis on powerful deeds that demonstrate God's power with Jesus. These versions of the story would focus on the people's opposition resulting in Jesus' death, portraying the resurrection as a vindication of Jesus as God's agent. This is not the only way the story could be told.

Paul's letters, our earliest Jesus literature, contain little that can be properly called a story of Jesus. That is not what the letters are about; they are not proclamation. They serve, rather, as instruction to those who have already heard and responded to the proclamation. However, we can catch some glimpse of Paul's proclamation in these words to the Galatians:

Now before faith came, we were imprisoned and guarded under the law until faith would be revealed. Therefore the law was our disciplinarian until Christ came, so that we might be justified by faith. But now that faith has come, we are no longer subject to a disciplinarian, for in Christ Jesus you are all children of God through faith. As many of you as were baptized into Christ have clothed yourselves with Christ. There is no longer Jew or Greek, there is no longer slave or free, there is no longer male and female; for all of you are one in Christ Jesus. (Gal. 3:23–28. See also the synopses in Rom. 3:21–26 and Phil. 2:5–11.)

There is obviously much left unsaid in this excerpt, and the story grows even more complex when we look at the related passages, which speak of Jesus as "a sacrifice of atonement" and as "emptying himself," taking "the form of a slave" and becoming "obedient unto death." If we try to imagine how these motifs might be fitted into the story chart, we might find something like this:

	Paul's Story of Jesus
Task/Lack	All people lack righteousness
Agent	Jesus
Conflict	
Opponents	Power of sin
Proponents	Jesus' death; faith
Resolution	Righteousness is available to all

God wishes to send righteousness to all people—Jew and Gentile, slave and free, male and female; Jesus becomes the agent of that righteousness; he was resisted by the power of sin but triumphed through his death. This is very elementary, but even so we learn something by this exercise.

If we compare this pattern with the one from Acts given above, we can draw several conclusions. This story about Jesus being God's agent to bring righteousness to all differs somewhat from the one we deduced from Peter's preaching. In Paul's story God wishes to bestow something on "all," not just on Israel but also on the Gentiles. What is to be bestowed is spoken of as "righteousness" rather than as forgiveness. And the power of the story lies in Jesus' death rather than the resurrection. It seems that people told the story in different ways right from the earliest times, depending in part on their purpose in telling the story.

The other major force in this early period was James. We have a letter that might be from him (see Chapter 7 for a discussion), but it says virtually nothing about Jesus. We also have a short speech attributed to him in Acts 15:13–21. I'll abbreviate:

> *My brothers, listen to me. Simeon has related how God first looked favorably on the Gentiles, to take from among them a people for his name. This agrees with the words of the prophets. . . . Therefore I have reached the decision that we should not trouble those Gentiles who are turning to God, but we should write to them to abstain only from things polluted by idols and from fornication and from whatever has been strangled and from blood.*

There is not enough here to reconstruct a story, but we can see that the elements we can identify are different yet.

	James' Story of Jesus (from Acts)
Task/Lack	Gathering a people for God from the Gentiles
Agent	(unstated)
Conflict	
Opponents	Those who require circumcision
Proponents	Simeon's previous speech
Resolution	Require only basic purity laws

Again, a different context and concern produces a different story. Different contexts and insights probably lie behind the various models or paradigms discussed earlier. Each represented a distinctive way of telling the Jesus story. Each would characterize him and his task in its unique way, providing great flexibility and variety in the verbal delivery. This variety alerts us to be constantly concerned, not only with the story but also with the tellers of the story and their historical and social settings. Their charter stories, which provide the basic justification for how they live, will exhibit strong correlations with their community stories and personal stories.

These stories of Jesus responded to the same concerns as the other stories of the time: What is freedom? How can fate be overcome? How can we live happily in the world?

Now let us try to imagine how these storytellers told their stories. Some of you will prefer to go directly to the stories of Jesus recorded in the four Gospels. You can proceed straight to Chapter 8. This has the advantage of showing how the stories of Jesus grew over time. I prefer a more historical approach, beginning with our earliest writings. So if you proceed directly to Chapter 3, you will meet first the great apostle, Paul, whose letters traveled to his communities when he could not. Written to be read aloud in the assembly, these letters must be heard as well as seen. As we hear them, we must listen for the underlying story of Jesus in Paul's proclamation and try to grasp the basic story of the world as he and his followers understood it (Chapters 3–5). For as these people heard the story of Jesus, they became participants in it, creating in turn a larger story that included their own lives. Next we will consider other letters, written by those who looked to Paul and those who did not (Chapters 6–7). Then we will turn to the narrative literature, the Gospels and the Apocalypse (Revelation), to see the many ways the Jesus story developed in the late first century (Chapters 8–13). Finally, we will bring our discussion full circle and consider the story after the writings, studying the processes of collection and exclusion that produced the New Testament canon (Chapter 14). At that point, we will step back from the immediacy of the individual writings to view their underlying unity. We will raise the question of history more abstractly, especially as it pertains to the historical Jesus, and discuss the relation of history to story. This is a lengthy endeavor. Yet we may regard it not so much as work as a mystery to be explored, a story to be heard. All that follows is designed to help you hear the story more clearly than you otherwise might. Listen.

LEARNING ON YOUR OWN

REVIEWING THE CHAPTER

Names and Terms

apostles	Neo-Pythagoreans	Stoics
Cynics	parable	suffering servant
Epicureans	prophet	teacher
final prophet	Son of God	Wisdom
Messiah		

Issues and Questions

1. How do the stories told about the great philosophers reveal their understandings of how a person could obtain freedom?
2. How did the early Christians' stories about Jesus reflect the practices of storytelling in their culture?
3. What forces shaped the form and content of these earliest stories about Jesus?
4. How do the five early paradigms each interpret a vital aspect of Jesus for his earliest followers? Why was no one paradigm completely satisfactory?

Scholars have invested an enormous effort in attempting to reconstruct the understandings of Jesus that were current before the writing of the Gospels; I will discuss their methods of reconstruction in detail in Chapter 8, where you will find further resources listed. The effort to go behind all these reconstructions and say something about what Jesus himself was actually like is called "the quest for the historical Jesus"; for a discussion and bibliography see Chapter 14.

TAKING THE NEXT STEP

Reconstructing how early followers interpreted Jesus in the time before the Gospels and before Paul is a difficult task, with only a general consensus among scholars. Three very helpful attempts, each quite different, are Dahl, 1976 (see also Dahl, 1991); Fredriksen, 1988; and Crossan, 1998. They would make a very interesting comparison.

For general resources and information on how to begin New Testament research, see Appendix A, "Doing Your Own Research."

Topics for Special Studies

Nearly any aspect of the ancient world could be profitably studied for the insight it might give into the lives of early Christians. Browsing through general works like the following will provide many leads: Balsdon, 1969; Brilliant, 1979; Carcopino, 1940; Garland, 1989; Jenkins, 1986; Robbins, 1989; Shelton, 1987; and Veyne, 1987.

Orality Studies

How do oral cultures work? How is oral speech different from written literature? What changes accompanied the shift to written tradition? When, where, and why did writing develop?

The theory that the oral preaching of the early believers shaped the story of Jesus is argued by Dodd, 1951. Kelber, 1983, highlights the power of the oral gospel even while challenging the easy continuity between the oral and the written. The topic was summarized in Dewey, 1995. See also the references on rhetoric at the end of the Introduction (page 24).

The seminal works on orality include the following. On theory: Ong, 1982 (see also Ong, 1967, 1977). On Greece: Havelock, 1963, 1982, and 1986. See also Lentz, 1989, and Havelock and Hershbell, 1978. For a more recent overview see Achtemeier, 1990. For a substantive discussion of the issues see Silberman, 1987.

Other helpful works include Wansbrough, 1991; Boomershine, 1979; Cullmann, 1950 (on Jesus); Bauman, 1975; and Kelber, 1987 (on oral communication); and MacDonald, 1986 (on miracle stories). Gerhardsson, 1961, argues for a more memorized tradition.

On writing: Boorstin, 1983, provides a broad overview. More specialized works include Clark, 1990; Roberts and Skeat, 1984; Reynolds, 1974; and Cameron, 1990. For a modern view see Bolter, 1991.

On literacy and illiteracy: start with Harris, 1989, and the wide ranging responses to Harris in Beard et al., 1991, and Hanson, 1991. The broader concern of how books were used is addressed in Gamble, 1995. For the Greek era see Lentz, 1989.

History of the Jesus Tradition
How was Jesus viewed by his earliest followers? How did the Jesus tradition develop over time? How far back can specific traditions be traced? What did it mean to call Jesus a Messiah (or one of the other paradigms)?

I know of no good introductory treatment. See the specific studies in tradition criticism by Fuller, 1980, and Hultgren, 1979.

In addition to the works listed at the beginning of "Taking the Next Step," others have tried to trace the developing understanding of Jesus: Cullman, 1963; Dunn, 1980; and Hengel, 1983.

The theory that the shape of the Gospels was determined by the structure of early Christian sermons is known as the *kerygmatic* (care-rig-MA'-tic) *hypothesis*, from the Greek word for preaching, *kerygma*. See Dodd, 1951.

Paradigms and Models of Righteous Deliverers
General issues and a variety of paradigms are traced by Nickelsburg and Collins, 1980. See also Dunn, 1980. On the influence of ideas about angels on the developing understanding of Jesus, see Gieschen, 1998, and Stuckenbruck, 1995.

On expectations about the **Messiah**: Perhaps the best overall work is Collins, 1995. On the messiah in the scrolls, see also Priest, 1963. For a critical Jewish analysis, see Neusner, 1984b, and Neusner, Green, and Smith, 1987. Older works that are still useful include Klausner, 1955, and Mowinckel, 1956.

The symposium edited by Charlesworth, 1992, provides a useful overview of what is agreed on and what is contested.

On the **suffering servant**: Manson, 1966; Page, 1985; Hooker, 1959; Zimmerli, 1965; and de Jonge, 1991. See also Bellinger and Farmer, 1998.

On the **final prophet**: Davies, 1945; Horsley and Hanson, 1986; Hooker, 1997; and Webb, 1991. For Paul's view see Moessner, 1983; see also Moessner, 1982, 1990; de Jonge, 1990; and Longenecker, 1981.

On the **Son of God**: Byrne, 1979; Hengel, 1976; and Lindars, 1984.

On **Wisdom**: Hammerton-Kelly, 1973; Kloppenborg, 1987; Suggs, 1970; Sandelin, 1986; Johnson, 1974; Scott, 1992; and Schüssler Fiorenza, 1994.

Philosophers and Their Ideas
Analyze the life of a philosopher. How did a particular philosophy address the concerns of the era? How did the various philosophies compare and contrast on a particular issue?

For a general overview see Grant, 1953; Long, 1974; MacMullen, 1966; Warner, 1958; and Jordan, 1987.

On **Stoicism**: Rist, 1978; White, 1983; and Hazlitt and Hazlitt, 1984.

On **Epicureanism**: Clay, 1984, and Dewitt, 1954.

On **Cynicism**: Malherbe, 1984, 1970; O'Neil, 1977; and Downing, 1988.

On other schools: Bowersock, 1969; Vogel, 1962; Gorman, 1979; and Wolfson, 1947.

History of the Era

What did the Roman historians say about early Christianity? See Talbert, 1987; Wallace-Hadrill, 1984; Bruce, 1974; and Wilken, 1984. See also the primary sources: Tacitus, *Annals*; Suetonius, *Lives of the Twelve Caesars*.

How did ancient historians view the period? See Josephus in: Rhoads, 1976; Stone, 1984; Schwartz, 1990; and Feldman and Hata, 1989. For a bibliography see Feldman, 1986.

On Philo: Stone, 1984; Wolfson, 1947; and Kasher, 1985.

On Eusebius: Chesnut, 1977; Grant, 1980; and Williamson, 1965.

Additional Books and Articles

For an additional bibliography on Jesus and the development of the tradition see Theissen and Merz, 1998, and the resources at the end of Chapter 14.

3

THE EARLIEST JESUS LITERATURE

 True understanding of an oral culture pulls one out of our typographic culture.

WALTER ONG, PRESENCE OF THE WORD

Why no literature about Jesus from the first two decades after his death has come down to us remains a mystery. Perhaps none was written. Perhaps what was written was of inferior quality. Perhaps the oral tradition, discussed in Chapter 2, was so strongly felt that it seemed inappropriate to write. Perhaps some archaeologist will yet turn up something from that age.

The earliest such literature we have was written around the year 50 CE. It is not a story but a letter written out of the very practical concern of a traveling teacher who was unable to return to some of his followers. It is not a story, but notice that to explain it I have to begin to tell you a story about who wrote it and why. As discussed in the Introduction (pages 10–12), every letter implies a story that we can think of as having three levels: the explicit story about the occasion of the writing (the story of the audience), the implicit story of the life of the writer (the story of the author), and the underlying story on which the ideas and advice of the letter are based (the story of Jesus). We will seek to uncover these story levels as we examine the letter. We begin by examining the letter for its literary structure, its historical context, and its major teachings; we will then consider its relation to a second letter addressed to the same group but possibly written by someone else. This possibility will lead us to discuss the meaning of authorship in the ancient world.

Now for the first level of the story. The traveling teacher was Paul, who had been a follower of this new way for about fifteen years. Paul was a tradesman, a leather worker, who traveled from city to city, and as he did he spread the word of this new tradition. He had founded an assembly (as they called their meetings) in Thessalonica, a thriving seaport city in northern Greece (Macedonia) (see Figure 3.1). Paul felt uneasy about these new followers. He had not been able to spend as much time in Thessalonica as he had wanted to, and, even more serious, most of his converts had been Gentiles who lacked the Jewish background necessary to understand Paul's teachings. Unable to return, he sent one of his companions, Timothy, to check on the Thessalonians. When Timothy returned, probably to Corinth (about two hundred miles to the south), Paul was moved to write this letter, sometime in the late 40s or very early 50s. (We have no secret source of information about these details; they are all either stated or implied in the letter itself. See 1 Thess. 2:17–3:10.) We will return to this level of the story below, but first let's look at how the letter itself is constructed.

A LITERARY ANALYSIS OF FIRST THESSALONIANS

Our study of Paul's first letter to the Thessalonians begins with a close look at its literary aspects. First we will examine its structure in relation to other ancient letters, then consider its rhetoric and listen for the story behind the words.

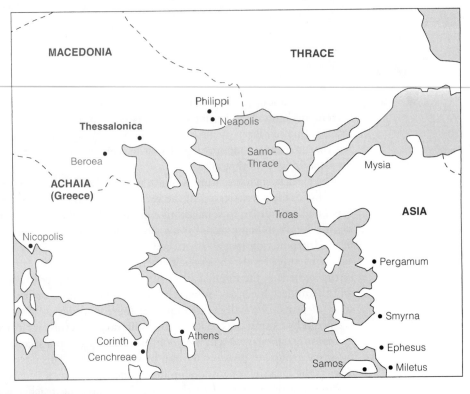

FIGURE 3.1 HELLAS What we call Greece, the ancients called Hellas. In Paul's day it consisted of two Roman provinces, Achaia and Macedonia. Unable to revisit Thessalonica, Paul sent Timothy. When Timothy returned (probably to Corinth) with a report on the situation there, Paul was moved to write them the letter we know as I Thessalonians.

THE SHAPE OF THE LETTER

The general structure of a letter in antiquity was fairly fixed, though there was some variety in kinds of letters (personal, business, government, and literary letters being the major types). Letters always began with the name of the sender, followed by the name of the receiver, and a greeting (often simply "health"). Then followed a personal section, often recalling some past association, and only then the reason for the letter, usually a request of some sort. Letters regularly ended with greetings to mutual friends and a closing wish. Here are two typical examples of personal letters: the first is written by a husband away from home on business and the other by a homesick military recruit trying to reassure his mother that he is well.

Damas, assistant, to Artemidora my sister [wife] greeting.
    Before all else I make supplication for you every day. Please come up to the metropolis at the New Year, since I am coming up to the city. Salute your mother and your father. I pray for your health.

ROMAN LEGIONARY STONE   Also known as a milestone, these 6-foot pillars were the ancient equivalent of the billboard. They were set up by the legions in honor of the emperor, extolling his greatness. This one, from Capernaum, dates from the late second century and honors the divine Emperor Hadrian. (Can you make out the end of his name in the last line?) The Romans built an awesome system of roads, connecting every part of their empire and greatly facilitating travel.

Apollinarius to Taesis, his mother and lady, many greetings.

Before all I pray for your health. I myself am well and make supplication for you before the gods of this place. I wish you to know, mother, that I arrived in Rome in good health on the 25th of the month Pachon and was posted to Misenum [to join the fleet] though I have not yet learned the name of my company; for I had not gone to Misenum at the time of writing this letter. I beg you then, mother, look after yourself and do not worry about me; for I have come to a fine place. Please write me a letter about your welfare and that of my brothers and of all your folk. And whenever I find a messenger I will write to you; never will I be slow to write.

> *Many salutations to my brothers and Apollinarius and his children and*
> *Karalas and his children. I salute Ptolemaeus and Ptolemais and her children*
> *and Heraclous and her children. I salute all who love you each by name.*
> *I pray for your health. (Hunt and Edgar, 1932:333, 303)*

Both letters follow a common pattern: there is a standard opening with the salutation "greeting." After alluding to praying for the recipient, the sender launches into the main reason for writing. A section of salutations to others precedes the formal closing, which concludes with another allusion to prayer. We can see a very similar pattern in 1 Thessalonians:

Paul began with the standard opening and greeted them (with "grace to you and peace" in place of "greetings," 1:1);
he alluded to praying for them (1:2);
he reminisced about their past association (1:3–3:13);
and then taught and exhorted them (4:1–5:22)
before closing with the wish for sanctity and grace (5:23–28).

The salutation to mutual friends, almost nonexistent in 1 Thessalonians (5:26), will be expanded in later letters.

It is possible to sketch a "standard form" for Paul's letters (based on Doty, 1973:27):

Opening
  Sender
  Receiver
  Greeting
Thanksgiving
  Often with a prayer
Main body
  Often begins with a formula ("I would not have you be ignorant" or "I appeal to you")
  Often ends with a reference to the near or ultimate future
Exhortations to good behavior
Closing
  Standard benediction ("The grace of the Lord Jesus be with you")
  Sometimes mentions the writing process

Two conclusions are evident. First, Paul's letters were similar to ancient letters generally. The hearers of these letters would have known what to expect and what to listen for, and they would have been guided by these expectations.

Second, there is a certain distinctiveness and innovation about Paul's letters. In addition to the specific references to Jesus introduced in the opening and closing, two major features stand out: the ethical exhortations at the end and the **thanksgiving** at the beginning (usually beginning with the expression "I [or we] give thanks"). Modern studies of these thanksgiving sections demonstrate that they are carefully crafted introductions to the main themes of the letters.

Finally, we should note that letter writing was taught as part of one's education, so that the patterns of rhetoric were also expected in letters. The Introduction outlined some of the patterns of rhetoric common in Paul's world (pages 13–14). Paul's letters are not formal rhetorical compositions, but as oral performances they needed to be effective. Thus we might expect to find rhetorical patterns overlaid on the letter pattern, especially the sequence: introduction, narrative, arguments, appeal, and conclusion (see Table 1.3 on page 16).

As you now read 1 Thessalonians, listen with ears attuned to ancient rhetoric. Pay particular attention to the introduction (the thanksgiving) for the way it sets the tone and themes of the letter. There is a particularly fine narrative review of Paul's interaction with the Thessalonians; try to figure out what purpose it serves.

READING AND REFLECTION

Read through the letter using the reading guide below.

1. For what does Paul give thanks?
2. What motifs or themes from the thanksgiving recur in the body of the letter?

READING GUIDE TO FIRST THESSALONIANS

Opening   1:1
Thanksgiving   1:2–5
Narrative review   1:6–3:13
Main body   4:1–5:11
   Preliminary exhortation   4:1–12
   Teaching section   4:13–5:11
      Beginning with a formula ("I would not have you be ignorant")   4:13
      Ending with reference to the ultimate future   5:1
Exhortations to good behavior   5:12–22
Closing   5:23–28

For a more detailed analysis see the perceptive study by Jewett (1986:71–78), which has influenced my own understanding of the rhetoric of the letter.

THE RHETORIC OF THE LETTER

Timothy's report on the developments at Thessalonica after Paul left had been encouraging, and Paul was exuberant that these new followers were doing so well. The dominant note of the letter is joy, and its primary literary feature is the thanksgiving. Paul gives thanks for three characteristics, their: (1) work of faith, (2) labor of love, and (3) steadfastness of hope (1:3). Faith-love-hope is a triad we meet often in Paul. Here the three characteristics provide the framework for the rest of the thanksgiving and the solution to two problems emerging at Thessalonica. Notice how they look to the past (faith), the present (love), and the future (hope), and how each of these joyful words has a companion of a different tone: faith/work, love/labor, hope/steadfastness (or endurance). This interplay between work and joy provides the moving force of the letter.

Paul used two similes (comparisons using the word *like*) to describe his relation to these Thessalonians; they echo this same duality and provide the dominant emotional orientation of the letter. On the one hand, he is "like a father with his children" (2:11). In Greek and Roman society a father was a stern taskmaster who demanded that his children fulfill their duties, learn their lessons, live up to their station in life. A father in this society had absolute control over his children, even the power of life and death. On the other hand, Paul described himself as being "like a nurse taking care of her children" (2:7). The nurse was the loving, self-sacrificing caretaker in this society. Paul sought to embody a gentle sternness and to elicit a labor of love.

This labor involves both the suffering with which the people embraced the faith (2:1–2, 14) and the physical labor required to earn one's keep (2:9 and 4:9–12). Paul bragged about the way they had accepted both his suffering and their own to attain this new faith. They had

> turned to God from idols, to serve a living and true God, and to wait for his Son from heaven, whom he raised from the dead, Jesus who delivers us from the wrath that is coming. (1:9–10)

Notice again the three temporal references: they turned in the past, serve in the present, and wait for a future. But there is more than one way to wait, and some at Thessalonica were waiting in ways that Paul viewed as destructive. What their problems were is not completely clear to us, but they were basically of two kinds: a passive waiting for the end that involved abandoning work and other normal activities (4:11; see also 2 Thess. 3:6), and something Paul refers to as ignorance—probably a faulty understanding of the end (4:13). Before we examine what that understanding was, we should consider the source of their information, the oral Jesus stories.

The Oral Tradition in the Letter

In responding to these concerns, Paul cited a fragment of the Jesus tradition about the coming end of the age. We can see how Paul used this tradition because another version of it has been recorded by another writer in the Gospel of Matthew. Writing much later than the time of Paul, Matthew included an extensive tradition, whereas Paul only alluded to a specific point. Yet we do find parallels:

1 Thessalonians 4:15–17	Matthew 24:29–35
For this we declare to you by the word of the Lord, that we who are alive, who are left until the coming of the Lord, will by no means precede those who have died. For the Lord himself, with a cry of command, with the archangel's call and with the sound of God's trumpet, will descend from heaven, and the dead in Christ will rise first. Then we who are alive, who are left, will be caught up in the clouds together with them to meet the Lord in the air; and so we will be with the Lord forever.	Immediately after the tribulation of those days the sun will be darkened and the moon will not give its light, and the stars will fall from heaven, and the powers of the heavens will be shaken; then will appear the sign of the Son of Man in heaven, and then all the tribes of the earth will mourn, and they will see the Son of Man coming on the clouds of heaven with power and great glory; and he will send out his angels with a loud trumpet call, and they will gather his elect from the four winds, from one end of heaven to the other.

Clouds, trumpet, angels, descent from heaven, and gathering of the elect all point to a common, though not fixed, tradition. Paul's use of that tradition is free, citing not quoting. (Of course, quotation marks were not invented till the fifteenth century, and even Matthew may have used the tradition freely.) Both Paul and Matthew employ the same tradition of the unexpected coming, "like a thief in the night" (compare 1 Thess. 5:2 with Matt. 24:42–44).

We might note in passing that the Greek word Paul used here to refer to Jesus' coming has become a technical term in scholarly literature. The word **Parousia** means to be present or, more specifically, to be present in an official way to exercise authority.

This comparison shows that aspects of the Jesus tradition were widely known in the world of Paul and his congregations, even if we cannot say in just what form. These traditions about the Parousia had probably been used in Paul's proclamation at Thessalonica and were now causing problems for the congregations. What really was the problem?

One intriguing suggestion is that the issue at Thessalonica stemmed from this same oral tradition about the end. That tradition, as preserved in Matthew, includes the assertion: "this generation will not pass away till all these things take place" (Matt. 24:34). This saying may have various interpretations but might raise an important question: If the end were so near, why should one continue to work? Also, some may have understood it to mean that believers would not die before the return of Jesus and the end of the age. Perhaps they thought that those who died had fallen from the faith or committed secret sin (compare 1 Cor. 11:30, where it is said that unworthy participation in the Lord's Supper can result in sickness or even death).

Further, these Gentiles would assume that those who die either cease to exist or pass on to another life. In either case they would not participate any longer in any events on earth. The Greeks generally considered humans as spirits or souls that escaped the body at death and went to a heaven or hell—a view we call belief in **immortality**. The Jews, by contrast, understood humans as a living union of body and soul and did not originally believe in a life for the soul beyond death until it was reunited with the body (of course, by Paul's time many Jews had been influenced by Greek ideas). Because this notion of **resurrection** was foreign to most Gentiles, they may have assumed that all who had died had missed out on the reign of God on earth.

Still, Paul had been gone from them less than a year, so it is unlikely that many had died or that there was any disillusionment caused by the failure of the end to come. We simply do not know the exact cause of their problem. However, their concern seems to have been with the fate of the departed rather than their own waiting. Thus, Paul started his explanation with the exhortation "that you may not grieve as others do who have no hope" (4:13). Paul assures them the dead will not miss out on the Parousia. But how did he know this?

It does not seem to be included in the Jesus tradition, at least not in the Matthean version available to us. And if it were already in the tradition, it would not have been a problem. Paul's logic seems to have worked like this: The tradition says that the Parousia will be a public event in which all the elect will be gathered (see Matt. 24:31). Since Jesus rose from the dead (4:14), we can now conclude that dead believers will also rise to join in the Parousia (4:16). This is a good example of how belief in Jesus' resurrection transformed the way these early followers understood his words and deeds. The sayings of Jesus take on a genuinely new meaning because of the conviction that Jesus rose from the dead. In this way the Jesus tradition was a living tradition, continually applied to new situations. It was this living and dynamic character of the oral tradition that made it so valuable to the early church, and so problematic for the modern historian who is trying to understand what Jesus originally said.

The Demands of the Future

Paul proceeded to build two further ideas on this oral tradition, both of which shift attention from speculations about the future to the more immediate concern of life in the present.

The first is a traditional idea, even commonplace. Since the day of the Lord will come unexpectedly, like a thief in the night, the people ought to be always prepared, living moral and faithful lives (5:1–3). This moral demand was common in writings about the coming end of the age (compare Matt. 24:42–51 and Rev. 3:3). It is a safe, if not inspiring, moral exhortation, resembling the warning to children that they had better be good because their parents may return from running errands at any moment.

The second idea is more daring and more inspiring (and, it turned out, more dangerous). Paul became captivated by his metaphor: the day of the Lord. He played with the ideas of night and day, darkness and light, boldly exhorting:

> But you, beloved, are not in darkness, for that day to surprise you like a thief; for you are all children of light and children of the day; we are not of the night or of darkness. So then let us not fall asleep as others do, but let us keep awake and be sober; for those who sleep sleep at night, and those who are drunk get drunk at night. But since we belong to the day, let us be sober, and put on the breastplate of faith and love, and for a helmet the hope of salvation. (5:4–8)

Notice how the ethical enterprise now depends not on some future event but on the present event of a transformed life. People are no longer asked to be good just because they might get caught at it. Goodness is now based on the transformation that occurs in those who are already children of the day. That future day is already present in the transformed lives of these Thessalonians, according to Paul. This is Paul at his finest: imaginative, innovative, centrally concerned about ethics, blazing new trails, and saying more than he intended to. For if taken literally, his teaching implies that that day has already come. We will return to this passage when we discuss 2 Thessalonians.

This literary analysis has shown that Paul's letter has a two-part structure, reflected in the duality of ideas (work/faith, labor/love, endurance/hope), the duality of experience (present/future, night/day, death/resurrection), and in the two basic aspects of the letter (thanksgiving/exhortation). Its dominant note is joy and its main demand is to "do so more and more" (4:1, 10). There is little mention of controversy or of failure. The problems revolve around the congregation's expectations of the coming end. Paul responds to these concerns with a creative use of the Jesus tradition, then quickly moves on to practical concerns for the present life of his new congregation. We have also encountered several unusual ideas that are remote from our time. Now let us examine more closely the general and specific historical circumstances surrounding this letter.

A HISTORICAL ANALYSIS OF FIRST THESSALONIANS

We turn now from a consideration of the letter itself to an investigation of the life context in which it was written and read. Here we are trying to eavesdrop on the story of Paul and of his followers at Thessalonica. How much of their stories can we discern from a careful reading of this letter?

PAUL AT THESSALONICA

Though we tend to imagine Paul as a modern pastor or missionary who devotes full time to his religious work, this was not the case. Like the Jewish synagogues, the earliest assemblies of Jesus' followers were organizations run by ordinary business and professional people. Neither institution employed a professional clergy, and, even much later, rabbis worked at some trade to support themselves.

Copyright Alinari/Art Resource, New York

THE GRANDEUR THAT WAS ROME   This artist's reconstruction shows something of the magnificence of Rome and, to a lesser degree, of all major cities. In the background is the emperor Caligula's palace (about 40 CE). Directly in front of the palace (center) is the home of the vestal virgins, containing the altar and Temple of Vesta (the round building). This was the central "hearth" of the Roman people whose fire the vestals were never to let go out. To the right is a typical Roman temple to Castor and Pollux. The arch of Titus stands to the left. Such enormous public buildings, each richly ornatmented with statues and paintings, were the pride of ancient cities.

THE EARLIEST JESUS LITERATURE   87

Paul seems to have been a tent maker, which we should probably understand in the broader sense of leather worker (just as the modern term *cabinetmaker* means woodworker or carpenter). As a tradesman, Paul would have worked long hours, doing much of his teaching while at work at his bench: "We worked night and day . . . while we proclaimed to you the gospel of God" (1 Thess. 2:9). Even a century later a good deal of Christian instruction seems to have taken place in such workshop contexts. One opponent derided the Christians as "uninstructed," "rustic," and "foolish" folk who tell young people

> *they must leave their father and their instructors, and go with the women and their playfellows to the women's apartments, or to the leather shop, or to the fuller's shop, that they may learn perfection;—and by words like these they gain them over (Origen Against Celsus 3.55; quoted from Ante-Nicene Fathers, 1981:4.486).*

What we must imagine, then, is that Paul has come to this major seaport city and either rented a workshop or gotten hired as a worker in an established leather shop. We are uncertain how long he was there; the story in Acts implies a brief stay of two to four weeks (17:1–10), but this hardly seems long enough to establish a business. Nor are we sure of who and how many converts Paul made. Again there is some tension between Paul's account (which suggests the converts were primarily Gentiles, for 1:9 describes them as having turned away from idols) and the account in Acts 17 (which implies that these followers were drawn from the **synagogue,** the Jewish house of prayer and study). Acts is probably oversimplifying in the interest of a compact narrative. (Such differences between Acts and Paul's letters cause most scholars to prefer to reconstruct Paul's career independently of Acts, turning to Acts only for verification and elaboration. For a discussion of Paul's place in Acts see Chapters 6 and 11).

What seems clear, and somewhat shocking to us, is that Paul formed this new community around himself; he reminds them, "you became imitators of us and of the Lord" (1:6). It is important to understand this dynamic to understand this letter. The notion that the disciple should become like (imitate) the teacher was a commonplace in Paul's world. As Seneca, a Roman contemporary of Paul, remarked, "the way is long if one follows precepts, but short and helpful, if one follows patterns" (*Letters* 6.5–6). We must imagine this from the Thessalonian side. A new teacher had come to town and these (few?) people converted to his new teaching, losing much in the process: family, friends, status, honor. Now he has left, taking this model of their new way of life with him. In his now-extended absence, Paul has found two ways to make his presence felt there, first by Timothy and then by this letter.

So the first context within which we must read the letter is the strong bonds that developed during a relatively brief but intense visit of a powerful traveling worker-teacher who had persuaded many to adopt a radically different course of life than they had previously followed. This warm rapport permeates the letter.

The next context is the city itself. Thessalonica, capital of the Roman province of Macedonia, was a cosmopolitan city with a fair-sized Jewish community and a diversity of Greek, Roman, and local religious rites. Coins show a variety of deities: Apollo, Artemis, Athena, Heracles, Dionysus, Poseidon, Pan, Zeus, and Roma. This last indicates the existence of the imperial cult (worship of the emperor) in the city. In Paul's day the temple of Roma would have contained images of Julius and

Hirmer Verlag, Munich

THE DEIFIED AUGUSTUS, ABOUT 25 CE The emperor Augustus died in 14 CE and was deified that same year. This deification proclaimed that Augustus did not descend into the underworld, as all mortals did, but that he ascended into heaven where, like the other starry presences, he exerted his influence. The practice of Tiberius, and most later emperors, recognized such deification only for their deceased predecessors.

Augustus. An archaic fertility cult still survived, whose formerly violent God was now transformed into a protector of seamen. The diversity of this list reminds us that the religious experience of Gentiles in that age was quite unlike our own. Rather than choosing one "best" religion, people usually combined elements from several religious systems, a process called **syncretism**. Generally, these deities provided only the public expression of religion; private religious needs were met in other ways, such as mystery religions, magic, and astrology. But all citizens would be expected to participate in these public rites.

A city in this time was more than just a location; it was the center of a region and the center of one's cultural identity. The tradition of the Greek city, though politically eclipsed by the emergence of empires, still provided the model of citizens striving together to create economic prosperity and a rich intellectual life. Many new cities were founded, and old cities grew in this period. The populations for these cities were drawn from surrounding areas, caused both by economic dislocation and the lure of city life. Many in the cities had left behind the stability of their past and were open to new ideas.

Thessalonica possessed a good gulf, which made it an important seaport and, combined with its location on the Egnatian Way (the main road between Rome and the East), a prosperous trade center. Politically, Thessalonica was a free city ruled by its own assembly of free citizens. In these ways it is typical of the kind of city to which Paul was attracted and in which he proclaimed the Jesus story. This social context of an urban, metropolitan center with a diverse population, many religions, combining Greek, Roman, and Eastern ways of life is important for understanding Paul and his letters.

Now let us examine more closely what this letter reveals about Paul's story. In Chapter 2 we learned that the story of Jesus was expanded into the past, by seeing the Hebrew Scriptures as telling about Jesus, and into the future, by seeing Jesus as God's agent for the time of the end. First Thessalonians focuses on the latter, and to understand how Paul related Jesus to the coming end, we need to investigate what people thought about the **end of the age** in his day.

One preliminary point is to differentiate their view of the end from views of the end of the world common today. Most of the ancients saw the world as evolving through different ages, with the dominant view being of a continual decline. The Greeks thought of an age of gold, followed by ages of silver, bronze, and iron. The arrival of a new age did not mean some catastrophic end of life but a new beginning. Some Romans even believed that the arrival of Augustus constituted the beginning of a new age, one far better than the old. As Virgil rhapsodized:

> *Now comes the last age of the song of [the Sibyl of] Cumae; the great line of the centuries begins anew. Now the Virgin returns, the reign of Saturn returns; now a new generation descends from heaven on high. And do thou, pure Lucina, smile on the birth of the child, under whom the iron brood shall first cease, and a golden race spring up throughout the world! (Virgil, Eclogue IV)*

Paul and the early followers of Jesus had their own version of a coming new age, but they shared Virgil's notion that it really was a new beginning and that it had already begun.

PAUL'S VERSION OF THE END OF THE STORY

Some of Paul's descriptions of the future probably sounded a little odd, like science fiction or fantasy literature today. Heavenly trumpets, calls of archangels, resurrections, heavenly descents, meetings in the clouds—hardly the stuff of everyday reality. Actually, Paul culled these descriptions from a unique kind of literature, a genre as removed from the letter as science fiction is from normal life today. Modern scholars have named this genre after its most popular representative, the Apocalypse of John (also called the Book of Revelation). The first word of that work is *Apocalypsis*, whose root meaning is "to take off the covering, to lay bare, to make naked," and thus by analogy to reveal, a revelation. An **apocalypse** is a written account intending to unveil the events of history, to see behind them to their true (spiritual) causes and effects. The apocalypses regularly achieved this unveiling by means of strange, often bizarre, symbolism: animals with multiple heads, angelic visitors, trips to heaven, and the use of symbolic numbers (see Chapter 13, pages 439–44).

This way of writing rests on a dualistic **worldview** (a general way of looking at life) that sees history as a battle between good and evil (to review the origins of this worldview, see Chapter 1, pages 47–49). Although tales of this struggle and its ultimate outcome are told in many ways, a single general plot underlies apocalyptic thinking.

The Plot of the Apocalyptic Story

Apocalypticism revolves around the core idea that there are really two ages to the world: this age and the age to come. This **dualism** is the central feature of apocalypticism. The future age will be the time when God rules, when justice and righteousness prevail, but the present is a time of great wickedness, ruled over by the Prince of Darkness. Because the evil one is in control of the powers of this age, righteous people must expect to suffer; as the end of this age approaches, wickedness will exert itself with the desperation of someone drowning. Thus, the increase in wickedness is evidence that the end of the age is near. In this way we could say that for the apocalypticist the worse things became, the better they were: for when wickedness has reached its zenith, God will intervene, bring this age to an end, and establish divine rule on earth, the reign of God—that is, God's perfect rule, when justice, peace, and prosperity would abound as God intended. This sequence is shown in Figure 3.2 (see also Table 1.2).

Apocalypticists differed greatly on how they envisioned the coming of God's kingdom, but there was widespread agreement on the basic pattern: (1) there are two ages; (2) the new age is near; (3) evil will increase as that age approaches; and (4) God will suddenly and unexpectedly intervene to overthrow evil. The details of how they told their stories of the end varied, but there was general agreement on this basic plot.

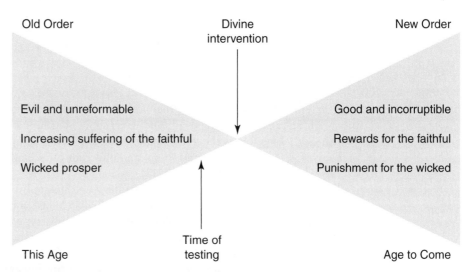

FIGURE 3.2 **APOCALYPTIC VIEW OF HISTORY** The apocalypticist viewed the present era as a time of evil, ruled by the powers of evil and those humans who had embraced evil. To be faithful to God in such a time was to expect to suffer. However, present suffering was also testimony that this era was drawing to a close, for the new era would be preceded by a time of testing. Some decisive act of divine intervention would soon bring this age to an end and launch the rule of God, a new order of justice and righteousness, the mirror image of the old.

Read 1 Thessalonians and, using the elements of Figure 3.2, note the apocalyptic elements you discover.

Paul's Revision of the Apocalyptic Story

Though Paul was no apocalypticist and his letters are far from apocalypses, he did share much of the apocalyptic worldview. Specifically, he agreed with the basic plot: Paul believed that this age would end soon and that he would be alive to see it (1 Thess. 4:17, "then *we* who are alive"; compare 1 Cor. 15:51–52 and 7:25–31). Paul warned the Thessalonians that the end would be unexpected, and he advised them how to live in this evil age (5:1–8). The role of the evil one and the increase of evil are not clearly stated in this letter, but they were part of Paul's concept (see Gal. 1:4 and 2 Cor. 4:4; note the emphasis on the suffering of the Thessalonians in 1:6; 2:9, 14).

But these apocalyptic motifs are not his central ideas; they are simply assumptions he makes about the world. Unlike the apocalypticists, Paul does not dwell on these last events but on their implications: Knowing that the end could come soon, how should they live now? The strongest tendency of this letter is its diversion of concern about the end into concern for the present. But then Paul did not make as strong a distinction between the two as was usual. Paul asserted that in some way the people already participated in that new day (5:4–5). Christ had delivered them from this present evil age, as Paul would remind the Galatians (Gal. 1:3). This meant that Paul could never abandon the world but was forced to live in and try to change it. For Paul the future, past, and present all met in Christ. In his version of the story, the crucial act of divine intervention had already occurred in the death and resurrection of Christ. This meant that the new age had already begun. But it was not yet fully come. Paul lived in the gap between this **already and not yet** and developed his ideas about life and action accordingly.

IN SUMMARY

The threefold notion of living in the world in love, with the faith that Christ has already been raised from the dead, and in the hope that he will soon return to establish God's kingdom is the letter's major theme. It is woven into the thanksgiving (1 Thess. 1:3, 9–10; 2:2; 3:8, and so on) and underlies the seemingly random admonitions with which Paul closes (5:12–22).

This letter also reveals Paul's general strategy and method. He traveled continuously, spending only enough time in a city to establish an assembly; he traveled with companions who acted as his agents and shared his ministry; he used the Jesus tradition in an oral form and assumed that his followers were familiar with it; and he wrote letters, real letters for specific purposes to specific people, that are also well crafted and thematically integrated. We may illustrate this integration thus:

Thanksgiving (1:2–10) for their
    1. work of faith,
    2. labor of love, and
    3. steadfastness of hope,
elaborated in a narrative of past labors (2:1–3:10)

and leading to instruction on

1. how to live in marriage and in community (4:1–12 love/labor),
2. knowledge about the fate of the dead and the nearness of the end (4:13–5:11 hope/steadfastness), and
3. exhortations to respect workers and to work (5:12–22 faith/work).

We see here not only Paul's rhetorical skill but also the needs of these men and women who so strongly anticipated that coming day that they encountered problems with their marriage vows and community love, misunderstood about the fate of the dead, and disparaged work. Can we learn more from 2 Thessalonians?

A COMPARATIVE ANALYSIS OF SECOND THESSALONIANS

Second Thessalonians is most notable for its strong similarities and basic differences from First Thessalonians, which are so great that an increasing number of contemporary scholars conclude that Paul could not have written the second letter. We will use this question of the likelihood that Paul is its author to analyze the basic ideas of the work. First we will examine the understanding of "author" in Paul's world, then consider the arguments on both sides of the issue. This will allow us to wrestle with the meaning of the work, and will demonstrate the tentative nature of all interpretation.

At first glance it might seem peculiar to ask whether Paul wrote 2 Thessalonians, since the letter clearly lists Paul as its author (2 Thess. 1:1); and in our world it would be unthinkable to write a letter in someone else's name. We would usually call that a forgery, and our copyright and libel laws are supposed to prevent such things. There are, however, some special circumstances in which we recognize the propriety of writing in someone else's name. Occasionally I am asked to write something for the dean or provost that they either sign and send on or deliver orally as if the work were theirs. Also, on occasion, our departmental administrative assistant writes a letter for me, as if I were requesting a publication or some such thing—and even signs my name. And it is not uncommon for Christmas cards to be sent from the whole family, even though only one person sends them. So there are a few cases where pretended authorship does not upset us even in the modern world. The ancients were still more accepting of such **pseudonymity** (just as an anonymous writing is by an unnamed author, a pseudonymous writing is by a falsely named author).

THE QUESTION OF AUTHORSHIP

One of the more charming letters to come down to us from antiquity is known as Plato's Second Letter. The letter discusses his writings and his great debt to his teacher, Socrates. He felt, the letter tells us, so dependent on the master that he could only write in his name:

> That is the reason why I have never written anything about these things, and why there is not and will not be any written work of Plato's own. What are now called his are the work of a Socrates embellished and modernized. (Letters 2.314c)

Plato wrote nearly thirty dialogues on a great range of philosophical ideas, but in all of them the main speaker is Socrates. Plato himself enters the dialogues only once, to ask a rather obvious question in the *Republic* and then fade into the background. This attribution of his work to Socrates becomes even more remarkable when we consider how far beyond Socrates Plato actually went. He was certainly the greater thinker, and his later dialogues introduce ideas never hinted at in the early ones, which depend more on Socrates. There is the further irony that the *Letters* of Plato were almost certainly written after the time of Plato by one of his disciples.

For a disciple to write in the master's name was a common and expected tradition in the ancient world. This practice may be observed in the Jewish heritage in the works of the prophets. Nearly all the writings of the prophets that we possess contain later additions by their followers. This is quite clear in the case of Amos, whose oracles are wholly pessimistic: he believed it impossible that Israel would avoid God's judgment. Will God not rescue Israel? Yes, Amos declared, like a shepherd rescues a lamb from a lion: "two legs, or a piece of an ear" (3:12). Israel's doom is sure, like a man who runs away from a lion and directly into a bear. Or, if he should escape and reach home, he would lean against his wall only to have a serpent come out and bite him (5:19).

In contrast to this pervasive pessimism, the book of Amos ends on a very promising note: "in that day I will raise up the booth of David that is fallen" (9:11). Most scholars regard this as the work of a later hand; the tone is radically altered from the earlier pessimism, and even the presuppositions have changed. The rest of the book presumes that Israel is prosperous and mighty and does not realize the nearness of judgment, which was the situation in Amos's time. But the ending presumes that this prosperity has come to an end and that, in fact, the house of David has fallen (an event nearly two hundred years after the time of Amos). Thus many conclude that the ending to the book of Amos was written after the time of Amos not because it prophesied something later, but because it assumed that something much later had already occurred. The ending to the book was likely added by some follower of Amos long after the prophet's death.

Such later additions are typical of the prophetic tradition and could be duplicated from nearly any of the writings of the prophets. The prophetic tradition was a living one, and, as circumstances changed, the tradition changed, expanded, adapted, and spoke to the new situation as if the prophet were still speaking.

A different but analogous situation exists with the Pentateuch, the first five books of the Bible, which are attributed to Moses, though one of them recounts his death (Deuteronomy 34). Even more telling, these supposed words of Moses discuss situations and institutions that did not arise until centuries after his death, such as the monarchy (Deuteronomy 17). Further, when the monarchy did arise, there is evidence that conservatives resisted the idea as an unnecessary innovation, apparently unaware of the Mosaic tradition in Deuteronomy (1 Samuel 8). It is generally agreed that Deuteronomy was written hundreds of years after the death of Moses, to address the religious and political needs under the late monarchy.

Now this is quite different from the case of Plato or Amos, for the author certainly never knew Moses. But the author wrote in Moses' name to give validity to ideas he just knew Moses would have endorsed. This may seem dishonest to us, but we should not be too quick to assume that it seemed so to the ancients. All three of these instances—producing imitations of Socrates, Amos, and Moses—share something closely related to **authorship**: *author*ity. Plato saw himself acting with the authority of Socrates and therefore spoke in his name. The writers of Deuteronomy were drawing on genuinely Mosaic ideas and applying them to the new situation of their day and probably saw no difficulty in writing them in Moses' name. The schools of the prophets assumed a similar authority.

Not all pseudonymous writings stood on such authority. A whole class of writings, the **pseudepigrapha** (sude-a-PIG-graf-a, false writings), were written in the names of ancient worthies without any valid claim to their authority: the books of *Enoch*, the *Ascension of Isaiah*, the *Apocalypse of Adam*, and many more. Also, literary forgeries were widespread, though they usually took the form of plagiarizing someone else's writing. We must remember that there were no publishers in the modern sense. Authors would read their works aloud, then have scribes copy them, making handwritten scrolls to be sold at the local market. There was little to prevent someone from purchasing a copy and making unauthorized use of it. The Roman poet Martial regularly complained that much of the poetry sold in Rome was his, but most of the profits went to the pirates, who were selling it as theirs. A whole series of oracles, the *Sibylline Oracles*, written in the name of the Sibyl of Apollo at Delphi, are in fact Jewish religious propaganda. Nor were Christians above such forgery: there are gospels written in the names of nearly all the outstanding leaders of the first century. Some pious soul produced a whole series of correspondence between Paul and Seneca, the two great first-century letter writers (see J. K. Elliott, 1993:549–53; Hennecke and Schneemelcher, 1992:2:46–53). The range of possibilities concerning the meaning of authorship may be shown as a continuum (see Figure 3.3).

Paul himself did not write any of his letters in the sense of setting quill to parchment; he used a secretary to whom he dictated (for example, Rom. 16:22). A very useful system of shorthand had been invented by Cicero's secretary about a century before Paul and was widely used. In addition, letters continued to be produced in Paul's name for over a century. Several are still extant: *3 Corinthians, Laodiceans,* and the series of letters between Paul and Seneca (these can be found in J. K. Elliot, 1994:380, 546; or Hennecke and Schneemelcher, 1992: 2:128, 375). The question

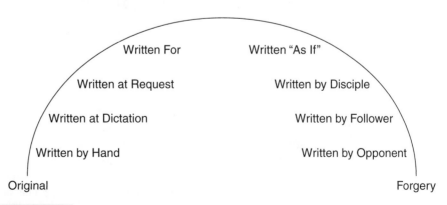

FIGURE 3.3   THE MEANINGS OF AUTHORSHIP

of where on the continuum of authorship a given work ought to be placed can be answered only by a careful examination of that work.

READING AND REFLECTION

Although the majority of New Testament scholars continue to regard 2 Thessalonians as Paul's work, nearly all recent studies of the problem have come to the opposite conclusion. The problem stems from the fact that the second letter is so like, and yet so different from, the first. Use the following reading guide to read 2 Thessalonians and consider these issues:

1. Note anything that reminds you of 1 Thessalonians.
2. What elements of the Parousia are definitely future?
3. How does the understanding of the Parousia in 2 Thess. 2:1–12 differ from that in 1 Thessalonians?

READING GUIDE TO SECOND THESSALONIANS

Opening   1:1–2
Thanksgiving   1:3–12
Main body ("Now concerning")   2:1–3:5
    Discussion of the day of the Lord   2:1–12
    Second thanksgiving and prayer   2:13–3:5
Exhortations to good behavior   3:6–15
Closing   3:16–18
    Novel benediction ("Now may the Lord of peace")
    Claims to be Paul's own handwriting

Given the nature of authorship in that era, we must take seriously the possibility that 2 Thessalonians may have been written by a follower of Paul who used 1 Thessalonians as a model. If it does postdate Paul, it would be telling Paul's story in a new way.

SECOND THESSALONIANS AS A NEW STORY

Those who doubt Paul wrote both letters have three main concerns.

1. Second Thessalonians exhibits a strong dependence on First Thessalonians, repeating the same ideas and even the same words and phrases. These two letters overlap more than any other two of Paul's letters—perhaps as much as a third of the letter repeats material from 1 Thessalonians. (For example, 2 Thess. 3:8 = 1 Thess. 2:9; 2 Thess. 3:10 = 1 Thess. 3:4; 2 Thess. 2:1 = 1 Thess. 5:12; 2 Thess. 3:7 = 1 Thess. 2:1.) This could indicate that someone was trying to imitate Paul, especially when we become aware that several of these repetitions use similar words but express different ideas. In the first letter, for example, the believers are admonished to stand firm "in the Lord" (3:8), while in the second they are to stand firm in the traditions taught in the word and letters of Paul (2:15). In a similar way, both 1 and 2 Thessalonians rationalize their suffering, but the first letter relates it to past commitments and the near end (2:14; 1:6–10), whereas the second relates it to future reward (1:5).

2. The tone of this letter is too somber for it to have been written near the same time as the joyous first letter, unless some major disappointment had occurred. Those who argue for a major change point to 2 Thess. 2:1–2, which may indicate that new opponents had come to Thessalonica, teaching that the end of the age had already arrived. On the other hand, the reference to forged letters is problematic, since imitations of Paul's letters were far more likely in the late first century than during Paul's lifetime.

3. The central issue is that 2 Thessalonians seems to have a different understanding of the approaching end of the age (or **eschatology**, to use the technical term). We saw that in 1 Thessalonians 5 Paul followed the common apocalyptic motif that the end would come "like a thief in the night," so one must be ready at any time. But in 2 Thess. 2:1–12, a detailed scheme of final events is spelled out, implying that the end is not at all near. A whole agenda of events must occur first, making it unlikely that the end will take anyone by surprise. This difference is so blatant that some who think the rest of the letter is from Paul suggest that 2:1–12 is an **interpolation** (a later insertion into the letter by someone else). If so, the most interesting part of the letter is an addition.

These three arguments cause many to regard 2 Thessalonians as a late work of the Pauline school, from a time when the expectation of a sudden end had waned but when there was renewed interest in speculation about the end. On this reading, the letter is aimed at refuting enthusiasts concerned with the imminent end of the age, for such speculation was undermining the need to live responsibly in the world as it was (see Koester, 1983). Or perhaps the real concern of the letter is not to refute apocalyptic enthusiasm but to persuade the readers to accept the authority of one particular interpretation of Paul, one oriented toward the end of the age (Holland, 1988:156–58). Or perhaps the letter aimed to refute those followers of Paul who discounted the idea of a real end to the physical world and thought instead of a spiritual end (Hughes, 1989). Viewing the letter as written by a disciple of Paul would be in line with the writing practices sketched above. On this reconstruction we encounter the story of the heirs of the Pauline tradition in a time when concern about the near end of the age had waned. To test this thesis, you will need to reread 2 Thessalonians after you have studied this later period (Chapter 6). But we should not understand too quickly. Other scholars continue to argue that Paul actually wrote this second letter.

SECOND THESSALONIANS AS THE STORY OF PAUL

Instead of merely contrasting 2 Thessalonians with 1 Thessalonians, scholars who argue that Paul actually wrote both seek the relationship between them. The second letter implies three changes: persecution has increased (1:4, 6; 3:3); a new revelation has occurred, saying that the day of the Lord has come (2:2); and someone has delivered this message by a word or letter allegedly from Paul (2:2). Thus the dramatic setting of the letter is that Paul has received word (though we are not told how) that his Thessalonian followers have been "shaken" in their faith and have come to believe that they already live in the new age, based on some word or forged letter claiming to be from him. That people might think they already live in the new age may seem incredible, but we will encounter similar beliefs at Corinth (1 Cor. 15) and Philippi (Philippians 3) and in later Pauline writings (Ephesians 2).

Given these changes, these scholars argue, we can explain the three concerns listed above. Paul might repeat the words and ideas of his first letter so that they could differentiate between a genuine and a forged work (point 1). He would emphasize his teaching and letter rather than the oral tradition (2 Thess. 2:15). Suffering might be better seen as a contrast with future reward (1:5) than as a part of the end of the age. The new situation could explain both the similarities and the differences between the two letters.

These aberrant ideas about the new age and the implication of fraudulent teachers working in Paul's name could also account for the more somber tone (point 2).

Point 3, concerning a different understanding of the end, is more complicated. This second letter provides a detailed schema of events that must occur *before* the coming of the day of the Lord, though with great ambiguity and without a timetable:

> The "man of sin" must come first (2:3).
> "He who now restrains" will be removed (2:7).
> "Jesus will slay him" when he comes (2:8).

Many question whether the person who reveled in the nearness of the end and its unexpected coming "like a thief" could also postulate such a series of prerequisites. The answer seems to be yes, for we find the two notions—immediacy and signs—repeatedly coupled in apocalyptic writings, including the tradition Paul drew on in 1 Thessalonians (now found in Matthew 24:43, 29–31, which includes both the thief metaphor and the detailed signs). Consistent or not, apocalyptic literature regularly combined both the notion of the nearness and unexpectedness of the end with the idea of cosmic signs before the end. But is not such an agenda in tension with Paul's sense of urgency, a sense so strong that he will advise other followers to abstain from marriage (1 Cor. 7)? Perhaps. But Paul also sketches an agenda of events before the end in Romans (9–11), a section surely his own.

What Paul may have meant by these arcane references to a "lawless" man taking a seat in the temple and the one "restraining" is very difficult to decipher. One suggestion is that this terminology grew out of the attempt of the Roman emperor Caligula to have his statue set up in the Temple in Jerusalem in 40 CE. Only the restraining influence of Petronius, the Roman governor of Syria, and a timely assassination prevented this desecration. Surely such an event left an impression on people's imaginations and provided grist for the mills of apocalypticists. (Josephus tells the story in *Wars* 2.10, and Philo, who was part of an official delegation dispatched to Rome to persuade Caligula [officially named Gaius] not to complete his plan, gives an account in *Embassy to Gaius*.)

Another suggestion, by those who conclude that the letter was written after Paul's time, identifies this figure with the mysterious "Antichrist" or "beast" mentioned in Revelation 13—a late first-century writing.

The new situation implied in 2 Thessalonians has another interesting feature: the Thessalonians claim to base their understanding on the teachings of Paul (2:2). Here the letter is emphatic: Paul denies he ever taught that the day of the Lord had already come, and promises to sign his letters so there will be no future misunderstandings (2 Thess. 3:17). On the one hand, forged Pauline letters were a much greater problem at the end of the first century than during Paul's lifetime. On the other hand, we do have some evidence that Paul taught that the day of the Lord had come, or at least something that could be understood in this way: in 1 Thessalonians he boldly declared that they already live in "that day," so they should live like day people (see 5:5 and the discussion above; consider that 1 Thess. 2:19 and 3:13 could also have been understood in a present sense). And this in a letter "purporting" to be from Paul!

Perhaps the Thessalonians so misunderstood Paul's metaphor about belonging to the day that when he heard a report of what they thought he had written to them, Paul no longer recognized it as his own letter. Thinking they had gotten a forgery instead, he wrote a new letter using many of the words and ideas of the previous letter that he had sent some months before.

We do not know whether this is what happened; it is merely one hypothesis that could explain the available data: the strong dependence on 1 Thessalonians, the new somber tone, and the emphasis on the future aspect of apocalyptic expectation, correcting a misunderstanding of the sense in which Paul thought they already lived in the coming day of the Lord.

Those who argue that Paul wrote the letter raise other questions: Why would anyone address such a letter to Thessalonica? And why would someone writing a letter in Paul's name condemn such letters? Why the emphasis on authenticating the letter in his own hand? Why would a later writer risk being found out by such a ploy (especially if it could be checked against another letter like 1 Cor. 16:21)? All this is comprehensible if we imagine a scenario like the one described above. On the other hand, perhaps the author protests too much, knowing there would be a problem attributing the letter to Paul. (And it is unlikely anyone had the original copy of 1 Corinthians to check the handwriting.)

Those who see Paul as the author of both letters make another argument. If a belief in salvation as an entirely present experience was held by some at Thessalonica before Paul wrote, it would explain why they became concerned for those who had died: those who died would be excluded from salvation. In 1 Thessalonians, Paul addressed the symptoms (concern for the dead); in 2 Thessalonians he dealt with the illness (a faulty understanding of the day of the Lord). Possible. But again, we must avoid understanding too quickly.

Strong arguments on each side point to different aspects of the literature. Able scholars disagree on the issue. How, then, do we decide? First we must be sure we understand the arguments that each side advances and carefully examine the evidence each points to in the text of the letters. We must also exercise our imaginations and see the two quite different stories implied by the two different readings of 2 Thessalonians. One reading sees it as a continuation of the story of the first letter; the other sees it as a reflection of the conflicting stories of the next generation. To test these two possibilities we need to become more familiar with both stories. It will be best to reserve judgment until we have completed our study of the Pauline literature, for the authorship of several other letters is disputed. We will consider these letters and more formal criteria for determining authorship in Chapter 6. Ultimately, only a careful and imaginative reading of the letters themselves will allow us to decide their setting and purpose.

THE THESSALONIAN STORY

We have now studied the earliest surviving literature about Jesus. In many ways it is what we might have expected. Its main concern is determining what it meant to live in relation to the Jesus story. There was no universal agreement, indeed there was considerable confusion, about how Jesus was to be understood.

In other ways this literature is perhaps surprising in the concern it shows for the end of the age. First Thessalonians reveals a Paul radically oriented toward the coming end; Second Thessalonians (if from Paul) shows him intensely concerned about the end but more reserved about its present significance. In either case we encounter a worldview very different from the modern one. Our study of other letters will show that this future orientation to the coming of Jesus had profound effects on Paul's way of life, thought, and ethics.

We have also considered important issues of method. We have deliberately analyzed both the literary and historical issues involved in understanding these writings. We have raised the issues of context: both the context of the oral stories of Jesus and that of first-century culture. We have tried to get some feel for the shape of a letter in this ancient culture and for the expectations with which letters would be heard. These same issues will continue to occupy our attention as we examine the rest of Paul's letters.

LEARNING ON YOUR OWN

REVIEWING THE CHAPTER

Names and Terms

already and not yet	eschatology	resurrection
apocalypse	immortality	synagogue
apocalypticism	interpolation	syncretism
authorship	Parousia	thanksgiving
dualism	pseudepigrapha	worldview
end of the age	pseudonymity	

Issues and Questions

1. Be able to outline the basic pattern of a Pauline letter and show how it is similar to other ancient letters. How are Paul's letters distinctive?
2. Be able to describe the nature of the oral traditions about Jesus and show how they evolved to meet the needs of the earliest communities.
3. How does Paul connect the ideas about the coming end of the age with concerns about how one should live in the present?
4. How do the issues discussed in these letters relate to the historical and social setting of first-century Thessalonica?
5. Be able to define apocalypticism and show how an apocalyptic worldview explains the nature of suffering.

6. How does Paul's version of the apocalyptic story differ from that of many other apocalypticists of the time?
7. Be able to discuss the various meanings of authorship in the ancient world.
8. What are the main arguments for and against Paul's authorship of 2 Thessalonians?

TAKING THE NEXT STEP

For a very interesting study of Paul's relation to the Thessalonian community see Malherbe, 1987. A fine but somewhat challenging study of the rhetoric and social setting is Jewett, 1986. Donfried and Beutler, 2000, is an excellent collection of essays on rhetoric and methods of interpretation.

Good short **commentaries** include Best, 1972, and Collins, 1984. Three good conservative commentaries are Marshall, 1983; Bruce, 1982; and Morris, 1959. Wanamaker, 1990, comments on the Greek text.

Topics for Special Studies

Among the many possible topics that will reward further study are the following. Unless otherwise stated, the sources are listed in general order of usefulness.

The Practice of Letter Writing

Klauck, 2006, provides the best discussion of the techniques of letter writing and transmission in antiquity, with a good bibliography. Doty, 1973, summarizes letter writing in the ancient Greco-Roman world and analyzes Paul's place in that tradition. On the general context and types of letters see Stowers, 1986, and White, 1986. On the theory of letter writing see Malherbe, 1977. On Roman practice see the short treatment in Shelton, 1987. Aune, 1987b and 1988, survey the place of the letter in its literary environment; see also chapter 2 of Richards, 2002. Richards, 1991, discusses the role of the secretary. Hughes, 1989, provides an excellent summary of the relation of letters and rhetoric. Anderson, 1996, looks at Paul's rhetoric.

The classic studies of the **thanksgiving** in Paul's letters are O'Brien, 1977, and Shubert, 1939. More generally see Malherbe, 1977, and White, 1983, 1984. On the **endings** see Weima, 1994, and on the **greeting** see Lieu, 1985. Boers, 1975, studies the typical forms in the letter.

A good introduction to the **rhetoric** of the Thessalonian letters is provided by Smith, 1995. You could then proceed to Jewett, 1986; Holland, 1988; Hughes, 1989; and (for a rather technical analysis) Johanson, 1987. For an analysis based on communications theory see Reece, 1979.

The **role of letters** in Paul's mission practice is addressed in Kee, 1980:129–33, and Meeks, 1983:109, 113–15. Important studies of the social setting of the Thessalonian letters include Malherbe, 1987, 1983. On the process of **collecting** the letters see Trobisch, 1994.

For the case against Paul's **authorship** of 2 Thessalonians see Holland, 1988; Bailey, 1978; Hughes, 1989; Koester, 1982; and Perrin and Duling, 2003.

For the case for Paul's writing 2 Thessalonians see Jewett, 1986; Kümmel, 1966; and Marshall, 1983. Nicholl, 2003, makes an argument for the unity of the two letters.

The practice of **pseudonymity** in the Greco-Roman world is given a good overview in the masterful work of Meade, 1986; see also Aland, 1961, and Donnelson, 1986. Additional resources are listed in Chapter 6.

On the process of writing and **publishing** see Gamble, 1995; Boorstin, 1983; Kenyon, 1932; and Hadas, 1950.

Apocalypticism

The best introduction to the shape and tenor of an **apocalyptic worldview** is Collins, 1984. See the extensive bibliography in Chapter 13.

On Paul's apocalyptic outlook see the important studies of Beker, 1980, 1982. More broadly see Minear, 1981, especially chapter 7.

On views of life beyond death there is an excellent overviews by Segal, 2004, and by Avery-Peck and Neusner, 2000; see also Cullmann, 1958; Nickelsburg, 1972; and Stendahl, 1965. Also see the resources at the end of Chapter 4 on the Hellenistic understanding of the body.

The expectations of the **Parousia** are treated by Harrington, 1987, and Kreitzer, 1987.

The role of **ethics** in Paul's mission practice is studied by Furnish, 1979; Sanders, 1975; and Westerholm, 1984. Special studies of Thessalonians include Best, 1972, and Marshall, 1983. For a more general study of early Christian ethics see Countryman, 1988. Also see the resources for Chapter 5.

The City of Thessalonica

On the physical environs of Thessalonica and its later churches see Thessaloniki, 1985.

On the religious dimensions of city life see Donfried, 1985; Edson, 1948; and Lightstone, 1989. For a nuanced discussion of syncretism see the introduction to Martin, 1987. On the social setting see De Vos, 1999.

Meeting Places

For an overview of sacred architecture in the Roman world see White, 1990. On **house churches**, the best study is Osiek, MacDonald, and Tulloch, 2006; for the case of Philemon, see J. K. Elliott, 1984. Brad, 1994, explores the setting in Acts. See also Ascough, 1998. Fine, 1996, explores the emergence of the **synagogue**; for an overview of its evolution see Kee and Cohick, 1999. On synagogues in Palestine, see Levine, 1996. Burtchaell, 1992, discusses the liturgical connections between synagogue and church in antiquity. For studies of the connection of both synagogue and church to the broader **voluntary associations** of antiquity see the excellent collection of Kloppenborg and Wilson, 1996.

Paul and Jesus

For the role of the **oral Jesus tradition** in Paul's work, start with the classical study of Dungan, 1971; and see also Hurd, 1984; Dewey, 1995; Allison, 1985; Tuckett, 1983; and (for a feminist reconstruction) Schüssler Fiorenza, 1983.

For Paul's relationship to Jesus see Wedderburn, 1989; Cousar, 1990; and Wenham, 1995.

Additional Books and Articles

Significant chapters on Thessalonians are included in Beare, 1962b; Ellis, 1982; and Patte, 1983. See also Malbon, 1980. You might also consult the one-volume commentaries listed in Appendix A, "Doing Your Own Research."

For a review of issues involved in **translating** these works see Ellingworth and Nida, 1976.

For an extensive **bibliographic** essay on the Thessalonian letters see Richard, 1990.

4

PAUL'S LETTERS TO HIS FOLLOWERS

 Now indeed it is possible for Hellene or non-Hellene, with or without his property, to travel wherever he will, easily, just as if passing from fatherland to fatherland. . . . For security it suffices to be a Roman citizen, or rather to be one of those united under [Roman] hegemony.

AELIUS ARISTIDES, ORATION 26.100

In spite of all he wrote and all that has been written about him, Paul remains something of an enigma to us. In the earliest of his letters (Chapter 3) we saw him as a concerned teacher, writing endearingly to his former associates at Thessalonica—profoundly interested in the coming end of the age, yet cautiously shifting attention to the present as a time of hope and hard work. In this chapter we will see him in many moods: happy, confused, outraged, charming, professorial, bitter, witty.

As we read each of these letters, we will focus first on its literary and rhetorical design, for that will tell us what to expect from the letter. Then we will reconstruct, as carefully as we can, the historical setting in and for which it was written. Though we are rarely certain of the exact dates, all the letters considered here were probably written in the mid-fifties.

We begin with a study of two letters written while Paul was in jail, probably at Ephesus in 53 CE but perhaps at Rome in 62. Whether or not they are early letters, these are marvelous examples of the intimate relationship between Paul and his followers.

WRITTEN FROM JAIL

Once, when Paul had been challenged by some other apostles who questioned his performance, he listed his accomplishments in this ironic way:

> *[I have] greater labors, far more imprisonments, with countless floggings, and often near death. Five times I have received from the Jews the forty lashes minus one. Three times I was beaten with rods. Once I received a stoning. (2 Cor. 11:23–25)*

The stoning referred to would have been an attempted execution, though not necessarily a legal proceeding (see Acts 14:19). The punishment of forty lashes was a disciplinary procedure connected with the synagogue; it was administered to troublemakers who could not be controlled in any other way. That Paul submitted to such a discipline indicates that he considered himself within the synagogue. (Only thirty-nine of the forty lashes were given, to ensure staying within the limit prescribed in Deut. 25:3 even if one miscounted.) Beating with a rod (a stick or a cane) was a Roman punishment.

Paul does not number his imprisonments but implies that they were many. Being imprisoned in the ancient world was not, in itself, a form of punishment. There was nothing comparable to our prison system. One might be imprisoned in one's own house or in some public building; according to Acts, Paul was imprisoned in Rome in an apartment he rented (28:30). Such imprisonment (more like being in jail or house-arrest today) had two major functions: to detain the suspect for trial or until punishment could be meted out, and to humiliate and intimidate unruly persons who annoyed the authorities. In either case, the stay would be short. In fact, accused persons were often left at large in the hope that they would flee into self-imposed exile, thus ridding the city of the problem. Banishment was one of the most severe punishments. Some of Paul's imprisonments resulted in the beatings he cited; at other times he was simply ordered out of the city; sometimes he was probably released unharmed. Acts 13–20 provides an authentic report of such encounters, though it is by no means complete according to Paul's own account.

At least two of Paul's letters, Philemon [fy-LEE-mun] and Philippians, were written from such imprisonments. While it has been widely assumed that they were written from his imprisonment in Rome, that need not be the case. In fact, the extensive interaction assumed between Paul and Philippi, including trips by Epaphroditus [ep-afro-DYE-tus] and Timothy, argue that Paul was not too far away (see 2:19–30), probably somewhere in Asia Minor (modern-day Turkey; see the map on page 120). These two letters, though they are poles apart in their content and their reflections of Paul, may well have been written closely together.

THE WHIMSICAL PAUL: PHILEMON

This is the shortest of Paul's letters and the last one in the collection. It is also the most personal, addressed to a particular person rather than to the whole community (but notice in verse 2 that the community is included). Still, the function of the letter—to represent Paul when he cannot be there in person—and its form follow Paul's standard practice.

READING AND REFLECTION

Read this short letter through quickly, and try to determine what has happened that caused Paul to write it. The letter is written for an unusual reason: something has happened in Paul's life that affects the community, rather than the other way around.

 READING GUIDE TO PHILEMON

Opening (sender/receiver, greeting)   1–3
Thanksgiving (with a prayer)   4–7
Main body   8–20
  The appeal for Onesimus   8–14
  No longer as a slave   15–20
Travel plans   21–22
  (Exhortations included in body)
Closing (with mutual greetings)   23–25
  (Writing process mentioned in 19)

The Story of Paul behind the Letter

While he was being detained, it seems, Paul encounters a slave from the household of a wealthy friend. Whether this slave, Onesimus [oh-NESS-eh-muss], was also imprisoned, we are not told. If so, his captors have not guessed his slave status. In the Greco-Roman world, slaves were not distinguished by any physical or educational

HOUSE OF POMPEII This spacious interior courtyard marks the style of the grand Roman household. This atrium was sometimes partially roofed and might have been used for entertaining large groups. Public and private rooms surrounded the atrium, including dining, sleeping, and storage areas. Wealthy patrons provided early Christians with meeting places for worship and dining together, and housing for the traveling apostles, prophets, and other workers. For a floor plan of a typical house see page 38.

differences from the general population; they represented all strata of society, from the farmers and miners to medical doctors and tutors. Most were used in manufacturing and household maintenance. The most common route to slavery was from war, as prisoners were often sold into slavery; piracy was also a major source of slaves. Children of slaves remained slaves, and even free children were sometimes sold into slavery, especially females. One could also become a slave by failing to pay personal debts. Instead of filing claims against bankrupt assets, creditors had the right to sell the debtor to regain their investment. Such slavery was usually for a set term (seven years seems to have been the average), and slaves were given a stipend that might be carefully saved and invested until they had accumulated the price of their freedom. The class of freedpersons consisted of former slaves who did not have full rights as citizens but who were often economically better off than many citizens. (For further discussion see page 34.)

But Onesimus was not a freed slave; he was either a runaway (as has been commonly held) or he has been sent to serve Paul in prison (as has been recently argued). It is even possible that he fled directly to Paul, hoping he might intervene with his master. And it is possible he didn't leave empty handed (18). In any case, the situation was further complicated by the slave's conversion (10). Paul decides to send Onesimus back, and he writes a letter to send with him.

The addressee of the letter was a wealthy friend of Paul, Philemon, whose spacious house was the meeting place of the assembly in that area (verse 2). He probably employed many slaves (for a large household in this era could employ hundreds, with perhaps twenty to thirty being common). Though the letter does not tell us Philemon's exact location, Colossae would be a reasonable guess; at least some of the people mentioned here are associated with Colossae (see Col. 1:7; 4:10–14; Philem. 23). The two others joined with Philemon in the address, "Apphia [AP-fee-ah] our sister" and "Archippus [ar-KIP-us] our fellow soldier," are probably the two overseers of the congregation, perhaps a wife and husband team. Curiously, the whole church is included in the address. (Actually the letter is not completely clear about the roles of the persons named in verse 2. Some think Philemon was the pastor and that Archippus was the wealthy patron. See Knox, 1935.)

But what is Paul's purpose in writing? What does he want Philemon to do? The most common suggestion is that Paul wanted Philemon to accept Onesimus back as his slave without punishment, to be a good master. Runaway slaves were often subjected to severe punishment, including being branded with the letter F (for fugitive). Did Paul write to forestall such harsh treatment? We have a nearly parallel incident involving a freedperson in the *Letters* of Pliny (61–112 CE), who wrote:

> You did well to take back into your heart and home the freedman who was once dear to you, as I asked you to do in my letter. You'll be glad you did; I certainly am, first because I see that you are so ready to listen to advice and that you can be in control of yourself even when angry, and then because you have paid me such a great tribute by yielding to my authority or granting my request. (9.24)

But is Paul asking for Onesimus to be readmitted to the household? John Knox (1935) has argued just the opposite: that Paul was seeking the slave's freedom so that he could join Paul in his mission. This argument is possible because the letter never says what Philemon should do. It operates by implication and indirection—and not a little humor. Philemon may have had to read the letter several times to figure out what Paul wanted (and so may we), but in the end he would understand. This short letter is filled with puns, ironic statements, and double entendres, the implication of which is that Knox was right.

The Story in the Letter: Reading between the Lines

First, we should know that the name *Onesimus* means "useful" or "profitable" in Greek. How inappropriate, for Onesimus had proven useless indeed. But Paul plays with the words, for now Onesimus is useful "to you and to me" (11). He goes on to pun on the name, "I want some benefit [*onaimen*] from you in the Lord" (20). In fact, it is just Onesimus that Paul wants; Paul frankly confessed that he had "resolved with myself to retain [Onesimus] in order that he might minister on your behalf to me in the bonds of the gospel" (13, literal translation). Here Paul clearly states his preference: he would have kept Onesimus not in the bonds of slavery or of jail but in the bonds of the Gospel. Instead, he sent him back, "sending my very heart" (12). Of course, Philemon has already been praised as one who refreshes the hearts of the saints (7), so that Paul can appeal directly: "Refresh my heart in Christ" (20).

Perhaps Paul was doing more than using a common expression when he said Philemon should receive Onesimus "no longer a slave . . . but as a beloved brother" (16). Perhaps he meant it literally. A literal reading of Paul's request to "receive him as you would receive me" (17) reveals Paul's true purpose. This would match the severe irony of Paul's promissory note embedded in the letter, written in his own hand, to repay any debt Onesimus has, even while reminding Philemon that he owes his very life to Paul (19). Paul does everything but command Philemon to free Onesimus to return to Paul (8). He appeals to him as an "old man and one in bonds" (9). But the bonds are those of the Gospel, and the word for "old man" can also be understood as "elder" or "ambassador." Finally, Paul calls on his status as a *partner* to Philemon (17), a designation that if taken literally would make Paul co-owner of Onesimus (see pages 37, 143). And so Paul concludes that he is confident of Philemon's obedience to the command he never issued, "knowing that you will do even more than I say" (21).

If the Onesimus who is later reported to be Paul's traveling companion (Col. 4:9) is the same fellow, Philemon was able to understand and to do more than Paul had requested. It is intriguing, but might only be coincidence, that the bishop of Ephesus at the end of the century was named Onesimus (see Ignatius *Ephesians* 1).

How did such a charming personal letter come to be included in Scripture? There is no clear answer. The importance of Paul, and possibly of Onesimus, might be a factor. Also, this is not entirely a private letter; it is addressed to the church as well (Philem. 2). But none of these factors is sufficient to explain its preservation. We will see that some of Paul's other letters could be lost (1 Cor. 5:9 refers to a previous letter now lost). Somehow this letter continued to be read long after the original problem had been solved. Knox went on to conjecture that it was Onesimus himself who collected and published the Pauline letters near the end of the century. That could explain the presence of this letter, but it remains no more than a guess.

More than a guess, however, is the way this short letter reflects Paul's larger story of Jesus. In a basic and profound way the story of Onesimus—his failure, return, release, and ministry—mirrors the experience of Paul and his followers. The story implied in this letter is one of freedom and partnership within a new community. These are, as we will see, basic themes of Paul's larger story. In Paul's story, all are slaves of Christ (1 Cor. 7:21–23) and all are free (Gal. 5:1).

This letter also reveals an aspect of Paul we see only vaguely in the other letters. A deep sense of serious humor runs through Philemon, revealing a Paul whom we would be delighted to know, far removed from the bitter sarcasm we encounter in Galatians. Again, we are reminded of the need to interpret each letter in its historical context and to interpret Paul only in relation to all of his letters. He was far too complex a personality to be expressed in any one way.

THE REFLECTIVE PAUL: PHILIPPIANS

This letter presents a couple of special problems, including the basic question of whether at least two letters might have been combined into one. We will consider this question as we first examine the organization of the letter, then turn to its historical setting and basic teachings.

One Letter or Two?

The basic reason for questioning the unity of Philippians is the curious trick played on the reader about halfway through. The writer says, "Finally," but then we are told that it is better to repeat a few things (Phil. 3:1). But even that promise is not kept. Instead of repeating earlier topics, the letter moves on to new ones. And the whole tone of the letter changes at this point. Whereas a mood of joy and even playfulness prevailed earlier, a new harsh note is introduced: "Look out for the dogs" (3:2).

There is also a problem with the assumptions made about a messenger sent from Philippi to Paul: in one reference he has been there some time, long enough for a report of his near-fatal illness to get back to Philippi (2:25–27); in another, he seems to have just arrived (4:18).

It seems plausible then that whoever published Paul's letters had two (or more) letters to the Philippians that were joined together for publication. Alternatively, Paul wrote one letter that has two distinct parts. Either way, our interpretation of the letter we read has to take account of duality.

READING AND REFLECTION

As you read Philippians through, you will find some things discussed twice. Ask yourself these questions:

1. What interactions existed between Paul and this community?
2. What sort of people opposed Paul, and how did he react to their opposition?

READING GUIDE TO PHILIPPIANS

The Story behind the Letter: Historical Setting

Again we find Paul imprisoned, and again we cannot be sure where. According to Acts (16), Paul was even in jail briefly at Philippi. The references to the imperial guard (the emperor's personal bodyguard, Phil. 1:13) and to the emperor's household (4:22) may suggest Rome but not necessarily so. The word translated "imperial guard" could as well refer to the residence of a provincial governor (the King James Version translated it "in all the palace"). The emperor's "household" probably refers to the slaves and freedpersons who were responsible for administering imperial affairs. Like bureaucrats in every age, they could be found everywhere. It is difficult to imagine Rome as the source of the letter because of the frequent travels it mentions to and from Philippi. (See the map on page 120.) A location in Greece or Asia Minor seems more logical. There Paul would be accessible in a matter of weeks rather than months.

The Philippians had sent Epaphroditus to minister to Paul's needs while he was confined (4:18; 2:25, 30). (Unlike those in charge of modern prisons, the ancients did not provide meals or do laundry, so one depended on friends.) Paul was now sending him back (2:25). He planned to send Timothy soon (2:19) and hoped to follow not long after (2:24). In the meantime, word had already reached Philippi that Epaphroditus was ill (2:26), and Paul had learned about certain problems there (for example, 4:2), implying that the Philippians had communicated with him by letter or another messenger.

PAUL'S FRIENDS AT PHILIPPI

This extraordinary effort of the Philippians to provide for Paul's support while he was incarcerated points up the special relationship that existed between this assembly and him. Philippi, named after the father of Alexander the Great, was a coastal city located in northern Greece. Typical of many cities, it remained relatively small until Antony (an associate of Julius Caesar) chose to settle a group of retired Roman soldiers there (about 40 BCE), causing it to flourish as a Roman colony. Its religion, like its population, was a mixture of ancient Thracian and Greek, with a strong overlay of Roman elements. We would expect such a city of Roman veterans to have a temple for the worship of Roma (the embodiment of Rome), the emperor, and such strong Gods as Jupiter (king of the Gods) and Mars (God of war). The city had these as well as temples to the female deities Athena, Isis, and the Thracian Cybele. The Jewish community there was small and was perhaps required to worship outside the boundary of the city proper (Acts 16:13). Acts indicates that Paul's primary contact in the city was with women, and the one convert named is Lydia, a businesswoman.

Apparently Paul had to leave Philippi and go on to Thessalonica, Corinth, Ephesus, and Galatia (Acts 17–18). (See the map on page 120.) In this letter Paul thanks God for the "partnership in the gospel from the first day until now" (Phil. 1:5), alluding to the continued financial support of those in the assembly. Twice they sent him support in Thessalonica (4:16), and now they have sent Epaphroditus. All this implies an extensive mutual contact between Paul and his followers at Philippi. If we try to fill in the gaps, we may imagine the following sequence:

1. Paul visits Philippi and then moves on to Thessalonica.
2. His followers twice send emissaries after him with gifts (4:16).

3. He probably responds to these gifts; at least the returning emissaries bring news of him.
4. They learn that Paul is imprisoned, perhaps at Ephesus.
5. They send Epaphroditus with support (2:25, 30).
6. Paul likely sends thanks and a report that Epaphroditus is ill (2:26; 4:18 may be part of this letter).
7. His followers write Paul expressing concern for Epaphroditus and giving news of their own situation.
8. Paul writes the present letter and sends it with Epaphroditus (2:25).
9. He plans to send Timothy soon to assist them and then to bring a report back (2:19).
10. Paul plans to come himself as soon as he is released (2:24).

This foundation of mutual interaction makes Philippians one of the warmest and most personal of Paul's letters. Even the rebuke of his opponents is milder and more playful in Philippians, at least toward some of those opponents.

PAUL'S OPPONENTS AT PHILIPPI

In his first reference to opponents Paul seems more bemused than concerned. Some preach Christ out of envy and rivalry, he alleges, yet Christ is being proclaimed (1:15–18). But his tone shifts in his next reference: "Look out for the dogs, look out for the evil-workers, look out for those who mutilate the flesh" (3:2). It seems unlikely that these two references allude to the same opposition. This latter group may be further described as those "who live as enemies of the cross of Christ. Their end is destruction, their God is the belly, and they glory in their shame, with minds set on earthly things" (3:18–19). Paul seems to have little objection to the first group but to regard the latter as enemies of Christ.

Paul's description of these enemies is so allusive that we cannot be certain of their stance. They urged **circumcision** (cutting off the foreskin of the penis), which might be seen as a symbolic denial of the world. Yet they seem more given to good food than to self-denial (3:19). Apparently they focused more on Christ's resurrection than his death and perhaps believed they were already perfect. This would account for Paul's assertion that he is not yet perfect (3:12) and for his absolute emphasis on the cross of Christ (3:8–11). Their requirement of circumcision and Paul's emphasis on his Jewish past suggest that, like Paul, they were Jews.

Paul took pains to show that his rejection of circumcision was not due to some failure on his part to keep the Law (a very common misunderstanding of Paul). His autobiographical recital here is instructive for understanding his attitude toward things Jewish. He was, he says,

> circumcised on the eighth day,
> a member of the people of Israel,
>   of the tribe of Benjamin,
> a Hebrew born of Hebrews;
>   as to the law, a Pharisee;
>   as to zeal, a persecutor of the church;
>   as to righteousness under the law, blameless.
>
> (3:5–6)

This self-portrait utterly shatters the common portrayal of Paul as one tormented by a failure to keep the Law. His own judgment on his guilt under the Law was sweeping, if unbelievable; he says he was "blameless." Whether his mother would have agreed or not, we must at least concur that Paul felt no dread before the Law. He was, as Krister Stendahl phrases it, one with a "robust conscience" (1976:90). Further, this positive evaluation of his Jewishness suggests that Paul's relationship with other Jews need not have been hostile.

In addition to this problem with opposition, Paul is also concerned with divisions in the church. Near the end of the letter Paul admonishes two women, Euodia [you-OH-dee-ah] and Syntyche [SIN-tih-kee], "to be of the same mind in the Lord" (4:2). We are never told the basis of their disagreement, but they are described as significant people, and we should, therefore, imagine a significant disagreement. These women had "labored side by side" with Paul in ministry; they were his "coworkers" (4:3). Whatever their disagreement and the nature of the partisan preaching Paul alluded to in chapter 1, he does not seem too upset with them. If we sometimes get the impression that Paul insisted that people always agree with him, it is because his letters usually address problems he regarded as integral to the Gospel. Incidents like this show that in other matters Paul recognized that differences were inevitable.

The Story of Jesus as Community Story

Although Philippians may not be a unity of discourse, it is a unity of rhetorical images. The dominant image of the whole work is that of mutuality. There is a common sharing of a common life, a mutual participation by Paul in his followers' lives, by them in his, and by both in Christ's life.

READING AND REFLECTION

Reread Philippians, noting all the images used to express this mutual participation. What relationship is assumed between the Philippians, Paul, Christ, and God?

They are partners, partakers, fellow workers, fellow soldiers, imitators, having the same mind, the same love: counting others better than themselves. All these images of reciprocity and mutual service reach a climax in the central poetic section of the letter. Having given his own case as an example of his suffering on their behalf, by his imprisonment and his release (1:12–26), Paul urges them to engage in the same conflict (1:29–30). He grounds this appeal in the work of Christ, citing what was probably a hymn chanted in their worship:

who,
   though he was in the form of God,
   did not regard equality with God
   as something to be exploited,
but emptied himself,
   taking the form of a slave,
   being born in human likeness.
And being found in human form,
   he humbled himself
   and became obedient to the point of death—
      even death on a cross.

Therefore
   God also highly exalted him
   and gave him the name
that is above every name,
   so that at the name of Jesus
   every knee should bend,
      in heaven and on earth and under the earth,
   and every tongue should confess that Jesus Christ is Lord,
to the glory of God the Father.

(2:6–11)

The poetic language, the regularity of the words, and the lack of any of Paul's usual vocabulary all indicate that this is most likely a hymn that Paul is quoting. Two questions arise: Why did Paul use this poem in this letter? What did these early believers understand when they heard or sang it? The most common interpretation of the original meaning of the poem understands it as a reflection on the **incarnation,** the process of God becoming human in Jesus of Nazareth. In this view the poem is about the preexistent divinity of Christ (form of God), which he laid aside ("emptied himself") when he took on human form. This is an ancient and very influential interpretation, of great beauty and intellectual daring, going back perhaps to the second century CE.

But some scholars have difficulty seeing this as the poem's original interpretation, for such explicit talk about preexistence was not common in Pauline circles. It became widespread, they think, only after the Gospel of John, late in the first century. These interpreters suggest another understanding of the hymn.

There was a popular ancient view that all life existed along a great chain of being, which stretched from the divine to the lowest form of animal life. The universe would be harmonious when each creature kept its proper place, neither grasping for a higher place (pride) nor sinking to a lower one (corruption). Humanity, however, was thought to occupy an ambiguous middle ground, sharing not only the divine nature ("made in the image of God") but also an animal nature, being bodily creatures. If we suppose such a context, the poem takes on a new meaning. Christ now appears as the true example of humanity, who, resisting the temptation of **Adam** to "be like God" (see Gen. 3:5), became the obedient servant. On this reading Christ is like a second, but obedient, Adam. (Paul developed the analogy between Christ and Adam more fully in Romans 5; see pages 164–65.)

We should not be surprised that the poem is capable of more than one interpretation, for that is the real wonder of poetry. But whether we understand it as talking about incarnation or about a second Adam, it is important that we see *why* Paul used it.

For Paul, this poem also reflected the mutual service that he found between himself and the Philippians, which was a reflection of the mutuality of the gospel: even as Christ served them, so they serve each other. They are to have the same mind as Christ (2:5). This theme of mutual service and sharing is the keynote of Philippians.

Philippians also shows how Paul's own life story reflected the larger Jesus story. In fact, Paul saw his own preaching, suffering, and labor as an imitation of Jesus' giving himself for the world (3:17–22; 1 Cor. 11:1). Paul, imitating Jesus, gave himself for the Gentiles. There is a direct correspondence between the sacred story of Jesus and the life story of Paul. That is why the sacred story is also a charter story, for it gives warrant to the lesser story. Thus, these two stories express two facets of the same reality.

Let us proceed now to the other letters, considering some of the problems faced by these Gentiles as they sought to be followers of Paul and of Christ.

WRITTEN FOR GENTILES

The place of the Gentiles (all the non-Jewish peoples) in Paul's self-understanding is central. His mission is to persuade the Gentiles (Rom. 1:13; Gal. 2:9), perhaps a mission he was engaged with even before his call to serve Christ (Gal. 5:11). Many

SPORTS STADIUM, APHRODISIAS   The Greek stadium was essentially a racetrack, typically 200 yards long, with seating all around. This well-preserved example in modern-day Turkey would seat about thirty thousand spectators. The Roman amphitheater was much larger (seating about 250,000) and devoted to more diverse entertainments, including gladiatorial combat and animal fights.

others of that time undertook a similar task, so Paul was not unique. He was simply a traveling Jewish tradesman and philosopher, who spread the word of his faith to the people among whom he traveled: Gentiles.

The status of the Gentiles who adopted this new faith was not clear. Some of Paul's followers in Galatia became confused about their new obligations and looked to other teachers for answers, prompting one of his most scathing letters. But before turning to that letter, we need to understand the general context of this problem with Gentiles. Many other Jews, men and women, were successfully engaged in similar travel, business, and witness, attracting a multitude of Gentiles to the Jewish way. One such success story is related by Josephus, a Jewish historian living in Rome in the late first century.

THE OUTREACH TO GENTILES

It seems that a traveling Jewish merchant by the name of Ananias [ann-ah-NYE-us], probably in the process of selling his goods, had been teaching Jewish religion to the women in the household of Izates, the son of the king of the small country of Adiabene [ah-dee-AB-en-ee] in northern Mesopotamia (north and far to the east of Palestine). Ananias succeeded in convincing many of these women of the superiority of the Jewish way. Through their intercession he was introduced to Izates [ih-ZAH-tays], whom he also persuaded to embrace the Jewish faith.

Meanwhile, in the king's household, his mother, Helena, had also been instructed in and attracted to the Jewish faith. When Izates succeeded to his father's throne and saw his mother's approval of the Jewish customs, he decided to make a full conversion by being circumcised and joining the Jewish people. However, his mother advised against this, fearing it could lead to insurrection among his people. (He had an older brother who would have liked to be king.) Partly convinced, Izates sought the counsel of Ananias, the Jew who had first instructed him. Ananias made an eloquent appeal for him to remain uncircumcised, citing not only the practical reasons that the queen mother had given but also arguing that he could worship God without being circumcised and that such worship was superior to circumcision. Izates was convinced and continued to worship God without being circumcised.

This situation did not change until another traveling Jew, Eleazar, arrived from Galilee. Eleazar was a scholar, and when he found Izates reading the **Torah**, the scroll of the Law (what we think of as the first five books of the Bible), Eleazar accused him of hypocrisy, of pretending to follow the Law but breaking the principal law by refusing circumcision. Convinced of his impiety, Izates immediately sent for a surgeon. His mother and Ananias were alarmed, but apparently the feared rebellion did not take place. (For the full story see Josephus *Antiquities* 20.2.)

This rare glimpse into Jewish outreach to Gentiles in the first century reveals several important clues for understanding Paul. First, we get the impression that this kind of appeal to Gentiles was widespread and reasonably successful. Despite a good deal of anti-Jewish sentiment among Gentiles, there was also a strong attraction to this ancient, monotheistic, and highly ethical religion. Second, the story reveals two major obstacles to the conversion of Gentile men: social stigma and circumcision. The need for circumcision was a great barrier; the thought of cutting off that excess skin elicited deep fears (as Sigmund Freud explained) and struck those who had embraced Greek culture as barbaric. The Greeks were deeply fascinated by the beauty of the body, especially the male body, and this deliberate mutilation appealed to them about as much as the incision rites of Australian Aborigines appeal to us. Civilized people, they felt, did not do such things.

However, and third, the uncircumcised convert is placed in the untenable situation of confessing the truth of the Torah, the Law, and denying one of its obvious demands: that males be circumcised (for example, Gen. 17:10–14). Fourth, we can see why women were more apt than men to convert fully, for they faced no such requirment. Fifth and finally, it is obvious that there were various opinions among Jews regarding Gentile circumcision without any reference to Jesus. The man of the world, Ananias, did not think it was very important; the scholar Eleazar deemed this ritual to be the most important of the laws, without which the pretense of keeping the others would be impiety.

A more subtle aspect of the argument is worth noting. The new convert has to remain uncircumcised day by day, a condition that can always be changed. Thus, though Ananias would have to win the argument repeatedly, Eleazar only had to win it once.

Jewish Responses to Gentiles

The difference between Ananias and Eleazar was not only that between the pious merchant and the legal scholar but also that between the Palestinian and the diaspora Jew. Eleazar was from Galilee, from the homeland. Though the contrast between Jews in the land and those outside (in the **diaspora**) can be exaggerated, significant differences in experience existed in the two groups. Jews had lived abroad in large numbers at least since the time of the exile (587 BCE), when military conquerors had carried many of the Jewish leaders off to Babylon, and probably even earlier.

By the time of Paul, diaspora Jews outnumbered Jews in the land by at least two to one. Literally millions of Jews lived in Egypt, Asia Minor, Mesopotamia, Greece, Italy, and farther north. Ties were closest between the Jews of Babylon and Palestine; both spoke Aramaic. Everywhere else Jews spoke Greek, the common language of the day. The Scriptures had been translated into Greek since at least 150 BCE, parts of it much earlier. Paul regularly cited Scripture from the **Septuagint**, a Greek translation that originated in Alexandria, Egypt. Diaspora Jews regarded it as just as authoritative as the Hebrew original.

These diaspora Jews not only spoke Greek but also gave their children Greek names, dressed like Greeks, and observed Greek customs. They became Greek in every aspect of their lives except religion, and some abandoned even that to some extent. Thus, we should not imagine that only two distinct classes of people existed in Paul's world (Jews and Gentiles). There was a whole continuum of experience, with pilgrimages in both directions. At one extreme you might have strongly nationalistic Jews who tried to avoid all Gentile influence, like the Essenes who withdrew from society to live a holy, separated life; at the other, you would have Gentiles who were anti-Jewish, some viciously so. But between these extremes the more frequent experience was a great deal of mutual influence and accommodation. Jews in Alexandria enrolled in the gymnasium (the primary school for Greek education) and sought full citizenship in this Greek city, which would surely involve some token honor to the Gods. Many Gentiles were attracted to, and no small number affiliated with, the Jewish worship of God, as the story from Josephus illustrates. Conversion to Judaism was so common that the Roman satirist Juvenal mocked it as one cause of Rome's decline. Here he reveals the probable process by which a Gentile family would come to be incorporated into Israel:

> *Some who have had a father who reveres the Sabbath, worship nothing but the clouds, and the divinity of the heavens, and see no difference between eating swine's flesh, from which their father abstained, and that of man; and in time they take to circumcision. Having been wont to flout the laws of Rome, they learn and practice and revere the Jewish law, and all that Moses handed down in his secret tome, forbidding to point out the way to any not worshipping the same rites, and conducting none but the circumcised to the desired fountain. For all which the father was to blame, who gave up every seventh day to idleness, keeping it apart from all the concerns of life. (Juvenal Satire 14.96–106)*

From Juvenal's jaundiced perspective, it all starts with a father who keeps the Sabbath and abstains from eating pork. The son moves on to study the Torah, neglecting Roman law, and is soon circumcised. Juvenal's contempt for circumcision, for the dietary laws, for worshipping an unseen God, for anything not Roman, is obvious and typical of the Roman upper class—yet obviously not typical of all Romans, or he would not have been moved to mock them.

Perhaps the most famous incident of conversion is the report by Dio Cassius that Flavius Clemens, cousin and heir to the emperor Domitian, was executed in 96 CE on the charge of atheism, along with "many others who were drifting into Jewish ways" (*History* 67.14.1–3).

Religion among the Gentiles

That Gentiles were open to Jewish proselytizing should not surprise us. The ancient world had changed dramatically in the three centuries before Paul. In the classical age of Greece the basic unit of civilization was the city, whose people, politics, Gods, and laws were at the center of life. But Alexander the Great and his empire changed all that. The city became far less important and only rarely autonomous. The forces controlling life had shifted to faraway places. Though local customs and deities were still honored, they no longer held sway. The religious writings of this period show a longing for salvation and deliverance from sin, a search for immortality, and, above all, freedom from fate. Fate (to which even Zeus was bound) bound all. One senses an overwhelming feeling of powerlessness. As one writer lamented:

> *We are so much at the mercy of chance that Chance herself, by whom God is proved uncertain, takes the place of God. (Pliny the Elder Natural History 2.5.22)*

Various religious impulses emerged to deal with these feelings. In the **folk traditions** there was strong emphasis on ways to understand and manipulate the fates: magic and astrology flourished. These probably comprised the primary religious experience of the masses of this age, but they were by no means limited to the masses. The emperor Tiberius never went anywhere without his personal astrologer, who continually cast his horoscope. **Astrology** rested on the premise that everything in the universe is interconnected, so that the movements of the stars revealed (perhaps indeed caused) events to happen on earth. One who could read the stars could read the future, it was believed.

And there were other means to read the future, and not popular only among the common folk. Generals would not march into battle without consulting oracles and priests, who examined the entrails of sacrificial animals for favorable signs. Even a political historian like Suetonius could not resist describing to the reader all the signs that foretold the death of each emperor.

Magic rested on the premise that certain people can manipulate the forces of the other world to produce effects in this world—if you just know the right spells. Elixirs, charms, or prophecies were available for everything from love potions to poisons, curses to healings, fortune-telling to business ventures. One old folk spell, for example, was supposed to cure sore feet: "I think of you; heal my feet. Let the earth retain the illness and let health remain here." This was to be recited nine times, touching the earth and spitting, and it would only work if one was sober (Varro *On Agriculture* 1.2.27). But magic was also believed to have power to subjugate others, even to kill them. When Germanicus, the adopted son of the emperor Tiberius, died mysteriously, his home was excavated, and magical paraphernalia were found: human body parts, curses on lead tablets, blood, ashes (Tacitus *Annals* 2.69). Nearly everyone believed in magic, and most people probably practiced it to some extent. Its influence among the people was very strong.

Among the more well-to-do, the **mystery religions** offered the hope of salvation from such fates. Unfortunately for our study, the mysteries were just that: mysterious and secret. Their essence was some saving rite through which the initiated found enlightenment and salvation, usually involving a personal experience with a particular deity. In this rite the initiate would reenact the saving story of the God or Goddess and thereby gain freedom. Two of the greatest mysteries of the ancient world centered on wine (Dionysus) and bread (Demeter), while others focused on the stars and sacrifice (Mithras) and resurrection of the dead (Cybele, Orpheus). One of the most moving descriptions of this process is found in a semicomical novel, *The Golden Ass*, written in the middle of the second century by Apuleius, a Roman aristocrat from North Africa. (For more on the novel see Chapter 1, pages 43–45.) We can see in Apuleius' novel not only the conviction that Isis can deliver her devotees from Fate's uncertain powers but also his own warm devotion to Isis, involving a lengthy process of initiation. This initiation was a rigorous affair requiring both study and moral purity. It was also an expensive endeavor, eventually costing the equivalent of many thousands of dollars. The masses could worship and experience the initiation from a distance but could never hope to be initiated themselves.

Beyond even the mysteries lay **philosophy**, which was a religious movement rather than an academic discipline in this age. There were a variety of philosophical schools, each pursuing its own vision of truth. What they shared was the conviction that such truth would liberate them from the mundane world. Whether by reason (Stoicism), self-denial (Epicureanism), mystical practices (Neo-Pythagoreanism), nonconformity (Cynicism), or some other means, the philosopher rose above the common experience (see Chapter 2, pages 56–58).

A strong movement in philosophy during this period, typified by **Stoicism**, was toward understanding the divine as one rather than many. Stoicism used a method of symbolic interpretation by which the various Gods and Goddesses represented various aspects of the one God. While being a philosopher was nearly a full-time pursuit of only the intellectual elite, all cultured persons studied philosophy and were influenced by it.

These options were not mutually exclusive. Typically, a person would continue to participate in the traditional religious rites of the various Gods and Goddesses, perhaps worship especially Isis or one of the other saviors of the mysteries, learn as much philosophy as permitted by his or her station in life, and not neglect to heed omens and astrology. The dominant experience of that age was **syncretism**, combining elements from various religious systems in a pragmatic or useful fashion. After Alexander the Great had conquered the East, Greek culture spread and mixed with the cultures of Egypt, Persia, Babylon, Palestine, Syria, and the rest. The new civilization that arose is called the **Hellenistic age**, a blend of East and West. Their religions, too, were blended so that the various national divinities were identified with each other, and we find names like "Apollo-Helios-Mithras-Hermes" and "Zeus–Ahura Mazda." The hallmark of the Hellenistic age was the conviction that the Gods of all the nations were just different names for the same divinity. (Review the discussion of religion in Chapter 1, pages 42–45.)

Against such a diverse background we must read Paul's letter to the Galatians. Some Jews were exclusivists; many more were active and successful missioners, who demanded varying degrees of conformity to Jewish ways from their converts. Gentiles were sometimes anti-Jewish, especially the Roman upper classes. Many more were attracted to the Jewish faith to some extent, some recognizing it as an honorable and ancient tradition, others converting to it, and many not actually converting but adopting Jewish ways to some degree. The Jewish tradition spoke to the deepest needs of the age. Its one God promised freedom from sin and fate, and offered life beyond death.

As we saw in the Izates story, Gentiles who accepted the Jewish way had to decide how diligent they would be in keeping the Law. In the two letters of Paul that we will now examine we find Gentiles taking opposite approaches.

GENTILES WHO OBEY THE LAW: GALATIANS

Unlike all Paul's other letters, this one is addressed to many churches in a broad geographical region known as **Galatia** (see Figure 4.1) The trouble seems to be widespread, infecting several cities. Paul is clearly alarmed, writing his most vigorous letter and taking a harsh and insulting tone. Much about the letter is controversial, including the exact location of the area known as Galatia, the nature of the underlying problem, the identity of the opponents, and the reasons for Paul's hostility. Our approach will be first to review the harsh language, then clarify the rhetorical structure, and finally examine the historical setting and meaning of this letter.

Rhetorical Insults

If this letter were all we had of Paul's work we could only regard him as a rather uncharitable radical. When he launches the main part of his argument, he addresses his hearers as "*O anoetoi Galatai*," which J. B. Phillips translated as "O you dear idiots of Galatia" ([1972] 3:1; literally "mindless"). Paul frankly admits to his listeners that his tone is unpleasant but explains that he is perplexed by what they have done (4:20).

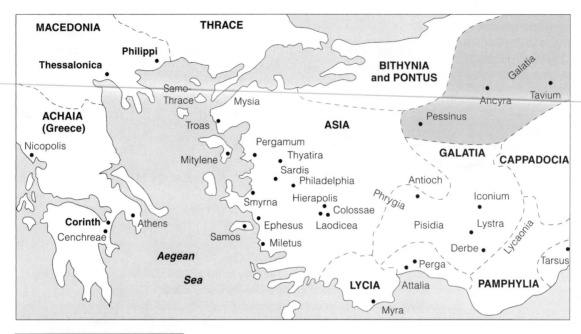

FIGURE 4.1 GREECE AND ASIA MINOR Born in Tarsus, Paul continually moved west (eventually to Rome and perhaps on to Spain). Most of his work and all but one of his letters centered on the large cities of Greece and Asia Minor, which became major hubs of Pauline influence. Whether Paul visited Galatia proper (the shaded portion) where actual "Galatians" lived is debated. The Roman province of Galatia extended much farther south. But calling the Hellenized inhabitants of this southern area "Galatians" would have been insulting.

This is the only letter in which Paul found nothing flattering to say about his readers in an opening thanksgiving. There is no thanksgiving. Where the audience might expect to hear "I give thanks for you" they hear instead:

> I am astonished that you are so quickly deserting the one who called you in the grace of Christ and are turning to a different gospel—not that there is another gospel, but there are some who are confusing you and want to pervert the gospel of Christ. (1:6–7)

There is some debate about whether the "one" they are said to desert is Christ or Paul, but it may be an intentional ambiguity. Clearly Paul, under personal attack by some group of opponents, was forced to defend himself as well as his message. Also, in the rhetoric of that time, no clear distinction was made between speaker and message. A primary task of the rhetorician was to present his own character to the audience.

Paul bows to no human authority. Repeatedly he refers to the Jerusalem leadership at the time of his visit as "those who were of repute" (2:2, 6, 9) and cannot resist adding: "what they were makes no difference to me." He calls Peter a hypocrite, perhaps even a sinner (2:14–17). His rhetoric is extreme: "Now I, Paul, say to you that if you receive circumcision, Christ will be of no advantage to you" (5:2). In a bitter metaphor he describes circumcision as being "severed" from Christ (5:4), and adds that he wishes that those who insist on circumcision would "mutilate themselves" (5:12). (One of the more repulsive forms of religion in Galatia involved the Galli, priests of the Goddess Cybele, who, in a frenzied rite of devotion, castrated themselves.) He attributes the desire to circumcise to a desire to "glory in your flesh" (6:12–13), as if those who opposed Paul were making little trophies or collecting scalps. He curtly compared their scars to his (6:17).

The Rhetorical Structure

The insults, hyperbole, and ferocity give the impression of a passionate letter, dashed off in a moment of anger. In places, the letter lends itself to this interpretation: Paul begins a sentence in 2:4, which progresses through verse 5 but never actually goes anywhere: it never reaches a main clause. That Galatians has often been interpreted as a passionate letter is a tribute to Paul's rhetorical skill, for it can be shown that it is a carefully organized, systematic work.

Yet its organization is not that of the standard Pauline letter. Though we can still find many of the formal sections we have observed in other letters, that pattern does not seem to determine the logic of Galatians. Consider the following:

Opening   1:1–5
Thanksgiving (none in Galatians)
Main body (no formulas or future plans)   1:6–5:25
Exhortations to good behavior   5:25–6:10
Closing   6:11–18
   Writing process   6:11
   Standard benediction   6:18

Recent interpreters have suggested another approach to the structure of Galatians, viewing it as a judicial argument. Ancient rhetoricians had several ways to organize an argument, but the preferred scheme in Paul's day was a five-part appeal (see Clarke, 1953:23–37). The form of the rhetorical defense was deeply influenced by its origin in the law courts. (See the general discussion of rhetoric in the Introduction and Tables I.2 and I.3, pages 15–16.) Various Greek and Latin technical terms were applied to the different parts of the speech. Rough English equivalents would be

1. *Introduction*—primarily to state the case but to get the listeners' attention as well. The normal means for gaining the allegiance of the audience were appeals to the character of the speaker, the lack of character of opponents, the nature of the audience, or the facts of the case.
2. *Narrative*—to review the facts of the case and put them within the proper historical context. Although both sides would agree generally on this narrative, each presented it in a way that would support his later argument.
3. *Argument*—to clarify the issues by showing the points agreed on by the two parties and those that separate them—a sort of summary of the case.
4. *Proof*—to establish the truth of the speaker's point of view by a series of arguments, usually proceeding from the strongest to the weakest. This would be the longest and most important part of the speech. Sometimes combined with

this, occasionally as a separate point, and sometimes even omitted was the refutation of the proofs offered by the opposing side.

5. *Conclusion*—to sum up the earlier argument and make an impassioned plea to persuade the listeners to accept the speaker's point of view.

The ancient listener, whether trained in the schools that taught such skills or not, had heard enough defense speeches to know what to listen for and what to expect. If we use this general pattern as a model, the course of Paul's argument will become clear.

Using the rhetorical pattern sketched above, and the reading guide, try to answer the following: 1. Why does Paul tell these stories about himself? 2. On which points do he and his opponents agree? What is their central disagreement?

 READING GUIDE TO GALATIANS

This narrative section is the most autobiographical passage in all of Paul's writings, but we must be cautious in interpreting it. Paul is not telling stories so we can know about his life; he tells these stories to support his argument about his authority. There is, for example, a direct contradiction in the sequence of events listed here and that given in Acts (contrast Gal. 1:17 with Acts 9:22–26). The point is not that either is wrong or that one or the other must be considered unreliable as a result of this discovery. Instead, both Paul and Luke are telling their stories in order to prove a certain point. Both are arguing a case. Within the literary conventions of their day, both might actually be correct. As we will see, Luke's case in Acts rests on his connecting Paul closely with Jerusalem; Paul's case is based on asserting his autonomy. Thus, we must expect that each will tell the story differently.

A rhetorically constructed argument required that every part contribute to the final purpose. Even the introduction lays the groundwork for Paul's later arguments. Notice especially the apocalyptic note of "the present evil age" and the deliverance already accomplished by Christ's death (1:3). This note of freedom will become the keynote of the letter. Notice too, the concise statement of the charges against Paul, charges related to the basic meaning of the gospel (1:6–7), implying that his gospel lacks divine sanction (1:11).

Even more revealing is the way Paul states the case in summary. He and his opponents agree on basic issues, including the key idea that being right with God does not originate in good works (2:15–16). Yet they disagree about what this means for the Gentiles. For Paul it meant that Gentiles were free from the Law (2:17–21).

The lengthy section of proofs divides into positive assertions, which prove Paul's case (3–4), and refutations of the implications of his opponents' position (5–6). He concludes with a recapitulation and an ironic comparison of scars (6:11–18). A final blessing (6:16) balances the opening curse (1:8). Before we analyze Paul's reasoning in detail, we must probe more deeply into the actual historical situation he confronted.

The Situation in Galatia

In the first century the term *Galatia* referred to two different but related areas. Broadly, it referred to the Roman province that stretched across central Asia Minor, but more precisely it referred to the northern part of this province where the ethnic group called Galatians (a relatively primitive people related to the Gauls) lived. The people in the southern part of the province were mostly Greeks; to call them Galatians (primitives) was not very nice; to call them mindless Galatians was even more insulting. But that is the point: Paul is not being especially pleasant in this letter. Though it is not impossible, there is no real reason to suppose that Paul traveled to this northern region. Ancient commentators who assumed he did were probably more influenced by the changes of the second century, which redrew this district and limited the name *Galatia* to the northern part. Thus, we should probably read the references to "Galatians" as light sarcasm aimed at the cultured Greeks in the southern region that we know Paul visited. The obvious similarity between the circumcised "Galatai" and the castrated "Galli" surely produced its rhetorical effect.

The opponents as reactionaries. A more serious question concerns the nature of the opponents confronted in this letter. In general it seems clear that some "Eleazars" have come along behind Paul and persuaded these new converts that circumcision was as necessary for Jesus' followers as for Jews (for example, 5:2–10). It was, after all, demanded in the Bible. Who might have done such a thing? One possibility is that they were simply other Jews, like Eleazar, with no connection to Paul or to the Jesus movement. It is not unlikely that if a man like Eleazar came upon a assembly reading the Torah and claiming to follow it, he would have admonished them for not following its principal precept: circumcision. This may have happened, but it does not explain Galatians. The phenomenon was too widespread, affecting the whole province, and the agreement between Paul and his opponents was too specific (2:15–16). They also proclaimed Jesus; they preached "another gospel" (1:6).

We meet such people in one of the stories Paul told in the narrative section. In fact we meet an interesting variety of people in his stories.

READING AND REFLECTION

Reread the four stories: 1:11–17; 1:18–24; 2:1–10; and 2:11–14. How many different attitudes toward Gentiles can you discern in these stories?

The first story recounts the revelation that turned Paul from an opponent of the church to a proponent of the Gentiles. Notice the intimate connection between the revelation and the mission to Gentiles (1:16). This link leads many to speak of it as Paul's call (a divine summons to a new mission) rather than his conversion (a changed religion). Paul himself speaks of it in a manner similar to the prophetic calls in Isaiah 6 and Jeremiah 1. Paul completely isolates this event from Jerusalem because he wants to emphasize its divine origin.

The second story recounts Paul's trip to Jerusalem to visit with Peter for fifteen days. The verb *to visit* (*historeo*) means to become acquainted with or to get information from, and it indicates that Paul was conscious of depending on Peter for information, but not for his gospel.

The third story involves an official trip to Jerusalem "by revelation," to present his gospel to the authorities there and gain their approval. This is probably (though not certainly) the same trip reported in Acts 15, where many additional details are provided. In the Acts version the explicit purpose is to decide the issue of circumcision, and Peter is the primary defender of Gentile liberty. Acts says the authorities decided to exempt the Gentiles from circumcision but imposed certain dietary regulations (Acts 15:19–20). This may be so, though Paul nowhere indicates that he knows of such dietary restrictions for Gentiles. Paul's account clearly shows that there was no absolute victory for his position at this conference. The most he can report is a kind of compromise, an agreement to disagree, in which Paul goes one way and Peter another (2:7–10).

This leads to the final story, in which Peter visits Paul's work in Antioch (2:11–21). The sequence of events (if not their meaning) is clear: Peter ate with the Gentiles until "certain men from James" arrive, then he drew back and refused to eat with the Gentiles "for fear of the circumcision faction." Paul challenged him publicly, labeling his behavior "hypocrisy." What is not clear is why Peter withdrew, as there were no prohibitions of eating with Gentiles per se. Of course, eating with Gentiles was always liable to involve one in idolatry, as we will see below. Gentiles often ate meat that had been sacrificed (see page 459). But that would not likely be a concern here. What is more likely at issue is not the dietary laws but the implications of sharing a sacred meal at a common table with Gentiles as Gentiles: the implication that they did not need to be circumcised and become Jews (see Nanos, 1996:337–71). Sharing a common table is a sign of inclusion, and although Peter was willing to do this earlier, he was apparently persuaded by these delegates from James to cease.

What is also not clear is whether Peter accepted this rebuke. The skill with which Paul tells this story, causing the reader to cheer for Paul and to assume the correctness of his position, must not be allowed to obscure the probable outcome. For he never says he persuaded Peter (and it would strengthen his argument if he could say he did). On the contrary, Barnabas, Paul's partner, actually went over to the other side (2:13) and no longer traveled with Paul (see Acts 15, especially verses 36–41).

A full spectrum of attitudes toward Gentiles is evident in these stories: from the "false brethren" who insist on circumcision on one side to Paul on the other. The "men from James" (and probably James himself) seem far more insistent on Gentile observance than Paul, and Peter and Barnabas seem to occupy a position halfway between James and Paul.

Do the opponents in Galatia fit on this same spectrum? Perhaps they are like the "men from James," Palestinian missioners claiming to represent the more authentic Jesus tradition of the Jerusalem church. Or perhaps they resembled those Paul labeled "false brethren," Jewish followers of Jesus who insisted on Gentile circumcision. They may well have set out deliberately to follow up Paul's preaching, which they would have considered flawed and incomplete. After all, the very same Law (Torah) that Paul cites to support his gospel explicitly demands circumcision of God's people. One can almost hear them urging these Gentiles: "You have made a good start with your faith, but now let's go on to perfection. Keep the whole Law of God" (Gal. 3:3 and Acts 15:5).

One difficulty with thinking that his opponents are connected with Jerusalem is that Paul takes pains to deny that he depends on Jerusalem for his authority (1:17–2:7). Is their argument that Paul ought to be dependent on Jerusalem but is not, and therefore that his gospel has only his own, human authority? Or do they accuse him of having to depend on Jerusalem while they have some higher authority?

The opponents as radicals. The latter possibility is argued by those who regard these opponents not as more conservative than Paul but as more radical. In this view, the opponents were promising a cosmic freedom to the Galatians. Freedom is the dominant theme of this letter. Such freedom was the purpose of Christ's death (1:3). Many of Paul's metaphors contrast with freedom: bondage (2:4; 4:8), confinement (3:23), custodianship (3:24), minor child (4:1), slavery (4:22). More particularly, Paul speaks of a bondage to "the elemental spirits of the universe" (4:3) and to "beings that by nature are no Gods" (4:8). Such language seems characteristic of Hellenistic philosophical speculation rather than of conservative Palestinian Jews.

In the Hellenistic view, the universe consisted of a few basic elements, "which are not simply material substances, but demonic entities of cosmic proportions and astral powers which were hostile" to humanity (Betz, 1979:205). These elements controlled human destiny, for they worked within the individual and within the cosmos (hence, astrology). The purpose of magic, prayers, rituals, and rites (or "laws") was to control and contain these forces to prevent harm. If this was the thinking in Galatia, then circumcision would be a sort of talisman to protect one from the powers of the elements (which Hellenistic Jews often identified with angels).

Nothing in the letter allows us to decide with certainty whether the opponents were more conservative or more radical or even whether they were Jews or Gentiles. But given the tenor of the Hellenistic era, the Galatians probably saw their rites and laws as a means of triumphing over the limitations of fate. It is no coincidence then that Paul presents himself as the great apostle of liberty. Let us look more closely at how Paul argues his case.

The Reasoning of the Letter

The lengthy section of proof and rebuttal begins in 3:1 and runs on to 6:10; basically, chapters 3 and 4 are the positive proofs, and 5 and 6 the rebuttal. Hans Dieter Betz's analysis of this section maintains that Paul offers six major proofs (1979: 19–21, 128–252). Use these summaries to reread Paul's arguments.

1. *The argument from past experience: the Spirit (3:1–5).* Paul makes good use of rhetorical questions: Did you begin by keeping the Law or by the experience

of the Spirit? Are miracles worked among you by keeping the Law or by the Spirit?

2. *The argument from Scripture: Abraham (3:6–14).* Scripture attributes righteousness to Abraham on the basis of faith (the words *believe* and *faith* share the same root in Greek) and further promises to bless the Gentiles through him (that is, through a similar faith). Other passages are quoted (some out of context) to show that Law and faith are opposites.

3. *The argument from common human experience: wills (3:15–22).* Just as a will cannot be altered once it has been put into effect, so God's promise to Abraham cannot be altered by the giving of the Law 430 years later. (Digression: Why, then, the Law? It was a temporary restraining order until the coming of the Messiah.)

4. *The argument from Church tradition: baptism (3:23–4:11).* Paul compares the situation before the Messiah to that of minor children who, although they are heirs to the estate, are controlled by slaves. Baptism makes all believers children of God, but those children must not now turn back to "the weak and beggarly elemental spirits" of the universe who ruled through the Law. The sign of adoption is possession of the Spirit.

5. *The argument from friendship: love (4:12–20).* Paul defends his character, reminding them of the exalted reception they gave him, "as an angel of God, as Christ Jesus" (4:14). He presents himself as a model for imitation (4:12) and compares himself to a mother in childbirth (4:19).

6. *The argument from story: allegory (4:21–31).* Strictly speaking, neither this nor the previous point is an argument. It is a convincing story designed to move the feelings of the audience already persuaded (it is hoped) by the earlier arguments. Paul reads the story of Abraham's two wives as an **allegory**, a symbolic story in which the characters and events really mean something else, often an idea. Paul read the story of Abraham's two wives as showing two ways of serving God: by relying on the Law (Hagar, the slave wife whose son did not inherit) or by relying on the promise (Sarah, the free wife whose son became heir). The implications for Paul's argument are obvious.

I have one final word on this section. Paul admonished his hearers with the Scripture, "Cast out the slave and her son" (4:30). Though this has been a text of many anti-Semitic preachers through the centuries, it has nothing to do with Jews. In the context of Paul's letter, it meant something like "reject the way of trying to please God by relying on the Law" (with perhaps the additional sense of rejecting those opponents of Paul who preach otherwise). Its meaning is captured in Paul's closing maxim:

For freedom Christ has set us free. Stand firm, therefore, and do not submit again to a yoke of slavery. (5:1)

These arguments are designed to show the need for depending on the Spirit rather than on rules, be the opponents conservative and Jewish or liberal and Hellenistic. Now Paul deals with their counterarguments. Against whatever positive arguments they might muster, Paul launches a tirade on the dangers of depending on the Law (5:1–12). Against their logical arguments that his position leads to lawlessness, he warns about "the flesh" (5:13–24), building an ethical exhortation on the contrast between flesh and spirit. Finally, he combines the idea of Spirit and of obligation in an appeal for mutual spiritual freedom and sharing, now obedient to the "law of Christ" (5:25–6:10).

In summary, Galatians represents Paul's attempt to present the story of Christ to Gentiles who felt constrained by fate, bound by powers beyond their control. For these Gentiles to be circumcised in an effort to protect themselves from such powers was, Paul felt, to miss the essential point of the gospel, namely, that Christ has already delivered his own from the powers of this age (1:3). This case is presented in an elaborately organized rhetorical argument, appealing to experience, Scripture (Law!), ritual, life, and story.

All together, Galatians is a grand argument for freedom that retains its persuasive powers nearly two thousand years later. But it was also a dangerous argument, as his opponents no doubt pointed out, because moral behavior left to spiritual promptings could lead to some strange aberrations. In fact, certain followers of Paul at Corinth who experimented with the limits of freedom in Christ soon discovered another side to Paul.

GENTILES WHO IGNORE THE LAW: CORINTHIANS

The ancient city of **Corinth**, strategically located on the narrow midsection of Greece, had been an important and prosperous city in the ancient world—a center of industry, trade, and vice. However, Corinth made the mistake of trying to stand up to Roman power and was completely destroyed in 146 BCE. The city lay desolate for a hundred years before Julius Caesar reestablished it as a Roman colony in 44 BCE.

Like Philippi, it was a place for army veterans who had served their twenty years and received a grant of land as part of their discharge. Officially, veterans were entitled to a grant of three thousand denarii (the equivalent of about ten years' pay) at retirement, but they often received a grant of land of equal value. In addition, about half their pay was withheld during their service as a kind of forced saving. Thus, these men in their early forties approached their new life with a sizable endowment. It did not always work out well because the land was sometimes not the most desirable, and old soldiers did not always make good farmers. But the settlement at Corinth was a success.

A thriving seaport city, Corinth attracted many other settlers as well. Situated on the isthmus and possessing two good harbors (one facing east and one west), the new Corinth became as prosperous as the old. (See the map on page 120.) It was a much more diversified city than most, attracting inhabitants from all quarters and all ethnic groups. A strong Jewish settlement existed there, though we know little about it. Corinth was a meeting place of East and West where one could hear half a dozen languages in addition to the dominant Greek and Latin.

This diversity was stimulated even further by the great athletic contests, the Isthmian Games, which Corinth sponsored every two years. Ranking only below the Olympic Games, these contests attracted competitors from all over the Greek world. The huge crowds were a stimulus to the local economy (including tent making, as many of the visitors stayed in tents). We get some impression of what Paul would have experienced from this somewhat dour description by a late first-century observer:

That was the time [the time for the Isthmian Games] when one could hear crowds of wretched sophists [philosophers] around Poseidon's temple shouting and reviling one another, and their disciples as they were called, fighting with one another, many writers reading aloud their stupid works, many poets reciting their poems while others applauded them, many jugglers showing their tricks, many fortune-tellers interpreting fortunes, lawyers innumerable perverting judgement, and peddlers not a few peddling whatever they happened to have. (Dio Chrysostom Discourses 8:9)

This mixture of peoples brought a multitude of religions into Corinth. The classical Greek deities were all worshipped in various shrines and temples, with Poseidon, God of the sea, taking first place in this sailors' town. A major temple to the Goddess Roma and devotion to the emperor would be expected in a city founded by former legionnaires. Greek and Eastern rites were combined in the worship of **Asclepius** (Greek God of healing), **Isis** (Egyptian Goddess of life), and Aphrodite (Greek Goddess of love), who had major temples here (see Figure 4.2). Aphrodite was also the patron of prostitutes. Strabo claims that her temple at Corinth employed a thousand sacred prostitutes (probably slaves), but whether he was referring to the old Corinth or the new is unclear (*Geography* 378). Sacred prostitution, common in the East, derived from prehistoric fertility rites whereby union with the priestess of the Goddess would make the land fertile. It remained popular for other reasons. Corinth is the only city in the Greek world where we hear of such a temple, casting some doubt on the accuracy of Strabo's report. Accurate or not, it illustrates Corinth's reputation as a freewheeling seaport city.

Paul's Contacts with Corinth: Piecing the Story Together

According to Acts 18, Paul's visit to Corinth was turbulent. He went into business with two other traveling Jews and stayed in the city a year and a half. He became so contentious in the synagogue that he was forced to leave it and meet in the house next door, which was owned by "Titus Justus, a worshipper of God," obviously one of those Gentile men who were almost converted to Jewish religion. Just as obviously, Titus Justus was wealthy, since only the wealthy owned homes. Ordinary citizens, and even the moderately well-off veterans, would have lived in apartments or condominiums. Although a few Jews joined Paul in his withdrawal, his major success was with these Gentiles (Acts 18:111).

Reconstructing the further course of Paul's interaction with the Corinthians is not simple, but it reveals how Paul operated. What follows is hypothetical, having the merit of explaining the data available in Paul's letters to Corinth.

The evidence of 1 Corinthians. First Corinthians reveals an ongoing relationship between Paul and Corinth, as we might expect. Not only has he sent his assistant Timothy back to Corinth (4:17), but he has also received a report from Chloe's people about the situation there (1:11). We know nothing else about Chloe. This reference to her people indicates that she was a woman of some importance, perhaps a wealthy member of the church whose business required some travel (in which case her "people" would be her employees). Or possibly she was a local teacher (in which case they would be her disciples; see verse 12). This report alone might have prompted Paul to write, but he had also received a letter from Corinth asking his advice on a number

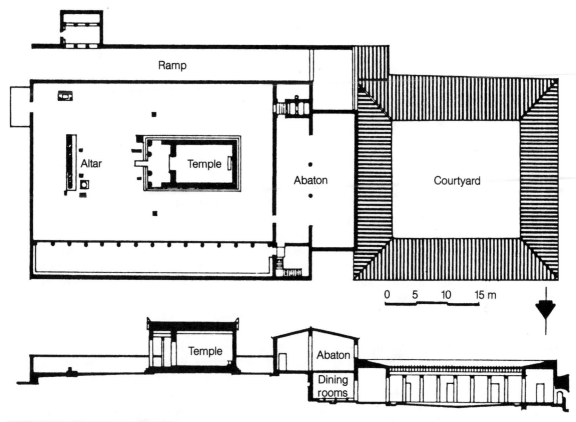

FIGURE 4.2 **TEMPLE COMPLEX OF ASCLEPIUS AT CORINTH** A floor plan (top) and a side view of the Asclepion. The temple and its altar were enclosed and would accommodate large crowds of worshippers. People sought healing from Asclepius, often spending nights here hoping for a healing vision. The dining rooms and courtyard, with its fresh spring, would have been used for religious and private purposes (guild meetings, family celebration, parties). We can imagine the dilemma of a recently converted Corinthian invited to a family gathering in such a place (see 1 Cor. 10:14–11:1). (From *St. Paul's Corinth* by Jerome Murphy-O'Connor [Michael Glazier, 1983:163], used by permission.)

of topics (7:1). Even more surprising, we learn that this is not his first letter to the Corinthians. For Paul declares, "I wrote to you in my letter not to associate with immoral" people (1 Cor. 5:9). This reference to an earlier letter means that Paul had written them sometime before "First" Corinthians. We no longer have this first letter, but a fragment of it may be preserved in what we call *Second Corinthians*, for a careful reading of that letter reveals that it is probably a composite of several separate letters.

The evidence of 2 Corinthians. The hypothesis that 2 Corinthians is a composite letter has been increasingly accepted since it was proposed about a century ago. This assertion is based on a problem in the text of the letter: at two points the thought breaks off sharply, jumps to an unrelated topic, then abruptly shifts back to the original thought. The suggestion is that the intruding material originally belonged to a separate discourse.

READING AND REFLECTION

Try reading the following verses in 2 Corinthians: 6:13 and 6:14, then 6:13 and 7:2; read 2:13 and 2:14, then 2:13 and 7:5. What connections do you see between these pairs of verses?

The ideas in 7:2 seem to belong to those in 6:13, and all the discussion about separation from evil (6:14–7:2) seems to be spliced into the middle of a completely unrelated topic. This fragment on separation is not easy to relate to anything else in 2 Corinthians. Some have noted that this topic is similar to Paul's lost first letter (see 1 Cor. 5:9), but others point out that it calls for the precise kind of separation Paul says he did not advocate: separation from the world.

So too, Paul's anxious search for Titus in 2:13 is interrupted without warning and resumed without cause in 7:5. All the intervening material is irrelevant to this quest. It seems more likely that the narrative about meeting Titus in Macedonia was originally connected and that this is another fragment from yet another letter.

Paul also referred to a painful letter that he had written out of much affliction (2 Cor. 2:4), one that he initially regretted writing (7:8). This does not accurately describe 1 Corinthians or either of the fragments. There seems to be yet another lost letter, though again some argue that it is partially preserved in 2 Corinthians.

Chapters 10 to 13 match this description rather well. The tone of these three chapters is far harsher than the rest: in them Paul directly confronts his opposition and rails at the Corinthians for listening to these other teachers. After bragging "as a fool," he says they will have no trouble accepting him, "for you gladly bear with fools" (11:17–18). He chides them: "I robbed other churches . . . to serve you" (11:8). He threatens: "I fear that perhaps I may come and find you not what I wish, and that you may find me not what you wish" (12:20). "If I come again I will not spare them" (13:2). The most obvious point of these chapters is that the conflict has not been settled; the outcome is still in doubt, which explains their painful tone.

Yet the early part of the letter is relatively tranquil and presumes that the crisis is past. Titus has already returned with the comforting news of reconciliation (7:6). Paul even asks mercy for the offending party (2:5–9). Either chapters 10 to 13 were written before these comforting words or we are to imagine that the conflict raged again at Corinth and that Paul learned of it while writing the letter, then dramatically shifted his tone at chapter 10.

A more logical hypothesis seems to be that there are three basic letters in 2 Corinthians, each of a somewhat different kind: there is the letter before the crisis (2:14–7:4, minus the addition on separation); there is the letter during the crisis (10–13), written in the genre of the fool's discourse; and there is the letter of reconciliation after the crisis (1:1–2:13 and 7:5–16). Chapters 8 and 9, both dealing with the collection, may have been attached to this last letter, or they may have been a separate letter or two (because 9:1 seems to reintroduce the idea of a collection as if it had not been mentioned earlier).

Thus the Corinthian correspondence seems to have been extensive, comprising a whole series of letters over several years' time. These letters also contain references to three visits by Paul himself and others by his associates, Timothy and Titus. A possible reconstruction of the course of events follows.

1. Paul establishes the church and spends more than eighteen months there (Acts 18).
2. He writes his first, now lost, letter regarding church discipline (1 Cor. 5:9, perhaps = 2 Cor. 6:14–7:1).
3. He sends Timothy to visit them (1 Cor. 4:17).
4. He receives reports from Chloe's people of divisions and immorality (1 Cor. 1:11).
5. He receives a letter from the Corinthians concerning questions they need to have answered (1 Cor. 7:1).
6. He writes another letter to answer them and to respond to Chloe's report (1 Cor.).
7. He sends Timothy on another visit (1 Cor. 16:10).
8. He hears of opposition at Corinth from outsiders with letters of reference. He is concerned but does not yet realize how serious the situation will become (2 Cor. 3:1).
9. He writes a third letter to warn and admonish them (2 Cor. 2:14–7:4, minus 6:14–7:1).
10. This letter is used against him, and real danger to his leadership emerges (2 Cor. 10:10).
11. Contrary to earlier plans (1 Cor. 16:7), he pays a brief visit to Corinth, where he finds open rebellion and insult (2 Cor. 2:5; 7:12).
12. He writes an angry letter (2 Cor. 7:12; 2:4; = 2 Corinthians 10–13).
13. He sends Titus to check on affairs (2 Cor. 12:17).
14. He learns from Titus of the success of his letter and of Titus's visit (2 Cor. 2:13; 7:5–6).
15. He writes a letter of reconciliation (2 Cor. 1:1–2:13; 7:5–16).
16. He arranges for a "gift" (2 Corinthians 8–9).
17. He visits a third time (proposed in 2 Cor. 12:14; 13:1).
18. He writes Romans from Corinth (Rom. 15:25–27; 1 Cor. 16:3).

If this is an accurate reconstruction of the events (and I emphasize that it is a hypothesis), we can readily understand Paul's anxiety about meeting Titus in Macedonia (see item 13 above) and much more about these writings. Paul's letters are not the reflections of an armchair philosopher; they are very specific communications, forged from conflict and controversy. Paul honed the letter into one of his most important tools. Let us proceed to examine the contents of these two letters more closely.

Problems of Gentile Converts: First Corinthians

From the lost first letter we learn that the assembly at Corinth was having difficulty with moral issues; for Paul admonished them to keep themselves separate from the immoral members of their assembly (1 Cor. 5:9–12). Although Corinth was well known for its vices, so that to "corinthianize" became an expression for debauchery, the moral standards at Corinth were probably not far different from those elsewhere in the Greco-Roman world. Most of the bad reputation really belonged to the old Corinth, which had been destroyed two centuries earlier. Like other places, the moral standards of Corinth were mixed. Generalization is dangerous but necessary.

Morality among the Gentiles. In this era, Gentiles asserted all sorts of moral standards, from the Cynic's lack of concern with morality to the Stoic's moral seriousness. In their effort to live according to nature, Cynics deliberately offended all social and moral conventions. When Demosthenes was rebuked for masturbating in public, he replied, "Would that I could relieve my need for food by just rubbing my belly" (Diogenes Laertius *Lives of Eminent Philosophers* 6.69). But the most popular philosophy of the day, Stoicism, defined a clear sense of duty that one must fulfill at all costs, even one's life. Epicureans, too, lived by very clear and demanding standards, being largely vegetarians, ascetic, and reclusive. The mystery religions demanded a strict moral standard from the would-be initiate, who had to prove worthy of being initiated.

The situation with popular religion was less clear, for there the central idea was not morality but **purity**, and there was no consensus as to what made one impure. One clear example of the lack of moral depth in the traditional religions is an inscription from a temple to Athena at Pergamum (just north of Ephesus, where Paul was when he wrote to the Corinthians):

> Whoever wishes to visit the temple of the Goddess, whether a resident of the city or anyone else, must refrain from intercourse with his wife (or husband) that day, from intercourse with another than his wife (or husband) for the preceding two days, and must complete the required lustrations [ceremonial purifications]. (Grant, 1953:6)

Clearly this does not show the Jewish concern for the absolute demand of God. The Jewish God forbade all adultery, not simply because it made one impure but because it was wrong. As long as the new Jesus message was proclaimed in a context dominated by this Jewish idea, there was no need to develop a theory of ethics. But when the proclamation was primarily successful with Gentiles, so that a split developed between this new way and the Jewish community (as was apparently the case at Corinth), the issue of ethics had to be addressed directly.

READING AND REFLECTION

Using the reading guide, read through 1 Corinthians and list Paul's responses to their questions. Are all these rules consistent with the freedom Paul advocated in Galatians?

 ## READING GUIDE TO FIRST CORINTHIANS

Salutation   1:1–3
Thanksgiving   1:4–9
Body: responses to problems   1:10–16:4

Paul's problems with the assembly at Corinth   1:10–6:20
Factions   1:1–4:20

Four distinct groups had emerged in the assembly, each attached to the person who had baptized them: the Paul party, the Apollos party, the Peter party, and the Christ party.

Incest   5:1–13

A man is living with his father's wife.

Lawsuits   6:1–8

The public courts are being used to settle disputes between believers.

Prostitutes   6:9–20

Some believers are continuing to visit prostitutes.

Paul's answers to their questions   7:1–16:4

Marriage   7:1–40

Should one marry?

Should married people have sexual relations?

Should widows remarry?

Should a believer divorce an unbeliever?

Food   8:1–11:1

Should a believer eat meat sacrificed to the Gods?

Is one free to eat even if it offends others?

Is it permitted to eat what is sold in the market?

Is it permitted to eat in the home of an idolater?

Conduct of worship   11:2–14:40

Should women pray and preach without a head covering?

How should the Lord's Supper be eaten?

Should spiritual gifts be regulated?

Resurrection   15:1–58

Will there be a resurrection?

With what sort of body are the dead raised?

Collection   16:1–4

How should it be taken up?

When will Paul come for it?

Travel plans   16:5–9

Exhortations   16:10–18

Mutual greetings   16:19–23

Handwritten greeting   16:21

Blessing   16:22–23

Morality at Corinth. Although the answers to their questions may seem obvious to us, we must try to imagine the situation at Corinth in which these were considered pressing issues. What could have created the dilemma that forced the Corinthians to write Paul for answers to just these questions? And why did they apparently fail to ask about the problems he addressed in the first six chapters? How are we to understand that they had scruples about sexual relations between husbands and wives, yet saw no problem with visiting prostitutes? Not only did they not have a question about the case of incest, they were proud of it (5:1–2: literally, "you are ones who have become proud of it"; see 5:6).

Paul describes the issue as a man "living with his father's wife" (5:1), thus the likely background is a household in which an older man had taken a far younger wife, probably because his first wife died. This was a very common occurrence: the new wife could well be younger than his own children, perhaps married when she was only thirteen or fourteen years old. When the man died, one of his sons married the wife, his legal mother—a practice that the ancients considered incest. This cannot be attributed to a supposed low morality among Gentiles. It was absolutely forbidden in both Jewish and Greek culture. The Greek story of **Oedipus**, who inadvertently married his mother and suffered extreme humiliation as a result, gives some sense of the Greek abhorrence of marrying one's mother (whether natural or legal). Paul himself was shocked by this situation and contrasted it with even pagan morality (5:1; for a dramatic version of the Oedipus story see the play by Sophocles, *Oedipus the King*).

If we could discover the logic by which the Corinthians could be proud of this situation, we might have the key to understanding what was happening at Corinth. By what logic could these Gentile believers feel proud of incest and free to visit prostitutes, be dubious of sex in marriage, and uncertain of the resurrection (to cite only the more obvious questions)? Of course, the existence of factions could mean that various people had problems with only some of these issues.

The problem behind the problems. Let's start with the hypothesis that the Corinthians were confused about their bodies and the relation of their bodies to things spiritual. All the problems addressed in the letter—except for factionalism, use of the courts, and the collection—have an obvious connection to the body: incest, prostitutes, sex within marriage, proper food (including the Lord's Supper), ecstasy in worship, and questions about resurrection. Even the question of women's role in worship has something to do with male and female bodies. Now the ancients did not understand their bodies in quite the way we do.

This is a complicated topic ably explored by Dale Martin (1995). Here I will only highlight two fundamental differences between how we view our bodies and how they viewed theirs. First, for the people of Paul's time, the body was not synonymous with matter. In fact, the human being consisted of various levels of material reality, with body being the most rudimentary. Above the body was the soul, consisting of much finer matter, and above the soul was the spirit, the finest and most active aspect (not coincidentally, the Greek word for *spirit* also means "breath"). This breath-spirit is like an active force that shapes both body and soul. It exists both within and outside the body.

And this implies the second major difference: the body of each individual participates in and reflects the body of the world; each person is a microcosm of the whole. We carry over some of this meaning when we speak of the social body, but what is for us a metaphor was for the ancients a simple reality. The breath-spirit of the world is the same as the breath-spirit of the individual. And just as the spirit forms the soul to rule over the body, so the spirit forms certain finer persons to rule over the body politic. The hierarchy of soul over the body mirrors society, where the noble rule over the crude.

Because the group is also a body, it can be healthy or sick. Divisions within the group were a sign of sickness of the body. Both the collection (for the unity of the group) and the refusal to use the public courts are necessary for protection of the body. Viewed this way, all the problems addressed in 1 Corinthians are problems of the body. We need then to explore a bit more how different groups regarded the body.

All regarded the body as inferior to the soul, but some went even further. Hundreds of years before Paul, in the dialogue recounting the death of Socrates, Plato reported this interesting interchange. Socrates speaks first:

> "Do we think there is such a thing as death?"
>
> "Certainly," replied Simmias.
>
> "We believe, do we not, that death is the separation of the soul from the body, and the state of being dead is the state in which the body is separated from the soul and exists alone by itself and the soul is separated from the body and exists alone by itself? Is death anything other than this?"
>
> "No, it is this," he said.
>
> "Now, my friend, see if you agree with me; for if you do I think we shall get more light on our subject. Do you think a philosopher would be likely to care much about the so-called pleasures, such as eating and drinking?"
>
> "By no means, Socrates," said Simmias.
>
> "How about the pleasures of love?"
>
> "Certainly not."
>
> "Well do you think such a man would think much of the other cares of the body . . . ?"
>
> "I think the true philosopher would despise them," he said. (Phaedo 64c–e)

Paul was not the first to have to explain the relation of the body to the pursuits of the spirit. But he took a very different tack than Socrates. To understand this difference, we need to explore the different interpretations of being human evident in the Greek and Jewish cultures.

The essential difference between the two can be seen by going back to the archaic period in each tradition. Several scenes in the *Iliad* and the *Odyssey* depict the hero descending into the underworld to gain some information from the dead. Here he meets disembodied spirits,

> souls of the departed dead flocked up from Erebos—brides, God-like youths, old men who had endured much, innocent maidens who had only just put on grief, and many wearing the wounds of bronze spears, men slain of Ares [God of war], with armor all gory. (Homer Odyssey 11.40–50)

In a very primitive fashion, these souls need the offerings of the living, especially blood, and can foretell the future. By contrast, no concern for life after death appears in the writings of the Jewish classical period. (For a late and pessimistic view, see Eccles. 9:10.) There is only the grave to which all go. Only once do we find a medium conjuring a ghost (1 Sam. 28:3–20). When the ghost of Samuel appears before Saul, he says: "Why have you disturbed me by bringing me up?" Here the dead are gone; they no longer need the living.

When a concern for life after death did develop in Israel, especially during the religious persecutions, it was conceived of as a **resurrection** of the body. Thus, a dying martyr addressing the pagan king, who is having him killed because he refuses to worship his Gods, says: "You accursed wretch, you dismiss us from this present life, but the King of the universe will raise us up to an everlasting renewal of life, because we have died for his laws" (2 Macc. 7:9). Even Paul, a Jew who had been deeply influenced by Greek ideas, equated the ideas of a bodiless afterlife with the idea of nakedness (2 Cor. 5:1–4).

But among the Greeks, beginning with Socrates (died 399 BCE), there is a clearly articulated belief in **immortality** involving a bodiless afterlife, with separate destinies for the good and the evil. For Socrates the soul was not only deathless, it was birthless, preexistent-immortal (Plato *Phaedo* 70–77, 105e). Thus the soul returns to its true abode after death:

> *But those who are found to have excelled in holy living are freed from these regions within the earth and are released from prisons; they mount upward into their pure abode and dwell upon the earth. And of these all who have duly purified themselves by philosophy live henceforth altogether without bodies, and pass to still more beautiful abodes which it is not easy to describe.* (Phaedo 114c)

We must notice the condition, "such as have purified themselves sufficiently by philosophy." Earlier in the same dialogue we are told that the task of the philosopher "consists in separating the soul as much as possible from the body" (67c). In fact it had become a pun in Greek philosophical thought that the body was the tomb of the soul. (In Greek: *Soma estin sema*. Perhaps the closest we can come in English would be to say "the womb is a tomb.")

Certain conclusions follow from this basic dualism. If we are essentially spiritual beings, we have somehow fallen and become entrapped into materiality, into body. But surely the first step in transcending the body and gaining our rightful place is to recognize the truth of our condition, to know our true natures. As the philosophers put it: know yourself—and your true self is spiritual.

These ideas were widespread, but a distinctive way of thinking about them developed about this time: **Gnosticism** (from the Greek word for knowledge, *gnosis*). There were countless forms of Gnosticism, but all were based on this idea of an absolute dualism between matter and spirit. All sought the saving knowledge by which we could be freed from bondage to matter, usually through the secret revelations of a divine man who would descend into the world and reveal these truths. Many later Gnostics were Christians who regarded Jesus as being that heavenly revealer. The problems at Corinth could have sprung from a Gnostic-like interpretation of Paul's gospel.

For example, if one takes as a starting point the absolute separation of matter and spirit, marriage—and especially sexuality—becomes a problem. One should be above the body. Even what to eat becomes a problem; by far the largest number of Gnostics were ascetics, often vegetarians. Other Gnostics argued, with equal logic, that since the body is ever and always evil, there was no need to control it. Thus, it is no more evil to visit a prostitute than it is to eat; both are bodily, and therefore irrelevant, activities. Nor should one put any emphasis on the differences between men and women, because this is purely a bodily matter. Thus the Gnostics were more apt than most to insist on absolute equality between men and women. Certainly the Gnostics would favor spiritual gifts, because they regarded themselves as the truly spiritual ones. Much of what Paul said about the wise and spiritual in 1 Corinthians (1–4) seems appropriate to a Gnostic view of the world.

Still, we know of no Gnostic groups this early; they develop mostly in the second century. At most we see the development of a gnosticizing and spiritualizing interpretation of this new faith. This Greek mistrust of the body and fascination with the spirit will eventually lead to daring new interpretations of Paul and Jesus (which we will examine in Chapter 6).

Let us look at the problem from the opposite point of view. One of the ironies of Greek culture is that there existed alongside this very negative view of the body a striking validation of the beauty and utility of the body. The body was a good thing, both in its individual and corporate identity. Midwives, nurses, and mothers were given explicit instructions on how to form the body into its most perfect shape, through massage and swaddling. Literally half of one's schooling was devoted to perfecting the body in physical training. Medicine was highly valued, and many drugs, both curative and preventative, were developed—as well as poisons. The body (again both individual and corporate) needed to be protected.

This protection of the corporate body is at the heart of much of Paul's advice. The way the Corinthians are practicing the Lord's Supper causes harm to the "body of Christ"—both a term for the bread eaten and for the group eating it (1 Cor. 11:27). In fact, such unworthy performance of this ritual threatens also the health of individual bodies (11:30). Clearly the individual body and the corporate body have a connection, which raises other problems.

One of the most difficult sections of Paul's writings concerns the status of women in worship (11:2–16). The reasoning makes little sense with our modern assumptions about the body but becomes clearer when we remember these ideas. The individual body mirrors the corporate body. What defiles one defiles the whole. The body is inferior to and under the control of the soul and spirit. Some bodies were more inferior than others, the softer the body the more inferior, thus women's bodies were inferior to men's bodies. And we need one more idea.

First, consider the story. Women at Corinth clearly participate in worship, both praying and prophesying (best understood as delivering a word from God rather than foretelling the future). Apparently no one questions their right to do so, but some are offended by their failure to cover their heads. Now given Paul's grand defense of freedom in Galatians and his bold declaration there that "in Christ" there "is no longer male and female" (Gal. 3:28), we might expect him to side with those who reject the covering. He does not.

Instead, he repeats a whole series of arguments supporting women's inferiority: the husband is the head of the wife; woman is the reflection of man; woman was created from man; woman was created for the sake of man (1 Cor. 11:2–10). All of these points agree with ideas about bodies current in Corinth, and most are based on the creation story in Genesis 2. But then Paul switches his base: nevertheless, in the Lord, woman is not independent of man or man independent of woman, and, whatever the case with creation, now man comes through woman (11:11). Here is the issue, then. What is the relationship between the natural order (in creation) and the new order (in Christ)? This is the problem behind the problems.

We can now understand the case of incest and, more importantly, their being proud of it (5:2). They were simply applying a theme of Paul's preaching that he once articulated as: "if anyone is in Christ, he is a new creation; the old has passed away, behold, the new has come" (2 Cor. 5:17). The Corinthians apparently understood this in a radical fashion: if the old has passed away, then the old relationships no longer apply. As a spiritual participant in the new order, one is freed from all the constraints of the old order, including family ties. The Corinthians were proud of their new freedom, so proud and so free that they endorsed this incestuous marriage.

Paul, the law, and the Gentiles. Paul was deeply shocked when he heard this interpretation of his teaching; he could scarcely believe it. He demanded a solemn handing over of the person to Satan, presuming he would die as a result (1 Cor. 5:5). Faced with a group that took his radical call to freedom literally, Paul quickly retreats. He even declares: "Neither circumcision counts for anything nor uncircumcision, but keeping the commandments of God" (7:19), striking a different note from that in Galatians, where he declares: "For neither circumcision counts for anything, nor uncircumcision, but a new creation" (6:15). Precisely such talk about freedom and new creation had caused the problem at Corinth.

Evidently Paul adapted his teaching to his circumstances. In Galatia, faced with a challenge to freedom by those who insist on using the Law as a means to control their fates, Paul sounds like one who would abolish the Law. In Corinth, confronted by those who would abolish the Law in their new freedom, Paul sounds like one who lived according to God's demands. As interpreters of Paul, we must always remember that we are hearing only part of the story at any one time and must seek to know the whole story before interpreting its parts.

Paul and women. Failure to notice how Paul must always be read in the context of the community to which he writes has done enormous damage to women. The popular image of Paul as a typical first-century misogynist seems very far from the truth when one looks carefully at what he actually says about women and in what context. In fact, women seem to have held the full range of church offices, to have exercised real authority in teaching and organization, and to have been treated with a remarkable evenhandedness in the early Pauline churches. But there is some tension in the tradition, related to the situation of the churches to which Paul wrote.

Thus in Galatians, the letter designed to protect the freedom of the new order, Paul makes his most sweeping generalization regarding women:

> *There is no longer Jew or Greek, there is no longer slave or free, there is no longer male and female; for all of you are one in Christ Jesus. (Gal 3:28)*

In the new order the old distinctions of ethnic identity, social location, and gender no longer apply; being "in Christ" obliterates these distinctions. This is such a radical idea that there is little wonder it caused problems. After all, if circumcision was no longer required as a sign of the covenant, then not just Gentile men but women too would be full members. No wonder problems arose. And when those problems arose at Corinth, Paul retreated to a more conservative position because of his overwhelming interest in preserving the unity and harmony of the community.

The exact nature of those problems and how they emerged at Corinth, I cannot confidently reconstruct. They seem to involve a requirement that women have some sort of "covering" (veil? hairstyle? haircut?) on their heads when they lead worship (praying or prophesying, 1 Corinthians 11). But the letter also requires that women maintain silence in the assembly (1 Corinthians 14). One problem is the obvious contradiction between these two requirements: one cannot both give someone directions on *how* to speak and require silence. Scholars are divided over whether the "silence" demanded in chapter 14 refers to something other than conducting the service or whether the passage is a later interpolation into the letter (see Walker, 1975). In fact, the sentiment expressed in chapter 14—that women would be married and should not be permitted to speak—seems rather more like what we will find in the later Pauline tradition (see Chapter 6). We will deal with the effort to silence women when we discuss these later works, but the limitations advanced in 1 Corinthians 11 are sufficiently serious to warrant discussion.

In a lengthy, convoluted passage from 1 Corinthians 11 that is difficult to translate, Paul seems to adopt the standard ancient view on the inferiority of women to men, even asserting that only males were made in the image of God, whereas females were made in the image of the male (11:7).

Now this sounds like the standard patriarchal worldview in which the great chain of being stretches down from God to men to women to animals. It echoes the widely held view of Aristotle that women result from embryos that did not develop quite fully enough to be men.

> *Just as it sometimes happens that deformed offspring are produced by deformed parents and sometimes not, so the offspring produced by a female are sometimes female, sometimes not, but male. The reason is that the female is as it were a deformed male. (Aristotle* On the Generation of Animals *737a 25–27)*

But more surprising than Paul's general participation in the dominant patriarchalism of his time is his obvious effort to resist it. Even in this passage, where he admits that the creation order in Genesis 2 supports the priority of men (women come from men), he immediately adds the converse:

> *Nevertheless, in the Lord woman is not independent of man or man independent of woman. For just as woman came from man, so man comes through woman; but all things come from God (1 Cor. 11:11–12).*

Paul here reverses the logic of the creation story to argue for the mutual interdependence of the sexes in the new order of being in Christ. This conviction is reflected in Paul's practice of addressing men and women in shockingly equal ways, as he does in 1 Corinthians 7, for example. And we can learn a lot by looking at Paul's actual practice in regard to women. Paul mentions numerous women who, like Euodia and Syntyche, "worked side by side" with him (Phil. 4:2–3). At Corinth itself, Paul worked, both in his trade and in his ministry, with a couple named Aquila and Prisca (1 Cor. 16:19). Years later, when they have moved to Rome, Paul will even send greetings to them, mentioning the woman first—a clear violation of the expected custom of male dominance (see Rom. 16:3). In fact, Paul greets seven women in Romans 16, indicating that they are coworkers with him in the mission task. In addition, Romans 16 indicates that the emissary trusted to deliver that letter to the Roman congregations was a woman named Phoebe, called a deacon of the church at Cenchreae, Corinth's eastern seaport. She thus would act as Paul's voice to the community.

In practice, then, Paul seems to have accepted women as coworkers. In theory, he articulated an idea of equality "in Christ" that could have far-reaching implications for male-female relations. But when problems arose, as they did at Corinth, Paul's strategy of finding a middle ground led to compromises (including even omitting the male-female dichotomy in his reference to the way baptism obliterates social distinctions; see 1 Cor. 12:13). At Corinth everything is said to foster community harmony (see Mitchell, 1991). Only a careful study of the full range of Paul's writing, with each letter related to its specific social and historical setting, can reveal with any confidence what Paul thought on any topic. One cannot simply quote Paul's words and imagine one knows what Paul meant.

The Rhetoric of Concord: 1 Corinthians

Perhaps the key to understanding Paul's argument in 1 Corinthians is not the specific problems or even his creative answers to those problems, but rather his strategy for answering them. Paul is consistently more concerned to find agreement and concord than he is in finding the right answer. He makes his agenda clear from the beginning:

> *Now I appeal to you, brothers and sisters, by the name of our Lord Jesus Christ, that all of you be in agreement and that there be no divisions among you, but that you be united in the same mind and the same purpose. (1:10)*

Although this is often taken as applying only to the discussion of factionalism (chapters 1–4), Margaret M. Mitchell (1991:111–83) has shown that the vocabulary of factionalism pervades the rest of the letter as well. Clearly the harmony of the community is threatened by the factions (chapters 1–4), but it is also threatened by outside (primarily sexual) defilements (chapters 5–10) and by their own practices when they "come together" for worship in ways that are divisive (chapters 11–14).

This concern for the harmony of the community colors all of Paul's arguments. Thus, although he agrees with those within the community who think there is no harm in eating sacrificial meat, he still urges them not to eat it in the interest of the good of the community (8:13; 10:31–11:1). He clearly believes that "in the Lord" men and women are mutually interdependent, but he still admonishes women to cover their heads (11:11). He clearly believes it is better not to marry, but he still urges marriage and conjugal relations (7:9). The rhetorical aim of 1 Corinthians is to foster community. The rhetoric of 2 Corinthians is quite different.

The Rhetoric of Controversy: 2 Corinthians

We saw earlier that 2 Corinthians is probably a collection of parts of several letters. Yet these letters focus primarily on one problem: opponents have appeared at Corinth and have succeeded in turning many of Paul's followers away. Thus, in a real way, 2 Corinthians is concerned with the same issue as 1 Corinthians: the unity of the community. But now threats to the unity come from outside.

READING AND REFLECTION
Use the reading guide to read through 2 Corinthians.

1. What charges did the opponents bring against Paul?
2. What means did they use to commend themselves?
3. How does Paul reclaim the allegiance of the Corinthians?

Clearly new missioners have come to Corinth. They claim to be servants of Christ (11:23), possess written testimonials to their excellence (3:1), and claim to be superior apostles (11:5, 13), and they have attacked Paul directly (10:10). He is charged with weakness (10:10), inferiority (10:7; 11:5), lack of good speaking skills (11:6), and perhaps with irregular handling of his finances (11:7, 9; 12:17). They probably also claim miraculous powers (12:12), visions (12:1), and a Jewish heritage (11:22). Eventually they succeed so well in alienating the Corinthians from Paul that, when he hurriedly visits them, he is put to public shame (2:5 with 7:12 and 13:1–2).

We can learn much about Paul and his handling of controversy by comparing these three writings. In the first letter, when the controversy is discovered, the dominant metaphor is hiddenness, and there is an implicit contrast between insiders and outsiders. Whether it involves discerning the right fragrance (2:15), having intimate letters of recommendation (3:1), seeing the veil on Moses' face (3:13), finding treasure in clay pots (4:7), discerning the heavenly building behind the earthly tent (5:1), or knowing Christ from a human or a spiritual point of view (5:16), Paul continually implies that he is on the inside. He seduces the hearer.

The last letter, when the controversy was settled, is marked by contrasts between joy and sorrow, affliction and comfort, repentance and stubbornness. What is rhetorically enacted is the shift from stubbornness to repentance, with the corresponding shifts from affliction to comfort and from sorrow to joy. This is one of Paul's most gracious works, asking mercy even on the one responsible for the insult to him on his hurried second visit to Corinth (2:5–11).

The middle letter, written in the heat of controversy, after the insult but before the apology, is the most dramatic. Here we find the ironic Paul. Here we see him mocking his opponents (11:5), his audience (11:19–21), and especially himself (10:8, 18; 11:1, 16, 21–33; most of chapter 12). Paul readily admits all the charges brought against him, and in so doing he ironically turns their charges into badges of honor. His sufferings actually identify him as the servant of Christ (11:23 and following). This whole section is a delight to read if we remember that here Paul is writing "like a madman" (11:23) and do not take him literally. Paul offers us another glimpse of his sense of humor, moderating to some extent the harsh reflection of him in Galatians.

The Corinthian correspondence displays some of the problems Gentiles had with the new faith Paul preached. Corinth itself was a prosperous city that, despite its bad reputation, was probably no more wicked than any other large city. Paul had spent a year and a half there and exchanged numerous letters and several visits with his Corinthian followers.

Although these letters deal with a host of individual problems, two stand out: the difficulty of translating Jewish ethics into a Gentile context, a context that deprecated the body, and the issue of loyalty to Paul in the face of opponents who were probably more at home in the Gentile world than he was. These are the major themes of the two letters we know as 1 and 2 Corinthians. Taken together, they illustrate the range of issues Paul confronted in his mission as apostle to the Gentiles.

PAUL AND HIS FOLLOWERS

There is a great danger for those of us who deal with Paul from these texts alone, since his world was infinitely larger. Because the text is all we have left, the danger is that we will let it fill our whole canvas. But how much our image of Paul must shift from letter to letter. How distinctive is the image in Galatians from that in Philemon. How different his teaching seems in 1 Corinthians from that in Galatians. How little continuity we discern between 1 and 2 Corinthians. What tantalizing hints we come across: near death in Asia (2 Cor. 1:8), frequent opposition, dramatic adventure (2 Corinthians 11). Yet we know almost nothing else about these events.

Still, the letters are a treasure trove, and it has been truly said that one meets Paul face to face in the reading of these letters. They are some of the most intense and personal writings we have from the Greco-Roman era, presenting us with an enormous range of feelings: rage to humor, endearment to sarcasm, poetry to incomplete prose. Strikingly well organized, according to the intended purpose, they are works of rhetoric and imagination as well as of spirit and idea. They are well worth many readings.

The letters do allow us to reconstruct a little about the men and women who became Paul's followers and friends. They seem to have been mostly Gentiles with strong sympathies for the Jewish tradition. They were city folk; three of these five letters were written to large and important cities, two Roman and one Greek. And Galatians, written to a region, obviously addressed cities. The audience included a variety of social classes, from the wealthy patrons and benefactors to the common citizens and slaves. The one letter to an individual (Philemon) shows the social dynamics at work. And the problems associated with the Lord's Supper in Corinth stemmed in part from the separation of the social classes.

One other dynamic is worth noting. Two of the letters include a rhetoric of bearing suffering: the Thessalonians are commended for bearing suffering from their compatriots (2:14) and the Philippians are praised for having "the privilege not only of believing in Christ, but of suffering for him as well" (1:29). But there is no such allusion in Corinthians. Instead we find clear evidence of cultural acceptance and integration. They were making use of the city courts (6:1–8); they were eating sacrificial food, both in the temples and in homes where they were invited (10:14, 25–27); outsiders were attending their services (14:24); some were still visiting prostitutes (6:9–20). Not only are these activities signs of cultural involvement, they are typical actions of wealthy males in Greco-Roman society. These issues of tension with and accommodation to culture would take generations to resolve.

The letters also show that Paul forged strong emotional ties with these people but spent surprisingly little time with them. Brief visits had to be reinforced by sending emissaries and, especially, letters—both of which substituted for Paul and represented (re-presented) him to the community.

Paul's central metaphor for this community is the family—the extended Hellenistic family of parents, children, slaves, and business partners. It is important to notice, however, that Paul does not conceive of this new family in the hierarchical manner of the typical Roman, Greek, or Jewish family. Typically, a family was organized under the highest ranking male (the lord or **paterfamilias**) who was like a king over his wife, children, wives of married sons, slaves, hired servants, live-in guests, and associated freedpersons (see Stowers, 1986:31). But Paul does not generally address his communities as a father; rather, his most common salutation is "Brothers." Fellow believers are to be treated as brothers even if they are rebellious (2 Thess. 3:15; see 1 Cor. 5:11; 6:1). A female coworker is addressed as a sister (Rom. 16:1). At other times Paul assumes a more parental tone, addressing believers as his children (1 Cor. 4:14 and 2 Cor. 12:14). Twice he describes himself as the father: he became father of Onesimus while imprisoned (Philem. 10) and exhorts the Thessalonians like a father with his children (1 Thess. 2:11). But he is also gentle among them, "like a nurse taking care of her children" (1 Thess. 2:7). Once he describes himself as a mother giving birth to her children again (Gal. 4:19). Once he describes a congregation as his virgin daughter, for whom he has arranged a desirable marriage (2 Cor. 11:2).

Two other family metaphors are more remote from us: the slave and the partner (for example, 1 Cor. 4:1; 9:19; Phil. 1:5). As Paul is the slave of Christ, he becomes the slave of all (1 Cor. 9:19). And each is to serve the other (Gal. 5:13, literally "be a slave to"). This metaphor of the household slave whose task it is to serve the needs of others captured for Paul some of the meaning of the cross of Christ, who himself became a slave to serve others (Phil. 2:7). The terminology of redemption and of purchase price (1 Cor. 1:30; 6:20) derives from the slave trade. There is, of course, some tension between these images and Paul's metaphor of freedom. But that tension is partly resolved by another image, that of voluntary association in mutual contractual obligation: partnership.

Partnership in Roman law created, in effect, an extended family; the earliest partnerships were those of brothers who inherited their father's estate but were not allowed to divide it. Paul Sampley (1980:103–8) has examined Paul's partnership imagery and found four distinct uses:

1. Paul understood himself to be in partnership with the church at Jerusalem, and in response undertook to collect an offering for their support (Gal. 2:1–10).
2. Paul entered into a unique partnership with the church at Philippi, the only church from which he received financial support (Phil. 1:5; 4:10–20).
3. Paul used his partnership relation to Philemon to induce him to treat Onesimus as he would treat Paul (Philem. 17).
4. Paul regularly used the terminology of the partnership even when formal aspects of support were lacking. "Be of one mind," "agree with one another," "fellowship," and, on the negative side, "fraud" were drawn from the partners' relation of mutual obligation.

These obligations exist both between Paul and his congregations and between members in their congregations. It is one more way of expressing their familial relationship, respecting both their absolute freedom and their absolute obligation to each other. Representing his communities as a family allowed Paul to tread a narrow path between the mutual responsibilities he saw as necessary and dependence on the Law that he saw as dangerous.

Of course, much about Paul remains unstated in these letters; they were written to friends with whom he shared a common stock of knowledge and experience. We surely miss much. But we are fortunate to have one letter that was not addressed to his friends; it was written to a community with whom he had not had previous contact. This is his most elaborate letter, presenting a long and carefully organized argument. With it, we will conclude our study of Paul.

LEARNING ON YOUR OWN

REVIEWING THE CHAPTER

Names and Terms

Adam	diaspora	incarnation
allegory	folk traditions	Isis
Asclepius	Galatia	magic
astrology	Gnosticism	mystery religions
circumcision	Hellenistic age	Oedipus
Corinth	immortality	partnership

paterfamilias	resurrection	syncretism
philosophy	Septuagint	Torah
purity	Stoicism	

Issues and Questions for Review and Discussion

1. Be able to reconstruct the relationship between Paul and Philemon and tell the story that leads to the writing of this letter.
2. Give a brief overview of the nature of slavery and prisons in Paul's time.
3. Develop a thesis concerning Paul's underlying purpose in writing the letter to Philemon, and cite evidence from the letter to support your claim.
4. Be able to reconstruct the relationship between Paul and the Philippians and tell the story that leads to the writing of this letter.
5. Be able to discuss the meaning of the poem/hymn that Paul gives in Philippians 2 and to relate it to the theme of the letter.
6. Show the relationship between the intertwining stories reflected in these letters: the stories of Jesus, of Paul, and of the communities that follow Paul.
7. Sketch the various means by which Paul stayed in communication with his followers, using data from Philippians and the Corinthian letters.
8. Be able to summarize the argument of Galatians as an example of the rhetoric of defense.
9. Be able to discuss the issues raised by the success of Paul's preaching among Gentiles, especially the religious and ethical issues.
10. How does the ancient family structure provide the metaphors for describing Paul's view of the community?

TAKING THE NEXT STEP

For a basic introduction to Paul and his thought you might start with Sanders, 1991; other good introductions include Beker, 1982; Fitzmyer, 1989b; Hooker, 1990; and Ziesler, 1983. For alternative views of Paul see Gager, 2000, and Scroggs, 1977.

Probably the best substantial introduction to Paul is Murphy-O'Connor, 1996; Beker, 1980, and Best, 1988, are also very helpful. The older works of Davies, 1980, Bornkamm, 1971, and Bruce, 1977, remain valuable.

Topics for Special Studies

Paul has become such a pivotal figure for later Christians that you can be confident of finding resources to study nearly any aspect of his life and thought that might intrigue you. You might begin by consulting an introduction to Paul's letters. One of the best is Roetzel, 1998; other good introductions include Ellis, 1982; Keck, 1979; Keck and Furnish, 1984; and Meeks, 1972. Patte, 1983, is an advanced study, analyzing the letters with a structuralist methodology; see his 1985b also.

Works on specific letters include:

- *Philemon*: Barth and Blanke, 2000; Bruce, 1984; Getty, 1980; Lohse, 1971; Martin, 1991; Patzia, 1984; and Petersen, 1985. Also interesting is J. H. Elliott, 1984. For an alternate reading that sees Onesimus as Philemon's brother rather than his slave, see Callahan, 1997.
- *Philippians*: Getty, 1980; Portefaix, 1988; Hubbard and Hawthorne, 1983; and Martin, 1987.

- *Galatians*: The commentary of Betz, 1979, is now the standard work; it is especially provocative on the rhetoric of Galatians. The focus on rhetoric is taken up by Brinsmead, 1982, and challenged by Kennedy, 1984:144–52. See also the major work of Martyn, 1998. Other commentaries include Boers, 1994; Conzelmann, 1979; Dunn, 1993; Ebeling, 1985; Guthrie, 1981; Matera, 1992, Osiek, 1980; and Williams, 1997. Hays, 1984, seeks to discover the story implied in Galatians. Wiley, 2005, considers how women are affected by the discussion of circumcision. Howard, 1979, explores the nature of the crisis in Galatia. Nanos, 2002, presents a stimulating Jewish reading.
- *Corinthians*: Barrett, 1974, 1975c; Conzelmann, 1975; and Furnish, 1984. Mitchell, 1991, and Witherington, 1995, explore Paul's deliberative rhetoric with somewhat different emphases. Adams and Horrell, 2004, collect an excellent sampling of scholarly essays on issues in the Corinthian letters. On the nature of the opponents at Corinth, see Barrett, 1971b, and Georgi, 1985. Martin, 1995, is a very provocative study of Corinthian notions of the body; it can be profitably paired with Deming, 1995, which traces the background of Paul's ideas on marriage and celibacy. On the religious context of Corinth see DeMaris, 1995 (baptism for the dead). On Paul's apocalyptic worldview see Brown, 1995. Two special studies on the social setting at Corinth have appeared: Murphy-O'Connor, 1984, is a valuable, comprehensive collection and interpretation of ancient writers and a review of archaeology relating to Corinth; and Theissen, 1982, provides a provocative look at the relation between the Corinthian problems and the social, economic, and cultural conditions of Corinth. On the composite character or unity of 2 Corinthians, see Furnish, 1984:30–41; also compare Barnett, 1997, and Taylor, 1991. On the ideas of 2 Corinthians see Murphy-O'Connor, 1991, and Martin, 1986.

The Social World of Paul
Grant, 1977; Hengel, 1974b; Judge, 1982; Malherbe, 1983b; and Meeks, 1983. De Vos, 1999, carefully examines the social settings at Thessalonica, Corinth, and Philippi to explore the reasons for social conflict evident in these letters. On Corinth see the collection of Adams and Horrell, 2004, and Theissen, 1982.

Paul's Occupation
The most useful discussion is Hock, 1980; see also Jenkins, 1986. More generally on work in the Roman world, see Grant, 1977; Cohen, 1993; Lefkowitz and Fant, 1992; Lewis, 1994; MacMullen, 1974; and Jenkins, 1986.

Funding for the Pauline Mission
Donaldson, 1997; Nickle, 1966; and Georgi, 1992, all treat the significance of Paul's collection. On patronage and benefaction, see Gellner and Waterbury, 1977; Wallace-Hadrill, 1989; and Eisenstadt and Roniger, 1984. J. H. Elliott, 1987, provides a useful reading guide to patronage and clientism.

Paul's Opponents at Philippi, at Corinth, or in Galatia
Barrett, 1982; Brinsmead, 1982; Gunther, 1973; Marshall, 1987; Barrett, 1971; Malherbe, 1970.

Views of the Body and of Life after Death
Martin, 1995; Brown, 1987; Williams, 1996:116–38; Deming, 1995; Laqueur, 1990; Rousselle, 1988; Saller, 1994; Bernstein, 1993; Wagnar, 1982; Black, 1984; Bernstein, 1993; van der Horst, 1991; Robbins, 1989; Rice and Stambaugh, 1979.

Paul's Attitude toward Slavery

On slavery generally, a good beginning would be the three books by Bradley (1987, 1989, and especially 1994). See also Garnsey, 1996; Vogt, 1975; Yavetz, 1988; Veyne, 1987; Finley, 1980; Wiedemann, 1981; and Tucker, 1982.

On slavery and Paul's letters see the excellent collection by Callahan, Horsley, and Smith, 1998. Braxton, 2002, provides a reading of Galatians from an African American perspective. See also Bartchy, 1973; Martin, 1990; Glancy, 1998; Lewis, 1991; and a related article on slavery in parables, Beavis, 1992.

For an extensive bibliography on slavery, see Osiek, 1992.

The Problems of Pauline Chronology

Compare the different approaches and conclusions of Jewett, 1979, and Ludemann, 1984. See also Knox, 1987. Finegan, 1998, provides a handbook on biblical chronological issues.

Paul's Metaphors for the Communities

Banks, 1980; Martin, 1990; Bossman, 1996; and Schweizer, 1965. See also Best, 1988b.

Williams, 1999, treats numerous metaphors in their cultural context.

The Nature of the Family in Antiquity

See the resources for Chapter 1.

The Role of Women in Paul's Churches

See the excellent overview of Osiek and MacDonald, 2006, and the introductory works of Gillman, 1992, and Bristow, 1988.

On a more advanced level: Schüssler Fiorenza, 1978, 1983; Gillman, 1990; Cotter, 1994; Wire, 1990; Abrahamsen, 1987; MacMullen, 1980; Scroggs, 1972, with Pagels 1974; and Brooten in Collins, 1985.

MacDonald, 1987, provides a balanced analysis of the ideas about women in Galatians and 1 Corinthians. Wiley, 2005, considers how the debate about circumcision affects women.

For a daring reconstruction of women's roles in the synagogue see Brooten, 1982; on the broader context see Kraemer, 1992. See also the resources section for Chapter 5.

On the issue of veils and hair at Corinth, see Martin, 1995; Thompson, 1988; Oster, 1988; and Murphy-O'Connor, 1988.

Poetic Material in the Pauline Collection

See Fowl, 1990. For the Philippian hymn see the contrasting views of Dunn, 1980, and Wright, 1993.

The Nature and Extent of Jewish Missionary Activity in Paul's Time

See van der Horst, 1990; Feldman, 1950; Goodman, 1994; Watson, 1986; McKnight, 1991; Reynolds, 1987; Theissen, 1982; Cohen, 1983; and McEleney, 1973. On *conversions* in this period, see MacMullen, 1985. Crook, 2001, is an excellent reexamination the paradigm of conversion in antiquity.

Donaldson, 1997, provides an excellent analysis of how contemporary scholars are rethinking Paul's basic convictions and practices.

The Jewish Historian Josephus

The place to begin is Mason, 1998. Other helpful works include Schwartz, 1990; Rhoads, 1976; and Mason, 1991. You can find the original writings of Josephus in the

Loeb series or in the handy volume from Hendrickson Publishers, 1987. For other works see the bibliography of Feldman, 1986.

The Nature of Gentile Religions in Paul's Time

Rose, 1959, is a good introduction to Greco-Roman religion. See the bibliography at the end of Chapter 1. There are three good overviews that reveal the texture of Greco-Roman religion: Ferguson, 1970; MacMullen, 1981; and Teixidor, 1977. On religious diversity, see Cohn-Sherbok and Court, 2001.

On the relations between Jews and Gentiles, see the balanced account of Gager, 1983, and the older work of Sevenster, 1975. On conversion to Judaism, see Cohen, 1983; and on the various attitudes of Jews toward Gentile circumcision, see McEleney, 1973.

On religious conversion, start with Crook, 2004, then see Gaventa, 1986, and McKnight, 1991. See also Feldman and Hata, 1989; Lofland, 1966; Nock, 1961; Cohen, 1983; and MacMullen, 1985. On the Roman view of Christians, see Wilken, 1984.

On **Gnosticism**: Start with Perkins, 1993; then Roukema, 1999; Rudolph, 1983; Wilson, 1968; Finegan, 1989. For a clear interpretation of Gnosticism see Wink, 1993. For the situation at Corinth try Pearson, 1973, and Wilson, 1968. For a major rethinking of categories, see Williams, 1996. For a history of its development, see Roukema, 1999.

On **philosophy**: Start with Warner, 1958, and Long, 1974. On individual philosophies, see Havelock, 1963 (Plato); Rist, 1978 (Stoics); Clay, 1984 (Lucretius and Epicurus); Dewitt, 1954 (Paul and Epicurus); Inwood and Gerson, 1994 (Epicurus reader); Gorman, 1979 (Pythagoras); Phillip, 1966 (Pythagoras); Malherbe, 1984 (Cynic epistles); O'Neil, 1977 (Cynics); Wallis, 1972 (Neoplatonism); Wolfson, 1947 (Philo). A fine study could be built on the materialist philosophy of Lucretius' *On the Nature of the Universe*.

On **magic**: Start with Aune, 1980, and Kee, 1986. For an overview see Graf, 1997. Meyer and Mirecki, 1995, is a collection of essays on magic from Mesopotamia to Rome. Collections of magical texts with some interpretation can be found in Faraone and Obbink, 1991, and Luck, 1985. On magic in early Christianity see Benko, 1982, and Arnold, 1989.

On **astrology**: Start with Cumont, 1960, and Barton, 1994a, 1994b. Then see Mac-Mullen, 1966, 1971, and MacMullen and Lane, 1992.

On **army religion**: Start with Wilkes, 1972, and Ulansey, 1989 (on Mithraism). Also see Cumont, 1956; Nock, 1937; Meyer, 1981; and Speidel, 1980. For some comparisons today, see Helgeland, 1989. For a summary of research and bibliography, see Birley, 1978.

On **Jewish religion**: A good place to begin would be Jaffee, 1997, and Stone, 1982. Good treatments of the diaspora include Lieu, North, and Rajak, 1992; Barclay, 1996; Cohen, 1993; Cohen, 1987; Smallwood, 1976; Goodenough, 1961; and Feldman, 1993. Special studies include Finkelstein, 1972 (Pharisaism); Frankfurter, 1998 (Egypt); Vermes, 1993 (Jesus the Jew); Harrington, 1993 (Paul and Judaism); Sanders, 1993 (sectarians); Wilson, 1995 (Jews and Christians); and Bockmuehl, 1997 (Revelation). A review of scholarship and a good bibliography can be found in Kraft and Nickelsburg, 1985. See additional resources at the end of Chapters 1 and 13.

Collection of Primary Sources on Religion

Ferguson, 1980, *Greek and Roman Religion: A Source Book.*
Grant, F. C., 1953, *Hellenistic Religions: The Age of Syncretism.*
Jonas, 1963, *The Gnostic Religion.*
Rice and Stambaugh, 1979, *Sources for the Study of Greek Religion.*
Luck, 1985, is an excellent collection on magic and the occult in antiquity; see also Aune, 1980b.

The role of religion in everyday life is displayed in the novel by Apuleius, *The Golden Ass*, and the essay by Lucretius, *On the Nature of the Universe*.

Additional Books and Articles

For good bibliographies on Paul, see Fitzmyer, 1993; Borchert, 1985 (annotated); and Petersen, 1984.

5

PAUL'S ADDRESS TO THOSE OUTSIDE HIS CIRCLE

Romans

LITERARY ANALYSIS OF ROMANS

HISTORICAL ANALYSIS OF THE CONTEXT

THE THEME OF ROMANS: TWO VIEWS

IN CONCLUSION: IMAGINING PAUL'S STORY

LEARNING ON YOUR OWN

 It was Paul who delivered the Christian religion from Judaism. . . . It was he who confidently regarded the Gospel as a new force abolishing the religion of the law.

ADOLF VON HARNACK

 In this letter the good news of Paul's gospel for Gentiles is not part of a polemic against Torah or Israel. Without at all excluding Jews, he is able to argue very effectively and very passionately that the inclusion of Gentiles was always the goal of the Torah.

LLOYD GASTON

As you begin to read Romans, you may find that it seems to be a different kind of writing from what you are accustomed to; it differs from Paul's other letters, though explaining how it varies is not an easy task. Our first impression perhaps is that it is longer. It is the longest of Paul's letters (which may be why it was placed first when the letters were collected as a set). But it is not that much longer than 1 Corinthians. The standard Greek text of Romans is thirty-four pages; 1 Corinthians is thirty. But whereas 1 Corinthians is a virtual list of topics to which Paul needed to respond, Romans does not jump from one topic to another. No other letter even approaches this length for one sustained argument.

The next thing we may notice is that the argument is hard to locate. Just what is the point? Paul never attacks anyone in Romans, never says any particular point of view is wrong, never indulges in name-calling. Though it seems to be one long argument, it is not easy to discover the major concern of that argument. This is due to a third difference. The letter never explains why Paul wrote it.

Certainly, he is planning a trip to Rome (15:22–29), but that is hardly sufficient cause for such a major letter. Also, Paul is evidently trying to drum up support for his trip to Spain. Some have suggested that gaining such support is the real purpose of Romans (which might make it the earliest surviving example of proposal writing). Other scholars make two telling points against this idea: First, if Paul were trying to gain support he could have done so much more directly and simply. But, second, it is unlikely that such was his purpose. We have seen that Paul was very reluctant to accept financial support even from the assemblies he himself founded (excepting only Philippi). How much less likely would he be to solicit support from an assembly founded by someone else. We should consider, then, that Romans differs to some extent from the other letters we have examined. Its length, determined pursuit of a single argument, and lack of a clear historical purpose all point away from the letter toward the essay as its genre.

First, let us examine the literary features of this letter-essay, then explore its historical context, before turning directly to its possible meaning.

LITERARY ANALYSIS OF ROMANS

READING AND REFLECTION

Quickly read through Romans and try to discover the main contours of Paul's argument. I have found it useful to pay special attention to

1. Paul's point of view. When does he speak about *them*, about *us*, or about *you*?
2. Paul's introduction of a dissenting voice. When does Paul imagine someone might raise an objection or infer a conclusion?
3. Paul's use of explicit logical indicators. When does he use words like *therefore*, *but*, *so*, *then*, or *however*?

THE FORM OF THE ARGUMENT: THE POINTS OF VIEW

Any writer finds it necessary to address the reader occasionally, usually by saying "you" or "we." Though Paul does this in Romans, he also does something else. At two places in the argument he shifts his basic **point of view** (the perspective from which he looks at things). After a lengthy introduction, he begins to discuss the "wickedness of *those* who by their wickedness suppress the truth" (1:18) and continues in the third person for some time. Even when he addresses the reader and hearers as *you* (as in 2:1 and 2:17) it is still clear that he is talking about them. He is talking about humankind, the human species and its specific manifestations as Jew and Gentile. Not until chapter 5 do we encounter a different point of view. Beginning at 5:1, Paul shifts his stance from considering *them* to talking about *us*. It is *we* who are justified; *we* who were sinners; *we* who are baptized; nothing can separate *us* from the love of God. This way of speaking continues through chapter 8 and surely represents a new stage of the argument. In the next three chapters (9–11) Paul seems to revert to the third person. But while the *them* in chapters 1–4 refers to the universal *them* of humanity, here it refers to the Jewish people. Chapter 12 marks the beginning of another shift—this time to the second person, *you*. The mood also changes. The address is now in the imperative: a demand.

Whatever the topic of this argument, then, its form seems clear enough. It begins with the universal, focuses on the particular instances of Paul and the Roman community and the people of Israel, and proceeds to the demands that such understanding brings to the hearers.

THE NATURE OF THE ARGUMENT

For us, the argument of Romans seems long, convoluted, and difficult to follow because we rarely encounter anything written in this style. But it was a popular style in the ancient world, especially among the philosophical schools where it served as a teaching technique. Actually, it may be considered an extension of the Platonic dialogue. In a **dialogue** a philosopher enters into formal exchange of ideas with students and adversaries. Consequently, the argument takes many turns, and even detours, before it reaches its conclusion. But in the writing style we see in Romans the formal partner in the dialogue has disappeared, leaving the questions and objections behind. This style is called the **diatribe**. Primarily it was a style of speaking in which the lecturer would raise questions or implications of the argument, which would then be pursued. Thus it would wander into alleys and byways rather than proceeding straight to a conclusion.

The writer of a diatribe imagines that his or her hearers are present, deals with any objections they might raise, and suggests related ideas to pursue. One objection might lead to another and the argument detour through much unexpected terrain before returning to the main point. The purpose of this method is to form a bond between speaker and hearer and lead them to a common conclusion.

In reading or hearing a diatribe, pay very careful attention to the specific topic at hand, and watch closely for the turns and returns of the argument. It is crucial in reading Romans always to be clear about exactly what question Paul thinks he is answering at any given point in the work. We must not be like the unscrupulous reporter who quotes a public figure without putting the quotation in context—just because it makes the reporter's point. The context of an answer is as important as the content of the answer. We must keep Paul's answers and questions together, for we understand an answer only when we understand the question for which it was intended.

In the best discussion of the diatribe and Romans that I know, Stanley K. Stowers (1981) explores the nature of this kind of writing and the features of Romans that correspond to it. He notes especially (1) the use of an imaginary partner in conversation, (2) the raising of objections, and (3) the inferring of false conclusions. Watch for these devices as we read; they are used repeatedly. Examples of addressing an imaginary hearer include

> Therefore you have no excuse, whoever you are. . . . (2:1)
> But if you call yourself a Jew . . . (2:17)
> You will say to me then . . . (9:19)
> Who are you to pass judgment? . . . (14:4)

Numerous objections raised to the argument include

> Then what advantage has the Jew? (3:1)
> Are Jews any better off? (3:9)

The objections raised usually result from drawing a false conclusion from Paul's argument, such as

> Do we then overthrow the Law? (3:31)
> Are we to continue in sin? (6:1)
> Is the Law sin? (7:7)
> Is there injustice on God's part? (9:14)
> Has God rejected God's people? (11:1)

These questions are designed to guide the argument; they must be carefully mapped, along with other logical indicators—such as the use of *therefore, but, so,* and *for*—for the modern reader to follow Paul's meandering argument.

A COMPARISON OF THE ARGUMENT

Another valid impression you may have had while reading Romans is that you have read some of these things before in the earlier letters. The lengthy discussion of eating food offered to idols (chapters 14–15) echoes the earlier advice to the Corinthians (1 Corinthians 8–10). Why has Paul chosen to introduce this topic again? Were the Romans having the same kinds of problems that caused the Corinthians to inquire about this subject? Yet we miss in Romans any sense that they have asked for Paul's advice. Other parallels have also been noticed (Bornkamm, 1971:93–94). You may wish to compare the following:

Topic	Romans	Other
Justification by faith	1–4	Galatians 3–4
Abraham as example	4	Galatians 3
Adam-Christ analogy	5	1 Corinthians 15
Slave of sin	7	1 Corinthians 15
Flesh and spirit	8	Galatians 4
Body of Christ and gifts	12	1 Corinthians 12
Food to idols	14–15	1 Corinthians 8–10

There is only one section that discusses a topic unparalleled in the earlier letters, Romans 9–11, a lengthy discussion of the role of Israel. Nevertheless, such extensive parallels imply a sense of summing up, a synthesizing of Paul's earlier ideas—perhaps another reason why Romans was put first in the collection of his letters.

The most extensive parallels are between Romans and Galatians, but significant differences also exist in both the tone and the specific arguments of the two letters. Although Romans defends much the same ground staked out in Galatians—that only faith makes one right with God—a sympathetic reader might well wonder what has happened to Paul in the interim. Gone are the sarcasm, coarse humor, and ironic belittling of his opponents. Here Paul is conciliatory, entreating rather than demanding, disagreeing without being disagreeable. The very style of the diatribe is meant to include and to persuade. And not only the tone has changed.

The substance of the argument in Romans represents a refinement of the ideas presented in Galatians. In Galatians the dying with Christ was left undefined (for example, 2:19–20; 5:24); in Romans Paul defines this death by the ritual of baptism (6:3–4). In Galatians Paul left his hearers with a paradoxical sense of self—the "I" died with Christ (2:20)—but in Romans he differentiates this "I" into an I slain by sin and an inner self that lives and wishes to please God (7:9, 22). In Galatians the example of Abraham is asserted without any demonstration of the priority of faith over Law (3:6); in Romans Paul develops an elaborate argument based on the priority of time, the lack of boasting, and the effect of promise or grace (4:1–16). Clearly, Paul has continued to reflect on these ideas. (For a discussion of these and other points see Betz, 1979:123–24, 140–41.)

The most important difference between Romans and earlier works is the shift in attitude on Paul's part. He now goes out of his way to stress his continuity with the past, with things Jewish; he even defends the validity of the Law. Compare these two essentially similar passages (italics added):

Galatians 3:19–26

Why then the law? It was added because of transgressions, until the offspring would come to whom the promise had been made; and it was ordained through angels by a mediator. Now a mediator involves more than one party; but God is one. *Is the law then opposed to the promises of God? Certainly not*! For if a law had been given that could make alive, then righteousness would indeed come through the law. But the scripture has imprisoned all things under the power of sin, so that what was promised through faith in Jesus Christ might be given to those who believe. Now before faith came, we were imprisoned and guarded under the law until faith would be revealed. Therefore the law was our disciplinar-

Romans 7:7–12

What then should we say? That the law is sin? By no means! Yet, if it had not been for the law, I would not have known sin. I would not have known what it is to covet if the law had not said, "You shall not covet." But sin, seizing an opportunity in the commandment, produced in me all kinds of covetousness. Apart from the law sin lies dead. I was once alive apart from the law, but when the commandment came, sin revived and I died, and the very commandment that promised life proved to be death to me. For sin, seizing an opportunity in the commandment, deceived me and through it killed me. *So the law is holy, and the commandment is holy and just and good.*

ian until Christ came, so that we might be justified by faith. *But now that faith has come, we are no longer subject to a disciplinarian*, for in Christ Jesus you are all children of God through faith.

Both excerpts are struggling to make sense out of one facet of the old story, the story of God giving the Law to Israel, in light of the new story in which God has acted to bring redemption to all people through Jesus. But the passage in Romans portrays the Law in a far more positive light. No longer do we hear about its transitory use. It is not now the Law that restrains but sin. The Law indeed had promised life, even though the power of sin overruled it.

These, and many similar changes, show us that Paul has taken a different approach in Romans: he is far more intent on proving his case. He is more careful in his argument, more tolerant of other points of view, and less inclined to dismiss those who differ from the fellowship. To understand these changes and to find a basis for interpreting the work as a whole, let us consider the historical situation of Paul and the Roman assemblies.

HISTORICAL ANALYSIS OF THE CONTEXT

All the letters of Paul we have studied thus far were written to assemblies located in the eastern Roman Empire, in Asia Minor (modern-day Turkey) and Greece. This letter is addressed to "all God's beloved in Rome" (1:7), the center of power and influence over the Mediterranean world. Because there were probably several assemblies in so large a city, we need not visualize one central church. But unlike all Paul's other letters, this one is addressed to assemblies he had no hand in founding. Rome was not in Paul's mission territory. He had probably never been there (1:13). Surely he must have felt some reserve in addressing those who owed their existence to others (see 15:20; 1 Cor. 3:10). This basic situation would certainly shape Paul's rhetoric and purpose.

THE SETTING AT ROME

It is one of history's little ironies that the origins of what was to become the most important church in Christendom are lost to us. Later generations, anxious to enhance the status of this center, could only boast of the ministry there of Paul and Peter, even claiming that the latter eventually became head of that church. Even then they could make no claims to a grand beginning. The likely inference is that the beginning was not grand.

Jesus Comes to Rome

The one clue we have to how and when the story of Jesus spread to Rome comes from the *Lives of the Twelve Caesars*, by the Roman historian Suetonius. In this rather gossipy work, while reporting the *Life of Claudius*, who ruled from 41 to 54 CE, he makes a strange reference to the Jews:

Because the Jews at Rome caused continuous disturbances at the instigation of Chrestos, he expelled them from the City. (25.2)

That one sentence is all there is; what are we to make of it? There are two possibilities. Perhaps it means just what it says: riots in the Jewish community led by someone named Chrestos led to a decree of expulsion. Or perhaps Suetonius, or his source, has garbled the account. One possibility is that he wrote *Chrestos* when he should have written *Christos* (Christ). The two words would have been pronounced the same in the first century, and though Chrestos was a common Greek name (meaning something like Goodfellow or Fairchild; it was often given to slaves); **Christos** (the Greek equivalent of **messiah**, meaning the "anointed one") would be wholly unknown and unintelligible to a Roman unfamiliar with Jewish lore. Serious outbreaks of trouble may have occurred in the Jewish community at Rome in the late forties CE, caused by the arrival of representatives of this Christos—trouble serious enough for some sort of expulsion to be the result.

On this reading, Claudius expelled (some) Jews from Rome because of unrest in the Jewish community caused by the appearance of Jews proclaiming Jesus to be the messiah in the late forties, about a decade before Paul wrote. An incidental support of such a reading is found in Acts 18:2, which reports that Paul encountered Jews at Corinth who had been expelled from Rome by Claudius. Such an expulsion so early in the development of the movement there would have serious consequences. It would mean that in the crucial early years the assembly at Rome was entirely Gentile, and that even later Jews and Gentiles probably formed separate assemblies in different homes at Rome—raising the specter of division and alienation.

The Jewish Community at Rome

Our first reference to the Jewish community at Rome is from 139 BCE, when Jews and followers of other Eastern religions were expelled from Rome. But the first significant increase in the size of the Jewish community there seems to have occurred in the time of Pompey, a general who brought many Jewish slaves back to Rome around 60 BCE. They attracted Roman attention both by the peculiarity of their religion (especially Sabbath observance, which seemed to the ancient Roman to be a terrible waste of valuable time) and by their otherwise industrious behavior. Their rapid establishment can be seen in Suetonius's special mention that Jews came in great numbers to the grave of Julius Caesar in 27 BCE for several nights in a row (84). This was probably more an organized show of support than a spontaneous response of grief.

It reveals a large and free Jewish community in Rome. More than a dozen synagogues from the imperial period have been found all over the city, indicating that Jews there were not confined to one quarter. The serious anti-Jewish feelings manifested by Juvenal in the next generation (see pages 116–17) show that not all Romans welcomed these foreigners—other grounds for possible antagonism between Jews and Gentiles at Rome. Would Paul have been aware of these possible problems?

Paul's Relation to Rome

One puzzling feature of Romans is the number of individuals Paul salutes by name in chapter 16—so many in fact that some argue that chapter 16 must be a fragment of a separate letter, perhaps to Ephesus (MacDonald, 1969:369–72). In support of this view, these scholars point out that some manuscripts of Romans do not include chapter 16 and that 15:33 would be a suitable ending ("Now the God of peace be with you all. Amen."). Nevertheless, most scholars do agree that it makes good sense to regard

Copyright Alinari/Art Resource, New York

ROMAN APARTMENT HOUSE   Only the very wealthy could afford the grand homes of the Roman period. Most people lived in apartment houses resembling this reconstruction from Ostia. The Hellenistic era was a time of rapid growth for cities, and an expanding population confined by city walls could only go up. As in our own time, living conditions in apartments might range from comfortable to squalid.

chapter 16 as part of the original letter. Paul's extensive greetings section is matched by his extensive travel plans in chapter 15, the most detailed of all his surviving letters. The omission of chapter 16 from some manuscripts probably indicates that the letter was circulated in a more universal form (without these salutations and without the address to Rome) as a summary of Paul's thinking. If Romans was widely circulated as a general letter, this would have produced some confusion in the arrangement of the ending. The only real reason we have to doubt the authenticity of chapter 16 is the unlikelihood that Paul would have known so many Roman believers.

Yet we must remember that first-century Jews were a truly international people who traveled widely and established relations with other Jews in the cities to which they went. The arrival and acceptance of Prisca and Aquila at Corinth reflect this interconnectedness, as do Paul's own travels. Acts (18:2) tells us that Aquila was a native of Pontus (in northeastern Asia Minor) who had been living in Rome when forced out by Claudius's decree. We could imagine that Prisca and Aquila returned to Rome when Claudius died in 54, a couple of years before Paul wrote. Such a return may explain other names in the list; and the presence of Epaenetus and Andronicus, who were associated with Asia Minor (16:5, 7), remind us that there was probably a good bit of traffic from the provinces to the capital.

If the people addressed in chapter 16 are at Rome, indicating that many Jews did return there after the death of Claudius, it may have created some problems for

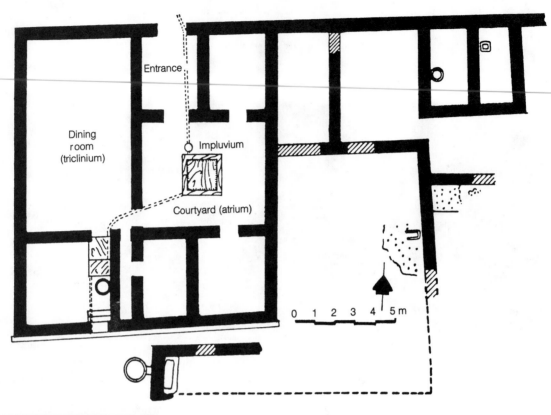

Entrance

Dining
room
(triclinium)

Impluvium

Courtyard (atrium)

0 1 2 3 4 5 m

FIGURE 5.1 ROMAN VILLA AT ANAPLOGA   This floor plan shows the layout of a typical Roman house (see also Figure 1.2, page 38, and the photo on page 106). One entered through a vestibule, on the floor of which were inscribed sentiments such as *havetis intro* (greetings to the arrivals) or *cave canem* (beware of the dog). This led directly to the atrium (courtyard) from which one could enter the public parts of the house, including the dining room and the washroom (the Romans had indoor plumbing and central heat). The atrium itself was a sacred space containing the hearth and the altar to the family Gods. The impluvium (pool) in the center of the atrium held rain water brought to it by a system of channels from the roof. It was adorned with statues and fountains. A kitchen, wine room, plant room, and various bedrooms completed the building, which would be surrounded by solid, high walls. Houses differed in some details. In some, the part facing the street might contain small shops. Larger houses had two or three courtyards and perhaps four dining rooms. (From *St. Paul's Corinth* by Jerome Murphy-O'Connor [Michael Glazier, 1983:154], used by permission.)

those Gentile believers who had remained in the city. They would now have to work through the meaning of their faith in relation to a significantly different community. In fact, chapter 16 seems to reflect several different groups at Rome, probably different assemblies meeting in different homes, perhaps five (notice how several greetings include a group: 16:5, 10, 11, 14, 15). The private homes of this period were spacious, including both public and private quarters (see Figure 5.1). Yet a typical home could accommodate only thirty to thirty-five guests, especially if a meal were involved. Inevitably then, the believers in a given city would soon be divided into different groups and would tend to evolve in somewhat different ways (recall the divisions at Corinth discussed in Chapter 4). It is remarkable, but not impossible, that Paul knew the leaders of several such assemblies.

It is also likely that officials from these Roman congregations traveled to other places, because being the capital implied having influence beyond Rome. The people greeted in chapter 16 were leaders, most of them having some sort of title (servant, apostle, kinsman, fellow worker, and so on). The presence of a significant number of women in this list, including Junia, who is listed as an apostle, and Phoebe, who is listed as a *diakonos* (literally "servant" or "minister") of the assembly at Cenchreae (what we might call a suburb of Corinth, where Paul was when he wrote this letter), reminds us of the contribution of women to this early period. Phoebe was the carrier and thus the first reader of this letter. Like Paul, these leaders were mobile people; Paul may well have met them without ever visiting Rome. This extensive greeting, if a part of the original letter, would mean that Paul was aware of the problems between Jew and Gentile that had arisen in Rome when Jews returned after the death of Claudius. Part of the explanation of Romans lies in this situation of Jewish and Gentile controversy at Rome.

THE SETTING IN PAUL'S LIFE

An additional explanation may be found by shifting our attention from the Roman scene to the immediate situation in Paul's own life. The most obvious reason for trying to build bridges to Rome was Paul's plan to visit there and, perhaps, use it as a base for missions to the West (15:24–32). This would certainly be a reason to write to Rome but not a sufficient reason for the letter we actually have. This is too magnificent a work to be explained as a letter of self-introduction to prepare for a brief visit after celebrating Passover in Jerusalem.

As the plan to go west indicates, Paul regarded his work in the East as nearly finished. He had planted assemblies in all the major cities and was looking for new territory. Having fought desperately to regain the confidence of his followers in Corinth, Paul had returned there to wait for a ship to take him to Jerusalem for Passover. In this precise situation, he wrote Romans (compare Rom. 15:25–27 with 1 Cor. 16:3–6).

The Politics of Paul's Mission

Paul described the purpose of this trip: "to minister to the saints" (15:25). By this he meant he was going to deliver a substantial relief offering to the Jerusalem community from the assemblies of "Macedonia and Achaia," his Gentile congregations in Europe. This was an event of greater significance than appears on the surface. We saw earlier that two chapters of 2 Corinthians (8 and 9, perhaps originally separate letters) concerned this collection and Paul's trip to Jerusalem. Paul worked diligently to collect this money, taking more than a year to do so (2 Cor. 9:2; 1 Cor. 16:1–2). He sent special messengers to collect it and arranged for envoys from each congregation to accompany him on the trip to Jerusalem (1 Cor. 16:3–4).

The significance of this offering may be seen in the logic by which Paul explains:

If the Gentiles have come to share in their [the Jews'] spiritual blessings, they [the Gentiles] ought also to be of service to them [the Jews] in material things. (15:27)

Although this logic has been exploited by many who would profit from their spiritual ministry, for Paul the meaning of the statement worked backward: it was the monetary contributions of the Gentiles that would demonstrate to the Jerusalem community that they had become partakers of the spirit. Because the first statement was true (if spiritual blessing, then material blessing) then the reverse must also be valid: because there is material blessing, there must be spiritual blessing. This collection is far more than a charitable deed; it is a political act. If the Jerusalem assembly accepts it, they implicitly recognize the validity of Paul's Gentile followers. Paul was fully aware of its political nature, for he asked the Romans to pray "that I may be delivered from the unbelievers in Judea and that my service for Jerusalem may be acceptable to the saints" (15:31).

On one hand, such acceptance had already been granted at some sort of meeting in Jerusalem. According to Paul's report, the leaders there had given Paul "the right hand of fellowship" (Gal. 2:9), apparently a rite of association. But it is important to notice the limitation they placed on this association: Paul would go to Gentiles while Peter would go to Jews. In other words, they envisioned a separate but equal situation that proved unworkable. For as Paul went on to recount in Galatians, the agreement broke down when Peter visited Antioch (see the discussion on page 124). In the actual lives of Jews and Gentiles in the diaspora it was impossible to be separate, and, consequently, equality was threatened. In refusing to share a common meal with the Gentiles at Corinth, Peter implicitly denied their equality (Gal. 2:11–13). The acceptance of the offering would confront the Jerusalem community with the acceptance of the equality of the Gentile communities of Paul.

The Community at Jerusalem

The development of the Jesus movement in Jerusalem is not well documented, probably due to the destruction of Jerusalem in 70 CE and again in 135. What evidence we do have indicates that a rather conservative, Law-observing tradition predominated there. Jesus' brother **James** soon became head of the community and, according to tradition, was followed by another relative, Symeon, a cousin of Jesus (Eusebius, *Church History* 3.11). James was known in later Jewish Christian tradition as "James the righteous," and various legends developed about his piety and Law observance (for example, that he was permitted to enter the temple because of his extraordinary holiness; Eusebius, 2.23.4). Although such claims are surely not historical, they reflect the attitude of those who held James in high regard. More directly relevant is the description the author of Acts attributes to James when he welcomes Paul to Jerusalem:

> You see, brother, how many thousands of believers there are among the Jews, and they are all zealous for the law. They have been told about you that you teach all the Jews living among the Gentiles to forsake Moses, and that you tell them not to circumcise their children or observe the customs. (Acts 21:20–21)

Notice the deep suspicion about Paul and the description of the **Jerusalem community** as involving people "zealous for the law." When he wrote Galatians, Paul seemed little concerned with what they thought of him at Jerusalem (see page 120–21).

There is even a slight mockery in his description of the leaders as those "reputed to be something" (Gal. 2:6). Yet even there we see the seed planted that is now being harvested. For Paul also reported that the Jerusalem conference had urged him to "remember the poor, which very thing I was eager to do" (Gal. 2:10). Perhaps this collection would have been nothing more than an act of charity had not subsequent events cast a shadow over the legitimacy of Paul's ministry and of the inclusion of the Gentiles. Or perhaps it was always intended to be what it now became: a symbolic statement of the unity of Jews and Gentiles in the new movement.

Just as the Gentile assemblies dramatize their dependence on Jerusalem by delivering the offering to Jerusalem, the Jerusalem community will dramatize its acceptance of Gentiles when it accepts the offering. To receive this gift from the Gentiles will be to recognize the unity of the new movement and the place of Gentiles as Gentiles in that movement. In the process, they will be forced to validate Paul's apostolic mission to the Gentiles—something at least some of them were not eager to do.

In contemplation of this approaching crisis, Paul sits in Corinth, writing Romans and preparing to sail to Jerusalem with the offering from his Gentile assemblies. Uncertain of the outcome, he asks those at Rome to pray for the acceptance of the collection (Rom. 15:31). Notice how strikingly different is the attitude toward Jerusalem implied here from that of Galatians.

As we turn to the actual interpretation of the letter, both these contexts must be kept in mind, the life of the Roman assemblies and the life of Paul.

THE THEME OF ROMANS: TWO VIEWS

The **theme** of a work of literature is the total impression it makes, the sum of all its images, characters, plot, and structure (or, in nonnarrative literature, its images, rhetoric, and structure). We have considered the literary features of Romans and examined its historical setting. Let us turn now to the central question: What is it actually about? The many different interpretations of Romans may be divided into two basic approaches, suggesting very different themes for the work. The traditional interpretation of Romans argues that its theme is the salvation of the individual. Another view, advanced by certain Scandinavian scholars, but having some precedent in the earliest interpretations of Romans, argues that its theme is the salvation of the world. Before examining these two themes more closely, we will briefly trace the major contours of Paul's discussion.

THE LINE OF ARGUMENT

Earlier we saw that the argument of Romans is a diatribe rather than a simple logical progression. We observed further that the viewpoint of the argument shifts from third to first to third to second person, giving us the following major sections:

Chapters 1–4:	they
Chapters 5–8:	we
Chapters 9–11:	they
Chapters 12–16:	you

Reread Romans, using the reading guide and the following very brief summaries of each major section. Compare your own reading of each section with that given in the summaries, trying to get a clear grasp of the logic of each section and of the logic that connects the sections to each other.

 ## READING GUIDE TO ROMANS

Understanding the Human Situation

The conclusion Paul reaches in this section, that all are sinful, has given him a reputation as a pessimist, but we should not miss the happy note on which he begins:

> For I am not ashamed of the gospel: it is the power of God for salvation to everyone who has faith, to the Jew first and also to the Greek. (1:16)

It is crucial for us in all that follows to remember that Paul's purpose is to explain how all may find salvation. Now we will trace the contours of this lengthy and involved argument.

Idolatry leads to pervasive sinfulness (1:18–32). Paul demonstrates that the wrath of God falls on all by means of two arguments that are very nearly **syllogisms** (a logical statement consisting of a major premise, a minor premise, and a conclusion). The first, stated in 1:19–23, should be carefully studied. The argument here is both simple and profound: something of God can be known through nature, namely God's awesome power and hiddenness. In other words, nature reveals only the mystery of God. Yet the human race has perversely persisted in resolving the mystery, reducing God to an image of the visible world, worshipping the creation rather than the creator. The logic here is straightforward:

> Since *the divine power and majesty can be known from nature;*
> and since *people persist in worshipping nature instead of the divine;*
> therefore, *they are without excuse.*

Ironically, Paul locates the root cause of human sinfulness in religion, or more precisely in a religious error.

Then Paul illustrates how this perversion affects every aspect of human life: perversion of the "heart" (what we would call the spiritual) results in idolatry; perversion of the "passions" (what we refer to as desires or drives) results in "unnatural intercourse"; perversion of the "mind" (the will) results in evil behavior ranging from murder to disobeying one's parents (1:24–32). The logic of all these conclusions is that of a **natural order**—the assumption that certain things are given in nature and could not be otherwise. Thus, the natural order of worship is revealed in creation; that of sex is revealed in procreation; and the natural order of behavior is revealed in culture (recall that in 1 Corinthians Paul argued that "nature" teaches a woman to have long hair; 11:14).

We should be careful not to confuse Paul's assumptions with the actual practices of other cultures: Hindus use images in their worship but insist that they are worshipping the divine not the image. Homosexuals have intercourse with same-sex partners but insist that for them this is natural. And the degree of obedience expected towards one's parents in American culture diminishes dramatically when the child becomes an adult. It did not in Roman culture. And in that culture the dominant form of same-sex relations is closer to what we call pederasty, sex between older married men and teenage boys. (See the recent study by Wink, 1999.) Paul is not here arguing that same-sex relations are wrong; he assumes they are wrong (because they are unnatural) and, like idolatry and parental disobedience, exemplify human sin.

All who judge stand under judgment (2:1–29). Having condemned the perversities of the world, Paul's next sentence is shocking: "Therefore you have no excuse" (2:1). Certain people can claim exemption from the first argument, namely those who live by the proper order (by the Law). Jews, in particular, whose rejection of idolatry is evident, seem to be acquitted in this argument. But now Paul raises a second point. Even good people stand guilty, convicted by the very evidence that they find *others* guilty, for in passing judgment on others they condemn themselves. Though much more rhetorically developed, the essence of this second argument is that all people set standards of behavior that they fail to live up to. Hence, in judging others, each condemns one's self as well.

These two points constitute a radical indictment and raise serious objections: Are moral Jews really no better off than immoral Gentiles (3:1)? Has God's plan to create a holy people failed (3:5)? If all are wicked, is there any sense in trying to do good (3:8)? These are the first detours through which the diatribe style leads the reader, but we shall bypass them to follow the main road.

Scripture declares all to be under the power of sin (3:9–20). Paul brings his argument for universal sinfulness to a dramatic conclusion by citing a medley of psalms: none is righteous; all have turned aside. The curious thing is that we sense no sadness here in Paul's argument, no lamenting. In fact, his argument rushes on to new conclusions.

Righteousness now comes through faith in Christ (3:21–31). Soon we realize that this argument about universal sinfulness was only the prelude; Paul's real thrust is to show that righteousness for all has appeared through faith in Jesus Christ (3:21–26).

Paul spends very little time developing this argument; clearly it is something he expects his hearers will agree with. Yet it raises new objections: Is there no basis for boasting (3:27)? Are Gentiles really included (3:29)? Does this faith overthrow the Law (3:31)? Then what about Abraham (4:1)? The story of Abraham is found in the Law and helps Paul show the degree to which his own understanding of salvation can be supported by the Law.

The Law itself teaches salvation by faith (4:1–25). This last question leads Paul into a lengthy discussion of the relationship between faithful trusting and faithful acting (usually referred to as faith versus works). The point here is that the election of Israel rests on the promise of God, not on the Law or on circumcision, both of which are later than Abraham's faith—the Law centuries later. As he has done earlier (3:10), Paul clinches his case by quoting Scripture: that is why his faith was "reckoned to him as righteousness." Just so, he argues, "It will be reckoned to us who believe in him that raised from the dead Jesus our Lord" (4:22–25). Faith counts as righteousness. This argument is easier to follow in Greek, where both the noun we translate "faith" and the verb we translate "believe" are built on the same root (*pistis* and *pistuein*), and both mean primarily trusting someone or being loyal to someone. Trusting in God through Christ now counts as righteousness in the same way as did Abraham's trusting. Paul now shifts his argument to "we who trust," shifting to an insider's view.

Understanding the Results

In chapters 5–8, Paul explores the implications for himself and the Roman believers (*we*) of this new situation, which has revealed both the wrath and the righteousness of God (1:17–18). We have peace (5:1). "We are now justified by his blood" and will "be saved by him from the wrath of God" (5:9). Paul explains how this comes about by an extensive analogy between Adam and Christ. A near contemporary of Paul had lamented:

> *O Adam, what have you done? For though it was you who sinned, the fall was not yours alone, but ours also who are your descendants. For what good is it to us, if an immortal time has been promised to us, but we have done deeds that bring death? And what good is it that an everlasting hope has been promised to us, but we have miserably failed?* (2 Esd. 7:118–20, also numbered as 48–50)

But Paul saw more. Read 5:12–21, noticing the parallels Paul draws between the two. We can diagram the ideas:

Adam → Disobeyed → Sin → Death → All → Condemnation

Christ → Obeyed → Righteousness → Life → All → Acquittal

This daring comparison reveals why Paul thinks that a new situation now pertains. God has worked to reverse the disobedience of Adam; Christ as the "second Adam" begins the process of the new creation. This is the closest we come in any of Paul's letters to what his actual proclamation may have been, for we see here the outline of a charter story in which the primeval deed of Adam is repeated and perfected in the cosmic work of the Christ. The obedience of Christ, as we have seen in earlier letters, was his death.

New questions and objections are raised: If God overcomes sin with grace, are we to continue in sin that grace may abound (6:1)? If we are not under the Law, can we sin without fear (6:15)? Is the Law sin (7:7)? If sin is only counted where there is a Law, did the Law bring death (7:13)? All are answered with an emphatic negative. If they remind us of the things his opponents in Galatia may have said, that is probably appropriate. They reveal just how agonizing is the line between freedom and anarchy on the one side and between obedience and legalism on the other.

The argument resumes in chapter 8 with an extensive contrast between life "in the flesh" and life "in the spirit." This is not a contrast between body and spirit (see verse 10), as some of Paul's followers assumed, but between life under Adam and life under Christ. This section ends with one of the most moving assertions of faith (trust) in all literature (8:31–39).

Paul now shifts his attention from the group he designates as *us* to another group, his "kindred" according to physical descent. The argument here is partly a return to the objection raised in 3:1, now dealt with more fully, and partly a response to the previous assertion of trust: Can God's word to Israel be trusted? It is also a continuation of the main line of the argument: What are the implications of the revelation of God's wrath and grace? Paul struggles mightily, though perhaps unsuccessfully, for answers. None of the earlier letters has any parallel to this section.

Understanding the Salvation of Israel

Paul first responds to the question of whether God has failed. This question is at the heart of Paul's dilemma, for his assertion that God now justifies all through faith in Christ seems to imply that God's covenant with Israel was worthless. The faithfulness of God in Christ seems to imply God's unfaithfulness to the chosen people of Israel. Paul answers that God is absolutely free to do whatever God wishes to do. But when Paul recognizes that this raises more questions than it answers (9:14, 19), he modifies his answer, asserting that the present situation is not unique; it has always been only a "remnant" who were faithful (9:27). So too, there is now a remnant, to which Paul himself claims to belong (11:1). The intervening material, chapter 10, is really an anguished rehearsal of Israel's "zeal for God" (verse 2) coupled with its rejection of the gospel (verse 16). Realizing perhaps that the ideas of election and of a remnant do not deal with the real issues, Paul tackles the question of Israel's salvation directly (11:11).

His solution, which proved to be romantic and unrealistic, displays the strength of heart that made Paul a great human being: Israel's trespass has resulted in the inclusion of the Gentiles; the inclusion of the Gentiles will make Israel jealous; the return of Israel and its full inclusion will usher in the reign of God (11:11–12). Paul describes all this vividly, with an intricate analogy to an olive tree that is well worth careful study (11:17–24). His rapt conclusion declares God's ways to be a mystery: "a hardening has come upon part of Israel, until the full number of Gentiles come in, and so all Israel will be saved" (11:25–26). This is Paul's ultimate hope.

We must also note here the audience Paul is addressing. His speaking of Jews in the third person (they) and his explicit address ("I speak to you Gentiles," 11:13) reveal his underlying purpose: Gentiles must feel no superiority to Jews, not even to those Jews who do not receive Paul's proclamation (11:18). Had later Christians heeded this admonition, much human suffering could have been avoided. Paul's conviction was that ultimately both Jew and Gentile would be redeemed.

Unfortunately, later Christians have only heard the first half of Paul's paradoxical assertion about Jews and have used it as a basis for repeated persecution. But we must hear the whole of the mystery:

> As regards the gospel they are enemies of God, for your sake; but as regards the election they are beloved for the sake of their ancestors; for the gifts and the calling of God are irrevocable. (11:28–29)

Paul admits he does not understand this but is willing to leave it to the judgment of God (11:33). Paul's understanding of God's grace forced him to embrace more than one paradox. We glimpse the absolute position of God's mercy in Paul's understanding of life by his almost Zen-like declaration that even universal sinfulness leads to life, "For God has gathered all together in disobedience, so that God may be merciful to all" (11:32, literal translation).

The Implications for Behavior

This brings Paul to the final phase of his extended argument: "I appeal to you therefore, brothers and sisters, by the mercies of God, to present your bodies as a living sacrifice" (12:1). The rhetorical *therefore* points back to the entire preceding argument. Paul based his ethical demands on his understanding that God has already worked to accomplish salvation. This is what Rudolf Bultmann meant when he declared that for Paul the imperative rests on the indicative: the demand rests on what God has done. There is nothing original about the ethical instruction offered here. Such actions were the common property of all persons of good will. What is original is the *therefore*: the basis of ethics rests in the charter story of what God had done through Jesus. Now let us consider more carefully what *therefore* suggests: how ought we to interpret Paul's argument?

TWO INTERPRETATIONS

The process of interpretation is always circular. We begin with some general notion of what a piece of literature is about and modify that notion in the reading of the literature. Our general notion shapes the way we perceive the details, and the details in turn shape the general notion. At its best, this is an ongoing process that continually refines our understanding and brings us closer to the full meaning of a text. At worst, a basic mistake will cause us to misread completely the original meaning of a work (as when one fails to realize that a certain article in the student newspaper is a satire). Most of our reading of literature falls between these two extremes, with varying degrees of correct interpretation. For Romans, two general notions are proposed as the correct context for interpreting the work.

Romans and the Salvation of the Individual

The traditional view, going back at least to Martin Luther and the Protestant Reformation of the sixteenth century, is that Romans concerns the salvation of the individual. According to this view the question Paul addresses deals with how a person is saved. Generally, those who hold this view see Paul as presenting his basic gospel to the Roman assemblies to gain their support for his mission to the West.

The question "What must I do to be saved?" (Acts 16:30) is one that all religions and all philosophies must answer, though many would phrase it differently. It is a version of the more general question: How does one achieve the highest possible good in life? This question raises others: Why do we not now possess the good? What is wrong? What is our true nature? What is the true nature of the ultimate reality? How can the individual apprehend this ultimate reality? According to the traditional view of Romans, Paul is addressing questions like these.

Martin Luther (1483–1546), father of the Protestant Reformation, established this reading of Romans. Luther was a person extremely oppressed by the notion of his guilt before God. Much to his father's dismay, he forsook his pursuit of law to enter an Augustinian monastery. There he prayed, fasted, and performed penance, but derived no satisfaction. He could not feel anything but God's wrath. But Luther was a scholar-monk, a professor of Old Testament. His study of Romans convinced him that because all are sinners, it is only the unconditional grace of God that brings forgiveness and salvation. He expressed it in Latin as *sola gratia*, "only grace" (1516). This interpretation of Romans, coupled with Luther's experience and great skill, certainly changed the face of Christendom.

The influence of this traditional view may be seen in the various outlines of Romans, nearly all of which divide the first section (chapters 1–4) into two; the first dealing with the problem (sin), the second with the answer (justification by faith). This leads logically to the next section (5–8), seen as a discussion of life in the spirit that culminates in the final section (12–15): practical instruction in living. The traditional view tends to neglect chapters 9–11, regarding them as a kind of parenthesis or diatribal detour.

Some modern interpreters go even further. Günther Bornkamm, for example, argues that chapters 9–11 relate to the earlier discussion as problem does to answer. Following the general line of Protestant interpretation, Bornkamm argues that Romans is written to refute all those who depend on good works for their salvation. He views Jews as Paul's opponents, for they taught the keeping of the Law whereas Paul taught salvation by God's grace alone. He goes so far as to pronounce:

> In a way the Jew symbolizes man [sic] in his highest potentialities; he represents the "religious man" whom the Law tells what God requires of him, who appeals to the special statute granted him in the plan of salvation, and who refuses to admit that he has failed to measure up to God's claim on him and is in consequence abandoned to sin and death. (1971:95)

According to this reading, the Law-observant Jews are worse off than the immoral Gentiles, for they refuse to admit their sinfulness. These anti-Semitic implications of the traditional interpretation have caused some modern interpreters to question this approach.

Romans and the Salvation of the World

Their uneasiness with the traditional interpretation has other bases, too. Such a strong emphasis on the individual seems anachronistic, they argue, for overwhelming concern with the inner self is uncharacteristic of Paul. So too, they point out, in

Romans Paul is trying to build bridges between Jewish and Gentile believers, not to divide them. He faces the need to explain his mission in terms acceptable to the conservatives in Jerusalem and is, therefore, unlikely to be thinking of contrasts. These interpreters point out that Paul does not speak of the forgiveness of sins in Romans but rather of justification by faith—an objective and historical fact rather than an inner, subjective experience. The theme of Romans, they assert, is not the salvation of the individual but the salvation of the world. In Romans, Paul is sketching God's plan for the ages and thus validating his mission to Gentiles.

On this reading Romans 1–4 is designed to show that something new has occurred in history: in the present time God is both the just one and the one who makes just (3:26). This means that both Jews and Gentiles may be found acceptable to God: there is no distinction between them (3:22); both sin; both find salvation. The next section (5–8) addresses this newness by the contrast between Christ and Adam and by the new experience of being "in Christ," that is, in the Spirit.

Rather than receding into the background, chapters 9–11 stand out as the central section of the letter, its climax (Stendahl, 1976:4). In these chapters Paul deals with the relationship between two communities of faith. He forbids Gentile believers to feel superior to Jews (11:17–18) and predicts salvation for "all Israel" (11:26). He does not say, Krister Stendahl observes, that they all become Christians. In fact, these interpreters generally agree that the major concern Paul has for his audience is their arrogant assumption of their superiority over Jews.

Both interpretations view the final section (12–16) as ethical exhortation based on the whole preceding argument. (For an actual reading of Romans from this perspective see Stendahl, 1995.)

READING AND REFLECTION

We saw above (see pages 152, 161) that the form of the argument can be traced in the point of view used: them (1–4), us (5–8), them (9–11), and you (12–16). Imagine how someone who held the view that Romans is about the salvation of the individual would title these sections. Now imagine how someone who held the other view, that Romans is about the salvation of the world, would title them.

Charter Stories: Being God's People

It is impossible here to reconcile these two interpretations of Romans or even to choose between them. Each offers insights into Paul; each interprets portions of the text as more important than others; and each must in turn be tested by reading Romans. To what extent does each interpretation explain the specific data found in Paul's letter? Only you, as an informed and careful reader, can answer that question.

We can, however, ask a related question: To what extent do the descriptions of Jewish life presupposed by these two views correspond to first-century realities? In the traditional view Judaism is seen as the paradigm of legalism and self-justification; in the second view, Judaism is quite similar to Christianity. What was early Judaism like? How did other Jews in Paul's day conceive of their salavation?

It is not a simple question to answer because we have very few contemporary sources to turn to for information. The primary Jewish evidence is derived from the **rabbis**, those scholar-teachers of the Jewish people who came to leadership in the second century. (For a discussion of their emergence, see pages 335–42.) Their works are not separate writings by specific individuals but an amalgamated collection of the views of various rabbis, without regard to when they lived, organized into a vast collection of material—rather several collections, the earliest dating from a century and a half after Paul (the **Mishnah**, about 200 CE). Another body of Jewish material was preserved by Christians, though not without change. This material consists of individual works, though dating them is extremely difficult because many pretend they were written by the pious ones of ancient Israel. These works, the **Apocrypha** (meaning "hidden works") and the **pseudepigrapha** ("forged writings"), were actually written over the course of centuries, some as early as two hundred years before Paul, many much later. All were continually revised by later hands.

This puts the historian in the uncomfortable position of depending on writings that are later in time and filtered by the concerns of later Christians and Jews (and both groups wanted to remember the first century in their own ways). There is, however, one exception: we now have access to a body of literature that was unaffected by these later concerns. It was put into a sort of time capsule shortly after the time of Paul and was not opened until the twentieth century.

The time capsule in this case consisted of huge stoneware jars, sealed and hidden in caves in the nearly inaccessible hills along the Dead Sea in southern Palestine. A group of Jewish ascetics, living in a commune in the area, apparently hid their sacred writings when the Roman army was invading the land to put down the rebellion of 66 CE. Why they never reclaimed them we do not know, but the scrolls were only rediscovered in 1947, when a Bedouin goatherd threw a stone into one of the caves while looking for a lost animal. The breaking jar prompted further exploration, and, years later, the discovery of many more scrolls in several caves. (The full story of this fascinating discovery is recounted by Vermes, 1977. For a photograph of the caves see page 321.)

These **Dead Sea Scrolls** reveal one type of first-century Jewish religion in its original form, uncensored by later Christian or Jewish concerns. Consequently, they are a suitable place to begin if we want to learn how some other Jews dealt with the issues that concerned Paul in Romans. A word of caution is necessary, however: these were surely atypical Jews who had forsaken society and family in their quest for holiness.

Rather than comparing the specific ideas of Paul and these other Jews on this or that subject, we wish to evaluate the general pattern of their religious conviction. The most fruitful comparison to date has been that of E. P. Sanders (1977), whose analysis is extensive and systematic (and highly recommended). What follows is indebted to his analysis but is considerably simplified. Here we will address only two aspects of their system: What did they believe God was doing to redeem God's people? And how did one become part of (and stay part of) what God was doing?

For the community at **Qumran** who produced the Dead Sea Scrolls, the great thing God was doing in their day was creating and sustaining their community. They understood themselves to be a community of the end time, those whom God had called out to inaugurate the kingdom of God. They understood themselves to be those prophesied by Isaiah who would "in the wilderness prepare the way of the Lord" (40:3).

What they were doing in the wilderness was keeping the Law as perfectly as they could. This is only logical. Because the kingdom of God and the rule of God are the same thing, the way one actualizes the kingdom is to obey God's rules. Thus,

Courtesy of the Israel Antiquities Authority

A Scroll from the Caves of Qumran Now known as the Dead Sea Scrolls, these writings were originally the library of a strict, ascetic Jewish sect. Containing both biblical writings and sectarian documents, they reveal much about first-century Jewish life. They were stored in large earthen jars, apparently hidden when the site was abandoned during the Roman invasion in 66 CE, and they were preserved unmolested until the twentieth century. This is a Psalm scroll found in cave 11 (thus designated 11QPsa; see page 504); the bottom edge was damaged from standing on its end in the storage jar.

we are not surprised to find an extraordinary emphasis on rules at Qumran. One stayed in this community by obeying these rules. Even minor infractions resulted in disciplinary action (usually exclusion from the common ritual meal and a reduction in rations). Major infractions resulted in expulsion from the community. Consider the following:

> *If one of them has lied deliberately in matters of property, he shall be excluded from the pure Meal of the Congregation for one year and shall do penance with respect to one quarter of his food.*
>
> *Whoever has answered his companion with obstinacy, or has addressed him impatiently, going so far as to take no account of the dignity of his fellow by disobeying the order of a brother inscribed before him, he has taken the*

law into his own hand; therefore he shall do penance for one year [and shall be excluded].

If any one has uttered the [Most] Venerable Name even though frivolously, or as a result of shock or for any other reason whatever, while reading the Book or praying, he shall be dismissed and shall return to the Council of the Community no more.

After several more serious offenses, it continues:

Whoever has spoken foolishly: three months.
   Whoever has interrupted his companion while speaking: ten days.
   Whoever has lain down to sleep during an Assembly of the Congregation: thirty days.
      (From the Community Rule *VI and VII; quoted from Vermes, 1995:78–79)*

There are many more such rules, but these suffice to show that the community regulated every aspect of the life of its members, including a pledge of obedience to all who had entered the community before them.

Getting into such a community was equally difficult: "Every man, born of Israel, who freely pledges himself to join the Council of the Community, shall be examined by the Guardian at the head of the Congregation concerning his understanding and his deeds" (*Community Rule* VI; Vermes, 1995:78). Only males, only native-born Jews, only those with proper understanding and proper deeds could join, and then only by examination—though others, perhaps even women, could be affiliated with the community. Joining was a multi-stage process. First, candidates lived in the community for a year (but without participating in the central meal); then, if they passed muster, they were admitted. At this point they gave all their property to the community. However, they spent another year on probation before they were fully accepted and their property merged with that of the community, and then only if they passed further examination. All of this suggests a very legalistic community, of the kind the traditional interpretation of Romans presumes for all Jews of this period. Yet it is not quite that simple.

If we also look at the hymns and liturgies of the community we find that in their self-understanding they did not think of these laws in a legalistic way. They did not understand them as earning their salvation. They saw themselves as redeemed by the mercy of God, despite their sins. Consider:

As for me,
   my justification is with God.
In his hand are the perfection of my way
   and the uprightness of my heart.
He will wipe out my transgressions.
As for me,
if I stumble, the mercies of God
   shall be my eternal salvation.
If I stagger because of the sin of flesh,
   my justification shall be
   by the righteousness of God which endures forever.
      (Community Rule XI; Vermes, 1995:86–87)

Righteousness, I know, is not of man,
* nor is perfection of way of the son of man:*
to the Most High God belong all righteous deeds.
The way of man is not established
* except by the spirit which God created for him*
* to make perfect a way for the children*
* of man. . . .*
I lean on Thy grace
* and on the multitude of Thy mercies,*
for Thou will pardon iniquity,
* and through Thy righteousness*
* [Thou will purify man] of his sin.*
                    (Hymn 7; Vermes, 1995:202–3)

Thus it seems fair to say that while the Qumran community placed great stress on keeping the Law, the men gathered there understood that their ability to keep the Law depended on the grace of God. God would create in them a spirit that would enable them to become obedient to God's entire will. Sanders has shown that a similar pattern obtained in rabbinic circles, which later became mainstream Judaism, and in the more esoteric circles that produced the Apocrypha and pseudepigrapha (1977:419–428).

This means that structurally, there was a strong resemblance between Paul and the Qumran community, even while they disagreed on nearly every particular point of content. This structural similarity may be portrayed thus:

grace → Spirit → obedience to God → reign of God

God's grace has resulted in granting the Spirit to those who would be faithful, and this Spirit enables them to be obedient to God and leads the faithful into God's kingdom.

Certainly, Paul and the Qumran community understood the nature of that kingdom, the kind of obedience required, the experience of that Spirit, the basis of that grace in radically different, perhaps antithetical, terms. Only the pattern is similar.

If this understanding of God's grace was shared in some way by other Jews, then we would expect Paul's argument to focus on showing the way God works for the salvation of the world rather than combating a legalism. The great issue that Paul needed to address, especially in light of his approach to Jerusalem with the collection, was the place of his Gentile congregations in the divine plan. If we add to this the special problems that the Roman congregations had with the proper relation between Jews and Gentiles, it appears likely that the central theme of the letter concerns the divine plan for the salvation of the world.

But again, we must be careful. Surely some, even many, would have failed to grasp this pattern and would see their keeping of the Law as a legal transaction earning God's favor. One can point to such legalistic misunderstandings in the later literature of the rabbis (and of the Christians), even as one can find this same pattern of grace alone at work. Perhaps we must conclude that Paul is responding to both concerns to some extent, to the ultimate question of how God is at work in the world to bring about the kingdom and to the immediate question of how one joins in that work. For these first-century Jews, to know what God is doing in the world would be to know what one must do to be saved.

TWO VIEWS OF PAUL

As scholars have begun to reread Romans and Galatians and reconsider Paul's relation to other Jews, a new view of Paul has begun to emerge. It is too soon to know if this new view will have a lasting effect on Pauline scholarship, but it is certainly commanding attention. The new view contradicts many of the basic ideas of the traditional view of Paul.

Traditionally, scholars have portrayed Paul as a Pharisaic Jew who cannot find peace with God by keeping the Law. Then Paul is converted. Paul becomes a Christian, ceasing to be a Jew. Paul then sets out on a mission "to the Jew first and also to the Greek"—that is, he aims to convert the whole world. In the process, Paul develops a law-free Gospel, claiming that the Law is no longer binding for all who follow Jesus. The traditional view of Paul's message is captured in this extract:

> It was Paul who delivered the Christian religion from Judaism. . . . It was he who confidently regarded the Gospel as a new force abolishing the religion of the law. (Harnack, 1901:190)

Two factors have caused some scholars to reconsider this image. First is the implicit anti-Semitism of this formulation. The long history of Christian oppression of Jews, along with the memory of the horrors of the Nazi death camps, demands a careful examination of all possible supports for such atrocities. But second, the reconstruction of ancient Jewish religion that underlies this view simply does not match up to any Jewish literature of the period, as our discussion of the Qumran community above shows.

Some scholars have tackled this problem head on and suggest a new solution: Paul is not addressing Jews in these letters. He is ever and only addressing Gentiles. Thus Paul's seemingly negative remarks about the Law must be understood within this Gentile context. Paul never suggests that Jews ought not to keep the Law; their covenant with God is not his concern. In fact, this new view argues that the underlying purpose of Romans—far from rejecting Jews—has as a central purpose the reaffirmation of the central importance of Israel, ending any sense of superiority by Gentile followers.

This new view of Paul sees him as remaining a faithful Jew all his life; he was not converted to Christianity. If we would stop misreading ancient Judaism, we would see how much Paul had in common with other Jews.

> What is new in the story, the mystery as Paul calls it, is that the redemption of the Gentiles and the salvation of Israel are intimately intertwined. (Gager, 2000:140)

SUMMARY OF ROMANS DISCUSSION

The Letter to the Romans represents a new venture on Paul's part. Although it is deeply rooted in the life setting of the Roman assembly (and its conflicts between Jew and Gentile) and in Paul's own life (especially his approaching visit to

Jerusalem, where he will have to defend his mission to Gentiles), it does not grow out of a specific crisis. In fact it is not addressed to one of his communities but to a community founded by others. In Romans Paul transcends the letter genre and produces a letter-essay in the style of a diatribe. The hallmark of a diatribe is its dialoguelike style, in which an invisible listener is made to pose various questions and objections—usually as a result of a misunderstanding of the argument. The purpose of this style is to persuade the hearer to adopt the same conclusions as the speaker.

Paul in Romans is at his most congenial, even as he summarizes and refines arguments that he presented in a heated way in earlier letters. Romans contains the longest sustained argument of any of Paul's writings as it wrestles with this issue of salvation, both the salvation of the world and the salvation of the individual.

This ends our discussion of those letters that are indisputably written by Paul, his central letters. Before we proceed to consider other letters, whose authorship is disputed, we must pause to explore the possibility of hearing Paul's own story as it echoes through these central writings.

IN CONCLUSION: IMAGINING PAUL'S STORY

There's an insult that says: "You remind me of a ranch-style house. Nothing upstairs." In quite a different sense, this is an apt metaphor for the age in which we live: the upstairs (God and company) is no longer an integral part of the structure. Although individuals continue to worship God, the structures of modern life (politics, education, labor, the economy, and so on) operate solely on one level: the human. The ancients, and not so ancient, lived in trilevels: there was not only an upstairs but also a downstairs (for example, Phil. 2:10). Each level was thickly inhabited with various beings, and each penetrated and influenced the others. In the general literature of this period we encounter a multitude of nonhuman characters, not only Gods and Goddesses, but witches, demons, ghosts, and dozens of minor divinities, such as the God laughter and the Goddess sleep. When the ancients told their stories, they portrayed far more characters than we are apt to have in our stories.

Paul did this too. In the story in which Paul lived it made sense to order one's behavior with regard to those who lived upstairs: Women were to cover their heads because of the angels (1 Cor. 11:10; see also 4:9). One could act on behalf of the dead (baptism for the dead is mentioned in 1 Cor. 15:29). Paul described his inability to revisit Thessalonica as having his way blocked by Satan (1 Thess. 2:18). He even claimed a journey into "the third heaven," though he admitted he was unsure whether this was a bodily or visionary experience (2 Cor. 12:2).

More universal than these references, the presence of the Spirit pervaded Paul's story. The Spirit "sealed" the believer, providing a "down payment" on the experience of God's kingdom (2 Cor. 1:22; Rom. 8:16; Gal. 4:6). The Spirit manifested itself in various gifts, from the mysterious to the mundane (1 Corinthians 12–14). This presence of the Spirit was not just a private experience for Paul; it was visible evidence of the dawning of a new age.

But Paul never tells us his story, not even his version of the Jesus story. We must infer those stories from what he does tell us in his letters. In what follows we will try to identify the basic images and metaphors used in the letters when Paul speaks of the universal order, then examine the metaphors for the community, and, finally, consider how Paul pictured himself.

IMAGES OF THE WORLD

Two powerful images Paul used to describe life are "waiting" (for example, 1 Thess. 1:10; Phil. 3:20) and "freedom" (for example, Gal. 2:4; 3:23; 5:1). These two ideas are related, although they are in some tension with each other; they reveal Paul's basic story. Paul understood himself to live in the mysterious gap between two antithetical epochs. (For a general discussion of the understanding of these two epochs in apocalyptic thought see the discussion of Thessalonians on pages 90–92.) The old order was passing away; the powers of evil had been defeated; those in Christ had been liberated from the powers of that evil order. This is what Paul meant by being "saved" or rescued (Rom. 5:9; 1 Cor. 1:18). Yet the new order was not fully here; it had begun with Christ's resurrection; Paul daily awaited its consummation.
Consider:

Formerly, when you did not know God, you were enslaved to beings that by nature are not gods. (Gal. 4:8)

For freedom Christ has set us free. Stand firm, therefore, and do not submit again to a yoke of slavery. (Gal. 5:1)

You turned to God from idols, to serve a living and true God, and to wait for his Son from heaven, whom he raised from the dead—Jesus, who rescues us from the wrath that is coming. (1 Thess. 1:9–10)

But our citizenship is in heaven, and it is from there that we are expecting a Savior, the Lord Jesus Christ. He will transform the body of our humiliation that it may be conformed to the body of his glory, by the power that also enables him to make all things subject to himself. (Phil. 3:20–21)

I consider that the sufferings of this present time are not worth comparing with the glory about to be revealed to us. For the creation waits with eager longing for the revealing of the children of God; for the creation was subjected to futility, not of its own will but by the will of the one who subjected it, in hope that the creation itself will be set free from its bondage to decay and will obtain the freedom of the glory of the children of God. We know that the whole creation has been groaning in labor pains until now; and not only the creation, but we ourselves, who have the first fruits of the Spirit, groan inwardly while we wait for adoption, the redemption of our bodies. (Rom. 8:18–23)

"Groaning in labor pains" was a common but wonderful metaphor for the birth of the new order out of the old. Like the onset of labor, the beginning of the distress would be mild, but constantly increasing until—just before the birth—the intensity would seem unbearable. Then, release! Paul lived very near this end. He lived in the time of the distress (1 Cor. 7:26 and Rom. 8:18–23, quoted above). This brief period of affliction was the preparation for the eternal kingdom (2 Cor. 4:17; Rom. 8:18).

Twice in his letters he describes the end and assumes he will be alive when it occurs (1 Thess. 4:17; 1 Cor. 15:51). He advised the Corinthians not to marry because there was so little time left in this age (1 Cor. 7:25–31).

This age is still the time of sin and death, still ruled by hostile powers (1 Cor. 2:8; 2 Cor. 4:4; Gal. 1:4). But all those in Christ have been liberated from these powers (Gal. 4:8; 5:1; quoted above); they have been made a new creation (2 Cor. 5:17). This new creation began with the resurrection of Christ, who is the "first fruits" of a general resurrection, which will be consummated at his coming, for which Paul waits (1 Cor. 15:20–23). But this waiting is in hope, for Paul already possessed a foretaste of this new creation in the Spirit.

As we have seen from the Thessalonian and Corinthian correspondence, this *already* and *not yet* of Paul was hard for his followers to grasp. They easily overemphasized one side or the other. Later followers of Paul also had this problem. But in Paul's story the basic nature of the world had been changed by the death of Christ, whose obedient death had reversed the disobedience of Adam. Those in Christ are freed from the power of sin and the power of this evil age.

IMAGES OF THE COMMUNITY

Paul's images of the community are naturally drawn from this story but seldom in an obvious way. Thus the community is the perfume of the new order, the fragrance of life to those being saved, the scent of death to those perishing (2 Cor. 2:14–16). We see here the dual experience of the community: living in this evil period and living beyond it.

Another metaphor drawn from this story represents the community as the body of Christ. Paul backed into this image. He began with the general metaphor of an organization as a collective body whose various members fulfill various functions (1 Cor. 12:14–26) but concluded with the declaration "you are the body of Christ" (1 Cor. 12:27). Paul never developed the potential of this image the way his later followers would; for him its primary significance remained the interconnectedness of the various members of the assembly (so Rom. 8:3–8, the only other use of this image in Paul's letters). Yet it had a wonderful potential, reflecting as it did two contrasting experiences of the community: suffering and resurrection. It was an image that would profoundly affect future generations. (For a discussion of a related metaphor of the community as a family, see pages 142–44.)

More revealing is a metaphoric image, which Paul shared with another group of his time, that of the believers as the temple of God:

Do you not know that you are God's temple, and that God's Spirit dwells in you? If any one destroys God's temple, God will destroy that person. For God's temple is holy, and you are that temple. (1 Cor. 3:16–17)

On the surface this idea is remarkably parallel to what we find in the work of a Stoic writer of the late first century:

But you are a being of primary importance; you are a fragment of God; you have within you a part of Him. Why then are you ignorant of your own kinship? Why do you not know the source from which you have sprung? Will you not bear in mind, whenever you eat, who you are that eat, and whom you are nourishing? Whenever you indulge in intercourse with women, who you are that do this? Whenever you mix in society, whenever you take physical exercise, whenever you converse, do you not know that you are nourishing God, exercising God? You are bearing God about with you, poor wretch, and know it not. Do you suppose I am speaking of some external God, made of silver or gold? It is within yourself that you bear Him, and do not perceive that you are defiling him with impure thoughts and filthy actions. Yet in the presence of even an image of God you would not dare to do anything of the things you are now doing. But when God himself is present within you, seeing and hearing everything, you are not ashamed to be thinking and doing such things as these, O insensible of your own nature, and object of God's wrath! (Epictetus *Discourses 2.8.9–14*)

Ethically, these two declarations are very much alike. Both Paul and **Epictetus** admonish their hearers to certain forms of behavior based on the conviction that God is within them. Paul may even have heard such Stoic preachers as he grew up, for they had a major school in his native Tarsus and conducted all their classes outdoors. (The name *Stoic* is derived from the *stoa*, the porch, at Athens where they got their start when they were not allowed inside the Platonic academy. After that, the Stoics never conducted their affairs indoors.)

But we must probe beyond the surface resemblance and ask what each writer meant by having God within. In the Stoic story, God was an elemental part of the universe itself and therefore part of human nature. Their favorite word for God was **Logos**, which they understood to mean reason, manifested in the world as natural order and in the individual as the intellectual life. Thus, the reason that we each carry within ourselves is the divine, in the Stoic view.

Just how far this is from the Pauline view will be clear if we pursue the ethical implications of this way of understanding the divine. For the Stoics, the moral life is a life lived according to this divine reason, and ethics becomes a matter of the power of will. Even happiness must be attained by willpower.

What is happiness? One of the simplest observations is that we are happy when we get what we want. But the weakness of such an approach is immediately evident: we never get all we want. As soon as we have one thing, we want another. Reason then dictates that we stop trying to get all we want (an impossibility) and learn instead to want what we get (the Stoic answer). This demands an absolute mastery of the will, a lonely enterprise far removed from Paul's community of the Spirit.

In the quotation from Paul above, the community rather than the individual is the temple of the Spirit (all the *you* pronouns in this quotation are plural), because it experiences the indwelling of the Spirit. Having God within is not a natural condition of the human species, as in the Stoic story; it is a new creation of a new community in a new age, which is just now dawning in the resurrection of Jesus and the gathering of his elect. For Paul the community is central; it is no accident that all his letters (including even Philemon) are addressed to communities.

It is important to see what is original about Paul's ethics; both the basis (God within) and many of the practical details can be found in **Stoicism**. The originality lies in his story: the new community of the new age, living in the freedom of Christ's victory over the powers of sin and death. But then, the difficulty is not knowing what is right but having the resources to do it. (For more details on Stoicism and the nature of the Logos, see the introduction to John's Gospel in Chapter 12.)

SELF-IMAGES

Our earlier discussion of the Pauline community has already pointed up several of Paul's images for himself: father, mother, nurse, brother, partner (see page 143). These highlight the ways that Paul participated in the lives of these communities. Here we will consider three other images that point not to relationships but to identity: weakness, the cross, and correspondence.

Paul was not a weak person in any sense. There is a popular though unfounded tradition that he was habitually ill; yet his rapid and wide travels belie this notion. No one in poor physical shape could have survived the perils listed in 2 Corinthians 10, including being adrift in the sea for twenty-four hours. Nor would anyone who has read Galatians think his personality weak. Intellectually, socially, religiously, Paul had great strength. More than once he mocks this strength in his mad boasting (2 Cor. 11:21–30; Phil. 3:4–11).

In spite of (and maybe partly because of) this strength, Paul portrayed himself with the image of weakness: "To the weak I became weak, that I might win the weak" (1 Cor. 9:22). But the real reason for his weakness is that he saw himself in contrast to Christ: "I will . . . boast of my weakness, that the power of Christ may rest upon me" (2 Cor. 12:9). Paul used a happy metaphor to describe this contrast, that of holding a treasure in a clay pot (2 Cor. 4:7).

Paul's central metaphor for understanding himself derived from his identification with Christ:

> *I have been crucified with Christ; and it is no longer I who live, but it is Christ who lives in me. And the life I now live in the flesh I live by faith in the Son of God, who loved me and gave himself for me. (Gal. 2:19–20)*

This extravagant metaphor is hard to decipher, but it affected all that Paul did. It provided the framework for his understanding of the baptismal initiation rite (Rom. 6:1–4). It provided his definition of the believing community as the community of those "in Christ" (1 Cor. 12:13; Gal. 3:27). It even provided the context for his understanding of his own suffering: "we share abundantly in Christ's suffering" (2 Cor. 1:5; Phil. 1:29). Paul lived his life under the image of the cross (1 Cor. 1:23; 2:2; 4:9; 2 Cor. 11:24; Phil. 1:21) and participated in the story of Christ: even as Christ's suffering was redemptive for the world, so Paul's suffering was redemptive for his communities. And their suffering would in turn redeem their cities.

To this process Paul gave the names *example* (Greek *typos*, designating a sculptor's creation of a likeness) and *imitation* (Greek *mimetes*, from *mimesis*, designating a poetic creation). Both images point to a quality of correspondence between art and reality. For Paul they indicated the correspondence between human life and the divine world, between his story and the charter story. Paul and his congregations lived in, and helped shape, the cosmic story of redemption in which God was overthrowing the powers of evil and bringing God's kingdom into existence in this world.

The initial phase of the story was a failure. God wished Adam to communicate God's love and joy to the creation, but Adam failed because of the power of sin and the weakness of the flesh.

Using the model of story relationships discussed in Chapter 2 (pages 70–74), we can diagram this part of the story as follows:

	The Story of Adam
Task/Lack	The creation lacks love and joy
Agent	Adam
Conflict	
Opponents	Power of sin, weakness of flesh
Proponents	(none stated)
Resolution	Failure: unrighteousness and death

Adam, the subject of this story, had the task of nurturing God's creation, but because his opponents were stronger than he, he failed to carry out the divine contract. That story aborted, and a new need arose. Something had to be done about Adam's failure, for now all creation stood under the power of sin and death. Thus the Christ has come to fulfill a new contract to communicate God's gift of righteousness to humanity:

	The Story of Christ
Task/Lack	Righteousness needs to be given to all
Agent	Christ
Conflict	
Opponents	Power of sin
Proponents	His death; faith
Resolution	All are made righteous, given life

Unlike Adam, Christ proved obedient, and through his obedience all may be made righteous. (For this basic story see Romans 5, especially verses 15–21.) But that is not the end of the story. A new contract remains to be fulfilled: this salvation must be communicated to those for whom it is intended. God's love must be delivered to the creation. The agents of this new action are Paul and his hearers:

	The Story of Those in Christ
Task/Lack	The creation lacks love and joy
Agent	Those in Christ (Paul, the communities)
Conflict	
Opponents	Power of sin, weakness of flesh
Proponents	Spirit
Resolution	(still in process)

We might summarize thus: because Adam (or humanity) failed in obedience and thus was unable to communicate the blessings of God to the world, it was necessary that a new hero arise. This hero is the Christ who, through an act of obedience unto death, brought righteousness to all, overcoming the opposition of sin. Now all those in Christ participate in that story and extend that story in their own lives. By their obedience in the Spirit they bring the blessings of God to the whole world—indeed, to the whole creation (Rom. 8:19). In this way the ordinary lives of believers are taken up into the cosmic story of the redemption of the world.

Thus, for Paul, Christ's story is the crucial middle phase between the story of humanity in Adam and the story of humanity in Christ—including Paul's own life and ministry. Given these interlocking story structures, we can perhaps better appreciate Paul's shocking declarations: "I have been crucified with Christ," "Christ . . . lives in me," "I live by faith" (Gal. 2:20). Paul's story does not merely follow the story of Christ; the two overlap. Paul is in Christ, and Christ is in Paul.

The details necessary to give substance to this story are lacking; at least our present methods of analysis are not sufficient to discover them. Yet this kind of story is the basis for the letters, and we must endeavor to hear it whenever the letters are read.

LEARNING ON YOUR OWN

REVIEWING THE CHAPTER

Names and Terms

Apocrypha	Logos	pseudepigrapha
Christos	Martin Luther	Qumran
Dead Sea Scrolls	messiah	rabbis
dialogue	Mishnah	Stoicism
diatribe	natural order	syllogism
James	point of view	theme
Jerusalem community		

Issues and Questions

1. Describe ways that Romans is like and unlike Galatians.
2. What do scholars think the Roman congregations were like in Paul's day?
3. How is Romans related to what was happening in Paul's life when he wrote it?
4. Be able to summarize the main line of argument in Romans.
5. Compare and contrast the two major interpretations of Romans.
6. Describe how one got in, and stayed in, the Qumran community.
7. Compare and contrast Pauline and Stoic ethics.
8. What is the relation between the Jesus story (as Paul understood it) and Paul's own story?
9. Write Paul's obituary.

Taking the Next Step

There are a few good **introductory commentaries**: Achtemeier, 1985, is perhaps the best; but see also Barrett, 1977; Jewett, 1982a; Maly, 1979; Smart, 1975; Throckmorton, 1961; and Ziesler, 1989. Part 1 of Bryan, 2000, is good for treating preliminary concerns about the letter's form and approach; part 2 analyses each section of Romans rhetorically.

For **other standard commentaries** start with Fitzmyer, 1993, which has an extensive bibliography, divided by topics; and see Barrett, 1957; Best, 1967; Black, 1973; Bruce, 1963; Byrne, 1996; Dunn, 1988; Heil, 1987; and Maly, 1979. Käsemann, 1980, will benefit those who know Greek. Also see the introductory works on Paul in Chapter 4.

Topics for Special Studies

A variety of scholarly opinions on various facets of Romans is admirably covered in Donfried, 1991, which is an excellent place to begin further study. The introduction will suggest many possible topics for further research, and it contains an extensive bibliography.

Term project topics growing out of this chapter include the following:

The Purpose and Setting of Romans
See Jervis, 1991; Smiga, 1991; Jewett, 1982b; and Wedderburn, 1991.

For a stimulating attempt to read Romans in the social context of Paul's life see Esler, 2003.

Those who wish to pursue the question of the theme of Romans could begin with the short discussion of Stendahl, 1976, and Espy's response to it, 1985. Kaylor, 1988, does a consistent reading from this perspective. Stendahl, 1995, provides an updated summary of his views. Stowers, 1994, presents a major rereading of Romans as a document addressed to Gentiles about Jews. Compare Nanos, 1996.

The new view of Paul, with a major discussion of Romans, is well presented in Gager, 2000, with a good bibliography.

The works of Bornkamm, 1971, and Käsemann, 1971, convincingly present the traditional view of Romans, which centers on the doctrine of justification by faith; see the response of Soards, 1987, as well. See also Fitzmyer, 1993, and Boers, 1994.

Paul's Relation to Israel
For an overview of current issues see Harrington, 1993; see also the overview in chapter 1 of Donaldson, 1997. Grenholm and Patte, 2000, have collected a variety of stimulating essays. Nanos, 1996, advances the daring thesis that Romans operated entirely within a Jewish context. Comprehensive treatments of the relationship between Paul and other Jews can be found in the classic work by Davies, 1980, and in the magisterial work by Sanders, 1977, 1983. Sanders is especially strong in his mastery of the Jewish sources, although his discussion of Paul must be read in conjunction with Davies, especially the latter's discussion of Christ as the new Torah (Law). See also Räisänen's careful study, 1987. Esler, 2003, presents a useful social analysis, based on a careful reading of Romans. Paul's Jewish background is also explored by Schoeps, 1961, though with less positive conclusions. See also Gaston, 1987; Getty, 1988; and Kaylor, 1988. For modern Jewish responses to Paul see Rubenstein, 1972, and Segal, 1990.

Paul's Relation to Rome
On the women Paul mentions see the fine study of Junia by Epp, 2005; also Cotter, 1994; Gillman, 1992.

On Paul's relation to empire, see the excellent social study of Horsley, 1997; also Castelli, 1991, and N. Elliott, 1994.

The Dead Sea Scrolls as a Window into First-Century Jewish Religion

For recent scholarship on the scrolls see VanderKam, 1994, and Collins, 1997. The older work of Vermes and Vermes, 1977, is still useful. For their context see McNamara, 1983; for a translation of the scrolls see Vermes, 1995, or Wise, Abegg, and Cook, 1996. Garnet, 1977, discusses the idea of salvation in the scrolls; Priest, 1962, and Evans, in Collins and Kigler, 2000, discuss their idea of the Messiah; Vermes and Goodman, 1989, explore the broader category of the Essenes.

Various connections between Paul and the Qumran community are explored in Murphy-O'Connor and Charlesworth, 1990; see especially chapter 5 on the question of justification. Lim, 1997, compares ideas on Scripture. A specific study of Paul's notion of purity in comparison with Qumran can be found in Newton, 1985. For a basic bibliography on the Dead Sea Scrolls see Fitzmyer, 1990.

Rhetoric and the Diatribe Style

Rhetorical analysis of Romans has been done by N. Elliott, 1990; Fiore, 1990; and Wuellner, 1976. Byrne, 1996, has produced a major commentary using rhetorical criticism. Also see the chapters by Jewett and Aune in Donfried, 1991. Related literary concerns are addressed by Jewett, 1982c (on genre); Little, 1984 (on analogy and structure); and MacDonald, 1969 (on chapter 16). Given, 2001, examines Paul's relation to philosophical traditions of ambiguity and deception in rhetoric (technical).

On the diatribe style see Stowers, 1981, 1994; the original work by Bultmann, 1910; and Donfried's critique of Bultmann, 1991:112–21. For a history of the form see Kustas, 1976.

History of the Assembly at Rome

Leon, 1960; Lampe, 1999; Jeffers, 1991; and Judge and Thomas, 1966, review the origin and development of the Roman assembly. Schäfer, 1997, discusses anti-Jewish attitudes in antiquity. Cohen, 1993, looks at diaspora Judaism more broadly. Grabbe, 1992, traces the history of Judaism in the Roman period.

The Significance of Paul's Collection for the Poor

The special studies of the collection by Nickle, 1966, and Donaldson, 1997, provide useful insights into Paul's mission strategy. Other studies relating Romans to its cultural and life context include Kaylor, 1988, and Wedderburn, 1987.

Other political issues are taken up in Castelli, 1991 (power); Bristow, 1988 (women); and Gillman, 1992 (women).

The Nature of Houses and House Assemblies

On the household as setting start with Osiek and MacDonald, 2006; see also Banks, 1980, and Branick, 1989; more generally see MacIver, 1971. Also see the discussion in Meeks, 1983, and Stambaugh and Balch, 1986.

Paul's Sense of Ethics

See Barclay, 1988; Enslin, 1957; Furnish, 1968; Hays, 1987; Mohrlang, 1984; Walters, 1993; and Westerholm, 1984; more generally see Sanders, 1975. For a case study on Romans 13 see Botha, 1994.

On homosexuality in antiquity see Dover, 1989; Scroggs, 1986; Brooten, 1996; Wink, 1999; and Balch, 2000. On sexuality more generally see Laqueur, 1990; Sissa, 1990; Veyne, 1987; Brown, 1987; and Rousselle, 1988.

Paul's Story

Of the few works that take the narrative element in Paul seriously start with Grieb, 2002; then see Hays, 1983, 1989; Petersen, 1985; Keesmaat, 1999; and Witherington III, 1994. Brondox, 2006, attempts a substantial reconstruction of Paul's story as an essentially Jewish story. Works that attempt some overall perspective on Paul include De Boer, 1988; Cousar, 1990; and Fowl, 1990.

The apocalyptic aspect of Paul's worldview is discussed by Beker, 1982; see also Branick, 1985.

The Christ-Adam Image

Paul's image of Christ-Adam is explored by Hooker, 1990; see also the theological treatment of Barth, 1956. For related discussion see Cousar, 1990 (death of Jesus); Black, 1984 (view of death); and De Boer, 1988 (view of death). Also see Chapter 4.

On the Life of Paul

Begin with the insightful work of Murphy-O'Connor, 1996. See also Sanders, 1991, and Becker, 1993; Donaldson, 1997, chapter 11, posits interesting ideas about Paul's early life, contrasting with Hengel, 1991. For the general social context see MacMullen, 1974. On Paul's occupation and chronology, see Chapter 4.

Additional Books and Articles

For additional bibliography see Borchert, 1985 (annotated); Petersen, 1984; and Fitzmyer, 1993.

6

PAUL FOR A NEW DAY

Colossians, Ephesians, Timothy, Titus

 No Roman would hesitate to take his wife to a dinner party, or to allow the mother of his family to occupy the first rooms in his house and to walk about in public. The custom in Greece is completely different: a woman cannot appear at a party unless it is among her relatives; she can only sit in the interior of the house, which is called the women's quarters [gynoeceum]; this no male can enter unless he is a close relation.

CORNELIUS NEPOS, *LIVES* PREFACE 6

It has never been much of a secret that a great deal of early Christian literature was written in the names of people who did not actually put the words on paper. One standard reference work lists more than fifty documents, written in the names of Peter, Paul, Thomas, Mary, Andrew, and others, even Judas (*ABD*, 1:295–96). Obviously literature continued to be produced under the names of that first generation of believers long after these people were dead. But most of these works represent an esoteric kind of tradition, whose adherents, it has been generally assumed, had fewer reservations about such false claims than their more mainline counterparts.

It is difficult to determine what the ancients thought about such imitations, for there are at least three categories into which they fall. Some imitated the work of others for personal profit. Some wrote in the name of their teacher, because they humbly felt that everything they wrote really derived from the teacher. Some wrote in the name of a famous person to attract attention to their work—folks were more likely to read a medical treatise by the great physician Galen, for example, than by some unknown doctor. And there is perhaps a fourth option: some wrote in the name of someone famous because they claimed to know what that person would say. (See the discussion of these motives in Chapter 3, pages 93–96.) It is probably best to think of authorship in antiquity as existing along a continuum from writer to forger, with many intermediate options (see Figure 3.3).

The question of authorship is complicated by other problems caused by the growing diversity of early Christianity in the second century. Many argued that only works written by apostles, or by their close associates, could be considered sound. Consequently, it became necessary to attribute even anonymous works to apostolic authorship, so that the gospels were each attributed to a disciple or a disciple's companion, Hebrews to Paul, and the Apocalypse to John the apostle, even though none of these works claims such authorship. We will see that there is rarely any good reason to think that these anonymous works were actually written by the famous authors. But there was also a converse side to this argument: if one rejected the authority of a work, one way to undermine it was to question its authorship. In antiquity, to question the authorship of a work was also to question its validity.

The modern study of the Bible has recognized the fallacy of identifying validity with authorship. Not everything Paul wrote proved to be of enduring value; some of his letters were lost. Hebrews is no less powerful a writing simply because it was not written by Paul. Thus, modern scholars have been able to approach the question of authorship in a more neutral fashion; to dispute the authorship of a work no longer means to dispute its teaching. Still, many people have trouble when scholars suggest that a biblical work was not written by the person named in the work. Deceiving about authorship seems to imply that the writer would deceive about other things as well. But such a conclusion represents a great misunderstanding of the ancient world, imposing our modern concepts of authorship and copyright most inappropriately.

We need a clear distinction between deception and imitation, and some appreciation for how much the ancients valued imitation. Whereas we strive for and value originality, the ancients valued repetition. Imitation was taught in school; a standard rhetorical exercise was to compose in the style of some ancient author. It is not enough to ask whether a given writing is an original (to some degree) or an imitation (to some degree); we also have to inquire about whether the writer had a legitimate claim to the authority of the named author. In this chapter we will examine the claims of several ancient writings to the authority of Paul, realizing that this is a subtle matter. It is worth noting that of all the letters of Paul we have studied so far, only Galatians is written exclusively in his name. In each of the others he is joined by Timothy, Sosthenes, or Silvanus. And Galatians is largely a defense of Paul's authority.

The modern quest to define more precisely how various biblical works came to be written is undertaken not to undermine their value but to describe more accurately the historical development of early Christianity. This chapter will first review the kinds of evidence scholars use to determine authorship and will then discuss various writings that claim Paul's authority. These writings are diverse and reveal the various directions taken by Paul's followers in the century after his death.

EVALUATING CLAIMS TO AUTHORSHIP

Since the ancient concept of authorship as authority is so much broader than the modern definition, how can we distinguish works actually written by Paul from works written by someone else in his name? For example, given that both Paul and Timothy are listed as the authors of 1 Thessalonians and of Colossians, how can we estimate the contribution of Paul to each? Also, Paul is listed as the sole or joint author of the following letters: 1 Thessalonians, 2 Thessalonians, 1 Corinthians, 2 Corinthians, 3 Corinthians, Galatians, Philippians, Philemon, Romans, Colossians, Ephesians, 1 Timothy, 2 Timothy, Titus, Laodiceans, and a series of letters to Seneca, the Roman philosopher. How can we determine whether each of these was in some way produced by or for Paul (an original), was produced in Paul's name by one of his disciples after his death (an imitation), or was produced in Paul's name to advance ideas contrary to Paul (a forgery)? Scholars have devised a series of tests, based on both external historical data and on internal literary data.

Two kinds of external evidence are useful, citations by other writers and ancient evaluations of authenticity. The latest possible date for a letter would be the first instance of direct citation by another author, and if that author is located some distance from the destination of the letter, we must also allow some time for its circulation. Further, if it has been distributed over a broad geographical area (especially in the widely separated centers of Rome, Antioch, and Alexandria), we know it has been circulating for some years.

Another external factor is the judgment of earlier investigators. About 150 CE a Christian leader in Rome, **Marcion**, established a list of what he considered truly divine writings, namely the letters of Paul and one gospel. But he included only ten of the thirteen letters now in the New Testament (omitting 1 and 2 Timothy and Titus); he also included one or two other letters that were eventually rejected from the New Testament. A later list from Rome, now called the **Muratorian Fragment** (because it is a partial document and was discovered by a Renaissance scholar by the name of Muratori; see pages 475–77), includes the same Pauline letters as the New Testament (but does not include 1 or 2 Peter or James, among others). This list is generally dated to around 200, but some think it is as late as 400. Another source of information is the fourth-century church historian **Eusebius**, who included the debates about the acceptance and rejection of various writings in his history of the development of Christianity (about 325). Somewhat earlier, a Christian philosopher, **Clement of Alexandria**, had analyzed the question of authorship.

Yet we should not rely too heavily on these external testimonies. They often reached decisions on grounds that seem to us inadequate, and frequently their decisions were influenced by their endorsement of, or antipathy toward, the ideas contained in the letters. All such external evidence is secondary. Of primary importance is the evidence that can be drawn from the letters themselves.

Three different kinds of internal evidence are useful in answering the questions about authorship: literary, intellectual, and historical. Literary evidence includes the style and typical vocabulary of a known author. In Paul's case this involves comparing the disputed letters with those that are clearly from Paul in a direct sense. His style may be characterized as intense and dialogical, personal and hyperbolic. While we must admit that different situations may elicit different styles (as Galatians and Philemon illustrate), Paul's letters are always vigorous expressions of his person. In the same way, vocabulary varies but exhibits a remarkable continuity from letter to letter. Not all topics are covered in all letters, but when a particular topic is broached, Paul uses a certain vocabulary to talk about it. Thus, in the undisputed letters, Paul always calls Peter "Cephas"; the evil one is always called "Satan" and never "the Devil" (*Satanas* rather than *Diabolos* in Greek); he speaks of Christ's appearing but never of his epiphany (*parousia* rather than *epiphaneia*). This consistency in Paul does not extend to some of the disputed letters. Obviously, the passage of time, moving into a new social context, and even employing a new secretary may all affect style and vocabulary.

All writers have the privilege of changing their minds, but when we find evidence of changed ideas we may have a clue to authorship. Three kinds of changes are interesting: omissions of characteristic ideas of the writer, development of ideas beyond their earlier formulations, and contradictions of earlier ideas. None of these would automatically resolve the issue of authorship or of Paul's actual participation in the writing. Evolution of an idea may suggest primary authorship by a disciple, especially if the extent of change is considerable, but it may simply mean that Paul continued to think about an issue (as his thinking about the Law evolved between Galatians and Romans).

The final kind of evidence useful for determining authorship is historical. Unfortunately, the disputed letters are not laden with historical references; this is part of the reason they are disputed (for all the undisputed letters have a clear historical setting). Still, we may glean two kinds of historical data to help determine the kind of authorship.

First, we seek evidence of historical change in the situation and institutionalization of the church. Although we have no detailed information about the development of the early organizational structures of churches, we can presume that they evolved from simple to more complex and that it became increasingly clear that the church assembly was not just another kind of synagogue. Thus we can ask: What is the relationship envisioned between Jews and Gentiles? What degree of organization has been achieved? Are there independent, paid pastors? Is there someone with authority over several churches (an unofficial bishop)?

Second (and perhaps most useful), we ask: What are the historical presuppositions of the writer? It would be easy for one well acquainted with Paul to imagine being in Paul's place and to say what Paul would say if confronted by this new situation. But it is very difficult to do so without presupposing the new situation. A crucial question to ask about the disputed letters is whether they presuppose a historical situation that did not exist in Paul's time.

In applying these criteria to certain letters written in Paul's name, we discover why their authorship has been disputed and gain richer insights into the development of early Christianity. The writings left to us in Paul's name, or in which Paul plays a major role, allow us to reconstruct several trajectories of Pauline influence in the late first and early second centuries. Each trajectory lays valid claim to some facet of Paul; each ignores other aspects of this complex person. All testify to his significance.

THE TRAJECTORY OF THE NEW COMMUNITY

Colossians and Ephesians share much, including their concern for the relation between Jews and Gentiles in the new community. This was, as we saw in the last chapter, a genuine concern for Paul. Yet there are things about these letters that seem unlike Paul. Let's consider the evidence.

THE AUTHORSHIP OF COLOSSIANS AND EPHESIANS

READING AND REFLECTION

Read through Colossians and Ephesians looking for evidence of their historical settings. Do you notice anything about these letters that seems unlike the Paul you have encountered in the earlier letters?

Both of these works have strong external support. They were regarded as Paul's letters by Marcion (about 150 CE) and were included in the Muratorian Fragment (between 200 and 400 CE). They were not questioned by any of the ancients. Similar language, though not direct quotation, appears in the letter of **Clement of Rome** to the Corinthians (about 95 CE). The modern concern about their authorship arises only from data within the letters themselves. Each of the three kinds of internal evidence raises questions.

Much of the literary evidence points away from direct authorship by Paul, though more so in the case of Ephesians than of Colossians. Forty words in Ephesians are not found in the rest of Paul's works, though many appear in late New Testament writings; the evil one is referred to as the "Devil," unlike Paul but like late works; the uncharacteristic phrase "in the heavenlies" occurs repeatedly. Certain prepositions (*en* and *kata*) are used much more frequently than in the other letters. Unlike Paul, the author of the thanksgiving did not pursue a single theme; unlike Paul, the author adopts a solemn liturgical style.

We may question whether either Colossians or Ephesians was directly written by Paul, but Colossians resembles his style more closely. In fact, it can be argued that the author of Ephesians must have regarded Colossians as being from Paul, since he (or she) depended on it heavily. Fully a third of Colossians is found in Ephesians (73

VIEW DOWN THE MARBLE ROAD, EPHESUS This sacred way led from the Temple of Artemis, about a mile north of the main city, past the theater and the business agora (central market plaza), then up the hill to the state agora (civic plaza). It was lined with shops, fountains, and monuments.

of the 155 verses have parallels in Colossians). Parallels are also apparent between Ephesians and 1 Peter, Acts, and John. The literary evidence suggests that Colossians probably derives in some direct way from Paul, but Ephesians goes further afield, deriving from Colossians and other sources.

A similar result follows an examination of the ideas of the letters. Paul's ideas are everywhere, but with significant development and omissions. When Paul discussed the church in his other letters, he referred primarily to individual local assemblies (as in Col. 4:16). In Ephesians, however, the church is a universal entity: one church over the whole world (for example, 5:23). Whereas Paul considered his work to be built on the one foundation of Christ (1 Cor. 3:11), it is now said to be based on the foundation of the apostles and prophets (Eph. 2:5), and the apostles are regarded as "holy" figures from the past (3:5). Whereas the divine mystery in Colossians is Christ, who reconciled Jews and Gentiles (1:27), in Ephesians the reconciliation itself is the mystery—the church rather than Christ (3:3–6). This emerging concern for the church is characteristic of major strands of the Jesus movement from the late first century on.

On the other hand, the writer of Ephesians has a more fully developed understanding of Christ and more nearly equates him with God. In Colossians (1:20) God reconciles the world; in Ephesians (2:16) Christ is said to do so. Whereas Paul said that God appoints officials in the church (1 Cor. 12:28), in Ephesians (4:11) Christ is said to do so. Paul's earlier writings dwell on the death of Christ; the author of Ephesians, however, is more concerned with his resurrection (see 1:15–2:10). This writer actually declares that believers have already been "raised with Christ" (2:6), which Paul carefully avoided saying in Romans (6:4). None of these ideas is foreign to Paul, but each is developed in ways that are not typical of the earlier letters; and the development in Ephesians goes beyond that of Colossians.

We find no problem imagining the historical situation in Colossians. Its close ties with Philemon seem to be good evidence of Pauline authorship (both associate Timothy with Paul in the address; both send greetings from Aristarchus, Mark, Epaphras, Luke, and Demas [4:10–14 and Philem. 23–24]; both call Archippus a minister [4:7 and Philem. 2]; both mention Onesimus [4:9 and Philem. 10]). Although Colossians addresses no obvious crisis, the situation assumed is realistic. Epaphras, it seems, had preached the gospel in Colossae, an interior city in southwest Asia Minor (1:7) (see Figure 6.1) where Paul was unknown (2:1). Yet Epaphras apparently acted as Paul's deputy (1:7; most manuscripts read "on our behalf"). The purpose of this letter seems to have been to report on Paul's situation, which would be described more fully by Tychicus (TIK-e-kus), the implied carrier of the letter (4:8). In the process a vague warning is given not to let anyone deceive them or judge them for their religious observances (2:8–23). This warning is not sharp enough to demand that we think of it as the primary reason for the letter, yet something definite seems to be envisioned, involving the occult (2:8, sometimes erroneously translated "philosophy"), questions of diet and Sabbath (2:16), self-abasement (2:18), and **asceticism** (that is, avoiding bodily pleasures, often including abstinence from meat, wine, and sexual relations) (2:21). These practices were so widespread that it may well be impossible to identify clearly the nature of the opponents. Though there are strong parallels to the Dead Sea Scrolls and to later Gnosticism, the cosmic allusions and asceticism rejected here were typical of astrological speculations widely practiced throughout the Greco-Roman world. We cannot even be certain if the dangers warned against stem from within or outside the church at Colossae. Though the historical setting is not as clear as in other letters, it is not vague enough to make it difficult to imagine as possible for Paul's time.

For Ephesians, on the other hand, we cannot easily imagine the historical context. First, the letter contains almost no historical references. There is no evidence in this letter that it was written to a concrete situation or with any specific problem in mind. More an essay than a real letter, it lacks even a formal addressee (the older manuscripts omit the words "who are at Ephesus" from verse 1). Although we cannot deduce much concerning its assumptions about the institution of the church, we can see the letter assumes that the controversy about the status of Gentiles in the church has been settled: the unity of Jew and Gentile in the church is a given rather than a present struggle. This probably reflects a situation beyond Paul's lifetime.

All in all, Colossians is an ambiguous letter on the boundary of Pauline authorship. It was written either by Paul to a congregation he had not founded but that belonged to his circle or tradition (having been established by one of his disciples), or by one of his disciples to clarify what the great apostle would have taught. In either case this letter is less personal, less idiosyncratic, less surely stamped with Paul's own hand. It has moved some distance from the kind of discourse we have become

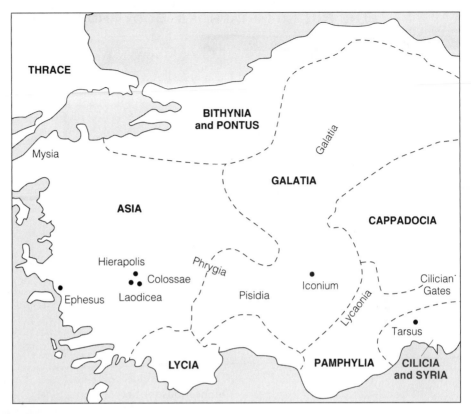

FIGURE 6.1 **THE PROVINCES OF ASIA MINOR** Much of the Pauline literature comes from the provinces of Asia Minor: Ephesus and Colossae were located in Asia; 1 Timothy is associated with Ephesus; the *Acts of Paul and Thecla* takes place in Galatia.

accustomed to in Paul but not so far as to make it impossible to imagine Paul making the journey—perhaps with a little assistance from Timothy, whose name is also on the letter. The ties with Philemon may indicate that it was written during the same imprisonment as that letter (about 56), though we miss dearly any sign of the humor and irony evident in Philemon.

Thus, it seems reasonable to conclude that whereas Colossians stands on the boundary of Pauline authorship, Ephesians passes beyond the boundary into the territory of the Pauline school after the death of the apostle. There is genuine continuity but a new agenda. The purpose of Ephesians seems to have been to present a summary of Paul's teaching, perhaps to assert that here (and not with other interpreters) lies Paul's true heritage. As we will see, others were making similar claims.

Although the majority of scholars today seem to regard Colossians as a work of Paul, only a minority think Paul actually wrote Ephesians. Years ago, Edgar Goodspeed conjectured that Ephesians may have been written as a sort of cover letter when Paul's letters were published as a collection, perhaps a decade or two after his death. Although that was and remains a theory, it does express something about the kind of writing we have in Ephesians.

THE RULING METAPHORS: BODY AND FAMILY

Reread Colossians and Ephesians with the aid of the reading guides. If time does not permit a complete rereading, choose similar parts of both letters to read. Pay particular attention to the way each author uses the metaphor of the body.

 READING GUIDES

Colossians		Ephesians
1:1–2	Salutation	1:1–2
1:3–12	Thanksgiving and prayer or praise	1:3–23
1:13–2:5	Message of rescue and release	2:1–3:21
1:13–20	The work of Christ	2:1–10
1:21–23	The work of the church	2:11–22
1:24–2:5	The work of Paul	3:1–13
1:24–25	The suffering	3:1–3
1:26–27	The secret	3:4–13
1:28–2:5	The labor	—
—	The prayer	3:14–21
2:6–3:17	Exhortations based on union with Christ	4:1–5:20
2:6–8	General principles	4:1–7
2:9–15	Christ as a cosmic conqueror	4:8–16
2:16–19	Implications for life	4:17–5:20
2:20–23	Christ's death and freedom	—
3:1–11	Christ's resurrection and freedom	—
3:12–17	General exhortations	—
3:18–4:1	Exhortations to household duties	5:21–6:9
3:18	Wives	5:22–24
3:19	Husbands	5:25–33
3:20	Children	6:1–3
3:21	Fathers	6:4
3:22–25	Slaves	6:5–8
4:1	Masters	6:9
4:2–6	Final exhortations	6:10–20
4:7–9	Travel plans	6:21–22
4:10–17	Greetings	—
4:18	Benedictions	6:23–24
4:18	Written with his own hand	—

To a remarkable degree these letters have essentially the same pattern. Both begin with the standard opening and thanksgiving, with poetic descriptions of Christ as the head of the cosmos and, especially, of the church. Both then draw out the implications of this headship for the lives of the hearers (in the exhortations) and close with salutations and travel plans. Colossians alone has a realistic discussion of some actual problems with food, drink, festival days, and worship practices (2:16–23). Both letters depend on standard rhetorical devices: lists of vices, lists of virtues, and instruction to the household, all built on the root metaphor of the congregation as a body.

This general organization and dependence on lists reveals a new kind of rhetoric, different from the judicial and deliberative rhetoric of the earlier letters. Here the rhetoric is demonstrative, seeking to show the wisdom of a particular point of view in the present. (See the discussion and chart on pages 13–16.) It seeks to move the hearer away from vice and toward virtue. That we have not encountered such rhetoric in Paul earlier can be evaluated two ways: it may be evidence that Paul did not write these letters, or it may help explain why these letters differ to such an extent from the others. However we explain it, there is no denying that these devices are rare in Paul's letters. The **household instruction** (listing specific tasks for each member of the household—Col. 3:18–4:1; Eph. 5:22–6:9) is unparalleled: Paul has shown no interest in children, and his advice against marrying (1 Cor. 7) would surely not win him any awards as an ardent supporter of the traditional family. Paul's earlier use of family imagery has been limited to the assembly as the household of faith (see pages 142–44).

In addition to this use of lists, both works repeatedly employ the **metaphor of the body**. In Colossians Christ is the head of the body (1:18); as his body, the church bears his suffering (1:24); the contrasting body of the flesh has been buried in baptism (2:11–12), a new body having been raised with Christ (2:12); they must not now submit to other heads (2:18–23). Works of the earthly body are to be put to death (3:5), but the new body is to be dressed in virtue (3:12). This hierarchical view of the church carries over into family relationships: as Christ is to the church, so the husband is to the wife, the father to the children, and the master to the slave. The metaphor reinforces the social world of traditional Greco-Roman society.

Ephesians shares this metaphor and draws these same lessons, even expanding them. Not only are believers raised with Christ, they are seated with him in the "heavenlies" (2:6). The notion of one body becomes a call to unity (4:4) and portrays dramatically the union of Jew and Gentile in the covenant and commonwealth of Israel (2:11–16). This genuine concern of Paul achieves new eloquence here.

Such concerns indicate one path the traditions of Paul followed, a path we might define as the creation of a new community. They carry forward Paul's concern for the one people of God, including both Jews and Gentiles. The Paul remembered here shares several traits with the Paul portrayed in Acts.

THE PAUL OF ACTS

We will reserve our study of Acts until Chapter 11 when we can treat it with its other half, the Gospel of Luke. Here we consider only the characterization of Paul in the story. Paul is a (perhaps *the*) central figure of Acts. He is introduced in chapter 8 and becomes the sole focus of attention by chapter 13. Peter, whose action predominates in the early chapters, is gotten off stage with the rather vague, "he departed and went to another place" (12:17). If character is revealed by actions and choices, as Aristotle taught, Paul is the one who carried the new way to the Gentiles while remaining a faithful Jew, trying to maintain the unity of the church.

Paul's Jewishness is highlighted. He is a Pharisee (regarded as the most important of the Jewish parties, 23:6). He studied in Jerusalem (22:3). He always goes first to the synagogue (17:1–2). He circumcises Timothy (16:3). He takes vows and offers sacrifice in the temple (21:26). The author even has him return to Jerusalem immediately after his experience of the risen Christ on the way to Damascus (9:19–26), something Paul himself denied (Gal. 1:17). This difference between Paul's letter and the story of Paul in Acts rests on the very different purposes of the two works. Whereas Paul is at pains in Galatians to establish his independent authority, the author of Acts needs to establish his close connection to the Jerusalem leaders, showing a unified church.

The portrayal of the unity of the church in Acts is a major theme. The believers shared everything in common (4:32); they grew and prospered in this unity (2:46–47). Paul himself promotes it by accepting the compromise concerning food regulations for the Gentiles (15:19–29), and he himself is Law observant (21:24). Paul mentions none of this in his letters.

The Paul of Acts is an obedient servant of the church, its representative to the Gentiles. Thus Acts, Colossians, and Ephesians all fall along a common trajectory. (For more on Paul's characterization in Acts, see pages 375–76, 379.)

THE DOMESTICATED APOSTLE

Although it is impossible for us to be sure that Paul did not write Colossians and Ephesians, we can be certain that the Paul personified there is far tamer than the Paul of the early letters. No longer do we find the demand for absolute freedom, the intense expectation of the near end of the age, the fiery enthusiasm of the Spirit. The life of faith is rationalized and moralized. Visions are distrusted (Col. 2:18). Faith itself becomes less a passionate commitment than a designation for proper thought and practice (Col. 2:7; Eph. 4:13; but contrast Eph. 2:8). Believers should conduct themselves with respect to the impressions they make on outsiders (Col. 4:5). There is no felt discrepancy between the demands of the gospel and the demands of the family (Col. 3:18–4:6; Eph. 5:21–6:9). There is even the admonition to obedience based on the Law (Eph. 6:2). This tendency toward cultural accommodation and moral accomplishment represents one of the dominant directions in which the traditions of Paul were carried by many of his followers.

THE TRAJECTORY OF THE EMERGING INSTITUTION

We have seen that Paul had numerous associates, some intimate enough to join him in his authorship (Timothy, Silas, and Sosthenes). Out of the lengthy list of associates two merit special attention, having had letters addressed to them in the name of Paul. Obviously this presumes that they are no longer traveling with him; he has left them as settled overseers in Asia Minor and Crete according to the perspective of these letters. Apparently, he neglected to instruct them in the details of church operation, for he writes them letters on the subject. Yet it is far more likely that Timothy and Titus knew all about Paul's practice of church organization. Most scholars today conclude that these letters represent a later generation putting into writing the teachings of the great apostle as they understood them to apply to their own time. They present Paul's pastoral advice for the care of the church and are thus called the **Pastoral Letters**. First we will consider the question of authorship, then examine more closely the portrait they paint of the emerging church and Paul's role in the development of that church.

THE AUTHORSHIP OF TIMOTHY AND TITUS

Sections of these letters, especially 2 Timothy, read like fragments of real letters from Paul. The last part of 2 Timothy 4, beginning at verse 6, contains either words from a letter of Paul or the work of an extraordinary imitator. The reference to the books (scrolls) and parchments (either loose sheets or sheets bound like our books) is perhaps too clever for an imitator (4:13). The end of chapter 1 and the first part of chapter 2 may also be from Paul. Some have guessed that a real letter stands behind these three compositions, providing a sort of model and inspiration, and that some late first-century or early second-century follower of Paul used Pauline tradition to create a kind of last testament of Paul (2 Timothy) and then a sort of handbook of church order (1 Timothy and Titus). This hypothesis remains a guess. Had we a sim-ilar handbook among the undisputed letters, or even specific information on how Paul organized his churches, comparison would reveal much about the development of early Christianity. Lacking such information, the best we can do is carefully read these letters and try to reconstruct the situation and the story behind them.

READING AND REFLECTION

Read through these three letters (begin with 2 Timothy; proceed to Titus, and then to 1 Timothy), making a list of the various church regulations they pro-pound. Pay particular attention to regulations for the clergy, attitudes toward differing points of view, and the role envisioned for women.

All three letters are very loosely organized, more a collection of ideas than an argument. They assume that the authority of Paul is such that no argument is needed; it is enough that the author gives instruction.

 ## READING GUIDES TO THE PASTORAL LETTERS

2 Timothy
Salutation   1:1–2
Thanksgiving   1:3–5
Admonition to courage   1:6–10
Paul's example and situation   1:11–19
Exhortations   2:1–4:5
  Take strength
  Remember Christ
  Remind people
  Turn from wayward impulses
  Know that the last days are evil
  Stand by the truth
  Proclaim the message
Paul's plight   4:6–18
Greetings   4:19–21
Blessing   4:22

Titus
Salutation   1:1–4
Titus' commission   1:5–16

Instructions for others   2:1–14
    Men, women, slaves
Instructions for Titus   2:15–3:11
    His themes, treatment of heretics
Travel plans   3:12–14
Greetings   3:15
    Blessing

1 Timothy
Salutation   1:1–2
Timothy's commission: guard against heresy   1:3–20
    With a thanksgiving   1:12–14
Instructions for church order   2:1–6:2
    Prayer, with roles for men and women   2:1–15
    Leader's qualities   3:1–13
    Bishops and deacons
Purpose of the letter   3:14–16
Warnings about heresy in the last days   4:1–10
Instructions to be passed on   4:11–6:2
    Men, women, widows, elders, slaves
Concluding admonitions   6:3–21
    Instructions to the rich   6:17–19
    Blessing

It is sometimes said that whether Paul wrote these letters makes no difference, for the letters remain the same and are powerful writings in their own right. Though this is true to some extent, whether these letters come from the apostle himself or from a later disciple makes a great deal of difference in our understanding of the development of the early church and our interpretation of Paul. For example: if what the pastorals teach about the role of women is the same as Paul taught, then we have badly misconstrued the evidence of the other letters. Before pursuing these differences, we need to consider the question of their authorship.

The evidence for authorship consists of many separate observations, and no single observation is compelling. Each could be explained in some way as a conceivable deviation from the Pauline norm. After a while, however, the process of explaining away the evidence becomes self-defeating, because everywhere we look something requires an explanation. Each of the separate kinds of evidence challenges the conclusion that Paul actually wrote these letters.

Even the external evidence raises doubts. These letters were not included in the list of Marcion, an ardent second-century follower of Paul. This implies that either he did not know of them or did not regard them as authentic. In either case, we are warned that their status is ambiguous. (They were included in the later, more orthodox, Muratorian Fragment, and followers of Marcion had included them by the third century.) But the really challenging evidence is in the letters themselves.

Except for the few passages in 2 Timothy referred to above, which echo Paul, the literary evidence points away from direct composition by Paul. Over one-third of the vocabulary of the Pastorals is not shared by the earlier letters. Those who count such things claim that of the 848 words used, 306 (36 percent) are not found in the

WRESTLERS This stylized view of Greek wrestling is from the inside of a drinking bowl. The purpose of ancient wrestling was merely to throw one's opponent to the ground. Greco-Roman culture was pervaded with athletics, celebrated in various games. The best known were the Olympic Games, held every four years; second in importance were the Isthmian Games, held every two years near Corinth. The Greeks showed no embarrassment over the nude male body, though such displays were an offense to many Jews. Paul may have witnessed the games at Corinth and used an athletic metaphor from racing to stress his points to the Corinthians (1 Cor. 9:24; see also Eph. 6:12).

other ten letters. Most of these unique words, 211 of them, are part of the general vocabulary of second-century writers. Further, of the 542 words shared between Paul and the Pastorals, only 50 are not shared by other writers in the New Testament (these statistics are taken from *IDB* 3:670). Even the shared vocabulary raises problems, for words Paul used in one way are used differently by our author. *Righteous* (*dikaios*), for example, is here used in the sense of being upright and moral rather than in the sense of justification, characteristic of Paul (compare Rom. 3:21–28 and 1 Tim. 1:9, where the NRSV translates it "innocent"). The most striking similarities in vocabulary are not between the Pastorals and Paul, but between the Pastorals and **Polycarp**, an early second-century follower of Paul. Some have even suggested Polycarp wrote them in Paul's name. (There are many interesting parallels of words and ideas in Polycarp's *Letter to the Philippians*, probably written about 110.)

Style is a rather abstract concept, but those who point to stylistic differences call attention to a basic dissimilarity between our writer and Paul. Paul's style may be characterized as passionate, argumentative, involved. One always has the sense that Paul is there, face to face. Our writer, in contrast, is cool, dictatorial, above the battle. His distance from the reader is all the more shocking in light of Paul's personal relationship to Timothy.

Those who would discount this evidence usually point to the lapse in time, attributing this new style to the aging Paul waiting in prison for his appointed end (as 2 Timothy implies but not 1 Timothy or Titus). They also suggest that the new subject matter would dictate a new vocabulary, or that Paul's secretary was given unusual latitude in the writing of these documents. It is not impossible.

The ideas of these letters are also not typical of Paul. As noted above, some of the altered vocabulary seems to be based on changed ideas: *righteousness* no longer means justification; *faith* no longer means trust but a position to be held (1 Tim. 3:9; 4:1). Christ is interpreted in terms of his epiphany, a common Hellenistic idea, rather than in terms of his death (2 Tim. 1:10; also used for Christ's coming, 1 Tim. 6:14; Titus 2:13; Paul would have said *parousia*). The attitude toward the Law lacks the dynamic yes and no of Paul (1 Tim. 1:9; contrast Romans 7). Young widows are now urged to marry (1 Tim. 5:14; contrast 1 Cor. 7:8). In fact, our writer completely reverses Paul's advice and insists that candidates for church office be married (1 Tim. 3:2). Women are forbidden to speak in church (1 Tim. 1:9; contrast 1 Cor. 11:5). Further, in the earlier letters Paul never spoke of special requirements for church office; he expected all to live up to the same standards. Nothing in Paul's letters indicates that he expected more from the leaders than from the followers.

Those who dissent argue that these changes are not so great; they are more a matter of degree. Other sentences can be quoted from the Pastorals that are more in accord with what we find in the other letters. Besides, they point out, Paul was not always perfectly consistent—even in the undisputed letters. Or perhaps the situation had changed sufficiently to account for these changed ideas. It is not impossible.

There is universal agreement that the historical situation has changed. The question is, has it changed so much that it reflects the next generation after Paul? The whole issue of the acceptance of the Gentiles, for example, seems a moot point. There is no struggle with keeping the Law, nor even reference to those issues that so preoccupied Paul, except for mention of a "circumcision party" that "must be silenced" (Titus 1:10–11). The struggle with opponents also seems different. Whereas Paul struggled with others in his own assemblies, there seems now to be a clear line between the faithful insiders and dangerous outsiders. And the danger of these unacceptable views now seems acute (for example, 4:1–5).

But the greatest change is in the organization of the church. A regular ministry, with specific qualifications, has been established. There is probably a paid clergy, to judge by the warnings against bishops and deacons being fond of money (1 Tim. 3:3, 8; Titus 1:7). The requirement that the bishop be "not a recent convert" (1 Tim. 3:6) seems quite out of place in Paul's time, when everyone was a recent convert. Although our author does not regard this bishop as holding the monarchic authority that **Ignatius of Antioch** claimed in the early second century (Ignatius demanded obedience to the bishop as to the Lord), still the concept of a ruler over the congregations in a city or region is evident. (Ignatius' letters can be found in the *Apostolic Fathers*.) In fact, Timothy and Titus are imagined to be such regional superintendents, acting as apostolic delegates (Titus 1:5; 1 Tim. 1:3). The bishops they appoint will soon claim a similar authority. The requirements for bishop and deacons are also revealing: they are not specific to the office but are very general and overlap considerably. Actually, little about them is specifically Christian; these are the traits expected of good upstanding leaders, traits that will make them respected by outsiders. Compare the requirements given in 1 Timothy (3:1–13) and Titus (1:5–9) with the similar list of characteristics set down for the good general by Onasander, a writer in the time of Paul:

> We must choose a general, not because of noble birth as priests are chosen, nor because of wealth as the superintendents of the gymnasia [schools], but because he is temperate, self-restrained, vigilant, frugal, hardened to labor, alert, free from avarice, neither too young nor too old, indeed a father of children if possible, a ready speaker, and a man with a good reputation. (Strategikos 1.1)

Also revealing are some of the assumptions our author makes. He assumes gospels are *written*, citing a Jesus tradition from the Gospel of Luke as a writing rather than in the manner of Paul, who always alludes to a word or command of the Lord—an oral tradition (1 Tim. 5:18; contrast 1 Cor. 9:3–14 and see the discussion on pages 59–63). He has Paul include himself with the Gentiles, "we" who were once disobedient (Titus 3:3); Paul always said "you." A pervasive assumption throughout these writings is that the church must settle down and be at home in the world, appoint respectable leaders, be above reproach, be well thought of by those outside, support the traditional family, and not allow women too much authority.

Those who remain unconvinced point out that our knowledge of church organization in Paul's day is scant, but both bishops and deacons were known (Phil. 1:1; 1 Thess. 5:12). The bishop is not yet the one ruler of the church, as in Ignatius. The situation regarding **heresy** (deviant views) may have changed quickly. Perhaps on his return from his intended trip to Spain, Paul found he had to deal with a new situation. Perhaps he cited an earlier written gospel than Luke, containing the same tradition. None of this evidence is strong enough to demand that we abandon belief in Paul's authorship, these scholars claim.

They are right. It is, as is every historical judgment, a matter of probability; the likelihood that Paul could not have changed in any one of these ways is not great. But the probability that he changed in all of them simultaneously is much less. Not only are we confronted with a myriad of details that seem dubious for Paul, but a different story underlies these works.

THE NEW STORY OF THE PASTORAL LETTERS

When we think back to Paul's story (sketched on pages 91–92, 174–80) we wonder: Where is the sense of the Spirit? Where is the sense of waiting for the near end? Where is the sense of freedom? Where is the sense of suffering that redeems the world? Where is the body of Christ? Where is the community as a family of brothers and sisters, slaves and partners? Where is the Paul who lived only "in Christ," who suffered, as Christ had, to redeem his communities? Paul lived at the end of the age, so intensely that he could advise against marriage so that full time might be devoted to the great task at hand. The time was short.

How different is the story of the author of the Pastorals. Attention to the present has eclipsed concern for the future kingdom. Church as organization is replacing church as family. The desire to be well thought of by those outside has eroded freedom. Women have to be reassigned to the roles traditional in their culture: wives and mothers (how, we might wonder in passing, would those women Paul advised not to marry be saved by bearing children? 1 Tim. 2:15). Concern about the cosmic conflict that heralds the end of the age has been replaced by concern for proper church organization. The angels have gone.

THE AUTHORITATIVE APOSTLE

The great issues dealt with in the Pastorals concern order:

> ordered teaching: 1 Tim. 1:3–20; Titus 1:10–16
> ordered worship: 1 Tim. 2:1–15
> ordered leaders: 1 Timothy 3; Titus 1:5–9
> ordered teachers: 1 Tim. 4:1–10; Titus 3:8–11
> ordered lives: 1 Tim. 4:11–6:19; Titus 2:1–3:7

These issues imply divergence. There must be those who teach falsely, whose worship is not orderly, whose lives are a scandal, women who are not submissive. Our writer represents that trajectory of the Pauline tradition that chose order over ardor. He (almost certainly a he) drew on that aspect of Paul that also strove for order. He gives us Paul the apostle, preacher, and teacher (2 Tim. 2:11). He gives us a Paul created in the image of the bishop, pointing ahead to the church as a hierarchical organization. It is a compelling portrayal, perhaps the dominant picture of Paul in Western consciousness. Yet it is not the only way Paul was remembered.

If the two trajectories we have examined represent the taming and the harnessing of the apostle for the work of the church, the next three represent the highlighting of the impetuosity and the radicalism of Paul. Some of his followers emphasized Paul's rejection of normal worldly pursuits (especially the family); others emphasized his intense spirituality. We will explore these two approaches to Paul and then consider a trajectory that saw nothing worthwhile in the traditions of Paul.

THE TRAJECTORY OF WORLD DENIAL

A Christian work written in the middle of the second century contains the following story about Paul and a young woman by the name of **Thecla**. I summarize:

> *While Paul was speaking to the assembly in the house of Onesiphorus, a virgin named Thecla, daughter of Theocleia and fiancée to a man named Thamyris, sat at a nearby window and listened day and night as Paul spoke the word and extolled the virgin life. She never left the window but pressed on by faith, with extreme joy. When she saw many women and virgins going in, she too desired to be counted worthy to stand before Paul's face and hear the word of Christ. For she had only heard Paul's words and had not yet seen him. After three days her mother sent for Thamyris, hoping to break the spell.*

When he arrived she reported what had happened, adding, "I wonder how a maiden of such modesty can be so troubled. Thamyris, this man is upsetting the whole city, for besides your Thecla all the women and young people go to him and are taught that they must fear only one God and live chastely. And my daughter, like a spider at the window, is bound by his words and is taken captive. Go and speak to her." Thamyris went to her both loving her and also fearing her fascination with this stranger. He chided her for her behavior and begged her to come to him. But she never moved. Her mother added her reproach, but she never turned from listening to Paul.

Thamyris left in great despair. He bribed two companions of Paul to learn more about this man who was deceiving young men and women into renouncing marriage, discovering that Paul spoke against marriage and demanded complete chastity. Thamyris succeeded in having Paul imprisoned, but Thecla bribed her way in to see him. Finally meeting him she came to complete faith. When her family learned of this, both she and Paul were brought before the governor. The governor demanded to know why she would not honor her marriage contract. When she did not answer but only stared at Paul, her own mother called for her condemnation as an example to all brides who would forsake their sacred duty. Greatly moved, the governor consigned Paul to be beaten and banished from the city, but Thecla was condemned to be burned. She was carried off to the theater where the execution was to take place. Like a lost lamb looking for the shepherd she looked about for Paul and was comforted to see not Paul but the Lord sitting in the form of Paul. The place of execution was prepared, wood was gathered, Thecla was brought in naked, causing even the governor to marvel at the power that was in her. When told to mount the pyre, she made the sign of the cross and climbed up on the wood. They lit the fire, and a great flame blazed up but did not harm her. God caused a sudden rainstorm to extinguish the fire, and Thecla was saved. She left the city and found Paul, who was praying for her rescue. She became, like Paul, one who traveled and spread the word of Christ.

There is much more to the story of Paul and Thecla that this summary omits. (You can read the full account in J. K. Elliott, 1993a:364–72, or James, 1924:272–81. Several versions are available online, such as at http://gbgm-umc.org/umw/corinthians/thecla.stm.) But this sample of this mid-second-century work shows that some of Paul's followers remembered him in a way markedly different from that of the Pastorals.

THE LEGENDARY ACTS OF PAUL

In fact, some of the views of those regarded as false teachers in the Pastorals correspond rather closely to the Paul of this story: forbidding young people to marry (1 Tim. 4:3), encouraging unsubmissive women (1 Tim. 2:11), telling strange and marvelous tales (1 Tim. 4:7). People "who make their way into households and capture weak women, burdened with sins and swayed by various impulses, who will listen to anybody and can never arrive at a knowledge of the truth" (2 Tim. 3:6–7) sounds like something Thamyris might say about Paul. Curiously, one of the companions who betrayed Paul to Thamyris is named Hermogenes, who is also known from the

Pastorals as among those in Asia, the westernmost province of Asia Minor, turning away from Paul (2 Tim. 1:15). (This story, by the way, is set in Iconium in Galatia, the next province east of the province of Asia. See the map, Figure 6.1, on page 191.) Onesiphorus is also mentioned in both (2 Tim. 1:16). If we studied the whole story of Thecla, numerous other parallels and contrasts could be drawn.

It has even been argued that the Pastorals were written, at least in part, in reaction to the developing picture of Paul that came to fruition in the Thecla story: Paul as a social radical (MacDonald, 1983). This Paul rejects the ways of the world: **virginity** is the highest virtue; married people should refrain from sexual activity; only the continent will hear the voice of God; only the chaste will participate in the resurrection (*Acts of Paul* 3:5, 12). The social dynamics of this way of thinking imply freedom for women and a challenge to the traditional family and social order.

Women in antiquity were usually married in their mid- to late teens and could expect to be raising a family until they passed childbearing age. Very little birth control was practiced, although the Romans had invented a rudimentary condom. Population was controlled through abortion and abandonment (and even infanticide), both widespread among Gentiles. The father's absolute authority is seen in the birth ritual wherein the newborn would be laid at its father's feet. If the father picked it up, it was welcomed into the family. If not, the baby would be exposed and left to die—or perhaps to be rescued by slave traders who might raise it to a saleable age. (See the section on family in Chapter 1 for more information.) Women's status is also seen in the aphorism of Poseidoppos (c. 250 BCE):

> *Everyone raises a son, even if he happens to be poor, but exposes a daughter, even if he is rich. (Fragment 11 in Stobaeus 4.24.40)*

Not only the enormous distraction of having a family would have limited the ministry of women. Although generalization is difficult, because the status of women differed considerably among classes and times, in Greek society women were never autonomous. They belonged to their fathers (or if the father died, to a brother or some other male protector). The father would give his daughter to her husband (a vestige of this custom is still a part of the traditional wedding ceremony). In classical Athens, the wife was expected to stay almost entirely at home: her tasks were to raise children and produce clothing. Roman women had more freedom, including the right to own property, but they too were expected to be submissive to their husbands.

One of the many slanders Octavian (later called Augustus) alleged against Antony, who had fled to Egypt and married Cleopatra, was that he allowed a woman "to make herself equal to a man" (Dio Cassius *Roman History* 50.28.3). Women remained under the control of men throughout their lives; widows were controlled even by their sons. In the Roman period numerous advances were made toward some basic equality for women, especially in the philosophical schools. Educated women were not uncommon; Juvenal mocks their independent ways in his derisive *Sixth Satire*. Yet the lot of most women was marriage and subordination to men. A philosopher of the Pythagorean movement (a movement more open to women than most) declared:

> *A woman must live for her husband according to the law and in actuality thinking no private thoughts of her own. . . . And she must endure her*

husband's temper, stinginess, complaining, jealousy, abuse, and anything else peculiar to his nature. (Thesleff, 1965:142–45; quoted from Pomeroy, 1975:134–36)

In the earliest communities, however, there were orders of widows who moved beyond these social constraints (Acts 6:1; 9:36–42). It is a short step from an order of widows to an order of virgins, especially if leaders are encouraged not to marry. The requirement of the Pastorals that only "real widows" be enrolled (1 Tim. 5:5) is probably meant to exclude virgins from this emerging order.

This freedom for women would be purchased at the price of radically challenging the central social institution of the Hellenistic world, the family. So sacred was this institution that it was considered a sacrilege not to marry, and in fact marriage was required by law in many cities. Augustus issued several marriage laws to prevent the decline of the Roman population. This tension between family and freedom for women may be seen in the provision of one of his laws: a freeborn woman who bore three children was freed from her dependence on the man (Balsdon, 1969:83). Women were seeking such freedom, and some versions of Christianity promised to provide it.

It was possible to understand Paul's admonition to remain single, his attitude toward women, and his elaboration of the church as a "family" as an attack on the traditional family. Guarding against this implication, the author of the Pastorals advises:

Train the young women to love their husbands and children, to be sensible, chaste, domestic, kind, and submissive to their husbands, that the word of God may not be discredited. (Titus 2:3–4)

One of the common charges against Christians by Hellenistic writers is that they divide and disrupt the household. In fact, Christians created alternative households, as the practice of looking after widows already implies. The writer of the Pastorals saw such charges as a discredit to the gospel. The author of the Thecla stories in *Acts of Paul* thought such charges valid. For her (perhaps), Christ challenged the very foundations of sinful human culture.

THE RADICAL APOSTLE

The story of Paul and Thecla is part of a larger work, the ***Acts of Paul***, written late in the second century but based on oral traditions and legends that probably go back to the first century. It commemorates the more radical aspects of Paul, the side that advocated the single life in light of the approaching end (1 Cor. 7:25–26, but notice 27). These stories extend Paul's logic that in Christ there is neither slave nor free, neither male nor female (Gal. 3:27–28). The Paul portrayed here is the passionate Paul, who prays for and receives miracles, who prophesies in the Spirit. Such stories pursue the implications of the assembly of believers as the new household, living outside the social conventions of the day. The tellers of these stories stood in opposition to Greco-Roman culture. They would have understood the Jesus tradition that declares: "I have come to set a man against his father, and a daughter against her mother" (Matt. 10:35). In these ways, they are truly heirs of Paul.

But our story has also resolved the tension in Paul. Paul did not deny sexuality, as the full discussion in 1 Corinthians 7 shows. Though Paul lived in light of the coming end, he was too Jewish to neglect the goodness of the creation: "'For the earth is the Lord's and everything in it.'... Eat whatever is set before you without raising any questions on the grounds of conscience" (1 Cor. 10:26–27; also Rom. 14:14). Paul lived a rigorous life, but he was no ascetic. Whereas Paul represented the invasion of the larger world by the message of Christ, the *Acts of Paul* represents a withdrawal from that world in the name of purity. It is a world-denying and culture-denying asceticism that loses the dynamic of Paul's yes and no. It solves the paradox of Paul by turning him into a social radical.

This portrait of Paul was widespread in the second century and even much later. The *Acts of Paul* was used as Scripture in some Christian circles, known as Manicheans. Thecla was eventually made a saint, as the church harnessed the energies of the virgins in monastic orders. The portrait of Paul as the model ascetic profoundly influenced great Paulinists like Marcion and Irenaeus, and later **Augustine**, who shaped the thinking of the church throughout the Middle Ages.

THE TRAJECTORY OF MYSTICAL EXPERIENCE

Other followers of Paul remembered him not so much for his universalism, authority, or asceticism as for his religious sensibility. Paul's great emphasis on the Spirit and his understanding of his life in Christ suggest his intense, inner aspect. There is no doubt that Paul underwent profound religious experiences. He reports being caught up to heaven (2 Cor. 12:3), claims to speak in tongues more often than all the enthusiasts at Corinth (1 Cor. 14:18), and, above all, reports that he encountered the risen Christ (Gal. 1:16). In his own account Paul equates this latter experience with that of the earlier resurrection appearances to Peter and the others (1 Cor. 15:3–8). The author of Acts portrayed it as a visionary experience, but then the author of Acts believed that the risen Jesus ceased to appear to his followers forty days after the resurrection, when he ascended to heaven (Acts 1:3–9). We know that some Christians claimed to encounter the risen Christ very late in the second century. This claim seems to have been made particularly by the Gnostics.

From Mystical Experience to Gnosticism

We have encountered incipient forms of **Gnosticism** in Paul's letters, especially at Corinth and possibly at Colossae. These early experiments may be considered a gnosticizing trend in Pauline tradition, often abetted by things Paul said but often resisted by Paul himself. (See the discussion on pages 134–38.) This trend will eventually achieve the status of a self-conscious movement in the second century.

We should say *movements*, for literally dozens of different Gnostic systems were invented; one writer listed sixty different movements. Some of them found their primary inspiration in the Gospel of John; many looked to Paul. **Valentinus**, a major Gnostic thinker who came to Rome from Egypt about 150 CE, claimed that his teacher Theudas had been a disciple of Paul. Marcion, a Syrian deeply influenced by Gnostic thought, who came to Rome at about the same time as Valentinus, was so impressed with Paul that he excluded all non-Pauline writings from his collection of truly divine writings. Other Paulinists violently rejected their claims to Paul, but that is a polemical and not a historical judgment—that is, the rejection was based on a disagreement of ideas. (For a glimpse of the controversy see 2 Pet. 3:15–16.)

Like Paul, the Gnostics were overwhelmed by the experience of the Spirit. They believed that in their spiritual rapture they transcended their bodies and their senses and experienced union with the divine. Like Paul too, they sought to live in the Spirit rather than in the flesh. They could appeal to Paul's rejection of the authority of the church in favor of private experience (Gal. 1:12–16), to his claim to speak a secret wisdom to the mature (1 Cor. 2:6), to his distinction between law and grace (2 Cor. 3:6), to his teaching that Jesus' resurrected body was a "spiritual body" rather than a physical one (1 Cor. 15:44–46)—he actually said that flesh and blood could not inherit the kingdom of God (1 Cor. 15:50) and even Jesus took only the "likeness of flesh" (Rom. 8:3). In all these ways, and especially in the emphasis on spiritual experience, the Gnostics saw in Paul their true source.

This mysticism of experience was attuned to the spirit of the age. We have seen that the mystery religions sought to achieve transformation through mythic enactments (see pages 118–19). It was a mysticism of ritual. Philosophy sought the transformation of life and the attainment of enlightenment. It was a mysticism of the mind. Gnosticism, deeply influenced by both, was ultimately a mysticism of experience. Traces of such mysticism—of experience, of ritual, and of enlightenment—are found in Paul. But the Gnostics went far beyond Paul.

They created a new story, or rather, they incorporated the story of Jesus into a larger one derived from Greek philosophical speculation. Even as the mythic speculation of the Greeks derived the universe from the primeval pair, heaven and earth, so philosophic speculation saw the world as a dualism of spirit and matter. Gnosticism viewed the material world as real but deceptive. Humans are really spiritual beings, created in God's image (which they understood to mean that the primal human was the mirror image of God). We are all deceived into thinking we are material creatures; we identify ourselves with our bodies. This is because we lack knowledge. Gnostics understood the old Greek proverb "Know thyself" to mean "Know your true spiritual nature." But this knowledge (*gnosis*) is not intellectual attainment. One had to know in the depths of one's being, that is, experientially. This required a revelation, a revealer—Jesus.

The Gnostic understanding of Jesus was different from the traditional view: Jesus is the heavenly man, the second Adam, of whom Paul spoke in Romans 5. He is humanity in its true state, now descended into the world to reveal the truth to those ready to receive it. Not all are ready. And to those not ready, the common people, he speaks in parables that point toward the truth and might eventually make them ready. But to the elect he imparts a secret knowledge. Typical of the Gnostic approach is the scene reported by an anti-Gnostic writer; Jesus explains the parable of the sower to his disciples:

[The Gnostics claim that the sower in the parable] was not a good sower, asserting that if he had been good he would not have been neglectful, or cast seed "by the wayside" or "on stony places" or "in untilled soil;" wishing it to be understood that the sower is he who scatters captive souls in diverse bodies as he wills. In which book also many things are said about the prince of dampness and the prince of fire, which is meant to signify that it is by art

and not by the power of God that all good things are done in this world. For it says that there is a certain virgin light whom God, when he wishes to give rain to men, shows to the prince of dampness, who since he desires to take possession of her perspires in his excitement and makes rain, and when he is deprived of her causes peals of thunder by his roaring. (Paulus Orosius Con-
sultatio 154.4–18; quoted from Hennecke and Schneemelcher, 1991:1:376)

The secrecy, the playful mythology, and the notion of souls captive to bodies are all typically Gnostic. Here we glimpse the radical novelty of their approach. Consider:

Jesus said, "If your leaders say to you, 'Look, the (Father's) kingdom is in the sky,' then the birds of the sky will precede you. If they say to you, 'It is in the sea,' then the fish will precede you. Rather, the kingdom is within you and it is outside you. When you know yourselves, then you will be known, and you will understand that you are children of the living Father. But if you do not know yourselves, then you live in poverty, and you are the poverty." (Gospel of Thomas 3; quoted from Miller, 1994)

The Gospel of Truth is joy for those who have received from the Father of Truth the gift of knowing him, through the power of the Word [Logos] that came forth. . . . The one who is addressed as the Savior, that being the name of the work he is to perform for the redemption of those who were ignorant of the Father, while the name of the Gospel is the proclamation of hope, being discovery for those who search for him. (Gospel of Truth; quoted from Hennecke and Schneemelcher, 1991:1:117, and Robinson, 1977:37–38)

How like Paul this sounds; how unlike Paul it is. That Jesus has come forth to redeem the world sounds like Paul. But now you must understand the hidden meaning. You must make the discovery.

Gnosticism plunges below the surface meaning to ever deeper meanings. "But it came to pass, after Jesus was risen from the dead that he spent 11 years discoursing with his disciples and taught them only as far as the places of the first commandment and as far as the places of the first mystery" (*Pistis Sophia*; quoted from Hennecke and Schneemelcher, 1991:1:363). So much more remains to be revealed. In the quote above, from the *Gospel of Truth*, I used an ellipsis to avoid some of the technical language that has the logos (word, message, or reason) coming forth from the fullness, which is the thought and mind of God. In the system of Valentinus, perhaps the author of this work, the universe is a very complex place, with layer upon layer of realities. Each level is overseen by a pair of rulers.

First you must understand that the world as you commonly experience it is a delusion. Valentinians explained the origin of the world and of humanity by means of a very complicated story, in which redemption by Christ is the final phase. All proceed from the primal pair: the Deep and Silence, which was the Thought of the Deep. From them arise Mind and Truth, Word and Life, Humanity and Church, and numerous pairs of Rulers making up the Fullness of thirty. The youngest of these generations, Wisdom, desired to know the Deep itself. But acting without her proper consort, Willed, she strove upward toward him, with disastrous results: she conceived the monster Fancy, with whom she nearly perished in labor. The original pairs acted to save her by producing a single Ruler, Limit (also called Cross), who delivered her of the monster and restored the primal harmony. This Monstrous Form of Wisdom lay outside this harmony in places of shadow and void.

Mind and Truth then produce a new pair, Christ and Holy Spirit, who pity the Monstrous Form of Wisdom and descend to her through the Cross. Receiving form from them, she is then called Wisdom after her mother or Spirit after the companion of Christ who formed her. She becomes a Ruler of the lowest sphere, and Christ and Holy Spirit return to the Fullness.

Aware of her marginal position between the lowest and the highest, Wisdom (or Spirit) alternates between grief and joy. In her grief she brings forth Body; then aspiring toward higher things she brings forth Soul. Finally, having been touched by Christ and Holy Spirit, she brings forth Spirit. Now imitating the action of the Fullness, she sets out to create a world that imitates that cosmic world. As an image of the Deep, the First Father, she produces the Creator out of Soul. He then creates Heaven and Earth and all therein.

But the Creator worked blindly, imagining himself to be the agent rather than just the tool of Wisdom. Out of Body he created Humanity and breathed into it Soul. Unknown to him his mother, Wisdom, created other beings out of Spirit so that these three now are mingled. Some, dominated by Body, are so bound up with this perishable world that they can never be saved. The spiritual, in contrast, are so attuned to the Fullness that they need no salvation. They ascend to the Fullness. But the rest, dominated by Soul, are capable of salvation; it was for these that Jesus finally came from heaven. (This summary is based on the excellent discussion in Dodd, 1953:97–114.)

These Souls may be saved by knowledge (*gnosis*) of their true being. Jesus came to reveal this knowledge, and it can now be learned from those he taught. But it lies not on the surface of his teaching, such as the common people think, but in the secret depths. When the common Christians call Jesus "Son of man" they do not understand what they say: Son of Man, indeed, Image of that Primal Humanity. (For examples of other Gnostic myths see the discussion of John's Gospel on pages 421–23.)

A Gnostic work from a different school summarized the revelation of Jesus as a kind of password one must know to reascend safely through the spheres of the Rulers to the Father. When challenged by these Powers, one should reply:

I have known myself and I have collected myself from every side; I have sowed no children for the Archon [Ruler] but I have uprooted his roots and I have collected the members that were scattered, and I know who thou art; for I am one of those from on high. (Fragment of the Gospel of Philip; *quoted from Hennecke and Schneemelcher, 1991:1:180)*

Knowing oneself, gathering oneself, rooting out the bodily: by such means the Gnostic ascended. In practice these would involve asceticism (or, in a few cases, bodily indulgence), prayer and meditation, and attention to Gnostic stories and interpretations. These techniques were widely practiced in many diverse systems. The formula above is nearly the same as that given by the Neoplatonic philosopher

Porphyry a century later in a letter to his wife: "Study to ascend into thyself, gathering from the body all thy scattered members which have been scattered into a multitude from the unity which up to a point held sway" (quoted from Hennecke and Schneemelcher 1963:1:275). Porphyry was a strikingly unoriginal philosopher, and he represents here only what would be typical of the philosophical enterprise.

THE APOSTLE OF KNOWLEDGE

Gnosticism represented a serious attempt to bridge the gap between Christian preaching and the philosophical tradition, trying to integrate Christianity into the best intellectual endeavors of the second and third centuries. In so doing the Gnostics reused many of the elements of Paul's tradition, claiming especially his experience. Like Paul they claimed knowledge of things unspeakable (2 Cor. 12:1–4). They thought they perfectly understood Paul's despair with ordinary believers: "And so, brothers and sisters, I could not speak to you as spiritual people, but rather as people of the flesh, as infants in Christ" (1 Cor. 3:1). They understood Paul spiritually, rejecting the flesh.

But in recasting Paul as the man of knowledge, they distorted major elements of his self-identity as a Jew. Marcion, who shared much with the Gnostics, went so far as to deny any connection whatsoever between Christianity and Judaism, even rejecting the Hebrew Scriptures and the God they portray. He was convinced that the God revealed by Jesus and preached by Paul was the antithesis of the Jewish Creator. (All who are deeply influenced by Gnostic ideas will have trouble with the notion of God as Creator, as the Valentinian hierarchy in the Gnostic story above shows.) For Marcion, Paul was the one true apostle. His collection of authoritative writings consisted of the ten letters of Paul and a gospel, probably an abridged form of Luke, who was thought to be a traveling companion of Paul. That one could exalt the authority of a tradition this much while altering its meaning so extensively is a remarkable accomplishment of the human imagination, one that should caution all readers.

THE TRAJECTORY THAT REJECTED PAUL

When Augustine allegorized the parable of the good Samaritan, he imagined that the Samaritan was symbolic of Christ, descending to help fallen Adam, providing the oil and wine of the sacraments, setting him on his beast—his body—and carrying him to the inn—the church. The innkeeper, he thought, was Paul (*Quaestiones Evangeliorum* 2.19). By the 400s Paul had clearly become the dominant voice in the church. It was not always so.

THE EARLY OPPONENTS

We know little about the opponents of Paul who constantly flit about in the background of the letters. They have been the subject of much study, but the available information is slight. We know them only through the charges Paul leveled against them, and who among us would wish to be known by the word of our adversaries? Worse, Paul never treats them in an organized way. He presumed that he and his audience already knew these opponents; there was no need to explain. One confusing factor is that from city to city and, sometimes even within one city, the nature of the opposition to Paul seems to shift. The opponents of 1 Corinthians seem to have little in common with those of Galatians or of 2 Corinthians. We must not suppose that Paul's opponents were a homogeneous group. Some, perhaps most, were more conservative than he and reluctant to depart from the Jewish traditions. Some were more liberal and eager to do away with all law, as they seemed to do at Corinth.

Paul confronted both and stirred controversy wherever he went. Even Peter and Barnabas, his traveling companion, opposed him at one point (Galatians 2). We presume Paul and Peter made up, but we are not told this. Barnabas never rejoined him, and Paul ceased to use Antioch as a base of operations after this incident. We can be certain that many of his contemporaries disagreed with him on one or more points at one or more times.

ONGOING OPPOSITION

Tracing Paul's influence in the decades following his death (probably around 64 CE) is not an easy task. None of the literature that can be dated with reasonable certainty between 65 and 95 refers to him until we come to Acts. None of the Gospel writers seems indebted to him. But after 100, or perhaps we should say after the publication of Acts, Paul's increasing status is easily documented. He is quoted extensively, and some begin to consider his writings equivalent to Scripture (1 Pet. 3:16) or as the only Scripture (Marcion). We have seen that many diverse groups laid claim to the authority of Paul.

A revealing scene near the end of Acts probably portrays the attitude of one group of Jesus' followers toward Paul at the time Acts was written (perhaps around 90). In this scene Paul has come to Jerusalem and made a report to the leadership on his mission to the Gentiles. Their response is to warn him: "You see, brother, how many thousands there are among the Jews of those who have believed; they are all zealous for the law, and they have been told about you that you teach all the Jews who are among the Gentiles to forsake Moses, telling them not to circumcise their children or observe the customs" (Acts 21:20–21). This is a false charge, as the author of Acts makes clear. There is no evidence in any of the letters that Paul thought Jews should abandon their customs; his concern was that Gentiles not be compelled to observe Jewish customs. But its inclusion in the Acts story suggests that many regarded it as true.

And in fact, by the end of the first century we find followers of Paul asserting what Paul is accused of in Acts: teaching that Jews ought not to keep the Law. Ignatius of Antioch, one of the first to self-consciously identify Jesus' followers as Christians, wrote to those in Magnesia (a city about 50 miles north of Ephesus): "It is an abomination to follow Jesus Christ and to practice Jewish ways" (10:3). For Ignatius, the form of Christianity dominant in Paul's time had become unacceptable. This trajectory will culminate in Marcion's rejection of all things Jewish, even their Scriptures and their God.

When we find Paulinists adopting this attitude toward Christians who are Jewish, we must expect to find those Jewish followers of Jesus adopting negative attitudes toward Paul.

The development of what is usually called **Jewish Christianity** is very difficult to trace, for those who attempted to preserve both their Jewish identity and their loyalty to Jesus were the losers in the struggle; and the history of the losers is typically obscured by the winners who write the history. The movement to be faithful to both Jesus and the Law did not die out with the first generation, not even with the destruction of Jerusalem in 70 CE. References to such groups in and around Palestine can be found into the seventh century, when this whole area was conquered by Arab armies and eventually converted to Islam. In the fourth century, Epiphanius discusses Jewish Christians of his day, telling us: "They break with Paul because he does not accept circumcision" (*Parnarion* 28.5.3).

Actually, there was diversity within the movement we call Jewish Christianity. Around 150, a Gentile Christian living in Palestine wrote an imaginary dialogue between himself and a Jew named Trypho. It is a stimulating debate, leading only to an agreement to talk further. The author, a philosopher named Justin, was later to be called **Justin Martyr** because he died for his faith. He identifies several alternative views held by Jewish Christians: some keep the Law themselves but do not believe Gentiles need to do so; some insist on Gentile observance; some do not insist that the Gentiles observe the laws but will not eat with them unless they do (and thus cannot share the Eucharist); some have ceased to observe the Law themselves (*Dialogue with Trypho* 47). Surely the last and probably the first group would have had little difficulty with Paul. The other two probably, as Epiphanius says, broke with Paul.

Some went much further than simply not following Paul; they regarded him as the perverter of Jesus' true teachings. We have a letter, probably written around 200, pretending to be from Peter to James, which discusses someone called Simon. The allusion is to Simon Magus, mentioned in Acts (8:9–24), who was later regarded as the father of all errors. But in reading the letter it becomes obvious that Simon is a thinly veiled way of referring to Paul. Thus Simon is described as "going to the Gentiles" and as failing to present his gospel to James and receive the direction of the Jerusalem church, both of which apply to Paul but not to Simon. In this letter Paul is portrayed as Peter's direct enemy.

> *For some from among the Gentiles have rejected my lawful preaching and have preferred a lawless and absurd doctrine of the man who is my enemy. And indeed some have attempted, whilst I am still alive, to distort my words by interpretations of many sorts, as if I taught the dissolution of the law and, although I was of this opinion, did not express it openly [see Gal. 2:11–14]. But that may God forbid! For to do such a thing means to act contrary to the law of God which was made known by Moses and was confirmed by our Lord. (Letter of Peter to James 2:3–5; quoted from Hennecke and Schneemelcher, 1992:2.494)*

Later writings in this same tradition are even more pointed. There are several direct encounters between Peter and this Simon, always to the latter's disadvantage. Even the legitimacy of Paul's encounter with the risen Jesus is questioned, first by suggesting that even the pagans have such visions, perhaps prompted by demons, but then more ingeniously:

> *So even if our Jesus did appear in a dream to you, making himself known and conversing with you, he did so in anger, speaking to an opponent [see Acts 9:4–5]. That is why he spoke to you through visions and dreams—through*

revelations which are external. But can anyone be qualified by a vision to be-come a teacher? And if you say it is possible, then why did the Teacher remain for a whole year conversing with those who were awake? (Pseudoclementine Homilies 19.1; quoted from Meeks, 1972:182)

Here we see Christians claiming Peter but opposing and rejecting Paul. It is worth noting what they reject: there is no discussion of Paul's highly nuanced understanding of the Law nor of his concern for Gentiles. What we find is a rejection of those Christians who laid claim to the Pauline heritage. *The battle we see reflected here is not over the ideas of Paul; it is a struggle between two communities and two different visions of the Christian life.* If people like Marcion claim Paul, the only option Jewish followers of Jesus have is to reject Paul.

THE CONTINUING INFLUENCE OF PAUL

No one was able to capture Paul. Neither his enemies nor his friends seem to have understood his dynamic and paradoxical message. No one pays attention to the careful argument of Romans with its forceful no, and equally forceful yes, to the Law. No one asks how in one place Paul can declare: "For neither circumcision nor uncircumcision is anything; but a new creation is everything!" (Gal. 6:15), while in another he writes: "Circumcision is nothing, and uncircumcision is nothing; but obeying the commandments of God is everything" (1 Cor. 7:19). The paradox of Paul remained unexplored; no one attempted a historical interpretation of Paul.

Yet each of these communities found Paul an important influence, and all but the last drew significant inspiration from his work. At the very least this ability of Paul to appeal to very diverse elements ensured his continued influence. He became the most significant influence in the development of Christianity—the keeper of the inn.

CHRISTIANITY AFTER PAUL

We may now draw some preliminary conclusions about the developments within Pauline Christianity in the next generation. Four trends appear significant:

1. *A new emphasis on the church emerges in these writings.* The church is coming to be regarded as a hierarchical institution with an ordained ministry tracing its roots back to Paul or to other apostles such as Peter or James. A primary concern of this institution is to preserve what the hierarchy takes to be the true teaching of the apostles.
2. *There is a definite settling in and becoming acculturated.* The intense concern with the near end of the age seems to have faded, and with it the indifference to culture. There is a strong concern for what outsiders might think of the behavior of Christians, a longing to be respectable. This results in a certain moralistic element, extolling virtues and condemning vices, both common in the general literature of this era. Coupled with this concern is an increasing accommodation to cultural expectations, especially in regard to the family and the place of women. To be respectable the community must restrict the freedoms women gained in the early charismatic communities. When people spoke because they

believed the Spirit inspired them, who was to prevent a woman from praying or prophesying? Only the fading of the charismatic experience and the increasing routinization of these tasks could lead to the silencing of half the assembly.

3. *Related to this new attitude toward culture was an increasingly direct attempt to interpret Christ and Christian experience in terms of the religious experience of Gentiles.* The earlier generation adapted the Hebrew Scriptures to interpret Christ; this generation begins to appeal to the Gentile traditions, such as the epiphany of a God, and to the ideas of the philosophers. Gentiles are playing the dominant role. This results in the development of many new ideas, prompting a very dynamic era in Christian thought.

4. *There is an increasingly clear demarcation between the various kinds of Christians.* No longer is there any question about the legitimacy of the faith of the Gentile Christians; quite the opposite. Jewish Christians are being relegated to the fringes; Gnostics are being driven out; ascetics are challenged. A large group emerges, still diverse but sharing much, that regards itself as the orthodox tradition: the guardians of the teachings of the apostles. The authority of the apostles escalates the value placed on their writings, resulting in an increase of the number of writings attributed to apostles and in the beginning of the process to establish the true corpus of their works: a canon. (See Chapter 14 for a fuller discussion of the development of the canon.)

Finally, we have one small item of unfinished business left over from our study of the Thessalonian letters in Chapter 3. We saw that there are reasons to think 2 Thessalonians may have been written after Paul's time. Now that we have a clearer idea of the developments among Paul's followers in the next generation, it would be appropriate to reread 2 Thessalonians and ask whether it is more closely related to these developments or to the Paul revealed in the earlier letters. In fact one scholar has argued that 2 Thessalonians makes perfectly good sense as a response to the ideas enunciated in Ephesians (Hughes, 1989). Whereas the author of Ephesians sees Christians as already "raised up" and seated with Christ "in the heavenly places" (2:6), the author of 2 Thessalonians insists that the day of the Lord has not yet arrived (2:2). (See the discussion of the Thessalonians correspondence, pages 96–100.)

LEARNING ON YOUR OWN

REVIEWING THE CHAPTER

Names and Terms

Acts of Paul	heresy	metaphor of the body
asceticism	household instruction	Muratorian Fragment
Augustine	Ignatius of Antioch	Pastoral Letters
Clement of Alexandria	Jewish Christianity	Polycarp
Clement of Rome	Justin Martyr	Thecla
Eusebius	Marcion	Valentinus
Gnosticism		

Issues and Questions

1. Be able to describe the criteria scholars use to determine Paul's role in the production of these disputed letters and to apply those criteria to one specific letter.
2. What is the main concern of Colossians and Ephesians?
3. How does the characterization of Paul in Colossians and Ephesians differ from the Paul of the earlier letters?
4. What is the main concern of the Pastoral Letters?
5. How does the underlying story of the Pastorals differ from the story of Paul based on the earlier letters?
6. How did the writer of the *Acts of Paul and Thecla* reinterpret Paul's understanding of the body, and why might women have been attracted to this new principle?
7. How did the Gnostics both build on Paul's teaching and radically change it?
8. Why did many Jewish Christians completely reject Paul in the second century?
9. Compare and contrast Paul's story as reconstructed from the undisputed letters with the story reconstructed from the disputed letters.
10. What does the study of these writings suggest about the unity and diversity of Christianity in the second century?

TAKING THE NEXT STEP

Because Paul became an increasingly important, even dominant, voice in early Christianity in the two centuries after his death, there are many possibilities for further study.

Topics for Special Studies

The Collection and Publication of Paul's Letters

Trobisch, 1994; Hahneman, 1992; Knox, 1942 and 1987; Gamble, 1975; Ferguson, 1982; Lohse, 1981; and Munro, 1983.

Paul's Influence

Start with one of the broad movements discussed in this chapter and then focus on one particular individual or writing from that movement.

The concept of **trajectories** was introduced into New Testament studies by Robinson and Koester, 1971, especially 1–19.

An extensive literature traces the various continuities and changes within Christian communities in the late first and early second centuries. Start with Brown, 1984; see also Grant, 1967 and 1957, and Sanders, 1980. On Paul's contributions to this variety, see Dunn in Cohn-Sherbok and Court, 2001. Theological developments are traced by Ziesler, 1983:122–39.

Treatments of second-century movements drawing on Paul include:

On Marcion's radical Paulinism, see Knox, 1942; Tyson, 2006; and Hoffman, 1984.
On the ascetic vision of Paul, see Howe, 1980; MacDonald, 1982, provides a very provocative look at the conflicts within the various strands of the Pauline tradition.
On they mystical element in Paul, see Ashton, 2000.

The more church-centered strand is explored by Wilson, 1979. Richardson, 1967, explores Ignatius of Antioch, as do Wallace-Hadrill, 1982, and Schoedel, 1984. Bernard, 1967, considers Justin Martyr.

Paul's profound influence on Gnosticism is traced by Pagels, 1975. See also MacDonald, 1987, and Batey, 1963.

For a more general study of Gnosticism, you could begin with Roukema, 1999, or Wink, 1993, and the recent challenge by Williams, 1996. For a brief up-to-date discussion see Wilson in Cohn-Sherbok and Court, 2001. See also Perkins, 1980, or the popular account of Dart, 1976. The older work of Grant, 1966, is still useful. On the question of whether Gnosticism predates Christianity, see Yamauchi, 1983.

Collections of scholarly essays are found in Goehring et al., 1990; Logan and Wedderburn, 1983; and Krause, 1981. For more on Gnosticism, see the resources in Chapter 12.

The Importance of the Gnostic Library Discovered at Nag Hammadi
See Hedrick and Rodgson, 1986, and the popular account of Dart, 1976. There is useful information in Cameron, 1984; and Logan and Wedderburn, 1983. For the actual texts from the library, see Robinson, 1977.

Other Gnostic sources are collected by Layton, 1987; Foerester, 1972 (2 volumes); and Jonas, 1992.

The Early Development of Forms of Church Government
The evolution of church order is traced by MacDonald, 1988, and more broadly by Burt-chaell, 1992. See also Schweizer, 1961.

Developments in the Post-Pauline Era
Many of the changes in early Christianity will be discussed in monographs on one or more of these Pauline writings:

On the error at Colossae, see Arnold, 1995; Royalty, 2002; Francis, 1973; and Sappington, 1991. Crouch, 1973, treats the origins of the household code.

On issues at Ephesus, see Arnold, 1989.

On the social location of the Pastorals, see Verner, 1982; Kidd, 1990 (on wealth); and MacDonald, 1983 (on women's roles). For related developments see Meier, 1991.

Towner, 1989, looks at the structure of theology and ethics in the Pastoral Letters. Wild, 1985, argues that the biographical details in the Pastorals are meant to portray him as the ideal philosopher. Harding, 1998, studies the rhetoric and Greco-Roman traditions in the Pastorals. Porter, 2004, includes essays with differing points of view on the development of the Pauline canon.

Extracts from many sources in the Pauline and anti-Pauline traditions, from the first to the twentieth centuries, can be found in Meeks, 1972:149–444.

The Roles Women Filled
Choose one or more of these broad movements or some specific submovement.

The changing role of women in ministry is traced by Schüssler Fiorenza, 1983, especially part 3. King, 1988, traces women's roles in Gnostic movements. The roles of women in society are treated by Pomeroy, 1975. Cultural interactions are traced by MacDonald, 1996. For a source book, see Lefkowitz and Fant, 1992. See additional literature referenced in Chapter 4.

Roman Attitudes toward Sexuality, Love, and Marriage
See Laqueur, 1990; Blok and Mason, 1987; and on illicit sex, Rousselle, 1988. Bartchy, 1978, treats sexual identity among Christians; and Countryman, 1988, provides an excellent treatment of the logic and presuppositions of sexual ethics in the New Testament writings. For insights from ancient art, see Kampen and Bergmann, 1996; Koloskie-Ostrow and Lyons, 1997; and Clarke, 1998.

The Role of Asceticism in Greco-Roman Culture
See Brown, 1987; Blok and Mason, 1987; and Burrus, 1987.

The Question of the Authorship of Pauline Writings

Any good commentary will discuss the issue of authorship; see the selection below under "Additional Books and Articles." See also Collins, 1988.

The general question of anonymous and pseudonymous authorship is addressed by Aland, 1961; Meade, 1986; Goodspeed, 1937; Cannon, 1983; Koch, in *IDB* 5:712–14; and Charlesworth, in *ABD* 5:540–41. See the more technical work of Kiley, 1986.

On the ethical question of pseudonymity, see Donelson, 1986; Metzger, 1972, considers the range of reasons for writing such works. See also Kittredge, 1998.

Prior, 1989, studies 2 Timothy in relation to Paul's letter-writing practices. Holland, 1988, and Hughes, 1989, build the case against Paul's authorship of 2 Thessalonians. Bauckham, 1988, argues that Timothy wrote the Pastorals. Miller, 1997, argues that they are later elaborations built on original notes from Paul. Richards, 2002, makes a spirited case for the three Pastoral Letters being written by different authors to address different social situations and problems.

For a conservative defense of Paul's writing the Pastorals, see Johnson, 1996; Barker, Lane, and Michaels, 1969; Ellis, 1961; and Guthrie, 1990.

The Relation between Ephesians and Colossians

Any good commentary will treat this issue; see the list below under "Additional Books and Articles." For a more recent approach to the connection between Ephesians and Colossians, see Cope, 1985. See also Taylor, 1986, and Crouch, 1973.

Who Opposed Paul?

The nature of the opposition to Paul is treated extensively, with a large bibliography, in Gunther, 1973; Georgi, 1986, provides a more specific study of the opponents addressed in 2 Corinthians; see also Sumney, 1990. Lüdemann, 1989, traces opposition to Paul from Jewish Christians. On the whole phenomenon of Jewish Christianity see the resources in Chapter 7.

Pauline Tradition and Judaism

An excellent brief description of the variety and interconnection among various forms of Judaism in this era is given by Stone, 1980. The growing split is traced by S. G. Wilson, 1995. See also Lüdemann, 1989, and the resources in Chapter 7.

The Role of Astrology and the Occult in Greco-Roman Culture

See Luck, 1985 (on magic); Potter, 1994 (on prophets); MacMullen, 1966; Ulansey, 1989; Campion, 1994; and Barton, 1994. Also see the resources in Chapter 1.

Additional Books and Articles

For a brief treatment of each of the disputed letters, see Sampley et al., 1978; Collins, 1988; Krodel, 1993; and Stockhausen, 1989.

Commentaries include:

Colossians and Ephesians: Barth, 1974; Bruce, 1984; Houlden, 1970; Lincoln, 1990; Lohse, 1971; McDonald, 1980; Martin, 1973 and 1991; Mitton, 1976; O'Brien, 1999; Patzia, 1984; Perkins, 1997; Reumann, 1985; Swain, 1980; and Taylor, 1986.

Pastorals: Barrett, 1963; Dibelius and Conzelmann, 1972 (technical); Fee, 1984 (argues that Paul wrote the Pastorals); A. T. Hanson, 1982; Guthrie, 1990; Houlden, 1989; Kelly, 1987; and Quinn and Wacker, 1999. Gealy, 1951, is still an excellent introduction to the issues and themes of these letters. Fiori, 1986, does a special study of the use of personal example in such literature.

ECHOES OF OTHER STORIES

James, Jude, Hebrews, Peter

 It is equally unreasonable to accept merely probable conclusions from a mathematician, and to demand strict demonstration from an orator.

ARISTOTLE, *NICOMACHEAN ETHICS*

he New Testament is not a historically balanced document. More than one quarter of it is the work of one writer (Luke-Acts), a writer who exalts Paul. In addition, Paul's authority stands behind nearly half (thirteen) of the twenty-seven writings in the New Testament. This strong emphasis on the Pauline tradition means that many other traditions have been recorded less completely. Acts, for example, is often called the Acts of the Apostles, but we learn little from it about most of the apostles; there are brief accounts of Judas's suicide, James's martyrdom, and Peter's early ministry. Nothing is said of their careers or of their distinctive accomplishments or individual views. Concerning nine of the original twelve apostles we learn almost nothing. About dozens of others we know little more than their names: Matthias, Apollos, Nicanor, Nicholaus, Ananias, Aquila, Prisca, Mary, Lydia, James, Archippus, Sosthenes, Onesimus. Their stories remain untold. Of countless others we know not even their names.

From this silence a few voices do speak, briefly, hardly more than an echo of the living stories. They remind us of other trajectories of the traditions about Jesus—trajectories that did not flow through Paul. Five short writings made their way into the New Testament, preserving vivid impressions of diverse kinds of early believers. One of these works, Hebrews, is anonymous, but its very name reveals its close ties to believers with Jewish roots. Another claims James, brother of Jesus and head of the church in Jerusalem, as its author; both James and the Jerusalem church mark its Jewish orientation. A third, barely one page long, is written in the name of Jude, another brother of Jesus. Finally, two works are attributed to Peter, but they are themselves works of different orientations. We saw from our study of Paul that Peter was a mediating figure between the thoroughly Law-observant tradition of James and the more lax tradition of Paul and his Gentile followers. In Acts Peter appears as Paul's ally, whereas in the anti-Pauline trajectory we saw him portrayed as the enemy of Paul (see Chapter 6). The two letters preserved in his name represent a more positive response to Paul.

The older designation for James, Jude, 1 Peter, and 2 Peter (along with 1, 2, and 3 John) was the General Epistles (epistle is the older English word for letters; they were called "general" because they are addressed to the community in general and not to a specific church) or the Catholic Epistles (*catholic* means "universal," again because they are addressed to everyone). But they are hardly general or universal; rather, they speak from very specific and focused perspectives. They represent somewhat different versions of the Jesus story than we have studied so far and will help us appreciate the diversity and commonality among early Jesus movements. (You might review the section on Christianity after Paul in Chapter 6 for a general orientation to this period; pages 211–12.)

The perspectives of these writings is both more "Jewish" (attempting to maintain the traditions of the ancestors) and more "Christian" (one of these writings clearly uses this title as a self-designation—one of the earliest to do so; 1 Pet. 4:16). Thus, scholars often designate this movement as "Jewish Christianity," a useful if problematic title (after all, Paul was Jewish). Still it is useful to see how other Jews at some distance from Paul attempted to establish their identity by telling the Jesus story differently.

TRADITIONS OF THE FAMILY OF JESUS: JAMES AND JUDE

We find real ambiguity toward Jesus' family in early writings. Mark shows his family trying to suppress Jesus' activities (3:21, 31–35), and John explicitly states that they did not believe in him (7:1–5). Yet from Paul we learn that one of the resurrection appearances was said to be to James (1 Cor. 15:7), who was considered one of the apostles and a leader of the Jerusalem assembly (Gal. 1:19; Acts 1:14). Eusebius claims that James was the first bishop of Jerusalem, followed by Simeon, a cousin of Jesus (*Ecclesiastical History* 3.11.1).

According to the gospel traditions Jesus had four brothers, Jacobos (which nearly all English versions give as James), Joses, Judas, and Simon, and at least two sisters—never named (Mark 6:3 and Matt. 13:55). Like the name *Jesus*, these are Greek versions of traditional Jewish names: Jesus for Joshua, Jacobos for Jacob, Joses for Joseph, Judas for Judah, Simon for Simeon. In the early traditions they are said to be brothers, with no further explanation, and one assumes the writers meant actual brothers. However, in the middle of the second century, clear traditions regard these brothers as children of Joseph by a previous marriage (*Protevangelium of James* 9:2, in Hennecke and Schneemelcher, 1991:1:430). These traditions coincide with the increasing exaltation of Mary and the understanding that she remained a virgin throughout her life. In the fourth century Jerome argued that they were really cousins of Jesus, children of Mary's sister who was also, and confusingly, named Mary (see John 19:25). This rather unlikely hypothesis became the standard opinion in the Middle Ages.

Although we lack the historical sources necessary to trace these traditions, we may assume that Jesus' relatives, and especially his brothers, enjoyed significant authority within the early movement, at least within those segments of the movement that looked to Jerusalem for leadership. Writings in the names of these brothers would have carried far more authority than we might initially assume. Simon and Joses have left little mark, Judas only a trace, but an extensive tradition developed around James.

TRADITIONS ABOUT JAMES

Like Paul, James was not only a historical figure but also a legendary one, and the hero of one branch of the emerging Jesus movement. In Paul's time, "certain men from James" urged stricter Jewish practice at Antioch (Gal. 2:12). Acts identified him with those observant Jews who did not insist on Gentile observance of the Law (21:18–20; 15:13–21); others claimed him for the stringent anti-Paulinists who insisted on complete observance of the commandments (the anti-Pauline *Letter of Peter to James*, along with an endorsement by James, can be found in Hennecke and Schneemelcher, 1992:2:493–96; for the anti-Pauline tradition and the various tendencies within Law-observant Christianity, see pages 208–11). He is often called James the Righteous, which implies his faithful observance of the Law. The *Gospel of Thomas* refers to him as "James the Just, for whose sake heaven and earth came into being" (12). In the *Gospel of the Hebrews*, and probably in the tradition behind 1 Corinthians (15:7), he was the first to encounter the resurrected Jesus (7; in Hennecke and Schneemelcher, 1991:1:178). Hegesippus, a Jewish Christian living in Palestine about 150, described James thus:

> *James, the Lord's brother, received control of the Church, together with the apostles. He is called James the Righteous by everyone from the Lord's time till our own, for there were many named James. This one was holy from his birth; he drank no wine or intoxicating liquor and ate no meat; no razor came near his head; he did not smear himself with oil, and did not go to the baths. This one alone was permitted to enter the Temple sanctuary, for he did not wear wool but linen. And alone he would enter the Temple and be found on his knees, praying for forgiveness for the people, so that his knees grew hard like a camel's. (Quoted by Eusebius* Ecclesiastical History *2.23.4 from a lost work of Hegesippus,* Memoirs)

How early this legendary portrait of James took shape is not clear, but certainly those who preserved it regarded James as Law-observant, vegetarian, teetotaling, ascetic, and so extraordinarily pious that he was allowed to dress in priestly garments and enter the temple. These are the extreme expression of motifs found throughout the James traditions.

Five writings come down to us in the name of James: two with the title *The Apocalypse of James*; two letters, one in Coptic (Egyptian) and one in Greek; and a *Book of James* more commonly known today as the *Infancy Gospel of James* or the *Protevangelium of James*. This last-mentioned work recounts the birth of Mary and has no connection with James other than the use of his name (translation in Hennecke and Schneemelcher, 1991:1:426–37). The two apocalypses and the Coptic letter are late works, perhaps from the third century. Though they contain many Jewish Christian themes, they have been deeply influenced by Gnostic ideas. Most of the texts of these three writings had been lost until the great discovery, in 1946, of a Gnostic Christian library from the fourth century at Nag Hammadi in Egypt. These texts have been published, and an English translation is available (Robinson, 1977). It is unlikely that any of these has a direct connection with James, though their incorporation of legendary material about James indicates that they stem from one trajectory of the James tradition.

THE LETTER OF JAMES

The Greek Letter of James eventually became part of the New Testament. Scholars generally agree that it stems from the first century but disagree on whether it was actually written by James. One issue is that early writers did not seem to have regarded it as from James. Origen, around 200, and Jerome, around 400, thought it was written by someone else in James's name and only gradually gained authority (see Eusebius *Ecclesiastical History* 2.23.24–25, 3.25.3; *IDB* 2:795; *ABD* 3:621). It is possible, however, that these negative opinions stemmed from its Jewishness and its non-Pauline character, since neither Origen nor Jerome had much sympathy for a Jewish version of Christianity. (On the meaning of authorship in antiquity, see pages 93–96, 185–88.)

The internal evidence for authorship is indeterminate because we have no other James tradition against which to measure it. We could argue that its excellent Greek style would be beyond a Palestinian Jew like James, but that would surely indicate some prejudice on our part. Many Palestinian Jews were fluent in both Greek and Aramaic. Besides, a significant number of Hebraic expressions underlie the Greek (*IDB* 5:469; but see *ABD* 3:627). Our understanding of what the letter means will be different, depending on whether we decide it was written by James (who died in 62 CE) or by one claiming James's traditions in the next three or four decades. Our only basis for deciding will be the content of the letter itself.

The Meaning of the Letter

As you read the Letter of James, you will notice that it is not a letter in our sense. It is not a communication sent on some specific occasion from one person to another. The concern of the writing is not some specific historical problem but the general issue of ethical **exhortation**: advice on how to recognize what is good and act accordingly. It is a moral essay dressed up like a letter; such letters on morality were common in antiquity, as the letters of Cicero and Seneca show.

The organization of the letter is very loose, but again, it is typical of this kind of writing. Seeking to move the hearers to certain kinds of action in the present, this kind of exhortation was labeled **demonstrative rhetoric**. Such rhetoric was seldom formally organized and consisted chiefly of an ordered series of topics. Rhetorical effect is achieved by repetition, amplification, comparison, and striking statement rather than by a well-ordered argument. (For a comparison with other types of rhetoric see the Introduction, pages 14–17, and Chapter 6, page 193.) It is possible to imagine continuity to the argument (Davids, 1982:27, is a good example), but the force of the rhetoric depends more on cumulative effect than continuity. Our reading guide to James only suggests the flow of the thought.

 ## READING GUIDE TO JAMES

Facing trials: maturity   1:1–4
  Wisdom from God through faith   1:5–8
  Lowly faithful and the rich   1:9–11
  Temptation is not from God   1:12–16
  Generosity is from God   1:17–18
Doing good: need for action   1:19–25
  True religion: controlled speech and protection of the weak   1:26–27
  True neighbor: impartiality   2:1–13
  True faith: works   2:14–26
Duties of teachers: to guide   3:1–5
  Dangers of the tongue   3:6–12
  Works done with gentleness   3:13–18
  Conflicts from inner desires   4:1–12
False confidence of the rich   4:13–5:6
Final advice   5:7–20
  Patience, truthfulness, prayer
  Rescue the wanderers

Read the Letter of James, and then make a list of the *specific* problems it addresses. Were such problems more likely to arise in a Jewish, Gentile, or mixed community?

The letter opens with a common rhetorical device, a chain of virtues: people should rejoice over their trials, for trials lead to endurance and endurance leads to maturity. (The Greek word here is ***telos***, sometimes translated "perfection" or "end"; it has the sense of a proper or intended outcome, 1:2–4.) Such a chain, even these specific virtues, was commonly urged in Jewish, Stoic, and Christian writings. The basic impulse of Stoicism was to meet all life's developments with steadfastness, achieving that inner calm of the rational creature. Actually, little about this letter is distinctively Christian. Put another way, Christian morality for our author is not very different from any other kind of morality.

This exhortation also provides the foundation for all that follows in the letter; the remainder may be regarded as more specific instructions on how to achieve the steadfastness that leads to maturity. Within this basic framework of trials, steadfastness, and maturity, the author's mind seems to wander freely from topic to topic: wisdom, faith, and a grasp of one's mortality are the prerequisites for steadfastness (1:4–15); these come from God (1:16–18) and lead to a practical, moral doing of good deeds (1:19–27). This morality is most evident when expressed toward the poor and powerless (1:27–2:13). Faith without good works is false (2:14–26). Even higher standards are demanded of teachers (3:1), who must be able to control their tongues (3:2–12) and possess the heavenly wisdom (3:13–18) that leads to peace rather than the passion that leads to strife (4:1–12). Merchants and the rich, especially, fail in such matters (4:13–5:6). Patience, truthfulness, and prayer are necessary as they await the coming of the Lord (5:7–18). Those who wander from the truth should be rescued (5:19–20). Surprisingly, the work has no formal conclusion, final summary, or letter characteristics to mark the end.

In these seemingly random exhortations, we find various rhetorical flourishes that indicate a keen ear for Greek, including repetition, rhyme, word play, puns, alliteration, sequences, parallelism, and the diatribe. Even in English the rhetorical polish of passages such as 5:7–11 and 2:14–26 is evident. The ability to use such devices suggests that our author knew Greek rather well.

James versus Paul?

Ethics is a dangerous enterprise. For, on the one hand, one can mistake the understanding of virtue for its accomplishment (like the person who is proud of achieving humility), and, on the other, the very struggle for ethical achievement may become an end in itself. This last is known as **legalism**, in which attaining the good is understood as a matter of keeping certain rules. Such rules bind the believer to lesser powers than God, according to Paul's argument in Galatians, but they also bind God: God, too, must play by the rules and duly reward those who are good. Thus, one may, indeed must, earn one's salvation by performing good works. In our study of Romans (pages 166–73), we learned that legalism was a constant temptation for early believers—both Jews and Gentiles.

Paul met the challenge of legalism by insisting on the absolute freedom of the believer (Galatians) and by asserting the absolute priority of faith over good works

(Romans). In Abraham he found a clear example of this priority. James saw the Abraham story differently.

READING AND REFLECTION

Compare Gal. 3:6–9, Rom. 4:1–25, and James 2:14–26. Of what is Abraham an example? What is the relationship between faith and works?

The points of contact and the striking points of contrast between Paul and James have led some interpreters to think that James was attacking Paul. And, if taken in an abstract or absolute sense, they do contradict each other. Paul argued that Abraham was put right with God through faith (hence, keeping the Law was unnecessary), but James responds that Abraham was put right with God by his works (thus, faith alone is inadequate). Both claim Abraham as the model of righteousness, but they draw opposite conclusions. How, then, shall we understand the relationship between these two?

First, we find that they appeal to different aspects of the Abraham tradition. For Paul, Abraham's trust in God led him to leave his homeland and to seek an heir from Sarah. For James, his sacrifice of Isaac perfected his faith by his works. Paul focused on the inaugurating events whereas James looked to climactic events. Because they are speaking in different contexts, we naturally expect them to say different things.

Second, although they use the same words, they seem to have different definitions for them. In fact, if we probe beneath the words, their meanings are very much alike. James equates faith with believing in God (2:19), but Paul understands faith to be a solid trust in God that influences the course of one's life. In other words, Paul includes in faith what James defines as faith and works. Both assert that only this life-changing response to God is adequate. Rather than attack Paul, James seems to be opposing someone who is using Paul's words with a different meaning than Paul attached to them.

Finally, however, we must not minimize the distance between James and Paul. The very fact that they emphasize different aspects of the Abraham story indicates that they themselves lived in different versions of the Jesus story. Paul stood on the boundary of Israel, reaching out to the Gentiles, inaugurating a new event as surely as did his model Abraham. James stood within the establishment, observing the ongoing life of the community. James belonged to those who were more impressed by the continuity of Jesus with the past work of God in Israel than with the novelty of including the Gentiles. Thus, James represents a more Jewish version of the emerging tradition.

The Context of James

Little can be said with certainty about the authorship or date of this moral tract. It could have been written by James or by someone who felt attached to his tradition, perhaps one of his disciples. Arguments are possible on both sides: The very good command of Greek that our author displays might point to a setting in the Hellenistic world outside Palestine (thus, to an author other than James), but the number of underlying Semitic expressions probably indicates a native Hebrew speaker. On the one hand, the opening address ("To the twelve tribes in the Dispersion," 1:1) indicates that the geographical sphere of the letter is the Hellenistic world, far beyond the influence of James in Jerusalem. Yet on the other, the assumption of this very

SARDIS SYNAGOGUE COURTYARD This magnificent synagogue was built in the early third century. This is a view of the courtyard with its central pool; the doorway on the far side led into the sanctuary.

address, its implied point of view, is that the writer is living in the homeland. The references to Jesus are so sparse and so general that it is hard to imagine this work was written by his brother, yet there are strong echoes of those teachings of Jesus now preserved in the Sermon on the Mount, widely regarded as his most characteristic ideas, for example:

5:1–6	Matt. 6:19–20
5:12	Matt. 5:33–37
1:22	Matt. 7:24
2:8	Matt. 5:43–44, 22:39
2:12	Matt. 7:1
3:18	Matt. 5:9

James seems to demand rigorous keeping of the Law, even every point of the Law (2:10); yet he defines the Law by the very paradigm used by Paul: love your neighbor as yourself (2:8; Rom. 13:8).

The date of the writing remains elusive. The crucial issue is, how does what is said here relate to Paul? The analysis above implies that James was directed not against Paul but against an oversimplification of Pauline tradition. But when did such an oversimplification arise? We know that some of Paul's followers in the late first century reduced the definition of faith to belief, which is the sort of faith that James finds inadequate. We saw this precise use of faith as a noun rather than as a verb in the Pauline trajectory that led to the Pastoral Letters, for example (page 198). This might mean James was written near the end of the first century, long after the death of the historical James in 62.

However, the rhetorical questions that Paul included in Romans (for example, 6:15) indicate that such oversimplification was possible in his lifetime, at least by his opponents. This might mean that James was directed against the same oversimplification of his teachings that Paul himself fought. If so, it is surprising that there is not even a mention of those aspects of the Law over which James and Paul struggled (circumcision and the dietary laws, Gal. 2:12). This omission probably, but not certainly, points to a controversy after the time of Paul and James. Although we can be sure of neither date nor authorship, two other kinds of considerations will help us locate the situation of the letter more accurately.

First, we can observe the kinds of advice given and ask who would need this sort of exhortation. We have already learned that a good deal of the letter has a Jewish cast. The work is so completely in the Jewish tradition that some argue that it was originally a Jewish tract, now rewritten to insert a few references to Jesus. It refers to Jesus only twice (1:1; 2:1). If we deleted these two references and changed one or two other words, this letter would be wholly Jewish. The major concerns, such as the doing of the Law and the protecting of the weak, are typical of Jewish ethical exhortation. In addition, the designation of the assembly as "synagogue" (the Greek word translated as "assembly" in 2:2 is *synagoge*, not the usual *ekklesia*), the appeal to "Abraham, our father" (2:21), and the appeals to the wisdom tradition (1:5; 3:13) point to a Jewish milieu. The primary office in the community seems to be teacher (3:1), and there is little evidence of hierarchical organization; in both ways it looks more like a synagogue than a church.

The advice given in the letter also indicates that the community contains both the poor and the very wealthy: merchants are admonished (4:13–17); the rich are chastised (5:1–11); and the gold ring (2:2) marks the visitor as a member of the Roman aristocracy who alone were permitted to wear such rings in this period. It is, then, a mixed community in which our author is trying to instill some of the ideal of poverty. Such exhortation seems most appropriate to a Jewish community of the diaspora that includes Gentiles.

Gentile influence may also be seen in the conviction that God gives wisdom "to all" people (1:5), the reference to God as the "Father of lights" (1:17), and the definition of faith as belief in God (2:19). Some refinement of this point may be achieved by a second strategy, comparing the advice given in James with another writing, known to be addressed to a Gentile audience.

There is an early second-century work known as the **Didache** (DID-uh-kay), or the *Teaching of the Twelve Apostles*. This essay is slightly longer than James and seems to have been used by the Syrian churches in the early second century. The first half is an ethical exhortation based on the Jewish wisdom tradition of two ways: a way of life and a way of death. The last half gives instructions for baptism, celebration of the Eucharist, and the role of prophets. The *Didache* shares much with James, including the summary of the Law as the two great commandments (James 2:8; *Did.* 1:2) and multiple allusions to the Jesus tradition (*Did.* 1:3–6). But the specific exhortations differ markedly: the *Didache* admonishes against sexual acts with young boys and condemns abortion and infanticide (2:2); it forbids eating meat offered to idols (6:3). These are specific ethical problems that Gentiles would bring to Christianity; they would not have been issues for Jews, who did not openly engage in these actions (because they were already forbidden). Thus, the *Didache* is addressed explicitly as "the teaching of the Lord to the nations [Gentiles] through the twelve apostles" (1:1).

None of this is characteristic of James. The community to which James is addressed probably included Gentiles, but Jews and Jewish ethics still predominated. Gentiles seem to have been incorporated into Israel, becoming a part of the twelve tribes of the diaspora (1:1). The Letter of James seems to represent a version of the Jesus story that was itself substantially Jewish. That there were such Jewish versions of Christianity, and that they were associated with the name of James, has become increasingly clear from recent research.

THE LETTER OF JUDE

Although the Greek text of this letter names the author as "Judas, the brother of Jacob," later tradition has regularly shortened the name to *Jude*, perhaps because of the infamy of that disciple named Judas who betrayed Jesus. *Judas* was a common name of this period, being the Greek form of the Hebrew *Judah*. We know nothing else about the author other than his claim to be the brother of Jacob (James), and thus by implication the brother of Jesus. Whether he was so related, or merely claiming that tradition, is disputed.

Jude, like James, is a letter only in a formal sense; actually it is more of an exhortation. Its address could hardly be more general: "to those who are called" (1:1). There may be some irony here, for among Gnostics the "called" were the common believers as opposed to the "elect" Gnostic few. Lacking all traits of an actual letter aside from this stylized address, Jude is a tract or sermon in letter form. It is a particularly fine example of a type of an ancient rhetorical exercise known as **invective**, the dark side of demonstrative rhetoric, the opposite of eulogy. As eulogy intends to praise the worthy, so invective seeks to damn the unworthy (Matthew 23 is a good example of invective).

Jude is a very short work, only one page, and its structure is straightforward.

 ### READING GUIDE TO JUDE

Letter opening   1–2
Purpose: to contend for the faith   3–4
Exposition of Scripture   5–19
Exhortation to faithfulness   20–23
Final blessing   24–25

READING AND REFLECTION

As you read Jude, notice all the forms of vilification used to attack those regarded as unworthy, usually called the heretics.

Our author uses three devices to discredit those believed to have abandoned apostolic faith; they range from simple name-calling (4, 11–12, 16, 19), to disparagement of their morality (4, 8, 10), to powerful comparisons with biblical and apocryphal villains (5, 6, 7, 9, 11, 15). The power of this condemnation stems from the vividness of the language and the tying together of the various techniques. Thus the "ungodly," who are said to be "licentious" and to "defile the flesh," are compared to "Sodom and Gomorrah" (4, 7, 8). The series of metaphors in verses 12 to 13 are powerful and provocative.

On the positive side, the hearers are exhorted to "contend for the faith which was once for all delivered to the saints" (3). Although this appears to be a cogent appeal, we must realize that we are given no clue as to what this faith was thought to be. Instead, it is a general appeal to "apostolic tradition" (17). Much the same can be said about the rejected tradition: we find only vague generalities. "They" are ungodly; "we" are apostolic. But the identity and the teachings of the *they* and the *we* are left undefined.

The social function of this kind of writing is not to define and expel the heretic but to unify the group and make deviance from the norm less likely. This writing probably stems from a group conscious of its own identity and of its differences from other groups. The references to preserving the apostolic tradition (3, 17) probably place them in the late first or early second century. The claim to the Jude tradition and the citation of noncanonical writings like *Enoch* (14) and the *Assumption of Moses* (9) place them within the framework of Jewish Jesus followers. These writings were especially popular with the marginal movements among Jews, such as those at Qumran.

Jude seems to represent a more sectarian spirit than James and gives no evidence of including Gentiles. As we will see, it has close ties with 2 Peter (page 241). Jude's audience lived in a rich story world that not only looked to the angels as examples but ascribed honors to them (8–9). They saw themselves as heirs to the Exodus (5), now awaiting their final deliverance. Their main task in the interim was to be holy (20–21). In this way too, they resembled the Jews of Qumran.

TRADITIONS OF HELLENIZED JEWS: HEBREWS

Though commonly known as the Letter to the Hebrews and often attributed to Paul, this work is neither Pauline nor is it a letter. It even departs from the form of a letter, at least until the very end, for it lacks a salutation and greeting. In concluding the writer declares, "I exhort you, brethren, bear with my word of exhortation, for I have written unto you briefly" (13:22). This is the same expression associated with the speech given after a reading from Scripture in the synagogue. Acts reports Paul being invited to give such a speech:

> *After the reading of the law and the prophets, the officials of the synagogue sent them a message, saying, "Brothers, if you have any word of exhortation for the people, give it." (Acts 13:15)*

A "word of exhortation" (a lecture, homily, or sermon stemming from some reading) is a more accurate description of this work than "letter," though the writer must have smiled a little when adding the "briefly." Containing some twenty-five pages of closely connected argument, this is a lengthy work by ancient standards.

THE STRUCTURE OF THE ARGUMENT

Hebrews is a good example of **deliberative rhetoric**, a style that attempts to prove a case and move the hearers to a specific course of future action. Deliberative oratory did not adhere to strict organization; all that was required was an introduction and a conclusion, between which a proposition was stated and proven.

READING AND REFLECTION

Read Hebrews 1–2 and 12–13. What seems to be the thesis of this work? What do you take to be the thrust of the argument?

The basic structure of Hebrews consists of a series of passages alternating between the explanation of an idea and the elaboration of the implications of that idea. It begins by contrasting the former and current revelations of God, then draws the implications: "Therefore we must pay greater attention" (2:1). This is the constant pattern: first an idea is discussed, then there is the exhortation on the implications of neglecting this idea. The diagram in Figure 7.1 shows the shape of the letter.

In effect, our writer has interwoven two presentations: a theoretical argument about the superiority of the new revelation (in Jesus) to the old (from Moses) and an exhortation to greater moral accomplishment based on this claimed superiority. The ideas lead to the implications, and the implications in turn lead on to new ideas that have further implications. The underlying logic is what we call **a fortiori**: if the lesser is true, then how much more true is the greater. (To put it another way: if your dad was unhappy when you broke his lawnmower, how much more unhappy will he be when you wreck the car.) In Hebrews, the argument that the new way is superior to the old has implications that require *more* of the followers of that new way. The continual interaction between these two aspects of the argument, the superiority of the new way and the increased responsibility, gives the work a dynamic quality and an apparent complexity. The interaction is so pervasive that it is not always possible to be sure when the author passes from idea to implication, but the scheme reflected in the reading guide is widely adopted. As always, don't take the divisions too literally.

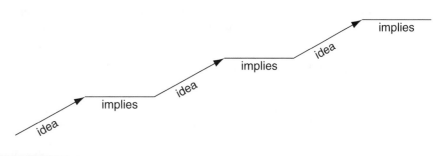

FIGURE 7.1 THE BASIC STRUCTURE OF HEBREWS

The revelation of a Son is superior to that through angels or prophets   1:1–14
　　Exhortation: pay more attention   2:1–4
As human, Jesus is superior not only to angels but also to Moses   2:5–3:5
　　Exhortation: do not miss the promised rest   3:6–4:13
Jesus the Son of God is the great high priest   4:14–5:11
　　Exhortation: go beyond the elementary   5:12–6:20
Jesus is high priest in the superior order of Melchizedek   7:1–10:18
　　Exhortation: draw near to God   10:19–39
The witnesses of faith   11:1–40
　　Exhortation: strive for holiness   12:1–10
　　Miscellaneous exhortations   12:11–13:21
　　Final exhortations in letter form   13:22–25

The major portion of the argument centers on Jesus as high priest (4:14–10:39), a startling idea. No other New Testament document calls Jesus a high priest, though certain priestly themes are associated with him (such as atoning for sins). In fact, the widespread tradition that Jesus is a descendant of David (of the tribe of Judah) would seem to preclude any priestly service, because priests had to be from the tribe of Levi (see 7:14). We will examine this priestly tradition more closely further on.

Preceding this major treatment of Jesus as high priest is a short section arguing the superiority of Jesus to earlier mediators: the angels, the prophets, and Moses (chapters 1 and 2, with the accompanying exhortation). Following the major argument, another short section portrays the great faith of the heroes of the earlier traditions (11, with the accompanying exhortations). Rhetorically, these constitute the introduction and the conclusion to the main argument. In Hebrews the main argument (4–10) concerns the establishment of Jesus' priestly service and the implications of that service for life and worship. Both the introduction and the conclusion center on the superiority of Jesus over the earlier heroes, and therefore the greater responsibility of those who would follow him (a fortiori). The priestly theme is introduced at 2:17 and culminates at 13:10–16. The basic line of the argument is given in the following verses, which provide a kind of synopsis of the book: 1:1–4; 2:1; 3:1; 4:14; 5:7; 6:1–6; 8:1–2; 9:6–11, 15; 10:19–25; 12:1–2; 12:18–29.

This argument may appear very strange to us, for it rests on ideas and a worldview not common today. We will be able to appreciate Hebrews more fully if we review briefly three other Jewish movements that share something of the same context. It is not necessary to think that the author of Hebrews was closely related to one of these groups, only that they shared a common world.

IMAGINING CONTEXTS

"To the Hebrews" occurs as a title on the earliest manuscripts we possess but is not a part of the text. It would have been added when this work was included with others in a collection. It rests, in part, on the way the work identifies with Jews (1:1; 2:11, 16, and so on). No author is indicated, nor can one be deduced. Some of the more interesting suggestions, in addition to Paul, include Barnabas, Apollos, and Priscilla—all are mere guesses. Although it was once attributed to Paul, it has nothing in common with the Pauline letters except an incidental reference to Timothy in the closing. That closing also contains the only geographical reference in the work: "They of Italy salute you" (13:24). This could mean the writing was sent from Italy, or it might only indicate people of Italian origin living elsewhere.

The only temporal reference in the work might imply that the priests still minister at the altar in Jerusalem (8:4). If taken literally, this might require a date before 70 CE, when the Jerusalem Temple was destroyed by the Romans. But perhaps we should not understand it this way, for our author never refers to the Temple but only to the tent or tabernacle, the portable shrine of the pre-Temple period in Israel. It is also possible that some priests continued to minister in the ruins of the Temple until it was utterly destroyed in 135. In fact, many Jewish and Christian writers write as if the Temple were still operating long after it was destroyed. The case against an early date is that the leaders of the community claim apostolic descent and belong to the next generation (2:3).

The internal evidence for establishing the setting of Hebrews is scant. The best we can do is hazard a guess based on the general nature of the work and on our knowledge of similar works. Three possibilities have emerged, and each contributes something to our understanding of Hebrews.

THE ALEXANDRIAN JEWISH TRADITION OF PHILO

Alexandria, in Egypt, was one of a hundred cities that Alexander the Great had founded and named in his own honor when he conquered the world from Greece to India shortly before 300 BCE. But it became *the* Alexandria, the intellectual and cultural capital of the Greco-Roman world. The library there surpassed all others, not only collecting but editing the texts of the classical authors and producing the first known critical editions, attempting to resolve conflicts between copies and to discover the most likely original reading. It was a spectacular city—its main east-west street was one hundred feet wide. Population figures are hard to come by, but it is estimated that one to two million people lived there in the first century. There were three main social groups: the Greeks, the native Egyptians, and the Jews. By the first century CE the upper classes in these separate communities had begun to intermarry. The Jews had the right to self-rule and constituted the largest concentration of Jews outside Palestine. This community translated the Hebrew Scriptures into Greek in the version known as the Septuagint (between 300 and 150 BCE). (For a first-century description of Alexandria see Strabo's *Geography* 17.)

From this community we know, especially, one person: **Philo of Alexandria** (about 20 BCE–45 CE). Born into a wealthy family, he received a thorough education in both Greek and Jewish culture, though he never learned Hebrew. Philo's immense scholarship (more than thirty-five of his works have come down to us) was built on one central assumption: Jewish tradition was a more perfect form of Greek philosophy. Both older and more precise than the philosophers, the Law contained all their central ideas. For example, philosophy taught the control of the passions through reason. So too did Moses, according to Philo, in the story of creation. For God first presented Adam with the animals (emotions) but found no suitable helper among them. Only the special creation of Eve (reason) produced a companion worthy of human creation (Gen. 2:15–24). Philo relied heavily on such allegorical interpretations of Scripture, always exploring what was taught by the philosophers, especially the

SHOPS ALONG SARDIS SYNAGOGUE WALL   These small shops, each about 12 to 15 feet square, were built along the outer wall of the synagogue. Immediately adjacent to the synagogue on the other side was a gymnasium, the basic educational institution of the Greek culture. It reminds us of how well integrated some Jews were into the larger society of the Greco-Roman cities.

Stoics. It was Philo's conviction that everything in Scripture had a symbolic meaning. Thus the Sabbath rest pointed to God, the unmoved mover; feast days symbolized gladness of the soul; circumcision portrayed the cutting off of excess pleasure and passions (*On the Migration of Abraham* 91–92).

Symbolic meanings are everywhere because this world itself is a reflection of the eternal. Following Plato, Philo viewed the world as a copy of the eternal forms (see Plato *Republic* Book 7). The tabernacle was a perfect example of the way this world is a copy of the divine:

> *When God willed to send down the image of divine excellence from heaven to earth in pity for our race, that it should not lose its share in the better lot, he constructs as a symbol of the truth the holy tabernacle and its contents to be a representation and copy of wisdom. (*Who Is the Heir of Divine Things? *112)*

Thus by studying the copy one could learn about the reality, for they correspond.

Philo went even further. He saw in the creation story and its declaration that God created humankind "after his image" not only a correspondence between divine and human wisdom but the existence of an independent heavenly wisdom that was itself the image of God (*Who Is the Heir?* 230–31). This divine image, the pattern from which humanity was made, Philo called the *logos*, a term the Stoics used for reason. This logos stands on the boundary between God and creation, revealing the One to the many and "pleading with the immortal as suppliant for afflicted mortality" (*Who Is the Heir?* 205). (See the discussion of logos on pages 400–404.)

This conception of the world as a reflection of the heavenly reality, as well as this vision of the heavenly mediator, helps clarify the meaning of Hebrews (see especially Hebrews 8).

THE ASCETIC JEWISH TRADITION OF THE ESSENES

A general introduction to the **Essenes** accompanied our discussion of the various Jewish movements of the first century (pages 169–73, 337–38). Two facets of the movement stand out in relation to Hebrews: their priestly nature and their strong asceticism. The Essene faction emerged from a struggle for the office of high priest. When the **Maccabees** were fighting against the religious suppression of **Antiochus Epiphanes** (shortly before 150 BCE), they were joined by many pious Jews who saw this as a struggle of light against darkness. But when the Maccabees eventually prevailed, they gravely disappointed many of their followers. For instead of purifying the temple and reappointing the legitimate high priest, who traditionally had to be a descendant of Zadok, they assumed that office themselves. In the view of some, this completed the defiling of the temple begun by Antiochus.

The historical sequence is vague, but many of these protesters seem to have retreated to Qumran, an ascetic community in the hills around the Dead Sea. At Qumran they established their version of the true Israel and the true temple, their community. Their spiritual worship and common meal became the true sacrifice. Within their community, the zadokite high priest ruled, and at the end of the age they expected both the princely messiah of common tradition and a second, priestly messiah (*Community Rule* 9 and the *Messianic Rule*). The priestly messiah was to be the teacher of the community, even as the living priest was the current teacher.

This understanding of the community as the temple resulted in a strong emphasis on purity, both ritual and moral. Because women were considered ritually unclean during their monthly menstruation cycles, their role in this community was severely limited; some have even wondered if they were permitted in the community at Qumran (though the cemetery there does contain females). In a striking departure from Jewish practice, the men at Qumran were celibate. (Other Essenes married, causing some to wonder whether the Qumran group was a different movement altogether.) They swore obedience to their superiors, all who had entered the order before them, and organized their day around work and worship so that some members of the community were always at prayer, day and night. They pledged themselves to keep the whole Law, as it was interpreted and expanded by the teacher of righteousness. Their interpretation of Scripture was literal and imaginative. They applied the laws directly to their own situation but also engaged in highly symbolic interpretation to show that the Scriptures were fulfilled in the experience of their own community. They believed they lived in the time of fulfillment and that God had established with them the new covenant prophesied by Jeremiah (Jeremiah 31; see *Community Rule* 1, 5). Their goal was nothing less than perfection, both individual and communal.

Like the Essenes, the community behind Hebrews believed themselves to be the true Israel, who served God with purity and true sacrifice (see especially Hebrews 13).

The Esoteric Jewish Tradition of the Mystics

The prevailing forms of Judaism and Christianity have been essentially rationalistic, and only scant attention has been paid to their more mystical aspects. This is especially true of Judaism, the tendency being abetted by the common Christian misconception of Judaism as a legalistic religion. More recently, especially because of the pioneering work of Gershom Scholem, it has become evident that there was a mystical strand even among the rabbis. This mysticism centered on the vision of God, or of the throne or chariot of God, in which the mystic felt transported into paradise.

Many surviving Jewish writings show traces of such mysticism. Enoch describes the ascent into heaven in mystic imagery of fire and ice (*1 Enoch* 14). The *Apocalypse of Abraham*, probably written about the same time as Hebrews, portrays Abraham's ascent to heaven, where he sees the throne of God, a throne of fire, and the chariot of God. He attains this vision through worship and the repeated recitation of a heavenly song, taught him by an angel (15–18):

> *You are he my soul has loved, my protector. Eternal, fiery, shining, light-giving, thunder-voiced, lightning-visioned, many eyed, receiving the petitions of those who honor you and turning away from the petitions of those who restrain you by the restraint of their provocations, redeemer of those who dwell in the midst of the wicked ones, of those who are dispersed among the just of the world, in the corruptible age. (Apocalypse of Abraham 17:14–17)*

The goal of this sort of mysticism was to ascend through the various (usually seven) heavens by means of mystical experiences, so that one eventually beheld the exalted throne of God (compare 2 Cor. 12:1–4 and Revelation 4).

So too, the hearers of Hebrews were admonished to go beyond the elementary (6:1–8), to ascend to the throne of grace (4:16), and to worship at the Heavenly Jerusalem, the true Mount Zion (12:18–29). With these three contexts in mind, let us examine the meaning of Hebrews in more detail.

Understanding Hebrews

The general meaning of Hebrews centers on the superiority of Christ, the Son, to the various messengers of God. But the specific meaning of this theme for its first hearers demands closer examination. We will examine two important, but somewhat varied, passages in order to illustrate the various ways Hebrews corresponds to these contexts. The first selection, the opening, is replete with technical words; the second, chapter 9, presents us with a clear portrayal of the worldview that underlies this writing.

The Opening

The following translation attempts to capture something of the structure and meaning of this passage.

> *In many parts and in many ways*
> *having spoken long ago to the ancestors by the prophets,*

> *God spoke in the last of these days to us by a son,*
> *whom he appointed heir of all things,*
> *through whom also he made the spheres who*
> *because he is the brightness of his glory*
> *and the imprint of his being,*
> *because he upholds all things in his powerful word,*
> *because he made himself a purification of sins,*
> *sat down on the right hand of the Majesty on High,*
> *having become so much superior to angels*
> *by as much as he has inherited a more excellent name than they.*
> *(Heb. 1:1–4, original translation)*

This is a marvelous example of the kind of sentence favored by an educated Greek audience: complex, balanced, protracted. The basic point is made by the subject and verb in line three: God spoke. The contrast between his former speaking (partial and piecemeal) and his latter speaking is evident. The son is then described by three relative clauses (whom, through whom, who) each of which employs a vocabulary remarkably reminiscent of Philo of Alexandria. He is said to be the heir, maker of the spheres, the brightness and the imprint of the divine—all terms characteristic of Philo. The heir may be understood in both messianic terms (Ps. 2:8) and wisdom terms (Prov. 3:35), which Philo developed by proclaiming wisdom to be the heir of the world and of all things (*Who Is the Heir?* 98; see also *On the Change of Names* 267, and *On Noah's Work as a Planter* 50).

Whereas Philo relates wisdom and logos, our author does not. In places where he might speak of the "logos of God" (1:3, 6:5, 11:3), he chooses a synonym and speaks of the "*rhema* of God." This might indicate lack of contact with the Philonic tradition, or it might represent a deliberate disagreement. In a key passage describing the logos, Philo places it among the angels:

> *If there be any as yet unfit to be called a Son of God, let him press to take his place under God's First-Born, the Word [logos], who holds the eldership among the angels, their ruler as it were.* (On the Confusion of Tongues 146)

But for our author, that one is far more than the first of the angels:

> *Having become so much superior to angels as he has inherited a more excellent name than they.* (Heb. 1:4)

Whereas Philo saw the logos as the chief of God's angelic creatures, our author painstakingly shows that the Son is superior to all angels.

Whoever composed this opening sentence of Hebrews was surely familiar with the popular Hellenistic philosophy, especially Stoicism and Platonism, which we see clearly reflected in Philo of Alexandria. Such familiarity can be demonstrated at many points in Hebrews. It can also be shown that the Septuagint, that Greek translation native to Alexandria, is the version of the Scriptures that is regularly quoted (for example, 2:7 quotes the Septuagint version of Ps. 8:5; the Hebrew is different). This does not mean our author depended on, or even knew of, Philo. But it does show that they lived in similar contexts.

The Priest

Hebrews represents both a radical reinterpretation of Jesus and a reinterpretation of the meaning of the priestly service. On the one hand, Christ is understood essentially as the high priest (rather than as the savior, Lord, servant, or Messiah of other traditions); yet the whole meaning of the priestly service is revised and interpreted so that it becomes a model for Jesus' life and death.

This passage describes the ministry of Christ in the true heavenly sanctuary, of which the earthly one was but a copy. Like Philo, our author considers the earthly tabernacle a copy of the heavenly original. But he goes far beyond Philo with an extensive analogy between the services of the two.

Just as Moses had sanctified the earlier sanctuary with the words "This is the blood of the covenant" so Christ shed his blood to form a new covenant (9:20, 15). More radical than Philo, our author declares that the new makes the old obsolete (8:13). Curiously, Philo had used the same observation of the correspondence between the earthly copy and the heavenly original to establish the opposite point, the validity of keeping the Law: keep the Law because it corresponds to ultimate reality.

In the ways that our author is more radical than Philo, this writing seems to share much with those from Qumran. They too believed that a new covenant had been given, making the old obsolete. They too believed that the actual service of priests in the sanctuary was inferior to the spiritual service of the community, a service of entering into the presence of God with the sacrifice of praise and obedience. If we add to this the shared concerns with angels, the contrast between the novice and the mature (5:12–6:2), the sense of Scripture as really applying to their history (for example, 3:5–6), the strong moral tone and the even stronger appeal to ascetic practice (7:26; 10:26–27), we get a strong sense of the affinity between Hebrews and Qumran. Even Melchizedek, an obscure figure in writings of this era, is known to have been a center of speculation at Qumran. In the *Melchizedek Scroll* he is portrayed as one who would proclaim release to the captives and atonement for their sins in the final year of release, known as a jubilee year. Many would turn to this context of sectarian and ascetic Jewish tradition for the proper context within which to interpret Hebrews.

The Entering

In addition to these specific parallels to Qumran, Hebrews shares much with the more general traditions of Jewish mysticism, especially in the exhortation sections. The hearer is admonished to be bold enough to enter the holy place (10:19). As Jesus has "passed through the heavens," so must the hearers (4:14–16). They enter the heavenly Jerusalem and worship with angels (12:22). Perfection is possible (6:1). If we try to translate the general admonitions of Hebrews into concrete practice, the picture emerges of a community intensely dedicated to prayer and holy living (see especially 13:1–17).

Conclusions

Our knowledge of this entire period is limited, and our information about minor movements is scant. The community behind Hebrews seems to share the most with the community behind the Dead Sea Scrolls, but that may be only because we know more about that community than any other. The similarities with Philo, the mystical implications, and the vague Platonism all point to a complex community of Hellenized Jews who interpreted Jesus in the light of ideas and aspirations evident in these contexts. It is more likely that these factors were widely shared than that Hebrews should be related directly to one group or the other. Hebrews seems to represent a kind of Jewish interpretation of Jesus quite at ease in the Hellenistic world. In this way the story of Hebrews is nearly the opposite of the story of the Apocalypse, and one suspects our author would have been much more comfortable with the woman John calls Jezebel than with John, for she too was open to Greco-Roman culture (see pages 450–51). Hebrews seeks a third way, following neither the Law-free gospel of many of Paul's heirs nor the Law-observant gospel of the James traditions. It demands serious moral striving while rejecting a direct reliance on the Law.

One final point: Hebrews stands at the beginning of a trajectory of anti-Judaism, viewing Judaism as an inadequate religion. Although Philo could argue that because the tabernacle was a copy of the heavenly reality, you could know the heavenly by studying the earthly, Platonists generally regarded the copy as deceptive. Thus, if the Temple and the Law are only "shadows" (8:5; 10:1), they are not inferior truths: they are not truth at all. It will be only a short step to see Judaism as a false religion. This step is already taken in a second-century work called the *Letter of Barnabas* (written about 130 and part of *Apostolic Fathers*, the text is available in Sparks, 1978). Like Hebrews, *Barnabas* sees all the stories of the Scriptures as symbolically referring to Jesus (especially chapters 10–16). God's covenant with Israel is ended (4:6; 14:1–4). Christians have replaced Jews in God's favor (14:1–4). It will be only another short step to anti-Semitism and the long history of Christian persecution of Jews.

TRADITIONS ASSOCIATED WITH PETER

We have encountered Peter many times in our study of other traditions. The earliest references to Peter are in the letters of Paul, in which he is regarded as a leader of the Jerusalem church whom Paul took special pains to get to know (Gal. 1:18); as someone opposed by Paul for his waffling stance on Jewish-Gentile relations (Gal. 2:11); and as the apostle to the Jews (Gal. 2:7). The author of Acts claims him for the Pauline school by portraying him as the predecessor of Paul and even as the originator of the mission to the Gentiles (Acts, especially 10–15). All the Gospels portray him as the leader of the disciples, though they also show him opposed to Jesus and denying him. Much of Mark's portrayal shows him faltering and uncomprehending. The tradition in John seems to consciously compare him to the unnamed "beloved disciple," to Peter's consistent disadvantage (for example, see John 13:23–24; for more details, see pages 418–19).

We have seen that in some Jewish-Christian traditions Peter is portrayed as the true apostle opposed to Paul "the man who is my enemy" (pages 208–11). In later traditions, Peter is claimed as the founder of the church at Rome, where Constantine (in the fourth century) built St. Peter's Basilica, presumably over his tomb. The tradition of his death during Nero's persecution and his burial in Vatican Hill may be traced back to the late second century, though there are earlier allusions that may support the tradition. The earliest of these comes from *1 Clement* (about 95 CE) implying that both Paul and Peter died in Rome (5:4).

As we might expect, numerous writings evolved around Peter. The *Acts of Peter* was written in the late second century and reports a miracle contest between Peter and "Simon Magus" and concludes with the story of Peter's death. In addition to the *Acts of Peter*, six other writings come down to us in the name of Peter: only two have been accepted into the canon, despite strong support for a third for a long time. We have already looked at the *Letter of Peter to James* (page 210). There also survives fragments of a work called the *Preachings of Peter* that, like the *Letter*, is a second-century document from a community with a strong Jewish orientation. There is also a *Gospel of Peter*, of which we possess only a section dealing with the death and resurrection of Jesus. This story represents a pious elaboration of the accounts of the four canonical Gospels. The Jews are treated rather poorly, and the point of view is that of a Gentile (for example, the writer limits the Law to "them" at paragraph 5). It was probably written in the early second century by followers of Peter. Late in the second century it seems to have been connected with Gnostics, but the fragment we have lacks Gnostic traits.

The *Apocalypse of Peter* was very popular for several centuries and a strong candidate for inclusion in the canon. The Muratorian Fragment accepted it but with the warning that some opposed it (see pages 475–76). It exists today only in an Ethiopic translation, a partial translation in another language, and a couple of Greek fragments. A major portion of the work consists of a vision of the damned built on the framework of the apocalyptic discourse in the synoptic Gospels (Mark 13 and parallels) and a vision of the blessed based on the transfiguration story (Mark 9 and parallels). These fanciful and sometimes grotesque scenes are designed to reinforce piety: blasphemers are hanged by their tongues, women who seduce by their braided hair, men by their thighs; those who have had abortions or exposed their children stand in a horrifying pit and see their children happily playing in a place of delight; special tortures are described for those who did not honor their parents, those who engaged in premarital sex, and for disobedient slaves. There is no concern with the historical future or with the coming of Jesus, as we might expect in an apocalypse. This devotional work was probably composed in the early second century.

Finally, there are the two Letters of Peter in the New Testament. Neither was included in the Muratorian Fragment, and Eusebius reports that 1 Peter was accepted in his day but 2 Peter was still disputed. The two works present somewhat different views of Peter.

PETER AS THE EXHORTING ELDER: 1 PETER

This short letter is written to "the exiles of the dispersion" in the provinces of Asia Minor, which overlapped the area in which Paul worked. This address is very general, raising the question of whether it is a letter at all. Many other aspects of the work are also disputed, including authorship, date, and purpose. The only available evidence must come from the letter itself, because we have no other writings indisputably from Peter. External evidence is of little help. The letter was not cited by name until the late second century, although Polycarp seems to quote it without naming it in his *Letter to the Philippians* (about 135).

First Peter is a practical letter, concerned with proper action in worship and in everyday behavior.

1. What aspects of worship are discussed?
2. How many times are terms like *revelation* or *revealed* used? Through what does such revelation come?
3. Make a list of the kinds of behavior encouraged.
4. To what social classes is the letter addressed?

READING GUIDE TO FIRST PETER

Salutation   1:1–2
Blessing on the newly born   1:3–9
The premise: salvation revealed through the prophets   1:10–12
The consequences: exhortations   1:13–5:11
   To a new lifestyle   1:13–2:10
   Advice to aliens: good conduct   2:11–17
   Duties of the household   2:18–3:12
      Servants   2:18–25
      Wives   3:1–6
      Husbands   3:7
      All   3:8–12
   Duty to suffer: Christ's example   3:13–4:19
      Suffer as Christ did   3:13–20
      Baptism   3:21–22
      General moral actions   4:1–11
      The present suffering   4:12–19
Closing personal section   5:1–14
   Elders to tend the flock   5:1–11
   Personal greetings   5:12–14

The Genre

"I have written briefly to you, exhorting and declaring that this is the true grace of God; stand fast in it" (5:12). So our author accurately describes his work. It is essentially a message of exhortation to patience, morality, and endurance in a time of persecution. Most of the letter seems quite conscious of the new status of the hearers (for example, 1:2–4, 14, 18, 22; 2:10; 3:21; 4:3). They have recently passed from the licentiousness of the Gentiles into the way of Christ. The means of their passing was baptism (3:21).

We do not know much about the liturgical rites of the early Jesus movement, which probably varied a great deal from place to place. However, an interesting story in Acts 8:14–25 recounts that the Samaritans had received the word and the baptism of Jesus. Then the Jerusalem authorities sent Peter and John to confirm their conversion, pray for them, and lay hands on them that they might receive the Holy Spirit. If this practice of baptism being followed by an apostolic confirmation represents a conviction of early Christianity, we have clear evidence of the genre of this work. For it seems to be an apostolic sermon confirming the newly baptized in their faith and admonishing them to moral behavior in the face of opposition. Much of the imagery of the letter makes sense within this context.

Baptism, Revelation, and Braided Hair

The imagery of 1 Peter is vivid and diverse, but overwhelmingly it portrays rebirth. Much of it is drawn directly from the ritual of baptism itself: new birth, resurrection, purification, and washing (1:3, 22, 23; 2:24; 3:21). Baptism is identified with the death and resurrection of Jesus (as in Romans 6) and thus is an event of revelation. This revelation both looks back at the death of Christ (1:18–21) and forward to the final revelation (*apocalypsis* in Greek) of Christ (1:7, 13). Both the past and present revelations exist in the baptismal rite; worship experience refuses to be bound by time, as we will see in our study of the Apocalypse of John (pages 465–66).

This understanding of ritual as revelation was widely shared in the Hellenistic world, finding its most dramatic representation in the mystery religions. Each mystery had its own central act of initiation, ranging from the viewing of the grain in Demeter's rites, to the wine of Dionysus, to the killing of a bull in Mithraism. These were life-changing events. One of our clearest presentations of the mysteries comes from a comic novel by Apuleius, the *Metamorphoses*, better known as *The Golden Ass*. It is the story of how a young dandy named Lucius makes an ass of himself, quite literally, in the pursuit of beautiful women and magic. Thus tragically transformed, he is forced to wander the world bearing other men's burdens, done in by fate. At the climax of the novel he returns to his human form as a result of his devotion to Isis, into whose mysteries he proceeds to be initiated. The process is complicated. Considerable time elapses, as he devotes himself to worship and to study. He is told that only the Goddess can select the time of initiation:

> The act of initiation had been compared to a voluntary death with a slight chance of redemption. Therefore the divine will of the Goddess was wont to choose men who had lived their life to the full, who were coming near the limits of waning light, and who yet could be safely trusted with the mighty secrets of her religion. These men by her divine providence she regenerated and restored to strength sufficient for their new careers. (11:21; Lindsay, 1962: 247)

The initiation of Lucius consisted of a ritual bath, worship in the temple of Isis, secret instruction, a ten-day fast from meat and wine, vows, and a nighttime ritual that all were forbidden to reveal but that is described as visiting heaven and hell, followed by a morning revelation of the initiate to the congregation. He is dressed as the sun, carrying a torch and wearing a wreath of palm leaves on his head. He describes the ensuing celebration "as if it were a birthday." (See the discussion of religion in Chapter 1, pages 42–45.)

We do not know whether early baptismal rites were equally dramatic. But we do know that baptism re-presented the death and resurrection of Jesus, required serious moral preparation, resulted in a new birth, and demanded a transformed manner of life from the initiate. All this is evident from 1 Peter.

The moral instruction of 1 Peter takes a form we have met in the writings of the Pauline schools, the household code. The household here includes slaves (2:18), wives (3:1), husbands (3:7), "all of you" (3:8). Later the author exhorts the elders (5:1), but this is a community, not a household, category. The instructions given are remarkable only for their conformity to the norms of the Greco-Roman world. They contain nothing radical and nothing specifically Christian. Slaves are to be submissive and suffer patiently (even if their master is crooked); wives are to be submissive to their unbelieving spouses and not braid their hair or adorn themselves; husbands are to be considerate of their wives; all are to have unity and love and are not to retaliate. These are the same virtues that a Stoic letter or an Isis exhortation would have extolled, only here the death of Jesus provides the model: he suffered quietly (2:21).

The Theme of Suffering

The connection between suffering and the rite that commemorates Jesus' death and resurrection is perhaps automatic. Much of the talk about suffering in 1 Peter is of this rather expected sort. Yet near the end, the tone seems to change, and the exhortation takes on a certain urgency. This change seems to occur at 4:12: "Beloved, do not be surprised at the fiery ordeal which comes upon you to prove you, as though something strange were happening to you." The present tense implies that this is a current experience of these communities. It is also described as religious persecution, not simply the general suffering that comes to all. It comes "for the name of Christ" and one is to "suffer as a Christian" (4:14, 16). Moreover it is an active persecution, for the adversary is said to prowl like a roaming lion "seeking someone to devour" (5:8). Unfortunately, the letter does not indicate who this adversary is (other than the Devil) or what form it has taken. Is it possible for us to reconstruct the social situation of the time?

The Social Implications

Some things we know. The setting is in the Jesus communities of Roman Asia Minor, all except those on the Mediterranean coast. These northern provinces were less permeated by Hellenistic culture than the coastal cities that had occupied most of Paul's attention. Resentment against Roman rule ran strong in these provinces. Roman conquest had brought with it a certain prosperity, but it was largely limited to the upper class: the rich became richer, and the poor became more hostile to the status quo. This hostility of the lower classes created an unstable political environment on Rome's eastern frontier. (For more details see the discussion of the setting of the Apocalypse, pages 458–64.)

We may also be reasonably certain that the hearers of this letter were from the lower classes. Slaves are admonished but not masters. There are no exhortations to the rich, as we found in James. They are addressed as exiles (1:1) and aliens (2:11), indicating people who, though free, lacked citizenship and thus had marginal social status. The strong theme of submission implies a specific problem: the conversion of parts of a household, especially the women and slaves. A household was supposed to manifest harmony and to worship at a common altar. As Gentiles now affiliated with this new religion, their social situation probably deteriorated further (4:4). (Review the discussion of class and status in Chapter 1 pages 32–35.)

Surprisingly, there is no hint of disaffection with Rome in the letter. Just the opposite occurs: the hearers are admonished to be subject to the emperor and the governor (2:13). Admittedly, this implies some need to so exhort. Some probably were not in subjection. Nevertheless, there is no expressed hostility toward Rome such as we find in the Apocalypse (which was also addressed to Asia Minor but only to the western and southern cities). If the "Babylon" of the closing (5:13) refers to Rome, as scholars generally assume, we may detect some underlying hostility. For the name associates Rome with that first destroyer of Israel. But we might also expect a more positive attitude toward Rome in a letter written from the capital.

The Author

This is the only Petrine work actually attributed to Peter by any substantial number of scholars. They relate it to the tradition that Peter traveled to Rome in the early sixties and died there during Nero's persecution (64–68 CE). Often they consider the last chapter and a half an addition based on the Neronian persecution. According to this hypothesis Peter would have written a general baptismal exhortation, which either he or one of his followers then composed as a letter by adding the more specific admonitions about suffering, then the entire work was sent to the Asia Minor churches. We know nothing else about the connection between Peter and these churches.

One problem with this view is the lack of evidence that Nero's persecution extended to the provinces. It seems to have been limited to Rome. It could be argued, of course, that with persecution of Jesus' followers as the official policy in the capital, their situation would have deteriorated in the provinces even without official Roman persecution. Peter may also have assumed that it would spread there, since he would not have known that Nero would shortly lose the emperorship.

Another problem is the excellent Greek style of our author. This is highly polished language with many constructions of a literary style (as opposed to the common style of spoken Greek). Yet Peter was a Galilean fisherman who, reportedly, could not even speak Aramaic without a northern accent (Matt. 26:73). He is described in another source as "uneducated" (Acts 4:13), an expression that actually means illiterate. That, of course, would have been more than thirty years earlier, but it is unlikely that such a man would have developed a fine Greek style so late in life. We would have to imagine that he used a very good scribe.

Those scholars who doubt that Peter actually wrote the letter point to a number of factors that seem to connect it with the late first century. Most notably, the letter seems to depend on some of the Pauline letters for its teaching. The advice on government (2:14–17), for example, seems based on Paul's teaching (Rom. 13:1–7). Strong echoes of Paul may also be heard in 1:18–19; 2:24; 3:16; 5:10, 14. The converse of this argument is that the letter reveals so little of Jesus; we expect more from the original disciple. Also, the teaching on female submission, the concern to live lives that outsiders will admire, the self-conscious reference to the community as "Christian" (4:16), and the development of the church as an institution all seem more in harmony with the late first century than with the time of Peter (see discussion, pages 211–12). Though Peter does not claim the authority of a bishop (5:1), he clearly acts like one. There is a paid clergy (5:2), and they can claim an absolute power, though our author urges them not to do so (5:3). The intellectual justification for hierarchy is already in place: Jesus as the chief shepherd with each pastor as an underling (5:4). All these factors connect it to the late first century.

The issue of authorship may be clarified by a curious statement at 5:12, "By Silvanus, a faithful brother as I regard him, I have written briefly to you." This expression is vague; it could mean anything from Silvanus having written (composed) the letter for Peter, to his acting as a scribe, to his serving as the messenger to deliver it. Whether this Silvanus was the same one who traveled with Paul (1 Thess. 1:1) remains a conjecture, but it would account for the strong orientation to Paul's thought. Also, the final greeting adds Mark and "she who is at Babylon" (5:13) to the letter and may point to the existence of a Petrine group at Rome.

It seems best, then, to consider 1 Peter as derived from Peter through this group. One possibility is that the source of much of the first four chapters was a contemporary Petrine baptismal exhortation, a kind of confirmation sermon. When real persecution developed against the Christians of Asia Minor, this general exhortation may have been expanded with the additional material beginning at 4:12 to produce the unified letter we now have. That the letter is a unified composition is indicated by the device of inclusion: compare 1:6–7 with 5:10 and with 4:12–13. We are unable to date it precisely because we know little about the actual situation in Asia Minor. As we note in our study of the Apocalypse (pages 462–64), Pliny found persecution in progress when he arrived there in 111. Some would relate 1 Peter to this event. This is probably the latest likely date; the earliest is perhaps around 75 (if it were written by an immediate associate of Peter).

PETER AS THE APOCALYPTIC PROPHET: 2 PETER

The Second Letter of Peter in the New Testament is quite unlike the First. It is too abrasive for modern sensibilities, too combative, too self-righteous, too gloomy in its detailing of the end of the world for our tastes. It is also a much-neglected letter. Yet this is all the more reason to study it, for it will help us to see more clearly the contours of the world it shapes and of our modern world. In addition, 2 Peter is a mediating work, on the boundary between the Jewish milieu of James and, especially, Jude and the Gentile traditions of Paul.

This work contains numerous correlations with Jude—too many to be coincidental. Consider these parallels:

2 Peter		Jude
1:2	Greeting	2
1:5	Need to write	3
1:12	Remind, though know	5
2:1–3:3	Extensive parallels	5b–19
3:14	Without blemish	24

(Adapted from Reicke, 1964:189; see also Sidebottom, 1967:65–67)

The extensive parallels in 2 Peter 2, particularly, demand some explanation. Either Peter used Jude as a source, or vice versa, or both used a common source. Whichever way the dependence worked (and scholars generally favor the dependence of 2 Peter on Jude), we may draw two inferences: First, the works have very different concerns. Jude shows no interest in the Parousia (central to 2 Peter; see 1:16); 2 Peter avoids the use of noncanonical Jewish writings so prevalent in Jude (omitting the citation of *1 Enoch* and the nonbiblical traditions concerning Michael, Cain, and Korah). Second, this creative use of previously existing tradition was a hallmark of writers in antiquity, demonstrating clearly that the claim to authorship was not a claim about the origin of the material.

On the Pauline side, we find something equally significant: our author cites Paul as Scripture.

So also our beloved brother Paul wrote to you. . . . There are some things in [his letters] hard to understand, which the ignorant and unstable twist to their own destruction, as they do the other scriptures. (3:15–16)

The author clearly knew Paul's letters as a collection and considereded them to be part of the canon of Scripture. He anticipated the later two-part canon ("Old Testament" and "New Testament"), when he spoke of "the predictions of the holy prophets and the commandments of the Lord and Savior through your apostles" (3:2). He is the first author to indicate that Paul is considered Scripture and the first to imply a twofold canon. In this endorsement of Paul, however, we should not overlook the implication that our writer claims for Peter the power to interpret correctly what Paul intended. The opponents also claimed Paul, but they twisted his meaning in our writer's judgment.

Second Peter represents an attempt to assert the authority of Peter in the face of other teachers with differing interpretations of Paul and different understandings of the coming end. This claim is embedded in a distinctive literary form.

Yet Another Genre

Second Peter is cast as a letter, addressed to no one in particular and consisting of general instructions and warnings. The letter form is part of its literary style, but it is not an actual letter. Written as if it were Peter's last words to his followers, it is a reminder of his lifelong teaching put forth on the eve of his death (1:12–15). In this regard it is similar to 2 Timothy, which claims to represent the last wishes of Paul, his testament. So too, 2 Peter claims to be the testament of Peter, a sort of farewell speech.

Such **testamentary literature** was widely known in the first century. The final speech of Jesus in the Gospel According to John (14–17) is rather like a testament. Our most extensive example, however, is an older Jewish work, which we know only in its Christian version, the *Testaments of the Twelve Patriarchs*. Modeled on the deathbed speech of Jacob (Genesis 49), this work claims to give the final wishes of each of the twelve sons of Jacob, the ancestors of the nation. Each of the twelve sections follows the same basic pattern: the patriarch calls his family together, recounts his life, warns them of vice and exhorts to virtue, predicts their future course, and finally dies. In 2 Peter this narrative has been transposed into a letter, and the biographical element is minimal. What remains is the notion of the last words of a great man of God who warns and exhorts, and predicts the future. Thus we may consider 2 Peter a testamentary letter.

Purity and the Parousia

To what does Peter testify? He testifies to the certain coming of the day of the Lord, admonishing his hearers to live pure lives in view of that coming day. He bases this conviction on the knowledge (a favorite word) of the prophets and of the Christ, alluding to the experience of Peter on the Mount of Transfiguration (Mark 9:1–8).

READING AND REFLECTION

Read 2 Peter, noting the motifs of purity, knowledge, and coming. How does this letter teach believers to triumph over evil?

 ## READING GUIDE TO SECOND PETER

Salutation   1:1–2
The testimony of Peter   1:3–21
   Peter's principles: sharing the divine nature   1:3–11
   Peter's reminder: approaching death   1:12–15
   Peter's claim to authority: eyewitnesses and prophetic word   1:16–21
False prophets and false teachers   2:1–22
   Their perversions   2:1–3
   Their predecessors   2:4–16
   Their doom   2:17–22
The predictions of Peter: scoffers to come   3:1–10
   Denial of Jesus' coming   3:1–7
   Rebuttal: God's timetable   3:8–10
Exhortations: what sort of persons ought you to be?   3:11–18

Addressed to Gentiles (1:1), this work uses a Gentile vocabulary and focuses on Gentile concerns. The vocabulary is evident in the first clause of the elaborate, and somewhat bombastic, first sentence of the letter proper (in Greek, 1:3–7): "divine power" has granted the things that pertain to "piety" that we may escape the corruption of "passions" and become "partakers of the divine nature" (1:3–4). These words represent distinctive ideas of Gentile religious thought; one, the idea of sharing in the divine nature, is alien to Jewish circles and even to other Jesus groups. It does not occur anywhere else in the New Testament but is frequently seen in Stoic thought, where human reason is considered a spark and fragment of divine reason. In addition, Stoics would readily understand the corrupting influence of the passions, for they regarded them as the source of delusion. The chain of virtues recounted in 1:5–7 is a typical Stoic device.

Second Peter differs from Stoicism in its understanding of how one escapes such passions and how one partakes of the divine nature. The answer begins with baptism (1:9), involves the knowledge of Jesus (1:16) and a proper interpretation of Scripture (1:20–3:2), and culminates in the coming of the Lord and of the new earth (3:3–13). The understanding of this approaching end is also distinctive. Our writer refutes a static view of history (a commonsense view also rejected by Stoics) and advocates a view of history as three ages: the time from the creation to the flood (when the world was destroyed by water); the time from the flood to the end (when the world will be destroyed by fire); and the time of the new heaven and the new earth (3:5–7, 13). Water and fire were two of the basic elements of Greek physics, the other two being air and earth (3:12). This notion of the earth destroyed by fire is not found in any other New Testament work but was a common Greek expectation. In fact, the successive dissolution of the world by water and then by fire was part of the cyclical view of history typical of Greek thought. Our writer differs in seeing these dissolutions as part of a meaningful story: God's rescue of his creation.

This grand vision of baptism, Scripture, and history underlies the basic concern of the writer: "Since all these things are thus to be dissolved, what sort of persons ought you to be?" (3:11, 14). The purity, patience, and peace required are derived from the divine nature itself and may only be acquired by overcoming the corrupting passions (1:4; 2:10). The vision of our writer is captured in a marvelous metaphor: the Scriptures are a lamp set in this dark world until that new day dawns (1:19).

In Peter's Name

Little about this rhetorically flamboyant and highly Hellenized letter convinces us that Peter actually wrote it. Given the practice of pseudonymity discussed earlier (pages 93–96, 185–88), this work has all the earmarks of an imitator. It depends either on Jude or on the same source used by Jude. Its language and much of its thought are closer to Stoicism than to Palestinian Judaism. It presumes that the first generation of believers has passed away (3:3) and responds to the loss of eschatological expectation common in the second and third generations. It even invokes the writings of Paul, now known as a collection and considered Scripture (3:15–16). Paul is used against other Paulinists, who are said to "twist" Paul. These are "lawless" people (3:17) who deny the coming of Jesus and, judging by chapter 2, have a false view of the Hebrew Scriptures. Though we cannot be sure, this reminds us of that Pauline trajectory that led to Marcion (page 208). Add to this that there are no early citations of the work and the ancient debate about its authorship, and we may reasonably conclude that it was written between 100 and 125. There is no hint about its geographical setting, unless we interpret the conscious reference to 1 Peter (3:1) to mean it was addressed to the same area in Asia Minor. If we are right in relating 2 Peter to developing Marcionite ideas, the choice of Peter as the voice of the letter would represent a conscious attempt to assert the authority of another apostle alongside Paul, on whom the Marcionites depended exclusively. Certainly, 2 Peter was part of the great debate of the second century: Who is the rightful heir of the apostles?

PETRINE TRAJECTORIES: SIMEON, SIMON, CEPHAS, PETER

We are not lacking in Petrine materials, but we are unable to demonstrate that any come directly from Peter. This is not unexpected. Peter was a Galilean fisherman, and it is likely that his entire career was oral. His impression was made on the minds of those who heard him, not on sheets of parchment. His audience was surely diverse. Even his names indicate that he traveled in more than one circle. Given the highly patriotic name of Simeon, he was more commonly referred to by the Greek name Simon (Simeon occurs only in 2 Peter 1:1 and Acts 15:14). Jesus gave him the added name of Cephas ("Rock"). We have no evidence that this word was used as a personal name before. The Aramaic Cephas was then adapted to the Greek world by turning the Greek word for rock (*petra*) into a proper name, Peter. This represents an accommodation to a new cultural situation, and the dominance of this version of his name implies that Peter moved into the Greek world. (Paul's practice of referring to him as Cephas was probably conditioned by his understanding of Peter's mission as limited to Jews; Gal. 2:7.) The name Peter is also an invention, although it is close to the Greek Petron, and Latin names like Petreius and Petronius were common. Peter continued to be claimed by different circles in the following generations. Let us examine two such claims.

The Law-Observant Peter

Both the *Acts of Peter* and that large body of material collected in the name of Clement (the *Pseudo-Clementine Homilies* and the *Pseudo-Clementine Recognitions*, known collectively as the **Pseudo-Clementines**) make Peter the centerpiece of a Law-observant version of Christianity. In both works Peter is the active opponent of Paul. He also opposes other understandings of being Jewish, for example, rejecting completely the notion of the temple and various segments of the Old Testament that support sacrificial worship. These are regarded as false prophecies wrongly inserted into Scripture by false prophets. These works envision an active mission to Gentiles but expect them to observe the Law and (it seems) be circumcised. Both works may be traced to sources from the middle of the second century and continued in active use for many centuries. While critical of other forms of Judaism and Christianity, the Pseudo-Clementines are remarkably open to both. Jesus is presented as a prophet, a sort of second Moses, but then in a rather surprising move, Peter is portrayed as teaching that:

> The Hebrews are not condemned because they did not know Jesus . . . provided only they act according to the instructions of Moses and do not injure him whom they did not know. And again the offspring of the Gentiles are not judged, who . . . have not known Moses, provided only they act according to the words of Jesus and thus do not injure him whom they did not know. . . . In all circumstances good works are needed; but if a man has been considered worthy to know both teachers as heralds of a single doctrine, then that man is counted rich in God. (Pseudo-Clementine Homilies 8.7.1–2, 5; quoted from Hennecke and Schneemelcher, 1992:2:525)

Hebrews (Jews) may be saved by following Moses, Gentiles (Christians) by following Jesus, but most blessed are those who follow both (Jewish Christians). Here we see the continuation of Peter's role as mediator, on the boundary between Jew and Gentile. To some degree this is a continuation of the portrayal of Peter in Matthew and in 2 Peter.

The Episcopal Peter

Perhaps because of this boundary position Peter was also vigorously claimed by later Gentile Christians. This is seen most clearly in the traditions incorporated into the *Ecclesiastical History* by Eusebius in the early fourth century. Peter is portrayed as the bearer of Christianity to Rome (2.14.6; 5.8.2), where he died as a martyr, having inaugurated the office of bishop (3.2). Thus, Peter is the one on whom Christ built his church (6.25.8).

This image of Peter as the rock on which the church is built derives from Matthew (16:18), but just what it meant in the Matthean situation, in which no one was to be called "father" or "master," or even "rabbi," is not entirely clear (23:8–10). It was, however, the image of Peter that became dominant. It owes something to 1 Peter (especially chapter 5) and was eventually taken up into the medieval papacy.

Perhaps this very trait of Peter—to be on the boundary between Jew and Gentile, between Paul and James, between ruling elder and scriptural expositor—made him such a valuable symbol for the emerging Christian consensus that resulted in early catholic Christianity.

HOW JEWISH WAS CHRISTIANITY TO BE?

We can see that the strand of early Christianity that scholars call Jewish Christianity was itself a diverse movement. Many of these writings were shunned and many nearly lost; only five were eventually included in the New Testament canon. Those included tend to be more mediating, more amenable to the dominant Pauline tradition (which reveals something of the process of canonization, as we will see in Chapter 14). And if we compare these writings with the literature associated with Paul we will learn something about the development of Christianity.

As suggested earlier (pages 211–12), the literary heirs of Paul exhibited four characteristics:

New emphasis on the church as a hierarchical institution
Fading concern with the end of the age and an increased concern for reputation, resulting in a new moralism
Use of Gentile religious thought to interpret Christ
Clear separation between accepted and deviant interpretations and interpreters

Similar tendencies may be found in this literature. Here too is a clear separation between the acceptable and the rejected, and a strong urge to hold fast to the "faith once delivered" (Jude 3). Related to this concern for true faith is the claim to apostolic authority. Only Hebrews fails to claim the authority (authorship) of a holy figure of the first generation—and it claims to be heir to their traditions (2:3). This claim to apostolic authority largely replaces the need to argue a case: opponents are simply labeled false teachers, who are known by the immoral lives they lead. True believers, in contrast, must live lives of moral excellence. This is typical of the kind of moralism and aspiration to social respectability that we saw in the Deutero-Pauline literature.

Nevertheless, real differences from Pauline traditions do emerge. There is less concern here with church organization and little evidence of a hierarchy (though some hierarchical focus may be discerned in the mediating work of 1 Peter). Whereas James and Hebrews share the general decline in eschatological expectations evident in the late first century, the coming end is a major theme of 2 Peter, and apocalyptic literature and ideas are evident in Jude. However, 1 Peter, Hebrews, and James share in the general move away from an apocalyptic worldview, a move characteristic of many at the end of the first century. Little attempt is made to interpret the world as a struggle between good and evil. And finally, the emphasis on the authority of Scripture is greater in these writings than in those of the Pauline schools. Second Peter is especially concerned with the proper interpretation of Scripture, and Hebrews is essentially an exercise in scriptural interpretation. Jude seems to employ a broader canon, which included *1 Enoch* and the *Assumption of Moses*. Only in 2 Timothy (3:16) do we find a similar concern in the Pauline heritage. So in comparison with the dominant Pauline trajectory:

The emphasis on hierarchy is evident only in 1 Peter.
The waning interest in the end coupled with increasing moralism is evident in 1 Peter, Hebrews, and James, but strongly resisted in 2 Peter and Jude.
The use of Gentile categories is evident in 1 Peter, 2 Peter, and Hebrews.
The separation from those who are different is evident in all these works, though less clearly labeled in Hebrews.

Finally we should note that these writings also help dispel the false understanding that to be Jewish was the opposite of being Gentile. At least two of them (Hebrews and 2 Peter) are deeply influenced by the Hellenistic world, as were many Jews in this era. (Neither is as thoroughly Hellenized as Philo of Alexandria.) Jew and Gentile were not exclusive options, only poles of a continuum of experience. While telling distinctive stories of Jesus, Jewish and Gentile followers of Jesus overlapped at many points.

LEARNING ON YOUR OWN

REVIEWING THE CHAPTER

Names and Terms

a fortiori	Essenes	Philo of Alexandria
Antiochus Epiphanes	exhortation	Pseudo-Clementines
deliberative rhetoric	invective	*telos*
demonstrative rhetoric	legalism	testamentary literature
Didache	Maccabees	

Issues and Questions

1. How does the Abraham story function in the debate about faith and works as Paul and James understand that debate?
2. Why did later Christian tradition need to explain the traditions about Jesus' siblings?
3. What features of the Letter of James suggest that it was written for a largely Jewish audience?
4. Briefly describe the contents of Jude's exhortation and place it on a continuum of Jewish-to-Gentile understandings of Jesus.

5. How does Hebrews reflect its cultural setting, especially the generalized Platonism of the era?
6. Discuss the treatment in Hebrews of Jesus as high priest, and explain why this is such a surprising idea.
7. Briefly describe the surviving works attributed to Peter and reflect on what this range of works suggests about the role of Peter in Christian tradition.
8. Be able to discuss the arguments for the authorship or pseudonymity of at least one of the works studied in this chapter.
9. How is the ritual of Christian baptism similar to practices in other Hellenistic religions?
10. What are some of the distinctive ideas of 2 Peter? What ancient tradition shared many of these same ideas?
11. To what degree does the movement known as Jewish Christianity appear to address issues also addressed in the literature from the post-Pauline traditions?

TAKING THE NEXT STEP

The only good overview of non-Pauline Christianity I have seen is Bruce, 1979. This whole area of early Christianity is less studied, perhaps because of the dominant voice of Paul in later centuries. Still there are ample resources to pursue a number of interesting topics.

Topics for Special Studies

The Rhetoric and/or Imagery of One of These Writings
Literary studies of these writings are only beginning, but see:

On Jude: J. D. Charles, 1993 and 1991.
On Hebrews: Cosby, 1988; Lindars, 1991; and Neyrey, 1991. See also Attridge's commentary, 1989.
On 1 Peter: Martin, 1992; Schutter, 1989; and Thurén, 1990.
On Jude and 2 Peter: Watson, 1988.

The Literary Relationship between Jude and 2 Peter
All the commentaries listed below under "Additional Books and Articles" treat this issue. See especially Watson, 1988; Bauckham, 1983; Kelly, 1969; Sidebottom, 1967; Neyrey, 1993; and J. D. Charles, 1993 and 1991.

The Authorship of One of These Writings in Relation to the Phenomenon of Pseudepigraphical Writing
All the commentaries listed below under "Additional Books and Articles" include some discussion of authorship. See also Charlesworth, 1987.

The Role(s) These Writings Imagined for Women
Not enough has been done on these specific works. See the general treatments of women in early Christianity listed in resources for the Introduction and Chapter 6. See also the treatment of these writings in Newsom and Ringe, 1992. On 1 Peter, see Balch, 1981.

The Social Location of the Implied Audience
Most of the work has been done on 1 Peter: J. H. Elliott, 1990; Balch, 1981; Talbert, 1986; and Hill, 1976. Maynard-Reid, 1985, studies poverty and wealth in James. On honor in Hebrews, see deSilva, 1995.

The Worldview of Hebrews in Relation to Hellenistic Philosophy, the Dead Sea Scrolls, or Jewish Mystical Traditions

Start with some of the general works, such as Chilstrom, 1983; Hagner, 1983; Johnson, 1980; Smith, 1984; and Käsemann, 1984. On Jewish mysticism, see Scholem, 1995. On Philo and Hebrews, see Dey, 1981, and Williamson, 1970. Both Yadin, 1958, and Bruce, 1963b, look at the parallels with the Dead Sea Scrolls. Good introductions to Philo include Sandmel, 1979b; see also Stone, 1984.

Most of the history of the Dead Sea community must be reconstructed from allusions in the *Damascus Rule* and the *Commentary on Habakkuk*. For a concise discussion, see Vermes, 1977:137–62. See also Kampen, 1988. Additional resources are listed at the end of Chapters 1 and 8.

Swetnam, 1981, looks at Hebrews in light of the Aqedah (sacrifice of Isaac).

The Noncanonical Writings Attributed to These Authors

Not a lot has been done yet, but see Cameron, 1984 (*Apocryphon of James*) and Van Voorst, 1989 (*Ascents of James*). See also Jones, 1984, and Kline, 1975, on the Pseudo-Clementine literature. In general, start by finding a scholarly translation and introduction. (The two best collections are J. K. Elliott, 1994, and Hennecke and Schneemelcher, 1991–1992; for the works found at Nag Hammadi, see Robinson, 1977; the older collection of James, 1924, is still useful.) Related works can be found in a collection known as the *Apostolic Fathers* (Sparks, 1978; Lightfoot, 1956; Goodspeed, 1950). Also consult a good Bible dictionary (see the list on page 499).

Views of Paul in the Petrine Literature

See Schmithals, 1965 (Paul and James), and Draisma, 1989.

Views of Peter in the Petrine Literature

See Smith, 1985.

What Can Be Known of the Historical Peter

Brown, Donfried, and Reumann, 1973, provides a careful comparative study with one eye on modern church relations. See also Perkins, 2000, and Cullmann, 1962.

Images of James in Early Christian Writings

Start with Chilton and Evans, 1999, and Painter, 1999; see also Carrol, 1961; Bauckham, 1999; and Kugelman, 1980. Most do not think Eisenman, 1986, has made a case for James references in the Dead Sea Scrolls.

Legends of Jesus' Brothers in Early Christianity

See Kugelman, 1980, and Bauckham, 2004.

Early Interactions between Jews and Christians

On Jewish identity, see Collins, 1999, and Hamerton-Kelly and Scroggs, 1976.

On various interactions, see Setzer, 1994; Klijn and Reinink, 1973; Sanders, Baumgarten, and Meldelson, 1981; Wilson, 1995; Schoeps, 1963; Klijn, 1974; and Horbury, 1998.

On anti-Jewish attitudes in early Christianity, see Gager, 1983; Schäfer, 1997; Feldman, 1993; Kee and Borowsky, 1998; Wilson, 1986; Lehne, 1990; and Lindars, 1991.

On the interactions between Greek-speaking and Hebrew-speaking Jews, see Hill, 1992.

On the use of Jewish Scriptures and traditions, see D'Angelo, 1984, and Hughes, 1979.

Additional Books and Articles

Important commentaries include:

> On James: Davids, 1982 (conservative, technical) and 1983 (popular); Dibelius and Greeven, 1976 (technical); Wall, 1997; and Reicke, 1964 (James, Peter, and Jude).
>
> On Jude and 2 Peter: Bauckham, 1983 (excellent, conservative), and Neyrey, 1993 (2 Peter, Jude; social science emphasis).
>
> On Hebrews: Attridge, 1989 (excellent); Bruce, 1990; and deSilva, 2000 (emphasis on social science and rhetoric).
>
> On 1 Peter: J. H. Eliott, 2000; Achtemeier, 1996; Beare, 1958; Buchanan, 1972; and Davids, 1990 (conservative).

Less technical works include:

> On James: Laws, 1981; Davids, 1983; Martin and Elliott, 1982 (James, 1 and 2 Peter, Jude); and Sidebottom, 1967 (James, Jude, 2 Peter).
>
> On Jude and 2 Peter: Kelly, 1969.
>
> On Hebrews: Casey, 1980, and Jewett, 1981.
>
> On 1 Peter: Best, 1971; Michaels, 1981 (conservative); and Senior, 1980 (1 and 2 Peter).

For a bibliography on 1 Peter, see Casurella, 1996.

8

STORIES TOLD

An Approach to Understanding the Gospels

 This [is the story] they tell, and whether it happened so or not I do not know; but if you think about it, you can see that it is true.

                                     Black Elk (Neihardt)

In those days Jesus came from Nazareth of Galilee and was baptized by John in the Jordan. And just as he was coming up out of the water . . .

This short, vivid scene comes at the beginning of the Gospel according to Mark. Immediately we recognize that it represents a different kind of writing from the letters we have studied so far. In this chapter we will explore the methods of study appropriate to this new kind of writing called **gospel**. One clue is found in the name itself. *Gospel* is from the Old English *godspel* (good spell). While *spell* implies a magical power, its root meaning is "story." A gospel, then, is a good story. Certainly the most important characteristic of these writings is that they are stories.

This clue will provide further insight if we consider the Greek term that *gospel* intends to translate: *euangellion* (or *evangellion*). The stem, *angellion*, means "an announcement" or "a proclamation" (thus an *angelos*, an angel, is one who delivers a message). The prefix of this word, *eu-*, means "good," "happy," or "well off." We meet this same prefix in English words like *euphoric* (a feeling of well-being), *euphonic* (a pleasing sound), and *eulogy* (good words spoken at a funeral). When used with a noun, *eu-* implies greatness or abundance. *Euangellion*, then, indicates an announcement of something favorable, an extremely happy event.

One use of this word in the Greco-Roman world was for the news of victory brought back from the battlefront (*TDNT*, 2:722). Such announcements were the occasion of great celebrations and festivals. Although the Christian usage probably does not derive from this secular usage, it does share some of the same connotations and feelings, connotations hardly evident in our word *gospel*.

Because gospels are stories about great good news of victory and triumph, we must endeavor to read them with some of the sense of expectation such a name implies. Our task is to hear them as they were originally heard, which also implies that we will hear them in the context of other ancient literature of a similar kind.

On the one hand, no ancient literature is exactly like the gospels, which seem to be a distinctive literary form invented by early Christian storytellers. On the other hand, the gospels do resemble other kinds of ancient writings. Probably the strongest parallels can be traced to the form known as a *bios*, the story of a famous politician, philosopher, or religious leader. Unlike a modern biography, the *bios* made no effort to explain its subject in terms of family, psychology, education, or motivation. It focused on showing the nature of the person through revealing anecdotes (and these brief stories are not necessarily told in chronological order). The gospels also share some traits with ancient histories, more with Hebrew history than Greek, and even with the *Dialogues* of Plato, especially the early ones that tell the story of the trial and death of Socrates. There are also numerous similarities to the stories about the lives of the prophets found in the Hebrew Scriptures and to Greco-Roman aretalogies (stories praising the lives of mystics and sages, often filled with magical deeds). Different readers probably heard in them echoes of, and expectations from, these various contexts. What is important to note is that one always reads literature in the context of whatever other literature one knows and that the ancients knew different kinds of literature than we do. Thus, our second clue for finding appropriate methods for studying the Gospels is that we must be conscious of the need to try to hear them within the literary context of antiquity. Striving to listen to them as gospels will require a new kind of listening on our part, different from the kind of attention we have given them as documents of our age, different even from the hearing we gave to the Pauline Letters.

A third and final clue is the simple observation that there are four Gospels—all very much alike—telling much the same story, though with significant differences among them. Thus, our study must be comparative, involving careful observation of their points of agreement and their differences.

A CASE IN POINT: THE EMPTY TOMB STORIES

Before reviewing the various methods that scholars have developed for interpreting the Gospels, we must become more familiar with what actually happens in a Gospel story. Familiarity with the specific details of an actual story will help us appreciate the issues involved and the strengths and weaknesses of the various proposals for interpreting the Gospels. For our purposes, the following exercise will suffice.

READING AND REFLECTION

Carefully study all four accounts below of the women coming to Jesus' tomb: Matt. 28:1–10; Mark 16:1–8; Luke 24:1–11; and John 20:1–18. Answer these questions for each version of the story.

1. Who went to the tomb?
2. What did they see when they arrived?
3. Whom did they meet?
4. What were they told about Jesus?
5. What was their response?
6. Who first saw the risen Jesus?

This task, and all your study of the Gospels, will be greatly aided by a study tool called a **synopsis** of the Gospels. Two of the best are the *Synopsis of the Four Gospels* (hereafter, *SFG*; Aland, 1972) and *Gospel Parallels* (hereafter, *GP*; Throckmorton, 1967 [RSV]). The former is more complete and less expensive, but the latter is somewhat better arranged. *GP* is also available for the New Revised Standard Version (Throckmorton, 1992). Each is divided into a series of individual stories, though they are numbered differently. I shall regularly give the number of the section in each version. For the empty tomb story, see *SFG* §352 or *GP* §253.

Matt 28:1–10	Mark 16:1–8	Luke 24:1–11	John 20:1–18
After the sabbath, as the first day of the week was dawning, Mary Magdalene and the other Mary went to see the tomb.	When the sabbath was over, Mary Magdalene, and Mary the mother of James, and Salome bought spices, so	But on the first day of the week, at early dawn, they came to the tomb, taking the spices that they had prepared. 2 They	Early on the first day of the week, while it was still dark, Mary Magdalene came to the tomb and saw that the stone had been removed from the tomb. 2 So she ran and went to Simon Peter and

Matt 28:1–10	Mark 16:1–8	Luke 24:1–11	John 20:1–18

Matt 28:1–10

2 And suddenly there was a great earthquake; for an angel of the Lord, descending from heaven, came and rolled back the stone and sat on it. 3 His appearance was like lightning, and his clothing white as snow. 4 For fear of him the guards shook and became like dead men. 5 But the angel said to the women, "Do not be afraid; I know that you are looking for Jesus who was crucified. 6 He is not here; for he has been raised, as he said. Come, see the place where he lay. 7 Then go quickly and tell his disciples, 'He has been raised from the dead, and indeed he is going ahead of you to Galilee; there you will see him.' This is my message for you."

8 So they left the tomb quickly with fear and great joy, and ran to tell his disciples. 9 Suddenly Jesus met them and said, "Greetings!" And they came to him, took hold of his feet, and worshipped him. 10 Then Jesus said to them, "Do not be afraid; go and tell my brothers to go to Galilee; there they will see me."

Mark 16:1–8

that they might go and anoint him. 2 And very early on the first day of the week, when the sun had risen, they went to the tomb. 3 They had been saying to one another, "Who will roll away the stone for us from the entrance to the tomb?" 4 When they looked up, they saw that the stone, which was very large, had already been rolled back. 5 As they entered the tomb, they saw a young man, dressed in a white robe, sitting on the right side; and they were alarmed. 6 But he said to them, "Do not be alarmed; you are looking for Jesus of Nazareth, who was crucified. He has been raised; he is not here. Look, there is the place they laid him. 7 But go, tell his disciples and Peter that he is going ahead of you to Galilee; there you will see him, just as he told you." 8 So they went out and fled from the tomb, for terror and amazement had seized them; and they said nothing to anyone, for they were afraid.

Luke 24:1–11

found the stone rolled away from the tomb, 3 but when they went in, they did not find the body.

4 While they were perplexed about this, suddenly two men in dazzling clothes stood beside them. 5 The women were terrified and bowed their faces to the ground, but the men said to them, "Why do you look for the living among the dead? He is not here, but has risen. 6 Remember how he told you, while he was still in Galilee, 7 that the Son of Man must be handed over to sinners, and be crucified, and on the third day rise again."

8 Then they remembered his words, 9 and returning from the tomb, they told all this to the eleven and to all the rest. 10 Now it was Mary Magdalene, Joanna, Mary the mother of James, and the other women with them who told this to the apostles. 11 But these words seemed to them an idle tale, and they did not believe them.

John 20:1–18

the other disciple, the one whom Jesus loved, and said to them, "They have taken the Lord out of the tomb, and we do not know where they have laid him." 3 Then Peter and the other disciple set out and went toward the tomb. 4 The two were running together, but the other disciple outran Peter and reached the tomb first. 5 He bent down to look in and saw the linen wrappings lying there, but he did not go in. 6 Then Simon Peter came, following him, and went into the tomb. He saw the linen wrappings lying there, 7 and the cloth that had been on Jesus' head, not lying with the linen wrappings but rolled up in a place by itself. 8 Then the other disciple, who reached the tomb first, also went in, and he saw and believed; 9 for as yet they did not understand the scripture, that he must rise from the dead. 10 Then the disciples returned to their homes.

11 But Mary stood weeping outside the tomb. As she wept, she bent over to look into the tomb; 12 and she saw two angels in white, sitting where the body of Jesus had been lying, one at the head and the other at the feet. 13 They said to her, "Woman, why are you weeping?" She said to them, "They have taken away my Lord, and I do not know where they have laid him." 14 When she had said this, she turned around and saw Jesus standing there, but she did not know that it was Jesus. 15 Jesus said to her, "Woman, why are you weeping? Whom are you looking for?" Supposing him to be the gardener, she said to him, "Sir, if you have carried him away, tell me where you have laid him, and I will take him away." 16 Jesus said to her, "Mary!" She turned and said to him in Hebrew, "Rabbouni!" (which means Teacher).

17 Jesus said to her, "Do not hold
on to me, because I have not yet
ascended to the Father. But go to
my brothers and say to them, 'I am
ascending to my Father and your
Father, to my God and your God.'"
18 Mary Magdalene went and
announced to the disciples, "I have
seen the Lord"; and she told them
that he had said these things to her.

The differences between these accounts are so vast that some have been tempted
to argue that they do not refer to the same incident. Yet because they share a number of common elements, including the presence of Mary Magdalene, we are left
with the task of making sense of them as different versions of the same incident.

The differences between the versions are stark: whereas in Mark the women approach the tomb "when the sun had risen" and find the stone already removed, in
Matthew they witness an earthquake and an angelic descent (both lacking in the
other accounts), and in John's version Mary arrived "while it was still dark and
saw that the stone had been taken away from the tomb." The number of women is
variously identified as one, two, four, or more, though Mary Magdalene is always
included. In one set of traditions they are told to return to Galilee (and in Matthew
they do); but Luke (aware of the Galilee tradition) keeps them in Jerusalem where
they encounter the risen Jesus. Only in Mark do they flee in fear and say "nothing to
anyone, for they were afraid." (The rest of Mark 16 after verse 8 is not in our oldest
texts of Mark's Gospel and probably was composed from the accounts in Matthew
and Luke. For a discussion, see pages 297–98.) In Matthew's version, the women encounter the risen Jesus as they leave the tomb; in John he appears after two male disciples come and go; in Luke he does not appear to the women but to two unnamed
male disciples far from the tomb; and in Mark he does not appear at all.

It would be inappropriate to try to explain these differences here. When we finish
our study of each Gospel, the reasons for their differences will be obvious. Here our
issue is the proper approach to dealing with such diversity. How should we proceed?

GOSPEL INTERPRETATION: A REVIEW

From earliest times the diversity of the Gospels and the differences—some would say
contradictions—between them have been a problem for serious interpreters. First I
will sketch some of the ancient ways of dealing with this diversity and then review
the development of the modern study of the Gospels.

THE ANCIENT APPROACH: REDUCTION

The ancient interpreters who became keenly aware of the differences between the
Gospels usually chose one of three solutions to the problem: elimination, combination,
or harmonization.

Various groups sought to achieve unity by eliminating all but one Gospel. Some of Paul's second-century followers accepted only the Gospel of Luke, because they thought Luke had been Paul's traveling companion (see the discussion of Marcion on pages 186, 208). Others kept only the Gospel of Mark because they felt more comfortable with a Gospel that did not show Jesus being born as a baby. Still others attempted to maintain a thoroughly Jewish Christianity, recognizing only Matthew. The Gospel of John also had its champions, as did other gospels that exist today only as fragments: the *Gospel of the Egyptians* was favored by Gentiles in Egypt; the *Gospel of the Hebrews* was used by Egyptian Jewish Christians.

Obviously each of these groups solved the problem of differences between the various gospels. By choosing to accept only one gospel as authoritative, that version of the gospel became the correct one; the others were simply ignored. Although these reductive attempts to achieve unity by rejecting multiple gospels never gained wide support in the churches, another kind of attempt did gain a wide following.

Sometime around 170 a church leader in eastern Syria set out to solve the problem of the disagreements between the gospels by combining the four Gospels into one blended account. **Tatian** did this by carefully extracting sentences from the various Gospels and weaving them together to produce one harmonious account of the words and deeds of Jesus. This monumental work of patience and ingenuity was called the ***Diatessaron***, which might be translated "Through the Four." Notice how cleverly he solves the problems of the empty tomb stories:

Matt. 28:1	Now on the evening of the Sabbath which is the dawn of the first
Luke 24:1	day, at very **early dawn**, behind the rest came Mary Magdalene and
Luke 24:10	the other Mary and the **other women** to see the sepulchre, **carry-**
Luke 24:1c	**ing with them the spices which they had prepared.** *And they said*
Mark 16:3	*among themselves, Who shall remove for us the stone from the door*
Mark 16:4b	*of the tomb? for it was exceeding great.* And when they said so, a
Matt. 28:2b	great earthquake took place; and an angel descended from heaven,
Luke 24:2	and came and rolled away the stone from the door. **And they came**
Matt. 28:2b	**and found the stone removed from the tomb,** and the angel sitting
28:3	upon the stone. And his appearance was as lightning, and his rai-
28:4	ment white as snow: and for fear of him the guards were terrified;
Mark 16:5	and became as dead men. And when he was gone away, *the women*
Luke 24:3	*entered the tomb,* **and found not the body** of Jesus: but *they saw*
Mark 16:5b	*there a young man sitting on the right side, arrayed in a white robe;*
	and they were amazed. And the angel answered, and said unto the
Matt. 28:5	women, Fear not ye: for I know that ye seek Jesus of Nazareth,
	which hath been crucified. He is not here; for he is risen, even as he
28:6	said. Come and see the place where our Lord was laid. **And while**
Luke 24:4	**they were perplexed thereabout, behold, two men stood above them**
24:5	**in dazzling apparel; and as they were seized with terror, and bowed**
24:6	**down their faces to the earth, they said unto them, Why seek ye the**
24:7	**living one among the dead? He is not here; he is risen: remember**
	what he spake unto you when he was yet in Galilee, saying, The Son
Matt. 28:7a	**of man is going to be delivered up into the hands of sinners, and to**
Mark 16:7b	**be crucified, and to rise again the third day.** But go quickly, and tell
Matt. 28:7c	his disciples *and Cephas,* that he is risen from the dead; and lo, he

Luke 24:8
Matt. 28:8

Mark 16:8b
John 20:2

goeth before you into Galilee; and there shall ye see him, where he said unto you; lo, I have told you. **And they remembered his words**; and they departed quickly from the tomb with joy and great fear, and hastened and went their way running; *for perplexity and quaking had come upon them: and they said nothing to anyone; for they were afraid.* But Mary ran, and came to Simon Cephas, and to that other disciple, whom Jesus loved, and said unto them, They have taken away our Lord out of the tomb, and I know not where they have laid him. Simon therefore went forth and that other disciple. . . .

(The only English edition of the *Diatessaron* is that of Hill, 1894 (2006), from which this is quoted: 253–54. But a number of modern works take essentially the same approach; for example, Thomas and Gundry, 1978.)

Amazingly Tatian achieved this agreement by omitting very little, changing only one word (the "but" before John 20:2, which in the original was a "so") and adding a couple of transitions (for example, the "when they said so" to Matt. 28:2; marked with shading above). He used the basic text of Matthew (given in roman type here), supplemented it with details from Luke (bold) and Mark (italic), and finished it with John (underlined).

Still, the effort is not as successful as might first appear. He hides the problems: the Lukan motivation of coming to anoint the body ignores the Matthean version that they come only "to see the tomb" (28:1) and is in some tension with the Johannine version in which the anointing was done before burial (John 19:40). Tatian is forced to blend what in his sources are alternatives: When and how to move the stone? Angels or men? Return to Galilee? To tell or not to tell? Although he eliminated the discrepancies, and the enormous historical difficulties they present, Tatian distorted the meanings of the individual Gospels.

It is easy to see why the *Diatessaron* became a very popular work. In some areas it seems actually to have displaced the four Gospels in public reading in the churches. It persisted throughout the Middle Ages, though its popularity declined somewhat when Tatian, on other grounds, came to be considered heretical (deviant from the true faith).

A third solution was to eliminate the contradictions and still preserve the autonomy of the four Gospels. Near the end of the second century the bishop of the French city of Lyon, **Irenaeus**, argued that there must be four Gospels—no more, no less. Although his arguments strike us today as less than convincing (for example, that the number four is divine), there is also a higher side to his argument, in which he speaks not of four Gospels but of a fourfold Gospel, the concept that prevailed in Christian thinking (*Against Heresies* 3.11.8). It is reflected in the way early canons were divided: the first section was never called *gospels*, but *gospel* with each work being called "the Gospel according to . . ." Thus, the church's intellectual solution to the problem of having four Gospels is to speak of a gospel within the Gospels, a unity in diversity, or as we might say, four versions of one gospel.

Believing in the unity of the gospel took several forms. At one extreme, it involved only the affirmation that a common faith in Jesus underlies all four; at the other there were those who sought to eliminate all discrepancies and harmonize the four on every point.

The most noteworthy of the many practitioners of this art is the fifth-century theologian and bishop, Augustine of Hippo, in North Africa. His *Harmony of the Gospels* was a comprehensive treatment that attempted to eliminate all inconsistencies. His favored solution was to imagine that the discrepancies stem from separate incidents, one not mentioned by any of the four writers. Thus Mark's young man in the tomb was just a second angel not mentioned by Matthew, whereas Mark in turn failed to mention the angel on the outside (3.24.63). An alternative strategy was to ignore certain differences, as Augustine ignored the problem of when the stone was moved. Some modern harmonizers adopt a similar approach, proposing additional incidents to account for discrepancies. Harold Lindsell, for example, gives us a sixfold denial for Peter (1976:175–76). Zane Hodges (1966) does a masterful job of explaining away the differences in the stories of the empty tomb by supposing that the Gospel writers simply choose to report different aspects of the event.

The difficulty with such harmonization is not that it is impossible, for if one is clever enough and willing to make enough assumptions, any item of Gospel tradition can be harmonized with the rest. The difficulty is the violence that such an approach does to the text. In order to harmonize Luke's version of the resurrection appearances, which happen only in Jerusalem, with Matthew's version, which takes place in Galilee, one must seriously distort the story Luke intended to tell. Because we assume that each Gospel writer told the story in a particular way for a purpose, our method must attempt to find that purpose. Certainly, these differences complicate our understanding of Jesus and of early Christians, but such complexity is more true to what actually happened. Our task, then, is to explain the differences between the Gospels, without explaining them away.

THE MODERN APPROACH: CRITICISM

The words *critic* and *criticism* have negative connotations in our society, but they are not negative endeavors. *Critic* is from the Greek word *kritikos*, one who is able to discern, to make distinctions. Thus a critic is a person of discernment. **Criticism** is essentially the positive endeavor to understand literature, or anything else for that matter, by asking disciplined questions designed to elicit the information we want to know. It is analogous to what happens in a court: the judge does not simply let the witness talk; instead the witness answers specific questions designed to bring out specific evidence. So too, the literary critic brings disciplined questions to bear on the literature.

If you are intent on just listening to the story, it can be annoying to have someone always interrupting to ask a question; yet we learn things by asking questions that we could not learn by just listening. And a good critic should be polite enough not to interrupt the story at an inappropriate time.

Unfortunately, biblical critics have not always been so polite. In fact, many of the earliest critics were adamantly opposed to the established Christianity of their time. They experienced this Christianity as a dogmatic restraint on their reason and worked to undermine it. Historically, the modern study of the Gospels may be traced back to the Enlightenment in the eighteenth century, and it is intertwined with the nineteenth-century invention of the modern idea of history. Both movements presented profound intellectual challenges to the traditional understanding of Christianity. Most regrettably, these controversies have colored the general perception of modern gospel studies. When stripped of all negative presuppositions and intentions, however, nineteenth-century scholars were confronted with a fact of enormous significance: there are discrepancies among the Gospels. Critics did not invent the various accounts of the empty tomb; they seek only to explain the great variety of such accounts. Their attempts may be traced through four distinct stages. Though these stages are chronologically successive, with later stages displacing earlier, each successive stage adopts and refines the conclusions of the earlier one(s).

Today a new way of approaching the problem is emerging, deriving from the study of oral traditional cultures. I will first trace the line of critical thought that operates from the perspective of a literary model (where each work is viewed as a document dependent on earlier documents in a linear development) and then suggest how the problem looks when viewed from the perspective of an oral model (where development is nonlinear and cyclical).

Variety from the Use of Different Sources

Most of us who heard these stories as children assumed that the Gospel writers simply recorded what happened. When we began to think historically, considering that one Gospel must have been written first and that the other Gospel writers may have read it before they wrote, we likely assumed that the Gospels were written in the order in which they occur in the Bible. Augustine proposed this view in the fifth century, and it remained the standard explanation until the rise of critical studies.

Later scholars examined the Gospels intently, trying every conceivable combination of interdependence. One thing became clear: three of the Gospels were so much alike that they must be related in some way, being either directly dependent on each other or all dependent on an earlier gospel. The fourth Gospel, John, was remarkably different—in the order of events portrayed, in the selection of events included, and in the interpretation of those events—so different that its dependence on any of the other three was considered doubtful. (These relationships can be seen in miniature by reflecting on the empty tomb narratives examined earlier.) Because three of the Gospels seemed to view things in the same way, scholars soon coined the term **synoptic Gospels** (from the Greek *opsis*, "view," and *syn*, "together)" to refer to them. The problem of their interrelation became the **synoptic problem**.

But which of the three was written first? Although each Gospel attracted some champions, the primary battle was fought between the proponents of the priority of Matthew as the first gospel (the traditional view) and the proponents of Mark, with Mark soon claiming a near-universal consensus. This consensus is questioned by some critics (notably Farmer, 1976b, and his former students), and some scholars feel a need to reexamine the problem. Still, it would be an exaggeration to suggest that the critical consensus has been shaken; the case for this agreement seems well founded.

To examine the problem in detail would lead us out of our way; readers desiring a greater familiarity with the arguments that attempt to prove Mark was written first are invited to read the following digression. Others may safely skip it. Though no one argument by itself is conclusive, taken together they convince most people of the priority of Mark.

Excursus on the priority of Mark

1. The subject matter of Mark is more extensively found in Matthew and Luke than either of them is found in Mark. Whereas Matthew contains over 90 percent of Mark, Mark contains only 50 percent of Matthew. Whereas Luke contains over 50 percent of Mark, Mark contains only 30 percent of Luke. In all but three cases, when a Markan passage is missing in Matthew or Luke it is found in the other one. This implies that Mark is the common element for both Matthew and Luke (see Figure 8.1).

2. The order of Mark is more clearly reflected in Matthew and Luke than the order of either of them is reflected in Mark. In most instances when either Matthew or Luke diverges from the Markan order, the other does not. More important, Matthew and Luke never share a common sequence unless it is shared by Mark. This is seen most dramatically in their beginnings and endings: neither the birth stories nor the resurrection appearances (both lacking in Mark) show any common order in Matthew and Luke. This also suggests that neither Matthew nor Luke had access to the other's Gospel.

3. Certain awkward expressions in Mark are either lacking altogether in the other Gospels or given in a form that is smoother or less troublesome. In Mark 10:17–18, for example, Jesus seems to draw back from attribution of divinity to himself, whereas in the same story in Matthew 19:16–17 the problem is avoided. Matthew (20:20–28) also reduces the disgrace of James and John by having their mother ask Jesus for their preeminence in the kingdom; in Mark (10:34–45) they ask for themselves. Yet Matthew leaves Jesus' reply in the second-person plural, which is appropriate only in the Markan form of the narrative. Numerous minor problems could be cited, but two stand out: Mark attributed a quotation from Malachi to Isaiah (Mark 1:2) and cited the wrong high priest (Mark 2:26, compare 1 Samuel 21), whereas Matthew was more precise in both instances. (Even some of the manuscripts have attempted to correct Mark's faulty citation.) Mark may well have been

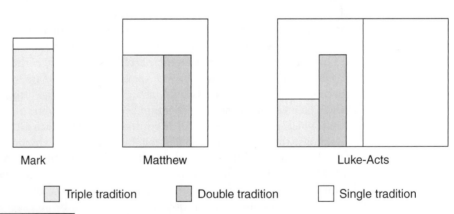

| Triple tradition | Double tradition | Single tradition |

FIGURE 8.1 **SHARED TRADITIONS** This figure shows what the (synoptic) Gospels share without regard to the source of the shared material. Mark shares most of its material with the other two; Matthew shares about half its material with the other two plus a sizable portion with Luke alone; Luke shares less than half the material in the Gospel with the other two, a large segment with Matthew, and an even larger segment with neither, having more unique material than either Mark or Matthew (including the whole of Acts). John is omitted from this comparison because his Gospel has so little in common with the others.

working from a list of prophetic testimonies, which had already combined the words of Malachi with those of Isaiah. Such lists, called *Testimonia*, were relatively common among Jewish scribes. In regard to the high priest, Mark located the David incident in the time of Abiathar, but the high priest when this incident occurred was actually Abiathar's father, Ahimelech (1 Sam. 21:1–6). Abiathar became high priest before David's reign ended (2 Sam. 15:35). David's son Solomon later deposed Abiathar because he had backed his rival to the throne, Adonijah (1 Kings 2:35). Other such difficulties in Mark do not appear in Matthew or Luke. (For a list, see Kee, 1977b:14–16. A complete examination was made by Hawkins, 1909:114–53.) Although we must also ask if Mark gained anything by these deviations, they have generally been viewed as primary evidence of Markan priority.

4. It is simply easier to imagine Matthew as an expansion of Mark than vice versa. If Mark were abbreviating Matthew, we would not expect him to omit completely such major Matthean features as the birth stories, the great blocks of teaching material (chapters 5–7, 10, 13, 18, 23–25), and the resurrection appearances. Nor would we expect him actually to lengthen many stories by adding incidental details; yet Mark's version of many stories is actually longer than Matthew's (compare Mark 2:1–12 with Matt. 9:1–8; GP §52, SFG §92). We face even greater problems if we imagine Mark abbreviating Luke or combining it with Matthew when we consider how much of Luke's work is missing in Mark—including the whole of Acts and the second half of Luke's Gospel (discussed in Chapter 11).

Other arguments are often made, but they are usually technical, often obscure, and always inconclusive. These are sufficient for our purpose: to understand the development of the modern study of the Gospels. Although conclusions of this kind must remain forever tentative, working hypotheses, conclusions are called for. The evidence adduced by scholars so far supports the view that Mark is the earliest of the Gospels, with Matthew and Luke depending directly on Mark. ■

Once the priority of Mark gained acceptance and Matthew and Luke could be printed in parallel columns, with Mark in the middle, a remarkable discovery emerged: the middle column was often empty. Matthew and Luke share quite a bit of material not found in Mark. Because this other material does not occur in the same order or context in Matthew and Luke, it did not seem probable that one writer simply copied it from the other. Compare:

Matt. 7:7–11	Mark	Luke 11:9–13
Ask, and it will be given you; search, and you will find; knock, and the door will be opened for you. 8 For everyone who asks receives, and everyone who searches finds, and for everyone who knocks, the door will be opened. 9 Is there anyone among you who, if your child	(No parallel in Mark)	So I say to you, Ask, and it will be given you; search, and you will find; knock, and the door will be opened for you. 10 For everyone who asks receives, and everyone who searches finds, and for everyone who knocks, the door will be opened. 11 Is there anyone among

asks for bread, will give a stone? 10 Or if the child asks for a fish, will give a snake?	you who, if your child asks for a fish, will give a snake *instead of a fish*? 12 Or if the child asks for an egg, will give a
11 If you then, who are evil, know how to give good gifts to your children, how much more will your Father in heaven give good things to those who ask him!	*scorpion*? 13 If you then, who are evil, know how to give good gifts to your children, how much more will the heavenly Father give the Holy Spirit to those who ask him!

Thus the **Q source** was born. *Q* is the symbol (from the German *Quelle*, meaning "source") that scholars use to designate the material shared by Matthew and Luke alone (it is also called the **double tradition**, in distinction from the triple tradition shared by all three). It is generally believed to have been a separate written source to which both Gospel writers had access. Remarkably, however, there is no other trace of its existence: not a single reference to such a document, let alone a copy, has come down to us. Those who do not see Q as a written document usually argue that it represents a widespread oral tradition, available to both Matthew and Luke, though perhaps not as a connected series. On the other hand, it is argued, Q can be reconstructed as an intelligible document. (For such a reconstruction see Kloppenborg, 2000:55–110.)

In fact, there has appeared a flurry of scholarship on Q since the mid-1980s, largely growing out of the Q Seminar in the Society of Biblical Literature. (SBL is the national professional organization of biblical scholars.) The Q Seminar was an ongoing research project of about twenty scholars who met yearly to discuss their work on the material thought to be part of Q. The most provocative aspect of this work has been the claim that Q represents an early Christian community that regarded Jesus as teacher but had little interest in his death (thus quite the antithesis of Paul). This view is based on the observation that Q, as reconstructed, lacks all the stories surrounding Jesus' death (called the *passion narrative*, with *passion* derived from the Latin word *passio*, meaning "suffering").

In addition to the material found in all three synoptic Gospels (the triple tradition), and the material found in both Matthew and Luke but not in Mark (Q, or the double tradition), we also find material unique to each Gospel. That found in Matthew is generally labeled M, denoting Matthew's private source or sources; that found in Luke is labeled L. There is also material unique to Mark, but scholars to date have taken little account of it.

This analysis of the origins of the material in the Gospels is called **source criticism**; Figure 8.2 represents the various conclusions proposed by scholars. I would stress how tentative such source conclusions must be. They represent scenarios that are not unlikely. Many other directions of influence have been proposed, including the influence of the oral gospel tradition and the influence of many smaller collections of miracle stories, sayings collections, and passion narratives. All in all, the influences on the Gospels were probably more complex that these simple charts suggest.

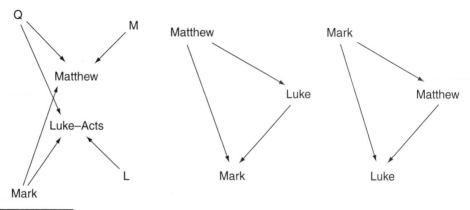

FIGURE 8.2 THREE VIEWS OF GOSPEL SOURCE RELATIONSHIPS

Even less convincing was the general assumption of source criticism that the older the source, the more reliable it must be. Scholars in this period had a tendency to prefer the synoptics to John, to prefer Mark to Matthew and Luke, and to value Q very highly. It was, of course, very congenial to nineteenth-century opinion, with its growing respect for science, that Mark made so little of the resurrection: no angels, no earthquakes, no appearances. And Q contains mostly sayings of Jesus, with only one miracle mentioned. We have learned, however, that simply finding the earliest source does not provide the full answer to the question of history.

The historical question led scholars to the next stage of Gospel criticism. For there was a great gap between the time of the events portrayed (before 30 CE) and the earliest possible written source (Q was dated after 50, Mark after 65). Scholars now sought to explore this gap.

Variety from the Oral Transmission of the Tradition

A technique had been elaborated by Old Testament scholars to deal with the tremendous time lapse between events like the exodus and the recording of those events centuries later. These scholars sought to determine the oral form and the typical social setting in which that form would be used for telling each story. Thus, the method is twofold: to determine the form of the tradition (legend, hymn, curse, lament, myth, example story, folk tale, and so on) and to determine the typical situation in which that form would have been used (hymns would be used in worship; example stories in education). For instance, the story of Abraham relinquishing Sarah to Pharaoh in order to protect his life can be shown to fit an early, nomadic situation, probably as a campfire tale (see Koch, 1969:111–32).

This method became known as **form criticism** (in German, *Formgeschichte*, the "history of the form"). New Testament scholars attempted to apply a similar method to the study of the Gospel traditions. Their goals were to determine the source of each tradition and how and why it was preserved (or created) in the period between Jesus and the Gospels. Again we notice an attempt to overcome the plurality of traditions and to get back to one supposedly best tradition.

We have seen that the Gospels came into being in an oral, storytelling culture and that traces of the oral tradition are clearly discernible in Paul's letters (pages 53–65, 84–85). Obviously, the story of the Last Supper (the oral form) already existed as a narrative within the context of the church's celebration of the Lord's Supper (the typical setting) before it was written down in any gospel (Paul actually recites part of the narrative in his letter to the Corinthians; see 1 Cor. 11:23–34).

Other typical situations proposed for the transmission of the oral Jesus traditions include missionary activity, instruction of new converts, disputes with other Christians or other Jews, the need for church order and discipline, and—above all—proclaiming the good news.

What we must imagine, then, is a rather complex process of transmission of the traditions about Jesus in a variety of forms. It is reasonable to assume that after 30 CE this material existed as a mass of stories and sayings that were used in a variety of contexts (sermons, debates, worship, and so on). This material would be selected and shaped to fit the contexts that transmitted it. Also, given the seeming lack of contact between the Gospel of John and the synoptic Gospels, we should probably posit at least two main channels of transmission: one flowing into the synoptic Gospels, the other into John. The emerging picture of the history of the traditions behind the Gospels may be shown in chart form (Figure 8.3).

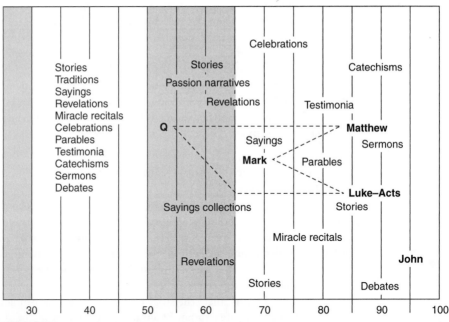

FIGURE 8.3   **THE GOSPELS AND ORAL TRADITIONS**   After the death of Jesus the traditions about him passed through three distinct stages. First was the stage of oral traditions, when the stories and sayings of Jesus were transmitted by those who retold them in sermons, debates, and liturgies. The second stage was the collection of similar stories and sayings into longer units. Probably the earliest was the passion narrative (stories about Jesus' death), but there were also collections of miracle stories and sayings collections. Some of these collections may have been written down during this stage; scholars believe that this was the case with Q. In the third stage written gospels appear, probably beginning with Mark.

Form critics sought to explain the diversity in the Gospels by tracing the history of each tradition. Thus the German scholar Joachim Jeremias, argued that in order to interpret the parables the interpreter must be conscious of the three different situations in which those parables have been used: the situation of the Gospel writer, the situation of the early church and the oral transmitters, and the situation of Jesus. He warned that the meaning of a parable could be different as it moved from one situation to another (1963). Form critics sought to transcend this diversity by uncovering the earliest and most reliable form of the tradition, even as Jeremias sought to discover the meaning of the "parables *of Jesus*" (the title of his book).

In the process, however, they discovered something about the Gospels that led in the opposite direction, not back toward a primal unity but forward toward increasing diversity. For the form critics discovered that when they isolated the various units of traditions and constructed their histories, there were things still left: editorial connections, expansions, and conclusions—what one scholar labeled "the framework of the story of Jesus" (Schmidt, 1919). A new method then evolved to deal with this framework.

Variety from the Editing Process

At the end of his monumental volume, suggestively titled *The History of the Synoptic Tradition*, form critic Rudolf Bultmann presented a brief sketch of each Gospel. He had begun to see that each writer was doing something unique with the Gospel traditions, though he still maintained that "Mark is not sufficiently master of his material to be able to venture on a systematic construction himself" (1972:350).

But as the attention of critics shifted from the tradition before the Gospels to the way each Gospel writer dealt with that tradition, a new method emerged to analyze the editorial activity of the Gospel writers—**redaction criticism** (*Redaktion* being the German word for "editing"). By means of this analysis of editorial and compositional techniques, these critics hoped to arrive at the specific perspective of each writer, what they called his *theology*.

Building on the priority of Mark as established by source criticism and alerted to the existence of editorial activity in the transitions, scholars began to examine the details of the stories and sayings more attentively. It became clear that each writer had a design that shaped the story of Jesus. This movement reached fruition in a brilliant and influential commentary on Luke's Gospel by Hans Conzelmann, in which he demonstrated the editorial process at work (1961). Conzelmann showed, for example, that the change Luke made in the geographical reference in the empty tomb narrative (from an appearance in Galilee to a saying in Galilee that he would appear—compare Luke 24:6–7 with Mark 16:7) is a deliberate reworking of the Markan tradition to fit the geographical scheme that Luke had followed from the beginning. Conzelmann argued that for Luke the culmination of God's saving activity centered in Jerusalem and that it was theologically impossible to shift back to Galilee at this point in his narrative (Conzelmann, 1961:93).

The excitement that many of us felt on our first exposure to redaction criticism is due to the ability of this method to take seriously the differences between the Gospels, to explain the differences without explaining them away. As scholarly attention to detail increased, so did appreciation of the abilities of the Gospel writers.

Soon it became evident that the Gospel writers were doing more than editing: they were creative authors. As one scholar wrote:

> At an earlier period in the history of New Testament scholarship the synoptic gospels (Matthew, Mark and Luke) were thought to be relatively uncomplicated documents which had been put together without careful planning and which told a rather straightforward story. Today the synoptics are understood to be enormously intricate products containing subtle and ingenious literary patterns and highly developed theological interpretations. (Dan O. Via, in Perrin, 1969:v)

Thus form criticism had shown that the Gospel writers had worked with a vast body of preexisting traditions about Jesus, whereas redaction criticism had shown that they used this material creatively, modifying and even inventing traditions. These two ideas may seem contradictory. They violate our neat distinction between fiction and nonfiction. But nearly all ancient authors operated in the ambiguous area between what their readers already knew about their subject and the new story they intended to tell. Homer, Aeschylus, Sophocles, Euripides molded the well-known stories of classical history and mythology into new patterns for their audiences. Their art was to tell a known story in a new way. The Gospel writers, too, included treasures, both "what is old and what is new" (Matt. 13:52). We should no more identify the Gospels with modern novels (fiction) than with modern history (nonfiction).

Redaction criticism has served a fruitful purpose in gospel studies. Even those who moved beyond it regarded it as a great advance over earlier methods, for it called attention to the specific purposes of each Gospel writer. Its scope, however, soon seemed limited. The redaction critic concentrated on what was unique to each Gospel, what had been edited. But it is possible that the material a writer adopted without change was as important as the material that was changed. The attempt to understand the Gospels as unified stories has led Gospel critics to explore a variety of methods commonly called **literary criticism**.

Variety from the Writing of Literature

Literary criticism attempts to explore the meaning of the Gospels as narrative entities, each with its own organic unity. Narratives differ in fundamental ways from other kinds of literature, creating worlds into which we must enter even before we understand them or decide whether we like them. They do not say; they show. They insist we meet them on their territory on their terms. Narratives involve characters and actions, not discussions of abstract ideas. To understand a narrative, we must discover the unity of its action, the nature of its world, the significance of its characters, and much more.

The means that Gospel critics have used to explore the narrative nature of the Gospels are extremely rich and diverse. It is not too much to say that every approach of general literary criticism has been applied to the Gospels in recent years, often with surprisingly insightful results. Rather than explore these approaches here (many of which will be illustrated in the following chapters) we must consider the central concern of this chapter: How does a literary method address the problem of diversity among the Gospels?

While accepting much of the results of earlier kinds of criticism, the literary critic is not content to explain the different versions of the empty tomb story as deriving merely from various sources, different channels of transmission, or different ideas. Though each of these may account for some of the variations, there are larger considerations. There is a story at work. Angels and earthquakes, for example, may appear quite natural in some kinds of stories but seem entirely out of place in others. The narrative role fulfilled by the women or the disciples may vary greatly among the different Gospels, and this would demand that they respond to the risen Jesus in ways appropriate to their character in a specific story. The logic of one plot may demand a return to the beginning (symbolized by Galilee), whereas another plot requires continual movement forward. These are the issues raised by literary criticism.

We expect variety in literature, and differences between the Gospels are thus not surprising. Aristotle (384–322 BCE) carefully distinguished between what he called "history" and "poetry," which is approximately what we mean when we distinguish between ordinary writing and literature:

> Poetry, therefore, is more philosophical and more significant than history, for poetry is more concerned with the universal, and history more with the individual. By the universal I mean what sort of man turns out to say or do what sort of thing. . . . By the individual I mean a statement telling, for example, "what Alcibiades did or experienced." (Poetics 1451b, Golden translation)

This, of course, is the basic distinction between art and life: art interprets; life simply is. Aristotle saw history more as a reporting of what is (or was) rather than as a creative interpretation of what might be. Many modern historians would question the absolute distinction, of course, for they intend to write meaningful history, an interpretation of the past and not simply a chronicle of what happened. With interpretation comes variety.

It is partly this effort of literature to go beyond the mere telling of an event to an interpretation of its meaning that accounts for differences among the Gospels. Because the Gospel writers sought to show the meaning of Jesus for their own communities, we must expect them to tell that story differently. In fact, a given writer might vary the telling of a story within a given work. For example, in Euripides' play *Ion*, the rape of Creusa is recounted five times, but each time it is told differently so as to shape the audience's reactions. Closer to our concerns, the story of Paul's inaugural religious experience is recounted in Acts not once but three times—and in three different ways.

READING AND REFLECTION

Carefully compare the stories given in Acts 9:1–30; 22:1–21; and 26:12–20, noticing all the differences among the accounts. A major thrust of this story is the commissioning of Paul to go to the Gentiles. How does this commission come to Paul in each case?

There is much overlap between the stories; and each one has significant elements added that are not in the other versions. There are also a few stark differences.

| 9:7 The men who were traveling with him stood | 22:9 Now those who were with me saw the | 26:13–14 When at midday along the road, your |

| speechless because they heard the voice but saw no one. | light but did not hear the voice of the one who was speaking to me. | Excellency, I saw a light from heaven, brighter than the sun, shining around me and my companions. 14 When we had all fallen to the ground, I heard a voice. |

It seems incredible that when these variations were first noticed they were attributed to the use of different sources, as if even the clumsiest of editors could not have made them agree. But Luke was not a clumsy editor; the writer was a creative author who introduced these changes for good reasons. Clearly the storyteller felt free to modify minor points of the story in order to make an impression on the audience. Modern scholars are convinced that the stories are told differently because they serve different purposes.

That purpose can be seen in how the author has made the mandate to go to the Gentiles fit the audience for whom the story is told. In the first telling, in chapter 9, the telling that the reader automatically regards as the authoritative version, the divine commission comes to Ananias in a voice from God (verse 15). This is probably the normal means by which people were called to service in the Lukan community (see 13:1–3). In the second telling, in chapter 22, the Jewish listeners hear that the divine commissioning came directly to Paul while he was praying in the Temple in Jerusalem, the central holy place of the Jews. In the third telling, in chapter 26, the secular ruler listens to a very abbreviated version of the story in which the divine commission is given in the inaugural vision itself by the epiphany of the risen Jesus (verses 16–18).

We have learned to speak of such changes as *literary license*, for we recognize that they are necessary for telling a story. In a sense each is true, for it does not change the basic meaning of the event; each is also appropriate for the place where it appears in the overall narrative. Unlike history, art does not need exact correspondence. As an ancient critic observed:

Now I am well aware that the greatest natures are least immaculate. Perfect precision runs the risk of triviality, whereas in great writing as in great wealth there must needs be something overlooked. (Longinus, On the Sublime 33.1)

Thus, in great art we must expect to find some imprecision, some disorder. If we refuse to overlook some of these inconsistencies, we will actually overlook a good deal of what the Gospels have to tell us. Luke's writing would be the poorer if he flatly repeated exactly the same story each time; just as our understanding will be the poorer if we refuse to accept the different versions of the story in their variety, insisting that they be harmonized. Instead, being aware of their differences leads us to a more fruitful interpretation of the intention and meaning of the writer. Careful study of the discrepancies between the Gospels, coupled with a literary analysis, will likewise lead us into a fresh understanding of what each writer was trying to say to the particular community addressed by each Gospel.

Variety Understood as Oral Performance

Although scholars appreciated the role of oral tradition already in the development of form criticism, a major shift is taking place today in our conception of an oral culture. This shift represents, in effect, a whole new way of thinking about the problem of how the Gospels developed. There is as yet no consensus on how this new approach should be pursued and certainly no agreement on the results. Nevertheless, the general contours of the new approach are clearly evident.

The premise of this approach is that the traditions about Jesus took shape and developed in an oral mode, and thus should be analyzed using the norms of research appropriate to an oral tradition. Studies of oral traditional cultures have shown them to be significantly different from literary cultures.

One basic difference is the model of transmission. In a literary model, we posit an original with lines of descent: version A, version B, and so on. This is the model that underlies the method of form criticism sketched above. In a simple transmission, there would be a straight line from the current version back to the original. In a complex transmission, there would be multiple lines of influence. Thus document A and document B might be combined to produce document C. This is the model that underlies the method of source criticism sketched above.

But this is not the way an oral culture operates. In an oral culture there is no original version of the story. Rather, different storytellers (or even the same storyteller on different occasions) tell the story differently on different days, at different events, and to different audiences. Scholars adopting this approach have suggested that linear charts, such as those in Figure 8.2, should be replaced by visualizing each story in a web of interconnected performances.

Thus, we should not think simply of Q influencing Matthew but also of Matthew's performance of Q as influencing Q itself. All is interconnected. Viewing Q this way, as a series of interconnected oral performances, avoids the question of whether Q existed as a source for Matthew and Luke. It is not a relevant question because in this model the Gospel writers do not work from sources so much as from a complex set of oral and written traditions, any one of which might be a source for any given story.

It is too soon to tell where this approach will lead or whether it will produce lasting changes in how we view the Gospels. Certainly it has begun to challenge some of the categories and easy assumptions of the earlier literary approaches.

OUR APPROACH

In the chapters that follow, the four Gospels will be studied using the results of these several kinds of criticism. Each has something valuable to contribute to our understanding as long as we are aware of what each is capable of doing. We must use the various methods as we would tools, to accomplish the ends for which each was designed. Here we will make only modest use of source criticism, because we will not focus on the origins of the Gospel traditions. In general, I accept the conclusions of source criticism, though I am not convinced that later writers necessarily used earlier written sources. The oral gospel was a potent source throughout the first century, and all the Gospel writers had some access to it. The hypothesis of Markan priority will be recognized when it reveals something interesting about the narratives studied, but the basic analysis that follows is not dependent on that or any other source theory.

Form criticism asks two kinds of questions: What is the literary form of a particular unit of Gospel tradition, and what is the pre-Gospel history of such a unit? Again, we will devote only scant attention to the history of the traditions but will often be interested in the literary form of a given tradition. The insights such analysis provides into the units of tradition will assist in our larger task: understanding the Gospels as a whole.

More useful for our purposes are the questions asked by *redaction criticism*—questions that concentrate on what each writer has done to shape the traditions used. Often we will study the individual Gospel traditions in detail, revealing (and trying to explain) their differences. However, our approach differs in two important ways from traditional redaction criticism. First, we are not primarily concerned with the ideas of the writers, because we do not view the Gospels as ideas presented in the form of stories. We are interested in the stories themselves. Second, we do not depend on the conclusions of source criticism as confidently as many redaction critics. It is not necessary, for example, to believe that Mark is the source of Matthew in order to be instructed by their differences. This demonstrates how redaction criticism shades off into literary criticism.

The variations among the Gospel accounts of a given incident reveal, at the least, different ways of telling the story. Viewed this way, Mark's differences from Matthew are just as significant as Matthew's differences from Mark, or from John's for that matter. It is not a question of sources and their modification, but rather of a close reading of the texts in comparison with other ways of recounting the incident.

Primarily, our approach will pursue the questions raised by *literary criticism*—the plots of the stories, their ways of portraying characters, their images, devices, and points of view. Our chief concern is to understand these writings as unified narratives. Thus, we will begin in each instance with the question of how each is structured, including the nature of its plot. Here, it will be useful to clarify some of the terms used to describe how the Gospels are organized. Some writers speak of outlines, others of structures or plots or narratives or stories.

The definitions of these terms vary somewhat from writer to writer. In general, an *outline* represents the formal ordering of ideas to show their logic and relationships. We use an outline when we write an essay or theme. One might outline a speech, sermon, or even a letter, but one would never outline a joke or a story, not in the formal sense of the concept at least. Thus, when the Gospels were viewed primarily as sermons or theological treatises, it seemed appropriate to outline them. But if the Gospels are stories, an outline is inadequate for grasping their significance. Our reading guides to the Gospels will therefore be somewhat different from our reading guides to the letters.

A *story* refers to a sequence of events, usually chronological, that form a pattern—an imitation of life as it is or might be. A story is told in a *narrative*, which recounts a story in a specific set of circumstances. This means that the narrative world is limited to the specific events narrated, whereas the story world is the larger reality that includes all that the narrative implies. Hence, a narrative that ends "and they lived happily ever after" implies a story world of indefinite duration and bliss that goes beyond the narrative itself. A narrative represents the plotting of the specific incidents of the story. A story is distinct from a **plot**, though it will always have a plot when it is narrated. The same story may be told through a variety of plots, each subtly shaping its meaning.

Plot refers to the sequence of events in a narrative, the movement of the action. Aristotle defined *plot* as the arrangement of the incidents (*Poetics* 1450a–b), the cause-and-effect logic that binds the incidents together and mandates that one follow the other. As one literary critic has suggested, the sequence "the king died and then the queen died" is a story that lacks a plot. "The king died and then the queen died of grief" represents a story with a plot (Forster, 1962:87). Now a causal relationship exists—or can be imagined—between the incidents.

Plots do not actually exist until we imagine them; readers must reconstruct them. This is so because an author never tells us everything; all narratives contain gaps, holes that must be filled in by the audience. Often an author does no more than put two incidents in sequence, and the obliging reader imagines some connection between them. These **narrative gaps** contribute to the indeterminacy of stories, as various readers fill them in in different ways. The audience makes the presumption that a story possesses unity and coherence, and will fill in gaps in the narrative in order to have a unified story.

A plot, again according to Aristotle, is marked by a beginning, a middle, and an end (1450b.27–32). The beginning is what we might consider an appropriate place to start, one that does not seem random or in need of justification. Middle incidents must then proceed in logical fashion from one to another, each growing out of the one before, until the plot reaches a conclusion—an appropriate place to stop. An end is a satisfying final incident that follows logically from what went before but that needs no further incident to be understood.

Structure is related to the concept of plot because it too deals with the ordering principle of a work. Yet it is a deeper sort of order than plot—the underlying pattern by which we intuit the meaning of a plot. One of the fascinating hypotheses of modern scholarship in several disciplines—from anthropology to literature, from history to linguistics—is that all human activity is structured.

Thus linguists talk of a structure to language that is deeper than word order, a grammar that allows us to make sense of words and sentences. So too, it will be argued here, a series of structures or patterns underlie the Gospels' narratives and help shape their meanings. Our approach to comprehending these structures will be indirect, using the correlative concept of plot. The goal for us is not to outline topics found in a given Gospel but rather to understand the organizing principles that shape and inform each of the Jesus stories.

Following the contours of their structures, we will examine each narrative in detail, focusing especially on those topics and concerns that scholars have raised in dealing with each work. Finally, we will try to place each writing in the social and historical context of the community for which it was written.

A word of caution is in order: The movement from narrative to history is a complicated one and not easily negotiated. We must attempt to speak historically about the Gospels without committing the historicist error of assuming they are merely telling us what happened. Though Jesus, Peter, Mary, and the others were real people with real personalities, we must be clear that we are not encountering these real people in the stories. Rather, we encounter characters shaped and defined by the various authors. The Jesus of Mark's Gospel may accurately reflect the Jesus of history (a topic we will address in the final chapter), but the two are certainly not identical. The Gospels present us not with candid snapshots but with artistic portraits, each characterizing Jesus in ways deemed revealing to the community for which it was written.

Similarly, we must not assume that the disciples in the stories are simply the historical disciples; nor should we readily identify the Jews portrayed in these stories with the historical community of Jesus' time, or even of the time of the author. As one literary critic remarked:

> We must keep in mind that the narrative is a form of representation. Abraham in Genesis is not a real person any more than the painting of an apple is real fruit. (Berlin, 1983:13)

We must be careful not to allegorize the stories, interpreting them as if they were about something outside the story. These stories are not windows on the real world; they are mirrors reflecting both that world and the author and audience they imply. These two views of the Gospels may be graphically represented (Figure 8.4).

Perhaps the best way to come to terms with the difference between a historicist and a literary reading of the Gospels is to take a close look at a particular incident. Study the following versions of the story of Jesus in the wilderness. What would be the reasons for viewing them as direct accounts showing what actually happened (historicist reading) or for viewing them as accounts (perhaps based on something that actually happened) but shaped by literary forces, such as plotting, symbolism, characterization, or point of view?

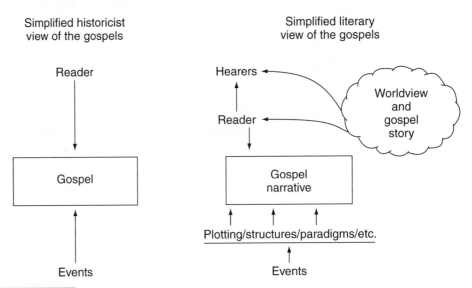

FIGURE 8.4 GOSPELS' RELATION TO EVENTS A historical reading of the Gospels imagines that the reader has direct access to the events of history by merely reading the Gospels: the Gospels are a window on the world. A literary reading of the Gospels imagines a number of intermediate stages. While real events stand behind the Gospel narratives, literary factors like plotting, and structures of story and perception determined how those events would be used in the Gospel narratives. On the other side, a reader would recite these narratives to hearers, in part shaping their perception. This reader and the hearers would also be influenced by their overall worldview and by a general understanding of the Gospel story, the overall story of Jesus with which they were familiar. With this in mind, we should not be too quick to assume that what these hearers heard can be equated with the actual events.

Matthew 4:1–11

Then Jesus was led up by the Spirit into the wilderness to be tempted by the devil. 2 He fasted forty days and forty nights, and afterwards he was famished.

3 The tempter came and said to him, "If you are the Son of God, command these stones to become loaves of bread." 4 But he answered, "It is written, 'One does not live by bread alone, but by every word that comes from the mouth of God.'"

5 Then the devil took him to the holy city and placed him on the pinnacle of the temple, 6 saying to him, "If you are the Son of God, throw yourself down; for it is written, 'He will command his angels concerning you,' and 'On their hands they will bear you up, so that you will not dash your foot against a stone.'" 7 Jesus said to him, "Again it is written, 'Do not put the Lord your God to the test.'" 8 Again, the devil took him to a very high mountain and showed him all the kingdoms of the world and their splendor; 9 and he said to him, "All these I will give you, if you will

Mark 1:12–13

And the Spirit immediately drove him out into the wilderness.

13 He was in the wilderness forty days, tempted by Satan; and he was with the wild beasts;

Luke 4:1–13

Jesus, full of the Holy Spirit, returned from the Jordan and was led by the Spirit in the wilderness, 2 where for forty days he was tempted by the devil. He ate nothing at all during those days, and when they were over, he was famished. 3 The devil said to him, "If you are the Son of God, command this stone to become a loaf of bread." 4 Jesus answered him, "It is written, 'One does not live by bread alone.'"

5 Then the devil led him up and showed him in an instant all the kingdoms of the world. 6 And the devil said to him, "To you I will give their glory and all this authority; for it has been given over to me, and I give it to anyone I please. 7 If you, then, will worship me, it will all be yours." 8 Jesus answered him, "It is written, 'Worship the Lord your God, and serve only him.'" 9 Then the devil took him to Jerusalem, and placed him on the pinnacle of the temple, saying to him, "If you are the Son of God, throw yourself down from here, 10 for it is written, 'He will command his angels

John 1:51

Matthew 4:1–11	Mark 1:12–13	Luke 4:1–13	John 1:51
fall down and worship me." 10 Jesus said to him, "Away with you, Satan! for it is written, 'Worship the Lord your God, and serve only him.'"		concerning you, to protect you,' 11 and 'On their hands they will bear you up, so that you will not dash your foot against a stone.'" 12 Jesus answered him, "It is said, 'Do not put the Lord your God to the test.'"	
11 Then the devil left him, and suddenly angels came and waited on him.	and the angels waited on him.	13 When the devil had finished every test, he departed from him until an opportune time.	And he said to him, "Very truly, I tell you, you will see heaven opened and the angels of God ascending and descending upon the Son of Man."

Even a casual look at these parallel versions of the story of Jesus' wilderness experience reveals how differently the four Gospels tell the story. As we come to expect, John's version is unique; in fact, John does not even report a wilderness experience following Jesus' baptism. (But then, John does not report Jesus' baptism either!) Mark's version, too, differs greatly, containing only the barest sketch of the action. Matthew and Luke share considerable material word for word, material not found in Mark, material that scholars conjecture came from a second source (Q). But a close reading will reveal differences even between these two similar accounts.

A historicist reading of these stories imagines that we are looking rather directly at reports of what actually happened. If you had been there you would have seen these things, they assume, and could know whether they happened in the order given by Matthew or in the order given by Luke. But even the existence of this divergent order ought to warn us that we are not reading direct historical reports. In fact, the oldest version (Mark) is vague and general, sounding for all the world like a period of testing that lasted the full forty days. Perhaps Matthew and Luke are simply elaborations of this rudimentary story.

This suspicion takes added weight when we notice that the three temptations are highly stylized, one for each element of the human person as the ancients understood it: body (food), soul (pride), and spirit (worship). Perhaps these three temptations are narrated because they symbolize the total temptation of Jesus, understood now as a representative human being (that is, the general Gospel story may be shaping the way individual incidents are narrated). And the differing order of the temptations may also stem from plotting devices by the writers, for we will see that Matthew treats proper worship as a major theme (so perhaps he puts the temptation to false worship in the climactic third position), whereas Luke has a strong interest in the Temple (which he puts in the third position). Each writer shapes the content and the sequence of the action to fit the story being told (and so one suspects that Luke's closing words foreshadow a return of the devil later in the story).

Reading with this literary paradigm in mind will alter our attitude toward the stories. It does not mean that these things did not happen. Surely many of the Gospel stories are rooted in the events of Jesus' life in first-century Palestine. But it does mean that we do not have direct access to what actually happened. We have Gospel narratives shaped by authors' purposes, by plotting devices, by ancient views of how humans work, by readers' expectations, and by overarching views of the real meaning of the Gospel story. We will eventually explore how we might move from these literary remains to historical realities (Chapter 14). But first it will be best to concentrate simply on the stories told, being careful not to confuse them with historical events or real people. When we read Mark we are seeing Mark's Jesus (not Jesus himself), Mark's disciples (not the real people), Mark's Jews (not the men and women of Jesus' time).

Now let us turn to the stories. We will study them in the order in which they were probably written, which is also a logical order, moving from the more simple narrative of Mark to the increasingly complex narratives of the other writings.

LEARNING ON YOUR OWN

REVIEWING THE CHAPTER

Names and Terms

bios	Irenaeus	source criticism
criticism	literary criticism	synopsis
Diatessaron	narrative gaps	synoptic Gospels
double tradition	plot	synoptic problem
form criticism	Q source	Tatian
gospel	redaction criticism	

Issues and Questions

1. What other kinds of ancient literature share common traits with the Gospels?
2. How did ancient interpreters deal with the diversity of gospels?
3. Describe the four stages of modern Gospel criticism.
4. What arguments lead many scholars to conclude that Mark's Gospel is prior to, and a source for, Matthew and Luke?
5. How did redaction criticism grow out of form criticism and into literary criticism?
6. How does a literary reading of the Gospels differ from a historicist reading?

TAKING THE NEXT STEP

An excellent introductory survey of the methods of biblical interpretation is Harrington, 1985. There is also a series of fine introductory works published by Fortress Press (the Guides to Biblical Scholarship series): see especially McKnight, 1969 (form criticism); Perrin, 1969 (redaction criticism); and Powell, 1991 (narrative criticism).

See also the works cited in the resources for the Introduction.

Topics for Special Studies

For general strategies and research tools useful for New Testament study, see Appendix A, "Doing Your Own Research." Each chapter concludes with a selection of topics and resources that will enable you to advance your study as far as your interest takes you.

What Was Tatian's *Diatessaron*?

You could focus on the nature of the work, the reasons for its popularity, or why it was ultimately banished; begin with Koester, 1990; then see Kahle, 1947. For the text see Hill, 1894 (2006 facsimile edition). The text can be found online at http://www.earlychristianwritings.com/text/diatessaron.html.

Which Gospel Was Written First?

Fitzmyer, 1971, is a good starting point; see also Sanders, 1968. Soards, 1987, provides a specific case study; Stoldt, 1980, reviews the history; and Farmer, 1964, argues an alternate solution. For the definitive study, see Streeter, 1924.

How Do Scholars Today Understand the Relationship among the Gospels?

There is extensive literature on the relationships among the gospel accounts; see the annotated bibliography of McKnight and Williams, 2000, and the older comprehensive bibliography of Longstaff and Thomas, 1988. For a simple introduction see Wansbrough, 1991. For a conservative view see Stein, 2001. A review of the common views can be found in Tyson, 1976, and Fitzmyer, 1971; Farmer, 1976b, represents a dissenting viewpoint. See also Tuckett, 1984, and Walker, 1978. For a vigorous response to Farmer's view, see Talbert and McKnight, 1972. A compelling case for a complex oral-written matrix in light of ancient writing practices is made by Derrenbacker, 2005. For a view of gospel relationships that includes all known gospels, see the works of Crossan, especially 1991 and 1988.

What Can Be Known about the Hypothetical Q Document?

Probably the best treatment of the formation and significance of the hypothetical Q document is Kloppenborg, 2000, together with his 1987 work. For an overview, see Catchpole, 1993, and Taylor, 1959. Less persuaded are Goulder, 1996; Hobbs, 1980; and Farrer, 1955. But see Downing's response, 1964 (also 1988); see also Kloppenborg, 1986. Both Farrer's critique and Downing's response are collected in Bellinzoni, 1985. Goodacre, 2002, argues the case against Q. Horsley and Draper, 1999, show how an oral performance would function. Allison, 1997, studies how Jesus is portrayed in Q.

How Might Oral Tradition Studies Change Our View of the Gospels?

For an overview, start with the popular work by Dundees, 1999. The basic theoretical work is provided by Ong, 1982, and Lord, 1960. The key work on the gospels is Kelber, 1983. See the important work of Dewey, 1995, 1991, and 1996, and Boomershine, 1987; see also Silberman, 1987. For an application to the study of the historical Jesus, see Dunn, 2000 and 2005.

What Other Kinds of Ancient Literature Are the Gospels Most Like?

On the question of the gospel genre, most see it as a form of the ancient biography (*bios*); see Aune, 1987; Talbert, 1977; Shuler, 1982; Collins, 1990; and Burridge, 2004. For other views, see, Smith, 1971; Kee, 1973; Smith, 1975; and Bruce, 1963c.

For Greco-Roman sources that have parallel themes or forms to gospel stories, see Cartlidge and Dungan, 1993.

How Did New Testament Criticism Develop?

Trace the historical development of one of the kinds of criticism (source, form, or redaction) or one of their leading proponents (such as Streeter, Bultmann, Dibelius, Conzelmann, or Jeremias).

The standard reference work, a virtual history of New Testament scholarship, has been Kümmel, 1972, but it is perhaps now surpassed by MacRae and Epp, 1987; see also Niell and Wright, 1988.

For a broad introduction to form criticism written on a popular level, see Lohfink, 1979.

An explanation and evaluation of these methods by religiously conservative scholars is the collection edited by Marshall, 1977; see also Green, 1987; Harrison, 1978; and Martin, 1975.

More advanced students will want to consult some of the original works:

Source criticism: Streeter, 1924.
Form criticism: Bultmann, 1931; Dibelius, 1935; and Taylor, 1935.
Redaction criticism: Bornkamm, Barth, and Held, 1963; Conzelmann, 1961; and Marxsen, 1969.

What Is the Literary Criticism of the Gospels?

One of the generative articles on the literary study of the gospels was Perrin, 1972. The work of Amos Wilder has been influential. For an early summary, see Petersen, 1978. For more recent work, see Powell, 1991; Beardslee, 1991; and Moore, 1989. On narrative criticism, see Merenlahti, 2002. On characterization, see the diverse collection by Rhoads and Syreeni, 1999. On story beginnings, see Smith, 1990. For a feminist view, see Dewey, 1992. For works on literary criticism, see the resources for the Introduction.

How Can We Distinguish Story and History?

Helms, 1988, challenges the notion that one can learn history from the gospels, whereas Theissen, 1987, attempts to tell a historical story about Jesus based on a literary reading of the gospels. Merenlahti and Hakola provide insight into the relationships between fictional and nonfictional narrative in Rhoads and Syreeni, 1999. Culpepper, 1984, and Freyne, 1988, seek to combine literary and historical conclusions. Bauckham, 1998, and Byrskog, 2003, present a more conservative approach, and Schüssler Fiorenza, 1983, provides a feminist critique. See the additional bibliographic suggestions at the end of Chapters 1 and 14.

How and Why Were the Noncanonical Gospels Written?

Explore one of the following: *Gospel of Thomas, Gospel of Peter, Dialogue of the Savior,* Jewish-Christian gospels,. For Thomas's relation to other gospel traditions see Risto, 1998.

The standard collection of "other" gospels, those that did not become a part of the canon, is volume 1 of Hennecke and Schneemelcher (1959) now available in a revised edition, Schneemelcher and Wilson, 2003. See also James, 1924, and J. K. Elliott, 1993a. Paperback collections of the more important gospels are now available in Cameron, 1982, and Crossan, 1985. For a broad treatment, see Koester, 1990. See also Borg, 1997. Ehrman, 1998, includes all texts produced in the century after Jesus' death, both canonical and noncanonical.

For examples of parallels between the gospels and other literature, see Cartlidge and Dungan, 1993, and Martin, 1988.

What Can Be Learned from the Study of a Particular Incident?
Choose one important gospel incident and apply one or more of these forms of criticism to it: source, form, redaction, literary.

For decidedly different applications of these methods to the resurrection narratives, see Perrin, 1977; Fuller, 1980; Osborne, 1984; and Lüdemann, 1994.

You can explore any passage in the commentaries listed at the end of each chapter in this book.

Additional Books and Articles

Of the many books on the gospels as collection, the following are especially recommended.

Introductory

Craddock, 1981; Green, 1987; Kee, 1977; Mays, 1981; Nickle, 1980; Powell, 1997; Rollins, 1963; and Sanders and Davies, 1989.

More Advanced

Donahue, 1988; Evans and Porter, 1995; Freyne, 1988; Goosen and Tomlinson, 1994; Koester, 1990; Moore, 1989; Mack and Robbins, 1990; Theissen, 1991; Vermes, 1981.

Malina and Rohrbaugh, 1992, is perhaps more useful as a clear explanation of the terms and models of a social science approach than as a commentary on the synoptics.

Tools

In addition to the synopses of Throckmorton, 1967 (now available with the New Revised Standard Version, 1992), and Aland, 1972, you may wish to use the specialized works of Funk, 1984, and Crossan, 1986a. Beginning students might also profit from Beare, 1962, which contains a brief analysis of the similarities and differences of the gospel accounts for each individual story or saying.

9

GOD'S KINGDOM IN A TRAGIC WORLD

 Every short story is essentially a story of revelation, either the hero's or the audience's.

THOMAS LEITCH, *WHAT STORIES ARE*

The Gospel according to Mark, the shortest and simplest of the Gospels, is also probably the earliest, marking the invention of the gospel genre. Thus it is a suitable work for beginning our analysis of this new kind of literature. Although its author had neither a good command of Greek nor a polished style, and although the work contains several awkward—even erroneous—constructions (as we discussed in Chapter 8; page 260), it has proven to be one of the most powerful literary works of the Roman era. Close examination will show it to be carefully crafted and engagingly written.

Here we will reflect briefly on how this work was written and then consider its plot and organization. A study of specific incidents in the story will lead to a discussion of major themes that have drawn scholarly attention. We will then turn to its characterization of the actors in the story and the sense that everyone betrays Jesus. Finally, we will attempt to relate that picture to the historical and social setting of its first hearers.

THE MAKING OF MARK'S GOSPEL

The Gospel we know as Mark is really an anonymous work; nowhere does it reveal the slightest clue to the identity of its author. When it became necessary to associate each canonical writing with a specific apostle, church leaders in the second century attributed this Gospel to a person named John Mark, declaring him to be a companion of Peter, the ultimate source of the Gospel. Peter and Mark are associated in Acts (12:25), 2 Timothy (4:11), and 1 Peter (5:13). But the evidence connecting either of them to this Gospel comes from a time long after the writing of the Gospel.

The fourth-century historian Eusebius summarizes reports from the second century that Mark wrote this Gospel in order to preserve Peter's teaching after Peter's death (*Ecclesiastical History* 3.39.15). But in another place Eusebius implies that Mark died "in the eighth year of Nero's reign" (64 CE), which would mean that he died before Peter (2.24.1). We simply do not know how soundly based these reports are, and nothing in the Gospel itself would suggest a connection with Mark or Peter. It might be more fruitful to consider why the Gospel makes no claim to authorship than to try to prove that it was or was not written by Mark. When I continue to call the author *Mark*, I mean no more than the anonymous author of the Gospel called Mark.

Anonymity is quite a different literary phenomenon from pseudonymity (see pages 93–96, 185–86). The pseudonymous work is claiming the authority of a particular teacher or tradition, but the anonymous work is claiming that the writing is simply the common tradition of the community. And in one sense all the gospels consist of community property. As we saw in Chapter 8, gospels are made up of small units of tradition (each of which scholars call a **pericope** [usually pronounced pur-RIK-uh-pee]) that circulated individually or in small collections in the period before there were written gospels. The creativity of the Gospel writers lay in their ability to shape these stories to their purposes, combine them in new configurations, and supplement them with their own writing.

Mark's Gospel consists of 106 (or so) pericopes, ranging in length from a single sentence to a couple of paragraphs. Most are connected together with the simple conjunction *and*, probably indicating the originally oral nature of the composition. Lacking indicators of the connection between incidents, members of the audience were forced to imagine their own connections. We must expect that different audiences might imagine different connections, and so might you and I. This is a good illustration of the modern literary thesis that every reader is also an author, creating with the writer the ultimate meaning(s) of the work. For every writer leaves what we call **narrative gaps**: elements of the story that must be inferred in order to make sense of the whole. For example, this story opens with the prophetic announcement about a messenger "crying in the wilderness" (1:3) and follows with the introduction of the first character: "John the baptizer appeared in the wilderness" (1:4). Is the reader to fill the gap and infer that John is the anticipated messenger? Or is the messenger Jesus, whom the Spirit drives "into the wilderness" (1:12)?

Some literary forms (Greek tragedies, for example) minimize these gaps, trying to connect each incident tightly to the ones before and after. Gospels often, though not always, seem to maximize the gaps. Without question the connections between incidents in the Gospels must often be inferred.

Most readers of Mark can agree that the opening sequence is connected: it introduces John the Baptizer (1:2–8); shows Jesus being baptized (9–11), tested (12–13), beginning his own proclaiming (14–15), and calling his own followers (16–20). But before long, most readers wonder whether the incidents are not coming in a random, or at least arbitrary, order. For example, Jesus heals a leper (1:40–45), cures a paralytic (2:1–12), calls another follower (13–14), takes dinner with him (15–17), and answers questions about fasting (18–22) and Sabbath observance (23–27). The only two incidents that have an obvious connection are the call of the disciple followed by dinner with him. For the other incidents, different readers may imagine different connections and thus construct somewhat different plots for this story (see the discussion of plot, page 271).

One way to focus on the issue of plot is to recall that plots involve conflict and resolution. The most obvious sort of conflict is between a hero and a villain (the western), but there are many other sorts of conflict: conflicts with supernatural beings (myths), with monsters (legends), with nature (hero tales), with the community (comedies), even with oneself (tragedies). Many stories will contain several types of conflict, and such is the case with Mark's Gospel.

To understand some of these conflicts, one has to understand one very basic difference between the way most modern people understand the world and the way the ancients did. We tend to interpret most things that happen in terms of impersonal cause-and-effect forces: storms are caused by low-pressure systems; illness is caused by germs; bizarre behavior is caused by chemical imbalances in the brain or by traumatic experience that causes psychological damage; people fail to understand something because they lack the requisite background or mental acumen; and so on.

Not so for the ancients. First-century people generally understood causality in personal terms. Bad things happened because of one's enemies—either humans, who could give one the evil eye or harm one through magic, or spirits. Good things happened because of God's blessings or because of some charm or spell. Storms are caused by God or by demons (see Mark 4:29, where Jesus rebukes the wind and talks to the sea); illness is the result of oppression either by some supernatural source or by an enemy using magic (see James 5:14–15; in Mark we see this clearly in Jesus' power to bring health, for example, 1:34; see also 6:5); bizarre behavior is likely caused by an evil spirit (see Mark 9:20; note that Matt. 17:15 attributes the behavior to madness); even not understanding something may be caused by external forces (see Mark 6:52).

SEEKING MARK'S STORY

READING AND REFLECTION

Read the entire Gospel of Mark, preferably out loud. Keep track of all the places in the story where Jesus comes into conflict using a chart like the following. Pay particular attention to conflicts with supernatural powers, illness, nature, opponents, and even the disciples.

Reference	Opponent	Outcome	How Resolved
1:13–	Satan	Unspecified	With angels (?)
1:23–	An unclean spirit	Expelled	By command
1:30–			

Tracing these conflicts allows us to construct a coherent plot to this story, a plot with several surprises. We are not too surprised at how triumphantly the story begins, since it is explicitly said to be "the beginning of the good news [gospel] of Jesus Christ, the Son of God" (1:1). This might lead us to expect that Jesus' contest with Satan in the wilderness will come out well (and note that in Mark it is a contest, not a temptation to sin). This expectation is confirmed by Jesus' first encounter with an unclean spirit. For Jesus orders it around as if it were a servant (1:23–27).

This very success causes problems—one of the paradoxes of this story. For some conclude that Jesus can order these spirits around because he is in league with their ruler, whom they name Beelzebul (3:22). The little story Jesus tells to refute this charge (3:27) is very important for understanding the basic thrust of Mark's story; we will return to it in a moment.

First we must note how unstoppable Jesus appears in the early part of the story. At 1:22 the disciples are astonished at his teaching; at 1:27–28 his exorcism miracle "amazes" them, raising the question of his authority and spreading his fame (demonstrated in a vignette in 1:32–34). After healing a leper, Jesus is so popular that he "could no longer openly enter a town" (1:45). At 2:12, after he heals a paralytic, the people exclaim, "We never saw anything like this." His next miracle produces the first opposition (3:6), but a great multitude follows him (3:7)—so great that he cannot even eat (3:20). A nature miracle prompts them to ask: "Who then is this that even the wind and the sea obey him" (4:41). More and more astounding miracles occur, coupled with increasing popularity (5:20, 42; 6:51, 55), until we learn: "They were astonished beyond measure, saying 'He has done all things well'" (7:37). This, the strongest expression of Jesus' popularity in this Gospel, marks the climax of the first movement of the plot. At this point it would seem that nothing can prevent Jesus from overthrowing the power of evil.

This leads to our second surprise: Jesus' truly shocking announcement midway through the story that he will undergo great suffering and be killed (8:31). This is the first indication from Jesus that he will suffer, and it will be twice repeated (9:31 and 10:33). Its mystery is highlighted by the fact that no one in the story understands it.

A third surprise in the story comes in the climactic scene in which Pilate is asked to condemn Jesus. Pilate sees through the motives of Jesus' foes and schemes to release him by calling on the crowd, who up to this point in the story have been on Jesus' side, protecting him (11:18; 12:12) and delighting in him (12:37). But the crowd turns against him (15:8–13).

A final surprise occurs at the very end of the story, a complex surprise. On the one hand we are surprised that the only people to stick with Jesus are the women, because women had very low status in this culture. But our surprise is compounded when even they seem to fail, in the very last words of the story:

> *So they went out and fled from the tomb, for terror and amazement had seized them; and they said nothing to anyone, for they were afraid. (16:8)*

Is this indeed good news? To answer this question requires a closer look at the details of Mark's story.

To summarize: Mark's story consists of two distinct movements, bound together by a scene of recognition and reversal. The first movement we can call the *movement of power*: Jesus seems to prevail against all opponents by his superior power. The final movement we can call the *movement of suffering*: Jesus seems abandoned by all. We can represent this graphically as a rising action, a reversal, and a falling action:

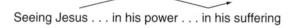

Seeing Jesus . . . in his power . . . in his suffering

There are many ways to sketch the sequence of the action in Mark's story, each revealing and hiding certain aspects. This reading guide focuses on the double movement of the plot and sees these two movements joined together by a scene of recognition and reversal. Do not be confused by the overlap between the sections; stories are not like logical arguments where one point has to be brought to a conclusion before a new point can begin. Stories are like tapestries with many interwoven threads. The aim of the reading guide is not to divide the writing into its parts but to reveal the connections between the parts. We will now examine more closely some of the pivotal scenes.

READING GUIDE TO MARK

> *The Gospel of Mark does not have a single structure made up of discrete sequential units but rather is an interwoven tapestry or fugue made up of multiple overlapping structures and sequences, forecasts of what is to come and echoes of what has already been said. (Dewey, 1991:224)*

THE PRESENCE OF GOD: KINGDOM AND POWER

The story opens with "the voice of one crying in the wilderness prepare the way of the Lord" (1:1). Because there was no punctuation in Greek in Mark's time, we may wonder whether Mark intended "in the wilderness" to describe where the voice was crying (thus describing John) or where the way of the Lord was to be prepared (thus pointing to Jesus' next action). I favor the latter, but in either case, we learn that preparations are under way for the coming of the Lord.

That God would one day come to the faithful and rule over them, establishing the **kingdom of God** on earth, was a dream of many from ancient times. That idea took on added significance in the centuries after the Babylonian exile (587 BCE) when there were no more kings to sit on the throne of David. The kingdom they longed for and dreamed of was a time when universal peace and kinship would prevail (for example, Isaiah 43, 49). Although *kingdom of God* has become established as an appropriate way to refer to this hope, the notion of the *rule of God* would be better, for it better expresses this hope for peace.

Although Jewish notions of both the nature of this rule and the means of its coming varied widely, from those who withdrew into the wilderness quietly awaiting God's time to those who took up arms in open rebellion, one main strand of tradition centered on the coming "Anointed One" (*Messiah* in Hebrew, *Christ* in Greek).

This **Messiah** was often seen as a second David, who would act with the power of God to establish justice and peace among the nations. Mark's use of the title *Christ* and his portrayal of Jesus' immense power raise the question of his view of the nature and coming of God's rule.

A Closer Look at the Opening

"The beginning of the gospel of Jesus Christ, the Son of God." So the story begins, with an incomplete sentence that functions as a title to the work. This identification of Jesus as the Christ and the Son of God warns us to expect no mere history of just what happened. Clearly this is history seen through the eyes of faith. It is history presented as gospel, though what Mark meant by that term is not completely clear. It had connotations of a victory pronouncement and of a story of happy news about a favorable event (see pages 252–53; Mark uses the term *gospel* at 1:14, 15; 8:35; 10:29; 13:10; 14:9).

The beginning that Mark chooses is itself curious, for the story starts neither with Jesus' birth nor background (though the writer knew at least some background information; see 6:3). Instead, it begins in the middle of things, not with Jesus but with John the Baptizer. To understand this, we need to study Mark's opening scene in relation to some of the expectations held by people at that time.

READING AND REFLECTION
Carefully study Mark 1:1–15 and try to answer the following questions.

1. Where do these events take place? Why?
2. How does Mark differentiate between Jesus and John?
3. Exactly what does Jesus proclaim?

James Robinson noticed a curious shift in Mark's language: though the beginning of the Gospel is announced in 1:1, the gospel is not *proclaimed* until after John is put in prison (1:14). Whereas verse 2 is cast in the future tense (what will happen), verse 15 uses the perfect tense to declare that the kingdom "has come." (Or perhaps, "has drawn near"—in either case something has taken place. See Robinson, 1982:24).

On the basis of this language, the events portrayed in verses 2–13 seem to be highly significant for understanding Mark's view of the kingdom of God. The events narrated here allow the kingdom to be proclaimed as an experience, not merely as a future expectation. Mark has carefully structured these events into a dynamic unit with its own logic, which reveals the basic purpose of his story.

The pattern that Mark adopts here is known as *inclusion* or **framing**: notice how the references to the gospel in verses 1 and 15 frame the whole incident. Another obviously balanced pair concerns John: his appearance (verse 4) and his arrest or disappearance (verse 14). In fact, each successive unit is matched with another so that the pairs form successive frames around a middle unit. You might visualize it as a series of parentheses: ((((_)))); or as an X, where the lines converge on a midpoint. In fact, the ancients called this *an X-like pattern*. The Greek letter chi looks like an X, so the pattern was called a **chiasmus** (pronounced kee-AS-muss). The passage could be visualized thus:

More simply, we can visualize three scenes: the first dominated by John, the last by Jesus, and the middle involving them both.

Now we must ask the crucial question: What logic binds these units together? What is their plot? Let us work from the middle out, as a chiasmus implies. The central scene may be taken as the empowerment of Jesus for his divine task, his inauguration. The Psalm quoted here was one used in the coronation of the king in ancient Israel (Psalm 2). This empowerment grows out of John's previous assertion that one more powerful is coming who will "baptize with Holy Spirit" (Mark 1:8). It leads directly to Jesus' encounter with Satan "in the wilderness" (1:13). We must not let our familiarity with other versions of this incident influence our interpretation of Mark. He says nothing of the nature of this experience, nor does he say Jesus fasted. He does not describe it as a temptation to sin or as weakness. Instead, he associates the experience with wild beasts and angels. The word translated "tempted" can equally well mean "tested," and it is no accident that this encounter is paired with the reference to Jesus as one "more powerful" (1:7) because here Jesus proves more powerful than his enemy. That Mark intended this scene to show Jesus' conquest of the power of Satan is made clear by an incident occurring a little later in Mark's story.

Jesus' mastery over demonic forces will lead to a severe charge being leveled against him by his opponents: he can expel demons because he is in league with their master. Jesus will reply to this charge with a little parable that also represents what Mark thinks happened in the wilderness encounter. The parable tells us no one can enter a strong man's house and spoil his possessions unless he is stronger and overpowers the strong man first (3:27). That Jesus is now freeing the demon possessed means that he has overcome the power of Satan: hence the victory pronouncement, the gospel, with which Jesus returned from the wilderness (1:14).

Now we can also see why Mark began with the quotation from Scripture, for this is the time of prophetic fulfillment:

> As it is written in the prophet Isaiah, "See, I am sending my messenger ahead of you, who will prepare your way; the voice of one crying out in the wilderness prepare the way of the Lord, make his paths straight." (1:2–3; I have omitted some punctuation.)

Although Mark appears to be quoting Isaiah, he has actually crafted three separate references from the Scriptures into one saying: the part about sending a messenger is from Malachi (3:1); the part about "ahead of you" is from Exodus (23:20); and the part about the voice and the preparation is from Isaiah (40:3). It was not unusual for writers in Mark's time to combine such sayings in a creative way, for they believed that each scriptural saying revealed the words of God and therefore need not be read in terms of the original context. It was unusual to attribute the combined quote to one source (Isaiah); more often the author would write "in the prophets" or some such general heading (some late manuscripts of Mark actually make this correction). Possibly, the three quotes were already combined before Mark, and he recognized the Isaiah reference. Or maybe he wanted to emphasize the Isaiah aspect of the quotation. Each of these three sources contributes something unique to the effect of the combined saying.

The Malachi prophecy in its original setting eventually identified the messenger with Elijah (Mal. 4:5). As we saw in Chapter 2, it was generally expected that Elijah would return as a final prophet who would prepare God's people for God's coming to them (page 69).

The Exodus passage shows the messenger to be both a guide and a protector who would bring the people to the promised land, the kingdom. It implies that the messenger leads the people, preparing their way.

The Isaiah passage, which Mark emphasizes, locates the place where salvation begins: in the **wilderness**. Though Jesus is already in the wilderness (1:4), he is driven "into the wilderness" by the coming of the Spirit (1:12–13). And for good measure, Mark adds, "And he was in the wilderness forty days, tested by Satan." As Scripture predicted, salvation has begun in the wilderness, a place traditionally associated with the demonic, and now the victory announcement can be made.

Further reading bears out this conclusion. The **exorcisms**, for example, are not struggles but a mere extension of the power of God's rule. When Jesus encounters the demons, their response is fear, even worship, and instantaneous obedience (1:24; 5:6–7). Although we should not make too much of these exorcisms—there are, after all, only five reported—they do reveal the kind of world Mark's story creates.

THE WORLD OF APOCALYPTIC EXPECTATION

Exorcisms are not, in themselves, unique to the gospels, or even to Jewish and Christian literature. A Roman writing about a Greek wonder-working philosopher includes an exorcism, and comparing the way this tale is told with the Markan exorcisms will highlight the way in which Mark viewed the world:

And when he told them to have handles on the cup and to pour over the handles—this being a purer part of the cup since no one's mouth touched that part—a young boy began laughing coarsely, scattering his discourse to the winds. Apollonius stopped and, looking up at him, said, "It is not you that does this arrogant thing, but the demon who drives you unwittingly," for, unknown to everyone, the youth was actually possessed by a demon, for he used to laugh at things no one else did and would fall to weeping for no reason and would talk and sing to himself. Most people thought it was the jumpiness of youth which brought him to do such things, and at this point he seemed carried away by drunkenness, but it was really a demon which spoke through him. Thus, when Apollonius began staring at it, the phantom in the boy let out horrible cries of fear and rage sounding like someone being burned alive or stretched on the rack, and he began to promise that he would leave the young boy and never possess anyone else among men. But Apollonius spoke to him angrily such as a master might to a cunning and shameless slave, and he commanded him to come out of him, giving definite proof of it. "I will knock down that statue there," it said, pointing toward one of those around the porch of the King. And when the statue tottered and then fell over, who can describe the shout of amazement that went up and how everyone clapped their hands from astonishment. But the young boy opened his eyes, as if from sleep, and looked at the rays of the sun [that is, at Zeus, who had delivered him]. Now all those observing these events revered the boy, for he no longer appeared to be as coarse as he was, nor did he look disorderly, but had come back to his own nature nothing less than if he had drunk some medicine. He threw aside his fancy soft clothes and, stripping off the rest of his luxuriousness, he came to love poverty and the thread-bare cloak and the customs of Apollonius. (Flavius Philostratus The Life of Apollonius of Tyana 4.20; quoted from Cartlidge and Dungan, 1993)

Apollonius was roughly contemporary with Mark, though this work about him was not written until about 200. Some influence from the gospel tradition cannot be entirely discounted. Such tales were common in that century, but we must also notice some crucial differences between this and Mark's accounts.

This account of Apollonius lacks any sense of two antithetical worlds, any cosmic conflict between the Spirit and Satan, any notion of the impending end of the old order now invaded by some outside force—all of which are primary themes in Mark. Apollonius's mastery over the demon is even compared to that of a master over his slave, the very charge leveled against Jesus in Mark's story (3:22).

In contrast, Mark's story is embedded in that view of the world we now call *apocalypticism,* the origin and basic notions of which we have already explored (see pages 90–92). Apocalypticism rests on the notion of a cosmic struggle between God and Satan, who, as the prince of this world (or this age), is seen to be in control of life. However, Satan's time is short, and his actions will grow increasingly desperate. Thus, the catastrophic events of "the present time"—sometimes called the "birth pangs" of the new age (13:8)—indicate the imminent arrival of the end.

Apocalypticism took many forms and displayed an amazing array of ideas. One form was Christian; for apocalyptic thought forms were useful to some Christians to interpret what was happening in Jesus of Nazareth. The opening scene of Mark's Gospel presupposes an apocalyptic view of the world but with one decided difference: it shows Jesus as already having overcome Satan. The "good news" of 1:1 and 1:14 is news of present victory. Thus, Jesus already possesses power and authority over demons (6:7), over disease (3:15), even the authority to forgive sins (2:10). See the amusing controversy story about Jesus' authority in 11:28–33.

All this is fairly easy to grasp. It is all played out by the time we reach chapter 8 of the story. Some such insight as this, we must imagine, is what Peter had grasped when he saw that Jesus was the Christ (8:29). Why, then, does Jesus respond with the demand that Peter not tell anyone (8:30)?

THE GREAT SECRET

When scholars first saw that Mark was doing far more than reporting the facts about Jesus, they noticed especially the editing of the material to introduce a theme of secrecy. Initially this was interpreted as a fault: Mark could no longer be considered a good historical source (Wrede, 1901). But this was to ask of Mark something never intended, for it did not intend to give us history. It is a gospel. (See Chapter 8, pages 252–53.)

Scholars now realize that our primary concern must be to find how the theme of secrecy functions in Mark's narrative. When we ask the question this way, we gain some insight into the meaning of the Gospel.

Two kinds of secrecy material first catch the readers' attention. Jesus enjoins strict silence on the demons and unclean spirits (3:11–12; also 1:25, 34; but not 5:6–13), and he also regularly demands silence from those he has healed (1:44; 5:43; 7:36; 8:26; perhaps 5:19; but not 9:14–29 or 10:46–52). A third kind of material is soon evident: Jesus repeatedly attempts to hide (7:24; 1:35; 3:7; 6:31; 10:1).

Mark seems to be trying to conceal the fact that Jesus is the Messiah, thus William Wrede originally called this the "**Messianic secret.**" He supposed Mark was trying to explain why Jesus had not been recognized as the Messiah: Jesus hid. But is that a Markan concern? Probably not. Mark is writing for an audience that has no difficulty in recognizing Jesus as the Christ; the issue is how they ought to understand that declaration.

Some progress is possible if we ask: From whom is the secret kept? Certainly not from the audience. We are let in on the secret from the opening words (1:1) and opening action (1:11). Nor does Jesus hide from the disciples; they are even privileged to a special divine revelation when Elijah, with Moses, appears to Jesus on a mountain (9:2–8). Jesus even tells them directly:

> To you has been given the secret of the kingdom of God, but for those outside everything is in parables. (4:11)

So the secret is kept from "those outside."

On two separate occasions Jesus cautions the disciples not to tell: just after Peter's confession (8:30), and again, when they are coming down from the mountain on which Jesus talked with Elijah and Moses, he admonishes them "to tell no one what they had seen until the Son of man should have risen from the dead" (9:9).

But why should they not tell? One answer derives from the "until" in that last admonition: there is a time before which it is not appropriate to tell. There is a secret time during which God's rule has entered the world incognito, so to speak. This hiddenness of God's rule points up the ambiguity of the miracle stories: the miracles only seem to reveal who Jesus is. Mark highlights this ambiguity in the other scene where the disciples are commanded not to tell, a wonderful scene of recognition and reversal that binds together the two halves of the story. Let us look at that scene in more detail.

THE REVERSAL

READING AND REFLECTION

Reread 8:21–9:1 several times, considering the following questions.

1. How does Mark characterize the way people understand Jesus?
2. Is Peter's understanding any better? Contrast the portrayal in Matt. 16:13–28 (*GP* §122, *SFG* §158, and K41 in Funk, 1995).
3. What does Mark suggest is the true understanding of Jesus' identity?
4. What is the connection of the very odd healing episode that forms the preface to this scene (8:22–26)?

A standard scene in literature reveals the true identity of the hero, followed by a reversal of the action. Such a scene occurs in Sophocles' *Oedipus the King* when the shocking news is delivered: Oedipus is the son of the king he has slain and of the queen he has wed. His identity precipitates his fate. So too, in Mark Jesus' identity engenders his fate. And a new understanding of Jesus as well as a new action begins in this crucial scene. But who achieves this new insight?

It is not the people, for they identify Jesus according to the old paradigms of Elijah or another prophet (8:27). In fact it is just such human understanding that Jesus condemns when Peter rebukes him (8:33; Mark uses the same term, *anthropoi*, "humans," in both verse 27 and verse 33). Nor is it, as we often find, the hero himself. Mark portrays Jesus as already knowing (see 1:11, where the voice addresses Jesus directly). The only other character in this scene is the disciples; do they achieve new insight into Jesus' identity? Mark's story is ambiguous.

On the one hand, Peter achieves a proper acknowledgment: "You are the Messiah" (8:29). As the title to this work shows, Mark regarded this as a true confession (1:1). But Jesus' response is not to congratulate Peter (as in Matthew); rather, he silences him. And when Peter waxes so confident of his correctly identifying Jesus as Messiah that he cannot accept Jesus' new teaching that he will suffer and die, Jesus rebukes him in the sharpest of terms: placing him on the wrong side of the great apocalyptic divide, on the side of Satan and human conception (8:33).

Rather than one of these characters, the implied audience gains new insight. The hearers of the Gospel story, having witnessed Jesus' power, must now see his weakness, must realize that the Jesus who worked miracles is the Jesus who suffered and died. Like the blind man whom Jesus cures, the audience achieves this sight in two stages.

This two-stage healing (the only story in any Gospel where Jesus fails to heal someone on the first try) seems like a small symbolic story, an allegory of the two movements of Mark's story. Jesus' use of physical means produces some sight, albeit distorted. Just so, the miraculous deeds of Jesus can lead to faith in him. But, like Peter's confession, such faith remains incomplete. Only in the second half, the portrayal of Jesus' death, will everything become clear and then only by looking intently (8:25). Only careful scrutiny will reveal what it means to be a follower of the Jesus who suffers and dies.

THE ABSENCE OF GOD: KINGDOM AND SUFFERING

To be sure, the once-popular dictum coined by Martin Kahler that *the gospels are passion narratives with extended introductions* fails dismally to see the great complexity of these works, but it does point to a worthwhile consideration: the large percentage of space devoted to the passion (suffering and death) of Jesus in each of the Gospels, but especially in Mark (see Kahler, 1988:80 n. 11.)

This emphasis is not unexpected, given the prominence of the theme of Jesus' death in early Christian preaching. (See Paul's radical statement in 1 Cor. 2:1–2.) We have seen that form criticism traces the Jesus tradition back to the oral preaching of the church, and it is only logical that a great deal of tradition about Jesus' death would be preserved. Many scholars think that all the stories connected with the death of Jesus (most of Mark 14 and 15) existed as a connected narrative long before Mark wrote. Certainly, the telling of the stories of Jesus' death was a central Christian concern long before Mark.

THE ABANDONMENT AND DEATH OF JESUS

Yet Mark went still further. As we saw above, after the reversal scene in Mark 8 everything converges on the suffering and death of Jesus. Thus, over half his Gospel is oriented toward the passion.

READING AND REFLECTION

As you reread 8:31–16:8, consider the following questions.

1. How does Mark portray the disciples? Do other characters fulfill roles you expect of the disciples?
2. Why do the Pharisees oppose Jesus?
3. What is the meaning of Jesus' death?
4. Is 16:8 a suitable ending for this story?

There are two sections to this final movement of the Gospel: Jesus' death is predicted and then enacted. The first section (8:22–10:52) is an artfully arranged series of three passion predictions (8:31; 9:31; 10:33), each with a response by the uncomprehending disciples, and each followed with a speech by Jesus that attempts to set forth a true understanding of discipleship. The whole section is framed by two miracles of sight that contrast with the lack of insight demonstrated by the disciples (8:22–26 and 10:46–52).

But if the disciples are slow to comprehend that Jesus must suffer, surely the audience is now prepared to witness the events of Jesus' final week in Jerusalem portrayed in the second section (11:1–16:8). This concluding section is divided into two lengthy and two shorter segments:

11:1–12:44	Confrontation with the Jerusalem authorities
13:1–37	Discourse about the end
14:1–15:47	Betrayal, arrest, and crucifixion
16:1–8	Empty tomb

Before looking more closely at the action of this section, it will be useful to reflect on the people involved and how our writer characterizes them.

THE CHARACTERS OF MARK'S STORY

It is customary to speak of characters in stories according to their degree of complexity, as either flat or round characters. A flat character is one who is adequately characterized by one or two dominant traits; they are readily understandable, even predictable. Round characters are more like real people; they may be known by several traits, even conflicting tendencies. We might say their personalities are more fully developed. Their actions are much harder to predict, for there is sufficient complexity to them that they can surprise us.

These are useful distinctions, as long as we do not blur too much the differences between modern and ancient ways of thinking about people. As we discussed in the Introduction, people in the ancient world were generally understood in terms of a few stereotypical traits rather than as complex psychological beings. They were seen as embedded in groups rather than as unique individuals. They were understood by what they did (especially the degree to which they preserved their honor) rather than by some inner character revealing their true identity. (See Table I.1 on page 7.)

In fact the most important characters in this story, besides Jesus, are characterized as groups: the authorities, the crowd, the disciples, and the women. Let's consider each of these in turn, focusing especially on their roles in the conclusion of the story.

The Characterization of the Authorities

From their first introduction, those associated with positions of authority question, accuse, and reject Jesus (for example, 2:6–7; 2:16; 2:24). They are soon conspiring to destroy him (3:6).

The events of Jesus' final week begin with a series of contests in the Jerusalem Temple with these authorities. The first group to confront Jesus is, not surprisingly, those leaders associated with the Temple, the **Sadducees**, a sort of priestly aristocracy in Jesus' day. Wealthy, conservative in both politics and religion, the Sadducees prided themselves on faithfulness to the Law of Moses. They were the sort of folk who demanded to see it in the Bible before they would believe it. Thus, they did not believe in resurrection, because there is no teaching about a resurrection in the Books of Moses. Their lack of concern about the afterlife probably indicates that they were unaffected by the persecutions of Antiochus Epiphanes, when the deaths of righteous Jews demanded some explanation and vindication. (For an example of such vindication, see 2 Maccabees 7. To review the persecution of Antiochus see the discussion on page 48.) This group was near the top of the social pyramid.

Characteristically, they challenge Jesus to defend the idea of a resurrection by proposing a riddle (12:18–27); Jesus offers a subtle argument that, though it seems strange to us, would have been quite compelling in that time. Jesus shows that his own orientation is much closer to the Pharisees than to the Sadducees.

The **Pharisees** were mostly laypeople, not priests, primarily artisans rather than aristocrats, scholars rather than administrators. But their primary difference from the Sadducees concerned their view of the Law (or better, the Torah). While having the highest possible respect for its authority, they did not regard the Torah as a closed book. *Torah* really means something closer to "instruction" than "law," and the Pharisees believed that God's instruction of the people was an ongoing process. Their duty was to take the Torah and use it to develop a life pleasing to God. A Pharisaic story about Torah goes like this:

> Both [oral and written Torah] were given at Sinai, as a king presents a gift to faithful servants. Once there were two servants, a wise one and a foolish one, and both received from their king a measure of wheat and a bundle of flax. The foolish one put them away in a chest, that they remain forever unchanged; the wise servant spun the flax into a cloth and made precious bread out of the wheat. Placing the bread on the cloth, he invited the king to be his honored guest. (Seder Eliyahu Suta 82; quoted from Trepp, 1982:219)

This adaptation of the Torah, which the Pharisees called **Oral Torah**, amounted to an oral expansion of the Torah by applying it to the new problems that arose from living. As we see in the story above, Oral Torah also was "given at Sinai"—a way of saying that it is as authoritative as the written word.

An example of this expansion of Torah may be seen in the Sabbath regulations. The Torah said to keep the Sabbath day holy, but what did this mean in daily living? Eventually, the heirs of the Pharisees spelled out thirty-nine different classes of work that would violate the Sabbath. The goal of this sort of expansion was "to build a fence around Torah" (*Mishnah Aboth* 1:1; see Herford, 1962)—that is, to protect the central commandment by numerous smaller commandments all around it. In the hands of some this could become a stern legalism, but the majority of Pharisees seem to have been open to debate, aware of different interpretations, and humane in their conclusions. We meet one such appealing character in Mark (12:28–34).

We know little about the other group, the Herodians, with whom Mark here allies the Pharisees (12:13). Herod was a client king of Rome, not well liked by the Pharisees.

Jesus meets each of these groups in debate and defeats them all, reducing his opponents to silence (12:34). But it is the silence before the storm.

The Characterization of the Disciples

Whereas the audience knows where the authorities stand and what attitude to take toward them, we are left wondering about the disciples. Clearly the disciples are presented as admirable characters, at least at the first. They follow Jesus immediately on his call (1:18, 20). They have a privileged position (4:34); they are given special powers and reenact Jesus' own conquest of evil (6:7–13).

But there is another side to the disciples. Already at their first appointment one of them is characterized as "Judas Iscariot, who betrayed him" (3:19). And later when Judas enacts his betrayal, he is characterized as "one of the twelve" (14:10). But perhaps the most telling incident occurs just before the scene of recognition discussed above. Not only does Mark repeat the story of the feeding of the crowds (with fewer people and more resources the second time) but the incident shows the disciples to be wholly uncomprehending—of both the sheer facts of the case and their significance (compare 8:1–5 with 6:35–38; see the following discussion in 8:14–21 and the comment by the narrator at 6:52). When Jesus clearly teaches them about his impending suffering, not only do they fail to understand but they take the *opposite* point of view (see 8:31–33; 9:31–34; 10:32–36).

And in these closing scenes they completely abandon Jesus: one of them betrays him; his three intimates fail him; all forsake him at the climactic hour, even as he predicted they would (14:27). It is astonishing that this portrayal of infidelity is the last we see of the disciples in Mark, their shadowy forms disappearing over a far hill—or, perhaps not so shadowy, as the humorous appendage to their desertion makes its impact (14:51–52). Mark's failure to rehabilitate the disciples, along with the consistent portrayal of them as uncomprehending, has led to a great deal of scholarly speculation about the writer's motives.

Perhaps the most revolutionary view is that advanced by Theodore Weeden, who argues that Mark was trying to undermine the authority of the disciples in the church (1971:23–51; see also Sandmel, 1970:52–54). These scholars point to the great ambiguity with which Mark treats the disciples. Although Jesus makes positive predictions about their future, the reader is never convinced they are paying attention. They never seem to understand what Jesus is really saying. Even the final promise to the women, that Jesus would meet his disciples in Galilee (16:7), is made indeterminate by Mark's closing words: they did not tell the message (16:8). Thus, the reader cannot be absolutely sure that the disciples ever understood and obeyed.

Yet neither can the reader be certain that they did not. Although we owe Weeden a debt for noticing the ambiguity, we must be careful not to overstate the case. One wonders whether Mark would have been so subtle if the aim were to overthrow the authority of the disciples. The positive characterizations of the disciples (for example, 1:18, 20; 2:14; 3:14; 4:11, 33; 6:1, 7; and so on), and more importantly the two-stage plot, coupled with the actual healing of the blind man after the second effort (8:25) and the candid reference to post-resurrection understanding in the transfiguration scene (9:4), imply the disciples' eventual insight (as do 14:28 and 16:7). Also, the very act of reading the Gospel demonstrates that we cannot take the remark about the women's silence too literally. Had they not told, Mark could not relate their story.

Another scholar, Howard Clark Kee, argues that the reason for the ambiguity toward the disciples is that within Mark's story they are surrogates for Mark's community (1977:43, 87–97). Their failure to understand merely illustrates the impossibility of grasping the meaning of Jesus' death until after they come to faith in his resurrection (96; Mark 9:9). Although this approach probably fails to take their negative image seriously enough, it is surely closer to the truth than the other suggestion. The more balanced view of James Robinson seems to consider both kinds of evidence: the real foe of Jesus is not the disciples but Satan (8:33). Yet the disciples are tempted by the Satanic suggestion that the kingdom can be had without suffering; to that degree they betray Jesus:

> Their opposition to Jesus' idea of suffering corresponds to their own unwillingness to suffer, and this in turn blocks their participation in the eschatological [ultimate] history which awaits Jesus in Gethsemane in definitive fashion. The sharpness of the debates of Jesus with the disciples is due to the fact that the issue at stake is Mark's eschatological understanding of history, which he sees advocated and exemplified by Jesus, but opposed in word and deed by the disciples. (Robinson, 1957:52; brackets added)

We should not identify the disciples either (literally) with the historical disciples or (allegorically) with Mark's community but seek to understand their narrative role in this story, where they seem intent on following Jesus in power but not in suffering. Only one group in this story follows Jesus all the way to the cross, exhibiting traits we expect of the disciples.

The Characterization of the Women

Just as the disciples' individual actions add to their characterization as a group, so too the actions of individual women contribute to the audience's image of the women as a group. It is late in the story before we encounter the women as a group. At the scene of Jesus' death we are told:

> There were also women looking on from a distance; among them were Mary Magdalene, and Mary the mother of James the younger and of Joses, and

Salome. These used to follow him and provided for him when he was in Galilee; and there were many other women who had come up with him to Jerusalem. (Mark 15:40–41)

We learn several important things from this brief characterization: it gives the names of specific women; they had a dual relationship with Jesus in Galilee, both followers and providers; there are many of them. It is very unusual for the tradition to preserve the names of women; even the name of the woman who anointed Jesus and whose story was to be told "in remembrance of her" (14:9) is forgotten. Following Jesus is Mark's regular designation for discipleship, and providing for Jesus indicates their control of considerable resources; they are both disciples and benefactors.

Though this is the first time the audience is encouraged to think of the women as a group, we have already met several significant women, women of faith and courage: the woman who manages her own healing (5:25–34); the woman who overcomes Jesus in debate and gains the health of her daughter (7:25–30); and of course the woman who earns such extravagant praise from Jesus by anointing him (14:3). Women come off very well in this story, with little negative characterization (the one major exception is the characterization of Herodias in the story of John's death; 6:17–29).

The women stand by Jesus at his death, learn the place of his burial, and return to the tomb to anoint him. But this remarkable faithfulness, contrasting so markedly with the absent male disciples whose tasks these rightfully are, is called into question in the final scene, where the women too seem to fail in their task. We will consider this final scene in a moment, but first we need to briefly consider Mark's characterization of Jesus and then reflect on the events of Jesus' death.

The Characterization of Jesus

A full analysis of the Markan characterization of Jesus is beyond the scope of this introduction, but we can briefly note its major orientation. First, we should note what is not said, because our familiarity with other stories might unduly influence our reading. Mark gives no story of Jesus' birth and no hint of divine descent. Jesus appears as a fully human character with no hint of the miraculous until he experiences a vision of God at his baptism. Second, we notice Jesus' enormous power: he is able to conquer Satan and to expel unclean spirits. Nothing seems beyond his power: he heals the sick and feeds the crowds without apparent effort, indeed, "even the wind and the sea obey him" (4:41). But, third, he cannot conquer the unbelief of his own disciples, just as he *could not* do any "deeds of power" in his hometown because the people there rejected him (6:5–6).

Perhaps the most revealing scene is the incident in Gethsemane, where Jesus struggles with his destiny (see 14:32–42). "All things are possible" with God and yet it is not possible for Jesus to be delivered from fast-approaching death. This severe irony underlies the whole of Mark's story and appears again with radical clarity in the crucifixion scene itself (15:25–39).

As Jesus hangs on the cross his opponents mock him with the ironically truthful taunt:

He saved others. He cannot save himself. (15:31)

The whole scene is cast in darkness as Jesus dies lamenting God's having forsaken him (15:34). They wait in vain for Elijah to come (15:36; recall the opening anticipation: 1:2). And yet it is in just this setting that the centurion recognizes who Jesus truly is (15:39).

Mark's Jesus is a deeply ironic character who is able to do anything except command human obedience.

THE ACTION OF THE STORY: ABANDONED

Following the contests in the Temple (which, like the contest in the wilderness, Jesus wins) events move rapidly to a denouement. Jesus is anointed, betrayed, deserted, tried, and sentenced to death. Once again we must face the centrality of suffering for this Gospel. Let us examine the crucial scene and see how Mark molds the story of the crucifixion, paying special attention to the action and characterization of Jesus (15:6–9).

It is startling that the last words spoken by Jesus in the Gospel of Mark are, "My God, My God, why have you forsaken me?" (15:34). Mark does nothing to relieve the stark realism of the crucifixion. In fact these are the only words permitted Jesus from the moment of Pilate's condemnation to the end of the story. It is an awful death, yet, Mark asserts, it is precisely the way Jesus died that leads to his recognition as God's Son. There is no need for us to speculate what a Roman centurion might have meant by calling Jesus Son of God (15:39). Mark is interested in the title for its own sake. (Luke felt free to report the centurion's statement quite differently, 23:47). The reader has learned of Jesus' status as Son of God in two crucial earlier scenes: the opening (1:11) and the midpoint (9:7). And now at the end this Gentile recognizes him without any voice from heaven. How can Jesus' death lead to such a confession of his divine sonship?

The answer seems to lie in the three incidents given earlier, in which Jesus predicts his end. There he indicates it is a divine necessity (8:31, *must* suffer), a necessity also laid on the disciples, who live in a "wicked and godless age" (8:38, as the New English Bible translates it). Here we must recall the apocalyptic concept of two ages, the present age being under the control of the powers of evil. Still, we may question why it is necessary for him to suffer, if he has already successfully overcome Satan in the wilderness (3:22–27). The closest we come to an answer in Mark is after the third prediction, where Jesus declares:

> *The Son of Man also came not to be served, but to serve, and to give his life as a ransom for many. (10:45)*

An implicit contrast is revealed here between two concepts of God's kingdom: the king who would be served, a person of power and authority, and the king who serves, even giving his life for the lives of his people. It is this servant messiah whose suffering brings life to many that characterizes Jesus in this story. For Mark, Jesus is the one who suffers.

It is also worth noting that each of the passion predictions foretells the resurrection (8:31; 9:31; 10:34). Although not emphasizing the resurrection (there are no resurrection appearances), the ending clearly shows that a resurrection has taken place. What are we to make of Mark's muted ending?

The Sense of an Ending

This ending requires closer examination. First of all, we have a textual problem. There are four different endings in the different manuscripts of Mark. In addition to the ending that became a part of the received text (printed in many Bibles as 16:9–20), there is a short ending, which reads:

> But they reported briefly to Peter and to those with him all that they had been told. And after this Jesus himself sent out by means of them, from East to West, the sacred and imperishable proclamation of eternal salvation.

This rather colorless, generalized ending seems designed simply to relieve the tension in 16:8. Its rhetorical tone and vocabulary are quite unlike Mark.

A third ending consists of an expansion of verses 9 to 20, by the insertion of the following between verses 14 and 15.

> And they excused themselves, saying, "This age of lawlessness and unbelief is under Satan, who does not allow the truth and power of God to prevail over the unclean things of the spirits [or, does not allow what lies under the unclean spirits to understand the truth and power of God]. Therefore reveal thy righteousness now"—thus they spoke to Christ. And Christ replied to them, "The term of years of Satan's power has been fulfilled, but other terrible things draw near. And for those who have sinned I was delivered over to death, that they may return to the truth and sin no more, in order that they may inherit the spiritual and incorruptible glory of righteousness which is in heaven."

Although this ending shares something of the apocalyptic tenor of Mark, it is clearly more esoteric, with a novel vocabulary and non-Markan tone that separates it from the Gospel itself. It also has scant manuscript support. Bruce Metzger's summary seems appropriate: "It probably is the work of a second or third century scribe who wished to soften the severe condemnation of the Eleven in 16:14" (1971:125).

A fourth ending is no addition at all; there is good manuscript evidence for regarding 16:8 as the ending of Mark's Gospel. The two oldest Greek manuscripts we have end here, as do numerous old Latin and Syriac translations. Several early church fathers, such as Eusebius and Jerome, say that their best manuscripts end at verse 8. And many of the manuscripts that have additional verses (9–20) indicate by some sign that they were not part of the original Gospel.

In addition, analysis of the passage itself indicates that these verses do not fit well. Eleven of the words and expressions are not found anywhere else in Mark, and the sudden change in subject from verse 8 (the women) to verse 9 (Jesus, but simply "he" in the text) is awkward. In addition, the existence of the shorter endings is an argument against the authenticity of the longer. What scribe would substitute the shorter for the longer unless he regarded the longer as unoriginal or (more likely) did not know of its existence?

Almost all textual critics agree: either 16:8 is the original ending of the Gospel or the original ending is lost. Those who argue for a lost ending do so for the same reasons that Mark has three spurious endings: 16:8 is a hard saying. Can a gospel end with fear and silence? A more proper question would be: Does it make sense for Mark's Gospel to end this way? One writer goes so far as to exclaim:

> *Considered from the viewpoint of dramatic composition, the conclusion of the Gospel at 16:8 is not only perfectly appropriate but also a stroke of genius. (Bilezikian, 1977:134)*

Gilbert Bilezikian stresses the dramatic appropriateness of such an ending. The story is told; now the author must end it. Above all, he must not introduce further ideas that will detract from the impact of his story; to narrate resurrection appearances would do just that. (Mark clearly knows such appearance stories, as his references to Galilee indicate: 16:7; 14:28).

Paul Achtemeier points to another important element of this ending, ambiguity (1975:109–10). The resurrection has taken place, but suffering remains (13:9–13). The kingdom has begun but has not come to completion. Even as Jesus' actions of power remained mysterious and fearful, so do his suffering and resurrection (for example, 4:35–41; verse 41 literally reads "they feared with a great fear"; see also 10:32).

This leads me to suggest a third point: the action of the faithful women is appropriate for anyone who understands this story. Jesus had three times predicted his death and resurrection; each time his disciples demurred. Each time Jesus added that his death would imply their own. Even the good news of the resurrection is now ominous, for as surely as it points to the death of Jesus, his death implies their own. Perhaps the women's fear should be understood not simply as their failure but also as evidence of their finally grasping the meaning of the second half of Mark's story.

Further sense can be made of this ending if we notice the way Mark uses geography to communicate meanings.

Symbolic Space: When Place Means Something

We have already seen that the wilderness in Mark's opening scene is not just a place; it has symbolic import. It is the signal of the preparation for the coming of the Lord, the place where a straight path is to be made. Scholars have understood for some time that Mark's locations are often more than just settings for the action, but one scholar has demonstrated just how complex is Mark's spatial symbolism.

Elizabeth Struthers Malbon's insightful work (1991) allows us to make sense of the two locations noted in the last speech of the story, the report of the young man in the tomb to the women:

> *Do not be alarmed; you are looking for Jesus of Nazareth, who was crucified. He has been raised; he is not here. Look, there is the place they laid him. But go, tell his disciples and Peter that he is going ahead of you to Galilee; there you will see him, just as he told you. (16:6–7)*

First, Jesus is said to be "going ahead" of them. This is an expression often used in the story (6:45; 10:32; 11:9; 14:28), and it is related to two other notions: being "on the way" or on the road and "following," itself a metaphor for discipleship (10:52). The notion of a road or way goes back to the opening declaration that such a way was to be prepared in the wilderness (1:2, 3). It was "on the way" that Jesus

OLIVE PRESS   Olive crushers like this were common in Palestine, where olive oil production was a major industry. Olives would be loaded into the stone basin and then crushed by rolling the stone weight over them (usually pulled by a donkey fastened to a pole inserted through the hole in the middle of the weight). The pulp would be loaded into sacks and left to drain before finally being pressed with weights. Olive oil was used for cooking (Lev. 2:5), fuel (Matt. 25:3), medicine (Luke 10:34), ceremonial healing (Mark 6:13), grooming (Matt. 6:17), social welcoming (Luke 7:46), consecration (1 Kings 1:39), and religious ceremonies (Exod. 29:40). A press like this would be shared by all the farmers of a village. Such a stone is envisioned in the saying at Mark 9:42.

asked the disciples who people were saying he was in the central scene of recognition and reversal (8:27). The tomb speech indicates another reversal: just as Jesus had led them on the way to Jerusalem (10:32) so now he leads them back to Galilee.

Second, **Galilee** is itself symbolically important. Galilee is the place of Jesus' proclamation (1:14), where the disciples are called (1:16), where huge crowds are attracted (1:28) by Jesus' teaching and power (1:39). The return to Galilee is a return to the beginning. And notice that the return to Galilee is not something that the disciples are told to do or even something that they will do in the future (as it was at 14:28). It is a present tense; it is happening now.

If we interpret this within the story world of Mark's narrative, rather than as a statement about the real disciples or about some imagined future, we might understand it as an invitation to return to the beginning of the story, to reread the story. For now we return to Galilee with new understanding. Having seen the power and the suffering of Jesus we now understand both in a new way. This is not the power of a despot or the suffering of a victim.

One remarkable thing about the power of Jesus now becomes clear. The one who could compel demons never compels obedience. Jesus overpowers the forces of nature and disease but never overpowers a human character. How then can the rule of God come? "He is going ahead of you to Galilee; there you will see." The blind do see, but they have to look more than once.

We conclude our discussion of Mark by exploring the audience that seems to be imagined for this story.

THE SITUATION OF THE MARKAN COMMUNITY

Telling people they must suffer would have quite a different significance depending on who the people are who are being told. To tell slaves they must suffer is to participate in their oppression; to tell slave owners might be to participate in the liberation of slaves. Significance depends on context, yet the Gospel of Mark tells nothing directly about its context.

SEEKING THE PROPER CONTEXT

Mark's Gospel is anonymous, undated, and makes no direct mention of its social, historical, or religious setting. Scholars have played a sort of detective game, discovering clues in the Gospel and in early references to it and then trying to deduce the time and place in which it was written. The evidence available is minimal and open to more than one interpretation, but historical reconstruction is always a matter of probabilities, and some conclusions seem more probable than others.

One complicating factor is that the story really has two contexts: it imitates the context of Jesus (here portrayed as Palestinian village society), and it reflects the context of its writer and earliest audience. Competent scholars will disagree over what counts as evidence for which context. There is, however, one place in the Gospel where the writer has Jesus address the supposed future, and what is future for Jesus may well be present for the audience of the story. Most of the evidence used to posit a context for the Gospel comes from this speech by Jesus on the eve of his betrayal.

Called the **apocalyptic discourse** by scholars, it takes the form of a farewell speech revealing what will happen after Jesus is gone (Mark 13). Its tone is warning, with expressions like "beware," "be alert," and "keep awake" repeated seven times. The dangers foretold include false reports of Jesus' return (5–6), official and familial persecutions (9, 12), the appearance of false messiahs (21), and uncertainty about the time of the coming end (32).

The premise of all this upheaval is the destruction of the Jerusalem Temple, which Jesus explicitly predicts at the beginning of the speech:

> "Do you see these great buildings? Not one stone will be left here upon another; all will be thrown down." When he was sitting on the Mount of Olives opposite the temple, Peter, James, John, and Andrew asked him privately, "Tell us, when will this be, and what will be the sign that all these things are about to be accomplished?" (13:2–4)

Forty years after the death of Jesus, in the year 70, the Romans did destroy the Temple, and scholars suspect that Mark found Jesus' words significant because that event had either just happened or was on the verge of happening. Thus most would date the writing of this Gospel sometime in the decade between 65 and 75.

There is far less agreement on the place of writing. Four general views can be identified: probably the majority favors Rome, but significant recent voices advocate Palestine and Syria. Others of us think it is impossible to specify the place of writing.

The traditional view, going back at least to the second century, is that Mark wrote at Rome under the influence of Peter. But that tradition is far from certain; it comes to us from Eusebius (writing around 325 CE), who was quoting an earlier writer, **Papias** (c. 120 CE), whose work is now lost and who depended on a report he had heard from "the presbyters" (apparently his name for people who had known the apostles). But Papias seems to have sometimes embroidered his accounts, and even Eusebius had some doubts about his abilities. (In *Ecclesiastical History* 3.39.15–16, Eusebius remarks: "He seems to have been a man of very small intelligence, to judge from his books.") In another place, Eusebius preserved a tradition that implies Mark's death occurred before Peter's (2.24.1). The tradition that Mark depended on Peter for his Gospel grew over the years from a mere acquaintance without any consultation to direct supervision of the project by Peter (the growth of this legend is traced by Kalin, 1975).

There is some evidence in the Gospel that can be used to support a Roman provenance, such as the occasional use of Latin words in the Greek at 4:21 (modius), 5:15 (legion), 6:27 (speculator), and 12:42 (quadrans) and the following of the Roman practice of dividing the night into four watches rather than three (6:48; 13:35). But of course these influences could be felt in many places besides Rome. There is nothing in the Gospel to suggest a location specifically in Rome.

Some who look within the story for clues have focused on the motif of the return to Galilee. If we assume that the disciples did return, perhaps the story was written in Galilee. This is certainly possible, but there is no reason to think that the return to Galilee was permanent. In fact the apocalyptic discourse envisions them proclaiming this good news to all the nations (13:10). It can also be argued that Mark was not very familiar with Galilean geography; the itinerary sketched in 7:31 would be a little like going from New York City to Chicago by way of Los Angeles (see also 8:10 and 5:1).

Others look within the story for different kinds of evidence; the rural character of the Gospel of Mark (revealed in its knowledge of agriculture, housing, employment, and land ownership and taxation) together with its use of Aramaic expressions (5:41; 14:36; 15:34) could point to southern Syria as the place of origin. Of course one faces the difficulty of distinguishing those traits that stem merely from the story world, for Jesus is shown to be active in just such village settings.

Rather than trying to specify a place, we would probably be better served to explore the general social setting.

A TIME OF TRAGEDY

Two momentous events occurred in the decade between 65 and 75 CE, events that profoundly altered the self-understanding of both Jews and Christians. The first was the madness of the emperor Nero's campaign to eradicate Christians from Rome; the second was the madness of certain Jewish radicals who thought they could free Israel from Rome through armed revolt.

ARCH OF TITUS, DETAIL OF MENORAH The great triumphal arch of Titus, still standing in Rome, shows many scenes from the conquest of Judea, including the deportation of slaves and (here) the removal of the treasures of the Temple. This is the only surviving representation of the great seven-branched lamp (menorah) that stood in the interior chamber of the Temple.

The squalid, overcrowded slums of Rome were a disaster waiting to happen. Huge wooden tenements housed the majority of Rome's population, for only an elite minority could afford houses of their own. Nero had plans to tear down some of the worst of these neighborhoods and build a more glorious city. But there was political resistance to displacing so many people. Then in 64 the problem was solved when a great fire destroyed a substantial part of the city. Because it was known that Nero wanted these buildings destroyed, and the fire department was the emperor's personal responsibility, rumors spread that he had started the fire. To allay these rumors, Nero needed someone to blame. He hit on the Christians.

Though short-lived (Nero committed suicide in 68), this persecution was intense. Tacitus, writing nearly fifty years later, described the events thus:

But neither human help nor imperial munificence, nor all the modes of placating Heaven, could stifle scandal or dispel the belief that the fire had taken place by order. Therefore, to scotch the rumor, Nero substituted as culprits, and punished with the utmost refinements of cruelty, a class of men loathed for their vices, whom the crowd styled Christians. . . . First, then, the confessed members of the sect were arrested; next, on their disclosures, vast numbers were convicted, not so much on the count of arson as for hatred of the human race. And derision accompanied their end: they were covered with wild beasts' skins and torn to death by dogs; or they were fastened on crosses, and when daylight failed were burned to serve as lamps by night. Nero had offered his Gardens for the spectacle, and gave an exhibition in his Circus, mixing with the crowd in the habit of a charioteer, or mounted on his car. Hence, in spite of a guilt which had earned the most exemplary punishment, there arose a sentiment of pity, due to the impression that they were being sacrificed not for the welfare of the state but to the ferocity of a single man. (Annals 15.44; also see Suetonius, "Nero," in The Lives of the Twelve Caesars 16.2)

The horror of this event surely made a lasting impression on Christians throughout the empire. They could not know it would not soon recur. In fact, given the lack of communications media, they could not be certain it had stopped; rumors would surely circulate for years. And we should note that even fifty years later Tacitus can assume that he does not need to explain his characterization of Christians as "a class of men loathed for their vices."

Mark's assertion that discipleship constitutes more than recognizing Jesus as the powerful Christ, that it involves inevitable suffering, may well be an attempt to make sense out of this senseless slaughter.

The second event too led to enormous suffering and death. When Jerusalem declared itself independent and refused to send tribute to Rome in 66, Nero responded by sending his best legions under the command of Vespasian to quell the rebellion. The Jews were no match for the might of Rome. We are fortunate to have a firsthand report of the war. One of the Jewish military leaders who was captured by the Romans, then defected and became an advisor to the Roman side, later wrote an account of the war that has come down to us. The man was Josephus, and the work is called the *Jewish War*. Written in the late seventies, this work is an invaluable source for this period. Josephus describes the beginning of Vespasian's conquest of Galilee as follows:

Vespasian's first objective was the city of Gabara, which he carried at the first assault, finding it deprived of effective combatants. Entering the city he slew all males who were of age, the Romans showing no mercy to old or young, so bitter was their hatred of the nation and their memory of the affront which had been done to Cestius [whose leniency had allowed the revolt to spread]. Not content with setting fire to the city, Vespasian burnt all the villages and country towns in the neighborhood; some he found completely deserted, in others he reduced the inhabitants to slavery. (3.7.1)

The conquest of Galilee did not take long, but the war dragged on for another seven years. It took three years to siege Jerusalem and literally starve it into submission and another four years to obliterate the last holdout in the desert fortress of

Masada. At war's end Jerusalem, center for both Jews and Christians, lay in ruins. Palestine was an enemy-occupied country, and Jews everywhere were under suspicion—as were those Gentiles who adopted Jewish customs. It might well have seemed like the end of the age had come, with "wars and rumors of wars" and many "false messiahs," accusations of family members, and the terrible "desolating sacrilege" of the Temple's destruction (Mark 13).

The devastating effect of this destruction of the homeland, together with rumors of Nero's persecutions (both Peter and Paul may have been caught up in the mass slaughter of Christians at Rome) would surely leave many Christians across the empire wondering: Were they right to follow this new way? Where was the power of God promised in the Gospel? Were they wrong to think a new age had begun?

Rumor had probably also carried the news that James, brother of Jesus and head of the mother church in Jerusalem, had been killed because of Saducean instigation in 62. Christians were, after all, part of a close-knit, mobile group. Perhaps it seemed like the community might be overwhelmed by the forces of evil.

The question that this community had to answer, then, was how to respond to that evil. And Mark mirrors this uncertain situation in telling the story of Jesus. The story encourages us to identify with Jesus, only to learn that his powers cannot rescue him from his suffering. We sympathize with the disciples and the women, yet this sympathy is increasingly complicated by the disciples' failure. While the reader hopes for a happy ending and a reconciliation of the disciples, Mark refuses to provide it, leaving their final choice as open and ambiguous as the real choices of Mark's audience.

The Gospel of Mark is far more than a simple retelling of the story of Jesus. It is a work of literature that attempts to portray Jesus, to illustrate his significance and meaning, to tell his story. To be sure this portrayal must be grounded in the Jesus who left footprints in the sand in Galilee, but Mark's intention is to show the relevance of Jesus for life in a time of suffering. It achieves this mimesis, this representation, by the way it structures the material, by shaping the characterization of the disciples and the women, by the development of the kingdom idea, by narrating Jesus' suffering in certain ways (and not others), and by many other devices. The story is written this way because it is written for a certain audience living in a certain situation to which and from which it spoke. We may be tempted to ask how someone in a different time and place might have told it differently. Fortunately, there is no need for speculation: we have four Gospels.

LEARNING ON YOUR OWN

REVIEWING THE CHAPTER

Names and Terms

anonymity	kingdom of God	Papias
apocalyptic discourse	Messiah	pericope
chiasmus	Messianic secret	Pharisees
exorcisms	narrative gaps	Sadducees
framing	Oral Torah	wilderness
Galilee		

Issues and Questions

1. How does the role of Satan and the theme of exorcism relate to the underlying apocalyptic worldview of Mark's story?
2. What do you take to be the plot of Mark's story?
3. Discuss various scholarly opinions about the characterization of the disciples in Mark and explain their narrative role in the story.
4. Discuss Mark's symbolic use of space and place, especially the significance of Galilee.
5. Explain the textual problem of the ending of Mark and either defend or refute the position that 16:8 is an appropriate end to the story.
6. How might the historical situation of Mark relate to the strong emphasis on suffering in the story?

TAKING THE NEXT STEP

The best introduction to the **narrative** character of Mark is Rhoads, Michie, and Dewey, 1999. For a brief and insightful introduction see Malbon in Anderson and Moore, 1992. The imaginative work of Juel, 1993, is valuable. Other useful studies of the story quality of Mark include Bergeson, 1996; Best, 1988; Bryan, 1993; Kelber, 1979; and Hedrick, 1987. Schildgen, 1998, is a sophisticated study of Markan narrative elements focusing on time, memory, and myth.

For an excellent introduction to and application of various methods to Mark, see Anderson and Moore, 1992.

Useful **introductory** works on Mark include Achtemeier, 1975b; Barta, 1988; A. Y. Collins, 1992; Gundry, 1993; W. Harrington, 1979; Hurtado, 1989; Kelber, 1979; Kingsbury, 1989; and Stock, 1984.

Standard treatments include Lane, 1974 (more conservative); Lightfoot, 1950; Marxsen, 1969; Nineham, 1964; and Schweizer, 1970. See also Marcus, 2000; Painter, 1997; and Telford, 1997.

Topics for Special Studies

Reconsidering the Plot of Mark's Gospel

Significant treatments include Rhoads, Michie, and Dewey, 1999; Kingsbury, 1989; Kelber, 1987; and Smith, 1996.

Another helpful discussion of Mark's **plot** and structure is Dewey, 1991; see also Dewey, 1989, and Cook, 1995. On irony see Camery-Hoggatt, 1992.

Characters and Characterization in Mark

For suggestions on Mark's **characterization of Jesus**, see Tannehill in Petersen, 1980; Slusser and Slusser, 1967; and Donahue, 1978. Some approach Jesus under the theological title *Christology*: Kingsbury, 1983; Schweizer, 1977; and Perrin, 1971.

An endeavor to develop a paradigm of a **divine man** in ancient writing by Hadas and Smith, 1965, has been critiqued by Kee, 1973b, and especially by Tiede, 1972; see also Corrington, 1986. Smith, 1978, traces the history of the idea, and Gallagher, 1982, examines its use in early anti-Christian polemic.

Characterization of the Disciples

The most pointed case for a negative view of the disciples is Weeden, 1971; see also Sandmel, 1970, and Kelber, 1974.

An effective response has been made by Tannehill, 1977; Dewey, 1982; and Boomershine, 1987. See also Malbon, 2000, as well as her earlier work in 1986 and 1993; Best, 1986; and Black, 1989. For a comparison with Matthew, see Barton, 1994.

The Role of the Women in Mark
Opinion is divided between those who see the women as sharing in the failure of the disciples (Munro, 1982) and those who see them as more positive models (Malbon, 1983, 1986, and 1991b). Also see Beavis, 1988; Swartley, 1997; and Kinukawa, 1994.

The Theme of Secrecy in Mark
The secrecy theme in Mark was first explored by Wrede, 1901. Originally understood as a historical issue, it is now more often seen as a literary phenomenon; see Fowler, 1981a, and the collection by Tuckett, 1983. See also Räisänen, 1990; Kingsbury, 1986; and Watson, 1985. For a very interesting literary study of Mark under the theme of secrecy, see Kermode, 1979.

The Political Implications of Mark's Story
Perhaps the most stimulating political reading of Mark's story is Myers, 1988. Another political reading is Waetjen, 1989. Both treat the apocalyptic worldview of Mark, as does Kee, 1977. A Marxist perspective can be found in the rather difficult work of Belo, 1981. See also Rohrbaugh, 1993; Kealy, 1990; and Theissen, 1991.

Mark's Apocalyptic Worldview
For a good summary see Kee, 1977; Myers, 1988, emphasizes this setting. For a general introduction to apocalypticism see J. J. Collins, 1984, and the resources at the end of Chapter 13.

The history of the **kingdom** idea is traced by Bright, 1953. For a general survey and a symbolist interpretation of the kingdom in the Gospels, see Perrin, 1976.

The Audience of Mark's Gospel
See Beavis, 1989, and the contrasting view of Rohrbaugh, 1993. See also Bryan, 1993; Senior, 1987; Kee, 1977; Marcus, 1992; Tolbert, 1989; van Iersel, 1980; and Marcus, 1992. Malbon, 1989, and Donahue, 1995, are conscious of the problem of drawing historical inferences from literary data. Mack, 1987b, tries to place Mark in the larger context of the emergence of Christianity.

The Oral Setting of Mark's Gospel
See the contrasting views of Kelber, 1983; Dewey, 1991; and Botha, 1991. See also Bryan, 1993, and the works of Boomershine, 1974, 1987, and 1988. For an overview, see Silberman, 1987.

Those who wish to experience an oral performance of Mark can view the videotape of David Rhoads, 1984 (Select, c/o Trinity Lutheran Seminary, 2199 E. Main St., Columbus, Ohio 43209; tel. 614-235-4136; 109 minutes).

The Purpose of the Two Feeding Stories in Mark
Begin with Fowler, 1981b; consult the discussion in Beare, 1962, and several of the commentaries listed above under the heading "Taking the Next Step."

Mark's Use of Symbolic Space or the Meaning of Galilee in Mark
The seminal work on geography in the Gospels is Lightfoot, 1939; also see his 1950 commentary. For a balanced modern view, see Freyne, 1988. The most complete analysis

of Mark to date is Malbon, 1991; see also Malbon, 1984. And more generally on the geography of Galilee, see Sawicki, 2000; Horsley, 1996; and Reed, 2000.

Mark's Understanding of Jesus' Miracles

Mark's use of **miracles** is explored by Achtemeier, 1970 and 1978; McVann, 1991; Countryman, 1985; Best, 1978; and Matera, 1993. For a cross-cultural view of healing stories, see Guijarro, 2000. For a broad consideration of miracle stories in several contexts see Labahn and Peerbolte, 2006.

Mark's Understanding of Jesus' Death

For a narrative view see Dowd and Malbon, 2006. For more comprehensive treatments see White, 1987; Brown, 1998 and 1988; and Allison, 1985. On crucifixion, see Fitzmyer, 1978. For a bibliography on the passion narratives, see Garland, 1990. See also Hamerton-Kelly, 1994. Ulansey, 1991, sees cosmic implications.

Mark: The Original Ending

Start with Danove, 1993 (excellent but technical); Magness, 1986; and Waetjen, 1965. Consider also Trompf, 1972; Horst, 1972; Meye, 1969; and Reedy, 1972 (who argues for a lost ending). Farmer, 1974, is a lone voice arguing that the longer ending may come from the original author. He suggests that the non-Markan features of these verses could be explained by positing a pre-Markan narrative, which Mark edited to his Gospel. Farmer is also one of few to argue that Mark depends on Matthew and not vice versa, thus making the abrupt ending of Mark problematic.

The best source for analyzing the textual evidence for the various endings to Mark, and other textual problems, is Metzger, 1971; for his discussion of the ending to Mark, see pages 122–28. In this instance, Metzger's discussion can be followed by anyone, though his discussion usually requires knowledge of Greek.

Mark's Shaping of the Gospel Tradition

One could also do a significant research project by comparing Mark's version of some important incident with alternative versions in other Gospels. Revealing passages include the opening scene (compared with other openings or with other versions of Jesus' baptism and temptation), the confession of Peter, the death of Jesus, and the empty tomb story. Such a project ought to be pursued both inductively (based on your own careful comparisons) and by doing research on the conclusions of others (by reading appropriate sections of commentaries).

One of the most fruitful analyses of the **temptation** in Mark is that of Best, 1965; see also Keck, 1966. The traditional view that the **passion narrative** existed before Mark (Bultmann, 1972:275) has been contested by Donahue in Kelber, 1976:1–20; see also White, 1987. Important studies of the **trial narrative** in Mark include Donahue, 1973; Juel, 1977; and Beavis, 1987.

On the Genre of Mark

Compare A. Y. Collins, 1990 and 1992, with Bryan, 1993.

Additional Books and Articles

On the issue of **history** in Mark, see Robinson, 1982. On the issue of the historical Mark, see Black, 2001.

More advanced **literary** studies include the following: For two different applications of reader response criticism, see Fowler, 1991, and Heil, 1992. For rhetorical analysis, see also Fowler, 1985; Dewey, 1980; and Robbins, 1984. On language and style, see J. K. Elliott, 1993.

Petersen, 1980, is a special issue of *Semeia* devoted to literary approaches to Mark. See also vol. 32 of the journal *Interpretation* (Mays, 1978), which is likewise devoted to Mark.

Most will find Moore, 1992, to be a radical if playful interpretation.

Bilezikian, 1977, and Via, 1975, present contrasting views about the relation of Mark to ancient comedy and tragedy.

For **feminist** readings see Anderson in Anderson and Moore, 1992, and Kinukawa, 1994.

Bibliographic essays on Mark include Brooks, 1978; Humphrey, 1981; Kee, 1978; and Matera, 1987. Smith, 1990, also provides an extensive bibliography.

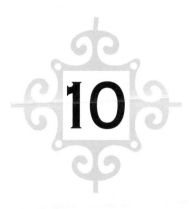

10

THE BOOK OF THE NEW COMMUNITY

 A story on the page is like a printed circuit
For our lives to flow through,
A story told invokes our dim capacity
To be alive in bodies not our own.

E. L. DOCTOROW, *CITY OF GOD*

The author of this Gospel said that a good scribe had to be like a person in charge of a large household, able to go into the storeroom and bring out things both old and new (13:52). By this definition, our author was a good scribe. We will find in this book many old things—some we have already found in Mark—as well as many new things and other old things used in new ways. In this chapter we will first explore what is unique to Matthew, in part by comparison with Mark, and attempt to achieve some sense of the overall pattern of the work. Then we will turn to specific incidents in the story, giving them a close reading. Finally, we will investigate the probable situation from which and to which this Gospel is addressed.

AN OVERVIEW OF THE WHOLE

It is remarkable that the Gospel according to Matthew contains over 90 percent of the material in Mark and yet is a dramatically different work. Whether the author actually used Mark as a source and consciously modified the text (as most New Testament scholars think), or whether both authors were simply heir to the same traditions, seeing the similarities and differences between the two works will lead to a better understanding of each.

REMINDERS OF MARK

Perhaps the easiest way to become aware of these similarities and differences is to compare a common scene. The scene of Jesus' baptism is important to both. Let us examine it closely.

> **READING AND REFLECTION**
>
> Compare Matt. 3:1–17 with Mark 1:1–11 (GP §1–6, SFG §13–18).
>
> 1. How does Matthew's telling of the story compare with Mark's?
> 2. What new material does Matthew add?
> 3. How does Matthew show that he does not regard this as "the beginning"?

The expression Matthew uses for a transition into this story is remarkable: "In those days John the Baptizer appeared" (3:1). But Matthew has just recounted the stories surrounding Jesus' birth. In those days? This expression allows Matthew to achieve two goals: first, it is an echo of a standard phrase in prophetic speech, for "in those days" God would establish a righteous kingdom on earth (for example, Jer. 3:15–18). Second, the expression establishes a tie to the earlier stories by implying that both belong to the same period. It is not that this happens in the time of Jesus' infancy but that the birth of Jesus is the beginning of a new time ("those days").

This conclusion is reinforced when we notice that John is already preaching the impending arrival of the kingdom (3:2), something that Mark reserved for Jesus after his baptism and wilderness testing, even after John's imprisonment (Mark 1:14–15). For Matthew the crucial event for the inauguration of the kingdom had already occurred before John appeared in the wilderness. The baptism of Jesus is *not* the beginning of the action in Matthew as it was in Mark. Before the baptism scene we hear stories of Jesus' birth, the visit of the magi, the attack of Herod, and the flight into Egypt. Unless we disregard these early narratives as mere decoration (and such has often been their fate), we must consider that the scope and structure of Matthew's action will be quite un-Markan. We must consider seriously that, for Matthew, the story began when "Abraham became the father of Isaac" (1:2) and that its first significant event is the birth of Jesus.

Matthew also introduced a new dialogue between John and Jesus, explaining why it was appropriate for John to baptize Jesus (one expects that ordinarily the greater will baptize the lesser). His explanation is short and ambiguous: the baptism is "to fulfill all righteousness" (3:15). Though John is convinced, I am not so sure the reader is. But this answer allows Matthew to anticipate what follows.

For in the next scene Jesus reveals his righteousness in the now-dramatized temptation scene. He does so by continual reference to Scripture, which Matthew has labored to show is being fulfilled in Jesus (five such fulfillments have already been indicated—1:22; 2:5, 15, 17–18, and 23). But Matthew becomes even more direct, soon explaining just what he means by the important terms *fulfill* and *righteousness*, combining them with a third idea, the Jewish understanding of the Law. His explanation follows:

> *Think not that I have come to abolish the law and the prophets; I have come not to abolish them, but to fulfill them. . . . For I tell you, unless your righteousness exceeds that of the scribes and Pharisees, you will never enter the kingdom of heaven. (Matt. 5:17–20)*

These statements provide the theme for what follows in Matthew, a long speech usually called the **Sermon on the Mount** (Matthew 5–7). The substance of that speech is an examination of the categories of **righteousness** (proper conduct), showing how they are fulfilled (brought to completion or perfection) in the teaching of Jesus. We will investigate these ideas presently, but first we must consider the close connection between this speech and the action of the narrative as a clue to the structure of Matthew's Gospel. It is not the only such speech in Matthew.

BEYOND MARK: THE FIVE SPEECHES

The Sermon on the Mount is not found in Mark; it is Matthew's creation (or perhaps in part the creation of an earlier collector). Someone has gathered sayings of Jesus and composed them into a continuous speech—at least much of the material in this speech is found in a variety of other settings in Luke and, in the case of three sayings, in Mark. (You can see this at a glance by examining the charts that show parallel references in *GP*, page xxi, and *SFG*, page 343. As we will see, Matthew was fond of collecting similar material into compact units.) Matthew has actually composed five such speeches, only one of which has a significant parallel in Mark.

That Matthew intended for each of these speeches to be seen as a special collection is indicated by the stereotyped expression with which he concludes them: "And it came to pass when Jesus had finished these sayings . . ." (In the Greek it is a six-word sequence: *Kai egenito hote etelesen ho Iesous*. It is repeated word for word at 7:28; 11:1; 13:53; 19:1; 26:1.) In addition, each speech is set off from the preceding context by references to "the crowds" or by the phrase "the disciples came to him"—usually by both. The disciples are mentioned at the beginning of each speech, four times by the stereotyped expression noted; the crowds are mentioned at the beginning of all but the fourth speech, where their presence would be inappropriate, because it is addressed to the disciples.

Thus, on the purely formal level, in considering the structure of the work, five long blocks of teaching material segment Matthew's Gospel: roughly chapters 5–7, 10, 13, 18, and 23–25. Further, each of these speeches grows out of a narrative context and is followed by a narrative. The formal arrangement of Matthew's Gospel, then, is an alternating sequence of narrative (N) and speech (S) sections in the pattern: N-S-N-S-N-S-N-S-N-S-N. It has been suggested above that the first speech served to explain and interpret the action of the first narrative by explaining the meaning of the phrase *to fulfill all righteousness*. There are, in fact, numerous interconnections between the narrative and speech sections. When these speeches were first discovered, they were viewed as comments on the prior narrative section. They are also comments on the succeeding narratives. The Sermon on the Mount, for example, demonstrates Jesus' authority in word (7:28–29), whereas the next section shows his authority in deed (8–9). It is worth noting that the phrase concluding each discourse ("And it came to pass when Jesus had finished these sayings") is a half sentence leading into the next narrative. Thus, we should see the speeches not as dividers but as connectors. Matthew's challenge was not to divide his narrative but to find ways to connect the diverse incidents. These speeches allow Matthew to reflect on the significance of Jesus' action in the preceding section and to prepare the reader for the action that follows.

THE STRUCTURE AND PLOT

As we saw in Mark, any particular incident in a work must be read in light of its place in the structure of that work and the shape of the narrative. Thus, any analysis of miracles in Mark should consider how Mark transforms that theme in the second half of his work. Any serious study of the disciples must inquire about their narrative role in the work as a whole. The same holds true for Matthew, but its structure is far more complex. Here is one way to visualize it.

 ### READING GUIDE TO MATTHEW

The Origins of Jesus the Messiah (1–10)

First narrative: Jesus, son of Abraham, is shown to be the one who fulfills Scripture's promises by the manner of his birth and by his actions. (1–4)

First speech: Jesus reveals his authority to redefine righteousness. (5–7)

Second narrative: Jesus reveals his authority in three cycles of three miracles each. (8–9:35)

Second speech: Jesus communicates his authority to the disciples and sends them on their mission as an extension of his. (9:36–10:42)

The Responses to Jesus (11–17)

Third narrative: Jesus is shown to be the "One Who Is to Come" because he performs "the deeds of the Messiah." (11–12)

Third speech: Jesus uses parables to show that the kingdom of God is mysterious and contains both faithful and unfaithful. (13:1–52)

Fourth narrative: Various characters respond to Jesus: Herod thinks he is John; the crowds are baffled; the disciples twice confess; the Pharisees and scribes question and are offended; the Canaanite woman persists in her confession; Gentiles glorify the God of Israel; Pharisees and Sadducees test him; Peter confesses him to be the "Messiah the Son of God," witnesses the events on the mountain, and pays the Temple tax. (13:53–17:27)

The Response of Jesus (18–25)

Fourth speech: Jesus explains the compassion and forgiveness required for the kingdom. (18)

Fifth narrative: Jesus debates his opponents and shows that one's status in the kingdom depends on how well one obeys God. (19–22)

Fifth speech: Jesus pronounces judgment on the Pharisees and scribes and on the whole world. (23–25)

The Death and Vindication of Jesus (26–28)

Sixth narrative: The obedient and righteous Jesus, betrayed by his disciples to the schemes of his opponents, dies as the Son of God and is raised from the dead to inherit the universal authority by which he commissions his disciples to make disciples of all the nations. (26–28)

READING AND REFLECTION

Read through the Gospel of Matthew, paying particular attention to the flow of the action and to the interplay between action and speech. Notice especially the interconnections that Matthew has woven into his art (see Tables 10.1 and 10.2.), and compare your observations with those below.

Matthew's story begins in the ancient past, with Abraham, and ends in the remote future, the end of the age (see 1:1–2 and 28:20). In between is Jesus, who when he is born is said to be Emmanuel—"God with us"—and who at the end promises to be with the disciples till the close of the age (1:23; 28:20). He is divinely named Jesus, "for he will save his people" (1:21). But the story does not seem to develop that way.

Although Jesus initially prevails, first over Satan (4:1–11) then over sickness and disease, so that great crowds follow him (4:23–25), as he elaborates his teaching (5–7) and manifests his powers (8–9), opposition begins to grow (9:34). He commissions his disciples to go to the lost sheep of Israel, endowing them with similar powers, but they do not go (10). Even John the Baptizer, who first welcomed him, begins to doubt (11:2–6). Controversies develop (12). The only explanation Jesus offers is a series of parables about how the rule of God is not what people might expect (13).

As opposition from scribes, Pharisees, and Sadducees continues to grow (14–15), Jesus encounters a Canaanite woman who wants him to heal her daughter. He refuses.

TABLE 10.1   VERBAL CORRELATIONS WITHIN MATTHEW'S GOSPEL (INTERLOCKING QUOTES)

	N_1 (1–4)	S_1 (5–7)	N_2 (8–9)	S_2 (10)	N_3 (11–12)	S_3 (13)	N_1 (14–17)	S_4 (18)	N_5 (19–22)	S_5 (23–25)	N_6 (26–28)
Jesus traveled/teaching	4:23		9:35								
Kingdom at hand	3:2, 4:17			10:7							
Good tree/fruit		7:19			12:33ff						
Fame—brought sick	4:24						14:35				
Voice: Beloved Son	3:17						17:5				
Right eye/pluck out		5:29						18:9			
Divorce/adultery		5:32							19:9		
Heaven/world pass away		5:18								24:35	
And when he had finished . . .		7:28		11:1		13:53		19:1		26:1	
Mercy/not sacrifice			9:13		12:7						
Alliance with demons			9:34	10:25	12:24						
Touch fringe/made well			9:20				14:36				
To lost sheep . . . Israel				10:6			15:24				
Take cross/follow				10:38–39			16:24–25				
Hated/for my name's sake				10:22						24:9	
Endure to end/saved				10:22						24:13	
Receive X/receive me				10:40ff				18:5		25:40	
Sign of Jonah					12:38–39		16:1ff				
Who has/more given						13:12				25:29	
Bind/loose							16:19	18:18			
Faith/move mountains							17:20		21:21		
Great/servant								18:1	20:26–27	23:11	
First/last									19:30; 20:16		
Blessed/he who comes									21:9	23:39	
Held John/Jesus to be prophet									21:26, 46		

	N₁ (1–4)	S₁ (5–7)	N₂ (8–9)	S₂ (10)	N₃ (11–12)	S₃ (13)	N₄ (14–17)	S₄ (18)	N₅ (19–22)	S₅ (23–25)	N₆ (26–28)
Fulfill all righteousness	3:15	5:20									
Dual responses		7:28–29	9:33–34	10:1		13:8, 24, 47					
Authority		7:29	8:9; 9:6–7	10:18					21:23		28:18
Suffer for Christ's sake	3:3; 4:14	5:11	8:17		12:17 (11:2–3)	13:21	15:17			24:9–10	
Prophecy of Isaiah						13:14					
Take offense					11:6	13:57 (13:21)	17:27 (15:12)	18:6		24:10	26:31
Faith			8:10; 9:2, 22, 29				17:20		21:21		
Gentiles in kingdom			8:11–12		12:18–19		15:27–28; 15:3; 16:12		21:43; 21:45	23:23	28:19–20
Pharisees condemned	3:7	5:20			12:7					23	
Brood of vipers	3:7				12:34					23:33	
Acts of obedience	1:24; 3:15; 4:19–20	7:21	9:9		12:50		14:29				26:29–30
Gospel of the kingdom	4:23		9:35				16:28			24:14	(26:13)
Imminence of the kingdom										24:34	
John the Baptizer	3:1; 4:12		9:14		11:2–3		14:2–3; 16:24–25		21:25–26		
Forgive to be forgiven		6:14–15						18:35			
Worship/kneel before Jesus	2:2, 8, 11; (4:10)		8:2; 9:18				14:33; 15:25		20:20		28:17; 28:9
To save from sins	1:21		(9:6)								26:28
Son of God	1:23; 3:17						17:5				27:54
To be "with" his people	1:23						(18:20)				28:20
King of the Jews	2:2–3										27:11, 37
Plot to kill Jesus	2:3–4										27:4
Return to Galilee	4:12–13						17:22				28:10, 16
Three temptations	4:1–2										26:38–39; 27:39–40
To make disciples	4:18–19										28:19

Correlations Between N₁ and N₆

He was sent "only to the lost sheep of the house of Israel," and she is a Gentile. But she convinces him, and he heals the girl, commenting on her great faith (15:21–28).

After more controversy, more parables, more opposition, Jesus travels to Jerusalem and enters riding on a donkey, in imitation of the ancient prophetic oracle about the entrance of the king (21:6–11). He further provokes the leaders by creating a disturbance in the Temple, overturning tables and driving out the merchants. When challenged, he refuses to say where he gets the authority to do such things (21:23–27). After further controversy and a long speech condemning the Pharisees and describing the coming end of the age and final judgment (23–25), he withdraws with his disciples for a final meal, where he tells them that they will all desert him (26:20–35).

The authorities decide that he must die, and the narrative grows ever darker as Jesus is arrested, tried, first by the Jewish priests and then by the Roman governor, condemned, and crucified, dying in a darkness that began at noontime and lasted three hours (26:36–27:54). But then, after the Sabbath, a new dawn breaks (28:1). The women not only find the tomb empty, they run to tell the disciples. In the final scene Jesus appears to the disciples on a mountain in Galilee. Once again he commissions them to go, only this time they are to make disciples of all the Gentiles. The story that began with Abraham (who was told he would be a blessing "to all the families of the earth," Gen. 12:3) has come to a fitting end.

Read this way, Matthew's story depicts Jesus as the creator of a new community, founded on his righteous words and deeds. Among the Gospels, only Matthew calls this new community a "church" (16:18; 18:17). In his story this new community is connected with the earliest call of God to Abraham (1:2) in the distant past and it will persist to the end of the age (28:20). With this structure and plot in mind, we will examine several important incidents in more detail and then try to place this community in its historical setting.

READING THE STORY: KEY INCIDENTS

For the modern reader, this story begins in an awkward way: a list of names, only a few of which we know and all of which are hard to pronounce. However, Matthew's genealogy takes on real life when we know something about the people mentioned. The list leads us through the whole history of Israel, connecting the story of Jesus with the story of God's past dealings with Israel. It may well have been this close connection with the earlier stories that cause Matthew to be placed first when the Gospels were collected.

THE ANCESTORS OF JESUS: A NEW BEGINNING

Matthew does not recite the history of Israel in a monotonous fashion but varies his presentation to emphasize certain points. The following exercise reveals these highlights.

READING AND REFLECTION

Read Matt. 1:1–17 aloud, trying to be conscious of the rhythm and movement of the words. You may also wish to compare this genealogy with that in Luke 3:23–38 (GP §7, also page 1, and SFG §19).

Matthew uses two literary devices to guide the listener's understanding of this genealogy: numerical symmetry and rhythmic interruption. The symmetry is first hinted at in the title sentence:

An account of the genealogy of Jesus the Messiah, the son of David, the son of Abraham. (1:1)

Unlike Mark, there is no declaration of divine sonship, nor is the proclamation called a *gospel*. Instead it is an "account" (*biblos*), a term as vague in Greek as it is in English. The word translated as "genealogy" is really a broad term for origin, source, generation, descent, and so on. We should probably understand this introductory phrase as a title, meaning an account of the origin of Jesus the Messiah, thus not too different from Mark's "beginning of the gospel."

By singling out David (the founder of the nation) and Abraham (the founder of the people), Matthew already implies a structure in his genealogy. He makes this structure explicit in verse 17, where he asserts that the genealogy consists of three sets of fourteen generations each. While this presents some problems historically, it served Matthew's literary purpose. Matthew has had to omit several kings known from the genealogies in the Hebrew Scriptures (compare 1 Chron. 3:10–16 with Matt. 1:7–11), and the only way one arrives at fourteen in the last section is to count Jechoniah again though he was already counted in the previous section.

To see the literary purpose, we need to consider the ways Matthew arranges this list in both rhythmic and arrhythmic fashion. The rhythmic pattern of the names is simple: A was the father of B; B was the father of C, and so on. This is the pattern of at least one of Matthew's sources (Ruth 4:18–22). But Matthew interrupts this smooth flow by the addition of nongenealogical material: mention of brothers, naming of mothers, and references to events. The events noted correspond to the major divisions of Matthew's genealogy: the kingship of David and the deportation to Babylon. Clearly, Matthew's understanding of the history of God's people moves in three epochs, marked by these two events.

At both points there was a radical shift in the self-understanding of Israel. With a king, Israel became a nation "like the other nations," no longer simply God's people under God's direct rule (1 Sam. 8:4–9). With the exile, all the major supports of Israel's faith were threatened or eliminated, including the monarchy (which some thought would last forever, 2 Samuel 7), the land, the Temple, even God's action in history seemed questionable. When we now see Matthew narrate other events about the origin of Jesus the Messiah (1:18), the expectation of another such crucial event occurring naturally arises, and the hearer is prepared for another radically new orientation to the meaning of being Israel.

References to "and his brothers" occur at two places in the genealogy: to differentiate the chosen line of Judah from the other sons of Jacob and to call attention to Jechoniah (here conflated with his father Jehoiakim), the end of the Davidic line. Just as Judah inherited the kingly promise (Gen. 49:5–12), so Jechoniah surrendered his kingdom to Babylon (2 Kings 24:12).

References to mothers, normally not included in Jewish genealogies, occur at four places, in addition to the ending reference to Mary. In each case we have a woman with a shady reputation involved in a situation requiring a striking act of loyalty to God and to the Law—and in each case a faithful Gentile is highlighted. [Tamar pretended to be a prostitute and became pregnant by her father-in-law (Genesis 38); Rahab was a prostitute (Joshua 2; 6:22–25); the wife of Uriah, Bathsheba, committed adultery with King David while her husband was away with the army (2 Samuel 11); and Ruth spent the night in the granary, after which Boaz proposed marriage (Ruth 3).] This is a tension that will pervade Matthew's Gospel: in the midst of his history of Israel, Matthew underscores the presence of faithful Gentiles.

The presence of Mary in verse 16 may also indicate an attempt to defend her reputation by showing that immediate reputations are no gauge of God's work, because the other four women were all vindicated in later Jewish tradition. This should not be pressed too far, however, for the focus of Matthew's account is on Joseph rather than Mary.

Instead of a birth story focused on Mary we hear the story of Joseph, "a righteous man" who is confronted by an awful dilemma: to obey the Law or to obey God. When a young woman promised in marriage turned up pregnant, the Law demanded at least divorce (Deut. 22:21). But instead the dream messenger commanded marriage. A book written a couple of centuries earlier, variously known as Sirach or Ecclesiasticus, warned against trusting such ephemeral messengers: "Dreams give wings to fools," "Dreams are folly," and "Dreams have deceived many" (Sir. 34:1, 5, 7; compare also 15:1). After all, how could God contravene the God-given Law? But Matthew does not yet allow these questions to emerge. The dream messenger is obeyed, and this culminates in the fulfillment of an ancient prophecy and the birth of *Emmanuel*, God with Us.

The story vindicates Joseph's decision by repeatedly showing that this birth inaugurates the time when all the ancient promises are being fulfilled. The manner of birth (1:22), the place of birth (2:5), the place of safety (2:15), the new residence in Nazareth (2:23), and even the horror of Herod's slaughter (2:17) are all seen as fulfilling prophetic promises. Whether Herod actually carried out such a slaughter is debated; there is no other record of it, but he was certainly capable of it. He was ruthless enough to kill three of his own sons when he thought they might threaten his rule, which led to the pun: "It's better to be Herod's pig [*hus* in Greek] than his son [*huios*]," because he attempted to keep the Jewish law that forbade eating pork.

Certainly, Matthew's audience would have had no difficulty believing such a thing, but we must ask a further question: Why include this kind of story in the Gospel? Only now does Matthew reach the point where Mark began, the stories of John and the baptism of Jesus. Why has Matthew found it necessary to go behind the beginning that Mark had found appropriate?

Raymond Brown's analysis of this new beginning is instructive. He shows that the writing of a gospel such as Mark represented a development over earlier thinking about Jesus. Both Paul's letters (in the mid-fifties) and Luke's report of the earliest preaching understood the resurrection as the event in which Jesus' divine sonship was manifested. "Designated son of God . . . by his resurrection" is probably an early creedal form that Paul quoted in Romans (1:4; see also Acts 2:32). Mark, however, recognizing that the deeds of Jesus' ministry already revealed his status with God, located the recognition of that rank at the baptism. But Matthew saw that such a formulation was inadequate for it could be understood as a sort of divine adoption. For Matthew, Jesus' status was already inherent in his birth (Brown, 1975:579–80). It is not so surprising, then, that the birth of Jesus provoked the same responses as his life, death, and resurrection, for in Matthew his birth is just as surely a revelation of his messianic role.

Jesus' birth, no less than his death and resurrection (Paul) and his deeds (Mark), evokes acceptance (the magi) and rejection (Herod). We might be tempted to say that Jews rejected him and Gentiles accepted him, but that is too simple. More precisely, certain leaders within the Jewish community rejected him. We must remember that in Matthew's story the pious ordinary Jew, one obedient to the Law, recognized this new work of God. The faithful Jew is represented by Joseph and by John.

Matthew's Gospel has sometimes been considered anti-Semitic (see 27:25). We will explore Matthew's possible relationship with other Jews when we investigate the situation of the community at the end of this chapter. But we note in passing that one of the main issues addressed in these birth stories (how can Jesus of Nazareth be the Messiah, when the Messiah must come from Bethlehem?) would be of concern only to other Jews. These birth stories already indicate a complex relationship with both Jews and Gentiles.

THE WORDS OF JESUS: A NEW MEANING FOR THE LAW

The early part of Matthew's Gospel reads like a meditation on themes from the exodus. Like Israel of old, Jesus was brought out of Egypt, crossed through the water, and led through the wilderness. Matthew has carefully molded the wilderness scenes to emphasize the faithfulness of Jesus: Matthew adds both dialogue (3:14–15) and drama (4:1–11); the dialogue declares his intention to "fulfill all righteousness," and the drama actually shows him resisting the temptations of the devil.

Jesus' faithfulness contrasts with the unfaithfulness of those who followed Moses in the wilderness; such unfaithfulness becomes attached here to the Pharisees. Matthew alone portrays Pharisees and Sadducees coming to John for baptism (3:7). This is Matthew's first mention of them; they played no role in the Herod episode (2:4), but Matthew's antipathy toward them is deep and is manifested here at their first appearance. We will explore the reasons for this hostility in the section on Matthew's situation at the end of this chapter. (For a preliminary discussion of these groups, see pages 292–93.)

The general thrust of Matthew's new material in the baptism and temptation stories is to present Jesus as eminently righteous, obedient to "every word that proceeds from the mouth of God" (4:4). Read the greatly expanded temptation story carefully (chapter 4), especially noting the motifs of son and obedience. It is noteworthy that worship is said to be due only to God, yet the magi came to worship Jesus (4:10; 2:2). This unprecedented claim to authority, seen in the call of the disciples, is explained and demonstrated in the first of Matthew's five long speeches.

READING AND REFLECTION

Study Matthew 5–7 and try to outline the material. Look for thematic or verbal ties to chapters 1–4.

Matthew has set the stage for this mountaintop instruction in two ways. First, there are the many echoes of the Moses-exodus stories. Though the category of new Moses proved inadequate to interpret Jesus, Matthew used it to good effect in this early section. We have seen that the idea of genesis dominates chapter 1, that

Joseph echoes the patriarch of the same name, and that the baptism and temptation sequence includes exodus themes. Now, like Israel of old, we come to the mountain of revelation, where God is present and the Law (Torah, instruction) is given (see Exodus 19–24 and Matt. 5:1, 21).

The second way Matthew has set the stage for this discourse is by the movement of the plot. The incidents of fulfillment, obedience, and righteousness narrated in chapters 1–4 require further explanation. These two terms, *fulfill* and *righteousness*, provide the keynote of the speech that could be entitled "The Meaning of Righteousness Fulfilled."

The discourse is a unified speech (though there is little connection between the various sayings in 6:19–7:12). W. D. Davies has suggested that the organization of the discourse corresponds to the sayings of a teacher called Samuel the Just, who taught a century or so before Matthew that the world was upheld by three things:

> *by the Law,*
> *by worship,*
> *and by the showing of kindness*
> (m. Avot 1.2; *Herford, 1962; see W. D. Davies, 1966:305*)

It is attractive to see Matthew's speech as structured by this pattern; we could paraphrase it as follows:

Introductory considerations (5:1–20)
    A new understanding of the Law (5:21–48)
    A new understanding of worship (6:1–18)
    A new understanding of deeds of kindness (6:19–7:12)
Concluding considerations (7:13–27)

Under this arrangement, each of the major sections ends with an appropriate summary statement (5:48; 6:18b; 7:12). Each represents what Matthew has earlier demanded, a righteousness that surpasses that of the Pharisees because the time of fulfillment has come (5:20, 17). It is crucial to see that this speech sets forth extraordinary demands, which make sense only in light of the conviction that the old promises are being fulfilled in the present time.

A comparison may be made to an extraordinary community of Jews who lived a monastic life at a wilderness place called Qumran, the community that produced the Dead Sea Scrolls (see pages 169–73.) These scrolls reveal a people who had a strict and radical ethic, so strict that they had to withdraw from contact with even the Pharisees lest they be polluted. (You may wish to read the scroll known as the *Community Rule*, sometimes called the *Manual of Discipline*; a good English translation is Vermes, 1987:61–80.) Like Matthew, these people believed they lived in the time of fulfillment.

They interpreted the Hebrew Scriptures by writing a kind of commentary called a *pesher* (Hebrew for "interpretation"). A **pesher** commentary moved directly from the scriptural sentences to the experience of the community, under the belief that the ancient books were written to explain the people's experiences. The typical method was to cite a verse, then give its application to the community by the expression "interpreted this means . . ." For example, the commentary on Hab. 1:4 reads as follows, first quoting Habakkuk, then interpreting it (the italic portion):

QUMRAN—SOURCE OF THE DEAD SEA SCROLLS   During the course of more than a century, around the time of Jesus, men gathered at Qumran and patiently copied their sacred writings, both the Scripture and the special writings of their brotherhood. Some think the scrolls were actually made in this long room, although that is not certain. What is certain is that they hid their scrolls in the nearby caves, which served as their homes and libraries. Given the nearly inaccessible nature of the caves, it is not surprising that the scrolls remained hidden for almost two thousand years—until 1947. The cave pictured here, which is directly across from this room, seems to have been the central library of this austere religious community, usually identified with the Essenes. For a photograph of one of the scrolls, see page 170.

> So the Law is weak and justice never goes forth. *Interpreted this concerns those who have despised the Law of God. . . .* For the Wicked encompasses the righteous. *The wicked is the Wicked Priest, and the righteous is the Teacher of Righteousness. (1QpHab; see page 504 on scroll citations)*

Because they believed they lived in the time of fulfillment, the Jews of Qumran developed an unprecedented community of celibate men who believed their prayers and holiness were bringing the kingdom of God. This radical community was based on an equally radical understanding of the Law, which they interpreted as requiring the lifestyle they had developed.

This conviction that the Scriptures were fulfilled in his own day motivated Matthew, with similar results: a radical reinterpretation of the Law. Because they too believed that they were living in this time of fulfillment, Matthew's community had to know how to apply the Law to their situation. This authority of Jesus that allows him to reinterpret the Law (7:28) will now be displayed in his actions (8–9). And just as Matthew painstakingly organized Jesus' teaching into a carefully crafted speech (5–7), so now he presents his deeds in an ordered series (8–9).

THE DEEDS OF JESUS: A NEW MEANING FOR MIRACLES

The next narrative section contains three cycles of three miracles each. Of these nine miracles, eight have parallels in Mark, but only four are found in the same sequence as here. In addition, the cycles are separated by two short stories, each raising two questions about discipleship. This artfully arranged unit can be displayed in the following format:

Cycle I
   A. Healing a leper (8:1–4)
   B. Healing a paralyzed servant of a centurion (8:5–13)
   C. Healing Peter's mother-in-law (8:14–17)
Two questions on discipleship: a radical forsaking of home and family (8:18–22)

Cycle II
   A. Rebuking a great storm (8:23–27)
   B. Expelling demons from two men into swine (8:28–34)
   C. Healing and forgiving a paralytic (9:1–8)
Two questions on discipleship: fellowship with sinners and proper fasting (9:9–17)

Cycle III
   A. Raising a dead girl and healing a woman of hemorrhage (conflated) (9:18–26)
   B. Healing two blind men (9:27–31)
   C. Expelling a demon from a mute (9:32–34)
Summary passage repeated from 4:23 (9:35)

A comparison with other versions of these stories in Mark and Luke will help us appreciate Matthew's accomplishment the more. If we examine this section in a synopsis (*GP* §45–57, *SFG* §84–98), we notice first that Matthew has arranged the material in his own way. Only IA and IIC (in the list above) follow the same context as in Mark. The sequence of miracles recounted in chapter 8 occur in a different order in Luke, where they come, respectively, in chapters 5, 7, 4, 9, and 8. This should caution those who wish to produce a sequential account of Jesus' ministry. Apparently a Gospel sequence relied more on the author's purpose than on chronology.

In addition, Matthew's version of every one of these stories is shorter than Mark's, often considerably so. One way he accomplishes this is by eliminating all third parties, creating a direct encounter between Jesus and the one healed. (Compare Matt. 8:5–13 with Luke 7:1–10, *GP* §46, *SFG* §85; Matt. 9:1–8 with Mark 2:1–12, *GP* §52, *SFG* §92; or Matt. 9:18–26 with Mark 5:21–43, *GP* §107, *SFG* §95.)

In Mark the miracles led to a false sense of understanding of Jesus' power and needed to be balanced with insight into his suffering. Mark's community seems to have been tempted to (mis)understand the miracles as the work of a "divine man."

Matthew's community apparently faces no such danger; rather, the miracles show Jesus to be the promised deliverer: they fulfill the prophecy of Isaiah: "He took our infirmities and bore our diseases" (8:17, end of Cycle I). For Matthew the miracles are not the opposite of Jesus' suffering; Isaiah's prophecy enabled Matthew to interpret the miracles as already a part of that suffering. Matthew is able to venture this new interpretation of the miracles because his hearers seem to operate more fully within a Jewish frame of reference.

Matthew has shown Jesus act with righteousness (1–4) and then speak with authority about that full righteousness (5–7) and also act with authority in these miracles (8–9). In fact, the crowds "glorified God who had given such authority to human beings" (9:8, unique to Matthew; see also 8:8–13). At the beginning of the next section Jesus invests his disciples with authority to heal (10:1).

At the end of this miracle cycle Matthew repeats the summary with which he closed the first narrative section (9:35 = 4:23). There it concluded the first calling of the disciples; here it precedes the special calling of the Twelve. Together they frame the authoritative words and the authoritative deeds of Jesus. The midpart of Matthew's story contains three speeches, explaining different aspects of the new community. We will consider them briefly.

THE RULES AND PARABLES: A NEW COMMUNITY

The three middle speeches are, like the Sermon on the Mount, collections of traditions drawn from a variety of sources and contexts. An examination of a synopsis will show the dexterity with which Matthew has adapted material (see also Beare, 1962:80–81). The discourse in chapter 10 combines material from both Mark and Q, and from different places in each. It draws on Mark's naming of the disciples (3:13–19) and his instruction of the disciples (6:7–11), and includes material from Q that Luke used as instruction to "seventy others" (Luke 10:1–2) and in other contexts (Luke 12:2–9, 51–53; 14:26–27; 17:33). There is also material Mark used in the apocalyptic discourse (Mark 13), and some material not found in any other Gospel (Matt. 10:23, 40–42).

As before, this material is carefully arranged, though in a novel way. It is arranged in the X-like pattern called a chiasmus (discussed on pages 285–86), in which the first and last items correspond, the second and next to last, and so on in the pattern A B C D C B A. Notice how this speech follows the pattern:

The setting of the discourse (9:35–10:4)
    A   Instructions for a mixed reception.....................................(10:5–15)
      B   Description of persecutions ....(10:16–23)
        C   Disciple treated as his master...........................(10:24–25)
          D   Do not fear—God knows ....(10:26–31)
        C   Discipleship is acknowledging Jesus .... (10:32–33)
      B   Descriptions of persecutions.....................................(10:34–39)
    A   Reception of disciples is reception of Jesus .... (10:40–42)
(adapted from Gaechter, n.d.:41)

By this scheme, the turning point is reached in verses 26–31, an exhortation to courage. This exhortation divides two kinds of material: Everything before the midpoint referred to an abstract master-disciple relationship; afterward it is the relation of Jesus to his disciples. Earlier, general persecution was described; now it is persecution because of Jesus. Earlier, this reception was seen as a general response to a message; now it is a reception of Jesus. This second half of the discourse is clearly "Christian": it depends on later reflections on the meaning of Jesus for the church. It is written for Matthew's own community.

One clue that the first more general admonitions are older is that they contain material that Matthew transforms. Matthew certainly did not support an exclusive mission to Israel (10:5, but contrast 28:19–20), nor did he seem to believe that the end would come before the gospel was preached throughout Israel (10:23, but contrast 24:14). Various solutions have been proposed for this complex problem. Perhaps the most common is to view the charge to go only to Israel as an early, conservative tradition that Matthew rejected in favor of a universal mission. But an equally important issue is how Matthew bridges the gap between the two. Matthew must motivate the change in instruction so that the reader is convinced the mission is now a universal one.

Several scholars have pointed to a scene where such a change seems to occur: Jesus encounters a Gentile and is persuaded that his initial reluctance to minister to her is mistaken (15:21–28). In that scene Jesus echoes the saying in 10:5: "I was sent only to the lost sheep of the house of Israel" (15:24, only in Matthew). The woman insists on her place at "the Lord's table," even if inferior (15:27), and Jesus immediately changes his mind (S. Brown, 1978).

This is a brilliant little scene that allows Matthew to show that Jesus himself made the shift to Gentile inclusion. Immediately after the episode with the woman in chapter 15, Jesus went into Gentile territory, where the people responded to him and "glorified the God of Israel" (15:31). But notice that in this scheme Israel remained at the center; Gentiles were now admitted into Israel. As the presence of Gentiles in the genealogy already implied, there has always been a place among God's people for faithful Gentiles. (Curiously, Matthew called the woman a Canaanite rather than a Greek as Mark referred to her in 7:24. The Canaanites were an ancient Gentile people whom the Israelites initially tried to destroy but who were eventually allowed to live in Israel.)

This discourse interprets the previous sections in two ways: it establishes the continuity between John, Jesus, and the early church by investing them all with the same message (3:2; 4:17; 10:7), and it extends the authority of Jesus to his disciples (7:29; 9:8; 10:1). Thus, as the second half of the discourse shows, the disciples stand in the same relation to the world as Jesus did. The references to suffering and rejection look forward to the rejection of Jesus that will become a major theme of the rest of the story. The message of John, Jesus, and now the disciples—the good news—is that "the **kingdom of heaven** has come near" (10:7). Just what is this kingdom?

The next discourse, chapter 13, elaborates Matthew's understanding of the coming of God's rule by means of a series of seven parables. As we might expect, Matthew's concept of the kingdom shares much with Mark's, because he uses a great deal of the same material. Both were strongly influenced by an apocalyptic worldview, looking forward to the imminent arrival of God's rule. (See the discussion in Chapters 3 and 9.) Yet we have already seen one way that Matthew deliberately digresses from Mark, by having John the Baptizer announce the kingdom (3:2).

Another striking departure from Mark is Matthew's addition to the story accusing Jesus of an alliance with Beelzebul. (Compare Matt. 12:25–37 with Mark 3:23–30; *GP* §86, *SFG* §117–18.) Matthew allows the charge to be made three times (9:34; 10:25; 12:24), choosing to answer only on the third occasion. To the answer we have already heard in Mark, he adds Jesus' declaration of the meaning of the exorcisms:

> But if it is by the Spirit of God that I cast out demons, then the Kingdom of God has come upon you. (12:28)

The verb translated "has come" here is past tense, and in the Greek a special kind of action is involved that indicates a completed action (an aorist tense). The coming of the kingdom, at least, is placed in the past. The presence of the kingdom should be seen in the exorcisms, because there the enemy Satan is overcome. We should not overlook the apocalyptic cast of this concept.

More than Mark, Matthew carefully explains the meaning of the kingdom, using seven parables (chapter 13). Parables are both easy and difficult to interpret: they speak directly to the reader, but they come to us preceded by a history of interpretations, including those of the Gospel writers.

Joachim Jeremias, in a masterful study of the parables, shows that the church sought to apply and reinterpret the parables chiefly by **allegorization** (1963:66–89), that is, by imagining that each item in the parable represented something else. Unlike a real story, an allegory does not make sense by itself; the reader must know the key, what each part of the story really refers to. (See the first chapter of Via, 1967.) A true **parable**, on the other hand, is a self-contained story that makes an impact on its hearers by the insight it provides. While we must expect that Jesus may have also used allegories, many of the allegorizations that we find in the Gospels seem designed to fit the situation of the church. For example, the allegorizations of the parable of the sower (13:18–23) and the parable of the weeds (13:24–30) seem to fit the situation of the church more closely than that of Jesus. (For more on these different settings of the parables, see pages 264–65.)

READING AND REFLECTION

Carefully study Matthew 13 and consider the following questions.

1. What is Matthew's understanding of the nature and function of the parables?
2. What are the characteristics of the kingdom?
3. What is the relationship between the present and the future?
4. Learn one of the parables so that you can tell it orally. (Don't memorize it; say it in your own words.)

A radical tension between present and future is evident throughout Matthew's Gospel (Bornkamm, 1963:15–51). Such tension is evident in these parables as the contrast between sowing and reaping, between present experience and final expectation. At every turn, the unexpected is found in the midst of everyday life. The long tradition of interpreting the mustard seed and leaven parables as the gradual growth of the kingdom should not be allowed to obscure Matthew's own view, which mentions not growth but its shocking result, not the process but the outcome.

These parables refer to something already begun, already planted, already hidden. This beginning is surely the church, for Matthew is the only Gospel to show Jesus consciously building a church (16:18), but it does not simply equate the kingdom and the church (for example, the parable of the weeds that shows good and bad growing together, and the parable of the net that catches all sorts of fish [13:47–48]).

Matthew avoids an overly idealized image of his community, never simply identifying it with the kingdom of God. Yet he does show that that kingdom has already appeared in the words and deeds of Jesus and has now become shockingly obvious in the community that seeks to follow Jesus. Hence, the closest possible connection exists between Jesus and the church. It remains for the story to explain how the church is to operate. Matthew does not hesitate to place such instruction on the lips of Jesus in another speech about the community (chapter 18).

Two themes dominate this (fourth) discourse: specific church laws for dealing with controversies within the community and radical provision for mutual support and forgiveness.

READING AND REFLECTION

Read chapter 18, making a list of the laws Matthew lays down. What are the characteristics of true citizens of the kingdom of heaven?

Perhaps the most surprising new rules are those that outline the process for expelling someone from the community: individual rebuke, group rebuke, corporate judgment, expulsion (18:15–17). These are clearly community regulations from Matthew's own time, and they reflect the realistic image of the community as containing both good and bad (as in the parables of chapter 13).

Matthew's argument that his community represents God's kingdom could easily lead to arrogance. Such arrogance is not unknown in church history. To recognize that the community includes both good and bad undermines any sense of conceit. The closing parable (18:23–35) especially—a real parable, not to be allegorized—establishes the basis of church discipline by recognizing the universal need for forgiveness (see 6:4–5).

THE RESPONSES TO JESUS

The middle narrative sections (11–17 and 19–22) have similar themes, portraying varying responses to Jesus. The question is set in the opening scene, a marvelous vignette drawn from Q, in which John the Baptizer has second thoughts about Jesus. John had been arrested (4:12), and now from prison he sends his disciples to ask Jesus, "Are you he who is to come or shall we look for another?" (11:2). Jesus' response here exactly matches Matthew's writing strategy; he does not say yes or no, rather, he recounts the "deeds of the Messiah":

> Go and tell John what you hear and see: the blind receive their sight, the lame walk, the lepers are cleansed, the deaf hear, the dead are raised, and the poor have good news brought to them. And blessed is anyone who takes no offense at me. (11:4–6)

That is, Jesus' deeds and words are answer enough. (For more on "the one who is to come" see the discussion of characterization below, pages 330–32.)

In this third narrative section (11–12) the Pharisees—offended at his lack of purity—do not understand (12:14), even though Jesus does the works of the Messiah (11:3–6; 8:17). It is all as Scripture foretold (12:17–21; note the emphasis on Gentiles). This section contains a kaleidoscope of responses to Jesus, of which Peter's confession is the highlight (notice 13:54, 57; 14:1–2, 33; 15:12, 27, 31; 16:1, 13–20; 17:4, 6). This confession now takes on the aura of an extraordinary accomplishment, quite unlike the Markan portrayal (*GP* §122, *SFG* §158). This is a beautifully wrought section, interweaving the defense of Jesus, the antagonism of the Pharisees, and the inevitable rejection. It should be studied as a unit, noting especially the materials unique to Matthew.

The fourth narrative section (19–22) heightens this tension with a series of controversy stories drawn largely from Mark. These controversies increase the tension between Jesus and the religious leaders until they decide to arrest him (21:46; which they do not act on till 26:4). They are afraid to act, however, and so seek to entrap him with a question about taxes, which would allow the Romans to arrest him (22:15). Jesus does nothing to defuse this hostility, in fact only enflames it with parables of judgment and rejection, which the leaders understand are directed at them (21:45).

This theme of judgment is explained in the final discourse (23–25). Although this is often labeled a judgment of Jews, or Pharisees, or of false Israel, the scope of the final discourse is a judgment on all the nations (25:32). This section differentiates true and false discipleship. It is, as H. B. Green suggests, a recapitulation and exemplification of some aspects of the Sermon on the Mount (1975:166); both disciples and Pharisees stand under judgment (19:25–30).

This echoes an earlier motif: the kingdom contains both true heirs and heirs of the evil one (13:38, 48) and that situation must persist until the "close of the age" (13:30, 40). Matthew takes a parable from Q and reworks it to introduce this theme of inclusion and exclusion (compare 22:1–14 with Luke 14:16–24; *GP* §205, *SFG* §279). Here we see the two aspects, the inclusion of "both bad and good" (22:10, only in Matthew) as well as the final judgment (22:11–13). Being in the church is no protection against the coming judgment. Matthew's account of the story of the man who sought eternal life sets forth the requirements (19:16–30 = Mark 10:17–31; *GP* §189, *SFG* §254). Besides moderating the difficulty raised by Mark's introduction (which seemed to question Jesus' divine status), Matthew's story differs in three important ways from the earlier telling: (1) he includes the radical summary of the law characteristic of his community, "love your neighbor as yourself" (19:19; 22:36–40); (2) he changes the subsequent question to show that even this standard is not enough (19:20); and (3) in Jesus' answer, he says, "if you would be perfect" (5:48) go, sell all, and follow me (19:21). This brings us to the crux of Matthew's argument with his fellow Jews (the topic of the next major section): obedience consists in more than keeping the Law; it consists in following Jesus. But this "following Jesus" is not simply identifying with him: Matthew thought that many would be turned away at the Last Judgment even though they preached and worked miracles in Jesus' name (7:21–23). Matthew calls them "evildoers" or, literally, "lawless ones." The "higher righteousness" (5:20) does not demand less than the scribes and Pharisees; it demands more. Disciples will fail unless they keep the Law as revealed in Jesus (24:35; 5:18). The Pharisees fail because they refuse to recognize the true heir to the vineyard (21:33–46, especially 43).

What, then, is the relationship between the church and the kingdom? In one sense the church is the kingdom, the seed planted in the earth, the leaven hidden in the lump. Yet it stands in paradoxical tension with the kingdom: the catch must be sorted; the weeds discarded. It is the maidens, wise and foolish, waiting for the wedding for which only some of them are prepared (25:1–13). Between the church and the kingdom stands the judgment, the theme of the final speech.

READING AND REFLECTION
Read Matthew 23–25.

1. List positive and negative things said about the scribes and Pharisees.
2. While this final speech of Jesus shares much with Mark's final speech (Mark 13), Matthew adds to it. Use a synopsis, beginning with *GP* §213 or *SFG* §287, and list the material Matthew has that is not in Mark and noting what is only in Matthew.
3. Based on the parable of the Last Judgment (*GP* §229, *SFG* §33), what determines whether a person is righteous?

An examination of the final discourse (23–25) will show how Matthew developed this concept of judgment. Over half the material in those chapters is unique to Matthew, revealing the importance of this theme for his work as a whole. Discussion of chapter 23 will be reserved for the next section, but its context as a message of judgment is to be emphasized. It is a judgment Matthew had seen fulfilled in the destruction of Jerusalem in 70 CE. If this chapter has a bitter tone, it is the bitterness of one who has seen the awful judgment.

The rest of the discourse shifts location (as did the third and fourth discourses—13:36; 18:21) but continues the theme of judgment, by using material from the apocalyptic discourse (Mark 13) and by adding Q and other materials concerning the coming end. The climactic scene is reached in a prophetic vision of the Last Judgment (25:31–46, only in Matthew). This important scene should be read and considered carefully.

If Matthew has written his book well and if we have read it well, there should be no need to elaborate on his judgment here. We ought to recognize his portrayals as easily as a shepherd recognizes a sheep or a goat. People are included on the basis of their fulfilling the law of love of neighbor, now focused as a response to Jesus. The crucial factor is not naming Jesus but responding to his demand for "higher righteousness." The one new twist is the innocence with which the righteous act, but even that was foreshadowed (19:13–15).

This parable confirms our earlier picture of the tension between the present of the church and the future of the kingdom. Matthew's church is in the process of coming to terms with living between the times; the kingdom has been inaugurated, but it has not been consummated. The church's task in this interim is to be faithful in doing the will of God, keeping the Law, following Jesus (see 7:21; 12:50; 19:17). In the final narrative section Matthew portrays the paradigm of such a life: the ultimate obedience of Jesus.

THE DESTINY OF JESUS: A NEW CONCLUSION

Jesus is the source of the higher righteousness that Matthew demands in two senses: he is its authoritative teacher (5:20) and its model (4:1–11). Now Matthew turns his attention to the latter, reworking the passion story to emphasize the themes of obedience and surpassing righteousness. The passion narrative was the most fixed part of the Jesus tradition, and Matthew's version is very similar to Mark's. Yet this also suggests that even minor variations may be important for Matthew. Before examining in detail the trial and crucifixion, notice how Matthew foreshadows both Jesus' burial (26:6–13) and death (26:20–29), carefully explaining their meaning: for the forgiveness of sins (26:28, only in Matthew). Matthew offers no fuller explanation, but he is sure that these are not accidental or unfortunate events. Jesus is deliberately fulfilling the will of God (26:52–54, only in Matthew). This is described in what may be called the climactic scene of the Gospel, the submission of Jesus to the Father's will in Gethsemane (26:36–46), a scene portrayed more intensely in Matthew than in Mark or Luke. The real struggle is not an agony in the face of death (as in Mark) but a struggle of the will; that accomplished, true obedience follows.

READING AND REFLECTION

Carefully study Matthew 27, both in relation to Mark's account and as a unified narrative. (Start at *GP* §242, *SFG* §334.)

1. Does Matthew emphasize the same points as Mark?
2. How does Matthew show that this is a cosmic event?
3. What is the role of the Pharisees in this event? Of the Jewish leaders?

Of the many observations possible, I shall limit myself to two that show how Matthew's interpretation of this event presents a radical new interpretation of Mark's notion that Jesus' death revealed his divine sonship (Mark 15:39). First, Matthew introduces cosmic phenomena into the text so that the centurion sees far more than the manner of Jesus' death (Matt. 27:51–54). Second, Matthew introduces the title *Son of God* into the crucifixion scene itself, in the form of a threefold taunt that is really a temptation to abandon the cross (27:40–44). This recalls the earlier threefold temptation by Satan in the wilderness (4:3, 6, 8) and perhaps echoes the threefold prayer in Gethsemane. In each of these scenes, the obedience of Jesus keeps him on the path of righteousness. By means of these and other modifications, Matthew transforms the story from one of suffering to one of obedience. Thus Jesus fulfills all righteousness (3:15).

In Matthew's version there need be none of the Markan reluctance to portray the resurrection, for it vindicates this obedience. At this point we may reflect back to the analysis of the four accounts of the empty tomb (pages 253–55). Perhaps the variations noted between Matthew and Mark are now more intelligible. Matthew's portrait of Jesus causes him to represent this scene differently. Thus, in his closing episode, which takes us back to the beginning and the promise of Emmanuel, Jesus appears to his disciples in Galilee and declares:

All authority in heaven and on earth has been given to me. Go therefore and make disciples of all nations, baptizing them in the name of the Father and of the Son and of the Holy Spirit, teaching them observe all that I have commanded you; and lo, I am with you always, to the close of the age. (28:19)

UNDERSTANDING THE CHARACTERS

Matthew presents us with vivid characters; they are recognizably the same individuals and groups as in Mark, yet they are characterized differently. An author may use several methods to reveal the nature of a person: the responses of other characters, the evaluative point of view of the narrator, the titles and attributes assigned to the person, and—most importantly—the deeds and words of the individual. We will examine these below, but before we do we need to consider another factor: an author must present the characters in terms of the expectations of the audience.

Matthew's audience lived in an age of expectation, even the Gentiles. The Roman poet Virgil (in 40 BCE) had proclaimed the beginning of a new era, a golden age of justice and men "sent down from heaven" (*Eclogue* IV). But the expectation among Jews was older and more highly developed—and more varied. Before considering more directly how Matthew portrays Jesus as **Messiah**, we will review some of the expectations of his contemporaries.

THE ONE WHO IS TO COME: THE VARIETY OF MESSIANIC EXPECTATIONS

It is erroneous to speak simply of Jews expecting a conquering king like David; that was only one strand in a tapestry of ideas not yet woven into a coherent pattern. For example, the concept of messiah in the Dead Sea Scrolls is certainly different from anything we might imagine on the basis of Rabbinic and Christian formulations. The community at Qumran seems to have expected two messiahs, one priestly and one royal, but neither was expected to play any significant redemptive role. God alone would bring in the new age; the messiahs would merely preside at the inaugural banquet (Vermes 1987:52–57; *Messianic Rule*, 100; and *The Community Rule*, 74 [1QSa 2 and 1QS 9:11]).

Several other messianic categories survive in the literature of this era, but we cannot always be sure how the various groups applied them. Some expected a final Prophet, usually identified with Elijah (Mal. 4:5) or Moses (Deut. 18:15), though Matthew seems to know a tradition that included the reappearance of Jeremiah (16:14). Others looked for a heavenly Son of Man (Dan. 7:13–14). Some expected a new David (Ezek. 34:23–24) or son of David (Jer. 23:5–6); there was even the radical idea that the Messiah was a Gentile king who would free Israel (Isa. 45:1). (For an overview of five types of expectation that were applied to Jesus, see Chapter 2, pages 66–70.)

It is unclear how intense and how widespread these expectations were in the time of Jesus, but the century after Jesus was a time of great change in Palestine, marked by two great wars with Rome, both fought with messianic fervor. For simplicity we speak of four movements: Sadducees, Pharisees, Essenes, and Zealots. In fact, of course, there was far greater diversity. If we characterize these groups in regard to their longing for God's kingdom, we may perhaps generalize in this fashion: Zealots strove most ardently for its coming, Sadducees the least, with Essenes and Pharisees somewhere in between. The Zealots appeared as a group around 50 CE; they believed in a literal kingdom and apparently also believed they could bring it about immediately. They stirred up active rebellion, with disastrous results. The Zealot movement seems to have been preceded by several messianic pretenders acting on similar convictions (see Acts 5:36–37). At the other extreme we find those content with the status quo, the wealthy priestly aristocracy, chiefly Sadducees. Apparently they had little interest in such notions. They cooperated with Roman rule and benefited from it.

The response attributed to Gamaliel in Acts (5:34–38) represents the attitude of the Pharisees: only God can bring about the kingdom. The Pharisees were not priests, but they banded together in religious associations, eating their meals in priestly purity, while waiting and praying for the coming of God's kingdom. The Essenes adopted a similar strategy but engaged in a more radical quest for purity—abandoning normal society to live a communal existence in mutual holiness. Their task was to wait, in patience and purity, for God to inaugurate the new age.

Whether prophet, priest, or king, whether teacher or son of God, whether human or heavenly redeemer, whether warrior or pious worshipper, the "one who is to come" would redeem Israel. With this confusing swirl of messianic ideas as a background, let us look at Matthew's Jesus.

THE MATTHEAN PORTRAYAL OF JESUS

Matthew's story is "an account of the origins of Jesus the Messiah," but we should not let later understandings (the world in front of the text) of this title influence our understanding too much, for the title *messiah* had no fixed meaning in Matthew's time. We should let the story define the title, not the other way around. The question is: how does this story characterize Jesus? Without doubt, the Matthean Jesus is a complex character; Matthew uses a variety of literary devices to reveal who Jesus is. Let's briefly consider four such characterization techniques: titles, response of other characters, the evaluative point of view of the narrator, and the actions portrayed.

First, certain titles are assigned to Jesus in the story, both by the storyteller and by other characters in the story. The magi approach him as king of the Jews (2:2), and the same title recurs at the end on the sign over the crucified Jesus (27:37); John calls him the "one mightier" (3:11), and then wonders if he is "the one who is to come" (11:3); the voice from heaven declares him to be "my son" (3:17; 17:5); demons also address him as "Son of God" (8:29), as do some who see his powers (14:33; 16:16; 27:54); yet claiming this title seems to be a temptation that must be resisted (4:3; 27:40); those needing healing address him as "Son of David" (9:27; 12:23; 15:22; 20:30; but Jesus seems to reject this title in 22:42); the centurion recognizes him as a person of authority (8:8); Jesus calls himself "Son of Man," an expression that meant roughly "a human being" (8:20; 12:8; 16:28), but could also be identified with Daniel's heavenly redeemer. This list could be extended. The titles are so varied as to offer little precision. A second strategy is to ask how other characters view him.

This list of titles already includes some of the responses of other characters, whose testimony shapes the reader's perception. Still, these other characters do not agree on the character of Jesus, and some, like John, vacillate. Others, primarily some Jewish leaders beginning with King Herod but including especially the Pharisees, regard Jesus negatively. One group slowly makes up its mind, and it is with them the reader most closely aligns, the disciples. I will discuss their views in the next section.

Although these various voices in the story are impressive, there is one voice that we listen to more than any other, the evaluative point of view of the narrator. What does the teller of this tale think of Jesus? There are several narrative asides in the story (for example, the narrator tells us that various events fulfill Scripture, 1:22), but the view of the narrator is especially clear in the opening and closing. Jesus is introduced as "Jesus the Messiah, the Son of David, the Son of Abraham" (1:1). This, followed by the genealogy itself, suggests Jesus is the culmination of Israel's long history—perhaps even the goal of that history. The final scene, in which the risen Jesus claims "all authority" and commissions his disciples to extend that authority over the Gentiles, also points to the centrality of Jesus in the history of Israel.

And surely the most important basis for a reader's view of characters is what we see them do and hear them say. If we focus our attention on what Jesus does and says, two characteristics seem to predominate: Jesus is one endowed with great authority, and, conversely, he is the supremely obedient one. Jesus is introduced with the quotation from Isaiah that points to "God with us" (1:23), and he is depicted as the one whose every action is oriented toward doing the will of God. Thus, his first deed and first word are explicitly to fulfill all righteousness (3:15 and 5:17–20). His final act, in Gethsemane, is to choose the divine will. It is a standard no one else in this story achieves.

Even Jesus' miracles, as we saw above, represent him as the coming one, bearing the infirmities of the people—thus they are part of his suffering. We also saw that the early stories echo the stories of Moses. Born under threat, preserved from harm, brought out of Egypt, crossed through the water, led through the wilderness, taught from the mountain. Jesus is not a new Moses (ironically, the Pharisees sit on Moses' seat, 23:2), but he is surely the coming one whose new words and deeds create a new people.

THE MATTHEAN PORTRAYAL OF THE DISCIPLES

Matthew presents a much more positive picture of the disciples than does Mark (for example, compare Matt. 14:32 with Mark 6:51). Or to put it another way, the disciples fulfill a different narrative role in this Gospel: they are the legitimate successors of Jesus, a common theme in biographies of philosophers in Matthew's time (Talbert, 1977:105–09). Matthew's legitimation of the disciples may be seen in the commission in chapter 10 and traced in the subtle variations in the material included in the next section (14–17). In the two feeding episodes, for example, the disciples clearly duplicate Jesus' own action, and the feeding itself becomes typical of the eucharistic meal (also called "communion" or the "Lord's Supper"). Now they understand Jesus' teaching (16:12). This new emphasis on the disciples is also evident in Matthew's recasting of Mark's central scene, Peter's confession, where Peter is now highly praised for his insight (16:13–23, *GP* §122, *SFG* §158).

Although Matthew does not delete the rebuke to Peter (as Luke will), he certainly emphasizes his preeminence (see also 14:22–33; 17:24–27; 18:21–22). Only in

Matthew is Peter given extraordinary power "to bind and to loose" (a power later extended to all the disciples, 18:18). In rabbinic literature this expression is used in connection with the rabbi ruling on a point of law, meaning to forbid or allow, but it also has a broader legal meaning to find guilty (or excommunicate) or to acquit (or forgive) (see Duling, 1987). The judgment of Peter or the church will be ratified by God. (See a similar bestowing of authority in John 20:23.) Such extraordinary power is in some tension with the faulty judgment immediately shown by Peter (16:22–23), a scene that Matthew expands.

The weakness of the disciples is not overlooked. When Judas arrives to betray Jesus, he is specifically labeled "one of the twelve" (26:47). Peter denies Jesus three times, clinching it with a curse and an oath (26:74). The disciples still forsake him in Gethsemane and do not appear at the crucifixion. However, unlike Mark's story, they do reappear at the end, meet Jesus on the mountain in Galilee, and receive his commission to be his agents.

Matthew's disciples, like Matthew's readers, struggle to understand Jesus. Unlike Mark's disciples, they succeed. With all their failures, including not standing by him in his suffering, they do forsake all and follow him (4:18–22 and 19:27); they confess him to be Son of God (14:33; 16:13–20); they worship him (14:33; even if with some doubt, 28:17). And most of all they stand poised to embark on a mission to the nations (28:16–20), even in the face of their own suffering (10:16–39; 13:20–22).

THE MATTHEAN PORTRAYAL OF OTHER CHARACTERS

We have seen repeatedly in this story that this trait of obedience to God, which Matthew typically calls *righteousness*, is a central concern. From the women of the opening genealogy, to Joseph, the magi, the disciples, and a host of minor characters (the centurion, the Canaanite woman, the woman who anoints Jesus, Joseph of Arimathea, the women at the tomb), Matthew portrays those who obey. This theme finds voice in a pronouncement of Jesus:

> *For whoever does the will of my Father in heaven is my brother and sister and mother (12:50).*

In fact female characters are nearly always portrayed positively in this Gospel. Two stand out. The bleeding woman (9:20–22) displays remarkable faith, even more noteworthy when contrasted with the men in the surrounding story who laugh at Jesus (9:24). The Canaanite woman (15:22–28) is portrayed even more impressively: she convinces Jesus to change his mind about healing her daughter. And the women at the tomb faithfully report to the disciples (28:8; contrast Mark 16:8).

By contrast other characters are portrayed as disobedient: Judas among the disciples, and to some degree Peter. The theme of disobedience is introduced already in the genealogy, for the faithfulness of women is implicitly contrasted with the unfaithfulness of others: Judah and David, leaders of Israel, failed to obey the divine command. We are not surprised then, when Herod and Jewish leaders in Jerusalem conspire against the infant Messiah (2:1–18). Matthew consistently gives a negative characterization of Israel's leaders, for he sees them as disobedient (see chapter 23).

We should not mistake this, as some do, for a rejection of the Jewish people as a whole; nearly everyone in this story is Jewish including Jesus. Matthew is concerned with obedience, not ethnic origin. This concern is found in Matthew's characterization of one other group: the crowds. Curiously Matthew overwhelmingly uses this term in the plural—as if the crowd were multiple, divided into parts. We first meet them as followers of Jesus (4:25; 8:1; 14:13; 19:2); they join the disciples in hearing Jesus teaching (5:1; 7:28; 11:7; 12:46; 13:2, 34; 22:33; 23:1); they respond to Jesus' triumphs (9:8, 33); they are the focus of Jesus' compassion (9:36); they struggle with faith (12:23; 21:11, 46). Yet they also join in the betrayal (26:55) and are persuaded by their leaders to ask for Jesus' death (27:20). These crowds are a conflicted character; struggling with Jesus, they yet fail to attain obedience.

The supreme model of this obedience is Jesus. Matthew's new telling of the temptation scene highlights this trait: Jesus, as Son of God, is tempted to act with independent authority—a temptation echoed in Gethsemane and on the cross. But he is supremely obedient, and thus he is given supreme authority (28:18). In this way Jesus becomes the leader of a new community and its chief model. The people too can now be children of God (5:9, 45; 13:38) and address God as "our Father" (6:9), one who negates the authority of every human father (23:9). Now let us investigate more directly the nature of that community.

THE SITUATION OF THE MATTHEAN COMMUNITY

Once again, we have a writing that is thoroughly anonymous—with no attempt to identify author, place, or time of writing—and again, we have little hope of recapturing these particulars. We must explore the document for clues to its social and historical setting, but the clues point in two different directions. As one writer lamented:

> The Gospel seems to contain so many contradictions, and to wear a double face. It is at once "Jewish" and anti-Jewish, "legal" and anti-legal, narrow and anti-Gentile and also catholic and universalist. (Montefiore, 1927:1:lxxiii)

Thus for example, Matthew has Jesus declare, "The scribes and Pharisees sit on Moses' seat, so practice and observe whatever they tell you" (23:2–3). The seat of Moses indicates their teaching authority and implies Matthew's acceptance of the Oral Torah. But he immediately goes on to condemn them in the most stringent terms, calling them "blind guides" (23:16; 16:6, 12). Both of these declarations are found only in Matthew; the other Gospels are neither so positive nor so negative.

We may summarize by saying that some clues point to a Jewish Matthew, a writer at home in the Jewish tradition. Our study of Paul revealed that many early followers of Jesus continued to worship within the synagogue, considering themselves Jews and being so regarded by other Jews. They probably considered themselves Jews who belonged to the party of Jesus as other Jews belonged to the party of the Pharisees or Essenes. This was not simply an early phenomenon; some Christian groups continued in this fashion for hundreds of years (Pines, 1966). Was Matthew such a person?

Or was he opposed to such a way of living, as other clues in the book might indicate? We do know that some, especially Gentile converts, rejected a Jewish understanding of life. Early in the second century a Gentile writer declared: "It is an abomination to follow Jesus Christ and to practice Jewish ways" (Ignatius *To the Magnesians* 10). By the middle of the second century Marcion, that ardent follower of Paul, declared that there are only contradictions between Jewish and Christian traditions (page 208).

We must review the relations between Jews and Gentiles in Matthew's time and try to discover the emerging consciousness of Judaism and Christianity as two separate movements. Only then will we be prepared to address Matthew's relationship to the Jewish people. First, let me address two logical but faulty assumptions: that people in Matthew's day were either Jews or Gentiles, and that Judaism in Matthew's time was a standard, stable religious movement to which all Jews adhered. Neither is correct.

JEWISH GENTILES, GENTILIZED JEWS

In Matthew's day Jews were a prolific and far-ranging people, sometimes estimated to comprise as much as 10 percent of the population of the Roman Empire, though this figure seems too high. Jews had lived outside their homeland at least since the exile (587 BCE) and, by Matthew's time, there were Jewish synagogues in every major city in the empire. In Egypt Jews were said to number one million (Philo *In Flaccum* 43), with the largest settlement in Alexandria—the leading intellectual and cultural center of that era. Two of the five sections of Alexandria were Jewish, though Jews lived and had synagogues in the other quarters as well (*In Flaccum* 55). Large Jewish communities also existed in Syria, Asia Minor, Italy, and even Parthia.

Several factors contributed to an increasingly large Jewish population. First, the Jews were nearly the only ancient people who did not practice *infanticide*, the abandonment of unwanted infants. More important, many Jews in this period sought to convert Gentiles, and many Gentiles were receptive (pages 114–19). Many Gentiles converted to Jewish religion (became proselytes), but others resisted full conversion. A fairly large contingent of near-converts gathered around the synagogue and became known as a special class: the devout or the God-fearers (Grant, 1962:105; Luke 7:1–5; Acts 10:1–2; 14:1).

Even as some Gentiles in Matthew's world had already moved toward becoming Jewish, many Jews had become Gentile in all but their religion. The majority of Jews lived in the diaspora, among Gentiles: they spoke Greek, read their Bible in Greek, adopted Greek names and dress—in many important ways they began to think like Greeks. This group is usually referred to as the Hellenists (from *Hellas*, the name for Greece). So instead of two antithetical groups, Jews and Gentiles, it is more accurate to speak of a continuum of identification with four recognizable concentrations (see Figure 10.1).

As might be expected, the middle groups had the most in common, and early Christianity apparently made its strongest appeal to them.

THE DIVERSITY OF JUDAISM IN THE FIRST CENTURY

The other faulty assumption would be to think there was one major form of Judaism in Matthew's time. This might be true by 150 CE, but it was not the case when Matthew wrote. We need some sense of the historical development in this pivotal period.

SYNAGOGUE FLOOR This mosaic on a synagogue floor from fourth-century Tiberias, in Galilee, shows the strong influence of Greek culture on the Jews. Not only does it portray the human figure, but the figure bears strong resemblance to images of Apollo. The figure here is said to be David, and he is surrounded by the twelve signs of the Zodiac, the whole encompassed by the four seasons—typical motifs in many Greek mosaics. These motifs are easily blended with strong Jewish motifs: the menorahs (light stands) and the ark that held the scroll of the Torah.

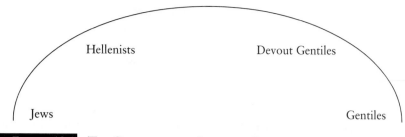

Hellenists   Devout Gentiles

Jews   Gentiles

FIGURE 10.1 THE CONTINUUM OF JEWS AND GENTILES

The outlines of the major religious sects of Jesus' time have been briefly characterized in the discussion above and in Chapter 9 (pages 292–93). Let us examine these groups more closely, because the history of all four was profoundly influenced by the political events that touched Israel.

Since the fall of the monarchy in 587 BCE, Israel had enjoyed only one century of virtual independence—the period of the Maccabees. This independence was brought to an end by the visit of Pompey to Jerusalem in 63 BCE. On the pretext of settling a dispute between two rival claimants to power, Pompey effectively asserted Rome's control over Palestine. At first Rome was content to rule through the appointed priest, then through puppet kings, the Herods, but eventually, in 6 CE, the emperor appointed a Roman governor. This direct rule, coupled with a census to determine taxes, led to the first Jewish revolt (First Judean War) and the founding of the new sect, the **Zealots**. These Zealots should not be viewed primarily as a political or nationalistic group; their first motive was religious. They considered recognition of Caesar as lord and the payment of taxes with coins bearing Caesar's image to be violations of the first commandment (Exod. 20:2). They were strictly observant Jews, as excavations of their mountain stronghold have shown (Yadin, 1966:164–67). They shared much with the Pharisees; they have even been referred to as left-wing Pharisees (Herford, 1952:51). But they differed on one essential point: for the Zealots, faithfulness demanded active resistance to Rome and the overthrow of the government. Consequently, they were hostile to the ruling aristocracy (the Sadducees) but immensely popular with the people. So popular, in fact, that in 66 CE they precipitated a war with Rome that lasted more than seven years. According to Luke, one of Jesus' disciples was a Zealot (6:15; Acts 1:13). Barabbas is characterized as a Zealot (Mark 15:7), and his popularity with the people is entirely believable.

Firmly opposed to this zealotry were the **Sadducees**, a wealthy priestly aristocracy that ran the domestic affairs of the Jewish people under the Roman governors (Reicke, 1968:155–56). The Sadducees represented the viewpoint of the **ruling elite**, the 1 to 2 percent of the urban population that controlled society. Like all rulers, the Sadducees were in no great hurry for the kingdom of God to come. They had little concern or respect for the common people, a feeling that was duly reciprocated.

A third sect, the **Essenes**, responded to Rome in yet another way. Like the Zealots, they believed that the foreigners polluted the land. So polluted had Israel become that even the Jerusalem Temple had been desecrated by unworthy priests appointed by Gentile kings. But unlike the Zealots, the Essenes adopted a completely quietist attitude: they withdrew from society to form a new holy society worthy to be called *Israel*. They followed a strict discipline and mingled only with each other, deeming even fellow Jews to be polluted. Apparently one group of these quietists withdrew to Qumran near the Dead Sea and produced the scrolls discovered in the mid-twentieth century (the Dead Sea Scrolls). Other Essenes formed enclaves within various villages. They maintained the strictest discipline of any of the Jewish sects. Some even refused to marry, because contact with women might contaminate them. Although Essenes are not mentioned in the Gospels, probably because of their seclusion, they represented one of the major religious options in first-century Jewish religion. Apparently, numerous other small sectarian groups of various kinds also existed, but we know little about them (Simon, 1967).

A moderate approach to Rome characterized the most influential of the groups, the **Pharisees**, who have the worst reputation of any of these groups—due in no small part to Matthew's writing. In English today to be a Pharisee means to be a hypocrite—precisely Matthew's opinion (23:13, 23, 25). There probably were Pharisees who were hypocrites, even as there were followers of Jesus who were hypocrites. But that is obviously not what they intended to be. The Pharisaic party of Jesus' time was in its period of growth and diversity, organized into local fellowships or associations that served both social and religious ends. Pharisees came largely from the social class we label **retainers**, people who serve the needs of the ruling elite and mediate their services (and demands) to the masses. Most would have been artisans, shopkeepers, or landowners. Though it is not right to think of them as a middle class on the model of the modern industrialized world, they were truly in the middle both economically and, more important, in terms of social power. They drew power both from the ruling elite (who needed their services) and from the peasants (who also needed their services and whom they were expected to control).

Again, however, we should understand the Pharisees as motivated primarily by piety. Their goal was to keep the Law and to teach others how to be observant. Their attempt to keep the ancient laws of purity caused them to avoid possibly polluting contact not only with Gentiles and Samaritans but also with less observant Jews. However, these associations were not rigid, closed communities; a great deal of variety of interpretation was allowed, and a consensus emerged only after prolonged debate. The leaders of the Pharisees seem to have developed the understanding of Jewish tradition that eventually became standard: **rabbinic Judaism**.

The Emergence of Rabbinic Judaism

The two formative teachers of Pharisaism before the time of Jesus were **Hillel** and Shammai, contemporaries whose dates are uncertain, though they probably both died between 10 and 20 CE. They represented divergent tendencies. For Hillel, the heart of the Law was love of neighbor, so he continually endeavored to adjust Torah to life. For example, the provision of Torah that required debts of fellow Israelites to be remitted in the seventh year (Deut. 15:1–6) had become a hardship for the poor because it was nearly impossible to obtain loans as the seventh year approached. Hillel created a new provision, whereby the law of release of debts could be expressly waived in a formal legal proceeding before the loan was made (Bruce, 1969:80). The common sense of this solution should not keep us from recognizing its radical nature: it effectively annulled the biblical law. We should also notice its intent: to serve the poor, the same intent as the original law.

Shammai represented a stricter interpretation of the Law, a more literal understanding. Against Hillel he argued that the Shema (a part of the daily prayer) must be recited while reclining in the evening but while standing in the morning, because the Scripture says to pray "when you lie down and when you rise" (Deut. 6:7; *b. Berakot 11a*; W. D. Davies, 1966:264). Such literalism characterized much of his teaching. F. F. Bruce considers it "probable" that the lawyers who "load men with burdens hard to bear" are Shammaites (Luke 11:46; Bruce, 1972:80). It is also worth noting that Shammai was from a wealthy family, whereas Hillel was more of a commoner and oriented more to the needs of the people. Their respective attitudes may be seen clearly in a famous rabbinic story:

> *A gentile once came to Shammai and offered to convert to the Jewish way but on a condition. It seems he found the Torah too complex and insisted that it be taught him "while standing on one foot." Shammai chased him away with a stick. The would-be convert went to Hillel with the same request. Hillel responded, "Whatever is hateful to you, do not do to your neighbor. That is the entire Torah. The rest is commentary; go and learn it." (See* b. Shabbat *31a)*

The striking similarity between Hillel's reply and Matthew's report of Jesus' summary of the Law (7:12) should not be overlooked.

Many similar stories illustrate the differences between Hillel and Shammai, and their personal antagonism was perpetuated by their disciples for at least the next century, and thus during the period of Matthew. Many of their differences are remembered even after a deliberate attempt to impose unity, and we must suspect that there was a good deal more diversity than just these two schools in the early period. The very nature of the Pharisaic approach would produce diversity, for although it drew upon an authoritative revelation, it depended on argument and analogy to prove new applications. It would take many years to achieve consensus by these means.

Just when the majority of the Jewish people began to regard themselves as "heirs of the Pharisees" is difficult to determine. Eventually one group, the rabbis, emerged as the intellectual and religious leaders of the Jewish people. The most decisive event in the evolution of rabbinic leadership was the publication of the Mishnah, a vast collection of rabbinic lore combined over many decades and published in final form about 200 CE. Certainly the rabbis, and Pharisaic leaders like Hillel, were influential long before then. But they were not the only influences. In the long period between the time of Herod and the Second Judean War (that is, between 6 CE and 135) the Zealots rivaled, and often surpassed, the Pharisees in popular support, leading the people in two wars of national liberation against Rome. Also, many sectarian movements (including the movements that became Christianity) struggled for recognition. Although the Pharisees, or their heirs, the rabbis, were eventually able to piece together a consensus that held and molded Judaism into its classical form, Matthew's Gospel was written during the struggle.

One of the most dramatic events of this long struggle occurred in 70 CE: the Roman conquest of Jerusalem and the destruction of the Temple. According to Josephus, Zealot activity rose sharply under the procuratorship of Felix (52–60 CE; *Jewish Antiquities* 20.185–86). This tumultuous period, marked by the ineffectiveness of Felix and the inattention of the new young emperor, Nero, culminated in open rebellion in 66. The war, surprisingly, lasted more than seven years and left the

Jewish people in a chaotic state. Soon after the war a few farsighted Pharisees under the leadership of Yohanan ben Zakkai gathered at **Yavneh** (also called *Jabneh* and *Jamnia*) to form a school for the study of Torah. From this center Pharisaic leadership eventually established its hegemony over the Jewish people, but not automatically. The Sadducees, like any wealthy aristocracy, did not lie down and play dead just because the Temple was destroyed. In fact, private sacrifices—though not the great public festivals—continued to be offered in the Temple ruins, and some pilgrimages were still made (Safrai and Sterns, 1974:1:211; Gaston, 1970:3; Clark, 1960:269–80). But their aristocratic policies were ill-suited to the new situation after 70.

The Zealots were temporarily discredited by the failure of the war. And the Essenes were ill equipped by their withdrawal to assume leadership. For the Pharisees, however, the time seemed ripe to inaugurate policies long believed in but heretofore blocked.

With the Temple at least temporarily removed, the Jewish people needed a new center. The answer was obvious to the Pharisees. Years earlier, Yohanan ben Zakkai had declared that Torah was the source and end of life (*m. Avot* 2:8). A story told about him reveals the ambiguous attitude of the Pharisees to the destruction of the Temple: both to mourn it and to surpass it with Torah.

> When a fellow rabbi mourned the loss of the Temple, lamenting that there was no longer a place to make atonement for Israel's sins, Rabban Yohanan ben Zakkai is said to have comforted him by saying there was another atonement as effective as the Temple, namely, deeds of kindness. "For it is said, I desire mercy and not sacrifice." (Avot de-Rabbi Nathan, A, ch. 4; see Neusner, 1986; Hos. 6:6)

Later rabbinic opinion would declare that whoever busies himself with Torah is equivalent to one who offered a burnt offering (Neusner, 1975:84; see *b. Menahot 110a*). As W. D. Davies notes, the Pharisees accepted the priesthood in principle but opposed it in fact (1966:258).

One problem confronting these postwar Pharisees was reconciling differences of opinion within their own ranks and refuting the opinion of those outside. They told an amusing story about the suppression of Shammaite opinion:

> Rabbi Abba said that Samuel told him that for three years the debate raged between the disciples of Shammai and the disciples of Hillel, both claiming their interpretation of the Law was the correct one. The debate did not end until it was interrupted by a voice from heaven, declaring: Both Shammai and Hillel teach the words of the living God, but the laws must be fixed according to the rulings of the disciples of Hillel. (b. Erubin 13b)

Such overcoming by incorporation seems to have been the preferred way of the rabbis. However, they were not averse to outright condemnation of opposing groups:

> All Israel will share in the world to come. For it is written, "Your people shall all be righteous. . . ." But these do not have a share in the world to come: anyone who says there is no resurrection of the dead prescribed in the Law [a teaching of the Sadducees], and anyone who says that the Law is not from

heaven and an Epicurean. Rabbi Akiba [c. 140] says: in addition, anyone who reads the heretical books. . . . (m. Sanhedrin 10:1)

Every social movement eventually reaches a stage of self-definition where it is necessary to say who belongs and who does not. This needed self-definition was especially acute in the turbulent period of Roman domination in the first century. Both the Qumran community (*Community Rule* 7; Vermes, 1987:70) and Matthew's community (see 18:15–20) had explicit procedures for expelling members (as apparently the earlier Pauline communities did; see 1 Cor. 5:1–5) It is not surprising then that leaders in Jewish synagogues made an effort to limit membership, using an ingenious approach. Around 90 CE a member of the Yavneh school known as Samuel the Small reworded one of the blessings recited daily in the synagogue, to make it impossible for those who refused to follow the Pharisaic line (including people like Matthew) to continue to worship there. The new prayer went:

> *Let there be no hope for renegades, And wipe out the kingdom of pride speedily in our days, and may all Nazarenes [followers of Jesus?] and heretics perish instantly. May their names be erased from the Book of Life and not be inscribed with those of the righteous. Blessed be Thou, O God, Who humblest the proud. (The Twelfth Benediction of the great official prayer, the* Shemoneh Esreh, *which consists in eighteen benedictions, most more positive than this. All eighteen are in Schürer, 1979:460–61, and Bonsirven, 1964:131–32.)*

Matthew versus the Pharisees

Matthew must have been written before this liturgical innovation became widespread (otherwise he could not have counseled obedience to the Pharisees; 23:2–3), but probably not much earlier. If, as is most likely, he used Mark as a source, sufficient time must have elapsed for that Gospel to have become popular and authoritative. There are also indications that Matthew knew the historical details of the fall of Jerusalem (21:43; 23:34–39; 27:35). Therefore it is reasonable to date the writing of the Gospel according to Matthew to around the year 85 CE.

It is also reasonable to see Matthew's community engaged in an activity similar to that of the Pharisees at Yavneh—a reinterpretation of the meaning of being Israel in a time of dissolution—but with this difference: Matthew believed the coming of the Messiah had inaugurated a new situation that, like the monarchy and the exile, must transform Israel's self-understanding. The essential difference of Matthew's community lies in its understanding of Jesus as "God with us," actually involving worship of him (2:2; 8:2; 9:18; 14:33; 20:20; 28:9, 17; contrast 4:10). (See Kilpatrick, 1946:107–8, and Kingsbury, 1975:40–83.)

In his vision of Israel Matthew tried to include the best from the past, especially the Law (5:17–19), and even much of the Oral Torah (23:2–3). He saw a continued Jewish piety (23:23), payment of the temple tax (17:24, 27), performances of private sacrifice (5:22), observance of the dietary laws (15:20; contrast Mark 7:19), and even the continued importance of the Sabbath (24:20). But he did not wish to understand all these as they were being defined at Yavneh. At Yavneh, *rabbi* (teacher) was developing into the central title of authority, but Matthew explicitly rejected this title (23:5–10). This rivalry with the rabbis at Yavneh produced Matthew's references to "their" synagogues (4:23; 9:35; 10:17; but see 6:2, 5; 23:6). But he never spoke of their Law (contrast John 15:25). (See Kilpatrick, 1946:110–11, and W. D. Davies, 1966:271.)

Matthew's strong endorsement of Gentiles probably marks him as a Hellenist, a Jew of the diaspora who saw his congregation as the proper continuation of historic Israel. So too, his concern with ethics rather than purity and his writing in Greek from Greek sources (Mark and Q) are evidence of a Hellenistic rather than a Palestinian orientation (Stendahl, 1968:xi–xiv).

An automatic authority of the rabbis over Hellenistic Judaism should not be assumed too readily (Goodenough, 1956:1:11–20). Synagogues were autonomous and independent institutions that varied greatly in different cities. If we imagine Matthew in the context of diaspora Judaism, rejecting the emerging authority of the rabbis of Yavneh, both the Jewish and the anti-Jewish material in the book makes sense. Matthew had not, as many suggest, converted from Judaism to Christianity. He saw himself as a Jew who was convinced the Messiah had come, thus changing the meaning of being one of God's people. What greatly disturbed him was that others claimed the same Jewish heritage, guiding the Jewish people in ways that seemed blind to him. The argument (one side of which we hear in Matthew) concerns the legitimate continuation of the heritage of Israel. Ironically, the very success Matthew's church had with the Gentiles ensured that his vision of things would never come to pass. The more Gentiles the movement attracted, the less firmly it retained its Jewish roots.

Thus W. D. Davies was essentially correct when he called the Sermon on the Mount "the Christian answer to Jamnia [Yavneh]" (1966:315). But we should not consider this a formal dialogue. Rather, it was the response of one living in the diaspora to something happening far away, something he did not entirely understand, which affected the Jews among whom he lived, worked, and worshipped. The purpose of Matthew's "book of the origin of Jesus the Messiah" (1:1) was to tell the story of how the coming of the Messiah has inaugurated a new phase in the history of God's people and to explain how they were expected to live in that new age.

Matthew may have lived in a large city, a city with many synagogues. Some were messianic; others were Pharisaic; still others were probably neither. Matthew wrote for his own people, showing them what he saw as their real heritage and differentiating them from the Pharisees. This seems to be a reasonable picture of the historical and social location of Matthew's Gospel. It is probably not possible to be more precise on the geographical location, but understanding this social and historical situation casts new light on the meaning of his Gospel.

LEARNING ON YOUR OWN

REVIEWING THE CHAPTER

Names and Terms

allegorization	kingdom of heaven	*pesher*
Essenes	Messiah	Pharisees
Hillel	parable	rabbinic Judaism

retainers   Sadducees   Zealots
righteousness   Sermon on the Mount
ruling elite   Yavneh

Issues and Questions

1. What implications for the meaning of the story as a whole can one glean by comparing the opening of Matthew's Gospel with the opening of Mark's?
2. Be able to describe the general content and significance of the five great speeches of Jesus in Matthew.
3. Describe and illustrate the ways Matthew characterizes Jesus.
4. Create your own title for Matthew's Gospel and then show how the story told is appropriate to your title.
5. Why is the portrayal of the coming of the magi appropriate to Matthew's story whereas the coming of shepherds would not be appropriate?
6. Be able to do a detailed comparison of one incident shared by Mark and Matthew and to draw implications for the meaning of Matthew's story based on their similarities and differences.
7. How does Matthew's treatment of the miracle tradition differ from Mark's treatment?
8. What similarities and differences can you detect between the community behind Matthew's Gospel and the community behind the Dead Sea Scrolls?
9. Why is the dichotomy Jew/Gentile false for the ancient world generally and for Matthew's Gospel particularly?
10. What is the most likely historical and social setting for Matthew's Gospel?

TAKING THE NEXT STEP

Introductory works include Edwards, 1985; P. Ellis, 1974; and Mounce, 1986. On a more advanced level, see Davies, 1993; Carter, 1996; Kingsbury, 1988; Meier, 1979; Riches, 1996; Montague, 1989; Stanton, 1983b; and Waetjen, 1976.

Topics for Special Studies

The Structure, Organization, or Plot of Matthew

The first to notice the structural significance of the five speeches and to elaborate an interconnection was Bacon, 1930, who argued that Matthew attempted to arrange his gospel into "five books," imitating the five books of Moses (the Torah, or Law). W. D. Davies, 1964:14–108, offers a thorough analysis and critique of Bacon's work. See also Rolland, 1972; Kingsbury, 1975; Barr, 1976; and Carter, 1992. Because Bacon associated the speeches only with the narratives that precede them, he designated the passion and resurrection narratives as an epilogue—hardly an adequate understanding of their role in the story. Bauer, 1988, is not as impressed by the speeches.

Branden, 2006, looks at the conflict of the plot. Kingsbury, 1992a; Matera, 1987; and Powell, 1992a and 1992b, all consider the plot of the story. A provocative view is taken by Rolland, 1972. Others who treat structure and patterns include Anderson, 1985; Murphy-O'Connor, 1975; Filson, 1956; and Keegan, 1982. For a detailed analysis of one segment see Heil, 1991b. On the broader issue of genre, see Shuler, 1982.

Problems or Issues Arising from the Birth Narrative

Issues include such ideas as the discrepancies between Matthew and Luke, the year, the meaning of the star episode, the census, and the trip to Egypt.

For an excellent discussion, complete with charts, of the historical problems of the birth narratives, see Brown, 1977:74–94, 225–28. Matthew's account of the birth of

Jesus is remarkably like Jewish expansions of the events around the birth of Moses, as seen in Philo's *Life of Moses* 1.8–22, and especially Josephus *Antiquities of the Jews* 2, 9.2. The place of Jesus' birth was also a problem for John (7:40–44), though he dealt with it in a radically different way.

An excellent discussion of the purpose of these birth stories in Matthew is Stendahl, 1964:94–105. The most insightful social analysis is Horsley, 1989. See also Smith, 1990, and Hendrickx, 1984. On the ethical issues of the slaughter of the infants, see Erickson, 1996.

For feminist interpretations, see Schaberg, 1985; Blomberg, 1991; and Anderson, 1987.

On the genealogies, see Johnson, 1969, and Davis, 1973.

On genre and sources, see Ashbeck, 1971, and Nolland, 1998. A succinct history of Herod's reign can be found in Schürer, 1973:287–329; more details in Richardson, 1996.

On the history of interpretation, see Trexler, 1997.

Jesus as a New Moses or Other Characterizations of Jesus

On the theme of Moses in Matthew, see Bacon, 1930:165–86; Davies, 1964, chapter 2; Green, 1975:18–19; Crossan, 1986b; and Stegner, 1967. For other characterizations of Jesus, see Malina and Neyrey 1988; see also Bauer, 1992, and Niedner, 1989. For a related resource, see Moessner, 1983. On the so-called seat of Moses, see Newport, 1990.

A History or Analysis of One of the Jewish Groups of the First Century: Pharisees, Sadducees, Essenes, Zealots

On the variety of sectarian groups of Jews in the first century, see Simon, 1967:85–107. See also Stone, 1980; Sanders, 1991; and Kealy, 1990. The evidence from Josephus is well summarized by Rhoads, 1976:32–42, 97–122 (though Josephus mentions other groups as well, for example, *Life* 11). The best detailed analysis is offered by Mason, 1991. A major new proposal has been advanced by Horsley and Hanson 1999, and Horsley, 1987. The best overview is probably Saldarini, 1989. Baumgarten, 1997, provides an excellent analysis of why these movements flourished at this time; see also Stemberger, 1995. Cohen, 1984, discusses the end of Jewish sectarianism in the period after the war.

For a discussion of John the Baptizer in relation to the Essenes, see Taylor, 1997; more broadly on John, see Kraeling, 1951, and Scobie, 1964; and for historical issues, see Tatum, 1994.

For a survey of the ancient accounts of the Essenes, see Vermes and Goodman, 1989.

The extensive literature on the Pharisees includes Cohen, 1984; W. D. Davies, 1967; Kampen, 1988; Mason, 1991; Neusner, 1971, 1979, and 1984; and Rivkin, 1978. And more broadly on law-observant communities, see Richardson and Westerholm, 1991.

A Study of Judaism in This Period

An excellent study of this period is Neusner, 1975b. More substantial treatments include Cohen, 1987; Bruce, 1972; and the reference volumes by Schürer, 1973–1987. A very interesting attempt at a parallel history of emerging Judaism and emerging Christianity is Shanks, 1992; chapters 2, 4, 5, and 6 seem especially well done. Other useful discussions of the politics and parties of this period include W. D. Davies, 1966; Herford, 1952; and Lohse, 1976. On the significance of rabbinic Judaism, see Moore, 1927, and, from a somewhat different perspective, Urbach, 1975. The standard English version of the Mishnah is that of Danby, 1933. For an overview, see the section on Jewish Literature in Appendix A, "Doing Your Own Research."

On the effects of Hellenism on the Jewish communities, see the excellent summary chapter in Tarn, 1952:210–38; Safrai and Stern, 1974:1:117–83; and Grant, 1962b. The classical treatment is Hengel, 1974a; see also Hengel, 1980b.

Part 1 of Glatzer, 1969, provides a good collection of primary sources. See also Neusner, 1995; Montefiore and Loewe, 1974; and Lipman, 1974.

Similarities and Differences between the Communities of Matthew and Qumran

Although both Matthew and the Qumran community believed that the Law was fulfilled in their community, what they actually did with the Law was quite different: the Qumran community practiced a radical legalism; Matthew radically transcended the laws. For a complete discussion of this *pesher* method in Matthew, see Stendahl, 1968:182–303. On the Sermon on the Mount, see Viviano, 1993. For an analysis of Matthew's community as antihierarchical, see Krentz, 1977.

For a survey of Jewish methods of Scripture interpretation, see Porton, 1979.

The Nature and Significance of the Dead Sea Scrolls

A very readable introduction to the life, history, and ideas of the Qumran community is Vermes, 1978; see also VanderKam, 1994. For an overview of scholarship, see Flint and VanderKam, 1998–1999. For an excellent collection of essays on religion in the scrolls, see Collins and Kugler, 2000. A very readable English translation is provided by Vermes, 1987; see also Wise, Abegg, and Cook, 1996.

On whether the sect behind the scrolls was Essene, see Fitzmyer, 1995; Boccaccini, 1998; and Vermes and Goodman, 1989.

An excellent bibliographical guide to the Qumran literature is Fitzmyer, 1990.

Types of Jewish Messianic Expectation in Matthew's Time

Recent studies have made it abundantly clear that there was no one Jewish expectation of the Messiah; start with J. Collins, 1995; see the useful introduction in Neusner, Green, and Smith, 1987. See also Charlesworth, 1992, and Horsley and Hanson, 1999. A cautious survey of the messianic views of various Jewish groups is found in Manson, 1966:1–35. See also Klausner, 1955, and Mowinkel, 1956. On the notion of two messiahs at Qumran, see LaSor, 1956; Priest, 1963; and Higgins, 1967. For a new view on the Messiah in the Dead Sea Scrolls, see Tabor and Wise, 1992. For the original sources, see Vermes 1968:47–52, *Messianic Rule*, page 121, and *Community Rule*, page 87.

Matthew's Attitude toward Other Jews

A detailed exposition of the Jewish aspects of this Gospel (though not sufficiently attentive to the negative elements) is Kilpatrick, 1946. See also Montefiore, 1927, and the excellent treatment of the setting of the Sermon on the Mount by W. D. Davies, 1966. A conservative treatment of the Sermon is Guelich, 1982. The question of the anti-Jewish (or even anti-Semitic) slant of the Gospel is discussed by Clark, 1947; Flusser, 1975; Garland, 1979; Hare, 1967; and van Tilborg, 1972. Ewherido, 2006, uses the parables to probe the two communities.

A more inclusive Matthew is envisioned by Howell, 1990, and Cargal, 1991. Stanton, 1992, surveys and updates the arguments.

Green, 1975:206, presents the view that Israel is excluded from the final "nations" to whom the disciples are to witness; see also Hare and Harrington, 1975. For an opposite view, see Meier, 1977:94–102.

For a balanced discussion of the issues between Matthew and other Jews, see Segal, 1991.

The Nature of Matthew's Community

For a good overview of the issues in identifying Matthew's community, see Stanton, 1992a and 1992b, and White, 1991a.

Specialized studies of various aspects of the social and historical context of Matthew include Balch, 1991; Levine, 1988; Overman, 1990; Weaver, 1990; and Clarke, 2003 (popular, with emphasis on how various groups have read Matthew). Both Garrow, 2004, and Sandt, 2005, consider the relationship to the *Didache*. Lawrence explains and tests the utility of an honor-shame model for understanding the community. Riches and Sim, 2005, explore the imperial context.

See also Able, 1971b; S. Brown, 1978; Cope, 1976; Farmer, 1976; Hartin, 1998; Isaac, 1984; Krentz, 1977; Malina and Rohrbaugh, 1992; Riches, 1983; Theissen, 1991; and Thompson, 1970.

Also note the listings in the previous and the next two topics.

The Separation of Jewish Christians from the Synagogue

See the discussions in Sanders, 1993; Katz, 1984; and Shanks, 1992. For an innovative Jewish analysis, see Boyarin, 2004. For a focus on Matthew's community, see Viviano, 2007; Overman, 1990; Stanton, 1992; Balch, 1991; and Segal, 1991.

On the role of the Twelfth Benediction in the process, contrast Kimelman, 1981, with Kilpatrick, 1946:109*ff*, and Frend, 1982:35*ff*. See also Kohler, 1970.

Gender Roles in Matthew's Community

See the influential article by Anderson, 1983; Wire, 1991; and the overview of the household by Love, 1993, which has a nice bibliography. On women in the opening and closing scenes, see McGinn, 1997; Baby, 2003; Longstaff, 1981; and Blomberg, 1991. For feminist readings, see Wainwright, 1991, and Levine and Blickenstaff, 2004.

Specific Themes or Topics in Matthew's Gospel

Miracle stories: See Bornkamm, Bath, and Held in Bornkamm, 1963:165–299, and Matera, 1993. For miracle stories more generally, see Kee, 1986, and Theissen, 1983.

Use of scripture: See the significant work of Stendahl, 1968; see also Menken, 2004; Nkhoma, 2005; Gundry, 1967; Goulder, 1974; and France, 1981. For broader issues, see Brewer, 1991, and Thomas, 1977.

Law and righteousness: See Sim, 1998; Meier, 1976; Przybylski, 1980; and Snodgrass, 1992. For a broad overview, see Richardson and Westerholm, 1991.

Wisdom ideas: See Suggs, 1970, and Burnett, 1981.

Parables: For a discussion of parables in chapter 13, see Kingsbury, 1969, and Donfried, 1974. Hedrick, 1986, compares Matthew and Thomas. For a discussion of Matthew's method of interpretation and a comparison with rabbinic parables, see Goulder, 1974:47–69. On parables in general, see Jeremias, 1963; Lambrecht, 1981; Perkins, 1981; or Stein, 1981. For a bibliography, see Kissinger, 1979.

Matthew's apocalyptic rhetoric: See Orton, 1989.

Repetition and redundancy: See Anderson, 1985.

The theology of Matthew: See Donaldson, 1985, and Kingsbury, 1975.

The Role and Character of Peter in Matthew's Gospel

There is considerable debate on whether the sayings regarding Peter and the church's divine authority (16:19; 18:18) stem from Jesus or were created by later followers. For a positive evaluation of their historicity, see Cullmann, 1962:182–85, 217; a negative judgment is registered by Bornkamm, 1970:37–50. See also Marcus, 1988, and Kingsbury, 1979. For further resources on Peter, see Chapter 7.

Additional Books and Articles

For an overview of how Matthew has been interpreted over time see Allison, 2005; Kealy, 1997; and Luz, 2007.

Standard commentaries include Beare, 1982; Davies and Allison, 1988 and 1990; Fenton, 1963; Filson, 1960; Green, 1975; Hill, 1972; Luz, 2007; and Schweizer, 1975. The conservative work of Gundry, 1982, is very provocative; see also Witherington, 2006; Bruner, 1987; and Mounce, 1986. The structuralist approach of Patte, 1985, is interesting.

The volume by Albright and Mann in the Anchor Bible series is somewhat idiosyncratic.

Textual and translation problems are discussed by Newman and Stine, 1988.

Other works with significant bibliography include Love, 1993; Ziesler, 1985; and Harrington, 1975.

A special issue of the journal *Interpretation* was devoted to Matthew: October 1992 (46, no. 4).

For an overview of the complex body of ancient Jewish literature, see Appendix A, "Doing Your Own Research."

11

THE GOSPEL AS HEROIC NARRATIVE

 Even the sophisticated are wont to listen to story-tellers.
PLATO'S SEVENTH LETTER

Mark began by announcing "good news" and Matthew spoke of a "book" for a new generation, but Luke acknowledges constructing a narrative and even outlines the process through which it was constructed:

> *Since many have undertaken to set down an orderly account of the events that have been fulfilled among us, just as they were handed on to us by those who from the beginning were eyewitnesses and servants of the word, I too decided, after investigating everything carefully from the very first, to write an orderly account for you, most excellent Theophilus, so that you may know the truth concerning the things about which you have been instructed. (1:1–4)*

A great deal can be learned about Luke's situation, purpose, and procedure from a careful reading of this preface, and we shall return to it repeatedly in our discussion.

In this chapter we will explore the shape and extent of Luke's narrative, showing that it includes both the Gospel and the book known as the Acts of the Apostles. We will trace the narrative through its major phases, from the birth of John the Baptizer to the imprisonment of Paul in Rome, then explore the historical and cultural setting implied in the writing. Our organizing image is that of the **witness**, already alluded to in the opening sentence where the author speaks of "eyewitnesses" (those who are witnesses *of* the events) and "servants of the word" (those who bear witness *to* the events, carrying the testimony to others). It is this double action that explains Luke's two volumes: witnessing as looking back (the Gospel) and witnessing as looking ahead (the Acts).

UNDERSTANDING LUKE'S NARRATIVE

The most striking thing about Luke's narrative is that, unlike Mark and Matthew, it is not limited to the time of Jesus. Matthew implied that the story goes on (with Jesus' promise to be with the disciples "to the end of the age," 28:20), and envisioned a period of worldwide witness before the end (compare Matt. 24:14 and Mark 13:10). Luke actually continues the story into a second volume, a sequel to the story of Jesus, which we know as the Acts of the Apostles. This is surely the most important observation we can make about the shape of Luke's narrative.

THE SIGNIFICANCE OF ACTS FOR UNDERSTANDING LUKE

That Luke-Acts is a two-volume work seems beyond dispute. The two volumes share a common understanding of life, a common literary structure, style, and vocabulary; both are addressed to the same person, both open with a distinct prologue—the second making explicit reference to the first—and the second volume takes up exactly where the first leaves off.

But the two do not merely come from the same author, they form a literary unity: one work in two volumes. This unity is implicit in the prologues (Cadbury, 1958:8*ff*).

Many ancient books began with a stylized **prologue**, a short formal introduction to the purpose of the work, and two-volume works had two interconnected prologues. Compare:

> In the first book, Theophilus, I wrote about all that Jesus did and taught. *(Acts 1:1)*

> In the first book, my most honored Epaphroditus, I have shown our antiquity. *(Josephus* Against Apion 1)

> Our first book, O Theodotus, was on the thesis that every base person is a slave. *(Philo* That Every Good Person Is Free 1)

Thus, Luke makes exactly the sort of connection one should expect for a single work in two volumes.

And notice that the second prologue explicitly labels the content of the first volume as "what Jesus did." But the first prologue does not limit the narrative to Jesus' work, referring more broadly to "the things which have been fulfilled among us" (Luke 1:1), thereby including the action of Acts. We have reason to suppose, then, that from the outset Luke envisioned the whole of Luke and Acts as a literary unity. This work is now usually referred to as Luke-Acts.

Luke consistently reshapes the telling of the story of Jesus so that it anticipates the story of the church in Acts. Consider, for example, how the story of Jesus' baptism is told.

READING AND REFLECTION

Carefully compare the versions of Jesus' baptism in Luke 3:20–23 and Mark 1:9–11 (*GP* §6, *SFG* §18), then compare it with Acts 2:1–4 and 1:14.

1. When does Jesus experience the divine voice in Luke's and Mark's accounts?
2. How much emphasis does Luke give to John the Baptizer?
3. What about this incident anticipates the story in Acts?

Although Luke's account of the baptism is recognizably the same event narrated in Mark and Matthew, even down to exact verbal correlations at certain points, this version dramatically transforms its significance. Its dramatic function in Luke concerns the reception of the Holy Spirit and the inauguration of mission. (Note also how the correlation of Spirit and mission is reemphasized at Luke 4:1.) The coming of the Spirit is connected with prayer rather than baptism, and Luke makes several changes to separate this event from any expectation of the coming of the kingdom. Not only does the story omit any mention of the kingdom in Jesus' subsequent proclamation (compare Luke 4:14–15 with Mark 1:1–15), it also separates the baptism from the temptation scene by interjecting a genealogy (Luke 3:23–38). Thus, unlike Mark, the baptism does not function as the prelude to Jesus' conquest of Satan (contrast "immediately" in Mark 1:12).

Luke's attitude toward the coming of the kingdom will be considered when we come to Acts; for now it is sufficient to observe how the story is changed. These changes illustrate what we might call Luke's **proleptic** view of Jesus, that is, the story of Jesus anticipates and foreshadows the story of the church. Thus the account of the coming of the Spirit upon the early church in response to prayer has cast its shadow before it in the account of Jesus' baptism.

LUKE'S LITERARY METHODS

These observations about Luke's handling of the baptism scene raise three related questions about Luke's way of writing: How does the writing of Acts influence and shape the writing of the Gospel? Are Luke's methods comparable to those of the ancient historians? How dependent is Luke on sources? We will consider these in reverse order.

Sources or Artistry?

One clue often used to identify various sources in Luke's writing is the varieties of style. Luke's Greek style varies from very good Greek to a thoroughly Hebrew-like Greek (usually called **Semitic Greek**, which uses grammatical constructions similar to those in the Semitic languages, such as Hebrew and Aramaic, rather than the constructions normally expected by a native Greek speaker). For example, the finest Greek in Luke-Acts is the opening prologue (Luke 1:1–4), consisting of a forty-two-word Greek sentence with one principal clause, one relative clause, three adverbial clauses, and three participial phrases. Delightful. (Contrast Mark's opening sentence, consisting of five Greek words without a verb.) However, as Greek readers would move from Luke's first sentence to the second (1:5), their stylistic sense would be jarred. This second sentence is one of the most Semitic constructions in the book, reading almost like a sentence out of the **Septuagint**, a rather literal Greek translation of the Hebrew Scriptures. (An impression of this style change is possible if you read Luke 1:1–4 in the Revised English Bible and proceed with verse 5 in the King James Version.) How can we explain this change in style?

One possibility, often advocated in the past, is that this variation stems from Luke's use of different sources: either the prologue was Luke's own composition, whereas verse 5 followed a Semitic source translated rather literally, or perhaps the opposite was true. Because prologues were rather easy, and could even be purchased, perhaps the author's real style emerges only in verse 5. A third alternative, probably the majority view today, is that Luke consciously adapted the style to suit the occasion. The opening prologue is meant to engage the reader (and is thus written in high style) whereas the beginning of the story is meant to sound "biblical" (and thus uses a style characteristic of the Greek translation of the Bible).

This phenomenon of suiting language to topic is widespread in Luke-Acts. H. J. Cadbury studied Luke's style extensively and drew these generalizations: Luke's most biblical language is found in the birth stories. The body of the Gospel is somewhat better Greek, yet Luke introduces Semitic constructions where there were none in the sources. The first part of Acts is similar, but with improved Greek, and as the book progresses the style becomes increasingly secular, climaxing in Paul's speech before Agrippa, which contains a half dozen classical Greek idioms in grammar alone (1958:223–25). Ernst Haenchen noted: "Luke is at his most literary in the four scenes where his subject matter demands it: 17:16–34 (Paul's speech at Athens),

19:21–40 (the riot and speech at Ephesus), 24:1–23 (Paul's accusation and defense before Felix), and chapter 26 (Paul's defense before Agrippa)" (1971:75).

Luke's pattern, then, seems to be to use Semitic Greek when Jews are involved and a more formal Hellenistic Greek when speaking to or for Greeks. Luke follows this pattern even in small things: the narrator in Acts 15 calls Peter by his Greek name, Peter (15:14), but has the Jerusalemite James refer to him by the Hebrew name, Symeon (15:14). When Paul is located in Syria-Palestine we hear only Paul's Semitic name Saul; at 13:9 we hear, "Saul who is also Paul," and from then on he is always Paul—a good Greek name. It is, Cadbury remarked: "When Paul's career is fairly started among Gentiles" (1958:225–30). Numerous other examples could be cited (see Creed, 1930:lxxvi–lxxxiv). This effort to fit the language to the character reveals a kind of conscious literary artistry not usually associated with the Gospel writers. Luke worked hard to find language appropriate to the narrative.

Method and Meaning

This attempt on Luke's part to be (or at least appear) authentic extends to other details as well. The city officials of Thessalonica, for example, are referred to by the unusual term "politarchs" (17:6), a designation confirmed by inscriptions found there. Numerous other local designations as well as navigational terms and cultural practices have been proved accurate (Cadbury, 1958:242–53). Such verisimilitude would have been appreciated by persons of culture in antiquity.

At least one school of ancient historiography allowed a writer great freedom of invention as long as what was invented was appropriate to the situation. Thus, Cicero (in 56 BCE) urged Lucceius, his would-be biographer, to embellish his accomplishments while giving the essential truth about his consulship (*Letter to Lucceius*). A more germane example may be cited from the historian of the Peloponnesian War (431–404 BCE), Thucydides, who made extensive use of speeches by his major characters. He explains his procedure:

> *With references to the speeches in this history, some were delivered before the war began, others while it was going on; some I heard myself, others I got from various quarters; it was in all cases difficult to carry them word for word in one's memory, so my habit has been to make the speakers say what was in my opinion demanded of them by the various occasions, of course adhering as closely as possible to the general sense of what they really said. (Peloponnesian War 1.22; also cited in Cadbury, 1958:185)*

Such a procedure was still being commended to the would-be historian a century after Luke's time. Lucian in his essay "How to Write History" (in *Works*) advises:

> *If a person has to be introduced to make a speech, above all let his language suit his person and his subject. (58)*

Something very similar to this is what Luke may be doing in Acts, a supposition that is supported by examining the speeches themselves. Each of the speeches follows a basic pattern, with the specific content changed to fit the dramatic situation (Dibelius, 1956:165; Haenchen, 1971:185; Kennedy, 1972:433).

Compare the two very different speeches of Peter (2:14–41) and Paul (17:22–34); then answer the following questions.

1. How does each speech begin?
2. What authorities are quoted?
3. What is the main focus of the speech? (Note that Paul's speech is cut off before he can develop his main point.)

It is true that some of the more objective historians of Luke's time rejected such free invention, partly because it was not always as carefully used as Thucydides claimed, but Luke was not an objective historian. Luke was, instead, what Haenchen calls a "dramatic historian" (1971:103–10). This writer did not simply report what happened but showed it happening, conjuring up scenes and speakers to make history live.

Such dramatic art fits well with the two recognized purposes of historical writing: to furnish pleasure to the reader and to make the subject intelligible (see Cicero *Letter to Lucceius*; Lucian, "How to Write History," 53). Lucian is often quoted as opposing the goal of giving pleasure. Indeed he says, "history has one task and one end—what is useful—and that comes from truth alone" (10). But that statement appears in a context in which he condemns an overdose of fictitiousness in history. He saw the task of the historian as resembling the task of a great sculptor: a sculptor does not manufacture the gold, but fashions and arranges it.

The task of the historian is similar: to give a fine arrangement to events and illuminate them as vividly as possible. (51)

The material to be shaped is the "bare record of events," which must be formed by a "historian of taste and ability" (16). Only thus will history "delight and instruct," as Horace (died 8 BCE) demanded of all poets (*On the Art of Poetry* 337). The preface of the Gospel reveals both the intent to order the material and to instruct the reader. His methods are not unlike those of other ancient historians.

Finally, these observations on Luke's literary methods, combined with the results of our study of the baptism scene, imply that Luke consciously molds the story of Jesus to the story of his earliest followers, and in turn carefully crafts the story of his followers to reflect the story of Jesus. Thus, we find a dynamic interaction between Gospel and Acts. This interaction is evident in the structure of the work.

THE STRUCTURE OF LUKE-ACTS

The structure of Luke's Gospel is perhaps more universally recognized than that of the other Gospels because the order of events differs markedly from the order in Mark and Matthew. The device Luke uses in this rearrangement is obvious to every careful reader of the Gospel: Jesus' journey to Jerusalem has become a major event. Thus 9:51 notes that Jesus set his face to go to Jerusalem, and everything that happens from then till 19:28 is portrayed as part of this journey. This is a uniquely Lukan idea. (Even a brief look at the index to *GP*, page xxiii, or *SFG*, pages 347–51, reveals this major shift.)

This supposed journey easily divides Luke's Gospel into three sections: before the journey in Galilee, the journey itself, and after the journey in Jerusalem. Even a casual acquaintance with Acts reveals that journeying—the journeys of Paul—is a major motif of that work. It seems reasonable, then, to ask if they perform a similar structural function.

A preliminary objection might be raised by those who find the structure of Acts indicated in 1:8 ("You will be my witnesses in Jerusalem, in all Judea and Samaria, and to the end of the earth"). Although there is some validity in this observation, 1:8 describes the progress and intention of the witness to Jesus, it does not seem adequate as a summary of the structure of Acts. First, Rome (where Acts ends) is not the end of the earth but its center. In addition, all these goals are accomplished by chapter 12, at least in a preliminary way (see 11:19–21).

On the other hand, there seem to be clear markers in the narrative that identify the various stages of the story. In the Gospel, Jesus indicates his resolve to go to Jerusalem (9:51); Paul in Acts also indicates his resolve to go to Rome (19:21). No less clear than the notion of Jesus' arrival at Jerusalem (Luke 19:28) is the indication in Acts that a new kind of mission involving journeys must be initiated (13:1–3). Other divisions in Acts represent subdivisions of these major sections, in my judgment.

Paul's journeys are the watershed of the action in Acts. Before the journeys (reported in Acts 13:1–19:20), the center of action is the Jerusalem church; afterward the entire focus is on Rome (see 19:21). Add to this the observation above about the parallels between the inauguration of Jesus' ministry and that of the church, plus the fact that each opens with a formal prologue, and a nearly perfect parallelism is evident between these two volumes. This structure may then be represented as follows.

 ## READING GUIDE TO LUKE-ACTS

Introduction to the two volumes   Luke 1:1–4
  The origin and spirit-indwelling of Jesus   1:5–4:13
    The gathering of witnesses in Galilee   4:14–9:50
      The instructing of the witnesses on the journey to Jerusalem   9:51–19:27
      The witnessing of the events in Jerusalem   19:28–24:53

Introduction to the second volume   Acts 1:1–5
  The origin and spirit-indwelling of the church   1:6–2:47
    The witness to Jesus in Jerusalem and beyond   3:1–12:25
      The journeys that carry the witness to the nations   13:1–19:20
      The progress of the witness to Rome   19:21–28:31

Notice that the basic pattern is geographical: Galilee-journey-Jerusalem—Jerusalem-journeys-Rome. Luke may have inherited the idea of a journey from Mark (who remarks that Jesus left Galilee and went to Judea, 10:1), but Luke has used it in a new and radical way. In Luke's story the journey expands to ten chapters. In these chapters Luke has gathered material found in different contexts in the other Gospels (plus some material not found in the others), carefully changing or omitting any geographical notations that do not fit the journey scheme.

This geographical structure will cause Luke problems, notably the location of the resurrection appearances, which we observed at the very beginning of our study of the Gospels (see page 255). It will also force him to be inconsistent about the route Jesus followed to Jerusalem, whether he took the shorter route through Samaria (9:53) or followed the alternate one through Jericho (18:35): the roads did not permit traveling through both Samaria and Jericho on the same trip. Thus some have questioned whether Luke knew Palestinian geography (Pritchard, 1972:116).

But Luke is not trying to teach us geography; we must see the literary importance of this structure. The journey is a literary device, the meaning of which is found in the declaration: "It cannot be that a prophet should perish away from Jerusalem" (13:33). It is not portrayed realistically and contains little that could properly be called a *travel narrative*, simply reminding the reader repeatedly that Jesus is on his way to Jerusalem (9:53; 13:22; 17:11; 18:31; 19:11). Luke uses geography not to teach about Palestine but to interpret history.

LUKE'S VIEW OF HISTORY

Surprisingly, Luke's Gospel also begins in Jerusalem, despite the fact that Jesus is associated with Nazareth (or Bethlehem) and John with the wilderness in the rest of the tradition. Luke's first incident occurs in the Temple in Jerusalem (1:9); even more shocking, the first appearance of Jesus is also in the Temple in Jerusalem (2:43, 46). Further, the Gospel closes with a command to stay in Jerusalem and in its very last words portrays the disciples as "continually in the Temple blessing God" (Luke 24:50–53).

In Luke's scheme of history, Jerusalem is the center of action: in the Gospel everything moves toward Jerusalem; in Acts everything moves away from Jerusalem. This was no easy task, given the fact that Paul, the major figure of Acts, was firmly associated with Antioch, not Jerusalem, in the tradition. Notice Luke's attempts to tie Paul to Jerusalem (8:1–3; 9:26; 12:25; especially 22:17) in spite of Paul's own reluctance to be so tied (contrast Gal. 1:15–23). This geographical scheme centered on Jerusalem provides a sense of inevitability; history is moving in a fixed direction. Thus, Luke is concerned in a way the other Gospel writers are not to interrelate this special history with general human history (Luke 2:1–3; 3:1–2; and so on).

This is a very ambitious goal, and Luke-Acts is a very ambitious work. Some thirty or forty years after Jesus, every major city in Asia Minor, Greece, and Italy had one or more assemblies. In this remarkably readable story Luke mentions ninety-five different people, fifty-four cities, thirty-two countries, and nine Mediterranean islands. Perhaps such rapid spread suggested to Luke the geographical concept that is the cornerstone of this work. This structuring according to geography produces an "orderly account" (1:3), though hardly the kind of order a modern reader expects. Let us now pursue Luke's plot in more detail by considering each section of the work in turn.

GATHERING WITNESSES IN GALILEE

It is remarkable that Luke uses the same kinds of material about Jesus' origins and early work in Galilee that we have encountered in Mark and Matthew, often the same traditions, but with dramatically different results. Part of Luke's novelty is the use of geography to interpret the meaning of the action.

Another Way to Begin

Mark (depending on Isaiah) portrayed the origin of salvation in the wilderness, but Luke places both the opening action of the Gospel and the first action of Jesus in the Temple in Jerusalem. Beginning and ending in the Temple (1:9 and 2:46), Luke has artfully structured the opening narrative into a series of six scenes, each celebrated with a short poem or hymn, interweaving the events surrounding the births of John the Baptizer and Jesus.

First Scene (1:5–25)	The angel appears to Zechariah in the Temple and announces the coming birth of John.	Poem to John identifies him with Elijah. (16–18)
Second Scene (1:26–38)	The angel appears to Mary in Nazareth and announces the coming birth of Jesus.	Poem to Jesus identifies him with David (32–33).
Third Scene (1:39–56)	Mary visits Elizabeth (Zechariah's wife), who blesses Mary and announces "the child in my womb leaped for joy."	Mary responds with a magnificent poem to the Lord who "has helped his servant Israel" (46–55).
Fourth Scene (1:57–80)	John is born to Elizabeth and named by Zechariah.	Zechariah responds with a poem to the Lord who "has raised up a mighty savior . . . to give light to those who sit in darkness" (68–79).
Fifth Scene (2:1–21)	Jesus is born to Mary and visited by shepherds.	Angels recite a poem to Jesus, "born this day in the city of David, a Savior" (10–14).
Sixth Scene (2:22–40)	Jesus is presented in the Temple, where he is praised by a righteous man named Simeon and a righteous woman named Anna.	Simeon is inspired and bursts into poem declaring that he has seen salvation, "a light for revelation to the Gentiles and glory to thy people Israel" (29–32).

This arrangement implies a special status for John and suggests a comparison between John and Jesus. In terms of design, notice there are two cycles of three scenes: the paired angelic announcements are synthesized in Mary's visit, and the paired birth accounts are synthesized in the final Temple scene, which returns, full circle, to the Temple scene of the opening. The immense literary skill manifested here recalls Luke's promise of an "orderly account" (1:3).

Luke alone of the canonical writers depicts a scene from Jesus' childhood, though the pious fancy of later believers created many such stories, some charming, some grotesque. (See *Pseudo-Matthew* and the *Infancy Gospel of Thomas*; both are in Elliott, 1993: 68–83, 84–99; and Hennecke and Schneemelcher, 1991:1:462, 439–61.) Whatever the source of Luke's story, it serves two purposes: to connect Jesus with the Temple at the very outset of the action and to provide a transition to the inauguration of Jesus' ministry, which forms the second part of this introductory section.

Carefully read 1:1–4:13, reflecting on these questions:

1. How does Luke use the following motifs: Temple, Holy Spirit, prayer, and Gentiles?
2. What points of comparison and contrast are established between John and Jesus?
3. How does Luke modify the Markan tradition of Jesus' baptism and temptation?
4. Compare the births of Samuel (1 Samuel 1–2) and Isaac (Gen. 18:1–15; 21:1–7) with those in Luke.

JOHN THE BAPTIZER AND JESUS

The figure of John remains somewhat shadowy in the Gospels. Before considering how Luke portrays him, let's consider the world behind the text, where such a figure was not quite as unusual as he may seem to us. There were apparently many such ascetics, people who abandoned ordinary life and withdrew into the wilderness to obtain purity, a quest that would require various kinds of ceremonial washings. For example, the historian Josephus, never modest, tells his readers of the great extremes to which he went to decide between the various Jewish sects, claiming to have, in turn, become a Pharisee, a Sadducee, and an Essene. Then he adds:

> Not content, however, with the experience thus gained, on hearing of one named Banus, who dwelt in the wilderness, using only such clothing as trees provided, and feeding of such things as grew of themselves, and using frequent ablutions [baths] of cold water, by day and night, for purity's sake, I became his devoted disciple. With him I lived for three years. (Life 11)

Even after we admit the substantial difference in the function of the washings (John's baptism seems to have been administered only once), the picture of Banus shares much with that of John, including the notion of gathering disciples around himself (see John 1:35). John, at least, appears to have been the same type of person.

Josephus also seems to have known about John the Baptizer; at least we find a reference to John in our text of Josephus. Some think that it may have been added by a later Christian copyist; if so, it is surprising that the image of John is so different from that in the Gospels—especially in the relationship depicted between John and Herod. Josephus's reference to John is set within the context of a battle that Herod lost to Arabia; some saw the loss as a divine retribution for his killing of John. He then describes Herod's handling of John:

> When others too joined the crowds about him, because they were aroused to the highest degree by his sermons, Herod became alarmed. Eloquence that had so great an effect on mankind might lead to some form of sedition, for it looked as if they would be guided by John in everything that they did. Herod decided therefore that it would be much better to strike first, and be rid of him before his work led to an uprising. (Jewish Antiquities 18.5.2)

The picture here is that of a charismatic leader, very popular with the common people, too popular for his own good.

Further clues about John may be gleaned from the Gospels. There are indications that the relationship between John and Jesus (or at least between their respective disciples) was not always as smooth as we usually imagine (John 3:22–27; 4:1–3). We also find evidence that disciples of the Baptizer remained active and independent of the early Jesus movement (Acts 18:24–25; 19:1–7). Some think that many of John's disciples regarded John as himself the redeemer, not simply the forerunner of Jesus. A small sect that believes this, called the Mandeans, exists in present-day Iraq, though it is debated whether they really derive from John. Whatever others may have thought of John, Luke portrays him in a subordinate relationship to Jesus.

Hans Conzelmann argued that Luke intended to separate John and Jesus completely. Leaning heavily on Luke 16:16 ("The law and the prophets were in effect until John came; since then the good news of the kingdom of God is proclaimed"), Conzelmann argued that John represented the old era, the time of Israel, separated from the new era, the time of the church, by the ministry of Jesus, which becomes the center of history (1963:18–27). His case is strengthened by careful observation of Luke's editing of material also found in Mark; for example, Luke edits John right out of the baptism scene (3:20–21).

Not all are convinced, however, and the case is considerably weakened by the interweaving of John and Jesus in the birth stories, which Conzelmann regarded as irrelevant (1963:22 n. 2; for a critique of Conzelmann on this point see Minear, 1966). The birth stories intimately link John and Jesus, even as they repeatedly subordinate John to Jesus (for example, 1:32 versus 1:76 and 1:17). By showing that John "proclaimed the good news to the people" (3:18, only in Luke), and stressing the same repentance-forgiveness theme that characterizes the Lukan Jesus (compare 3:3; 5:32; 24:47), this story binds the two close together. John even possessed the Holy Spirit (1:15, which is in some tension with the tradition behind 3:16).

Two tendencies seem evident in the way Luke handles the traditions about John and Jesus: their births and destinies are carefully intertwined; their work and mission are just as carefully separated. John is that "Elijah" who "will turn many of the people of Israel to the Lord" (1:16–17). Thus, he is not only the precursor of Jesus, he proclaims the "good news" and points to Christ (3:16, 18). He demands repentance (3:3), even as does Peter and those who come after (Acts 3:19).

USING TRADITION FOR NEW ENDS

Luke's power to transform tradition may be seen in the so-called baptism scene, which is actually no baptism at all. Luke has completely reinterpreted this event to display two dominant motifs: prayer and the Holy Spirit. As in Mark, the voice from heaven is addressed to Jesus. Now, however, this is not due to any secrecy, but because the scene is depicted as one of prayer the voice thus becomes the response to Jesus' prayer. Whereas Mark had portrayed the baptism-temptation as an eschatological event ushering in the kingdom (see pages 285–87), Luke separates the temptation from the baptism by a summary (3:23) and by inserting the genealogy. (That this genealogy has little connection with Matthew's in either function or content would seem clear evidence that Luke did not know Matthew's Gospel. For a discussion of the discrepancies, see Brown, 1977:74–94.) Dividing the baptism and the temptation enables Luke to link the wilderness encounter with Satan to what follows, making it the foundation of Jesus' public ministry, rather than considering it a result of the baptism. Luke's own understanding of that encounter is revealed in 4:13: Satan is no longer able to touch Jesus, and departs "until an opportune time"—until he uses Judas to betray Jesus (22:3).

The last temptation returns us to the Temple once again, marking the end of the introductory section. "Then Jesus, filled with the power of the Spirit, returned to Galilee" (4:14), where he stayed until he "set his face to go to Jerusalem" (9:51).

Luke begins the narrative of Jesus' Galilean ministry with the story of his rejection at Nazareth, thereby causing a few logical problems. The story involves the charge that Jesus has been healing in Capernaum but not Nazareth (4:23b); although in Luke's account, Jesus has not yet been to Capernaum or worked any miracles. (Mark used this episode in chapter 6, after a miracle section.) What, then, does Luke gain by placing this scene at the beginning of this part of the story?

Jesus' rejection at Nazareth is set in a **synagogue** (the Jewish house of prayer and study) and reflects what we know about synagogue worship in the first century, which apparently followed this pattern:

> recitation of the Shema ("Hear O Israel, the Lord is one")
> saying the eighteen prayers
> singing or recitation of Psalms
> reading a fixed portion from the Law of Moses
> reading a selection from the Prophets
> an explanation of one or both passages
> a closing blessing by a priest or a prayer by a layperson

There were no clergy, though various elders would be in charge of a given synagogue and a "head of the synagogue" would supervise the service. Various members of the congregation, or interesting visitors, might be asked to read and comment on the Scripture. According to later tradition, prayers were said standing and facing the Temple in Jerusalem; Scripture was read while standing but explained while sitting. (See Schürer, 1979:447–63; Herford, 1952:99–100; Bouquet, 1953:209–13).

A similar scene is portrayed in the other Gospels, but Luke has made major changes. (Read Luke 4:16–30, comparing it with the Markan (6:1–6) and Matthean (13:54–58) accounts; GP §10, SFG §33.) First, we learn what the prophetic reading for the day was the passage from Isaiah that says: "the Spirit of the Lord is upon me" (4:18). Indeed! The reader who has followed Luke's narrative knows this full well. Second, Luke provides a synopsis of Jesus' sermon: the claim that the Scripture is fulfilled.

Third, Luke represents the people as responding favorably to this proclamation, which leaves Jesus' sharp reply less than cogently motivated. Apparently we are to understand that Jesus is resisting their acceptance of the implication of the Isaiah prophecy that he would work miracles. In fact, Luke is carefully crafting this story to prepare the audience for the accounts in Acts, for Luke saw in Jesus' further reply—"No prophet is accepted in the prophet's hometown" (4:24)—an illustration of a major concern of this work, the mission's concentration on Gentiles.

This leads him to introduce a fourth change: Jesus continues his sermon by associating the Gentiles with the poor and lowly to whom the good news would be proclaimed, justifying this mission by reference to the works of Elijah and Elisha. "When they heard this, all in the synagogue were filled with rage" (4:28). A mob action ensues, in which they nearly throw Jesus off the edge of a cliff. Here one might expect that Jesus would leave Israel and go on to preach to the Gentiles. Instead, this leads directly to a string of miracles and the call of the disciples. Not until the middle of the Acts is such a withdrawal suggested:

> It was necessary that the word of God should be spoken first to you [Jews]. Since you thrust it from you, and judge yourselves unworthy of eternal life, behold, we turn to the Gentiles. (13:46)

Luke reiterates this sentiment in the final scene of the work. When Paul is in prison at Rome, he tries to convince "the local leaders of the Jews" concerning Jesus. Only a few respond. Paul summarizes:

> Let it be known to you then that this salvation of God has been sent to the Gentiles; they will listen. (28:28)

Luke has shifted the scene of Jesus' rejection at Nazareth to the very beginning of Jesus' ministry in order to foreshadow the whole course of the narrative. The end is known from the beginning; Acts is the rest of the story begun in the Gospel. This points to a major theme of Luke-Acts: the way in which the disciples of Jesus function as a bridge between Jesus and the church.

NEW CHARACTERIZATION OF THE DISCIPLES

Luke's new characterization of the disciples is evident already in his version of their call to follow Jesus, which is much more clearly drawn and better motivated in Luke than in Mark or even Matthew. (Compare Luke 5:1–11 with Mark 1:16–20; GP §17, SFG §41.) Luke picks up on the fishing image and turns the call into an allegory of the church itself—with a great catch to be taken as it launches out into the deep (Conzelmann, 1961:41–42). Yet Luke did not anachronistically portray Jesus as founding the church (as Matthew had, 16:18; 18:17). Luke reserves the word *church* (Greek: *ekklesia*) until well into the story in Acts, first using it almost incidentally (5:11). Such precise and realistic use of terms is one of Luke's characteristics.

Rather than transporting the church back to the time of Jesus, this story uses the disciples as the vital link between Jesus and the church. Thus, the fallen Judas must be replaced, and that replacement must be "one of the men who have accompanied us during all the time that the Lord Jesus went in and out among us, beginning from the baptism of John until the day when he was taken up from us" (Acts 1:21). For Luke the church stands on the sure foundation of eyewitnesses (1:2). Luke alone of the Gospel storytellers asserts that the disciples are witnesses even to the crucifixion (23:49).

This emphasis of the disciples as the true **apostles** of Jesus (special emissaries sent by him) was characteristic of the emerging orthodox consensus toward the end of the first century (see pages 211–12). It became a keystone of defense against the Gnostic version of the faith in the mid- and late second century. (On Gnostic interpretations of Christianity see pages 204–08.) Thus, Irenaeus (c. 185 CE) attacked the Gnostics who claimed to have a special private oral teaching from the apostles that justified their reinterpretations of Scripture. Irenaeus declared:

> We appeal to that tradition which is derived from the Apostles, and which is safeguarded in the churches through the succession of presbyters. . . . Those that wish to discern the truth may observe the apostolic tradition made manifest in every church throughout the world. We can enumerate those who were appointed bishops by the Apostles, and their successors down to our own day, who never taught, and never knew, absurdities such as these men produce. (Against Heresies 3.2.2; 3.3.1; from Richardson, 1953)

Luke's characterization is quite in line with this more exalted view, for the story consistently omits most of the negative incidents found in Mark and adds new positive portrayals. Their task is to be with Jesus. Though they still do not grasp what he means, they do not oppose him (compare 9:18–27 with Mark 8:27–9:1; GP §122–23, SFG §158–60). Notice the subtle changes in this discourse on discipleship: the cross is now something taken up daily rather than a reference to death; the contrast of this evil age is bypassed; they are promised to see the kingdom but not with power. These changes reflect Luke's concern for the ongoing life and witness of the church rather than for ideas connected with the coming of the kingdom.

And whereas Mark used a second feeding story to highlight the disciples' lack of understanding, Luke omits it—in fact, he omits a large section of material found in Mark (Mark 6:45–8:27 is not found in Luke). This not only portrays the disciples in a better light, it allows Luke to establish a close connection between three important events—the feeding, the confession, and the transfiguration—which now all point to Jesus' coming passion (see especially 9:30–31). In each of these the positive role of the disciples is emphasized. The confession scene, for example, is rewritten to omit completely the rebuke to Peter (compare 9:18–22 with Mark 8:27–34).

We will see this more positive image consistently throughout the rest of the story. By the end of this first section (9:50), the gathered disciples witness the coming of great events, yet they do not understand. They need instruction, which Luke will supply in the next section.

INSTRUCTING THE WITNESSES ON THE JOURNEY TO JERUSALEM

In the first section Luke softened the Markan theme of the disciples' misunderstanding (compare 8:25 with Mark 4:40; and 9:22 with Mark 8:31–34). At the close of the Galilee section, Luke deliberately introduces a reference to Jesus' passion into the healing-exorcism story, then adds:

> They did not understand this saying; its meaning was concealed from them, so that they could not perceive it. And they were afraid to ask him about this saying. (9:45)

Unlike the Markan ignorance, this is not natural or perverse. It is divinely ordained.

Now, in the second section of the narrative (9:51–19:27), Luke portrays a journey from Galilee to **Jerusalem**, the divinely appointed city, the city of suffering (13:33). In this Lukan portrayal, Jesus—by taking his disciples with him to Jerusalem—is performing a highly symbolic act, a movement toward understanding. Thus the primary activity of this section is the instruction of the witnesses, and the section properly closes with the declaration, "and when he had spoken these things" (19:28, literal). Luke focuses attention on these witnesses in the final words of the Galilee section, subtly modifying a traditional saying to read: he that is not against *you* is for *you* (9:50, emphasis added, in Mark it is *us*; see also 10:16).

Like the Galilee section, the journey section opens with a scene of rejection. In an incident found only in Luke, the Samaritans reject Jesus "because his face was set toward Jerusalem" (9:51–55). More than mere regional rivalry is involved; Jesus is in danger of rejection by all because of what will happen in Jerusalem. Luke moves directly from this rejection to three radical sayings about following Jesus (9:57–62; Matthew used these in a miracle cycle, 8:19–22). In Luke, the movement toward Jerusalem is a movement toward understanding the mystery of Jesus' passion.

THE INCREDIBLE JOURNEY

This so-called journey has occasioned much scholarly debate, and with good reason. For one thing the trip from Galilee to Jerusalem was considered a three-day journey (about sixty miles), yet Luke implies a much longer time. There is time, for example, for the seventy "others" to go on a preaching tour (10:1–17); a tour, incidentally, which presupposes a fixed center to which they "return" (10:17, contrast 10:1; Conzelmann, 1961:67). And however often we are reminded that Jesus is on the way to Jerusalem, we get no sense of progress and are given no itinerary. There are other confusing points: in 17:11 the geography is odd, both in the order of reference (from south to north) and by supposing a location close to Galilee even though the journey has been going on for seven chapters; the warning, to flee from "here" because of Herod, ignores the fact that Herod had no authority in Samaria where Jesus presumably was. Herod Antipas, son of Herod the Great, was tetrarch (subordinate ruler) only over Galilee and Perea in the north. Similarly, Luke suppresses the name of the village of Mary and Martha (10:38), probably because their village was Bethany, a scant two miles from Jerusalem—at least according to the tradition recorded in John (11:1).

These and other geographical irregularities prompt most commentators to wonder about Luke's map of Palestine. (See Conzelmann's curious attempt to draw a map to Luke's specifications, 1961:69ff.) Most assert that Luke is confused in matters of geography. But I think not: confusing, perhaps, if taken literally, but not confused. The suppression of place-names is too deliberate, the use of Jerusalem too intentional to suppose it is mere incompetence. We must take more seriously the deliberate fictitiousness (or, to use a more positive expression, the creative artistry) of this journey, the literary purpose of which is to point to Jesus' death:

> *It is impossible for a prophet to be killed outside of Jerusalem.* (13:33; 19:11–28; 18:31)

If we understand the meaning of Jerusalem, it will be clear that Jesus journeys to Jerusalem whether he moves north or south, or whether he does not move at all.

LEARNING ON THE WAY

There is a grave disparity within the journey section between form and content: the form is that of a travel narrative, but the content has almost nothing to do with a trip, being mainly instructional. Yet in another sense, form and content are perfectly congruent. The primary task of the disciples in this section is to be "with" Jesus (see Acts 13:31), for only then are they prepared to be witnesses to him. Being with Jesus "on the way" is a favorite metaphor of Luke for what God is doing to redeem the world. (See Acts 9:2; 19:9, 23; 22:4; 24:14, 22.) The "way" to Jerusalem becomes the paradigm of the church as it seeks to follow the way of God. Thus, teaching those who are with him on the way is a most appropriate activity.

You may wish to read through this section (Luke 9:51–19:27), using a synopsis to appreciate just how subtly the traditions are transformed to this new goal of teaching the disciples (beginning at *GP* §137, *SFG* §174) and studying a unit or two in detail.

A favorite technique used to interpret the tradition is the posing of questions that shape the reader's understanding of the teachings. For example, the final parable of this section, concerning the nobleman who went to a far country to receive kingly power, is expressly set in the twofold context of nearness to Jerusalem and of the disciples' (false) expectation of the nearness of the kingdom (19:11). By providing such a context, Luke shapes the way the reader understands the parable—accenting an important theme: that readers should not be surprised or concerned about the delay of the **Parousia**, the return of Jesus. (Other examples of this technique of framing Jesus' teaching can be found at 10:25; 11:1; 12:13; 12:41; 13:1; 13:23; 14:1, 3, 7; 15:2–3; 16:14; 17:20; 18:1; 18:9. All these settings are found only in Luke. This is a good example of the gospel writer providing a new context for the parables; see page 265.)

By this device Luke is able to give a different impression of the meaning of these parables from that of the same parable in another context. Compare, for example, the parable of the lost sheep in Matthew (18:12–14) with that in Luke (15:1–7; *GP* §172, *SFG* §219). Luke adds vividness, even a party, and shapes our understanding of the parable through two additions. We are told the specific setting in the life of Jesus (he is accused of attracting all the wrong kinds of persons, 15:2), and we hear two similar parables (the lost coin and the lost son). By these means a new value is placed on "lostness"; the lost recognize the salvation that has come to them, while the grumbling elder brother is unable to see the marvelous deed to which he might be witness. We see here, and throughout Luke-Acts, a striking concern for the marginal people of society: the sick, the poor, the powerless, and those regarded as sinful or unclean.

In this context, Luke's handling of the "Sign of Jonah" is instructive. Jesus' mere presence constitutes the sign, for one "greater than Jonah is here" (11:29–32; compare Matt. 12:38–42; *GP* §152, *SFG* §191). For Luke, the great act is to be witness to Jesus. It is the one necessary thing, as the charming story of Mary and Martha asserts (10:38–42, only in Luke).

LEARNING ABOUT THE WAY

Luke's understanding of the **kingdom of God** begins to come into focus in this section. The Pharisees are made to ask when the kingdom will come; to which Jesus replies that it is not coming with signs to be observed.

The kingdom of God is among you. (17:21)

This, then, becomes an occasion for teaching the disciples about the kingdom.

READING AND REFLECTION

Carefully study the instructions concerning the kingdom in Luke 17:20–37 (*GP* §183–84, *SFG* §234–35), noting all the ways Luke's version differs from that found in Matt. 24:26–28, 37–41.

Commentators are divided on the translation of the last phrase in Jesus' reply to the Pharisees: the Greek could equally well mean the kingdom is among you, is in your midst, or is within you. It may be understood existentially (Perrin, 1967:74), in an individualized and spiritualized sense (Perrin, 1976:43–46), or as a historical reference to the time of Jesus (Franklin, 1975:17). Whichever way we take it, it is important to realize that the saying is the positive side of a denial; it represents the reason there can be no signs: the kingdom is (already) among them or within them.

Even more interesting is the way Luke rewords the traditions about the coming of the Son of Man in the ensuing teaching to the disciples. It is not at all clear here that Luke is anticipating a future, apocalyptic appearance of the Son of Man. In fact, Luke explicitly links the suffering of the Son of Man with his appearing—the only such association in the whole of the synoptic tradition.

Luke's great reserve about the future coming of the kingdom is evident in the closing parable of this section, a parable for which Luke creates a context: they supposed that the kingdom of God was to appear immediately (19:11). Whereas in Matthew's version of the parable (25:14–30) the emphasis was on the judgment through which the church must pass on its way to the kingdom, Luke emphasizes the duration of the present time (19:11–27). The present is a time of faithful witnessing to the kingdom already in their midst, inaugurated by the suffering of the Son of Man. This brings Luke to journey's end: Jerusalem, the city of destiny.

THE WITNESSING OF THE EVENTS IN JERUSALEM

Luke's version of Jesus' time in Jerusalem is so different from Mark's that some argue he must have had an additional source (Taylor, 1926). But there is another possibility: Luke may have made conscious changes to the story.

IN COMPARISON WITH MARK

This argument was first put forward by Hans Conzelmann (1961:73–94), and many of the following observations are indebted to Conzelmann's careful analysis.

READING AND REFLECTION

Read 19:28–24:53, noting any major ways that Luke's version of these incidents differs from Mark's version, 11:1–16:8 (begin with *GP* §196, *SFG* §269).

1. Continue to notice Luke's emphases (especially Temple, prayer, Holy Spirit).
2. What aspects of Luke's narrative seem calculated to protect or defend the new way by making the followers of Jesus seem loyal to the Roman authorities?
3. Characterize Luke's portrayal of Jesus' death.

Mark carefully organized the time of Jesus in Jerusalem into a week, noting the passage of each day and night. Matthew followed the same scheme but moved the cleansing of the Temple story from Monday to Sunday in order to make a more positive point about the Temple (Matt. 21:10–13; Mark 11:11–15). Luke abandons this pattern of one week. The story shows Jesus teaching "one day" (20:1), teaching "every day" (21:37), and being "day after day in the Temple" (22:53). The Jerusalem mission thus becomes one of indeterminate length, something comparable to the Galilean activity or to the journey.

Nor does Jesus return to Bethany each night, as in Mark's version. Luke knows the Bethany tradition (19:29 and 24:50), but the significant place is the Mount of Olives (21:37), the place of prayer (22:39–48). (This symbolic use of space is also evident in Luke's version of the Sermon on the Mount, which no longer occurs on a mountain, the place of prayer, but "on a level place" (Luke 6:17; see Conzelmann, 1961:44–45). Without Bethany, there can be no anointing scene (Mark 14:3–9), but Luke has managed to use the scene earlier for other purposes (7:36–50).

These modifications illustrate for us the reorientation of the whole story in accord with Luke's basic view of Jesus. It is not surprising that some have felt the need for another source, especially if they were not prepared to view the Gospel writers as authors in their own right. Yet when we become aware of Luke's purpose, we can see the logic of this version of the story and will not be easily convinced by theories of other sources.

Consider, for example, Luke's handling of Jesus' withdrawal for prayer just before his arrest (Compare Luke 22:39–46 with Mark 14:26–31 and Matt. 26:30–46; GP §239, SFG §330.) There are enough differences to make the hypothesis of an additional source possible; yet if we examine the nature of these changes they all make sense in light of Luke's purpose. What in Mark is a crisis of one facing death, and in Matthew a temptation to disobedience, becomes in Luke a routine withdrawal for prayer "as was his custom" (22:39; 21:37). And prayer here is answered; an angel comes (22:43; notice that Luke earlier transformed the two incidents in which a voice spoke from heaven into times of prayer: 3:21; 9:28). Thus also prayer is admonished at the outset (22:40). In Luke the disciples are exonerated of any fault; they sleep "for sorrow" (22:45). This is in keeping with Luke's general elevation of the disciples into the primal eyewitnesses of the faith (1:2). Although such analysis does not prove that Luke did not use an additional source, it tends to make such a hypothesis redundant, for all the changes have already been explained. Far more important than any theory of sources is the way such careful observation can contribute to our understanding of the purpose and intention of Luke's narrative.

HE ENTERED THE TEMPLE

One who has followed Jesus on the long journey to Jerusalem may be surprised that he does not "enter" Jerusalem on his arrival. Luke omits the actual entry, saying only that he "entered the Temple" (19:45; compare Mark 11:11). Perhaps, as some suggest, Luke misunderstood and thought that one could enter the Temple without entering the city—as would be true in many Greco-Roman cities, where temples were often located outside the city walls. But in light of what we have observed about Luke's method of using place as a metaphor, it seems more likely that the city name is suppressed to focus attention on the Temple, where Jesus spends all his time until the Last Supper, which

THE TEMPLE This model of Herod's Jerusalem, located at the Holyland Hotel in Jerusalem, shows the Temple proper (the tall building) and its surrounding courtyards. Only priests could enter the Temple; the innermost courtyard was reserved for male Israelites; women could go as far as the walled area with corner towers in front of the men's courtyard. Gentiles were restricted to the very large surrounding courtyard, about the size of four football fields. In the background you can see the stadium where Greek athletic contests would have been held.

does take place in the city. The supper foreshadows Jesus' death, and Jerusalem is the place of destiny, the place of death (13:33). The **Temple** is the place of reconciliation.

Jesus' first act on arriving is to claim the Temple for his own, cleansing it to make it fit for prayer and teaching (19:45–48, a different scene from that of Mark; see *GPGP* §200, *SFG* §273). Luke has prepared the reader for this situation by introducing Jesus as one whose natural home is the Temple, conducting his father's business (2:41–51). Jesus now spends all his time in the Temple (19:47; 20:1; 21:1, 37), and "all the people would get up early in the morning to listen to him in the Temple" (21:38). This is the great opportunity, when the whole people gather to hear Jesus— a theme to which Luke will return. Jesus' early followers, also, will spend their days in the Temple (Acts 2:46; 3:1–10; 5:20).

Luke's abbreviated account of the cleansing lacks the air of impending crisis and imminent end that one finds in Mark, in accord with Luke's understanding of the postponement of the end. Even the great apocalyptic discourse is transformed by Luke: it no longer provides signs of the end time (compare Luke 21 with Mark 13; *GP* §216, *SFG* §290). Luke sees the desolation of Jerusalem as an act of retribution (21:22); having missed its time of visitation, Jerusalem must face the consequences (19:41–44).

Again Luke is working with an older tradition (the destruction of the Temple) to which he adds new details—in this case the details suggest that Luke knew how Jerusalem was conquered ("surrounded by armies," 21:20). And because Jerusalem is destined for destruction, the mission of the church must be traced beyond Jerusalem, even to Rome (the plot of the book of Acts).

But how could such a religion succeed in Rome? Founded by one crucified as an insurrectionist and propagated by one who spent a lot of time in Roman chains, this new way needed some defense.

THIS MAN IS INNOCENT

That Jesus was innocent is a conviction shared by all the Gospel writers. But Luke goes further, showing that the Roman authorities themselves recognized his innocence. In fact, three separate Roman officials proclaim Jesus' innocence: Pilate, who pronounces the official verdict three times (23:4, 14, 22), Herod (23:11), and the centurion who supervised the crucifixion. The latter declares, "certainly this man was innocent" (23:47; compare Mark 15:39). (In a similar fashion in Acts, Paul will be declared innocent by three separate officials: Claudius Lysius [23:29], Festus [25:25], and Agrippa [26:31].) Luke even offers what we might call an expert witness: the thief on the cross is made to testify that Jesus did nothing wrong (23:41). At one point the reader is actually forced to admit that Jesus is falsely accused. For when Jesus is brought before Pilate, Luke is careful to give the exact charges:

> We found this man perverting our nation, forbidding us to pay taxes to the emperor, and saying that he himself is the Messiah, a king. (23:2)

Yet the reader knows that Jesus did not forbid such tribute (20:19–26).

Such a miscarriage of justice raises another problem for Luke, since it seems to impugn the integrity of Roman officials. But they are shown to be largely at the mercy of their circumstances. In addition, much of the blame is laid on the Jerusalem leaders, who engineered Jesus' trial and constantly harassed Paul. In fact, in Luke's version one almost has the impression that they crucified Jesus (see Luke 23:22–26).

On the other hand, Luke is careful to show Jesus, the early community, and even Paul to be good, Law-observant Jews. Of the many examples, H. J. Cadbury summarizes:

> *The circumcision of John, of Jesus, and of Timothy, the attendance at the temple by Jesus' parents and admirers and by the early Christians, and the regular participation in the synagogue services of Jesus, Paul and others, the ritual observances of shearing or shaving which Paul made in connection with vows—these are some of the points which would indicate that Christianity is not anti-Jewish. (Cadbury, 1958:306)*

Cadbury also suggests one possible motive for this "Jewishness": if this new way were really a form of Jewish religion, it would come under the legal protection of the Roman Empire. The religion of the Jews enjoyed several important advantages including exemption from worship of the emperor, an issue that eventually became crucial for Christians. Jews were allowed to pray *for* the emperor rather than *to* him. On the other hand, if the Jesus movement were deemed a new religion it might be considered to have no legal standing and face official harassment. Yet our information on these matters is scanty, so it is difficult to say how seriously such distinctions as legal and illegal were taken or how perceptive Roman officials were about what they must have seen as the subtle distinctions between these two faiths.

The Roman historian Tacitus assumed the worst about Christians ("a class of criminals"; see pages 301–04). In addition, we know that in the early years of the second century Christians could be brought to trial and even executed simply for their allegiance to the Christ. (See the full discussion on pages 462–64.) Whatever their official status, followers of this new religion appeared subversive to many Romans. Luke's modifications of the trial narrative seem intended to dispel some of the basis for such a charge. We will see a similar strategy in the narrative of Paul's trials in Acts.

LUKE'S CHARACTERIZATION OF JESUS: MARTYR AND HERO

When the protagonist of a story dies, we expect that the recounting of the death will reveal much about how the author wants us to see the character. Such is the case with the death of Jesus in Luke.

READING AND REFLECTION

Carefully compare Luke 23:26–49 and Mark 15:21–41 (*GP* §248–50, *SFG* §343–48), and make a list of all the differences.

1. What new sayings are attributed to Jesus?
2. Who witnesses these things?

The contrast between Luke's account of the crucifixion and Mark's is striking because of their diametrically opposite tendencies. Mark sought to depict the starkness of the event, the reality of the suffering, whereas Luke sought to portray the death of the ideal martyr, a victor over evil. Mark's Jesus cries out: "My God, my God, why have you forsaken me?" Luke's Jesus declares: "Father, into your hands I commend my spirit." God's presence, not his absence, supports the death of the faithful. (Compare the death of Stephen in Acts 7:54–60.)

It has been suggested that there is something of a romance about Luke's work (Spivey and Smith, 1974:180). There is, as we say, a happy ending, and without too much complication of the plot. There is not (as in Mark) a reversal of the action but rather a steady growth from the birth stories to the resurrection. The action is an ever-ascending progression, ending in triumph and victory. The crucifixion is only one more stage in the upward progress of the story, an event that was necessary in the divine scheme of things revealed in the Scriptures. When two disciples encountered the risen Jesus on the road to Emmaus, they lamented the seeming catastrophe of the crucifixion. Luke gives this response:

> Oh, how foolish you are, and how slow of heart to believe all that the prophets have declared! Was it not necessary that the Messiah should suffer these things and then enter into his glory? Then beginning with Moses and all the prophets, he interpreted to them the things about himself in all the scriptures. (24:25–27; compare Acts 28:23–24)

Jesus' death was no catastrophe; it was arranged by God. Why God so arranged things Luke does not attempt to answer, but that all this happened according to God's will is clearly portrayed. Jesus thus becomes a model of proper behavior (as also 1 Pet. 2:21; 4:1). Luke's Jesus is heroic in a classical sense. He faced many trials but overcame them all; he conquered even death. Like that great classical hero Hercules he was exalted on high after performing the works assigned to him. Luke alone portrays the scene of Jesus ascending—describes it twice, in fact. It is the closing scene of Luke and the opening scene of Acts.

WITNESSING TO THE EVENTS IN JERUSALEM

In passing from the Gospel of Luke to the Acts of the Apostles we cross into new territory because unlike the Gospel, this writing is not limited by fixed and authoritative sources. Even if some sources were available for Acts, they had not attained the authoritative structure of the Jesus story or the likely status of Mark. This relatively greater freedom allowed for the telling of a compact, lively, and graceful story. As F. J. Foakes-Jackson reflects:

> We are often blind to the excellences of St. Luke and Acts, because, like the Aeneid and the Odyssey, we read them in short portions, and examine their every word, forgetting that they are not school exercises or fields for expert ingenuity, but literary masterpieces. (1931:xix)

We must attempt a holistic approach to Acts, concerned not so much with the bits and pieces as with the movement of the whole action and the way that action influences our understanding of Luke's gospel.

THE BEGINNING OF ACTS

Luke has chosen the difficult task of converting the closing scene of the Gospel into the opening scene of Acts. To do so required certain changes. The two accounts may be laid out as follows:

Luke 24:44–53
  Acts 1:1–14
Same day (13, 36)
  Forty-day period of appearances (3)
To preach repentance and forgiveness (47)
  No parallel
Beginning at Jerusalem (47)
  In Jerusalem and . . . (8)
Stay in the city (49)
  Do not depart from Jerusalem (4)
You are witnesses of these things (48)
  You shall be my witnesses (8)
I will send power from on high (49)
  You will receive power (8)
Led them to Bethany (50)
  Return from Mount Olivet (12)
Blesses them (50)
  Questions and answers about the kingdom (6)
Carried up into heaven (51)
  He was lifted up, a cloud received him (9)
Return to Jerusalem (52)
  Returned to Jerusalem (12)
Were continually in the Temple (53)
  Went to the upper room (13)

Much is the same; much is changed: their location (Bethany or Mount Olivet; Temple or upper room), the length of time (same day or forty days later), their dialogue. These changes are in line with the symbolic way Luke uses space and his concern to deemphasize apocalyptic ideas of the end. For example, in the short dialogue between Jesus and the disciples they ask him if the kingdom is to be restored at that time. Jesus' answer prepares the way for the story in Acts:

It is not for you to know the times or periods that the Father has set by his own authority. But you will receive power when the Holy Spirit has come upon you; and you will be my witnesses. (1:6–8)

Thus Luke shifts our attention from the ultimate goal of the Parousia (the coming of Jesus) to the more immediate goal of being his witness; that is, from an ultimate idea of God's kingdom to the intermediate idea of the church. Jesus' ascension into heaven and his enthronement at God's right hand (2:33) is the necessary prerequisite for this new idea of the church. Luke alone presents an ascension narrative, and Luke alone presents an account of the life of the church.

CROSSING THE BOUNDARIES

Earlier I argued that, like Luke's Gospel, Acts is structured into three parts: before the journey, the journey, and after the journey (pages 353–54). The first major section (Acts 1–12) shows the rapid and divinely led expansion of the witness "in Jerusalem and in all Judea and Samaria and to the ends of the earth" (1:8).

Photo by author

TEMPLE INSCRIPTION   This partial inscription, now in the Rockefeller Museum, was a part of Herod's Temple in Jerusalem. Written in both Latin and Greek, it forbade Gentiles to enter the Temple. This physical barrier corresponded to the social barrier between Jew and Gentile in the first century.

Skim through Acts 1–12, noticing how the witness to Jesus is carried across the various boundaries mentioned in 1:8. What stages are used in this section to accomplish the incorporation of the Gentiles into the church?

The first stage, beginning in the Temple (as we have come to expect), could be labeled the "struggle among the Judeans." It culminates in the death of Stephen (chapter 7). The witness to Jesus is shown to be remarkably successful. Many join the new way (2:41; 4:4), and these form a unified community (4:32), though not entirely without problems (5:1–11; 6:1). A Pharisee even intercedes on behalf of Peter and John (5:34). The real hostility seems to come from the Sadducees (4:1; 5:17–18; also pages 292–93, 337).

We are also introduced in this section to a group whom our writer calls **Hellenists**, a group he contrasts with the Hebrews (Acts 6:1). While we cannot be entirely clear about the significane of these groups, the difference seems to be primarily one of language and culture: the Hellenists speaking Greek and probably from the diaspora; the Hebrews speaking Aramaic and from Judea. Luke introduces the dispute between these Hellenists and the apostles as one of "serving tables," which should be understood in the context where sharing a common table was also sharing the Lord's table (2:42, 46). The qualification of these servants points in the same direction: they were to be "of good repute, full of the Holy Spirit and wisdom" (6:3).

Following the controversy between the Hellenist and the Palestinian disciples, another dispute breaks out between the Hellenist disciples and other diaspora Jews who had returned to the land. With typical concern for authentic detail Luke tells us the name of their synagogue: the Synagogue of the Freedmen. This is a likely indication that they had lived abroad as slaves, probably captives of some war. They now accuse Stephen, one of the Hellenists appointed to solve the earlier crisis, of blasphemy, speaking against "the holy place and the law" (6:13).

These two central aspects of Jewish life, Temple and Torah, would have had different meanings in the diaspora and in the land. The Temple in Jerusalem could play little role in the daily round of Jews living in Egypt, Asia Minor, Rome, or points further west. The real center of Jewish life in the diaspora had long been the synagogue, the house of prayer and study. Nor would the Torah be understood in quite the same way abroad. For one thing, major aspects of the Law applied only to life in the land, where issues of purity seem to have been paramount. Jews living among Gentiles could not possibly be so pure. Though we cannot be sure how many of these debates were already explicitly understood in the first century, we may be certain that Jews already disagreed about these things before the time of Jesus. Thus, some of the earliest divisions within the Jesus movement were simply the extension of earlier divisions within the Jewish people.

Stephen, despite a brilliant defense, is killed, but not before Luke introduces the next major character: "the witnesses laid down their garments at the feet of a young man named Saul" (7:58). Saul is introduced as an opponent, consenting to and then actively perpetuating a persecution of the church (8:1). Many were forced to flee Jerusalem, especially the Hellenists (the phrase "except the apostles" in 8:1 seems to imply that the more Law-observant Hebrew faction remained unaffected by this persecution). As they fled, they preached. Luke later lets slip that they preached directly to Gentiles at this time (11:19–20); for now, however, that fact is obscured in order to portray a more orderly progression.

And the expansion of the witness proceeds with vigor: first in Samaria, to people who were considered half-Jewish (8:5); then to an Ethiopian eunuch, a Gentile but a true worshipper of God, probably a full convert (8:27). Both **Samaritans** and converts were on the boundaries of Jewishness but still incorporated in the broader concept of the people of God. The dictum of the later rabbis was: "The usages of the Samaritans are at times like those of the heathens, at times like those of the Israelites, but most of the time like the Israelites" (*Kutim* 1, 2; quoted from Baron and Blau, 1954:68). Officially, Jews and Samaritans did not intermarry, but they were regarded equally in all civil law. A eunuch stood in a similar situation. Both Samaritans and eunuchs were forbidden to participate in the Jerusalem Temple activities. The social location of these groups is shown in Figures 11.1 and 11.2. They are boundary dwellers.

Now, before we are taken beyond the boundary, we encounter the first of Luke's three portrayals of the transformation of Saul from an enemy to a follower of the way (9:1–19; see the earlier discussion of this scene, pages 267–68, and of Paul's account, page 122). But it is not Saul who breaches the boundary; with delicate irony Luke reveals that it was Peter, the central apostle, a Hebrew and not a Hellenist, known in other traditions as the apostle to the Jews (Gal. 2:9). Peter, having already validated the mission to the Samaritans (8:14–17), now becomes the agent for spreading the word to the Gentiles (10:1–48).

The action in this carefully crafted story is divinely directed in every detail. Actually the story is told twice, once as it happens and again as Peter reports it to the Jerusalem church—not all of whom think it proper. In both versions, the decisive point is that the Gentiles too received the Holy Spirit (11:18). It is interesting to note

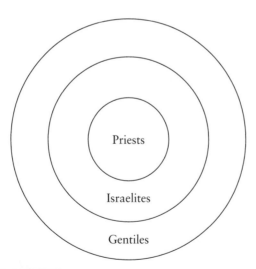

FIGURE 11.1 JEWISH SOCIAL SPACE   Like most people, Jews considered themselves above other peoples. To Greeks, the whole world was either Greek or barbarian; to Jews, the world was either Jew or Gentile. Gentiles were "those outside." For Jews this social distinction was also a religious one, and people were defined socially according to their status in the Temple. Only priests were allowed to enter the Temple's central shrine; Jews could enter the surrounding court; Gentiles had to remain outside.

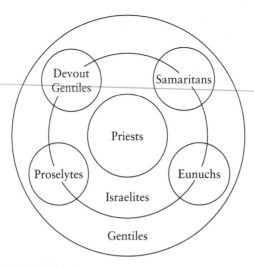

FIGURE 11.2 **JEWISH SOCIAL SPACE: BOUNDARIES** Certain groups did not fit neatly into the categories of Jew or Gentile. Proselytes, for example, were former Gentiles who had become Jews. In most ways they were regarded as Jews but not in all: a priest, for example, was forbidden to marry a proselyte. Jewish eunuchs were another marginal group, with obvious marriage restrictions. Samaritans, natives of northern Israel, were treated like Gentiles in regard to marriage and social interaction but like Jews in business. The most marginal group of all included devout Gentiles, those who worshipped the God of Israel but who had not become proselytes. For the most part, they were treated like Gentiles.

that in the second telling, Luke subtly shifts this decisive action of the story from near the end of Peter's preaching (10:34–44; see especially verse 44) to the beginning: "As I began to speak the Holy Spirit fell on them" (11:15). Luke's repetition marks this as an important story, for if we accept it the rest of the book will naturally follow. In fact, Luke will tell it in summary one more time (15:7–9), thereby confirming its meaning: God "has made no distinction between us [Jews] and them [Gentiles]."

At one point, at least, the story is perfectly historical. Cornelius is just the sort of **devout Gentile** to whom this new way made its greatest appeal. "A devout man who feared God" (10:2) surely marks him as a would-be convert to Jewish faith who does not fully convert because of the aversion to circumcision (see the discussion, pages 115–17). He is marked as one who "gave alms liberally" and "prayed constantly." It is precisely at his afternoon prayers (10:2–3) that he receives the divine command to summon Peter, which results in his receiving the Holy Spirit. This comes as no surprise to the reader of Luke-Acts, for Luke has reinforced this connection between prayer and Spirit from the opening scene. (See, for example, the reworking of the baptism of Jesus, discussed on pages 350–51.)

All that remains is for Luke to clear the stage so that the story of Paul's witness to the Gentiles can be told. This is accomplished through a story of Herod's persecution of the church (12:1), which resulted in Peter's flight: "he left and went to another place" (12:17). Admittedly it is not a very gracious exit, but it opens the way for the next stage of the story.

The journey section of Acts begins (13:3) and ends (19:21) as decisively as the journey section in Luke, even using the same technique of a resolve to go to the city of destiny: now Rome in place of Jerusalem. The theme of this section is vividly portrayed in the first two chapters: although there was some success among Jews, the overwhelming acceptance came from Gentiles. Chapter 13 closes with a scene that makes this explicit (13:46–48), and chapter 14 explores the acceptance among Gentiles.

In chapter 14 we have both high drama and comic relief in a story that illustrates how readily the Gentiles accepted this new way. We join the story in the city of Lystra (14:8), to which Paul and Barnabas have fled as a result of disturbances at Iconium; their preaching there had divided the city and led to stiff Jewish opposition. At Lystra Paul performs a miracle, which is followed by a great celebration (compare the parallel miracle by Peter, 3:2–8). Only gradually does Paul realize that the people, speaking their native language rather than the common Greek, are about to offer a sacrifice to him and Barnabas, whom they believe to be manifestations of the ancient Gods Hermes and Zeus. Try as he might, Paul only "scarcely restrained the crowds from offering sacrifice to them" (14:18; the story nicely illustrates the meaning of *Hellenistic civilization*: the cultural blending of native and Greek elements). At this point the scene is completely reversed. "But Jews came there from Antioch and Iconium and won over the crowds. Then they stoned Paul and dragged him out of the city, supposing that he was dead" (14:19).

In this graphic fashion, Luke contrasts the typical responses of Jews and Gentiles and justifies Paul's earlier resolve: "we are now turning to the Gentiles" (13:46). The Gentiles may not quite understand, but their openness and zeal are hard to match. Apparently, such Gentiles need someone to carefully tell them the full truth about the things of which they have been informed (Luke 1:4).

Luke mediates this simple dichotomy in two ways in the succeeding narrative: these new Gentile converts are closely tied to the Jerusalem church and to the traditions of the Jewish people (chapter 15), and not all Gentiles warmly embrace this witness, especially the elite (chapter 17). This last reminds us of Luke's earlier theme: it is the lost who are chosen (Luke 15). So little did the philosophers understand the witness that they supposed that when Paul proclaimed Jesus and resurrection he spoke of a new divine couple (*resurrection* being a feminine noun in Greek, 17:18). This is amusing to the reader, who knows more than these philosophers. In passing we must note that the way Luke's Paul uses the pagan tradition as a stepping-stone to Jesus is more typical of the approach of the church in the late first century than it was of Paul (contrast Romans 1–3, where Paul's argument is from nature rather than pagan philosophers; see Vielhauer, 1966). This is one of many ways that the Paul of this story differs from the Paul we meet in the Letters.

Another major way that Paul is made to fit the Lukan mold is the degree to which Paul is seen to depend on Jerusalem and adapt to the wishes of the more traditional Jews. In Acts, Paul immediately returned to Jerusalem after his experience at Damascus (9:26); Paul claimed otherwise (Gal. 1:17–18). So also the compromise struck by the Jerusalem council, that Gentiles should keep the most basic of the food laws, is unknown in the Pauline literature (Acts 15:19–21). These basic food and purity laws probably represent an application of a rabbinic notion that the whole law is only incumbent on Israel because it derives from the special covenant at Sinai, but the universal covenant that God made with Noah meant that even Gentiles had to adhere to certain demands (Genesis 9; C. S. C. Williams, 1964:32). This effort to relate the new way closely to the Jewish tradition is a consistent theme of Acts to which we shall return when we discuss the situation of the community.

The scenes of the journey section are richly textured and dramatic gems in the finest tradition of heroic narrative. They consistently portray Luke's major themes (such as prayer, Spirit, and the inclusion of the lowly). Overall, they dramatize the ever-expanding witness into the world. If we trace Paul's journeys on a map we will see that he went ever farther afield. Although this has the ring of historical probability, it precisely matches Luke's literary intention of showing the gradual, divinely directed spread of the witness to Jesus to the whole world.

This section closes with a scene at Ephesus depicting the conquest of Jesus over magic (19:11–20). Such magic, along with astrology and related practices, represented the primary religious experiences of the masses in the Hellenistic age. The dominant feeling of that age was powerlessness, lostness, and a sense of being at the mercy of fate. The traditional religions were not able to deal with these feelings. Philosophy offered a way out for the cultured elite. The mystery religions promised new birth and freedom from fate for the initiate, but the enormous cost of initiation limited such liberation to the wealthy. (See the discussion of religion in Chapter 1, pages 42–45.) Acts portrays, in a way that must have been very appealing to Gentiles of that time, the redemption of the common person who participates in the divine scheme of things. The ending note is appropriate:

So the word of the Lord grew mightily and prevailed. (19:20)

WITNESSING OPENLY IN ROME

The last section of Luke's lengthy work (19:21–28:31) opens on an ominous note: a near-riot in Ephesus led by the silversmiths, who are losing money because these new followers of the way (as Luke calls it) are no longer buying their icons. Although it may be unlikely that this economic impact would be felt as soon as Luke describes, there were economic implications of following Jesus. A provincial administrator, writing from this same region about three decades after Luke, describes how he successfully repressed the Christian "superstition" and comments on the renewed economic activity:

> *There is no shadow of doubt that the temples [of the Gods], which have been almost deserted are beginning to be frequented once more, that the sacred rites which have been long neglected, are being renewed, and that sacrificial victims are for sale everywhere, whereas until recently a buyer was rarely to be found. (Pliny Letter to Trajan; quoted from Bettenson, 1977:5–7)*

Notice how areas of life we regard as independent (such as economics, politics, education, religion) were all interconnected in that world. Culture was holistic, not segmented into different spheres; all activities were intertwined. Religious rites and allegiances had economic and educational implications. (For a more detailed discussion of the ancient economy see Chapter 13, pages 459–62.) The emergence of Christianity was not just the arrival of a new religion; it refused to blend in with the rest of the culture, and its success produced a serious challenge to that culture. The great opposition to Christianity manifested in the persecutions of the second, third, and fourth centuries represents a struggle to the death between two opposing views of reality. The economic roots of this conflict are clear in this first episode of the last section of Acts. Notice the implied exoneration of Paul. No wrong has been committed; the law is on their side; proper Roman officials protect them.

SOME DARING ADVENTURE

In a way more typical of the ancient novel than of a history, Luke has packed numerous scenes of adventure into this closing section: sea voyages, intrigues, riot, arrest, trials, mutiny, shipwreck, clairvoyant predictions, encounter with primitives. It is exciting reading. This technique is in keeping with Luke's heroic style, and Paul is always portrayed as completely in charge of each new situation.

One aspect of Luke's technique in this section has stirred great debate. Four times the narrative point of view suddenly shifts from the third person (he or they did) to the first-person plural (we did, 16:10–17; 20:5–15; 21:1–18; and 27:1–28:16). In each case the shift to and from the first person plural point of view is abrupt, and in each case it involves a sea journey. The most frequent explanation for the use of *we* in these passages is that the author must have been with Paul on these journeys.

But another explanation appears more likely. Vernon K. Robbins has shown that a regular feature of sea-journey narratives in the Greco-Roman world was the use of a first-person plural viewpoint, even in narratives written in the third person. The most exact parallel of the many he cites is from a second- or third-century BCE account of an expedition of one Hanno to found colonies:

> And he set forth with sixty ships. . . . After passing through the Pillars we went on and sailed for two days' journey. (1978:226)

Robbins concludes: "The evidence within contemporary Mediterranean literature suggests that the author of Luke-Acts used 'we' narration as a stylistic device" (1978:229). It is a way of involving the reader in the intimacy and danger of the travel by ship rather than a claim that the author is present. It is perhaps not unrelated to the author's claim in the preface to be narrating the things "fulfilled among *us*," not claiming thereby to be a witness to the Gospel events. Many of the other features of these sea narratives are also typical of this genre, including the shipwreck.

Travel was more extensive and safer in the Roman world than it had been for centuries before (or would be for centuries after), but it still entailed considerable risk. Travel by boat was especially risky and therefore also exciting. One ancient sage described it thus:

> What is a boat? A sea-tossed affair, a house without foundations, a ready-made tomb, . . . a prison in winged flight, fate bound up in a package, the plaything of the winds, a floating death, a bird made of wood, a seagoing horse, an open weasel-trap, uncertain safety, death in prospect, a traveler amid the waves. (Secundus the Silent Philosopher 14; quoted from Perry, 1964:87)

THE END IS THE BEGINNING

The question of the meaning of the ending of Acts is tied to the question of the date of Acts. Does the narrative stop because it has reached the present time of the author, or was there some other reason? The dramatic date of this last scene is about 60 CE: Paul is awaiting trial in Rome. If this could be shown to be the time of the composition of Acts, with the Gospel of Luke earlier and Mark earlier still, a whole new picture of the development of the Gospels would emerge. But I do not believe this can be shown. In fact, there is good reason to believe that the Gospel of Luke must have been written subsequent to the events of 70 CE, moving the date of Acts at least into the mid-eighties. This will be discussed in the next section.

But if Luke knows the rest of the story, why stop here? There may be several reasons. First, as Haenchen says, the really fitting end of Acts would be the Parousia (1971:98). Failing that, some intermediate end must be devised. Second, this end has a certain dramatic appropriateness. As John Chrysostom, a fourth-century Christian commentator, remarked:

> At this point the historian stops his account and leaves the reader thirsting so that thereafter he guesses for himself. This also the non-Christian writers do. For to know everything makes one sluggish and dull. (Homilies on Acts 55; quoted in Cadbury, 1958:322)

Third, in all probability Paul died at the hands of the Roman government, either at the end of this imprisonment or during Nero's persecution following the fire in 64 CE as early legend has it. (Haenchen argues that Luke presupposes Paul would die in Rome, basing his argument on 27:24; 20:25, 38; 1971:731–32.) But to recount Paul's death at the end of Acts would work against the interpretation of history that Luke has built up in this story. It would collapse the whole upward movement of the action that Luke has so patiently built and establish a false parallel between the death of Paul and that of Jesus.

Finally, this *is* the rest of the story, if we but understand what story Luke is telling. It is the story of the progress of the gospel, or more precisely of the witness to Jesus, from the initial gathering in Galilee through the climactic events of Jerusalem to the heart of the civilized world. (Notice that the way Luke tells the story obscures the fact that the church was established in Rome long before Paul arrived there. See also pages 155–59.) The witness has now been established in Rome, in undeserved chains to be sure, but with the witness being given "with all boldness and without hindrance" (28:30).

In one way the writing of a book of *acts*, a narrative of the witness to Jesus, is only a logical extension of what Matthew had already implied, namely a long period of witness—of the church's mission—till the close of the age. Matthew's final scene promises Jesus' continued presence in this interim period, but it seems implicit that he is present in a new way, a way unlike his life or even the resurrection appearances.

Luke makes this explicit, first by portraying the ascension of Jesus into heaven, from where he will return only at the end of time, and second by continuing to narrate the story of the witnesses. But in adding Acts, Luke really goes far beyond Matthew and Mark, shifting the focus from the past to the present. It is possible now to speak of the story of the church as something distinct from (though completely dependent on and parallel to) the story of Jesus. In this sense Luke really was the first church historian.

CHARACTERIZATIONS

No single character persists from the beginning to the end of Luke's story. Even Jesus is removed from the story. Luke's story is more like a James Michener novel or a TV miniseries that carries us forward into succeeding generations. Characters are important, for they move the story forward. But ultimately action predominates over character.

The previous discussion has already considered basic shifts in the characterization of Jesus, transformed by Luke from Mark's suffering servant into a noble hero, and the disciples, transformed from Mark's inept followers into the apostles who are the foundation for the true witness to Jesus (see pages 360–61). The story of these apostles, focused through Peter, is now expanded. Their success goes far beyond what we might imagine at the end of Matthew (let alone Mark!), carrying the witness to Jesus to the ends of the earth. Paul is so expertly inserted into this narrative that we easily accept him as heir to the apostles.

We have seen that Luke ties Paul closely to the Jerusalem church—he acts under its direction and stands with, not against, its leaders (see pages 375–76). Unlike the Paul of the previous generation, Luke's Paul does not fight for his independent apostleship. Whereas the Paul of the Letters is always directed to the Gentiles, the Paul of Acts always goes first to the Jews (see pages 142–45). In remarkable parallel to Jesus, Paul is now a heroic figure. It is recognizably the same Paul, but his portrait has been painted by a new artist.

Luke also redraws the secondary characters. We might first note just how many there are; even a listing of them would prove tedious. But we also note that like the other Gospel writers Luke melds individual characters into character groups (quite in keeping with the group-based identity of people in that culture). Let us look briefly at two such group characters that have appeared in earlier stories: the women and the Pharisees. In both cases the general scholarly consensus that Luke portrays these groups in a positive light is being challenged by some current interpreters.

Women

The heightened role of women in Luke-Acts is usually related to Luke's emphasis on the lowly because more than the other Gospels Luke portrays the inclusion of people of low status. Traditionally, scholars have read Luke as inclusive of women to such a degree that some have even suggested the work might have been written by a woman (Via, 1987:49–50). One example of this increased attention to women is Luke's practice of pairing stories of men and women; thus the centurion's slave (7:2–10) is followed by the widow of Nain (7:11–17); the good Samaritan (10:29–37) by Mary and Martha (10:38–42); the man with lost sheep (15:3–7) by the woman with a lost coin (15:8–10); the man with dropsy (14:2–6) by the crippled woman (13:10–16); the illustration of two men in bed (17:34) is followed by mention of two women grinding (17:35); and so on. Luke portrays women in unexpected roles: Mary Magdalene, Joanna and Susanna, and many other women travel with Jesus and serve as his **patrons**—and at least Joanna seems to have left a husband at home to do so (8:1–3).

Only in Luke does Jesus defend the right of a woman to neglect household duties in order to listen to his teachings (10:38–42).

More recently, however, some scholars have noticed that it is only the right to learn (not to teach) and that Mary is said to sit at the Lord's feet. And although Acts begins with the pronouncement from Joel that "your sons and your daughters shall prophesy" (2:17), in fact only the sons are featured in the story (but see 21:9). The prophet Anna may be paired with the devout Simeon in the story of Jesus' birth, but only Simeon's words are recorded (2:25–38). Women are silenced in this story.

Luke's characterization of women is ambiguous. They play a far more prominent role in this story, but their role is secondary. Scholars continue to debate the meaning of Luke's characterization of women. (See the resource section at the end of this chapter for details.)

Pharisees

Without question there is ample evidence for the traditional reading that emphasizes the positive characterization of the Pharisees. Luke curtails many of the harsher observations of Mark (compare Mark 3:6 with Luke 6:11), shows Jesus eating with Pharisees (7:36; 11:37; 14:1), even has the Pharisees warn Jesus of danger (13:31). They play no part in the passion story. In Acts, Pharisees comes to the aid of Peter (5:34–39) and Paul (23:9); some become believers (15:5); and in fact the hero of the last story segment is a Pharisee (26:5).

Nevertheless, there is strong warrant for another reading. In their first encounters with Jesus they raise questions of his blasphemy (5:21), of his eating with the wrong sort of folk (5:30), of his not fasting (5:33), and of his violating the Sabbath (6:2). They are specifically said to have "rejected God's purpose for themselves" (7:30). And while not as harshly or as thoroughly as in Matthew (23), Jesus pronounces a series of woes against them (11:39–44). And one can put some of the apparently positive evidence in a bad light. Paul was a Pharisee *before* he became a follower of Jesus; the Pharisees who are believers argue the losing cause.

Perhaps we can say that scholars who look for ways in which Luke's characterization differs from those of Mark and Matthew tend to see a positive portrayal of the Pharisees. Scholars who emphasize Luke's story as a consistent whole tend to see a negative portrayal. (See the resource section for specific references.)

It may be disconcerting to discover that scholars cannot agree on something so basic to this story as the meaning of the characterization of these groups. Such disagreement is testimony both to the difficulty of reading and to the complexity of Luke's writing. It warns each of us to approach our own reading with a bit more humility.

TRAGIC OR COMIC: HOW SHOULD WE READ LUKE'S STORY?

There are two kinds of ancient drama: tragedies and comedies. Even though tragedies were serious and comedies were funny, that was not the chief distinction between them. Here I am interested in one particular difference between the outcomes of the two types of drama. In a tragedy, the hero falls through some noble flaw and ends up exiled from society. (Think of the end of *Oedipus the King* when blinded Oedipus must leave Thebes and wander alone.) By contrast, a comedy ends by reintegrating the hero into the larger society or even the creation of a new society. (See the ending of Aristophanes' *The Birds* or *Lysistrata*, both of which end with marriages and new societies.)

The Gospels are not dramas and are neither tragedies nor comedies; however, this basic duality—what we might call the *structure* of tragedy and comedy—is a useful way to think about stories of various kinds. Clearly the Gospel of Mark tends toward the tragic; Jesus dies forsaken by all, alone on the cross. Matthew incorporates most of Mark's tragic elements yet transcends them with Jesus gathering a new community. Some interpreters refer to this as *tragicomic*. What of Luke?

Robert Tannehill (1985) has suggested that Luke-Acts is a tragic story, in part at least, because the new community envisioned in the opening fails to materialize; Israel is not included. The salvation promised to Jews at the beginning of the story (Luke 2:29–32) is at the end offered only to Gentiles (Acts 28:28), in Tannehill's reading. This is a complex issue, and Tannehill offers several lines of support for his reading. It leads us to a topic strongly debated by contemporary scholars: the role and status of the Jewish people in Luke-Acts.

The debate is too complex to enter into here; Joseph B. Tyson (1988) provides a useful overview of the range of views. Here I want only to raise the question of the overall tone and structure of this story. I have noted above the prevailing heroic style evident in the death of Jesus, the journey stories, and the daring adventures of Paul. One striking feature of Luke-Acts is the movement from one success to another; obstacles exist, but they are always overcome. Most readers have found the overall tone of Luke-Acts to be positive, often relating it to genres like the ancient romances (which were adventure stories in which all obstacles were overcome; see Pervo, 1987).

Although the centrality of Jerusalem in the story surely points to Luke's concern for Israel, the negative portrayal of Jews in the passion narrative qualifies any sanguine assertion about the vision of the future of Israel. The closing scene is itself ambiguous: Paul debates with Jews living at Rome. His final speech repeats the earlier assertion that God's salvation has been sent to the Gentiles. But Luke had already noted:

> Some were convinced by what he had said, while other refused to believe. (28:24)

Luke's social situation is probably more ambiguous than the question of whether Luke includes or excludes Jews. Luke's story creates a new community, but it includes only a remnant of Israel. Perhaps enough not to be tragic.

THE SITUATION OF LUKE'S COMMUNITY

Like both Mark and Matthew, this Gospel is anonymous, giving no explicit indication of its author's identity. Nor does it say where it was written or when. It is addressed to one Theophilus but does not locate him in space or time. Once again, these matters can only be deduced from clues in the writing itself.

GENERAL ASPECTS OF LUKE'S SITUATION

Several observations that bear on Luke's historical setting have been made in the course of this discussion. First, no one wants to place our author in Palestine; the geography is too befuddled (Kümmel, 1966:105). Yet this geographical confusion serves a literary purpose and is not a firm basis for identifying Luke's locale. Still, it seems safe to assume that Luke did not expect the audience to be familiar with the fine points of Palestinian topography.

Second, Luke probably lived some distance in time from the fall of Jerusalem; far enough to view it dispassionately as a historical judgment of the nation, yet close enough to know some of the details. So the earliest likely date is in the late eighties or early nineties; either date would be in harmony with Luke's belonging to the second or third generation of Jesus' followers (depending on the "ministers of the word," who depended on the "eyewitnesses," Luke 1:2).

Third, Luke's orientation is primarily toward Gentiles. The story not only justifies their inclusion but also shows a deliberate turning away from the mission to

THE ODEUM   Something of the grandeur and style of Greco-Roman culture can still be seen in these ruins of the Odeum (Music Hall) at Aphrodisias, a city not far from Ephesus. Music was an integral part of public life. The marginal status of Jews in this culture can be seen in the inscription here that reserved certain seats for them. They are both in the culture (they attend performances) and outside it (they have separate seating). The author of Luke-Acts seems to see Christians in a similar role.

Israel and a turning toward the Gentiles (especially Acts 13:48; 28:28). In this sense it may be relevant that the name Theophilus (Luke 1:1; Acts 1:1) means "one who loves God," a name that would be entirely appropriate for one of the devout Gentiles who appear so often in the story. In any case, this attitude toward Gentiles seems again to indicate a time late in the first century or early in the second.

Finally, we observed Luke's effort to make the Jesus movement appear innocent of the slanders urged against it before the Roman authorities and to present the Romans in a way that Luke's community could accept and admire. A concerted effort at the end of Acts attempts to show Paul's innocence, to such an extent that one commentator has called chapters 16–28 "a catalogue of Paul's acquittals" (Foakes-Jackson, 1931:xvii). Some have even imagined that the immediate purpose of Luke's work was as a brief for the defense at Paul's trial (Munck, 1967:lv–lxi). Such a proposal faces several difficulties, including the very nonjudicial character of the work. The proposal also views Acts in isolation from Luke's Gospel. Luke is just as concerned to show the innocence of Jesus as that of Paul, and there can be no question of influencing a judicial outcome in Jesus' case. Rather, the whole work is a general defense of the Jesus movement cause before a Roman public with a decidedly poor opinion of its members (see the malicious judgment of Tacitus, quoted on pages 302–03). One aspect of this defense is to present this new way as a legitimate form of Jewish religion, which Rome recognized and protected.

However, numerous first-century followers of Jesus had little use for Rome. The author of the Apocalypse, for example, labeled it the "great whore" (17:1). And the repeated admonitions in the New Testament to obey the government and pay taxes (Rom. 13:1–7; 1 Pet. 2:13–17; 3:13), indicate that some at least were not so inclined. Luke apparently wanted to establish good relations between these two parties; Luke is, as Robert Grant notes, the only Gospel storyteller "who takes such responsibilities [as fall to citizens of the empire] with full seriousness" (1977:46).

In short, Luke was coming to terms with Rome without recourse to the apocalyptic notion of evil governments whose overthrow must precede the coming kingdom. Many argue that Luke's positive attitude toward Rome was probably formed before the last years of Domitian (before 93–96 CE), who made it a crime for a Roman citizen to convert to Jewish religion (Dio Cassius *Roman History* 67.14.1–3), though some would date it well into the second century. Luke's story reflects a community that realizes it is going to have to settle down and live in the world. He seems more attuned to the woman John calls Jezebel than to the apocalyptic outlook of the Book of Revelation itself (see pages 459–62).

All this is in agreement with our impression of Luke as a person of some culture, who felt at home in the Greco-Roman civilization and wished to relate to it. Is it possible to be more definite on the identity of our author?

DID LUKE WRITE LUKE-ACTS?

The tradition that Luke-Acts was written by Luke, the physician and traveling companion of Paul, can be traced to the Muratorian Fragment (see the quotation on pages 475–76). But perhaps it was already regarded as from Luke in the mid-second century. At least Marcion, a confirmed Paulinist, chose only this Gospel for his canon, probably because of Luke's association with Paul (Thompson, 1972:4–5; on Marcion see pages 204–05, 208). The question we cannot answer is: Why did people think

Luke wrote it? Perhaps they had an older tradition or perhaps they made an informed guess. There are a couple of pieces of evidence from which such a deduction could be made. First, there are the "we" sections in Acts, discussed above. It is generally presumed that these prove the author of the book is with Paul at these times. Second, a reference in 2 Timothy, presumably written during Paul's Roman imprisonment, says that "only Luke is with me" (4:11). Since one of the "we" sections brings the author to Rome, Luke must be that author. If this is the basis for the ancient tradition of Lukan authorship, it rests on two tenuous presuppositions: that the presence of the first-person plural pronoun indicates the author's presence and that Paul actually wrote 2 Timothy from Rome. Few modern scholars defend Pauline authorship of 2 Timothy, and the change to the first-person plural may be for dramatic reasons rather than a personal account. (See the discussion on pages 195–99, 377. On the latter point, see Cadbury, 1958:357; on the former, see Kümmel, 1966:130–32.)

Of course, the strong interest in Paul, the claim to rely on the testimony of others, and the Gentile orientation are all consistent with Lukan authorship. Some have attempted to buttress these observations by arguing that Luke was a physician and that the story exhibits a medical language, but the argument does not hold up to examination. Cadbury has clearly shown that Luke shares this language with writers who are not physicians (1958:358; 1920:39–72).

Still, of those I surveyed on the subject, the majority support Lukan authorship (Thompson, 1972; Creed, 1930; Williams, 1957; Manson, 1930; Munck, 1967; and Fitzmyer, 1981:1:35–53, who accepts it after a lengthy and inconclusive review), whereas only one flatly denies it (Haenchen, 1971) and three believe it is not possible to reach a decision (Cadbury, 1958; Leaney, 1958; and Foakes-Jackson, 1931). The grounds for rejecting Lukan authorship center on the differences perceived between Paul and our author.

In addition to many specific points of difference, there is a basic difference in attitude between our author and Paul: between one in the heat of battle and one reporting the battle after a victory has been secured and the bitterness forgotten. Whereas Paul fights passionately for his apostolic authority and the freedom of his Gentile converts, for Luke these are matters long settled. Paul's apostolic authority is not defended; it is ignored. In fact, Acts 1:21–25 implies that Paul would not be qualified to be an apostle. Again we must imagine the passage of a considerable length of time. Whether it would be possible for a personal acquaintance of the great apostle to so transform him some twenty-five years or so after the apostle's death is not within the scope of our debate. The evidence does not seem compelling on either side. Clearly, however, the world of Luke-Acts and the world of Paul are very different, and Luke-Acts uses the story of Paul for a different purpose than that for which Paul himself fought.

THE PURPOSE OF LUKE-ACTS

We must give due weight to Luke's claim that the purpose of this story is to show the true significance of the facts about Jesus and his followers (1:1–4). The primary concern of Luke is not simply to present the facts of history (many of which Theophilus already knew) but to interpret history as well. What does it mean, Luke asks, that Jesus of Nazareth has lived, suffered, died, and been raised from the dead, and that a witness to him has gone out into all the world? The story suggests that it means a new era has dawned. It is not the eschatological kingdom. That kingdom will come in God's own time (1:6–8); in the interim, however, God has brought salvation to the Gentiles. This is a story for the interim.

Luke ignores the tension between his claim that a new age had dawned in Jesus and the imperial claim that a new age dawned with Augustus. For Luke does not wish to contest Roman culture; rather he sees Jesus and his church fully embedded within Roman history. He seeks to show the Romans that this is no subversive movement; and he seeks to show his fellow believers that a full knowledge of the things accomplished among them exonerates Rome of any fault in the death of Jesus and the leaders of the church.

Writing late in the first century (or perhaps early in the second), some writer of great skill and quite at home in the Greco-Roman world has presented a remarkable story of the dawning of a new age. The hero of this story is Jesus, a man of great compassion and unconquerable power. Endowed with the Spirit, this man called together a group of disciples and instructed them on their journey. After his death, he was exalted to heaven, from whence he reigns and brings God's plan to completion. His work is carried on by his followers, themselves now endowed with the Spirit. This work of God had its focus in the Temple in Jerusalem, the ancient center of God's revelation. But from Jerusalem, a witness to God's work has spread throughout the whole world, even to the very center of political power, Rome itself—where it continues quite openly and unhindered.

LEARNING ON YOUR OWN

REVIEWING THE CHAPTER

Names and Terms

apostles	Parousia	Semitic Greek
devout Gentile	patron	Septuagint
Hellenists	proleptic	synagogue
Jerusalem	prologue	Temple
kingdom of God	Samaritan	witness

Issues and Questions

1. How does seeing Acts as the continuation of the story of Luke's Gospel change our understanding of that Gospel?
2. Be able to describe and explain Luke's use of geography to structure the narrative.
3. Trace and explain a few of Luke's prominent themes, such as prayer, spirit, Temple, the lowly.
4. Compare Luke's characterization of the disciples with Mark's portrayal and discuss the role they play in Luke's narrative.
5. What relationship exists between John the Baptizer and Jesus in this story?
6. How and why does Luke characterize Jesus as innocent?
7. On your reading, how does this story suggest one understand the relationship between Jews and Gentiles? Between Jews and followers of Jesus?

8. Compare the characterization of Paul in Acts with that in the Letters.
9. Is Luke-Acts a tragedy, a comedy, a romance, or some combination of these?

Taking the Next Step

Good introductory works include Tannehill, 1996; Kurz, 1993; and Edwards, 1981. Other useful introductions include Danker, 1976; Juel, 1984; Talbert, 1982; and Tiede, 1988.

For detailed studies of the text, consult one of the major commentaries on Luke's Gospel: Caird, 1963; Craddock, 1990; E. E. Ellis, 1967; Leaney, 1958; and Marshall, 1978b. Probably the best now is Fitzmyer's two-volume work, 1981, 1985, and his 1998 volume on Acts. See also Nolland, 1990; and Trites, Larkin, and Comfort, 2006.

On Acts see Bruce, 1988; Conzelmann, 1987; Crowe, 1979; Haenchen, 1971; R. P. C. Hanson, 1967; Marshall, 1982; Munck, 1967; Talbert, 1984b; and C. S. C. Williams, 1957.

Topics for Special Studies

Because Luke-Acts relates its story to general history and situates it in the general cultural milieu, it provides numerous opportunities to study the relation between emerging Christianity and Greco-Roman culture. If you are interested in some aspect of culture (from art or politics to the way people dressed), you can probably find occasion to peruse that topic in relation to Luke-Acts. This is a particularly fruitful writing to study with social science methods, and considerable work has been done already. The headings below provide some general project topics.

Luke's View of History

The definitive study is Conzelmann, 1961; his understanding of Luke is clearly seen in the German title of his book, *Die Mitte der Zeit* (*The Middle of Time* or *The Center of History*). Conzelmann argued that Luke envisioned three historical epochs: from Adam to John, the time of Jesus, and from the founding of the church to the second coming. His argument relies heavily on Luke 16:16: "The law and the prophets were until John; since then the good news of the Kingdom of God is preached." There is much to be said for this view, though it ignores contrary evidence. For a summary critique with an excellent bibliography, see E. E. Ellis, 1972. Conzelmann's view is widely adopted; see Barker and others, 1969:281–300; Kee, 1977a:189–212; Duling, Perrin, and Ferm, 1994:378–82; and Spivey and Smith, 1974:151–80. Hengel, 1980, defends the essential reliability of the Lukan history.

Luke's view of history is often called *salvation history* (from the German *Heilsgeschichte*), or the history of redemption. As generally used, the term refers to a special sacred history distinct from the general history of the world. "These two run side by side, and at certain points they intersect, but salvation history is not exhausted in world history" (Perrin, 1974:201). However, salvation history is believed to reveal the true meaning of general history. For a commentary built on this theory, see Munck, 1967. For an introduction, see O'Toole, 1984; Tiede, 1980; and the related work of Sterling, 1992.

Luke's Attitude toward the Jewish Community

Related to Luke's view of history is the stance these writings take toward Jews, about which there is considerable difference of opinion. Much of the debate was started by Jervell, 1972, with responses by Brawley, 1987; Sanders, 1987, who argues that Luke-Acts is anti-Semitic; and Tyson, 1992, who takes a more nuanced view. On the related issue of the portrayal of violence in Luke and Philo, see Seland, 1995. On the legal status of Jews see appendix A in Novak, 2001.

For an overview, see the collection of essays in Tyson, 1988; see also Moessner, 1999; Tannehill, 1985; Juel, 1984; and Wills, 1991.

The Pharisees in Luke-Acts

Gowler, 1991, sketches Luke's various portraits of the Pharisees. For the older view that Luke is favorable toward the Pharisees, see Ziesler, 1979. For a challenge to that view, see Darr, 1989. Moxnes, 1988, traces economic aspects of the conflict. See also Hultgren, 1979. Mason, 1991, examines Flavius Josephus on the Pharisees; Richardson and Westerholm, 1991, provide a broader study of law in religious communities of the time. Saldarini, 1989, is perhaps the best introduction to Pharisees and other groups. See additional resources at the end of Chapter 10.

In addition to a historical study, one could compare Luke's characterization with another, such as that of Matthew, Mark, or Josephus.

Luke's Technique as a Historian in Comparison with Other Historians of That Time

Luke's methods, techniques, and even goals are much like those of his near-contemporaries, for whom history was a branch of rhetoric, the art of persuasively presenting a case (see Quintilian Institute 9.4; 10.1.3). For a good summary and comparison of the methods of ancient historians, see F. C. Grant, 1957:119–24. See also Hengel, 1980.

The most complete work on Luke's methods and purpose is still Cadbury, 1958; see also Drury, 1976. Tyson, 2006, challenges the traditional view and argues for a second-century date. Within this context of making a case, Luke has proven to be remarkably accurate in such things as use of political titles, navigational terminology, and local customs, as well as several incidents in Paul's life that can be confirmed from Paul's letters. On the other hand, there are a number of historical problems that do not fit well with our knowledge from Paul or other sources. (For a list, see Cadbury, 1958:366–67, and Haenchen in Keck and Martyn, 1966.) Still, in standards of accuracy, Luke compares well with the better historians of the time. Cameron, 1990, studies the writing of ancient history. For an analysis of modern historiography as rhetoric, see Carpenter, 1995.

Whereas Mark's references to the destruction of Jerusalem were vague, Luke's details correspond closely to those given by Josephus in his lengthy account of the destruction of Jerusalem (Jewish War 5 and 6). The siege, the bank works, the surrounding wall, and the terrible slaughter are all described in Jewish War 5.6.2; 5.12.1–3; 5.9.1–3. Josephus claims that 1,100,000 people perished during the siege and 97,000 were taken captive, though those numbers seem to be inflated; see 6.9.3 Josephus, too, regarded the destruction of the city as divine retribution; for example, 6.8.4. Holladay, 1999, compares other Jewish historians.

Luke's Portrayal of Jesus

See Rowe, 2006; Scaer, 2005; Jervell, 1977; and Moessner, 1999.

Luke's Portrayal of Paul

Moessner, 1983, examines Paul and the pattern of the prophets like Moses; see also Wall, 1991, and Gaventa, 1986.

For a discussion of Luke's theology in comparison with Paul, see Vielhauer, 1966; the numerous ways Acts differs from Paul's Letters are also traced by Bornkamm, 1971: xv–xx; Haenchen, 1971:112–16; and Kummel, 1966:102–5.

It would also be interesting to compare Luke's portrayal with Paul's own self-portrait.

The Genre of Luke-Acts

Discussions of the genre of Luke-Acts have tended to focus either on the Gospel or the Acts of the Apostles, the former usually favoring biography, the latter history. Important works include Alexander, 1993; Barr and Wentling, 1984; Barrett, 1961b; Callan, 1985; Hemer, 1977; Robbins, 1979; and Talbert, 1974. Praeder, 1981, relates it to the ancient novel or romance, as does Pervo, 1987; see also Pervo, 1999. Eerdmans' series, the Book of Acts in Its First-Century Context, includes several volumes, including Winter and Clark, 1993 (literary context); Gill and Gempf, 1994 (Greco-Roman context); Rapske, 1994 (Paul in Rome); Bauckham, 1995 (Palestinian context); and Levinskaya, 1996 (diaspora context).

Parsons and Pervo, 1993, challenge the consensus view of the unity of Luke and Acts. Bonz, 2000, examines the epic.

Luke's Portrayal of John the Baptizer

On John's baptism, see Creed, 1930:309–13, and Starr, 1932. On John, see Taylor, 1997; Webb, 1991; Scobie, 1964; and Kraeling, 1951. For an appraisal of the historical relationship between John and Jesus, see Tatum, 1994.

On the Mandeans, who claim to descend from John, see Kraeling, 1951, and Drower, 1962.

It would also be interesting to compare Luke's portrayal with that of other authors (Mark, Matthew, John, or Josephus).

Literary Parallels between Luke's Gospel and Acts

Among the modern scholars who have recognized various parallels between the Gospel and the Acts of the Apostles, I am especially indebted to Talbert, 1974; Perrin, 1974:205; Spivey and Smith, 1974:150, 167, 253; and Conzelmann, 961:17. See also Lane, 1996, and Tannehill 1990.

The Birth Stories

One could explore either the historical issues surrounding these stories or their status as literary compositions.

In addition to the sources mentioned in Chapter 10, see Derrett, 1973; Oliver, 1963; and Conrad, 1985. Anderson, 1987, and Schaberg, 1985, provide contrasting feminist critiques.

Luke's Portrayal of Women: Liberating or Dominating?

Luke's attitude toward women is hotly debated. For the older view that stresses Luke's inclusion of women, see Via, 1987. For the more recent but growing view that stresses Luke's subordination of women, see Schaberg in Newsom and Ringe, 1992; Schaberg calls Luke "an extremely dangerous text." O'Day, in the same volume, presents a more positive view of Acts, suggesting that we can learn much about women's lives by the "suggestive glimpses" provided in the story. See Schüssler Fiorenza's feminist reconstruction of the period covered by Acts, 1983:160–204, and D'Angelo, 1990. Reid, 1996, and Seim, 1994, are both aware of the double message of this work.

The Role of Miracle, Magic, and Spirit-Possession in Luke-Acts

See Achtemeier, 1975; Garrett, 1987, 1989; and Johnson, 1977. See also S. Davies, 1995.

Is Luke Tragic or Comic? The Meaning of the Ending

On the differences between tragedy and comedy, see Via, 1975; Buechner, 1977; and Exum, 1987. For a good translation of *Oedipus*, try Grene and Lattimore 1967. Aristophanes was the premier Greek comedian. On tragedy with implicit contrasts with comedy, see Aristotle's *Poetics*. Tannehill, 1985, sees Luke-Acts as a tragic story. It is more common to compare Mark to tragedy; see Bilezikian, 1977; Stone, 1984; and Walsh, 1989. On the ending, see Marguerat, 1999. On Luke's portrayal of Jesus' death as heroic see Scaer, 2005.

Further Study of Plot, Characterization, Point of View, or Structure
The most impressive study to date is Tannehill, 1990. Both Parsons, 2007 (by topics), and Borgman, 2006 (by sections), explore the story; see also Tannehill, 2005. See also Dawsey, 1986, on irony, and Moessner, 1989, on the travel narrative. Darr, 1989, and Heil, 1989, use reader response theory. On Luke's rhetoric see Spencer, 2007.

On characterization, see Gowler, 1989; see Darr, 1998, for the characterization of Herod.

The Social World of Luke-Acts
For an overview, see Neyrey, 1991b; for special studies see J. H. Elliott, 1991 (household and meals); Karris, 2006 (food); Gowler, 1991 (host, guest, enemy, and friend); Moxnes, 1988 (the economy); and Walaskay, 1984 (politics).

Other Acts and Gospels
The best collection of other works is J. K. Elliott, 1994; see also his abbreviated collection on Jesus, 1996; the collection of Hennecke and Schneemelcher, 1991–1992, is very good; the older work of James, 1924, is still useful. For good translations of selected other gospels, see Cameron, 1982, and Crossan, 1985. See also MacDonald, 1982, on the apocryphal Acts. Van Voorst, 2000, surveys what is said about Jesus outside the New Testament.

Additional Books and Articles
For extended bibliography on Luke-Acts, consult Segbroeck, 1989; Mills, 1986; and the older work of Mattill, 1966. See also the summary of Powell, 1992c.

Important monographs on Luke-Acts that point in new directions include Cadbury, 1955, 1958, 1969 (1920); Darr, 1989; Hengel, 1980; Jervell, 1972, 1977; Johnson, 1977; Talbert, 1974; and Tiede, 1980.

Three important collections of essays are Keck and Martyn, 1980; and Talbert, 1978, 1984b.

Kealy, 2005, surveys the history of the interpretation of the Gospel; on Acts see Gasque, 1989.

12

IRONY AND THE SPIRIT

 Often the predominant emotion when reading [irony] is that of joining, of finding and communing with kindred spirits.
WAYNE BOOTH, *RHETORIC OF IRONY*

Readers have long felt that John's Gospel is in some basic way different from the other three in the New Testament. A second-century writer expressed it thus:

> Last of all, aware that the physical facts about Jesus had been presented in the other gospels . . . John wrote a spiritual gospel. (Clement of Alexandria, about 200, as preserved in Eusebius Ecclesiastical History 6.14.7)

Clement's solution—that the synoptics presented "physical facts" (we might say "history") while John presented the "spiritual" (we might say "meaning")—does not quite work. Our study of the synoptics has shown that they were less concerned with "physical facts" than Clement suggests; like John they were concerned with the significance of Jesus. Still, the significance John saw differed markedly from that of Mark, Matthew, and Luke. This Fourth Gospel, as it is frequently called, does not often include the same stories and sayings we have come to expect from the synoptics (except for the stories of Jesus' death, which are remarkably similar). In addition, even when we find a parallel story or saying, the wording and the order of events vary considerably. Perhaps even more important, the general organization and story pattern of this Gospel are unlike anything we have encountered so far.

THE STRUCTURE OF JOHN'S GOSPEL

In this chapter we will explore the action and structure of the Gospel, read several of the major incidents, and then ask how, why, and where such a gospel may have come into existence. Looking for the setting of the Gospel will lead us to examine three other early writings that are remarkably like it, namely, the letters we know as 1, 2, and 3 John. First, let us trace the course of the action portrayed.

THE DEVELOPMENT OF THE ACTION

There are several problems with the arrangement of the stories in this writing:

Problem: At one point we are told, "After this Jesus went to the other side of the Sea of Galilee." One might expect Jesus to already be at the sea, but the previous incident was set in Jerusalem—sixty miles away. (Compare 6:1 with 5:1. This awkwardness was already noted by Tatian, who resolved it by placing chapter 6 before chapter 5 in his *Diatessaron*.)

Problem: Jesus seems to close a major speech by telling the disciples, "Rise, let us be on our way" (14:31); but he continues to speak for two more chapters, and nobody moves until 18:1.

Problem: The current ending (chapter 21) clearly represents material added to the Gospel by another hand. It presupposes the death of the original author (verse 23) and it claims to be written by his disciples who add their testimony

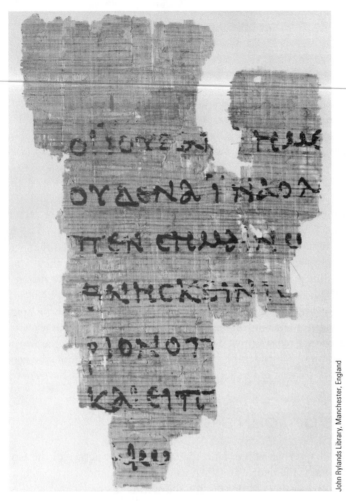

PAPYRUS FRAGMENT OF JOHN'S GOSPEL This small fragment is the oldest portion of the New Testament known to us, perhaps written as early as 130—just a generation after the Gospel itself. Only about 2½ by 3½ inches, there is writing on both sides, showing that it was part of a codex (book form) rather than a scroll. It contains what is now chapter 18 of John; the side shown represents verses 31–33, with verses 37–38 on the reverse.

to the trustworthiness of his word (verse 24: the "we" who know that "his" testimony is true).

Problem: The story of the adulterous woman (7:53–8:11) was not part of the original story but was later inserted into John's text. We find it in different places in different manuscripts: sometimes after 7:36, other times after 7:44, sometimes after 21:25, and still other times after Luke 21:38 (see the evidence in Metzger, 1971:219–22). Apparently, this story was never included in a gospel but was just too good to lose.

Problem: The little legend explaining why people could be healed by getting into the pool at Bethzatha (5:4) was not part of the original story. It is probably the work of some well-meaning scribe, perhaps originally written in the margin. A later copyist may have assumed that it was part of the story and so copied it into the text.

Clearly, John's Gospel has a history of revision, which we will return to at the end of the chapter. But whatever its earliest form and whenever these revisions were made, the author has arranged the material this way for a purpose, leaving us clues to the present order.

READING AND REFLECTION

On your preliminary reading of John's Gospel, look for formal indications of order. I have found it especially useful to note the following:

1. What kind of material is being presented (narrative, dialogue, monologue, transitions), and when does the text shift from one to the other?
2. What means has the author used to order the material (explicit statements of order, repetitions of similar incidents, use of numbers, references to time or to earlier incidents)?

In spite of the seemingly loose ends mentioned above, the plot of John's Gospel is more tightly organized than that of the other Gospels. It contains fewer incidents, elaborates each more, and connects them in explicit ways. For example, John organized the opening incidents into a week by the expression "the next day" (1:29, 35, 43), and then "on the third day" (2:1). The wedding thus occurs on the "seventh" day of the narrative (and both a wedding feast and the seventh day were powerful symbols for the kingdom of God). Jesus' action at this wedding is then labeled "the first of his signs" (2:11). But instead of a list of signs, as we might expect, only one more is numbered, "the second sign" (4:54), also performed at Cana. Because of this partial listing and because Jesus is reported to have performed other signs in Jerusalem (2:23), there has been considerable debate about whether John used a source that consisted of a collection of miracle stories, usually called the Signs Source (Fortna, 1970). He may well have used such a source, but we miss the more important point if we do not ask why these two incidents are linked by this numbering. They form a frame around one unit of material, marking one movement of the action: from Cana to Cana.

Besides these two signs, this section portrays one action of Jesus (cleansing the Temple) and two dialogue-monologues (with a Jewish ruler in chapter 3 and with a Samaritan woman in chapter 4). Responses of disbelief (2:18), wavering indecision (Nicodemus; 3:1–9), and wholehearted belief (4:42) are described. Unlike the characters, the reader has been given special access to the identity of Jesus, by direct testimony from the narrator, aided by the testimony of John the Baptizer, Andrew, and Nathaniel (chapter 1). The contrast between the readers' private insight and the struggle of people within the story to understand Jesus provides much of the dynamic of the plot.

Following the Cana section, Jesus returns to Jerusalem, where he heals a man on the Sabbath (5:1). The time markers are now the sacred year: the approach of

Passover (6:4), the Festival of Booths (7:2), and the Festival of Dedication (10:22). Otherwise time is only vaguely marked by the general temporal reference "after this" (5:1; 6:1, 66; 7:1). Time within these incidents, however, is sometimes more explicit (6:22 = the next day; 7:14 = midfestival; 7:37 = last festival day). The organization of each incident is similar: each begins with an action of Jesus, which leads to a dialogue with someone who misunderstands, and culminates in a monologue by Jesus, who explains the higher significance of what he does. Thus the healing of the invalid (5:1–9) elicits a controversy about Jesus healing on the Sabbath (5:10–18), which in turn becomes a speech by Jesus (5:19–47). A similar pattern is found in the narratives of the feeding of the five thousand (6:1–58), of Jesus at the Feast of Tabernacles (7:1–8:59), and of the healing of the blind man (9:1–10:21). C. H. Dodd, in an excellent discussion of the organization of John, has shown this scheme of action-misunderstanding-monologue to be a characteristic pattern of this Gospel (1953).

The healing of the blind man is remarkably like the healing of the invalid with which this section begins (compare 5:1–15 with 9:1–38). They both involve healing of long-term illnesses, take place in Jerusalem, involve a pool, occur on the Sabbath and cause offense to the Jewish leaders, comment on the relation of sin to sickness, spring from the need and not the faith of the recipient, are misunderstood, and end with lengthy speeches by Jesus. Yet they are different, especially in their portrayals of the response of the one healed. The second story (one might almost say second version of the story) carries us much further than the first. Jesus is vindicated, and the error of his opponents is clear, at least to the reader.

Once again we have a section framed by similar incidents, as Jesus' identity is explored in the context of the great Jewish holy days: Sabbath (5 and 9), Passover (6), Tabernacles (7–8), and Dedication (10:22–42). The reader learns that Jesus is the true bread, the living water, the true light, the good shepherd. The contrast of these symbols with ordinary bread, water, light, and shepherds and Jesus' bold declaration, "You are from the below; I am from the above" (8:23, literal) reveal John's dualistic view of the world.

Reality exists on two levels in John's Gospel, an ordinary reality and another true or good reality. So far, all the action has been directed downward, initiated by the descent of the "Word" into the world (1:14). The action of these first two sections shows the descending Word from above changing the world below—a metaphor of decent. The change is even more dramatic in the next incident, the raising of Lazarus, but the direction of the metaphor begins to reverse, as one from below is raised.

The Lazarus narratives are the climax of Jesus' earlier actions (his ultimate sign) and the foreshadowing of his ensuing suffering (and his own resurrection). It is the last of the signs of glory (compare 11:4 and 2:11) and the dramatic cause of Jesus' own death (11:46–53; 12:17–19). The section closes with a daring and isolated pronouncement of Jesus:

I have come as light into the world . . .
I speak just as the Father has told me. (12:44–50)

The prior narrative has shown the influence of that light on the world below (mostly misunderstanding). Now the story focuses on what Jesus has to say (he enlightens them, we might say; see 1:5, 9–11). He speaks no more to the world but concentrates all his energies on the disciples. Jesus' last meal with his disciples is turned into an occasion for extensive conversation that soon becomes a monologue (chapters 14–17). Dodd made the intriguing suggestion that John here reverses his normal pattern of action-discourse (1953:400). Earlier stories showed Jesus acting and then speaking to explain the action, now he speaks and explains the ensuing story of his death.

The story of Jesus' last days is usually called the **passion narrative**, but in John it would be better called the "departure narrative." It is remarkably like the three other versions we have already encountered: recognizably the same events yet with a distinctive Johannine perspective. It is the strong similarities in the four accounts that convince us that this part of the Jesus tradition was the most fixed and probably the earliest to be told as a connected unit. After retelling the story of Jesus' death and resurrection, John's whole work reaches its climax in a general declaration of its content and purpose:

> *Now Jesus did many other signs in the presence of his disciples, which are not written in this book. But these are written so that you may come to believe that Jesus is the Messiah, the Son of God, and that through believing you may have life in his name (20:30–31)*

This sounds like an ending, but the narrative continues with an additional resurrection appearance and the testimony of the Johannine community to the veracity of the account (chapter 21). This closing testimony balances the opening testimony of the narrator and of John the Baptizer (chapter 1). This balancing is also evident in the other units of John's narrative. We have identified five basic units of John's narrative: the progression from Cana to Cana (2–4), the progression from Sabbath healing to Sabbath healing (5–10), the raising of Lazarus (11–12), the speeches to the disciples (13–17), and the departure narrative (18–20). Actually, these seem to form a chiasmus, a series of concentric circles in the following pattern:

Testimony to the true identity of Jesus 1
   The glory of God revealed in signs.. 2–4
      The union of Jesus with God in action 5–10
         The ultimate sign 11–12
      The union of Jesus with God in Word 13–17
   Jesus is glorified in his death 18–20
Testimony of the community to the truth... 21

But there appears to be an even more basic underlying structure.

THE SHAPE OF JOHN'S STORY

These stages of John's narrative are also encompassed in a larger structural design, already hinted at in the above discussion—a design of descent and ascent. The underlying theme of the action in chapters 1–12 is the descent of the Word into the world (1:9), caught nicely in Jesus' pronouncement: "No one has ascended into heaven except the one who descended from heaven, the Son of Man" (3:13). Then, beginning in chapter 13 when Jesus recognizes that his hour has come, the Gospel reenacts the ascent of Jesus to the Father (13:1), again caught nicely in Jesus' pronouncement: "I came from the Father and have come into the world; again, I am leaving the world and am going to the Father" (16:28). This descent-ascent paradigm provides the basic organizing principle of the story. The actions sketched above are fitted into this structural framework, producing a story in two distinct movements.

The turning point between these two movements is a dramatic pronouncement by Jesus, unattached to any story; it begins:

> *The one believing in me believes not in me but in the one who sent me. And the one seeing me sees the one who sent me. I have come as light into the world. (12:44–50, literal)*

This is both a summary of the narrative to this point and the beginning of a new action. Several important changes occur now.

Jesus' orientation shifts from the world to his immediate followers: he speaks no more to the crowds but privately instructs his disciples (Dodd, 1953:390). His topic also changes. Earlier, Jesus had spoken of light and life; now he speaks of love. (By Dodd's count, the terms *light* and *life* are used eighty-two times in chapters 1–12 but only six times thereafter; *love* is spoken of thirty-one times in chapters 13–17 but only six times earlier; 1953:398.) Also, there are no more signs (miracles) after chapter 12; even the word disappears until the final summary. Finally, and most significantly, what happens in chapters 13–20 corresponds with what happens in chapters 1–12 as answer to question or as fulfillment to promise. Although the signs of 1–12 anticipate what Jesus will do once he is glorified, the substance of 13–20 is his glorification (R. E. Brown, 1966:541). Thus, whereas Jesus had demurred in chapter 2: "My hour has not yet come" (2:4), chapter 13 opens: "Jesus knew that his hour had come."

We recognize, then, that the structural form that underlies John's narrative is like the basic Johannine worldview: a **dualism**. It is a going out from the Father (1–12) and a return to the Father (13–20)—a descent and an ascent. We may be tempted to view these as two antithetical movements, but their relationship is more subtle. Each contains a basic irony. The glory of Jesus is both manifested and hidden in his signs, and his ultimate glorification and return to the Father is his crucifixion.

The first movement of the book is concerned with signs. Narrowly defined, these **signs** are mighty works, miracles, that have the power to reveal God in Jesus. That is, they function as revelations no less than the discourses of the second movement. They reveal Jesus' glory (2:11) but only to those with eyes to see it (6:26). The second movement of the book is concerned with the fulfillment of these signs, the coming of the hour that at first was only signified in the giving of wine. The ironic enthronement of Jesus (19:19–22) fulfills his promise to be "lifted up" (3:14); it is his exaltation (17:1).

These two movements shape the plot, as stated explicitly in the prologue:

> *He came to what was his own, and his own people did not accept him. But to all who received him . . . he gave power to become children of God. (1:11–12)*

Each incident in the story is linked to the others by this simple dynamic: Who sees the significance of the sign? Who receives this Word? Let us examine these two movements in greater detail.

Coming Down from the Father (1–12)

Testimony to the true identity of Jesus   1
    Narrator—the Baptizer—the disciples
Glory of Jesus revealed in signs from Cana to Cana   2–4
    Wedding at Cana: first sign
    Sign of the Temple cleansing
    Dialogue with Nicodemus: being born from above
    Controversy with John: the One from above
    Dialogue with the woman: living water, true worship
    Healing at Cana: second sign
Union of Jesus with the Father: Sabbath healing   5–10

Event	Controversy	Explanation by Jesus
Healing in Jerusalem	With the Jews	As the Father so the Son
Sign of bread	With the crowd	True bread from heaven
Teaching at the Feast of Tabernacles	With the Jews	Water and light from above
Healing in Jerusalem	With the Pharisees	Good shepherd gives his life; I and the Father are one

The Ultimate Sign: Death and Resurrection 11–12

Story of Lazarus: Jesus as life; one should die for the people
    Approach of Passover
    Anointing of Jesus
    World drawn to Jesus
    Jesus' pronouncement

Going Up to the Father 13–21

Jesus talks with his disciples 13–17
    Supper and service
    Jesus explains his glory
    Jesus prays for glory
Jesus performs his work 18–20
    Arrest
    Trials of Jesus and Peter
    Death of Jesus
    Appearances of the resurrected Jesus
Testimony of the community 21

THE DESCENT: THE WORD BECAME FLESH

Mark begins directly with a dramatic incident that immediately involves the reader in the action. Luke, after a short preface, also begins with a narrative event. Matthew starts with a genealogy, though that also has a dramatic effect as an interpretation of Israel's history. John does not open with a narrative incident of any kind. He starts outside historical time and space: "In the beginning."

THE PROLOGUE AS A LITERARY DEVICE

This opening section of John's Gospel (usually called the *prologue*) is unlike anything we have encountered in the Gospels so far.

READING AND REFLECTION

Read John 1:1–18 aloud.

1. What is the main theme of the passage?
2. What attributes and activities are portrayed for the Word?

This prologue is sometimes called a *hymn*, but it is very different from the Psalm-like hymns of Luke 1–2: it is abstract, philosophical, esoteric. Because the material about John the Baptizer (verses 6–8 and 15) interrupts the flow of the main declaration about the Word, most scholars think it was inserted sometime after the poem had been composed. (Some translations even put verse 15 in parentheses.) Before discussing the ideas of the prologue, we should first think about its literary significance: What does it do to John's story to begin with this prologue?

The primary literary effect of the prologue is to change what the story is perceived to be about. By setting the story of Jesus in the context of the descent of the Word, John fundamentally alters the audience's perception of the story. We know from the beginning that this is no story of a Galilean peasant prophet; this is the story of the Word made manifest in the life of such a prophet. There is an implicit challenge to the reader: Will you be able to see the story of the Word within the story of Jesus? Thus the prologue also functions to instruct the reader.

This secondary literary effect of the prologue creates distance between the reader and the narrative; it inserts an interpretive overlay between the audience and the action. The effect is similar to that of *allegorization*, in which an author first tells the reader the real significance and identity of the characters and action that follow. The closest analogy in the synoptic Gospels is Matthew's use of the speeches to interpret the actions of Jesus. The use of such material by Matthew and John represents a move away from the immediacy and drama of art toward the rational reflection of philosophy and theology. Yet John remains an imaginative work that skillfully interweaves narrative, dialogue, monologue, and a narrator's point of view into a readable unity.

We experience both these effects in the prologue itself. The juxtaposition of abstract philosophical generalizations about the Word and concrete historical references to John the Baptizer (1:6–8) both distances us from John (contrast Mark's immediacy) and lures us to see John's story as part of the story of the Word. This juxtaposition of the eternal and the historical exposes a basic paradox of this Gospel: by its very approach it is *ahistorical* (that is, philosophical or theological; concerned with things outside space and time, things that happened "in the beginning"). At the same time, however, John is telling a historical story about historical persons. John's story, paradoxical at its very heart, is guided by the basic idea that the timeless entered time, the Word became flesh (1:14–18).

All historical literature exists in the tension between history and literature. Literature by its nature refers only to itself, not to external events. Gospels are literature about actual events. (This conflict between the demands of literature and history will be explored more fully in Chapter 14.) John's prologue sets this tension in the starkest terms. John's strategy for resolving the tension between ultimate and historical realities is to construct a story on two levels, which we may call the *"apparent* reality" of the visible, tangible world and the *"true* reality" of the unseen world. John even designates these levels with names: the below and the above (8:23). If these two worlds were perfectly congruent, the literary form would be allegory. But for John the two are anything but congruent or harmonious; they are nearly the opposite. In John there is a paradoxical relation between these two worlds, and the literary form is irony.

THE IRONY OF IT ALL

Like all important concepts, **irony** means different things to different people. It is a form of comparison—an implied comparison, never stated. Irony forces the hearer or reader to consider a relationship between two dissimilar things. Were someone to say to you, "a fine friend you are," you would be forced to compare your action with that expected from a friend and—if the words were meant ironically—see your failure as a friend. We may regard such sarcasm as an elementary form of irony, where the speaker says one thing but the hearer knows that the meaning is the opposite.

Literary studies often distinguish two forms of irony: verbal and dramatic. *Verbal irony* is expressed through the use of sarcasm, double entendre, and ambiguity, when the real meaning of the words contrasts with (and usually destroys) their literal meaning. John's Gospel has examples of verbal irony that range from simple verbal ambiguities (such as 3:3–10, where "born anew" can mean both born again or born from above; 4:10–15, where "living" water means also simply flowing water; 7:8, where "going up" to Jerusalem may refer to a simple journey or to Jesus' ascending to the Father [see 20:17 and 12:23]) to profound interpretations of the meanings of Jesus' death (such as the "prophecy" of Caiaphas in 11:50–51 and the sign on the cross in 19:19–22).

Dramatic irony concerns the plot; it is a situational irony in which the action portrayed forces the reader or hearer to understand the opposite of what is being portrayed. The real meaning is the tragic reverse of what the participants think. Dramatic irony was a common device in Greek tragedy. Thus, for example, Oedipus accuses the blind prophet of corruption, when in fact it is he who is blind and corrupt, having unknowingly killed his father and married his mother. We see him pronounce a curse on the murderer and pledge to avenge the dead king "as if he were my father," all the while knowing what he does not know: that the king was his father and that he had killed him (Sophocles, *Oedipus the King*). Although Oedipus imagines that when he discovers the identity of the murderer all will be well in his land, the tragic opposite is true. Most of the irony of Oedipus turns on the audience's knowing what Oedipus does not, the identity of his parents. So too, in John's Gospel the irony depends on the hearers' knowing the true identity of Jesus, the Word from the above.

Such situational irony pervades John's Gospel, especially the portrayal of Jesus' death, which really means the opposite of what it appears. And the irony of the release of Barabbas, who *was* an insurrectionist, while Jesus is crucified on a similar charge, has not escaped John's notice (18:39–40). Eventually we will see that nearly every incident in John has an ironic dimension. At the risk of overgeneralizing, we may say that John writes in an ironic mode.

In his somewhat overcomplicated theory of literary modes, Northrop Frye describes the ironic mode of thematic poets (such as T. S. Eliot, Virginia Woolf, and Ezra Pound) as a "sense of contrast between the course of a whole civilization and the tiny flashes of significant moments which reveal its meaning" (1957:61). Without wishing to press the formula too literally, I suggest John is doing something similar. Consider, for example, John's use of the story of the cleansing of the Temple. (Compare John 2:13–25 with Mark 11:15–19, 27–33; *SFG* §24–26.) John saw in this "tiny flash" a far more profound meaning than any of the earlier writers. He saw an indication of Jesus' own death and resurrection (2:21). Such scenes with double meanings permeate this Gospel, though they are not always so clearly delineated.

A correlative theme of this irony and double meaning is the misunderstanding of Jesus by persons in the story, such as Nicodemus in chapter 3. In part, at least, such misunderstanding is a deliberate literary device. It allows the author to have Jesus explain his meaning, hence the long speeches. All this (speeches, misunderstanding, irony) follows directly from the worldview of the prologue.

THE SHAPE OF JOHN'S UNIVERSE

Translating the prologue from Greek into English is one of the most difficult tasks to confront an interpreter of John. This difficulty arises from several causes, the most basic of which is that John is talking about things for which we have no English equivalents. Thus the dominant concept of this prologue is that of the **logos**, usually translated as "Word":

> *In the beginning was the Word [logos] and the Word was with God and the Word was God.*

But *logos* means far more than the English term *word*; it can be used for any part of the process of communication or for the total act of communicating. It can mean a word, a saying, a statement, a speech, a conversation, a story, language itself, the process of communication, or reason as the presupposition of communication. We simply have no English equivalent—not even an adequate paraphrase. So it seems best to leave the word untranslated and force the reader to confront its alien character. A number of other ambiguities are evident in the prologue, which any good translation will seek to resolve. But part of John's effect stems from his lack of clarity. What follows, then, is not a good translation but a rather literal transposition into English, trying to preserve some of the (intentional) ambiguity of the original. You would do well to compare it with several of the standard English translations.

> *When things began the Logos was; the Logos was with God; and as God was the Logos. That one was with God when things began. All things through that one came into being; and without that one nothing came into being; that which had come into being in that one was life and the life was the light of humanity. And the light shines in the darkness and the darkness has not*

mastered it. It was the perfect light, enlightening all humanity, coming into the world. In the world it was and the world came into being through it and the world knew it not. To that akin to it it came and the kin were not receptive; but as many as received it to them it bestowed the prerogative to become children of God, to the ones trusting in the name of that one, the ones who, not from blood, nor from the desire of the flesh, nor from the desire of a man, but from God were born. And the Logos became flesh and pitched a tent among us, and we marveled at the glory of that one, glory as of a father's only child, full of grace and perfection. Out of the fullness of that one we all received, grace against grace. The Law through Moses was given; grace and perfection through Jesus Christ came into being. (John 1:1–5, 9–14, 16–18, literal)

The poem (if such it be) remains somewhat obscure to us, in part because we lack a sufficient context within which to interpret it. To begin with, we must ask in what context a first-century hearer was likely to understand the meaning of *logos*. But it is not quite that simple, for *logos* was used in a variety of contexts, three of which deserve special consideration. (For studies on *logos*, see the resource section at the end of this chapter.)

Logos as Torah

Greek-speaking Jews were familiar with the expression the *logos of God* as a way of referring to their Scriptures, for the **Septuagint** (the Greek translation of the Hebrew Scriptures) regularly used *logos* rather than its synonym *rhema* in phrases such as the *word of God*. Logos would thus imply revelation and would be equivalent to the Torah, God's instruction (Psalm 119). God's logos was the Law but also the divine word that came to the prophets—the same word by which God had created the world ("And God *said* let there be . . ."). Much of what John says about the logos makes perfectly good sense within this context. Reread the prologue above, imagining that the reader understood *logos* to be the divine revelation, the word of God.

Logos as Reason

Among Greeks *logos* had become the common philosophical term for that all-pervading order that underlies the universe (called variously *nature, providence, destiny,* or *God*). **Stoics**, beginning with Zeno (died about 263 BCE), taught that the stories about the Gods were really talking about this force of nature:

> *The General Law, which is Right Reason (Logos), pervading everything is the same as Zeus, the Supreme Head of the government of the universe. (Fragment 162; found in Barrett, 1971a:62)*

This move to identify God with reason was successful in part because educated people in late antiquity had grown uncomfortable with the Gods of Greek mythology. Zeus' penchant for seducing young maidens was hardly the sort of thing to inspire awe, yet by the Stoic reinterpretation even such antics were redeemed. If Zeus is now reason, perhaps the maiden is our human understanding, which is to be seduced and made pliant to the will of reason. Thus, by allegorization Stoicism transcended and rescued mythological religion for many. A prime example of this transformation is the widely quoted *Hymn to Zeus* by Cleanthes, which begins: "Thou, O Zeus, art praised above all gods" and includes the line "we are thy offspring," a version of which Luke has Paul quote at Acts 17:28. The hymn has been published in a number of works, including Barrett (1971a:63) and Grant (1953:152).

Further, we can know this reason/logos, because, like the universe, humans possess logos/reason. "The Nature of the Universe ought to be apprehended by Reason [Logos], which is akin to it" (Posidonius, a Stoic thinker of the first century BCE; quoted in Barrett, 1961a:65). Stoic purpose was to know reason/logos and to live in accord with it. "You are," says Epictetus, the great Stoic philosopher, "a principal work, a fragment of God himself; you have in yourself a part of him [the logos]" (*Discourses* 2.8.9–14). Stoic philosophy was not an academic exercise in John's time; it was a very aggressive popular movement advocated by wandering philosophers in the marketplace. Thus, we may presume that John's audience had already heard that they must live in accord with logos, believed to be both an expression of the divine will and even of divinity itself. (Reread 1:1–18, noting how the meaning changes when we imagine a Stoic context.)

Logos as Wisdom

There were three great intellectual movements in ancient Israel, each with its own class of leaders: priests, prophets, and sages (for example, Jer. 18:18). These sages, or teachers, were concerned with **wisdom**, a wisdom derived from close observation of daily life. The classic text of the wisdom tradition is the book of Proverbs (see Proverbs 6, for example, where wisdom about living is derived from watching an anthill). But these sages understood themselves not to be inventing wisdom but to be *discovering* it; thus, wisdom existed prior to their discovery. One of the grandest statements of this notion of preexisting wisdom is found in Proverbs 8, where wisdom is envisioned as God's coworker:

> I, wisdom, live with prudence, and I attain knowledge and discretion. . . .
> By me kings reign, and rulers decree what is just. . . . I love those who love me, and those who seek me diligently find me. . . .
> The LORD created me at the beginning of his work, the first of his acts of long ago. . . . [T]hen I was beside him, like a master worker; and I was daily his delight, rejoicing before him always. (Prov. 8:12, 15–17, 22–30)

Wisdom is here exalted to near-divine status as metaphor passes into mythology. A later work in this tradition, commonly known as Sirach (also as Ecclesiasticus) described wisdom thus:

> I came forth from the mouth of the most high and covered the earth like a mist. I dwelt in high places. . . . In every people and nation I have gotten a possession. Among all these I sought a resting place; I sought in whose territory I might lodge. Then the Creator of all things . . . said, "Make your dwelling in Jacob, and in Israel receive your inheritance." (Sir. 24:3–8)

This theme of homeless wisdom is most poignantly portrayed in *1 Enoch*:

> *Wisdom could not find a place in which she could dwell; but a place was found (for her) in the heavens. Then Wisdom went out to dwell with the children of the people, but she found no dwelling place. (So) Wisdom returned to her place, and she settled permanently among the angels. Then Iniquity went out from her rooms, and found whom she did not expect. And she dwelt with them, like rain in a desert like dew on a thirsty land. (42; quoted from Charlesworth, 1983:1:33)*

John seems to use similar ideas, though he speaks of Logos rather than Wisdom. Whether he made that change himself or drew on an earlier tradition is not certain. We do, however, see a similar shift in an earlier Jewish writer, **Philo** of Alexandria (c. 20 BCE–45 CE). Alexandria had replaced Athens as the intellectual center of the Greco-Roman world. It was a huge city with a strong and vital Jewish community, and the Septuagint was probably translated there. Alexandria also witnessed a lively interaction between Jewish and Greek thought: the primary Greek influences were Stoicism and Platonism; the main Jewish influence was from the wisdom movement.

For our purposes, Philo achieved two significant things with the wisdom concept. First, he developed it further so that wisdom actually appears as a separate identity, an intermediary between God and humanity. And second, he did not refer to it with the feminine name *wisdom* (*sophia* in Greek) but used the masculine term *reason* (*logos*), which, as we saw above, the Septuagint had used for divine revelation. (Notice the ambiguity of a declaration like Ps. 118:89, "Forever, O Lord, your logos [word, wisdom] is firmly fixed in the heavens.") Philo was able to accept much that the Stoics taught about logos but believed they erred in identifying logos with God; instead, logos proceeds from God and is God's revelation (see Dodd, 1953:54–73).

Thus, Philo could write that all should "endeavor to know the Self-existent [God] or, if they cannot, at least to see Its image, the most sacred logos" (*On the Confusion of Languages* 97). And in another place he declares, "For the logos is the God of us imperfect men, but the Primal God is the God of the wise and perfect" (*Allegorical Interpretations* 3.207). This logos is God's agent in creation and God's chief messenger:

> *To his Logos, his chief messenger [angelos], highest in age and honour, the Father of all has given the special prerogative, to stand on the border and separate the creature from the Creator. This same Logos both pleads with the immortal as suppliant for afflicted mortality and acts as ambassador of the ruler to the subject. . . . [He is] neither uncreated as God, nor created as you, but midway between the two extremes, a surety to both sides. (Who Is the Heir of Divine Things? 205–6, Colson and Whitaker translation)*

Readers familiar with Philo's thought would have no trouble understanding and would surely approve of what John said in this prologue: the creative power and divine status of the Logos, its enlightening function, its being in but not accepted by the world, all this was shared. (For more on Philo, see pages 229–31.) Now reread the prologue, imagining all three contexts.

One point of the prologue is not explained by these contexts. Although they all imagine that the Logos comes to the world, a world truly its own, accepted only by the few, yet only John dared draw the momentous conclusion:

And the Logos became flesh and pitched a tent among us. (1:14, literal)

And that is why John wrote a Gospel rather than a philosophical essay. He intended to show the outworking of this incarnation of the Logos by telling his story. As we might expect, the life of this Logos-become-flesh will be extraordinary, and remarkable things will occur in it.

AND WE BEHELD HIS GLORY

John recounts fewer miracles than the other Gospels, but there is something unusual about them. They are sometimes called *more miraculous*, an impossible expression that nonetheless captures the phenomenon. In John, the miracles of Jesus are spectacular: he turns water into wine (2:1–11), heals a boy "at the point of death" (4:46–54), heals a man "ill for thirty-eight years" (5:29), feeds five thousand with five loaves and two fish (6:1–14), walks on the sea (6:16–21), heals a man "blind from birth" (9:1–12), and raises Lazarus from the dead (11:1–44). It would be difficult to imagine more awesome events.

Yet John never calls them *miracles* or even *wondrous works*. They are always "signs." *Sign* is an ambiguous word. It was a synonym for *miracle*, but it could have another, deeper meaning. John used the term sparingly, but it is a key term in his conclusion (20:30–31), and he used it in connection with each miracle except the one in chapter 5 (2:11, 23; 4:48, 54; 6:14, 26; 9:16; 11:47; 12:18, 37; no further reference until 20:30–31). Curiously, in chapter 5 he explains why the miracles are "signs."

Being challenged for healing on the Sabbath, Jesus replies, "My Father is working still, and I am working" (5:17). This response is probably part of a larger Jewish argument about God and the Sabbath. For although the biblical tradition that God rested on the Sabbath was clear, Jewish scholars were reasonably sure that God never took a day off. Births occurred on the Sabbath; people died on the Sabbath. Surely these were works that only God could do. John's Jesus adopts this conclusion and applies it in a new way: because Jesus is the One from above who does the works of God, he too works on the Sabbath. In fact, he works on the Sabbath precisely because he does the work of God (5:19–47).

This is ironic, because working on the Sabbath was generally considered a sign of low spiritual aspiration. John declares that Jesus' Sabbath cure is just the opposite: a sign revealing his union with God. The meaning of these signs is not easy to grasp because we look at them "from below," as this Gospel would say. We confuse the event with its meaning. John expects the reader to be able to do more.

Consider the sign of Jesus feeding the five thousand. The people are so impressed that they want to make Jesus king. Nothing could better demonstrate that they failed to grasp the sign. When they eventually approach Jesus with the ironic question: "When did you come here?" he responds, "Very truly, I tell you, you are looking for me, not because you saw signs, but because you ate your fill of the loaves" (6:26). Yet how could they not have seen the sign? It was not, as a student once suggested, because they were in the back of the crowd. They saw the miracle; they did not see the sign. They did not realize that it signified something quite beyond ordinary food. John reveals this with a very clever maneuver. Still thinking of food, the crowd recalls the Exodus story when the people ate manna in the wilderness (Exodus 16). They knew that this was expected to occur again in the last days, when a new Moses would arise. Jesus challenges their reading of the text. They read: "He [Moses] gave them bread from Heaven" (John 6:31). Jesus shifted both the subject and the verb. Because Hebrew was written without vowels, it can often be read in more than one way. Later rabbis would delight in finding new meanings in old texts by supplying unexpected vowels. So Jesus says the text should be read, "He [God] gives them bread from Heaven" (6:32). That bread from heaven is "true bread." It is Jesus himself. That is the significance of the sign (Borgen, 1963).

Simply put, the sign reveals that Jesus is doing the work of God (or, more precisely, the work of the creative Logos *through* whom God created all things, 1:3). God multiplies the loaves every year in the harvest; God produces wine from water; God heals. For John the performance of these deeds should evoke faith not because they are spectacular but because they are significant. To the one who can see (like the blind man in chapter 9) they reveal the wisdom of God. We are expected to understand more than the characters in the story. When the crowds ask Jesus when he came here, they are puzzled only about how he got to the other side of the lake after the last boat left without him. But in John's ironic fashion that is the real question. The reader who understands the prologue knows the true answer.

John is fond of such irony. The story in chapter 9 is laden with it, often to humorous effect.

READING AND REFLECTION

Read the story of the healing of the man born blind in John 9 and 10. Why do the Jewish leaders reject Jesus? What examples of irony or sarcasm do you find?

The Jewish leaders had rejected Jesus because he was from Nazareth (7:41; a problem also faced by Matthew and Luke). But instead of using the Bethlehem tradition, John found an alternative one more suited to his purpose; he used a tradition about the hidden origin of the Messiah (7:27). Then, in chapter 9, he shows the Jewish leaders making just this confession about Jesus: they do not know where he comes from (9:29). How ironic, for they really do not know. They do not see the sign.

The final sign of Jesus is the climax of the signs, the ultimate work of God, and a sign of things to come. The ultimate work of God is to give life, and in chapter 11 Jesus raises Lazarus from the dead. This complex story is well worth our close study. It opens as Jesus is informed of Lazarus's illness. On one level, Jesus' response seems to be insensitive or even cruel: "But when Jesus heard it, he said, 'This illness does not lead to death; rather it is for God's glory, so that the Son of God may be glorified through it.' " (11:4). Is Jesus saying that God would kill someone just so Jesus could be glorified by raising him up? Is this a publicity stunt? If the reader asks such a question he or she has progressed no further than Nicodemus (3:4). To see the sign of Lazarus the reader must understand that in John's scheme of things the Lazarus incident leads directly to Jesus' death (11:47–53) and that his death is his glorification (12:23). In a symbolic way Lazarus's death and resurrection are Jesus' death and resurrection; it is "for the glory of God."

On this note the first movement of John's story, the descent, is complete. The Logos has become flesh and manifested the glory of God (1:14, 18). The reader must now witness his reascent to the Father.

THE ASCENT: THE HOUR HAS COME

One major purpose of this first movement of John's Gospel has been to teach the reader how to read the story, how to see the signs. Jesus performs the works of God (5:30; 14:8–11). This is the descent of Logos into the world. Now the hour has come for the ascent (13:1). In the rest of the narrative, there are no more signs in the sense of miracles. Yet all Jesus does and says is sign. Jesus' whole action becomes a visible presentation of his true nature and glory (2:11). The writer has now set the stage for us to encounter the familiar events surrounding Jesus' death, which John characterizes as his hour "to depart from the world and return to the Father" (13:1).

THE EVENTS BEFORE THE DEPARTURE

Perhaps the most striking thing about Jesus' last meal with his disciples in this Gospel is that there is no Last Supper, no eucharistic meal (13:1–30). The scene is familiar from the synoptic Gospels: there is the final gathering on the night before the arrest; Judas is revealed as the betrayer (as in Luke, Satan entered him; Luke 22:3 = John 13:27); they eat together. But novelties appear (a foot-washing ceremony); familiar events disappear (no agony in Gethsemane); there are special Johannine touches ("He immediately went out, and it was night," 13:30; see 1:5; 9:4; 11:10; note also 20:1).

The omission of the Last Supper is variously explained. A daring school of interpretation believes John is deliberately antisacramental (recall that there was no baptism scene either). Those who argue this way must see certain passages as later additions (such as 3:5; 6:51–58), and, as Robert Kysar recognizes, ignore a basic aspect of John's thought: that faith may be mediated through sensory experience (1976:109). Though radical, such a view must be given serious consideration in light of John's general divergence from the synoptic tradition.

Another attempt to explain the omission of the eucharistic meal derives from the differences in chronology in John and the synoptics. All four Gospels connect Jesus' death to the Passover festival, a spring ritual that commemorated the exodus from slavery in Egypt, a festival of freedom. A central aspect of the festival involved the killing of a lamb in the afternoon, which would be eaten at an evening communal meal involving at least ten people. In John, Jesus dies in the afternoon of the day of preparation, at about the time the Passover lambs were slain in preparation for the evening meal (John 19:31). In the synoptics, Jesus eats the Passover meal with his disciples and is executed the next day, which by Jewish reckoning would be Passover day (see Mark 14:12 and parallels; GP §234, SFG §308). However, Mark also reports that Jesus died on "the day of preparation" (15:42). Let us deal first with the historical and then consider the literary issue.

Some of the confusion, but certainly not all, may stem from different ways of relating days to nights. Ancient practice varied widely. Pliny the Elder noted:

> The Babylonians count the period between two sunrises, the Athenians that between two sunsets, the Umbrians from midday to midday, the common people everywhere from dawn to dark, the Roman priests and the authorities who fixed the official day, and also the Egyptians and Hipparchus, the period from midnight to midnight. (Natural History 2.79.181)

The official practice in Israel was like the Greek, counting from sundown to sundown: the evening is connected with the following daylight rather than the preceding daylight. Thus, what we call Monday night would, by Jewish and Greek standards, be Tuesday night (the night that goes with Tuesday). Similarly, Passover evening would be what we would normally call the evening of the day before, rather like our Christmas Eve. This may account for some of the confusion in the texts, for Mark probably followed a Roman system (in 11:11–12 he seems to regard evening and morning as representing two separate days; compare Matt. 21:17–18). In the Roman system, "Passover evening" would imply the evening *after* Passover day, whereas under the Jewish system it would mean the evening *before* Passover day.

The historical question then becomes: Did Jesus die on the day before Passover or on Passover day itself? If Jesus died on the day before Passover, as in John, and the next day was both Passover and Sabbath (Saturday), then he would have been crucified in either the year 30 or 33, because in those years the two holy days coincided. If Jesus died on Passover day and the next day was Sabbath (Saturday), as in the synoptics, Jesus was crucified in 27, a year in which Passover fell on a Friday. You can see these possibilities in Table 12.1.

This leads us to the literary issue: How does this chronology influence the way John told his story? Clearly, if Jesus died before Passover eve, he could not have eaten the Passover meal with his disciples because it was eaten that night. Consequently, John could not portray the Last Supper in its synoptic form. This would not mean that John's community did not celebrate the Eucharist (Communion). Jesus' death, understood as the death of the Passover lamb (1:29), would naturally point

TABLE 12.1	CHRONOLOGIES OF JESUS' DEATH	
	John	*Synoptics*
Day of Jesus' Death	Day before Passover	Passover day
Next day	Passover and Sabbath	Sabbath
Day of Passover	Saturday	Friday
Years when Passover came on this day	30 or 33	27
Symbolism	Jesus dies with Passover lambs	Jesus becomes the Passover meal

to a commemoration of that death in a Passover meal. Yet this would raise the serious question of whether it would then be possible for John's church to celebrate the Eucharist in anything like the Pauline form (see 1 Cor. 11:23–26).

A third explanation argues that sacramental teaching permeates the whole Gospel but that John does not portray the sacramental acts themselves because he "will not divulge the Christian 'mystery' " (Dodd, 1953:393 n. 1). As we learned earlier, the mystery religions were powerful and popular religious movements in John's day, and each centered on some secret ritual, often involving bread, wine, and blood (pages 118, 205). We know from other sources that the unbaptized (that is, the uninitiated) were not allowed to witness the Eucharist in some circles (for example, *Didache* 9:5 in *Apostolic Fathers*). Perhaps John hides the central rituals because they are too sacred to share with the uninitiated. Although the rituals are not portrayed, wine and bread are certainly strong symbols in the Gospel: 2:1–11; 15:1–11; 6:32–40; 51–59; 19:34 (R. E. Brown, 1966:cxiv).

We should notice how the same observation that neither the baptism nor the Last Supper is portrayed in John can lead to two opposite conclusions: John is antisacramental; John is wholly sacramental. This problem does not lend itself to a clear solution. Whether we regard John as sacramental or antisacramental (or something in between) depends on larger questions of interpretation, such as how we understand the meaning of the signs and, especially, how we understand the meaning of Jesus' death. For that too John seeks to instruct us.

The Words before the Departure

Nowhere is John's divergence from the synoptic tradition more radical than in chapters 14–17. Nothing like this exists in the synoptics; the final apocalyptic speech (Mark 13 and parallels; *GP* §214–22, *SFG* §287–94) is only a remote reflection of a similar idea: the farewell words of Jesus. But in both form and content John's speeches are unique.

READING AND REFLECTION
Read John 13:31–17:26 and try to answer the following questions.

1. In his final hours with the disciples in the synoptics, Jesus addressed such concerns as the betrayal, the denial of Peter, the coming persecution, the need for service, and his return to them. Which of these themes are addressed here?
2. The events discussed here are future from the viewpoint of Jesus in the story. Are they also future from the viewpoint of the narrator?
3. What is the Spirit called, and what is it said to do?

We can readily demonstrate that these speeches are not historical in any simple sense, especially if we consider the synoptic Gospels as historically grounded (for example, Schnackenburg, 1968:21–22). These ideas belong to a different thought world, and it is the world of the author, for we encounter the same ideas and even the same vocabulary in the remarks of the narrator. (The prologue, for example, reveals an identical worldview.) Even more revealing, it is the same thought world seen in the letter we know as **1 John**. Our author has not merely replayed the historical record, he has transposed the sayings and actions of Jesus into a new key; he has given us a new interpretation. This is, of course, also true of the synoptics but less radically, in a way that long remained undetected. Whether John's interpretation is a legitimate one depends on several factors, including what is meant by *legitimate*.

John chose a new means of interpretation. Whereas Matthew created speeches for Jesus by combining units of tradition into new patterns, John developed single ideas into long discourses. Most agree that these exact words were not spoken on the night before his death, but there is no consensus on whether the words spoken then are truly represented here. John and his community claim that they never truly understood Jesus until after his death, when they experienced his resurrection presence; as Dodd correctly asserts, these speeches would be more appropriate coming from the resurrected Jesus (1953:397). John apparently is not prepared to provide speeches for the resurrected Jesus, although later writers will (The *Gospel of Thomas*, for example, consists of sayings of the "living" Jesus to Thomas; see Hennecke and Schneemelcher, 1991:1:117–29 or the online translation at http://home .epix.net/~miser17/Thomas.html.)

But John's contention from the beginning has been that, for those who have eyes to see it, the real significance of Jesus' words and deeds is that he comes from above. The bare deeds themselves are meaningless, unless one sees the "sign" (6:26). We might say that these speeches are no less historical than the cleansing of the Temple. The event itself is probable, but John's interpretation is a claim that it means something specific. Certainly, Jesus said some things privately to his disciples. Dodd shows that the basic themes of these discourses are the same as those found in the synoptic tradition (1953:390–99). Common to both are teachings on the disciples' mission, precepts for living in community, warnings of persecution, promises of assistance and of the Spirit, and predictions of death. Yet what John actually tells us about those themes diverges greatly from the synoptics because he is interpreting Jesus for his own community—he narrates the meaning of these words rather than merely repeating what Jesus said.

John undertakes such revisionist history confidently, as he explains in these speeches. Jesus' word is like a seed planted in the believer; it grows and bears fruit (15:3–7). More importantly, John's community knows the presence of the Spirit, who reminds believers of what Jesus taught (14:26) and leads them into all truth (16:13). He has shown earlier that the proper understanding of events was remembered only after Jesus' resurrection (2:22; 12:22–26). Now he speaks for Jesus just as Jesus spoke for God (16:14; 14:10), or perhaps more accurately "the risen Christ speaks through the evangelist [Gospel writer]" (Cullmann, 1976:18). Thus, John shows Jesus speaking of the one who has ascended into heaven (3:13), introducing his own words and concepts into the time of Jesus. Only the scale is different, for we saw similar things in the synoptics. An abiding feature of the gospel form is its blend of past and present. The Gospels not only tell us what Jesus said to his disciples, they also relate what their authors believed Jesus was saying to their own communities.

One such revision is in an area we have been watching develop since Mark: the tension between the present and the future experience of God's kingdom (although *kingdom of God* is not an expression that John uses much; it occurs only at 3:3, 5). To appreciate what John does here it is helpful to recall the story of Lazarus. When

Jesus tells Martha, "Your brother will rise again," she replies, "I know that he will rise again in the resurrection at the last day." But Jesus declares:

> *I am the resurrection and the life. Those who believe in me, even though they die, will live, and everyone who lives and believes in me will never die.* (11:25–26)

Here Jesus shifts attention from a future orientation to a present orientation (Kysar, 1976:88). This is typical of the view of life expressed in these discourses and probably represents John's basic contribution (see 20:31, noting its emphasis on the present).

It will be helpful at this point to consider a few definitions widely used in writing about last things (**eschatology**). *Futurist eschatology* is used to refer to a conception of the kingdom of God and related events as entirely or essentially in the future. *Realized eschatology* refers to an understanding of the present as the time of fulfillment. In a fully realized eschatology there is no future element. *Inaugurated eschatology* is used to express the belief that although the kingdom of God has already begun to appear, it is not yet fully realized. This idea involves a future expectation. The synoptic Gospels present an inaugurated eschatology. Which viewpoint does John represent?

Clearly, a few references appear to envision a future fulfillment: 6:40; 12:48; 14:3, 18, 28; 20:17. Apparently, however, these future elements are not very important to John. His casual way of handling them (for example, it is not always clear whether by "coming again" he means the second coming or the resurrection; see 16:16–24) and their relative scarcity in the text indicate that the balance has shifted dramatically from the imminent expectation of the end (as in Paul and probably Mark) to the present life of the believer. John stops just short of the gnosticizing interpretation that Paul challenged at Corinth (1 Corinthians 15; see also pages 134–38); the present does not wholly swallow up the future. Clearly, however, those Corinthians would be very pleased with much that John teaches (Pagels, 1973). In John's view, eternal life is something one has now (17:3).

This is not so much a contradiction of the synoptic view as it is a novel approach. The synoptics, and Jewish tradition generally, approach the kingdom with what we may call a *horizontal metaphor*: the kingdom stands out ahead of them, beckoning them forward. John understands life with a *vertical metaphor*: the kingdom exists in a world above this one and descends.

The final prayer of Jesus with which John ends this section fulfills several functions. It summarizes and concentrates many of the important ideas of the book (Käsemann, 1968), and carefully explains the meaning of Jesus' coming death as the Son of the Father. It also completes the final metaphor of ascent (17:11) and represents Jesus offering himself to the Father, an offering actualized and accepted in the death of Jesus, which follows (see Dodd, 1953:420–23). It should be read carefully.

FINISHING HIS DEPARTURE

Although it is unlikely that John used any of the synoptics as a source, it is revealing to compare his account with theirs for two reasons: first, because the narrative of Jesus' death is the most fixed part of the Jesus story, we might expect strong similarities even between independent accounts. And, second, John's emphases will generally stand out when compared with other accounts.

READING AND REFLECTION

Read John 18 and 19 and carefully compare selected incidents with the synoptics' accounts, Mark 14:26–15:47 and parallels (the reading begins at *GP* §238, *SFG* §330; revealing incidents include *GP* §239–41, 248–50; *SFG* §330–32, 343–47).

1. List ten specific ways that John's account of the suffering and death of Jesus differs from the other accounts.
2. Try to explain one or two of these differences in terms of what you already know about John's emphases and techniques.

Although the stories surrounding Jesus' death are often called the passion narrative, this is not appropriate for John's version. The word *passion* is from the Latin, meaning "suffering," something that happens to one, something passive. But as John tells the story, this is actually something Jesus does; even Simon of Cyrene is eliminated; Jesus carries his own cross (19:17). The soldiers are powerless to arrest him (18:6); he sets the terms by which they take him (18:8). Jesus is the One from above (18:36; 19:9). He controls his own destiny and pronounces his own judgment on the affair: it is finished (19:30). This act of Jesus is a basic Johannine idea (12:27). The offering of himself to his Father is somehow an essential act—*the* essential act of Jesus (18:37). It represents no defeat; there is no power of darkness here (19:28; contrast Mark 15:33). This is the moment we have been waiting for (2:4), the exaltation of Jesus (3:14–15). Irony.

IS SEEING BELIEVING?

Like everything else in his Gospel, John's account of the resurrection goes its own way (20:1–30). Much here is typical of John, but two aspects deserve our attention. First, John has an alternate tradition regarding the giving of the Holy Spirit (20:22). He wishes to tie the experience of the Spirit directly to the experience of Jesus (see 7:39). Second, John uses the resurrection appearances to further his meditation on the relation between seeing and believing that is basic to his idea of signs.

The scene here is one of the famous scenes in literature. Thomas has missed the first appearance and expresses his doubts: "Unless I see . . ." (20:25). In the very next incident the risen Jesus appears and challenges Thomas to examine him and "not be faithless but believing" (20:27, RSV). Thomas then answers: "My Lord and my God."

What is the meaning of this? How is the reader to respond? John recognized that such evidence was no longer available, for he has Jesus say to Thomas: "Have you believed because you have seen me? Blessed are those who have not seen and yet have come to believe" (20:29). Here John is employing the ultimate irony of his book: no amount of miracles can ever produce faith, yet he recounts a story full of miracles, precisely to produce faith. Like the crowds at the feeding (John 6) one is always in danger of missing the sign—the insight produced by apprehending the meaning of Jesus, which points to faith.

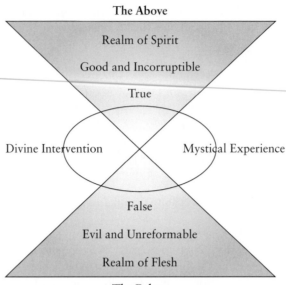

The Above

Realm of Spirit

Good and Incorruptible

True

Divine Intervention   Mystical Experience

False

Evil and Unreformable

Realm of Flesh

The Below

FIGURE 12.1   **GNOSTIC VIEW OF HISTORY**   The Gnostics turned the apocalyptic view of the world on end (compare with Figure 3.2); they did not look for a future transformation of the world but for a transformation of life below through absorption in the world above. For the Gnostic, the human realm, represented by the oval in the figure, involved both the above and the below, both the true and the false. But human nature was spirit and could transcend the flesh by means of mystical experience. They would have agreed with the statement, "You shall know the truth and the truth shall make you free" (John 8:32).

In this sense, everything in John's Gospel hinges on his characterization of Jesus. And the overwhelming trait of that characterization is that Jesus is the One from above. He is, quite literally, beyond us. He transcends the human situation in nearly every way. He is beyond time: "Before Abraham was, I am" (8:58); "In the beginning" (1:1). His existence extends forward into the life of the community after his death, and he will be there at the last day (14:18–19; 5:28–29; 6:39–40). Thus, while John's narrative is occupied with what we may call the life of Jesus, the story time extends both backward and forward to previous and later history, and even beyond history. Some of these themes are implicit in the synoptics, but John has attained a new clarity of expression.

John has quite abandoned the apocalyptic view of history. He no longer stands poised between the past and the future (see the discussion and Figure 3.2 on page 91). In fact, John shares much with the Gnostic view of the world, which emphasizes being (**ontology**) not time (history). We might depict the Gnostic view as in Figure 12.1. Like the Gnostics, John's Jesus is from beyond time.

This "beyondness" of John's Jesus raises acutely the question of his actual humanity. There are no birth stories; Jesus expresses few emotions; he is not surrounded by children; no one ever "touches" him (Culpepper, 1983:106–12). Only the profound assertion of the reality of his "becoming flesh" (1:14) and the reality of his death preserve his human quality. But precisely this other, divine dimension of Jesus points up Jesus' true identity: he is one with the Father (10:30). The question John posed to his hearers was whether they could "see" the real significance of all that Jesus had said and done. Such sight, he maintained, leads to eternal life. Even "those who have not seen" may attain such insight by hearing such a story as John has written (20:30–31).

The disciples clearly attain such insight, at least by the end of this story. They remain somewhat uncomprehending throughout, but only because they have not yet experienced the resurrection and the Spirit. Perhaps the most significant difference from the synoptic versions is that the disciples do not abandon Jesus in Gethsemane (compare Mark 15:50; *GP* §240, *SFG* §331). One of them, at least, stands at the cross and becomes the caretaker of Jesus' mother (20:26–27). This same disciple, sometimes known as the one whom Jesus loved, attains insight within the story, before the resurrected Jesus appears (20:8).

This brief study hardly does justice to this brilliant, witty, and ironic book, which merits many readings. However, we now turn our attention to the kind of community that provided the background for such a work.

THE SITUATION OF JOHN AND HIS COMMUNITY

Much energy has been devoted to the task of deciphering the kind of community to which, and from which, this Gospel is addressed. This scholarly work enables us to consider the likely process by which the Gospel came to be written, the supposed identity of the author, and the social and historical situation it presupposes. We seek to discover the kind of audience the author imagined. Before we turn to the audience, however, we must inquire about the author.

THE COMPOSITION OF THE GOSPEL

Three questions about the author concern us here: Was the writer of this Gospel acquainted with the other Gospels? Was the writer of this Gospel one of Jesus' immediate disciples? What else can be known about our writer from other early writings also connected with the name of John? We will consider them in this order.

Did John know the synoptic Gospels? Outside the narrative of Jesus' death and isolated sayings of Jesus, John shares only eight major incidents with the synoptic Gospels. These do not demonstrate the extensive verbal correlations that existed among the synoptics themselves. For our purposes, Table 12.2 will prove a convenient tool for noting these similarities and differences.

There are only a few verbal correlations between John and either Mark or Luke in these stories; they are relatively insignificant details but the parallels are striking. For example, both Mark and John estimate it would take more than two hundred denarii to buy bread for the five thousand, and they both appraise the perfume used in the anointing at three hundred denarii. In the latter incident both use the unusual expression "perfume made from pure Nard" (John 12:3; Mark 14:3). These, and a few other details, convince some that John knew and drew upon Mark and Luke at least. (Kümmel concluded that such dependence was "indisputable" [1966:144]). But this ignores the real problem: the degree of difference shown in even these stories, which differ in far more details than they agree. We may add to this the number of

TABLE 12.2   INCIDENTS SHARED WITH THE SYNOPTICS

Reference in John	Number in GP and (SFG)	Incident	Degree of Correlation
1:35–51	11–17 (21)	Call of disciples	A variant tradition
2:13–22	200 (25)	Cleansing of Temple	Same action Different words and context
4:46–54	46 (85)	Healing official's son	Same location and action "Son" in John "Child" or "servant" in Matthew "Slave" in Luke
6:1–21	112–13 (146–47)	Feeding five thousand and walking on sea	Same action and sequence Different words and characters (a boy's lunch)
6:66–71	122 (159)	Peter's confession	Different story
12:1–8	232 (267)	Anointing at Bethany	A variant tradition
12:12–19	196 (269)	Entry into Jerusalem	Different portrayal of the event
13:1–30	225 (309–10)	Last Supper	Foot washing replaces meal

incidents that John does not share with the synoptics; some of the most notable of which include:

The wedding at Cana (2:1–11)
The story of Nicodemus (3)
The story of the Samaritan woman (4)
Several long disputes with Jews (for example 5:10–46; 7:25–36; 8:30–59; and so on)
Healing miracles (5:1–9; 9:1–7)
The raising of Lazarus (11:1–44)
The extended farewell discourse (14–16)
The prayer for the disciples (17)

In addition, John omits several important synoptic accounts:

Jesus' temptation (and perhaps his baptism)
Peter's confession of Jesus as the Christ
The transfiguration
The Lord's Supper
The agony in Gethsemane (contrast John 12:27–33)
All Jesus' parables
All the exorcism stories
Numerous healing stories

The situation may be seen in miniature by carefully comparing John with similar synoptic material:

John 3:3	John 3:5	Matt. 18:3	Mark 10:15	Luke 18:17
Truly, truly, I say to you, unless one is born anew, he cannot see the kingdom of God.	Truly, truly, I say to you, unless one is born of water and the Spirit, he cannot enter the kingdom of God.	Truly I say to you, unless you turn and become like children, you will never enter the kingdom of heaven.	Truly I say to you, whoever does not receive the kingdom of God like a child shall not enter it.	Truly, I say to you, whoever does not receive the kingdom of God like a child shall not enter it.

In this example we see that the similarities between the synoptic traditions are great enough to posit a common source or mutual dependence, but the Johannine traditions are probably an independent reporting of what may once have been a common tradition. John has shaped the material to fit his own distinctive worldview and way of speaking. And, it must be added, it is rare for John to share even this much with the synoptic tradition. (I owe the example to Lindars, 1981.)

We must also consider that in the overall portrayal of Jesus there are significant differences in detail. John describes several trips to Jerusalem, with most of the action taking place in Judea in a period of about three years; the synoptics imply only one trip in one year and concentrate on Galilee. Also, the overall mythic pattern is that of the descent of the divine savior into the world, a pattern not found in the synoptics.

In short, it does not seem safe to presume that John relied on any of the synoptic Gospels. John represents a separate tradition, or rather a separate preservation of the same tradition. This would explain the presence of similar stories and even similar sequences (especially in the narrative of Jesus' death) told differently, in different words and with varying emphases. Perhaps the few verbal correlations represent points at which the traditions had contact in the period of oral transmission, as Raymond E. Brown suggests (1966:xlvi–xlvii). We should probably imagine the process of transmission as illustrated in Figure 12.2.

Or perhaps John knew one or more of the synoptics without relying on them. One strong indication that John knew at least some synoptic tradition is his rejection of the Gethsemane story. It is not just that John omitted the story; the image of Jesus in the Gethsemane story was so much at odds with John's characterization of Jesus that he had to refute it. At the place in the narrative where we might expect a Gethsemane story we find:

Now my soul is troubled. And what should I say—"Father, save me from this hour"? No, it is for this reason that I have come to this hour. (12:27)

The characterization of Jesus in this story as the Logos simply will not permit the very human shrinking from the hour of death that so fit Mark's story. Whether he knew it in the Markan version or from the oral tradition, John seems to have rejected the Gethsemane story.

One further note: if John did not know Mark or one of the synoptics, then he independently produced a work remarkably similar in type. Did John reinvent the gospel form? Perhaps, but there is no real reason to believe that John was unfamiliar

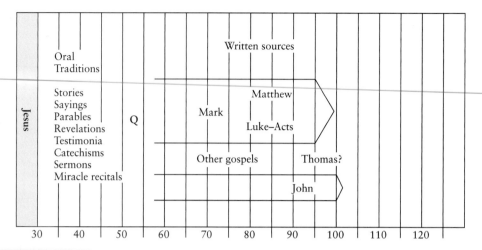

| | 30 | 40 | 50 | 60 | 70 | 80 | 90 | 100 | 110 | 120 |

FIGURE 12.2   CHANNELS OF ORAL TRADITION   Although our knowledge of the process of oral transmission in the Jesus traditions is meager, it seems clear that one major strand of tradition feeds all three of the synoptic Gospels. Paul also seems to have stood in this tradition. The Johannine traditions, however, seem to have followed a separate course for several decades before the writing of the Gospel of John. The similarities John manifests to particular synoptic incidents are probably best explained by imagining some contact between the two strands of oral tradition. There were probably other strands as well, and it is difficult to prove whether gospels like *Thomas* and *Peter* depend on the canonical Gospels or on similar oral traditions.

with Mark, Matthew, or Luke, even though he was not dependent on them for his traditions.

In fact there are reasons to think that the process of composition of this Gospel was more involved than our models of transmission and dependence can deal with. Based on observations of phenomena within the text, we can probably isolate five stages in the evolution of the Gospel. To answer our second question, whether the author was a disciple, we must explore the process of composition.

THE PROCESS OF COMPOSITION

Like the synoptics, this Gospel is anonymous, without explicit historical references, and surrounded by second-century traditions for which we lack convincing supporting evidence. Yet we have one advantage: chapter 21 is a very early postscript to the Gospel.

READING AND REFLECTION
Read John 21.

1. Why were these stories added to the Gospel?
2. What evidence does the last story about the other disciple provide concerning authorship and the process of composition?
3. Why do you suppose such attestation was necessary?

Although we have here an explicit claim that the authority of some never-named disciple of Jesus stands behind this Gospel (21:24), the traditions in the Gospel itself are anything but the simple recollections of an eyewitness. They represent thoroughly interpreted and highly developed reflections on the meaning of Jesus. Any adequate solution to the origin of this Gospel must consider both factors.

One cautious but imaginative theory of the origin of John's Gospel does just that. In his magisterial commentary in the Anchor Bible series, Brown suggested that we can reconstruct five stages in the composition of John (1966:xxxvi–xl).

> *Stage one*: the mere existence of a body of Jesus material, stories and sayings, in the life of some church. This is in an oral tradition, not dependent on the synoptic tradition though perhaps having some contact with it. This material may depend on an original disciple (R. E. Brown, 1966:cii).
>
> *Stage two*: the shaping and development of all this material into Johannine patterns of thought, probably under the influence of a dominant theologian-preacher, perhaps the same original disciple. Unified stories were developed at this stage (for example, chapter 9).
>
> *Stage three*: the organization of much of this material into a consecutive Gospel, the first edition of the Gospel of John, probably by the theologian-preacher who shaped stage two.
>
> *Stage four*: the reediting of the Gospel, primarily adding new material designed to meet new problems; the overwhelming problem seems to have been some sort of exclusion from synagogue worship (see 9:22–23), perhaps related to the Twelfth Benediction discussed earlier (see pages 340–41, 346).
>
> *Stage five*: the final reediting of the Gospel after the death of the original author, probably by one or more of his disciples. A primary motive of this editing is to preserve other material from stage two that had not been included in the earlier editions. This material produces the awkward junctures in the text, for example, 5:1 and 14:31 (the material in John 15 and 16 was probably an alternative version of that in 14 but is now simply added to it). Obviously, chapter 21 belongs to this stage, for the point of view has shifted from the original author to those who endorse his work (21:24).

At first glance such a theory may appear overcomplicated, yet it does not differ greatly from the process proposed for the composition of works of the Jewish prophets such as Jeremiah and Amos, whose disciples kept their words alive and reedited them long after their deaths. It may be possible to combine stages four and five into one reediting by friends or disciples of the author, as Cullmann suggests (1976:9–10), giving basically three phases to the material: collecting and shaping; an original Gospel mainly like the present work; a final edition published after the death of the author, adding material not included in the first edition.

If we now reexamine chapter 21, Brown's theory will help illuminate what is found there. Several purposes can be adduced for adding this material, including the desire to preserve a good story not included in the earlier version. But the overriding purpose seems to be to defend the work from a slander that had arisen: with the death of the author the validity of this Gospel was questioned, because some apparently had believed that he would not die until Jesus returned (21:22–23). The final editor seeks to squelch such a problem by carefully giving the original story: Jesus had not said he would not die but only that he might not. We note in passing that this legend implies that the community originally expected the return of Jesus in the near future, within the lifetime of the author. Can we know more about the identity of this author?

ON WHOSE AUTHORITY? THE DISCIPLE WHOM JESUS LOVED

It is perhaps germane to inquire what kind of authority this Gospel expects to rest on an anonymous disciple, for whom it consistently refuses to provide a name. Much effort has been expended to identify him, but no clear solution has emerged. All our real evidence comes from the Gospel itself.

The "**beloved disciple**" is first mentioned at 13:23–25 in the context of the last meal, at which he reclined close to Jesus. He is next mentioned in the crucifixion scene where Jesus entrusts his mother to him (19:26). In the empty-tomb narrative he raced Peter to the tomb and arrived first but entered last. Yet he "sees and believes" (20:2–9). In each of these incidents (as well as those in John 21) this disciple is paired with Peter, to Peter's disadvantage. (Peter is not mentioned in the crucifixion scene, but the faithfulness of this disciple implicitly highlights Peter's absence and contrasts with Peter's denial.)

It is less clear whether two other references are to this same figure. In the scene of Jesus' arrest Peter and "another disciple" follow him (18:15–16). Both his anonymity and his relation to Peter suggest that he is the same character. An unnamed disciple also appears in the opening section; two of the disciples of John the Baptizer follow Jesus, one unnamed and the other identified as Andrew, the brother of Peter (1:35–41). This would introduce our author at the very beginning, a handy device if the Gospel is going to depend on him. Cullmann (1976:73) suggests that all the references were originally to the "other disciple" and that the final editor added "the one whom Jesus loved." In fact, at 20:2, he is both the "other disciple" and "the one whom Jesus loved." (See also R. E. Brown, 1966:xliv.)

So the claim of the Gospel is that some anonymous disciple, probably with Jesus from the beginning to the end, transmitted the story to disciples who now have put it forth with their own endorsement. But who was he? Two later sources claim he was John, the son of Zebedee, one of the twelve: Irenaeus (*Against Heresies* 3.1.2) and the Muratorian Fragment. Irenaeus wrote around 180, and the Muratorian Fragment was written at Rome sometime between 200 and 400 (see pages 186–87, 475–77). Eusebius (about 325) followed Irenaeus (*Ecclesiastical History* 3.23.1–6), but apparently had no Papias tradition regarding John as he did the other Gospels (but see 3.39.1–2).

Some today are prepared to take this tradition at face value; others remain unconvinced. Alternative suggestions include that our author is some other John; that he was an otherwise unknown disciple, not one of the twelve; that he was Lazarus (the only other character Jesus is said to have loved, 11:3, 5, 36); or even that he is a symbolic figure, sort of a narrator (or implied author) invented by the collective authorship. In this view he represents the ideal disciple (Bultmann, 1971). At least this much can be said: the attempt to obscure the identity of the author has been successful.

But why was the author's identity hidden in the first place? Was it due to humility (R. E. Brown, 1966:xciv) or fictitiousness (Bultmann, 1972:484), or is it simply inexplicable (Cullmann, 1976:84)? We know that John's Gospel was not easily accepted outside its own circle (Eusebius *Church History* 3.24.5–18; Muratorian Fragment, 9–33, in Hahnemann, 1922). It is not quoted by mainstream teachers until near the end of the second century and is rejected by some as late as the beginning of the third century. But does an attestation such as that found in chapter 21 really help? The editors apparently thought so, but notice that they claim two kinds of authority: that of the anonymous disciple and that of the community in which he worked ("*we* know," 21:24, emphasis added).

Remember that all the other Gospels were accepted without such internal attestation, mainly because they were used by the churches. The editors of this Gospel verge on introducing a novelty, making the Gospel's reliability rest on the authority of its author. Clearly, by the middle of the second century it became necessary to associate a specific apostle with each writing to gain acceptance for the work. The claim of chapter 21 seems to represent the transition between the earlier anonymous tradition and the second-century tradition of apostolic authorship. We can learn more about our author by expanding our data to include some other writings.

THE JOHANNINE COMMUNITY

There is one more bit of evidence for reconstructing the Johannine community: three other short writings that bear striking resemblances to this Gospel. They too are anonymous (they claim to be from "the elder") but are attributed to John. They are relatively simple documents, as the following reading guides illustrate. After reading them, you will readily understand why these three letters have long been identified with the Gospel. What can be learned from these other Johannine writings?

 ### READING GUIDES TO THE JOHANNINE LETTERS

1 John
Prologue   1:1–4
Testimony to the message   1:5–10
Purpose of the letter   2:1–17
Warnings about antichrist   2:18–27
The marks of God's children   2:28–4:21
   Do not commit sin   3:4–10
   Love one another   3:11–18
   Keep Jesus' word   3:19–24
   Confess Jesus came in the flesh   4:1–12
   Possess the Spirit and love   4:13–21
Summary and conclusion   5:1–21

2 John
Salutation: elder to the elect lady   1–3
Plea for love   4–6
Warning about deceivers   7–11
   They deny Jesus "in the flesh"
   Do not receive them
Closing greetings   12–13

3 John
Salutation: elder to beloved Gaius   1–4
Commendation for service to strangers   5–8
Condemnation of Diotrephes: not receiving the brethren   9–10
Testimony to Demetrius   11–12
Closing greetings   13–15

Actually, the reading guide to 1 John implies more order to the material than one senses while actually reading it. It is an extraordinarily free composition, more like a free-form musical composition than a logical argument, themes and variations rather than thesis and proof. The following exercise is designed to explore what was happening in the Johannine community.

READING AND REFLECTION

Read 1 John, chapters 1 and 4.

1. How does the prologue in 1:1–4 resemble the prologue in John's Gospel?
2. What images of good and evil are shared between this letter and the Gospel?
3. Why does the writer urge the hearers to "test the spirits"? What is the test?

Anyone who has read the Gospel of John feels right at home reading 1 John. They share many images, ideas, and even forms (like the prologue). It is easy to agree that they come from the same basic circle. Yet something has changed. Although both insist "that Jesus Christ has come in the flesh" (4:2), the letter declares that all who do not subscribe to this view are "antichrist" (4:3). This is strong language, indicating a serious breach within the community (2:19). Such a basic division is not evident in John's Gospel, making it is likely that the letters stem from a later period in the life of the group, a period when some of the community have gone in a different direction. Let us first reconstruct what we can of the community and then consider the new direction that some have taken.

The Johannine circle, as scholars often refer to the authors responsible for these writings, seems to have participated in three distinct but overlapping spheres of influence: Jewish tradition, Greek tradition, and Gnosticism. The first is the world of Jewish tradition with some active relationship with Jewish people. John's attempt to explore the meaning of Jesus in relation to the major Jewish holy days (Sabbath, Passover, Tabernacles, and Dedication are all discussed in 5–10) and his concern for the exclusion of Jesus' followers from the synagogue (9:22; 12:42; 16:2) convince most commentators that this community had Jewish roots. They are less sure the community still thinks of itself as Jewish. Dodd, for example, concludes: "Though no one but a Jew would be likely to possess such knowledge of the Torah, the evangelist clearly feels himself to be outside the Jewish system" (1953:82). John consistently speaks of being put out of the synagogues (9:22; 16:2) and of "their law" (15:25; 10:34), referring to "the Jews" in a fashion that presumes psychological distance (for example, 5:16, 7:1; 19:7; Fuller, 1977; Barrett, 1975). So it seems that John's community is one further stage separated from Judaism than was Matthew's (pages 341–42). Yet unlike Matthew (though like Mark), John felt the need to explain Jewish customs (2:6; 4:9; 6:4; 9:7; 18:28), implying that many in the community had little connection with Jews. John's talk of "the Jews" as Jesus' opponents could easily lead to anti-Semitism, which has long been a blight on Christian history. But John's position is similar to that of certain Jewish sectarians who regarded the main body of the people as deceived (or perverse). John shares other features with some of the sectarians, and in particular with the Qumran community, especially his dualism and opposition to the Temple. At the same time, W. G. Kümmel has pointed out decisive variations: their different attitudes toward the Law; the role of a messianic redeemer (virtually ignored at Qumran); and the apocalyptic expectation of the imminent end, so strong at Qumran but virtually ignored by John. Nevertheless, it is easy to imagine people from Qumran, Samaritans, or other Jewish sectarians finding their way into the Johannine community. It is a community deeply influenced by Jewish tradition.

Second, the Johannine circle had been influenced by Hellenistic Jewish philosophy in the tradition of Philo of Alexandria. We have already seen some of the similarities of terminology and concept (pages 402–04). Whether this influence was through direct contact with Alexandrian philosophy (Dodd, 1953:54–73) or whether it represented a sort of parallel expansion of the biblical wisdom tradition (Brown, 1966:520–24), we surely must imagine a community in active dialogue with both its Jewish and Greek heritages.

Third, the Johannine circle has some connection with another movement in Hellenistic Jewish philosophy that we call **Gnosticism**. Although earlier scholars overemphasized this connection, there are many similarities between how this Gospel and later Gnostics speak about Jesus (see Bultmann, 1972, index entries on *Gnosticism* and *Archetypal Man*). Many complicated questions surround the origin and development of Gnosticism, including the precise meaning of the term. (See the resource section at the end of this chapter.)

Most scholars are convinced that Gnosticism, as a self-conscious movement, did not emerge until the second century but that most of the Gnostic ideas existed much earlier. Christianity often proved to be the catalytic agent needed to synthesize these Gnostic ideas into a system. (Something like this seems to have happened at Corinth in the early fifties, causing Paul to write 1 Corinthians. See Chapter 4.) Briefly, Gnostic ideas include that the world is essentially a dualism of matter and spirit; that only the spirit is really good; that humans in their essence are spirit and must transcend the flesh to realize salvation; that such transcendence is possible by special knowledge, mediated from above (see pages 204–08). For a clearer understanding of Gnosticism, consider this summary of a popular Gnostic story:

A father sends his son, a young man, on a dangerous mission. He is to go to Egypt to recover a magnificent pearl that had belonged to his father but had been stolen by a dragon. So the lad takes on a disguise: laying aside his royal robes, he dresses as an Egyptian and takes a room at an inn near the dragon's lair. But the Egyptians suspect him. They mix him intoxicating drinks, cloud his mind. He forgets his mission, forgets the pearl, forgets even who he is. Only a magical letter sent from his father rouses him from his drunken stupor and causes him to remember who he is, whence he came, and what he is about. Coming to his senses, he seizes the pearl and rushes for the border, re-ascends to his father. Shedding his filthy and impure rags, he regains his robe of glory and adores the glory of the father. (The complete "Hymn of the

Pearl" can be read in the Acts of Thomas, *108–13, in J. K. Elliott, 1993:488–91; in Hennecke and Schneemelcher, 1992:2:380–85; in Jonas, 1958:113–14; and online at http://www.gnosis.org/library/hymnpearl.htm.)*

Although there was a wide range of Gnostic systems, they usually shared an underlying worldview, basic elements of which are clear in the story above. First, something has gone wrong; humanity has somehow fallen; we have forgotten who we really are. Our wrong is not something we do; it is a flaw in the nature of the universe itself, for the visible universe was a mistake from the beginning. Second, there is a secret knowledge that will redeem. This is not knowledge in the ordinary sense, not philosophic insight or a correct understanding of the Law—this knowledge is mystical. One writer described it as knowing

Who we were; what we became;
Where we were; to where we have fallen;
Where we are going; from what we are redeemed;
What birth is, and what rebirth.
                    (Excerpts from Theodotus 78,
                    quoted from Antenicean Fathers *8)*

Line two is especially revealing, for it envisions a recollection of life before the fall. This is not the kind of knowledge one person can tell another; it must be achieved individually in an ecstatic experience. Third, there must be some way of mediating this knowledge to us, and that was usually accomplished through some divine savior who descended from that world above into this world below. In some Gnostic systems this savior is called *Anthropos* (Human), or sometimes *Son of Man*, and seems to represent a primordial humanity, eternal, unfallen, preexistent, who now descends into the world to redeem its fallen counterpart (Dodd, 1953:109–12). These three factors are also evident in the Gnostic-like story of the fall in a Jewish-Hellenistic work from the second century; I summarize:

The Human is created in the image of God: so alike that it would be impossible to tell the difference between the Human and the Divine. This Human lives and rules alongside God. Like God, Human desires to create and so fashions the seven planetary spheres, each ever farther from the Divine Mind. One day this Human descended through the spheres, desiring to rule all. Breaking through the vault of Harmony, he showed to Lower Nature the beautiful form of God. She, responding to that beauty, looked back in love. Passing over the water, he too sees the beautiful form of God reflected back to him. He could do nothing but love it and desire to dwell in it. And at once, with the wish came the reality, and so the Human came to inhabit the form devoid of reason. And Nature, having received into herself the beloved, embraced him wholly, and they mingled—inflamed with love. And this is why of all the creatures of earth, the Human is twofold, holding both the mortality of the body and the immortality of the Human. (The Poimandres of Hermes Trismegistus, *12–15; a complete version can be read in Jonas, 1958:150–51, or Barrett, 1971a:84–85; it can be found online at http://www.hermetic.com/texts/hermetica/hermes1.html.)*

This myth is mediated by Poimandres, a manifestation of the absolute, and is meant to impart the saving gnosis, whereupon the soul reascends to the Father. Such mythic speculation was a regular feature of Gnosticism, and Gnostics found it relatively easy to fit Jesus into this mythic framework, especially as Jesus is portrayed in the Fourth Gospel, as the One from above, the Logos. (For a more elaborate Gnostic myth of origins, see pages 206–07.) The first two interpreters of John's Gospel to leave a record were Gnostics, and this Gnostic use surely impeded its acceptance by orthodox Christians. That John's Gospel is open to such gnosticizing interpretations is evidence that it was almost certainly written before such thought was decisively rejected within the community, that is, before the letter known as 1 John.

Some have even characterized John's presentation of Jesus as a kind of "naive docetism" (Käsemann, 1968:26). **Docetism**, from the Greek *dokeo*, "to seem" or "to appear to be," was a belief that Jesus only appeared to be a human being but was actually a spirit being descended into the world incognito. An interesting exercise is to read through the Gospel of John, searching specifically for signs of Jesus' humanity: How does John show (or fail to show) that Jesus is a real human being? Although John may not be called a docetist, he (naively?) fails to present the human qualities of Jesus. Even so, by choosing to tell his story as a gospel, John has chosen an inherently anti-Gnostic form, one never used by the Gnostics, though they wrote many so-called gospels. The Gnostic gospels dwell on the resurrected Jesus and the teachings of Jesus; they do not portray the career of a real person. None of them could ever be mistaken for a biography or a historical account. Thus, even though the Gospel of John differs greatly from the synoptics in content, its literary form is closer to them than to the Gnostic gospels. (Compare some of the Gnostic gospels in Cameron, 1982; Crossan, 1985; and Hennecke and Schneemelcher, 1991, vol. 1, such as the *Gospel of Truth* or even the *Gospel of Thomas*.)

Thus, John's Gospel stands in an ambiguous relation to Gnosticism, sharing much of the same worldview and presenting Jesus in a mode that many Gnostics would find congenial. Nevertheless, John presents a real, human Jesus whose movements about Palestine can be traced in a Gospel narrative. Gnosticism, Hellenistic philosophy, and Jewish tradition all contribute to John's unique view of Jesus. This community is characterized by a selective syncretism, combining elements from diverse religious traditions into a new tradition. John's community is not afraid to appropriate key elements of alien religious movements, shape them according to its own faith, and produce a new synthesis. It is a strategy the church in late antiquity would make its own.

THE ELUSIVE PARTICULARS: TIME, PLACE, AND PURPOSE

If we reject the late second-century tradition that identified this Gospel with the apostle John and the city of Ephesus, then there is no way to locate the Fourth Gospel geographically. The above constellation of characteristics (Jewish tradition, Hellenistic philosophy, gnosticizing philosophy, syncretism) probably existed in every major city in the Roman Empire and in some not so major.

A bit more may be said about the date, or perhaps *dates* would be more accurate. The final edition of this Gospel was probably produced toward the end of the first century, so that the tradition about the immortality of the beloved disciple (21:23–24) was significant enough for his eventual death to cause a problem. This is supported by the traditions about eviction from the synagogues, which probably occurred in the nineties. But the writing of the Gospel cannot have been much later, because a fragment of John's Gospel, discovered in Egypt, is generally dated between 130 and 150, and sometimes "at the beginning of the second century" (R. E. Brown, 1966:lxxxii–lxxxiii). Known as P52, this is, ironically, the oldest surviving New Testament text (see photo on page 392). Thus, the most likely date for the final edition of the Gospel according to John would be the late nineties. Unfortunately, there is no way to judge the time lapse between this final text and the earlier edition (or, in Brown's scheme, editions). It could be a few years or a few decades. In the past, a frequent argument claimed that the high degree of Hellenization manifested by the Gospel required a late (possibly even a second-century) date. But this ignores the extensive Hellenization among some Jews before the time of Jesus (see Chapter 1). Certainly the process of shaping this material to Johannine thought patterns (Brown's second stage) must go back several decades before the composition of the Gospel. For John, surely, and probably for each of the other Gospels as well, it is too simple to ask when it was written. The Gospel was developed over a long period of time, achieving its final form near the end of the first century.

Finally, we might think it easy to agree about John's purpose, because he states it explicitly: "that you might believe that the Christ the Son of God is Jesus" (literal translation of 20:31). But it is debatable whether this means "might come to believe" or "might continue to believe," for the various manuscripts differ; some use the future tense ("come to believe") and some the present tense for *believe*. Every conceivable hypothesis has been argued by various scholars (see the summary in Kümmel, 1966:161–65, and the discussion in R. E. Brown, 1966:lxvii–lxxix). The future tense would imply that John aims to convert unbelievers; the present tense would indicate a focus on those who already believe.

The more serious purposes advanced for John include: to appeal to those who do not believe in the Christ; to refute those who believe in a more spiritual Christ (especially Gnostics); to encourage and confirm those who do believe the Christ is Jesus; to give confidence to Jews in the diaspora synagogues who believe in Jesus; to demonstrate the superiority of this new way to traditional Jewish piety; to appeal to Jewish sectarians, especially the followers of John the Baptizer and the Samaritans; and to interpret Jesus more adequately than the synoptics.

All these purposes are present to some degree in the Gospel, but not all are central. John lived in a very complex situation, propounding a version of the faith that differed significantly from other interpretations. We can construe various options along a continuum, with John very far to the left. The only group further left were the Gnostics, who viewed Jesus as the descending revealer who transcends the bounds of an earthly and historical person. He is known not so much by past traditions as by the immediate experience of those who have the Spirit (Woll, 1981). To the right stood a whole array of more conservative options, both those who followed Jesus and those who did not, both Jews and Gentiles. Brown (1979) identified six distinct groups on this side of the spectrum.

Three did not believe in Jesus:

The World: those who prefer darkness to light (for example, 9:39; 12:35–36; 16:20).

The Jews: those within the synagogues who opposed and excluded the Johannine community (especially 9:22; 16:2).

The **Baptists**: those followers of John who did not believe Jesus surpassed John (especially 3:22–26).

And three did believe in Jesus, but not in a way that John found adequate:

The **Secret Believers**: those who quietly believed in Jesus but also desired to remain within the synagogues (especially 12:42–43; and Nicodemus 3:1–9; 7:50; 19:38–39).

The Jewish followers of Jesus: those who had left the synagogue but who interpreted Jesus primarily on the basis of his miracles (6:60–66; 7:3–5; 8:31–32).

The Apostolic Believers: those who followed Peter and the Twelve but saw Jesus as the Davidic Messiah rather than the One from above (6:67–69; 14:9; and the contrast between Peter and the beloved disciple). Chapter 21 seems aimed at reconciliation with this group.

If we add the Gnostics, perhaps the Samaritans (4:39), probably apocalypticists, and divisions within John's own community, we begin to appreciate the tremendous diversity of the late first-century Jesus movement. Within this diversity, the community that is reflected in this Gospel struggles to identify itself and to proclaim its vision of Jesus in contrast to these others. In this sense, it is a sectarian vision. John's community stands in conflict with its surrounding culture rather than in easy accommodation to it. This community emphasized love and prayed for unity (17:20–21) even while it vigorously rejected those outside. John has drawn a portrait of Jesus that speaks to this situation of diversity and attempts to assert the truth of his own community's understanding of Jesus against competing claims.

LEARNING ON YOUR OWN

REVIEWING THE CHAPTER

Names and Terms

Baptists	Gnosticism	Secret Believers
beloved disciple	irony	Septuagint
docetism	logos	signs
dualism	ontology	Stoics
eschatology	passion narrative	wisdom
1 John	Philo	

Issues and Questions

1. Discuss the use of dramatic irony in the Gospel of John.
2. In what ways is John most like the synoptic Gospels? Where does it differ most radically?
3. Discuss the descent-ascent theme as an organizing principle of John's story.

4. How would a Stoic understanding of the meaning of logos differ from the concept as expressed in the Hebrew Scriptures?
5. Why is it so difficult to reach a conclusion about John's view of the sacraments?
6. Discuss the similarities between Gnosticism and John's worldview. In what important way does John's Gospel diverge from the Gnostic tradition?
7. How does John's description of events change after the story moves from its descending phase to the ascending?
8. How does John diverge from the other Gospels in the treatment of Jesus' humanity?
9. Be prepared to summarize Raymond E. Brown's five stages in the composition of John.

TAKING THE NEXT STEP

Kysar, 1976, and Brown and Maloney, 2003, are excellent; other competent introductory studies include Bruce, 1984b; Kysar, 1984, 1986; Talbert, 2005; Sloyan, 1988; and Smith, 1976. For an overview of the current scholarship see Sloyan, 2006.

Though dated, the finest commentary on this Gospel is R. E. Brown, 1966; the even older works by Dodd, 1953, and Lightfoot, 1956, remain extremely useful. Bultmann's important commentary, 1971 (1941), is both difficult and dated. Bultmann's source theories have been very influential, on which see Smith, 1965. Also difficult are Barrett, 1978; Haenchen, 1984; and Schnackenburg, 1968 and 1980; but they contain a wealth of insight into the text. See also the literary approach of O'Day and Hylen, 2006, and Lindars, 1990; perhaps the best conservative work is Beasley-Murray, 1987. Neyrey, 2007, applies social science insights. Levine, 2003, provides feminist perspectives.

Topics for Special Studies

A Study of a Literary Aspect of the Gospel

Useful topics include narrator, point of view, plot, characterization, implied reader, metaphor, and rhetoric.

Our literary understanding of John has been fundamentally altered by the work of R. Alan Culpepper; see especially his (rather technical) 1983 volume. For an exploration of the narrative see Kysar, 1984. Culpepper and Segovia edited issue 53 of *Semeia* (1991), which is devoted to a literary analysis of John; it includes studies of plot (Segovia), character (Staley), metaphor (Kysar), rhetoric (Wuellner), and narrative time (O'Day). See also Culpepper, 1997 (on plot), and Koester, 2003 (on symbolism).

For an overview on characterization see Malbon and Berlin, 1993. For John's characters see Conway, 1999, and Petersen, 1993.

Staley, 1988, presents a rather sophisticated argument concerning the effect that the medium (here, the print medium) has had on reading John.

A Study of One Section of the Gospel from One or More Literary Aspects

For an overview of recent work and an application of narrative and social methods see Stibbe, 1992, 1993.

On the prologue see Phillips, 2006; Botha, 1991, uses speech act theory to read John 4:1–42, showing how extensively the writer manipulates the reader's point of view. Borgen, 1981, has an insightful study of chapter 6; see also MacKay, 2004, and Webster, 2003.

Segovia, 1991, seeks an integrative interpretation of the farewell discourse based on modern narrative and rhetorical analysis. Stube, 2006, does a rhetorical reading. Other provocative studies of John 14–17 include Parsenios, 2005; Painter, 1981; and Woll, 1981, which relate what is said to supposed happenings in the Johannine community.

On the famous story of the woman caught in adultery see Toesing, 1995.

John's Use of Irony
A careful discussion of the uses of irony in literature is Booth, 1974; Duke, 1985, applies these insights to John, and O'Day, 1986, uses irony to explore John's notion of Revelation.

John's Characterization of Jesus
See Borgen, 1965; de Jonge, 1977 and 1993; Meeks, 1972a; Neyrey, 1988; Derrett, 1993; Käsemann, 1968; and Nicholson, 1984. Fortna and Thatcher, 2001, have collected diverse essays on various aspects of this characterization—especially its relation to history and to other literary traditions. On Moses as a character see Harstine, 2002.

The Meanings of Logos
Metzger, 1952, discusses translation issues; Borgen, 1972; Miller, 1983; and Evans, 1981, explore uses of the term. For an overview see Dunn, 1980, or Beasley-Murray, 1987. Perkins, 1993, discusses Gnostic usage.

The Relation of John's Language to the Social Setting of the Community
Important themes include light, descent-ascent, and Jesus as equal to God.

Social science concerns are addressed by Esler and Piper, 2006; Neyrey, 1988; Blasi, 1996; and Petersen, 1993; see also Meeks, 1972a.

The Historical Setting of the Story
The most important work on the setting of this story has been done by R. E. Brown, 1979, and Martyn, 2003; a comparison of their views would make an interesting study. See also Smith, 1989, and Klink, 2007.

The Idea of a Johannine School
Start with Culpepper, 1975; R. E. Brown, 1982; and Cullmann, 1976.

The Author of This Gospel
On the identity of the author, see Culpepper, 1994; also see the lengthy introduction to R. E. Brown, 1966, and the previous topic. For a more sociological view, see Kurz, 1989.

The Nature and History of the Signs Gospel
The basic work is Fortna, 1970 and 1988; Von Wahlde, 1989, traces two stages in the development of the tradition. See also Smith, 1989.

The Meaning of "the Jews" in This Story
John uses the term *the Jews* in a disparaging way, raising important questions concerning the relations between this community and actual Jews. For an introduction, see Barrett, 1975; for more detail, see Von Wahlde, 1993, and Jonge, 1993. Borgen, 1987, does a comparative study of Philo, John, and Paul. Sanders, 1993, surveys the first hundred years of Jewish and Christian relations.

The question of anti-Judaism is addressed by Bieringer, 2001, and Kierspel, 2006. For a Jewish reading see Reinhartz, 2002.

Connections between John and the Dead Sea Scrolls
See Charlesworth, 1972, and R. E. Brown and Charlesworth, 1990. See also Culpepper and Black, 1996, and Evans, 1992.

The Relationship of John's Gospel to Gnosticism
On John's use by Gnostics, see Pagels, 1973, and Sloyan, 1996. For related studies considering John's relation to Gnosticism, see Dodd, 1953; Nicholson, 1983; Thompson,

1988; Von Wahlde, 1990; and Countryman, 1985b. Good overviews of Gnosticism are provided by Wink, 1993; Perkins, 1993; and Roukema, 1999. For a discussion of the origins of Gnosticism, see Nock, 1964:xiii–xvii; Jonas, 1958; Yamauchi, 1973; Rudolph, 1983; and R. M. Grant, 1961. For a major reconsideration of how we think about Gnosticism, see Williams, 1996, and Hill, 1997; for a contrary view see Logan, 2006. A good summary is given by Wilson in Cohn-Sherbok and Court, 2001.

The Relationship of John's Gospel to the Other Gospels
On the historical question of the correlation of this story and actual events, see Dodd, 1963. See also Martyn, 1979, and Haenchen, 1970.

On the pregospel history of these **traditions**, see Fortna, 1988.

On the literary question of the correlation of John and the **synoptics**, the best overview is Smith, 1992. See also Kümmel, 1966:142; Talbert, 1977, chapters 2, 3; Painter, 1993; and Culpepper and Black, 1996. MacKay, 2004, compares the feeding stories in Mark.

On the relationship between John and **Thomas** see Pagels, 2004, and Dunderberg, 2006.

The Chronology of Jesus' Death
On the events surrounding Jesus' death, see Finegan, 1969:291–98, and Jeremias, 1955. Finegan treats a broad range of chronological issues in great detail, including the various calendars and ways of counting years. He generally takes a conservative approach to the ancient sources, trusting their literal meaning more than may be warranted.

The Relationship between the Gospel and the Letters of John
The extensive commentary by R. E. Brown, 1982, not only explains the letters but also shows their many relationships to the Gospel of John. Also valuable are Lieu, 1985 and 1991, and Smith, 1991. The commentaries of Bultmann, 1973, and Dodd, 1946, are also useful, as is the conservative work of Smalley, 1984, and Marshall, 1978c.

Additional Books and Articles
A useful (though somewhat dated) guide to the extensive literature on John is Kysar, 1975. Belle, 1988, surveys the period 1966–1986.

Recent discussions of the setting and sources of John are admirably summarized and evaluated by Smith, 1984. There are good bibliographies in Stibbe, 1992, and Koester, 1991.

Good anthologies covering a variety of topics include Lierman, 2006; Culpepper and Black, 1996; and Ashton, 1997.

13

THE DAWN OF A NEW DAY

The Apocalypse of John

 There is a theory which states that if ever anyone discovers exactly what the universe is for, and why it is here, it will instantly disappear and be replaced by something ever more bizarre and inexplicable. There is another which states that this has already happened.

DOUGLAS ADAMS, *RESTAURANT AT THE END OF THE UNIVERSE*

The Apocalypse of John is also known as the Revelation of John (*apocalypsis* being the Greek word for "revelation"). Its dual name is perhaps evidence of its ambiguous position in history. Although it is very popular with some people today, others rarely read it. Even those who are fascinated by this work rarely claim to understand it completely. Its history has oscillated between times of compelling concern and times of complete neglect. Already in the second century some considered it the ultimate revelation, whereas others condemned it utterly. As late as the time of Eusebius (about 325 CE), debate still raged about whether it should be included in the canon of works read as part of the public meeting of the church.

In this chapter we will review three approaches to interpreting Revelation, explore its relationship to other ancient literature of a similar kind, then carefully study its symbolism and plot. Finally, we will see how this work fits the social and historical situation in which it was written and read. Because considerable background is necessary to read and appreciate Revelation, we will read only short excerpts from it until late in this chapter.

THEORIES OF INTERPRETATION

> *And I saw a beast rising out of the sea. . . . It causes all, both small and great, both rich and poor, both free and slave, to be marked on the right hand or the forehead, so that no one can buy or sell who does not have the mark, that is, the name of the beast or the number of its name. This calls for wisdom: let anyone with understanding calculate the number of the beast, for it is a human number. Its number is six hundred sixty-six. (Rev. 13:1, 16–18)*

Wisdom, indeed. This seems to call for more than wisdom—perhaps a crystal ball. How shall we interpret such an image? Can we ever understand what John was referring to? Such a scene raises acutely the issue of how we make an accurate interpretation. We should begin by admitting that there is no ultimate and final interpretation of any work of literature. All works of literature elicit varying interpretations, and no interpretation ever exhausts the meaning in a work of art.

But with the Apocalypse there are not only diverse interpretations, there are diverse strategies suggested for making interpretations. Three different theories are advocated for making sense out of this work. Some argue that it must be interpreted entirely in terms of events in the first century (historical views); some argue that it actually predicts the future (prophetic views); and still others insist that it is best seen as a book of timeless symbols (symbolist views). Without judging the adequacy of each approach, let us try to understand what its advocates mean.

HISTORICAL: THE FIRST CENTURY IN CODE

The basic idea of the historical interpretation is that all the symbols in Revelation refer to people and events that existed in the first century. At first this may not seem very promising, but most of John's images may be interpreted as coded references to first-century events. That beast, for example, whose name or number is 666 may well have been a coded way of referring to Emperor Nero. To understand this we need to digress briefly to discuss ancient numbers.

Neither the Greek or Hebrew languages had numbers; more precisely, neither had a separate system of symbols for indicating numeric values. Both used the letters of the alphabet for this purpose. One of the great contributions of Muslim civilization was the invention of our present number system (thus *Arabic numbers*). Before that, the Romans had invented a separate number system, which, although a great improvement on earlier practice, was still cumbersome. But imagine how awkward it would be if there were not a separate number system so that letters were also numbers (see Table 13.1).

Whereas Hebrew had only twenty-two letters and Greek only twenty-four, and those in a different order, these English equivalents are reasonably analogous to their systems. Notice this is not a digital system. Twenty is not two (B) with a zero; there was no zero. Imagine trying to add NOPE + SQE (two ways of writing 185!).

Now we can understand what it means to get the number of a name: simply add up the letters of the name. In Table 13.1, the letters of the name David [4 + 1 + 400 + 9 + 4] would add up to 418; in Hebrew the value of the name was 14; in Greek 18. Thus, interesting possibilities develop. Scribbled on a wall at Pompeii, for example, was the less than bold declaration: "I love her whose number is 545," a cryptic reference only intelligible to the young man who wrote it and his circle.

A Christian work from the second century interprets the meaning of the Abraham story involving 318 men (Gen. 14:13). The number is divided into 300 and 18. In Greek the first two letters of Jesus' name add up to 18. Thus 18 stands for Jesus. And 300 is the value of the letter T, which represents the cross. Thus the meaning of *318* in the Abraham story is the cross of Jesus (*Letter of Barnabas* 8:8–9).

The strategy here involved finding similarities between diverse things just because their names added up to the same value, a practice that Jewish mystics called

TABLE 13.1	LETTERS AS NUMBERS VALUES			
A = 1	G = 7	L = 30	Q = 80	V = 400
B = 2	H = 8	M = 40	R = 90	W = 500
C = 3	I = 9	N = 50	S = 100	X = 600
D = 4	J = 10	O = 60	T = 200	Y = 700
E = 5	K = 20	P = 70	U = 300	Z = 800
F = 6				

gematria. Similar to this is a political slogan that Suetonius reports someone wrote on a wall in Rome:

Count the values: Nero has the same number as "murdered his own mother."
(Nero, 39.2)

In this case both words add up to 1,005. How then might Nero be the figure behind 666?

The process is a bit cumbersome: one takes the Greek form, *Kaisar Neron*, transposes the letters into Hebrew, and the sum is 666. Obviously, with such flexibility, other solutions are possible as well: some interpreters have suggested Gaius Caesar (Caligula), others Domitian. Clearly, no amount of wisdom would lead to a solution unless it was already known to the hearers, but this was probably the case. The historical interpretation insists that the sum referred to some first-century person whom John and his community regarded as the embodiment of evil, the beast from the sea.

Similarly, all the symbols and images of the book are interpreted to refer to events of the first century. The seven churches to which messages are written in chapters 2 and 3 are considered by historical interpreters to be real assemblies in these specific cities. Various first-century disasters are referred to in the earthquakes and fire, such as the eruption of Mount Vesuvius. According to the historical interpretation, then, all the symbols and actions of Revelation are really coded ways of referring to first-century realities. Others take a wholly different approach.

PROPHETIC: THINGS THAT ARE YET TO BE

Other interpreters assume that Revelation intends to tell about the future. Some believe it forecasts the whole future history of the church from John's day to the end of the age, others that it predicts only the events that will occur at the end of the world.

Those who take the more rigorous view believe that Revelation offers a kind of metachronology of the whole course of history. They view the work as being chronologically arranged from John's time (chapter 1) to the end of the age (chapter 22). Thus, the seven churches of chapters 2 and 3 are not individual congregations of the first century but predictions of the seven ages or epochs through which the church would pass from the first century to the second coming. They point out that the first church, the apostolic church in this view, is relatively pure. Succeeding churches have both vices and virtues. The last church by contrast is neither hot nor cold and is in danger of complete repudiation (3:16). To these interpreters, this wealthy church that has lost its zeal seems typical of the mainline churches of the contemporary United States.

According to this view the figure referred to under the symbol 666 must, because it occurs late in the Apocalypse, refer to some future figure, an antichrist who will appear on earth at some point in the future. These interpreters imagine that one can trace the whole course of Western civilization in John's Apocalypse.

Most who hold a prophetic view do not go so far. In fact, the most popular approach (popular in the sense that one is apt to hear it on the radio) makes some compromise with the historical view—but only a modest one. They hold that the first three chapters of Revelation are historical and refer to events in the first century, but beginning at 4:1, where the angel tells John to "come up here," there is a great gap that includes all the time between the first century and the end of the age. These interpreters assert that all of Revelation after chapter 4 refers to events at the end of time.

Thus, these interpreters agree with the historical view that the seven churches are real historical congregations, but they insist that the figure represented by 666 is a future person, properly designated as the antichrist, who will appear in the last days. Like the other prophetic interpreters, they believe that our own times are those just before the end (otherwise the work would be meaningless to us).

SYMBOLIST: TRUTH, NOT HISTORY

A third approach to Revelation argues that the two approaches discussed above are both right and wrong. The historical view is right in that these symbols represent first-century events, and the prophetic view is correct in applying them to future historical events; but both are wrong to believe that the symbols apply only to some specific event. In this third view, Revelation is a book of timeless truths in symbolic form. The symbols have no specific connection with historical events, though many such events may correlate with the symbols. The seven churches represent seven kinds of churches that exist in any age and any time. Some are pure; some are tepid; most are a mixture of success and failure.

Even more interesting is the symbolist interpretation of 666, now understood as a timeless truth, not a reference to some historical person. To begin, we might observe that the Greek text can be read two ways: either "it is the number of a human" or "it is a human number" (13:18). They suggest that we should see the number 666 as merely an intensification of the number 6, the number of the day of the creation of humanity and one short of the number of perfection, 7. Further, the symbolist can point to an early Christian tradition that found it significant that the numerical value of Jesus in Greek was 888 (*Sibylline Oracles* 1.324–34, in Hennecke and Schneemelcher 1992:2:656). Now 8 represents the beginning of the new week: the eighth day is the first day (and the day of resurrection). The symbolist interpreter, then, sees 666 as representing the arrogance of the human claiming the sovereignty that belongs only to Jesus as Lord of the new age. The antichrist, then, might well be Nero (or Hitler, or Mussolini, as certain prophetic interpreters have alleged), but he is all of us to the degree that we falsely claim to be ultimate. Thus, the symbolist approach attempts to uncover the timeless truths hidden in the symbols of the Apocalypse.

OUR APPROACH

In one way our approach differs from all of these views, for they are ways of interpreting the meaning of Revelation for today, whereas our purpose is to discover what it meant to its first hearers. With this goal in mind, some interpretations of Revelation advocated by certain interpreters today are not possible.

For example, shortly before the 1984 presidential election a flyer proclaimed that 666 pointed to Ronald Wilson Reagan, the only U.S. president with six letters in each of his names. Why is such an interpretation of Revelation 13 unconvincing?

Does it merely depend on our political sympathies? No. This interpretation makes three basic mistakes.

First, this interpretation rests on certain assumptions about Revelation that are not at all likely. It assumes that Revelation was actually talking about our time rather than the time in which it was written. It also assumes that the United States is so important that only its presidents should be considered candidates for this role.

Second, the author of the flyer was apparently unfamiliar with the relationship between numbers and names in the ancient world. Once we know that the ancients used letters for numbers, so that every name was also a number, we will see that the symbol 666 in Revelation has nothing to do with how many letters one has in one's name.

Third, such an interpretation would have meant nothing to the audience to which Revelation was addressed. They simply did not know Ronald Reagan. If we assume that the author was addressing a real message to real human beings in the first century, interpretations like this one become impossible. This does not mean that a prophetic interpretation is automatically ruled out, but it would have to be a prophetic insight able to be understood by the original hearers.

In fact, all three modern approaches (historical, prophetic, and symbolic) are instructive, for they were also the three modes of interpretation available to the original audience. Certainly the people of that early audience heard in Revelation an interpretation of their own history (as the historical approach would insist); surely they regarded it as in some way predicting the near end of the age (a prophetic idea); surely they appreciated the symbolic nature of the book and applied these symbols to their lives. We can be sure of these things because Revelation was not the only book of this kind at that time. There were many others not included in the canon, and becoming familiar with them will help us know how to read Revelation. Once again, the question is one of genre, or kind of literature.

THE NATURE OF THE GENRE

We have already encountered shorter examples of this kind of writing in 2 Thessalonians 2 and Mark 13, with its parallels in Matthew 24–25 and Luke 21. And we have seen that the apocalyptic worldview underlying this kind of writing was widespread in first-century Jewish circles (see the discussion on pages 90–92, 287–88). Works of this kind take their name from the Greek title of Revelation; they are called *apocalypses*, and the kind of literature is called *apocalyptic literature*. We can very briefly summarize our earlier discussion of the worldview of apocalypticism as a dualism: the heart and driving force of history is a cosmic struggle between God and Satan. At the moment, Satan is prevailing, but apocalypticism rested on the firm conviction that God would soon intervene, overthrow evil, and establish the new age of righteousness. This was the hope of the apocalyptic writers. The older view, stretching back to the time when Israel was an independent nation with its own king (roughly 1000–500 BCE), was strikingly different. (For contrasts with the older Israelite view see Table 1.2 on page 49.)

Yet this hope was rarely stated so directly, for apocalyptic literature is a literature of indirection. Let us now consider the literary features and typical characteristics of the various writings that are enough like Revelation to be called *apocalypses*.

THE LITERARY TRAITS OF APOCALYPTIC LITERATURE

The best way to gain an impression of this kind of literature is to read as many different examples as you can. One that is universally accessible is the book of Daniel (7–12) in the Hebrew Scriptures. Another is *4 Ezra* (also called *2 Esdras*), found in a collection known as the Apocrypha, which is in Roman Catholic Bibles. Other possibilities include *1 Enoch* 14–15 and 17–36; *2 Enoch*; *2 Baruch* 53–74; the *War Scroll* from Qumran; the *Ascension of Isaiah*; the *Apocalypse of Peter*. (See the resources section on other apocalypses at the end of the chapter for details on finding these writings.) The genre was vigorously pursued. Some writers reedited older apocalypses to make them explicitly refer to Jesus (4 Ezra); others wrote entirely new works, often in the names of apostles (in addition to those attributed to John and Peter, there is also one of Paul, one of Thomas, and at least two of James) but also in the names of earlier writers, such as the *Ascension of Isaiah*, written about the same time as Revelation.

This is just a sampling of the writing still available, which is only a small portion of the works written. The Book of Revelation was part of a major literary tradition in antiquity, the genre of apocalyptic writing. Two other conclusions may be drawn from even a glance at these writings. First, apocalypses traveled under many names. (And conversely, not all works called *apocalypses* are similar. Title is only one clue to genre.) Second, there was a great deal of variety exhibited within the genre. We can get an get an impression of the traits of this type of literature from the following excerpts:

> A. *And after [one thousand] three hundred and thirty-two days the Lord will come with his angels and with the hosts of the saints from the seventh heaven with the glory of the seventh heaven, and will drag Beliar with his hosts into Gehenna, and he will bring rest to the pious who shall be found alive in the body in this world . . . and to all who through faith in him have cursed Beliar and his kings.* (Ascension of Isaiah 4:14–16; in Hennecke and Schneemelcher, 1992:2:609)

> B. *And these things shall come to pass in the day of judgment of those who have fallen away from faith in God and have committed sin: cataracts of fire shall be let loose; and obscurity and darkness shall come up and cover and veil the entire world, and the waters shall be changed and transformed into coals of fire. . . . And the stars shall be melted by flames of fire.* (Apocalypse of Peter 5; in Hennecke and Schneemelcher, 1992:2:627)

> C. *And it came about, when I had spoken to my sons, the men called me. And they took me up onto their wings, and carried me up to the first heaven. And they put me down there. They led before my face the elders, the rulers of the stellar orders.* (2 Enoch 3:1–4:1; in Charlesworth, 1983:1:111).

> D. *Then a great angel came forth having a golden trumpet in his hand, and he blew it three times over my head, saying, "Be courageous! O one who has triumphed. Prevail! O one who has prevailed. For you have triumphed over the accuser, and you have escaped from the abyss and*

Hades. You will now cross over the crossing place. For your name is written in the Book of the Living. (Apocalypse of Zephaniah 9:1–3; in Charlesworth, 1983:1:514).

E. *After this I saw in the night visions, and behold, a fourth beast, terrible and dreadful and exceedingly strong; and it had great iron teeth; it devoured and broke in pieces, and stamped the residue with its feet. It was different from all the beasts that were before it; and it had ten horns. I considered the horns, and behold, there came up among them another horn, a little one, before which three of the first horns were plucked up by the roots; and behold, on this horn were eyes like the eyes of a man, and a mouth speaking great things. (Dan. 7:7–8)*

Remember this is a literary genre that lasted more than three centuries; variety should be expected. Nevertheless, certain typical features are found in many apocalypses:

1. The claim that a secret revelation has been given to some seer or prophet (as in all the examples above).
2. This revelation is imparted in a dream, a vision, or a transportation of the seer to heaven—often the three means are combined (see C above).
3. The revelation is usually mediated by some figure, such as an angel, who acts as guide and interpreter to the seer (C and D).
4. The revelation is usually not self-explanatory but consists of a variety of arcane symbols involving cosmic upheavals, animals (often composites of different animals, with multiple heads), mythological figures, and numbers (E).
5. The reception of the revelation is often attributed to some figure from the past: Moses, Enoch, Daniel, Adam, and so on. This practice of pseudonymity gives the name to the major collection of these works: they are called the **pseudepigrapha** [sood-eh-PIG-gra-fa] (all of the above).

An awareness of these characteristic features will help us to read Revelation. But to understand the genre better, we need to add one more dimension to our analysis. The central impulse of apocalypses brings together two diverse elements from the history of Israel: a concern for God's redemptive activity in history and a concern for the cosmic action of God in ritual and story.

THE PROPHETIC HOPE OF RESTORATION

The rise, development, and decline of prophecy in Israel is a fascinating topic, but it would take us too far afield to pursue it here. In the heyday of prophecy in the eighth to sixth centuries BCE, prophets in Israel acted as judges of the covenant, pronouncing divine blessings or curses on the people for their faithfulness or unfaithfulness to God's laws. These blessings and curses were to be carried out in history, which was considered to be under divine control. So intertwined were the prophets with history that they are often thought of as foretellers of the future; that was never their primary task. They looked to the future to explain the present. When Israel fell on hard times, when the divine judgment had fallen, the prophets began to look beyond the present distress to a time of restoration. They looked forward to a time when God would act to restore the people to their former glory. There would be a new exodus (Isaiah 40). A new David would arise to sit on his father's throne (Jer. 23:5). God would make a new covenant with the people (Jeremiah 31). The prophets saw these as historical events that would bring back the good old days, before Israel forsook God (Hos. 2:14–20).

However, things did not work out this way. As the years after the devastation of Israel in the exile grew into centuries, the prophetic hope waned. History seemed to have passed Israel by; all her energies were now directed inward. A few prophets persisted, also directing their attention to the inner life of the people (Malachi, for example). Soon even these ceased. There were no more prophets. The tradition arose that God had withdrawn the spirit of prophecy in the days of Haggai, Zechariah, and Malachi (about 400 BCE). (Thus, the reappearance of the Spirit among early followers of Jesus was itself considered a significant event, marking the dawn of a new age; see Acts 2:15–17.) This prophetic consciousness is the ground from which apocalyptic expectation grew, feeding on the hope of renewal.

MYTHIC ENACTMENTS OF RENEWAL

An even older pattern of renewal existed throughout the ancient Near East, from Babylon to Egypt, including Israel. This pattern also centered on the king, not as a historical hope but as a divine agent. The **Babylonian story of creation** (called *Enuma Elish*), enacted at the New Year's festival, is its clearest example. In this story the act of creation is God's victory over chaos, establishing the order of the world.

The story takes place in primeval time, before the creation of heaven and earth. Only the Gods exist. But the Gods have grown raucous and noisy, and their father, Apsu, conspires to have them destroyed. But he himself is killed instead. Then **Tiamat** (Chaos), mother of them all, is driven to avenge her husband. She makes plans to destroy all the Gods. Tiamat creates monsters to fight on her side—serpents, dragons, the sphinx, and others—and she works more magic. The Gods cower in terror. Finally Marduk is brought forward. Son of the Sun, God of the Storm and the Four Winds, wisest of the Gods, Marduk is made king. All the Gods invest him with their powers to determine destiny, and his word becomes supreme. Marduk and Tiamat meet in a raging battle. He drives a fierce wind into her open mouth, pierces her inflated torso with his arrow, and kills her. From her split carcass he creates heaven and earth. He fixes each of the Gods in his own sphere, orders the heavens, and then, from the blood of Tiamat's army commander, Kingu, he creates humanity to be the servants of the Gods. Marduk makes his home in Babylon, where he becomes shepherd of the human race. (The complete story in translation is in Pritchard, 1955: 60–72, and can be found online at http://ccat.sas.upenn.edu/~humm/Resources/Ane/enumaA.html and http://www.sacred-texts.com/ane/enuma.htm.)

Every year in Babylon they reenacted this story. Each year, as the old year wore out, Chaos reasserted herself. The king lost his throne, the family disintegrated, law ceased. Then once again the priest would enact the drama of God's conquest of Chaos (portrayed as a sea monster or dragon). This ritual battle between the divine warrior and the dragon and the ensuing victory resulted in the reestablishment of order and of marriage, the recoronation of the king, the preservation of society—or rather the creation of a new society in the truly new year.

In Israel this story was adapted and applied to their God:

Awake, awake, put on strength,
*   O arm of the LORD!*
Awake, as in days of old,
*   the generations of long ago!*
Was it not you who cut Rahab in pieces,
*   who pierced the dragon?*
Was it not you who dried up the sea,
*   the waters of the great deep;*
who made the depths of the sea a way
*   for the redeemed to cross over?*
So the ransomed of the LORD shall return,
*   and come to Zion with singing;*
everlasting joy shall be upon their heads;
*   they shall obtain joy and gladness,*
*   and sorrow and sighing shall flee away. (Isa. 51:9–11)*

Notice how the victory over the dragon is associated with the theme of the exodus: a cosmic event is linked to a historical event. The historical event is the same kind of chaos-overcoming act as the primordial battle with the dragon. Both are the work of the divine warrior. In Israel, this theme of the divine warrior seems to have been closely connected to the king and to worship in the Temple at Jerusalem. The power of the king to suppress chaos is his power to create a just society (see Psalm 72). These ideas also influenced the development of apocalypticism.

APOCALYPTICISM AS A MYTHO-PROPHETIC VIEW OF HISTORY

Paul Hanson argues persuasively that the blending of these two visions of God's victory in the increasingly pessimistic atmosphere of Israel after the exile resulted in the gradual dawning of apocalypticism (1979). The mythic story of God as the warrior who conquers Chaos provided the inner structure of apocalypticism that depicted the struggle between good and evil in cosmic dimensions. The prophetic hope of restoration within history was transferred to a cosmic redemption at the end of time (see Table I.2, page 49). But the prophetic concern with real history always remained, and the triumph of God was always envisioned to include the historical situation of the people. As apocalyptic thought developed, it evolved a specific view of how history works, which we may summarize as follows:

1. God has appointed a time for the end of the present world order and that time is imminent (see excerpt A above).
2. This age is under the control of the powers of evil, so we must expect that the good will suffer and the wicked prosper. This represented a complete shift from the earlier optimistic tradition that proclaimed that good would prosper and evil be punished, found, for example, in Proverbs (see excerpts A and D).
3. This age will soon be replaced by another, the age to come, which will be the exact opposite of this one. The new age will be accompanied by the judgment of evil and the reward of the righteous (see excerpts A, B, and D).

4. Between these two ages stands the decisive act of divine intervention. There was great variety in the ways different writers imagined this would take place. Some spoke of God sending the Messiah. Others spoke of two messiahs. In some visions, Michael would act as God's agent, perhaps alone or more often leading the armies of heaven. Others saw themselves as the human agents of the coming divine deliverance; some even advocated revolutionary violence. Others believed the final battle would be fought by God alone (see excerpt A).

5. As the end of this age approaches there will be an increase in the activity of evil and a period of intense suffering for the righteous. Usually called the *period of tribulation*, its most common metaphor was the labor of a woman in childbirth—birth pangs of the new age (see excerpt B).

The literary characteristics of apocalypses sketched earlier become logical once we understand the basic nature of apocalyptic thought. An apocalypse is symbolic because it claims to see behind the veil of ordinary experience, revealing this cosmic struggle between God and Satan. It is intended to transcend our common perceptions and reveal the ultimate causes of the events—a revelation of the cosmic processes underlying history. Only symbols could portray the interrelatedness of historical and cosmic events. The most commonly used images were numbers, animals, and heavenly signs (sun, stars, moon). Dreams, visions, and angels are the agents of this secret wisdom. And wisdom is required in the hearer to perceive the truth behind the symbol.

Even the pseudonymity of apocalyptic literature makes sense in this context, for the apocalypticist lived in a time after prophecy yet believed that he (or she) had a message truly derived from the earlier prophets. One advantage of this pseudonymity was that it allowed the writer to be an extraordinarily accurate predictor of the future course of events from the time of the ancient worthy to the writer's present, because of course it had all already happened. Often the fictional device employed was a "sealed book" that was revealed to the ancients but kept hidden until the last days, when it would be unsealed (Dan. 12:4). Here too the sense of unveiling what had been hidden is appropriate.

No one apocalyptic work contained all these literary and ideological characteristics; there was great variety. Examining these traits will help us experience Revelation as a typical example of a genre and will help us to appreciate the unique contributions of that work. Our ability to appreciate this literature will depend to a great extent on our ability to deal with its strange symbols.

SYMBOLS, IMAGES, AND MEANINGS

READING AND REFLECTION

Read chapter 1 of Revelation and make a list of all the symbols. Next to each, list what each might mean, based either on something the narrator says or on your own guess.

When you drive down the road and see a diamond-shaped sign at the edge with an S-shaped line on it, you instinctively slow down. You know it means danger. The road curves ahead. This is part of the common knowledge of all drivers. But what might you make of such a sign if you were an alien? Watch out for *s*'s? Scenic route? Snake crossing? We know such interpretations are ridiculous, yet they are no more so than some interpretations of Revelation. These three erroneous readings of the road sign symbol represent three types of errors commonly made in reading the symbolism of Revelation.

Mistaking curves for snakes is the kind of error that occurs when we lack the common knowledge of the original hearers, then imagine another context quite foreign to the original one—usually our own, modern context. Thus, for example, some interpreters will tell us that the symbol of the stars falling from heaven refers to nuclear missiles, for this is easy for us to imagine. But if you lived in a preelectric world, you would have seen hundreds of falling stars nearly every night of the year. We must always test our interpretations by asking whether they would have made sense to the original audience of Revelation in their context. Because neither John nor his hearers could have conceived of nuclear missiles, we must conclude that this is not a possible interpretation for the original meaning of the work.

To mistake the curve sign for the letter *s* and then imagine that it refers to a scenic route is the kind of mistake that results from a disregard of context altogether. The interpreter allows his or her own imagination to invent hidden meanings, which might be possible in the original context, but there is no evidence of that meaning in this particular case. Hence, we must seek a consistent, overall interpretation within which the individual symbols may be interpreted.

Imagining the *s* shape on the sign refers to real *s*'s stems from a misreading of the genre. It results from taking literally what was meant to be symbolic. This is an especially common error in reading Revelation, a book filled with symbols. A general rule for Revelation might then be this: never take the work at face value. Remember, it attempts to reveal a hidden reality, to produce insight. Revelation does not mean what it says; it means what it means. And to unravel what it means we must avoid taking symbols literally, keep a rein on our imaginations, and not ignore the historical context. We have to learn how to interpret the many symbols it uses.

A Guide to the Symbols

Many of the symbols used in Revelation were the common property of apocalypticists; they have a stylized meaning, which we have little difficulty interpreting. One example is the use of numbers, which the ancients generally regarded more mystically than we do. Numbers in Revelation must be read as symbolic statements instead of quantifiable amounts. The most obvious use of number symbolism is the number 7. The esoteric qualities of 7 were widely discussed in the ancient world, especially among the Neopythagorean philosophers.

Pythagoras (fl. 525 BCE) had sought to understand the harmony of the universe, pursuing his investigation through music and mathematics. He discovered the mathematical basis of harmony. In the Pythagorean system, certain numbers were considered masculine (3, 5, 7) and others feminine (2, 4, 6). For Pythagoras the great numbers were 1, the foundation of all that is, and 10, a perfect number. The number 10 is the triangle of 4: if you make a triangle with four dots on each side, the dots total ten. A square of a number originally meant the same thing, forming a square of dots.

Notice that our triangle is built on 1, the root of all, and contains the three dimensions and the three harmonies (the musical chords 1:2; 2:3; 3:4). The value of any two adjacent lines create masculine (odd) numbers; any two alternate lines create feminine (even) numbers. Four dots in three directions point to 7 and result in 10, both numbers of great significance. Such are the mystical qualities of numbers.

Another writer, Philo of Alexandria, described the mysteries of 7 as follows:

> So august is the dignity inherent by nature in the number 7, that it has a unique relation distinguishing it from all the other numbers within the decade [the first ten numbers]: for of these some beget without being begotten, some are begotten but do not beget, some do both of these, both beget and are begotten: 7 alone is found in no such category. (On the Creation 99)

By "beget" Philo means it generates another number from 1 to 10 by being doubled or tripled; being "begotten" is to be produced in such a manner. So 1 through 5 all beget; 6, 8, 9, and 10 are all begotten. Only 7 remains ungenerated and ungenerating. Thus, the Pythagoreans used it to symbolize the Unmoved Mover of Aristotle; the first cause, which is itself uncaused. This is admittedly a strange way to view numbers; but it was popularly accepted as true at the time the Apocalypse was produced.

We have learned, then, that not all numbers are alike. Each has its special significance, though some (8 and 9) were seldom felt to be symbolic. Like many apocalyptic writers, John used numbers to reflect the numbering of the creation story in Genesis 1. The first three days are associated with the cosmos, creating the elemental forms of light, air, earth, and sea. These are the forms that will contain the work of the remaining days. They are thus associated with the world above. Day four begins to fill these forms with actual things (sun, birds, animals). Thus, 4 is the number of the earth. Day six is the day humans are created. Day seven is God's day. Most of John's numbers are built on the symbolism of the basic numbers. Briefly, here are John's more important numbers:

3 stands for the spiritual order.	10 stands for totality.
4 stands for the created order.	12 stands for Israel (God's people; it is also the product of 3 and 4).
7 stands for perfection (contrast 6; it is also the sum of 3 and 4).	3½ stands for the number of evil.
Multiples and repetitions stand for intensification of the base number's meaning.	

John makes it appear that he has more numbers by using multiples of these numbers, especially squares. Such multiplication intensifies the meaning of the root number. Thus Christ rules 1,000 years: his full time (20:4). There are 144,000 redeemed (7:4) (that is, 12 × 12 × 10 × 10 × 10): all God's people. The new Jerusalem lies "foursquare," with multiples of 12 (21:16–17). Another derived number is 3½, which stands for the period of evil, being half of 7 but neither 3 nor 4. This 3½-year period can also be called 42 months or 1,260 days.

John used colors in a similar fixed way:

> White stands for victory (not purity).
> Red is the color of war and strife.
> Black is the color of famine and suffering.
> Pale (actually a gray-yellow, the color of rotting meat) is the color of death.

Animals too are used symbolically:

> Beasts are always satanic powers.
> The lamb is the animal of sacrifice.
> The lion is king.
> Eagles and oxen are the superior animals of their kind.
> Horns point to power and thus to rulers.
> Multiple heads point to multiple rulers.

These are all commonplace images that the first-century hearer would readily have known. We, however, will need to keep a scorecard.

In addition to these ordinary images, John helps the audience along by providing his own interpretations of several of his symbols. Revelation provides a dozen or more such explicit interpretations (see Table 13.2).

TABLE 13.2   SYMBOLS INTERPRETED IN THE STORY

Reference	Symbol (What It Says)	John's Interpretation (What It Means)
1:8	Alpha and Omega	The One who was, who is, and who is coming
1:20	Seven stars and lamps	Angels and churches
8:3	Angel with censer	Prayers of the saints
10:1–11	Little open book	Must prophesy again
11:8	Great city, Sodom	Where the Lord was crucified
13:6	God's tabernacle	Those dwelling on earth
13:18	Six hundred sixty-six	Number of (a) human
14:14–20	Winepress	Wrath of God
17:9–15	Seven heads	Seven mountains and kings
17:12	Ten horns	Ten kings
18:21	Angel with millstone	Babylon cast down
19:11–16	One on a white horse	Word of God

The meanings of several other symbols are obvious: the Lion-Lamb of 5:6 is surely Jesus; the earthquake in 6:12 represents judgment; the birth in 12:1 is surely that of the Messiah. The descriptions of Jesus in chapter 1 are derived from Daniel and the appearance of the high priest. With a little effort, we can decipher most of John's symbols.

Three aspects of this correlation between symbol and interpretation are intriguing. First, the use of symbols forces the hearer to operate on two levels at the same time. On one level we move in a fantastic universe of angels and monsters, whores and virgins, stars and temples, dragons and warriors, Christ and antichrist. Yet on considering John's own interpretation, we find that we are also operating on the level of ordinary experience. We are not hearing about stars but about churches (1:20). John is not really eating books, he is prophesying (10:9–11). It never would have occurred to me to picture a prayer meeting as an angel swinging a golden censer and throwing it upon the earth (8:3–5), but perhaps John's prayer meetings were livelier than those I have seen. And there is something maliciously appropriate in symbolizing the grandeur of Rome as a gaudy prostitute riding on a scarlet beast, at least from the provincial perspective of John (17:3–14). But late first-century Roman culture is under attack, not gaudy prostitutes. We must, then, learn to keep our heads as we travel through this esoteric terrain and exotic symbolism, most of which seems to refer to everyday realities. This does not imply that the book should be read like a codebook. John's story is about monsters and whores, and we must experience these as real images to feel the power of his work. Premature translation will destroy the story. But to fail to make the interpretation will destroy its meaning.

There is another sense in which the hearer is forced to think on two levels, for reality itself exists on two levels in John's book. Notice, for example, the analogy between the stars and the lamps. Lamps are earthly analogues to stars; they represent below what the stars are above. As one ancient observed about fortune-telling by looking into a fire:

It is not so very mysterious that this Flamelet, trivial as it is, and produced by human agency, should yet possess an awareness of that greater and celestial Flame as of its Sire, and that it should know and announce to us by divine intuition what the latter will be doing up on the crest of the sky. (Apuleius The Golden Ass 2, Lindsay translation)

Thus, there are connections between things below and things above. On the level of interpretation, too, there are angels and churches, an analogy more compelling when we recall that in Greek the word **angelos** means messenger. In this story there is an above and a below to the world, and John has ascended into the above "in the spirit" (4:2), where he sees behind the veil of ordinary experience to the true causes. This notion of the world as consisting of an above and a below that correspond to each other in certain crucial ways was widely shared in John's world. Deriving from the mild and diverse Platonism of ancient culture, it was popularly assumed that this world was an imitation, a copy of that other world of truth and reality. (For more discussion of this point see pages 229–31, 411–13.)

Closer inspection of John's use of symbols reveals a third, more shocking, point. John has disarmed a number of his most powerful symbols. He has, in fact, transformed images of power into images of vulnerability, symbols of conquest into those of suffering. The Apocalypse portrays at least three such reversals of symbolic value. The first and most dramatic of these occurs in chapter 5. Let us consider the scene.

READING AND REFLECTION

Read Revelation 5:1–6.

1. What is the basic drama of this short scene?
2. Why does John cry?
3. Note the contrast between what John "heard" and what he "saw." What emotional impact does this change in symbols cause?

REVERSING THE IMAGES

This is a very dramatic scene. John shapes the hearers' reaction to it by sharing his own: he wept when no one was found worthy to open the scroll (5:4). An angel comforts him with the news that "the Lion of the tribe of Judah, the Root of David" is able to open it. This is a standard prophetic symbol based on the description in Gen. 49:9–10, which depicted Judah as a lion and as ruler. It was elaborated in later traditions to show the lion tearing his enemies to pieces. If this is what the hearers expected, they would have been greatly surprised. For instead of the bloodthirsty

Hirmer Verlag, Munich

ROMAN COIN OF DOMITIAN, ABOUT 83 CE   This naked infant seated on a globe with his hands extended into a field of seven stars is a tribute to Domitian's son who died in infancy. The inscription refers to "the Divine Caesar." John saw such tributes as antichrist and pictured Christ holding the seven stars (see Rev. 1:12–20).

lion, what actually appears is a bloody lamb incongruously described as "standing as though it had been slain." What are we to make of this transformation of symbols?

On the one hand, this is simply creating images for historical events. Jesus just did not match up to the grand and regal messianic expectations commonly held; he was no second David. He did not overthrow the evil earthly powers. The pagans continued to dominate God's holy people. Instead of slaying the wicked, he was slain by them. This is history. But John also makes a more daring point. He asserts that the lamb *is* the lion. Jesus is the Messiah, a messiah who has conquered through suffering rather than by tearing his enemies to pieces. It is his suffering that enables him to open the scroll, for he has conquered and is worthy. Jesus does not conquer by overwhelming the enemy with superior force. Instead, he shows that the superior force overwhelming all is persistence even in the face of suffering. Hence, the sufferer is the conqueror; the victim is the victor.

There is a similar reversal of images in chapter 12, where we hear about a dark war in heaven. In a scene reminiscent of Marduk's battle with Tiamat, Michael and his angels defeat the dragon and his host, driving them out of heaven, casting them down to earth. In Jewish tradition, **Michael** was the "chief of the holy angels" (*Ascension of Isaiah* 3:16) and often performed messianic tasks (for example, Dan. 10:12; 12:1). Another apocalyptic work describes him as "the mediator between God and men for the peace of Israel. He shall stand in opposition to the kingdom of the enemy" (*Testament of Dan* 6:2). This image of cosmic warfare corresponds to the image of the lion and, like it, is immediately reversed. For when heaven celebrates this triumph, it is explained:

> *But they have conquered him by the blood of the Lamb and by the word of their testimony, for they did not cling to life even in the face of death. (12:11)*

Again conquest is attributed to faithful suffering. But this time it is not only the death of the Lamb but that of his followers who add their testimony to his. Not only does Jesus' suffering overthrow evil, so does that of his faithful followers. Once again, the victim is proclaimed the victor.

Another scene of cosmic war occurs later in the book with the appearance of the divine warrior, riding a white horse (19:11–21). Once again we have the traditional images of the eschatological battle, and again they are subverted. There is the battle setting, but no battle is ever portrayed. The narrative jumps directly to the victory pronouncement (verses 19–20). We are told that the hosts of the wicked are all killed (the traditional image), but their deaths are attributed to one sword, "the sword of the rider on the horse, the sword that came from his mouth" (verse 21). They are undone by the word of Jesus, which is the Word of God (his title in verse 13) as well as the word of his testimony (verse 10; note his other titles in verse 11: the Faithful and True, which point to his death). This symbol of "his testimony" is complex. The "testimony of Jesus" is his death, but it is also testimony about Jesus (see 1:9). This faithful witness about Jesus will lead to suffering: the *martys* (Greek for "witness") will become the martyr. Again, the death of Jesus and the suffering of his followers bring about the overthrow of evil. This is even more evident when we observe that Jesus appears before the battle with his robe dipped in blood (19:13). The blood is his. (Note that, earlier, Jesus was said to have tread the winepress "outside the city," a traditional way of locating where he died, 14:20. The probable source, and a more traditional use, of this imagery of the bloody robe and the winepress is Isa. 63:1–6.)

Jesus conquers through his death and the death of his faithful followers. It is not that the wicked have killed him and now he returns to kill them; the Lamb is not transformed into a Lion. John's symbol is more radical: the Lamb is the Lion. The death of Jesus overthrows evil (compare John 12:31). "The blood of the saints and the blood of the witnesses to Jesus" have caused the fatal inebriation of the great harlot (17:6; 16:6). The victims are the victors.

Thus, while John draws his images from the traditional apocalyptic stock, even using the central symbol of cosmic combat, his experience of Jesus has led him to radically reverse the value of these symbols in order to express the conviction that faithful witness brings salvation and judgment. But this conviction is not argued, or even stated; it is portrayed, enacted in a story. Let us turn our attention to that story and its action, plot, and structure.

THE PLOT OF THE APOCALYPSE

John seems to lead hearers by the hand until about halfway through this work. He carefully tells us there are seven messages, seven seals, and seven trumpets. Then he seems to abandon us near the end of chapter 11 and does not resume numbering his sequences again until chapter 16. This has produced a great variety of outlines for the work. Many interpreters have been unable to resist the urge to remedy John's deficient numbering, and various sequences of seven have been created out of the material John neglected to number. This does not seem wise. Before we proceed to help John in this way we should try to understand his own organization. Perhaps these sequences were not meant to be numbered. In part this urge to organize everything into a series of seven, perhaps even into seven such series, is the result of a rationalistic reading of the book. The modern urge has been to organize everything into an outline, hardly the best way to comprehend the structure of a narrative. The Apocalypse must be encountered as story, with imagination. We are almost ready to attempt such a reading. Having gained some perspective on the general kind of literature this represents and having explored the way it uses symbols, we must now examine the general methods it employs to weave together the diverse material this work contains.

PRINCIPLES OF ORGANIZATION

Revelation is presented as one vast vision that John experienced on an island called **Patmos**, off the coast of Asia Minor, while he was "in the Spirit on the Lord's day" (1:10). Thus, it is a book of ecstasy. Since by its nature ecstasy transcends the senses, ecstatic literature must not be expected to conform completely to rational analysis. In Revelation, as one commentator suggested, "we must reckon with an element of incoherence" (Sweet, 1979:44). Similarly, John's grammar does not conform to the proper Greek usage. Numerous grammatical "mistakes" occur in Revelation but not (as is often assumed) because John knew no better; a grammatical construction he misuses in one place is often correctly used in another. We must understand that ecstasy does not always follow the rules. These loose ends of grammar and event enhance the feeling of extraordinary experience. We must anticipate a bit of untamed order in this enthusiastic literature.

On the other hand, we should not assume too readily that John's narrative is incoherent simply because his organization is not immediately obvious to us. John employs two other principles that lend his work an aura of enthusiasm and complexity. One type of complexity results from John's practice of making later events and cycles mirror earlier ones and echo their meanings. Such **recapitulation** is not a matter of simple repetition, for the later symbols modify, intensify, and focus earlier ones. But the underlying meanings of the two are the same. Thus, for example, the relationship between prayer and judgment originally shown in seals five and six (6:10, 12) is recapitulated in the new image of the angel with the censer, full of the saints' prayers, which, when thrown on the earth, brings judgment (8:3–5).

Understanding this principle solves many problems, for we do not have to imagine that the narrative is always moving on to new events: it may be further explaining old events. Thus, for example, we hear the declaration in 11:15 that the kingdom of God has come. Rather, it seems to come and go, for chapter 12 opens with a new vision of conflict carrying us back in time to the birth of Jesus, and further to the exodus and the Garden of Eden. This flashback may be interpreted as John's attempt to provide a new image for the coming of the kingdom. It is as if he were saying, "Now that you have seen the coming of the kingdom, let me show you how it happened." He is recapitulating the meaning of earlier images by showing what brought about the kingdom: the birth of the Messiah. Such recapitulation does not preclude the possibility of progress within the narrative, but the progress will be on the level of the images rather than their meaning.

Another type of complexity is achieved by mingling material from separate scenes to interlace the two scenes, a technique known as **intercalation**. John often interweaves material from one section of his book into another section to bind the two more closely together. Thus, if we imagine two cycles that we designate A B C and 1 2 3, intercalation might produce a combined sequence: A B 1 C 2 3. This sandwiching of outside material into the first sequence forces the hearer to imagine a relationship between them, thus creating a unity. Most of the material that seems out of place in the Apocalypse may be explained by this device.

Whereas recapitulation echoes earlier meanings in new symbols, intercalation echoes the symbols themselves. Thus, for example, the symbol of the 144,000 who are sealed in the middle of the series of seven seals (7:1–8) really belongs to the battle scene (14:1) and ties the two scenes together. Intercalation applies to the repetition of symbols, recapitulation to the repetition of their meaning. It is possible for a scene to be both a recapitulation and an intercalation (for example, 8:3–5).

The use of these techniques has produced a complex work. It is no wonder that commentators seeking a simple outline or a linear development have produced divergent results. We must expect to find symbolic material from one section intercalated into other sections, binding them together. We must anticipate recapitulations of similar ideas under very different symbolic images, producing a sense of repetition and explanation. We must also expect to find some material that seems wildly out of place, enhancing the ecstatic nature of the book (16:15). Now we are ready to read the Apocalypse itself.

I find the easiest way to follow the story of the Apocalypse is to view it as having three interconnected acts. The first takes place on the island of Patmos, the second in heaven in the divine throne room, and the third takes place on earth. The changes in location correspond to basic changes in the action. In the first act on Patmos, John records the words of the heavenly visitor. In the second act in heaven, John observes the heavenly liturgy. And in the third act, the dragon makes war on the followers of Jesus. See Table 13.3 for more details.

READING AND REFLECTION

For your first reading of the Apocalypse (which should take about an hour) use Table 13.3 to read each act.

1. In the first act, what elements are numbered?
2. In the second act, what is intercalated into each series of seven? What is repeated in the second series (the trumpets) from the first series (the seals)?
3. In the third act, what is the cause and purpose of this war?

PATTERNS OF NUMBERS: 7-3-2

The first three chapters contain only one numbered sequence, that of the seven churches. It is universally agreed that these form a major segment of the work. The next numbered sequence occurs in chapter 6 and afterward: seven seals. This leads directly into another: seven trumpets. The last three trumpets are also separately numbered as a series of three woes. Closer examination shows that the author somehow marks each series of seven so that it consists of subsets of four and three. In the seals, for example, there were four horsemen and three heavenly signs. Here the four seem to relate to earth and the three to the spiritual world. The seventh trumpet, the final work of God, brings the proclamation that the kingdom has come.

TABLE 13.3 **THE THREE ACTS OF THE APOCALYPSE**

	First Act	*Second Act*	*Third Act*
Place	Patmos	Heaven	Earth
Characters	Jesus as Majestic Human John Churches	Jesus as Lamb-slain Elders and Heavenly beings	Jesus as Heavenly Warrior Dragon and beasts Woman and her children
Action	Letter writing	Worship	War
John Presented as	Secretary	Heavenly traveler	Seer/prophet
Mythic Paradigm	Theophany	Throne vision	Holy war
Chapters	1–3	4–11	12–22

There are many ways to view the organization of the material in the Apocalypse, but when viewed as a story it falls naturally into three acts, each containing a complete action. Part of John's artistry was to weave these three acts together into one larger story.

The next explicit numbering does not occur until chapter 16, where John reports seeing seven angels with seven plagues. How, then, are we to construe the material in chapters 12–14? Notice that John introduces these seven angels by saying he saw "another sign" (15:1). If we look for earlier signs, we find two. Chapter 12 begins with a reference to the "great sign" that was seen in heaven—a woman clothed with the sun—then immediately shifts our attention to "another sign" (12:3). This material may be understood as a series of three signs or as a great sign with two other subordinate signs. To support the dualistic view we have the double vision of the open temple (11:19 and 15:5). The triadic view would find evidence in the heavenly significance of the number three.

This last sign consists of seven angels pouring seven bowls of wine on the earth (the ancients drank their wine from bowls). The seventh is again climactic: "it is done" (16:17). Yet it is not done; the story continues. Now one of these seven angels presents John with two contrasting visions of two very different women: the whore of Babylon (17:1) and the virgin bride of Jerusalem (21:9). There is no other numbered sequence in the rest of the revelation. Apparently the remaining scenes are to be construed with these two visions of the feminine. Even though one can easily find a series of seven visions, each marked by the construction "I saw," in the scenes from 19:11–21:8, John did not number them. Nor should we.

John's explicit use of numbers would have been valuable in listening to this work, even though the numbers do not solve all the problems of its structure. This general structure will become clearer if we now turn our attention to the action portrayed.

THREE DRAMAS IN ONE

Aristotle observed that the action of a story is defined by its beginning and end. But the beginning and end of this work seem to stand outside the story. Revelation begins and ends by directly addressing the reader in the guise of a letter, a most unusual form for an apocalyptic work. There is a word to the reader and advice to the hearers (1:3 and 22:18–19). The work begins and ends in the real world and draws the reader into the story. The end corresponds to the beginning (see Table 13.4).

This technique of beginning and ending by directly addressing the reader serves as a bridge from the consciousness of the everyday reality to the consciousness of the reality created by this story. It is like the flight attendant who greets you as you enter and exit an airplane, easing your transition. It resembles the writing on the screen at the beginning and end of a movie, leading you into and out of the story. These two sections frame the whole work and help shape its meaning.

The Drama of the Messages

John has welcomed the hearers aboard his craft and now launches into his first drama: the risen Christ appears to John and dictates seven messages to seven angels of seven churches. (The angels are to the churches as stars are to lamps; 1:20.) This action, completed in 3:22, constitutes the first act in John's drama.

Each message follows the same pattern:

The addressee is named.
The sender is designated by referring to some of the symbolism used to describe the risen Christ in the earlier vision.

TABLE 13.4   PARALLELS BETWEEN THE OPENING AND CLOSING

Opening	Correspondence	Closing
1:1, 4, 9	John names himself	22:8
1:1	An angel sent	22:6
1:1	Will soon take place	22:6
1:1	The servants	22:6
1:3	Reader blessed	22:7
1:3	The time is near	22:10
1:4	Grace to you	22:21
1:8	The Alpha and Omega	22:13
1:10	The spirit	22:17
1:16, 20	Stars and angels	22:16
1:17	John falls at feet	22:8

The works of the church are diagnosed.
The appropriate praise or blame is given.
The refrain occurs: the one having an ear should hear.
The promise of future reward is given.

The only variation is that in the last four the promise and the refrain occur in reverse order.

If we focus on the praise and blame, we can see that John wrote to a deeply divided community. Some of these cities receive only praise and are wholly supportive of John (Smyrna and Philadelphia), some receive only blame and are lost to him (Sardis and Laodicea), and some receive both praise and blame, with one faction following John and others following other leaders (Ephesus, Pergamum, and especially Thyatira).

Thyatira was the least important city of the seven but receives the longest, central letter. The majority (John addresses his own followers as "the rest" 2:24) follow a prominent woman leader whom John calls Jezebel, a symbolic name. Jezebel was an ancient queen, wife of King Ahab and daughter of King Ethbaal, a Phoenician; she established the worship of Baal in Israel. Her story and great struggle with Elijah is told in 1 Kings (16:29–19:18). She is the archetype, the original model of one who seduces Israel to worship alien Gods. John's condemnation of his female opponent, who also claimed prophetic powers, could not be more complete. Curiously, in the one specific charge he makes against her (she teaches that they may eat things sacrificed to idols), she seems closer to Paul's position than does John (compare 1 Corinthians 8–10 and Romans 14, where Paul allows eating food sacrificed to idols, providing one avoids the idolatry; 1 Cor. 10:25–29). We begin to notice John's passion for avoiding entanglements with Greco-Roman culture, a theme that will expand in the rest of the story.

Each of these messages will repay close study. As the audience would hear each message read, the seventh is the expected end. Nothing said thus far would require any further narration, but it is only the end of the first act. The scene shifts, and a new action begins.

The Drama of Heavenly Worship

John is now transported through an open door into heaven, where he observes God's throne and the heavenly court at worship (4:1). While new, the scene has been anticipated in the messages with the promise of an open door (3:8; 3:20) and a call to join Jesus on God's throne (3:21). Applying Aristotle's principle of beginning and end once again, we find that the worship begun in chapter 4 culminates in chapter 11, where the twenty-four elders resume their worship of God (11:16). Act two portrays the heavenly liturgy, to which, we may suppose, the earthly liturgy of John's congregations would in some ways correspond.

The initial scene focuses entirely on God. John majestically describes the entire creation at worship before the Creator. The four living creatures include wild and tame animals, the flying eagle, and humanity. Ezekiel had used similar images (Ezek. 1:4–14). In later Jewish tradition they were understood to represent the chief of their kind: each king paying homage to the king of kings. The twenty-four elders may represent the twenty-four priestly families (1 Chron. 24:4–6), or they may represent the twelve tribes and the twelve apostles (Rev. 21:12–14), or both at once.

But this scene of primal harmony is soon disrupted by an angel calling for someone worthy to open a sealed scroll. When no one is found, John weeps. Here we feel the loss of the world as it might have been: a world in need of redemption, sealed off from God's revelation.

The subsequent scene focuses on Jesus, the one worthy to open the scroll. This strange scroll requires some discussion. Three suggestions have been made concerning its symbolic significance. First, it may recall the common apocalyptic theme of the sealed book. Because the apocalyptic revelation was intended only for the last days, the original book was sealed and hidden until the appropriate time (see Dan. 12:4 and compare Ezek. 2:8–10). To unseal such a scroll would then mean to reveal the message of the world's end. Judgment and salvation are at hand.

Second, a scroll with seven seals may reflect the Roman practice of sealing a will with the seals of seven witnesses. Only when the will was to be put into effect would it be unsealed. Thus, to unseal such a scroll would mean to put into effect the will of God. Salvation and judgment are at hand.

Third, the scroll may reflect the scroll of the Torah, the revelation of God. We know of other early traditions that spoke of the Law as "veiled" to those outside Christ (2 Cor. 3:14) and of Christ "opening" the Law to new understandings (Luke 24:27). To unseal such a scroll would mean to reveal the true meaning of the Hebrew Scriptures. Although John never quotes the Scriptures, he continually repeats their ideas and phrases. (These extensive echoes of Scripture may be conveniently studied in the Jerusalem Bible, where they are put in italic type.) But we should be in no hurry to make a choice among these three possibilities. All three images work; all three may be intended.

In any case, the meaning is much the same: Jesus as the Lamb-slain worthily reveals and actualizes the will of God. He brings God's rule into reality (5:13). Or we may translate more fully: the harmony of creation has been disrupted. The will of God no longer prevails. Only the death of Jesus reestablishes the harmony. Of course, such a translation loses much of the force and delight of John's images and cannot quite capture his meaning.

We come now to our first apocalyptic cycle (6:1–8:2), a series of seals, each producing a small dramatic scene. We also encounter the first major intercalation (all of chapter 7), which puns on the seals by a sealing of the righteous. Logically, the symbol of those sealed relates to future action, to the following series of trumpets (9:4) and to the coming battle (14:1). To encounter them here is to feel that these actions are related to each other.

Let us examine more closely how this series works, the logic by which the various scenes succeed each other. The first four scenes are an obvious unit, showing four horses with their riders. Interpreters differ on the meaning of the first rider on a white horse. Because Christ later appears on such a mount (19:11), many have argued that Christ is symbolized here. But others contend nearly the opposite: noting that the figure lacks all the identifying iconography of the Christ given in chapter 1, they propose that the rider of the white horse represents the conqueror, a military figure. More specifically, scholars have shown that the bow points to the Parthian warrior who made fearsome use of that instrument. Parthia was Rome's archfoe in this era, a constant threat to peace on the eastern frontier. Thus, the first rider is the harbinger of war. In a similar way these symbols can be directly related to Roman warfare. The God of the Roman army was **Mithras**, who was commonly symbolized as riding a white horse, carrying a bow, and crowned with the sun. Both interpretations view the first rider as conqueror, allowing us to make sense of the sequence. Each leads inevitably to the next:

$$\text{Conqueror} \rightarrow \text{War} \rightarrow \text{Famine} \rightarrow \text{Death}$$

War inevitably led to famine in the ancient economy because it disrupted the planting or harvesting of crops in that overwhelmingly agrarian society. The famine envisioned here is serious; a day's worth of wheat is going for a day's wages.

The logic of the four horsemen is straightforward—the simple lesson of history. What, then, makes it a revelation? To answer this question we must consider the rest of the sequence. Seals five, six, and seven have no inherent connection to these four horsemen. Their logic lies in their breaking the logic of the first four. They answer the questions: How shall we ever get free from the oppression of history? How can the awful work of the conqueror be arrested? The answer is wonderfully naive: by the prayers of the saints. For the prayers of the saints (seal five), sealed with their suffering, lead inevitably to the divine judgment portrayed as seal six. If the first four seals reveal only the logic of history, the last three pull aside the veil (*apocalypsis*) and reveal the hidden course of history in the divine will.

According to this logic, seal seven should reveal the kingdom of God. But it is far too early in the story for that. John delays (10:6). Instead of the end, seal seven opens out into a new sequence of seven trumpets. A short intercalation (8:3–5) recapitulates the power of the prayers of the saints to bring judgment to the earth.

The new sequence of trumpets recapitulates the judgment allusively portrayed in seal six. Multiple images portray the destruction of one third of the earth. Then another major intercalation intrudes between the sixth and seventh components (10:1–11:13).

This intercalation has three visions. The first portrays a small open scroll that John is to consume. The imagery repeats that of Ezekiel (2:8–3:3). As Ezekiel's message was both sweet and bitter, so John proclaims both salvation and judgment. The second shows John measuring the temple, a symbol of preservation. Notice that the true temple is to be preserved while the outward court is to be trampled by the Gentiles, just as John's communities will be preserved despite outward oppression. The third vision provides a new image for this proclamation and preservation, the symbol of the two final witnesses, Moses and Elijah returned as the Jewish traditions anticipated. These two "lamps" (11:4) enact the mission of the church, whose suffering brings judgment and vindication.

With that judgment John hastens on to the final trumpet. Great voices signal: "the kingdom of the world has become the kingdom of our Lord and of his Christ, and he shall reign forever and ever" (11:15). Heavenly worship resumes. Surely the hearer expects the end of the tale. Creation is redeemed. But the story does not end. John sees into the heavenly temple, and startling new action follows.

The Drama of the Woman, the Dragon, and the Warrior

John's final scene retells one of the oldest and most enduring stories in literature, stretching back some two thousand years before his time but alive and still interesting today. In ancient times this was the story of Marduk defeating the dragon Tiamat; in medieval legend it was the story of St. George and the dragon; today it thrives in fantasy literature and computer games. It provides the archetypal plot of many stories. And it is the most powerful part of Revelation. New characters are introduced. Woman holds center stage. Dragons, beasts, and warriors control the action. A decisive shift now occurs in the nature of the action, which to this point has been dominated by divine action. In Chapter 2 we discussed the basic structure of stories, involving a subject trying to deliver an object to a receiver (see pages 70–74). Using this model, the basic story contracts of the first two acts may be simplified thus:

	Basic Story Elements
Task/Lack	The world needs salvation and judgment.
Agent	Christ
Conflict	
Opponents	Unfaithful witnesses
Proponents	John, angels
Resolution	The message is delivered; all worship before the throne.

But in the third act the action shifts, as the beasts now become the agents of the action.

	Basic Story Elements
Task/Lack	War on and destruction of the woman and her children/witnesses
Agent	Beasts sent by the dragon
Conflict	
Opponents	The heavenly warrior and the faithful witnesses
Proponents	The harlot and the kings of the earth
Resolution	The dragon is defeated.

In this third act the dragon initiates the action, waging terror and warfare on the woman, attempting to destroy her child, persecuting the faithful. The only hint we have had of this new action is in the scene of the two witnesses, an intercalation in which this story pattern was foreshadowed (the beast was mentioned at 11:7, even though not formally introduced until 13:1).

The story portrays a dragon attempting to destroy a woman and her son. The woman is a complex symbol: she is Israel, mother of the Messiah; she is Eve, whose promised seed would destroy the serpent (Gen. 3:15). We cannot know whether first-century readers would have also thought of her as Mary, nor can we be sure they would have recognized motifs from Greek and Roman mythology: Leto is hidden on the island of Delos to protect her and the newborn Apollo from the dragon Python; Romulus and Remus, the founders of Rome, were threatened with destruction as infants; and the Goddess Roma was portrayed on coins as queen of heaven. John may intend to contrast Roma (Rome) with the true queen of heaven. There is also an Egyptian story in which Isis is pursued by Set (a red dragon), but her son Horus later kills Set—as Apollo later kills Python. Both Set and Apollo were sun Gods, and their stories reflect the perennial battle between light and darkness (see John 1:5).

Failing in his attempts to destroy the child or the woman, the dragon turns his attention to the rest of her offspring. Like Tiamat of old, he conjures a beast from the sea and a beast from the earth who attempt to coerce all people to worship them and the dragon. The Lamb and his 144,000 stand against them. Multiple scenes of judgment follow and culminate in the seven angels with the seven final plagues. The plagues parallel the motifs of the trumpets, but now the destruction is complete. Like the trumpet series, they end with a proclamation: "It is done" (16:17).

Just what is done is portrayed in two visions of two women: a monstrous prostitute and a virgin bride, each with accompanying scenes of judgment and of redemption, respectively. It is impossible to summarize adequately the action of the various scenes, but perhaps some clearer delineation of the characters and symbols will enable us to read them with greater understanding.

Ultimately, the image of the beast goes back to Daniel, where the contrast is between the animalistic character of the Gentile nations and the human quality of Israel. The seven heads and ten horns are allegorically related to the various Roman rulers (17:9–10); the first head whose death stroke does not kill the beast alludes to the assassination of Julius Caesar, which did little to stop the empire (13:3; in the Greek text it is not the head that is healed but the beast). For John the key to this conflict with the beast involves worship; the beast demands total allegiance. It is death to refuse such worship (13:15).

This demand of the beast is answered by the demand of the angel, flying in mid-heaven with eternal good news:

Fear God and give him glory, for the hour of his judgment has come; and worship him who made heaven and earth, the sea and the springs of water. (14:7)

This is the central concern of this narrative. The essential struggle is for the hearts and minds of men and women. To worship the beast is to bruise the heel of the son; to worship Christ is to crush the head of the serpent (Gen. 3:15). Notice the nice wordplay on *head*. A bishop writing to one of these same churches a couple of decades later admonished them:

Seek, then, to come together more frequently to give thanks [that is, to celebrate the Eucharist] and glory to God. For when you gather together frequently the powers of Satan are destroyed, and his mischief is brought to nothing, by the concord of your faith. There is nothing better than peace, by which every war in heaven and earth is abolished. (Ignatius To the Ephesians 13:1–2)

Thus, the real war of Revelation is a war to conquer the hearts and minds of the people of Asia Minor. Receiving the mark of the beast on the hand and forehead (13:17; 14:9) is probably a symbolic way of speaking about submitting to the economic (hand) and spiritual (head) domination of the Roman Empire. To worship at the shrine of the emperor was one thing, but even to buy one's daily bread required using coins that testified to his deity. (See the coin on page 89.)

Two harvest images complete this first sign: the wheat and, especially, the grape harvest (14:14–20). The results of this harvest are bread and wine, and the wine-blood covers 1,600 measures: the whole earth. The eucharistic themes are clear.

The second sign recapitulates and greatly expands the portrayal of judgment. Enlarging on the wine metaphor, seven bowls of wrath are poured out on the earth. Those who poured out the saints' blood are given blood to drink (16:6). They are drunk with wine (17:2). The Babylonian whore is drunk with the blood of the saints and the witnesses of Jesus (17:6). The logic of these judgments is to show that evil ultimately defeats itself, even as the beast ultimately turns on the prostitute, strips her naked, and eats her flesh (17:16). John may be remembering what Rome did to Jerusalem.

There follows a lengthy lament and ironic liturgy over the fall of Babylon: kings, merchants, and sailors all weep for the departed glory (18), while the multitude rejoices (19). This liturgy follows the ancient mythic pattern:

The appearance of the divine warrior (19:11–16)
The cosmic warfare (19:19–21)
The coronation of the proper king (20:1–6)
The fixing of destinies (20:11–15)
The divine marriage (21)

John might be accused of mixing his metaphors in this wedding between a lamb and a city. The city is a combined idealization of Jerusalem, the dwelling place of God, and the Garden of Eden. It represents the redemption of all creation, now including the city, a human creation. In this fantastic vision of the end, the work of humanity is taken up into and perfected in the work of God.

Use the following reading guide to browse through the Apocalypse, trying to follow the main contours of the action in the different acts. Write a short plot summary of either act two or act three.

READING GUIDE TO THE APOCALYPSE

Opening Address to the Audience   1:1–11
  Literary address to the seven churches   1:4–7

Writing messages on Patmos: the revelation of Jesus   1:12–3:22
  The risen Jesus appears to John   1:12–20
  Jesus sends messages to the seven cities   2:1–3:22

Witnessing worship in the heavenly throne room   4:1–11:18
  The liturgy of creation   4
  The liturgy of redemption   5
  Unsealing the scroll [intercalation: sealed servants, 7:1–13]   6–7
  Sounding the trumpets [intercalation: heavenly scenes, 10:1–11:14]   8–11

Seeing the signs of war: the dragon's attack   11:19–22:5
  The first sign in heaven: a woman pursued   12–14
    Eve/Israel/Messiah/Christ   12
    Satan/Rome   13
    Lamb/judgment   14
  The second sign in heaven: seven final plagues   15–16
  The vision of the prostitute   17–18
    Scenes of judgment   19:1–21:8
  The vision of the bride   21:9–22:5
    Scenes of restoration   21:22–22:5

Closing address to the audience   22:6–20
  Literary farewell to the churches   22:21

Notice also how John begins this vision "in the spirit on the Lord's day" (1:11) but then ascends to the heavenly throne room "in the spirit" (4:1), and finally is transported "in the spirit" to witness the closing scenes of the two antithetical female archetypes (17:3).

SUMMARY OF THE PLOT

Three separate actions are recounted in Revelation. The risen Christ appears and dictates seven messages to his churches. The Lamb appears in the heavenly throne scene and opens a sealed scroll that reveals the will of God and the judgment of evil. The dragon makes war on the elect but is overcome by the divine warrior, resulting in the replacement of the whore by the bride. Each action has its own scroll. There is the scroll on which the seven messages are written (1:11), the sealed scroll that must be opened by Christ (5:1), and the small open scroll that John must consume (10:2). This open scroll is described in the intercalation that foreshadows the action of act three, thus properly belonging to that final action. It may be that the open scroll represents the revelation of nature (which John sees by looking at the heavens; 12:1), whereas the sealed scroll represents the special revelation of the Hebrew Scriptures, which must be opened by Jesus to be known. The messages would then represent the new revelation given in Jesus.

Each action shows the realization of the coming of salvation and judgment, with subsequent acts being recapitulations, elaborations, and clarifications of earlier ones. In the messages, Jesus has promised to come to his churches in judgment (3:3) and salvation (3:20). The second act offers a fuller portrayal of this coming judgment (seal six and the six trumpets) and salvation (seal seven and trumpet seven). These are made possible by the Lamb slain, by the death of Jesus. The relationship of the third act to the second is evident if we see the link between chapter 11 (the declaration that God's kingdom has come and the resumption of heavenly worship) and chapter 12 (the birth of the Messiah and the struggle with evil). The new action of chapter 12 represents a recapitulation of the earlier action, explaining how the change of kingdoms has occurred historically.

These three acts do not represent one continuous action. The relationship between them is one of meaning, with later acts expanding the meaning of earlier ones. The three scenes do not grow out of one another in the way we anticipate in a modern drama. They more closely resemble three one-act plays on a common theme, performed in succession within a common frame. Each act reveals the hidden dimension of life in which the kingdom of God is realized: Jesus comes to his churches, enables the cosmic worship of God to persist, and overthrows the work of the evil one. These are three dimensions of the work of Christ, not three consecutive actions. Each reveals the meaning of Christ's death and resurrection. I am tempted to say they portray the work of Christ in relation to the church, in relation to the cosmos, and in relation to history. But that is perhaps clearer than John would wish to be. The unity of this work is achieved by using a common set of symbols in all three acts, by intercalating aspects of one act in another, and by presenting all three in a common setting.

THE FRAMEWORK OF A LETTER

We saw above that the opening and closing of Revelation correspond, that they employ the device of a letter, and that they address the hearer directly as a person in the real world. Such letters were often read in public worship, as were apocalypses (1 Cor. 14:26).

John's "letter" apocalypse certainly presupposes a liturgical context. The implication of the opening is a public assembly at which a reader presents a letter to the congregation (1:3–4); the experience takes place "on the Lord's day" (1:10); the work uses extensive liturgical material (for example, 1:5–6; 4–5; 7:12) with numerous allusions to the Lord's Supper. The closing invites the hearer to "come" and "take of the water of life" (22:17), having strictly separated insiders from outsiders (22:14–15), complete with a curse (18) and an invitation to "come Lord Jesus" (20). These elements are all associated with the Eucharist in other early Christian literature (for example, 1 Cor. 16:20–22; *Didache* 10:6; and Justin *First Apology* 66).

As we have seen earlier, the symbolism and the plot of Revelation both focus on the death of Christ, a death that proves to be his victory over the forces of evil. In the third major scene the focus on blood and wine is especially extensive. Overall, then, we may infer that the probable social setting of Revelation is an assembly for public worship, which culminated in the "coming" of Jesus to the communion table. On this reading, Revelation is a literary correlate to the worship service. It portrays, on a cosmic and symbolic level, what happens in the liturgy: in the spirit on the Lord's day, the risen Jesus comes to his congregation, examines their worthiness to receive him, reveals the will of the Father, and overthrows the powers of evil, thereby enabling the true worship of God and the coming of God's rule. The impact of such a reading of the Apocalypse is the topic of our final section.

SYMBOL, STORY, AND HISTORY: THE SETTING OF REVELATION

The Apocalypse tells us that it was written by John (1:1) during the reign of the sixth emperor in a series of seven (17:10). Unfortunately, none of this helps determine the precise historical setting of the work. We have at least four different ways to count the number of emperors. To make matters worse, John may not have intended this numbering to be taken literally, because the emperor is always a six claiming to be an eight in the symbolic way John used numbers—for 6 is always the number of the incomplete, the human, whereas 8 is the number of Jesus and of the beginning of new order.

Nor does the name John help; it was a common Jewish name and, without some further clue (like "son of . . .") it is impossible to establish his identity. Further, he does not claim to be John the apostle as later tradition assumed. (A living apostle would probably not have spoken of the apostles the way our author did in describing the heavenly Jerusalem; 21:14.) Even if our author had claimed to be John the apostle, we would have to test the claim, for so much of apocalyptic literature claims authorship that is feigned. Hence, we will have to find a less direct way to John's historical setting.

We are no better off concerning the date of the work. One would think that the references to Nero would allow us to date it in his reign (the late sixties), but John apparently knew a legend of Nero's return (17:8), necessitating a date after his death. The two emperors after Nero do not seem to have been inclined either to persecution or to claims of divine honors, according to the evidence available. The practice of the third emperor after Nero, **Domitian**, may be closer to John's concern, although he has traditionally been portrayed in darker hues than the historical record supports. Still, there does seem to have been some increase in emperor worship, attributing divinity to the living emperor, bowing when coming into his presence, and addressing him as Lord and God, especially in Asia Minor. In his reign, there was nothing similar to the persecutions under Nero, but it is likely that the general hostility toward people like John as atheists—those who refuse to honor the Gods and thus threaten the well-being of the community—focused on their refusal to ascribe divine honors to the emperor. (In fact, five emperors before Domitian had been declared by the senate to be Gods, perhaps pointing to Domitian as the "sixth"; 17:10.) This is not sufficient to justify dating Revelation to his reign, however, unless we accept external evidence.

The earliest external reference to the date of the book comes from one who grew up in Asia Minor but became bishop of Lyon in Gaul (France) in 178. Irenaeus declared that John wrote the Apocalypse near the end of the reign of Domitian, about 95 CE. Again, we do not know the basis for this tradition, but it is a reasonable date for the final composition of Revelation. Even so, the work might have existed earlier, for like other narrative works, such as the Gospel of John, it may have gone through several editions before it reached its final form. Its persistent popularity shows that Revelation continued to speak to the needs of the churches for decades. The situation envisioned in the Apocalypse existed from the middle of the first century into the fourth. It is not impossible that the work was originally composed under Nero and continually revised till the end of the first century.

CHRIST AGAINST CULTURE

We saw in the reading of the messages (Revelation 2–3) that there were factions in the Johannine communities. John deliberately opposes those he names Nicolaitans, as do some of the congregations. John seems to regard them as outsiders (2:6), although some within the church at Pergamum seem to hold Nicolaitan views (2:15). There was also the other prophetic voice accepted at Thyatira, whom John designates Jezebel (2:20). Although these may well have formed a separate group from the Nicolaitans, John lumps them together with prophets such as Balaam, whose teachings about cultural assimilation to Canaanite ways led to disaster for Israel as they prepared to enter the promised land (Num. 25:1–9; 31:16). John's opponents seemed to share a relaxed attitude toward Greco-Roman culture, for example, permitting believers to eat meat sacrificed to idols (2:14, 20).

We must not let John's bitter condemnation obscure the fact that this was a perfectly logical position for a follower of Jesus to hold. Paul held similar views, though with certain qualifications (1 Cor. 10:14, 25–28). We do not know whether these other prophets also had built-in safeguards, and John would probably not have told us if they did. Obtaining meat would have been a real problem for those living in cities. Nearly all the meat offered for sale in the marketplace would have been previously sacrificed to some deity. Unlike Jews, Greeks only burned a small portion of the sacrificial animal. An ancient story tells how Prometheus tricked Zeus into choosing the inedible portions of the animal for the Gods, leaving the rest for human consumption (Hesiod *Theogony* 535–57). Because most slaughtered animals would have been sacrificed in this way, those who ate the meat would have been understood to have communion with the deity to whom the sacrifice was made.

Jews avoided this problem by their strict dietary laws and by living in an extensive community that could provide its own meat. The Jerusalem church seems to have demanded that Gentile believers avoid such pollution (Acts 15:20); John belonged to this stricter school. Avoiding such meat, and other contacts with the religious aspects of Greco-Roman culture, would have been possible only as long as Jesus' followers could find shelter in the Jewish community. The difficulty in John's day, however, was that a gulf of hostility had developed between the Jewish communities and the Jesus communities of Asia Minor. John regarded them as a synagogue of Satan, not true Jews (2:9). They probably had a similar opinion of him.

Avoiding entanglements with the Gods affected more than what one could eat. Nearly every aspect of ancient culture was permeated by religious observance.

Photo by author

STATUE OF ARTEMIS, EPHESUS MUSEUM This traditional statue of Artemis (called Diana by the Romans) shows her as a Goddess of the wild, associated with the hunt. To the Greeks, she was the virgin sister of Apollo. Her sacrifices were birds and wild animals, and her priestess rode in a chariot drawn by stags.

Education began with reading Homer's ancient tales of Gods and heroes. Medicine was practiced in the name of Asclepius, God of healing. Entertainment consisted of sporting events (both the bloody arena and the Olympic Games) dedicated to the Gods and the theater dedicated to Dionysus. Each performance began with a sacrifice to Dionysus, whose altar stood at the front of every theater. To ply a trade meant to belong to a guild, but trade guilds were devoted to a patron deity regarded as the founder and protector of the craft. Mutual assistance societies (the ancient form of insurance) would gather in the name of some God or Goddess. The very coins by which one bought and sold, and paid one's taxes, testified to these Gods

Statue of Artemis Ephesia, Ephesus Museum How unlike the traditional Artemis is this statue from Ephesus. Hung with ripe fruit (variously interpreted as pomegranates, eggs, or breasts), she was a figure of fertility and life, far from the virgin huntress. Yet one of Artemis's traditional functions was to give and protect life, so that identification of this Goddess with the Greek Artemis (and the Roman Diana) was possible. Her monumental temple at Ephesus was one of the Seven Wonders of the Ancient World.

and Goddesses. One could not live, it seemed, without the mark of the beast on the head and hand (13:16).

The Jews had dealt with these issues by constructing alternative institutions. Cut off from this alternative, John's communities were feeling their way forward. Some believed that culture could be redeemed by participation. The Gods, they would have reasoned, are either nothing at all or simply faulty perceptions of the one true God. In either case, participation in occupations and meals carried out in their names was of no consequence. John disagreed and called for separation. Some, perhaps, began to create alternatives. We do know that the success of Christianity in Asia Minor had significant economic and social implications. Early in the second century **Pliny**, a provincial governor from Asia Minor, wrote to the emperor to clarify how he should proceed against the Christians. He concluded with the following assessment:

> *Persons of all ranks and ages, and of both sexes are, and will be, involved in the prosecution. For this contagious superstition is not confined to the cities only, but has spread through the villages and rural districts; it seems possible, however, to check and cure it. It is certain at least that the temples, which had been almost deserted, begin now to be frequented; and the sacred festivals, after a long intermission, are again revived; while there is a general demand for sacrificial animals, which for some time past have met with but few purchasers. (Pliny the Younger Letters 10.96)*

Here we see one concern of the new governor: Christianity had adversely affected the economic life of Asia Minor. This only added fuel to the Roman opposition. The churches of Asia Minor became locked in a bitter struggle not only with the Roman government but with the whole culture in which they lived. They saw life as Christ against culture.

CULTURE AGAINST CHRIST

The history of Roman persecution of Jesus' followers in the first century is not easy to trace, for little evidence remains. The persecution by Nero in the mid-sixties (see pages 301–04) seems to have been directly aimed at Christians but was limited to Rome and to the last four years of Nero's reign. There is no evidence that the new line of emperors beginning with Vespasian actively persecuted Christians. There is widespread evidence of local harassment in various places but none of official, government-sponsored persecution. There is some evidence of Roman action against all philosophers and against all so-called eastern cults, which would have affected Christians as well as others. Actually, the first definite evidence we have of Roman suppression of Christianity as a policy derives from just such a situation. Interestingly enough, it comes from Asia Minor and is reflected in the letter of Pliny quoted above.

In this letter we learn that Pliny had published an imperial edict forbidding all "political associations" (10:96). Asia Minor had continually resisted Rome's conquest, but it was especially important to maintain order at that time because Trajan was preparing for war with Parthia, and his supply lines would run right across this area. Pliny had been sent out as a special imperial legate to ensure the peace. The situation was considered so volatile that Trajan had forbidden Pliny even to form a fire brigade of 150 men for "that province and especially those towns have been troubled by bodies of this kind. Whatever name we give to those who are brought into association, and whatever the purpose, they soon become gangs" (Pliny *Letters* 10.34). Not surprisingly, the edict forbade all private associations.

Hirmer Verlag, Munich

THE DEIFIED VESPASIAN, ABOUT 80 CE We may see here an aspect of the ceremony of deification: the emperor is enthroned on a quadriga, a chariot drawn by four elephants. He holds a scepter and the Goddess Victory. The inscription bears witness to "the Divine Vespasian."

When Christians continued their clandestine meetings, they attracted Pliny's attention. He had already arrested, interrogated, and executed a number of Christians before he appealed to the emperor for guidance. He was uncertain, he says in the letter, whether they should be punished for the mere profession of Christianity or only for the crimes associated with it. (Crimes of atheism, cannibalism, and arson were common charges. Christians denied the Gods, said that they ate flesh and drank blood, and spoke of setting the world on fire.) He admits he has tortured a couple of deaconesses in order to learn more about their actions and that he has executed some because they refused to forsake their religion. He reasoned that whatever the nature of their belief, refusal to obey a direct order of the governor was sufficient grounds for execution. Those who recanted, cursed Christ, and offered adoration, wine, and incense to the image of the emperor were released.

The emperor Trajan's reply commends Pliny for the enlightened way he has handled the inquiry. Though reluctant to lay down strict rules for such cases, Trajan offers the following policies:

> No search should be made for these people; when they are denounced and found guilty they must be punished; with the restriction, however, that when the party denies himself to be a Christian, and shall give proof that he is not (that is, by adoring our Gods) he shall be pardoned on the ground of repentance. (Pliny Letters 10.97)

This is our first official word on Roman attitudes toward Christians, coming two or so decades after the traditional date of the writing of Revelation but probably reflecting earlier practice. Pliny begins by saying he has never been present at any trials of Christians, implying that such trials were already in process (but were not so common that a well-traveled Roman administrator had ever encountered one). The great revival of religious and economic activity he cites implies a serious recent effort to turn people away from this new religion, but he notes that some had left the Christians "as many as 25 years ago" (*Letters* 10.96). Trajan was apparently not too concerned with these Christians, because he left room for repentance and prohibited active searches. They were evidently not considered criminals.

The evidence in Revelation indicates that the community felt persecuted (1:9; 2:10, 13; 6:9–11; 14:12; 17:6) though it only mentions the name of one martyr, Antipas (2:13). John himself had apparently been banished rather than executed, if that is how we are to understand his presence on Patmos (1:9). There is one remarkable agreement between John's account and that of Pliny: the litmus test centered on ascribing divine honors to the emperor.

John had come to see this requirement as the embodiment of evil, a conspiracy between the demonic forces and the imperial government. How abhorrent he would have found Paul's earlier advice to honor the emperor (Rom. 13:1–7). How convenient those other prophets he calls Jezebel and Balaam may have found such advice.

THE JOHANNINE CIRCLE

We may then conclude that these communities represented a distinctive type of early Jesus community, at odds with the more conservative Jewish version and the more liberal Pauline type. Its worldview is separationist and sectarian. We saw a similar sectarian attitude behind the Gospel of John, though the issues seem to be different. In antiquity it was thought by some that the apostle John wrote both works. That seems unlikely, but it raises the question of whether these two works stem from the same circle.

Many scholars have concluded that they do, and there is considerable evidence to relate them. Both understand Jesus' death as his decisive victory over evil. Both have strongly negative attitudes toward Jews. Both speak of Christ in similar terms: Logos, Witness, Lamb, Shepherd, Judge, Temple, and so on. Both view the world as existing on two levels, above and below. Both acknowledge that some significant aspect of the end is already a present reality. Both use numbers symbolically. Both focus on worship, especially the Jewish festivals, to interpret Jesus.

Other scholars highlight the serious differences between them. A problem recognized as early as the third century is the vast difference in the quality of Greek in the two works. The Greek of John's Gospel is quite good; that of Revelation is poor. Both are anti-Jewish, but Revelation seems more intent on claiming the title of true Jew; in John's Gospel, *Jew* has become a term of derision. Both pronounce the climactic formula *it is finished* and *it is done*, but they do so in words as different as these two English translations (John 19:30, Rev. 16:17). Revelation seems to delight in the traditional apocalyptic language of Jesus' coming and the eschatological battle; John's Gospel rarely uses such language.

The thrust of these and similar observations gives us no reason to believe that the same person authored both works. It is unlikely that they even derive from the same circle, understood as a formal association of prophets. Yet there are too many correlations to believe that they originate from entirely separate arenas. Probably they do come from the same communities but are separated either by time (say, ten to twenty years), by having as their source different factions within the larger group, or by both. All the Johannine writings reveal a community with strong factions, ranging from Jewish to Gnostic. From the view of Jesus as preexistent (John's Gospel), it seems that some moved on to Gnosticism while others rejected such a view, insisting on a Jesus "in the flesh" (1 John 4:2). Some apparently assimilated to culture (Jezebel); others rejected that culture (the Apocalypse). The final question we will raise is how this writing functioned in the lives of men and women in first-century Asia Minor to enable them to live in opposition to their world.

THE APOCALYPSE IN THE REAL WORLD

Recent attempts to explain the social function of Revelation have turned to analogies such as what scholars of religion call *myth and ritual*. This is a difficult concept, made more so by the popular and pejorative meaning of *myth* in our culture. In popular usage, a myth is something that is not true; thus we might speak of the myth of equal opportunity in the United States. For we know in fact that people have very unequal opportunities, depending on where they were born, how much money they have, the color of their skin, their gender, and other factors. But this sense of a myth as something not true is the opposite of what the term means in scholarly discussion.

Scholars use the term **myth** to indicate a story so true that it determines the truth of other stories and events. It is a world-making story. Thus, it would be more proper to speak of the myths of democracy and freedom in the world today. For even while neither freedom nor democracy is perfectly achieved, our belief in their truth shapes how we understand our world and ourselves. A myth is true not because it corresponds to some previously existing reality but because it shapes the reality of people who come under its power. (So equal opportunity in America could someday become a myth!) You could imagine my delight, then, when I got a mailing from an atheist organization that included a bumper sticker that read: "God is a myth."

But a myth is more than just a world-creating truth; it is a story. One function of myth as it is told (and acted out in ritual) is to allow the believer to experience the world as it ought to be and to reshape the lived world so that it makes sense in terms of the mythic world. It is a bridge from the world of ordinary experience to the world of ultimate reality, taking the everyday up into the cosmic by means of a participation in the mythic story.

If we look back to our analysis of Revelation, we can see an analogous process at work. The hearers are first encountered in the world of ordinary experience, then they are taken on a fantastic journey into another reality. First, they meet the risen Jesus, then they ascend into heaven itself. Finally they witness the ultimate battle—the cosmic struggle between the dragon and the Lamb—a more uneven match would be hard to imagine. But things are not as they seem. Slain, the Lamb destroys the dragon and the beasts. In each cycle, symbolic expression is given to the coming of Jesus in salvation and judgment, but the images of violence are transformed into images of faithful suffering. The hearers experience a vision of life that makes the unintelligible meaningful; they are transformed as they comprehend that it is their suffering witness that brings salvation and judgment to the world—just as the suffering of Jesus was really the overthrow of evil.

We must not underestimate this experience. It is a real experience of the community, not just a glimpse of some future day that might give them courage to endure present suffering. They actually experience the "coming" of Jesus *in the present.* He comes to them through his prophet; he comes to them through the recital of the apocalyptic vision; and he comes to them in the liturgy of the Eucharist, of which this recital is a part. This present experience *looks back* to the "coming" of Jesus, which brought salvation to the world through his testimony and faithful witness (1:2; 1:18). It also *looks forward* to the "coming" of Jesus, when "every eye shall see him" (1:7). Yet the real power of the Apocalypse is not just this hope for a future coming of Jesus but the community's present participation in that coming.

It is the nature of ritual not to be confined to a time. Ritual transcends time. It takes place on "the Lord's day" (1:10). The Lord's day is the present day, which celebrates Jesus' victory over death, but also that past day of triumph itself, the day they believe it actually happened. Further, it is that (future) day of the Lord, which will mark the end of all things. In worship present, past, and future blend. The liturgical recital of the Apocalypse becomes a real experience of the kingdom of God because the worship of the community actualizes the rule of God. This is why the central theme of the Apocalypse is true worship (22:9). The struggle of the Apocalypse is the struggle between the worship of God and the worship of the beast. To worship God is to experience God's kingdom. To worship the beast is to fight against that kingdom.

We might think this experience would be short-lived, that when the people leave the service and return to the suffering of the real world they will be shocked back to their senses. Yet that is exactly the point: their "sense" has been changed. Having participated in the Apocalypse, they no longer consider their suffering as weakness or as something to be avoided. Now they understand that suffering rules. Their suffering will result in the fatal inebriation of the whore of Babylon. They cannot be shocked back to "reality," for they live in a new reality in which lambs conquer and suffering rules. The myth of the Apocalypse transforms victims into victors.

Although such a vision of life led to the excesses of some of the martyrs who rushed to their appointed end, it also provided a meaning in life for those who suffered helplessly at the hands of Rome. They no longer suffered helplessly; they were now in charge of their own destiny. By their faithful witness, they participated in the overthrow of evil and the establishment of God's kingdom—perhaps a greater victory than most people achieved in Roman Asia Minor.

READING AND REFLECTION

You are now ready for your second complete reading of Revelation. I suggest you read it aloud. If possible get together with several others, divide it up into sections, parts, voices, and read it with as much dramatic flair as you can. If you are well prepared, it will take just over an hour—and you will find the time goes by quickly.

LEARNING ON YOUR OWN

REVIEWING THE CHAPTER

Names and Terms

angelos	Michael	pseudepigrapha
Babylonian story of creation	Mithras	Pythagoras
Domitian	myth	recapitulation
gematria	Patmos	Tiamat
intercalation	Pliny	

Issues and Questions

1. How do the three basic approaches to interpreting Revelation explain the significance of the character symbolized as 666?
2. Be able to discuss the key characteristics of the literary genre of apocalyptic literature and give two or three examples of other writings of this type.
3. What does it mean to call apocalyptic thinking a mytho-prophetic view of history?
4. Explain the role of dualism in apocalyptic thinking and relate it to the notion of "two ages."
5. Be able to explain John's symbolic use of numbers and to relate that usage to the Pythagorean system of mathematical harmony.
6. How does John reverse certain traditional apocalyptic symbols so that they fit more with the experience of Jesus?
7. Be able to discuss the plot of Revelation and to summarize the three basic actions portrayed.
8. What evidence is there that John's Revelation takes place in a liturgical setting? What would be the significance of that setting for understanding the work?
9. Where in the broad spectrum of types of early Jesus communities would you fit the Johannine community? How different is it from a Pauline community?
10. What data would one consider to decide whether the Apocalypse and the Gospel of John share a common authorship? How are the Letters of John related?

TAKING THE NEXT STEP

There is an abundance of good introductions to Revelation, though I cannot resist recommending Barr, 1998, as the place to begin. Other suitable beginning points are Murphy, 1998; Schüssler Fiorenza, 1991; Knight, 1999; Michaels, 1992; Harrington, 1993; Trafton, 2005; Kealy, 1987; and R. Farmer, 2005. Aune's commentary in Mays, 1988, is also commendable.

More advanced but still very readable commentaries include those of Sweet, 1979; Boring, 1989; Roloff, 1993; Thompson, 1998; Boxall, 2006; Beckwith, 1919; and the conservative works of Wall, 1991, Mounce, 1977, and Trafton, 2005. Students who know Greek will profit from Caird, 1966; Beale, 1999; and Charles, 1920. An unusual but very interesting work is Corsini, 1983.

The best research commentary is Aune, 1997–1998; for a comprehensive evangelical commentary see Osborne, 2002. Two provocative but contrasting feminist works are Pippin, 1999, and Keller, 1996. R. Farmer, 1997, interprets through the lens of process philosophy with very interesting results, though difficult reading; see also his introductory commentary, 2005.

Topics for Special Studies

The Nature of the Apocalypse Genre

The place to begin is J. J. Collins, 1979 and 1984a; see also the introduction to his commentary on Daniel, 1984b. See also A. Y. Collins, 1986, and Vorster, 1988. Two classic works defining apocalyptic are P. D. Hanson, 1979, and Russell, 1964. Minear, 1981, surveys apocalyptic thought in other New Testament writing. More technical discussions include Aune, 1986; Tigchelaar, 1987; and the first three essays in Barr, 2006. Malina, 1995, sees Revelation related to astrology; contrast Chevalier, 1997.

A Study of Some Other Apocalypse

Analyze another work either in its own terms or in comparison with the Book of Revelation. For the study of other apocalypses, see J. J. Collins, 1984b and 1997; Collins, McGinn, and Stein, 2000; Stone, 1984; P. D. Hanson, 1983; Hall, 1990; and VanderKam, 1984. The most convenient collection of Jewish apocalypses is Reddish, 1995 (also has a good selection of Christian apocalypses), or, more comprehensively, Charlesworth, 1983. The old collection of Charles, 1913, may be more widely available. For Christian apocalypses, see Reddish, 1995, and Hennecke and Schneemelcher, 1992, vol. 2. Other apocalypses, mainly with a Gnostic inclination, may be found in the collection of material from the library at Nag Hammadi, in Robinson, 1977. Qumran materials can be found in Vermes, 1995.

For a broad and insightful study of the places connected with revelations and mysteries in the ancient world, see Bockmuehl, 1997.

A Study of a Literary Element of the Story

Topics include plot, characterization, symbolism, temporal distortion, and setting. Introductory works include Barr, 1998; Efird, 1978; Schick, 1977; and Blevins, 1984 (an interesting but unpersuasive attempt to see Revelation as drama).

On a more advanced level see Farrer, 1949, and especially 1964. Studies of particular aspects include Barr, 1995, and the first chapter in Barr, 2003 (plot); Boring, 1992 (narrative voice); Payne, 1989 (narrative voice); Moore, 1982 (characterization); deSilva, 1998 (persuasive stragegy); Schüssler Fiorenza, 1991 (rhetoric); Kermode, 1967 (the ending); Boring, 1994 (the ending); and Barr, 2001 (the ending). See also Good, 1984 (Daniel as comedy). On the rhetoric and politics see the essays in Barr, 2006.

Schüssler Fiorenza, 1977, explores a structuralist reading; Barr, 1984, explores the power of symbolism. Other studies of the symbolic include De Villiers, 1988; Babcock, 1978; and Dillistone, 1986. On the general use of symbols for social ends, see Lévi-Strauss, 1967.

Wilder, 1971, provides a general introduction to the distinctive ways of speaking characteristic of early Christianity.

On the characters see Johns, 2003 (Lamb); Barr, 2006 (Lamb); Boring, 1992; McWhirters, 2006; and Stuckenbruck, 1995.

The Composition and Publication of the Apocalypse

On John's use of earlier traditions, see Ruiz, 1989 (Ezekiel); Beale, 1984 (Daniel); Moyise, 1995; and Beale, 1999. Bockmuehl, 1997, explores various modes of revelation. On the oral setting, see Barr, 1986. On the related phenomenon of dreams, see P. C. Miller, 1998.

On the issue of authorship, see Culpepper's nice study of the legends surrounding John the apostle, 1994. The view of MacKenzie, 1997, has not attracted much support. See also Smith, 1995. Most commentaries will treat this topic; see especially Aune, 1997:1:xlvii.

The Treatment of Women in the Apocalypse

The two most comprehensive (and contrasting) treatments are Pippin, 1999, and Keller, 1996; see also the short commentary by Garrett in Newsome and Ringe, 1992.

On the issue of the characterization of women, begin with Pippin, 1993, who presents a vigorous case for seeing a negative characterization; other approaches include A. Y. Collins, 1987; Cameron, 1990; and the writings of Schüssler Fiorenza, especially 1983, 1985, 1991, 1992, and 1998. See also A. Y. Collins, 1993 (on feminine symbolism).

Rossing, 1999, and Humphrey, 1995, consider the feminine portrayal of the cities; see also Kim, 1999. Provon, 1996, looks at the interplay between economic and gender terms. McWhirter, 2006, examines the motif of Jesus as bridegroom.

The Apocalypse as Myth and Ritual

On myth, ritual, and liturgy, start with Rowland, 1982, and Ruiz, 1992; see also Aune, 1972; Ulfgard, 1989; Cabannis, 1970; Gager, 1975; Thompson, 1969; Hooke, 1935; and Shepherd, 1960. On the Apocalypse as spectacle, see Frilingos, 2004. On the related theme of magic, see Aune 1987a.

On the combat/holy war myth, see A. Y. Collins, 1976; Day, 1985; and Kang, 1989. Both Fenn, 1997, and Lesses, 1998, provide a broader perspective on rituals and social power. On the relation of myth and history, see Court, 1979.

On a general theory of social worlds, see Berger and Luckmann, 1966, and Eliade, 1959.

The Nature of Prophecy in Early Christianity

On prophecy in early Christianity, see J. J. Collins, 1997; Aune, 1983; and Hill, 1979. See also Forbes, 1995, and Potter, 1990. Bauckham, 1993, and Schüssler Fiorenza, 1998, focus on Revelation.

The Historical Context of the Apocalypse

Start with Court, 1979, and Sweet, 1979. For the setting of the Jewish communities see Barclay, 1996; and for John's relation to these communities, see Bredlin, 1999, and Duff, 2001. For John's theory of community see Pattemore, 2004.

A few scholars date Revelation early, in the time of Nero; see Bell, 1978, and Wilson, 1993. Marshall, 2001, presents an interesting reading in the context of the Jewish-Roman War. For the more common view, see A. Y. Collins, 1981.

Jones, 1984; Southern, 1997; and Pleket, 1961, provide useful studies of the emperors of this period. Frillingos, 2004, is an excellent discussion of how John reflects Roman culture.

A Study of One of the Cities Addressed

Ephesus, Pergamum, and Sardis probably have more written about them.

On the physical setting and archaeological remains, the standard reference works are Bean, 1966, and Akurgal, 1985. Overviews of the area are provided by Jones, 1971; Yamauchi, 1987; and Grimal, 1983. For specific cities, see Friesen, 1993 (Ephesus); Koester, 1998 (Pergamum); Kraabel, 1978 (Sardis); and Erim, 1986 (Aphrodisias, in the same area). The older work of Ramsay, 1906, has been updated by Hemer, 1986, and contains some useful information, but it is not very critical. For an excellent discussion on how to use archaeological data in interpretation, see Friesen, 1995. See also Trevett, 1989.

The Social Context of the Apocalypse

For somewhat different overviews of the historical and social settings, see A. Y. Collins, 1984, and Schüssler Fiorenza, 1985. On the social use of the reading of the Apocalypse see Barr, 1996. On the ideology of wealth, see Royalty, 1998.

For an examination of the conflicts within the Johannine community see A. Y. Collins, 1986, and especially Duff, 2001. For John's views of other Jews, see Mayo, 2006, and the essays by Duff and Friesen in Barr, 2006.

For a challenge to John's rhetoric of domination, see Carey, 1999.

On the social role of Satan, see Pagels, 2006.

There is debate about whether the Apocalypse was written in a time of persecution. Thompson, 1990, offers an outstanding treatment of the relation of the Apocalypse to the Roman government. For the older view that envisions imperial persecution, see Smalley, 1987. The definitive edition of Pliny's letters is Sherwin-White, 1966.

For a discussion of violence see Barr, 2003; Gibson and Matthews, 2005.

The History of Roman Persecution of Christians

The general question of Roman attitudes toward Christians is addressed in most of the commentaries and in many of the monographs mentioned above. The following are more specialized studies: Frend, 1967; Horbury and McNeil, 1981; Plescia, 1971; and Wilken, 1984.

The Nature of the Imperial Cult (Emperor Worship)

On the issues of emperor worship, the best treatment is Price, 1984; see also the excellent work of Friesen, 1983 and 2001, and Kraybill, 1996. For a good overview of the issues of imperial rule, see Wengst, 1987. See also Botha, 1988; Horsley, 1997; and the sourcebook of MacMullen and Lane, 1992. On the role of images in establishing reality see Zanker, 1990.

Revelation and Modern Cultural Studies

See the excellent introduction and collection of essays in Rhoads, 2005. See also Maier, 2002. See also the early and influential work of Segovia and Tolbert, 1994 and 1995, and the recent challenge of Schüssler Fiorenza, 1999.

Revelation and Modern Millenarian Movements

Social studies of contemporary movements that have been influential in interpreting the Apocalypse include Worsley, 1968; Thrupp, 1962; and Trompf, 1990; also see Gager, 1975.

On the modern context, see O'Leary, 1994 (United States); Boyer, 1992 (United States); Wright, 1999 (United States); Blount, 2005 (African American); Rhoads, 2005 (multicultural); Boesak, 1987 (South Africa); Richard, 1995 (Latin America); and Guthrie, 1987 (British, conservative). For a cogent analysis of the modern idea of the rapture see Rossing, 2004.

History of Interpretation

Wainwright, 1993, provides a fine survey of the history of the interpretation of the Apocalypse. Kovacs and Rowland, 2004, review the reception history in a chapter by chapter format. Weinrich, 2005, provides the surviving texts of ancient interpreters.

Additional Books and Articles

Special issues of *Interpretation* (40, no. 2, 1986) and *Listening: Journal of Religion and Culture* (28 no. 3, 1993) were devoted to the Apocalypse.

For the Apocalypse in art, see Grubb, 1997.

Important collections of essays addressing a broad range of topics include Hellholm, 1989; Collins and Charlesworth, 1991; Moyise, 2001; and Barr, 2003 and 2006.

Those wishing to consider issues in translation would benefit from Bratcher, 1984.

For further research see the annotated bibliography of Muse, 1996, and the specialized bibliography of Ford, 1993.

14

THE STORY AFTER THE WRITINGS

 To study and not think is a waste. To think and not study is dangerous.

CONFUCIUS, *ANALECTS*

In our close study of the various writings that make up the New Testament, we have savored the rich diversity and extraordinary variety of ideas, practices, literary genres, purposes, and abilities of the various writers. Now we must raise a new kind of literary question. The New Testament itself reaches us as one document—in a way it never appeared to its earliest hearers. Does it, then, make sense as a unified work? It hardly seems possible. We have all seen pictures that seem to consist of innumerable and random dots and shapes that, on close inspection, appear to have little connection. Yet when we step back from these pictures, hidden relationships appear. Suddenly they make a whole picture; we see it.

So too, the people who live in your city are extremely diverse; you may think they have nothing in common. Yet sociologists assure us that they do share many things. As easterners, southerners, westerners, or whatever, they share certain tendencies. As speakers of a particular language they understand the world in certain ways. As citizens of a particular country, they are committed to certain common values such as freedom and democracy, however much they may disagree as members of competing political parties.

This final chapter will focus on the unity that can be found amid the diversity of the New Testament writings. First, let us consider how the writings of the New Testament were collected into a common canon, then sketch in broad strokes the story that informs all the stories we have heard so far. Finally, we will consider the relation of the basic story—especially the stories of Jesus—to history.

THE MAKING OF THE CANON

I used to wonder, who decided what writings ought to be in the Bible? I have since learned that this is a faulty question, for no one ever decided, and the ancients did not have a "Bible." Rather than someone or some group making a clear decision, the process of the formation of the New Testament was gradual and proceeded only by widespread agreement, an agreement that held until the Protestant Reformation in the sixteenth century. We will trace the growing agreement below. But even as this agreement was emerging, it was not an agreement about what ought to be in the Bible. Our notion of a Bible, a collection of a large number of different works by different authors all in one book, simply did not exist in antiquity. Technology would not permit it.

Because these early writings were written on scrolls, and because scrolls could contain a very limited quantity of writing, the question was which scrolls should be collected for public reading. The writings in the New Testament would fill eight or nine scrolls, and if you add in the Hebrew Scriptures, you have many more. No one assembly could be expected to have them all, and, as you might imagine, it would take a long time to agree on the proper list.

Rather than asking which writings ought to be in the Bible, second-century readers asked which writings were profitable for reading when they assembled. As one writer commented about a disputed work: "it should be read, but it cannot be read to the people in church" (Muratorian Fragment 75; quoted in Klijn, 1980). Thus, it is not quite accurate to think that these early Christians set out to create a canon. No Christian writer even speaks of a canon in the sense of a list of sacred works until the fourth century. What is evident before then is a complicated, and often unconscious, process of excluding and including certain writings as reliable and authoritative witnesses to Jesus.

THE PROCESS OF EXCLUSION

Not all early writings were included in the canon. We have seen that even some of Paul's writing was lost. The preface to the Gospel according to Luke claims that "many others" had constructed similar narratives (1:1); surely this suggests more writers than Mark and Matthew. What, then, happened to all the other writings?

Some works were not saved through mere neglect; they were simply not powerful enough to outwit the enormous forces of destruction in a world where writing was an extremely expensive and time-consuming process. This is true of all kinds of literature from antiquity. As with Greek and Roman writings generally, so with early writings from the Jesus movement: only a small fraction of the originals survives. Some writings, however, were deliberately and consciously excluded.

As Christianity in the second and third centuries became an increasingly self-conscious movement, and people began to call themselves Christians, there emerged an ever-sharper distinction between various versions of Christianity. Our study of the individual writings shows that the movement was diverse from the beginning, but by the second century this diversity was threatening to create essentially different faiths, each calling itself Christianity. For the sake of simplicity, we may speak of the emergence of a spectrum of options, from a radical right wing to an extreme left wing.

On one side, we find those whose commitment to the biblical traditions of Israel was so strong that it completely shaped their understanding of the Christian faith, so that Jesus appeared rather like one of the prophets. Because of this strong connection to Jewish experience, scholars often call these people Jewish Christians, though in fact Jews and Jewish influence appear all across the spectrum. In order to emphasize their connections with the older traditions of Israel, I am going to call them the Hebraic Christians.

The other extreme included those whose commitment to Greek learning was so strong that this shaped their understanding of their faith, so that Christianity appeared as a variety of Hellenistic philosophy. Scholars generally call these people Gnostics. Yet a word of caution is appropriate here: Greek influence is evident even in the most conservative Jewish circles, and Jewish influence is strong among the Gnostics.

To name the middle group is not a simple task. They called themselves the **orthodox**, a word made up of the Greek words for "straight" (as in *ortho*dontist) and "praise" or "worship" (as in *dox*ology). They were the ones claiming to get God's worship straight, worshipping in the proper way. They also took the name *catholic*, a term meaning "universal," though in fact there was no universal version of Christianity. And in some places, such as Syria, it seems that the catholics were not even in the majority. Nevertheless, they emerged as the dominant body in the church and, like all the victors in history, got their choice of names. Here I will call them the orthodox and the catholics, framing them always with invisible quotation marks, indicating those toward the middle of the spectrum. (These two terms will eventually name the two great branches of the Medieval church: the Roman Catholic church in the west and the Eastern Orthodox church in the East, but that is a much later development.)

This middle group eventually ratified the canon. It is not surprising, then, that works that are clearly Gnostic works (such as the *Gospel of Truth*) or clearly Hebraic works (such as the *Gospel of the Hebrews*) are not to be found there. Further, works that tend toward Gnosticism (such as the Gospel of John) or Hebraic Christianity (such as James) had the greatest difficulty being accepted into the canon. A primary criterion for inclusion in the canon was whether a writing manifested orthodox teaching. This will simplify our quest to discover some underlying unity in the whole, for certain works have been excluded.

THE PROCESS OF INCLUSION

On Easter in the year 367, a Christian bishop of Alexandria in Egypt, **Athanasius** by name, published a festal letter in which he listed the writings he deemed canonical. This is the first such list to include precisely the twenty-seven books we know as the New Testament. Others before him had drawn up lists, but they were always partial and always included other works that were eventually excluded. And even after him, the scope of the canon was debated. That it took over three hundred years for this list to appear should caution us that the process of canonization was a slow and ill-defined one. It does not seem to have occurred to anyone to draw up a canon list until about 150, a century after Paul began to write. The scripture of these early communities continued to be the Hebrew Scriptures, which they knew primarily in their Greek translation (the Septuagint), and these new writings were not automatically added to it.

Our earliest clue to the development of a new canon comes from 2 Peter (written about 125). The writer refers to Paul's Letters in the plural, showing that they had been collected, and claims that they are being twisted by other interpreters, "as they do the other scriptures" (3:15–16). The *other* implies that Paul's Letters are gaining scriptural status. In another place this writer reflects the beginnings of a two-part canon:

> *You should remember the words spoken in the past by the holy prophets and the commandment of the Lord and Savior spoken through your apostles. (3:2)*

Notice that the parallelism is not complete: the words of the holy prophets (Old Testament) are not set beside the words of the apostles (New Testament). The new revelation is not the writings of the apostles but the word of Jesus, to which the apostolic writings bear witness. This emphasis on the word of Jesus, rather than the writing, appears to have prevailed in the period before 150.

The practice of Hebraic Christians seems to have reflected the practice of Jews generally; their primary authority was the Hebrew Scriptures, supplemented and interpreted by an oral tradition. But for them the oral tradition consisted of the words and deeds of Jesus. Eusebius quotes Papias (about 125), for example, who makes clear his preference for the oral tradition about Jesus; it is superior to the written word: "For I did not suppose that information from books would help me so much as the word of a living and surviving voice" (*Ecclesiastical History* 3.39.4). Yet writers like Papias used certain books as reliable sources of tradition about Jesus—one step on the long road to canonization.

The practice of Gentile Christians was not very different. Although they knew and used a collection of Paul's Letters—as the evidence from 2 Peter and the letters of Ignatius, Polycarp, and others show—and they cite these Letters as authoritative, they do not cite them in the way they do the Hebrew Scriptures. They have a collection of authoritative new writings, but they do not have a new Bible. The question for these second-century Christians was not so much whether a given writing was canonical but whether it was helpful. Did it build up the church? Was it useful for public reading? The writings that eventually emerged in the canon were those that a large number of Christians in many places and over a long period continued to read in their public services.

Opinions differed widely about which books were worthy of such reading. But in about 150 a crisis in the church at Rome gave a whole new impetus to the process of canonization. **Marcion** had concluded that the Hebrew Scriptures were incompatible with the new revelation of God in Jesus Christ. In his view, the loving (and always good) Father of Jesus was pure spirit; the just (and sometimes bad) Creator was tied to this material world (see pages 204–08). This wholesale rejection of the Hebrew Scriptures created a vacuum, which Marcion filled by publishing a purified New Revelation in two parts: The Gospel and The Apostle. He purged both Luke's Gospel and Paul's Letters of all Jewish elements and added certain writings of his own, creating a new scripture that he used instead of the Hebrew Scriptures.

We are more certain of the Roman church's reaction to his discarding the Hebrew Scriptures (they condemned it) than we are of their reaction to his creation of a new scripture. Yet it is probably no coincidence that the Roman church seems to have produced its own list of acceptable books sometime in the next generation after Marcion, perhaps around the year 190. This list was somewhat misleadingly entitled the Muratorian Canon. Both parts of the title are modern. L. A. Muratori discovered this badly preserved Latin manuscript from the eighth century in a monastery library at Milan in the early 1700s. Because the writing refers to a Roman bishop from the mid-second century as "recent," it is generally assumed that the original was written by the end of the second century—though some would date it as late as the fourth century. Even so, it is an anachronism to call it a canon because it is, as it states explicitly, a list of books recommended for public reading. Thus it is more common now to refer to it as the **Muratorian Fragment**. Because it reveals so much about the thinking of these early Christians, I quote the entire document:

> *The third gospel book according to Luke. Since Paul had taken him in as a competent writer, the physician Luke wrote it down after the ascension of Christ under his own name (but) according to his (Paul's) views. Yet he himself did not see the Lord in the flesh either and therefore he too began his narrative, as far as he was able, with the birth of John. The fourth gospel is by John, one of the disciples. When his fellow disciples and bishops urged him he said: Fast with me for three days from today and we shall tell each other what*

is revealed to each of us. That same night it was revealed to Andrew, one of the apostles, that John would write everything down under his name, and they were all to check it.

And therefore, although different prefaces (principles) are presented in the various gospel books, this still makes no difference for the faith of the believers, since everything is explained through the one leading Spirit in all of them: concerning the nativity, the passion, the resurrection, the association with his disciples, and concerning his twofold coming, the first time when, in lowliness, he was despised, which has taken place, the second time resplendent in regal power, which is to come. Is it surprising therefore if John so consistently brings the various things forward also in his letter, when he says of himself: what we have seen with our eyes and heard with our ears and touched with our hands, that we have written down for you. For thus he introduces himself not only as a spectator and hearer, but also as a describer of all the miracles of the Lord, in the (correct) order.

The Acts of all the apostles have been written in one book. Luke sums up for the excellent Theophilus what successively took place in his presence, as he makes clear by omitting Peter's martyrdom and also Paul's departure from the city for Spain.

The letters of Paul themselves make it clear, to anyone who wishes to know, what (they are), from where and for what reason they were sent. The first of them all to the Corinthians, forbidding the heresy of the schism; next to the Galatians, forbidding circumcision; then to the Romans, explaining that Christ is the rule of the Scriptures and their principle, he wrote rather extensively. It is necessary for us to discuss these one by one, since the blessed apostle Paul, following the rule of his predecessor John, wrote to only seven congregations mentioned by name, in this order: to the Corinthians, the first; to the Ephesians, the second; to the Philippians, the third; to the Colossians, the fourth; to the Galatians, the fifth; to the Thessalonians, the sixth; to the Romans, the seventh. For when (a letter is written) anew to the Corinthians and Thessalonians to reprove them, it is clear that there is one church scattered over the whole earth. For John also writes, in his Revelation, to seven churches, yet he speaks to all of them. But one to Philemon, one to Titus and two to Timothy (written) out of affection and love have been held sacred in honour of the catholic church for the regulation of ecclesiastic discipline. There is also in circulation a letter to the Laodiceans and another to the Alexandrians, fakes in Paul's name for the sect of Marcion and still others that cannot be received in the catholic church: for gall cannot be mixed with honey. In addition a letter from Jude and two with John's subscription are preserved in the catholic church; and the Wisdom which was written by Solomon's friends in his honour.

We have also included the Revelations of John and Peter, although some of us will not let them be read in church. Recently in our time Hermas wrote the Pastor [or the Shepherd] in the city of Rome, when his brother Pius was seated as bishop on the throne of the Church of the city of Rome. For this reason he should be read, but he cannot be read to the people in church, nor (be counted) among the prophets, whose number is complete, or among the apostles, until the end of time.

> *We accept nothing at all by Arsinous, or Valentine, or Miltiades. They com-*
> *piled a new book of psalms for Marcion, together with Basilides, of Asia*
> *Minor, the founder of the Cataphrygians. (quoted from Klijn, 1980:218–21,*
> *who also includes the Latin text)*

It would take a rather perverse logic not to think that the lost beginning talked about Matthew and Mark, meaning that the four Gospels were recognized at Rome. But there seem to have been serious questions about John, to judge by the obviously legendary story that supports not only its apostolic authorship but claims that the other apostles checked it. All Paul's Letters are included, though arranged in a curious order and believed to be written later than the seven letters of John in Revelation. Some writings are missing: Hebrews, James, 1 and 2 Peter; and there are doubts about Revelation. Yet there is support for another Revelation, that attributed to Peter, along with the *Wisdom of Solomon*, which is recognized as pseudonymous. There is also a conscious rejection of works associated with Gnostic teachers and an explicit distinction between books that are merely sound and pious (such as the Shepherd of Hermas) and those that should be read aloud in the assembly.

Even a century later many of these problems remained unresolved. Around 325, Eusebius provided a classification of these early writings, probably reflecting the discussion of the great school of Alexandria in Egypt. He writes:

> *We must, of course, put first the holy quartet of the gospels, followed by the*
> *Acts of the Apostles. The next place in the list goes to Paul's epistles, and*
> *after them we must recognize the epistle called I John; likewise I Peter. To*
> *these may be added, if it is thought proper, the Revelation of John, the argu-*
> *ments about which I shall set out when the time comes. These are classed as*
> *Recognized Books. Those that are disputed, yet familiar to most, include the*
> *epistles known as James, Jude, and 2 Peter, and those called 2 and 3 John, the*
> *work of either the evangelist or of someone else with the same name.*
>
> *Among the spurious books must be placed the "Acts" of Paul, and the*
> *"Shepherd," and the "Revelation of John," if this seems the right place for it:*
> *as I said before, some reject it, others include it among the Recognized Books.*
> *Moreover, some have found a place in the list for the "Gospel of the Hebrews,"*
> *a book which has a special appeal for those Hebrews who have accepted Christ.*
> *These would all be classed with the Disputed Books, but I have been obliged*
> *to list the latter separately, distinguishing those writings which according to*
> *the tradition of the Church are true, genuine, and recognized, from those in*
> *a different category, not canonical but disputed, yet familiar to most church-*
> *men; for we must not confuse these with the writings published by heretics*
> *under the name of the apostles, as containing either Gospels of Peter, Thomas,*
> *Matthias, and several others besides these, or Acts of Andrew, John, and other*
> *apostles. To none of these has any churchman of any generation ever seen fit to*
> *refer in his writings. Again, nothing could be farther from apostolic usage than*
> *the type of phraseology employed, while the ideas and implications of their*
> *contents are so irreconcilable with true orthodoxy that they stand revealed as*
> *forgeries of heretics. It follows that so far from being classed even among Spu-*
> *rious Books, they must be thrown out as impious and beyond the pale. (Eccle-*
> *siastical History 3.25; quoted from Williamson, 1965:134–35)*

We see here the slow, painful process of creating an agreed-upon canon. It was not enough that a work was not heretical; it had to meet the test of usage. The process of inclusion was the process of incorporating diverse works into a common tradition.

We should remember that the physical means of book production contributed to this piecemeal approach. Books were written primarily on **papyrus**, a paper-like material made from pounded reeds. Papyrus sheets were rather stiff, so they were not folded; instead they were rolled up. A short writing, like Philemon, would fit on a single sheet about a foot square. It would be rolled and tied with a string. Longer works were made by sewing many sheet of papyrus together and rolling them from each end around long sticks. A work like Romans would form a scroll about eighteen feet long. The longest works, such as Matthew, Luke, or Acts, would run up to thirty-three or thirty-four feet, about the limit of what was manageable for this form.

When a work would not fit conveniently on one scroll it was divided into "books"; thus Homer's *Iliad* took ten scrolls, and works like Samuel and Kings in the Hebrew Scriptures took two each. The whole Hebrew Scriptures might take twenty-five or so scrolls, and there are twenty-seven writings in the current New Testament. There were also many other writings vying for attention. A given congregation might possess a collection of some of these scrolls, but none would have a complete set of the writings available; they were very expensive.

A new technology came into use sometime in the first century. A finely crafted leather, called *vellum*, was used for the writing material. This vellum was sewn together along one edge, producing what we think of as a book, then called a **codex**. Early codices reflected the scroll conventions in manner of writing, width of columns, and length of documents. Gradually, however, these elements changed, and by the beginning of the third century the codex had replaced the scroll. This new technology allowed the combination of numerous works into a common book, so that collecting the writings that we consider the New Testament became technologically possible.

THE PROCESS OF TRANSMISSION

It is still a long way from the fourth-century canon to the New Testament that we read today. All the New Testament documents were written in Greek, though many were soon translated into other languages. The Greek method of writing strikes us as odd: Greeks wrote in all capital letters with no punctuation, not even spaces between words. Consider:

ITISANENORMOUSCHALLENGETO
READAWRITINGINWHICHALLTHE
USUALCLUESTOMEANINGAREMI
SSINGINCLUDINGWORDDIVISIO
NANDTHETASKISMADEHARDERBY
SLOPPYSCRIBESWITHBADHANDW
RITINGORPOORSPELLINGOREVE
NAREGIONALDIALECTANDIFYOU
WERENOTENTIRELYFAMILIARWI
THTHETOPICITMIGHTBEIMPOS
SIBLETOEVERMAKESENSEOFIT

About 900 CE cursive script replaced this style; and word separation and elementary punctuation were introduced.

In the West, Latin replaced Greek as the language of the Bible. Around 400, **Jerome** translated the Bible into Latin (the vulgar tongue, hence the name, the Vulgate) and this translation became the standard Bible in the West for the next thousand years. Only during the Renaissance, with its call to go back to original sources, was Greek reintroduced in the West, with scholars imported from Greece to teach it. This led first to the effort to produce the most accurate Greek text possible. **Erasmus** of Rotterdam, the great humanist priest of the late Renaissance, produced the first modern Greek text of the New Testament. It was very primitive by modern standards and based only on late manuscripts; the text was often "corrected" on the basis of the Vulgate. But it was a beginning.

There followed the long development of that discipline known as **textual criticism**, the effort to reconstruct, as precisely as possible, the original texts of these ancient writings. The first stage of text criticism was the publication of the Greek manuscripts currently available in cathedral and monastic libraries. These were generally late manuscripts from the tenth to fourteenth centuries. The next stage involved the discovery of much older manuscripts, usually from the libraries of ancient monasteries long closed to outsiders (though one such manuscript was found in the Vatican library itself). As a result of this late-nineteenth-century detective work, we now possess complete manuscripts from the 300s and numerous papyrus fragments going as far back as 135. (See the photograph on page 392). These contain many variant readings, and modern textual criticism compares all the variants of all these manuscripts along with citations in early writers and early translations, eventually arriving at the most probable reading in each case. The standard Greek texts available today, based on more than five thousand sources, provide us with the most accurate texts available since the first century.

This return to the Greek text also sparked an interest in translating the Bible into the languages of various people. When the Vulgate was made, Latin was such a language, but by the Renaissance it had long since become the language of the intellectual elite. The masses spoke the regional languages that evolved from Latin (Italian, French, Spanish, and so on) or from their native dialects (German, English, and so on), and now various translations began to appear in these languages. The most significant English translation, made in 1611, is known as the **King James Version**. It remained the standard English version for three hundred years and is the direct ancestor of several twentieth-century translations, including the New Revised Standard Version.

Only as a result of this long historical process are we able to study the New Testament as one document. Now let us explore how that document fits together and produces its own meaning.

THE MEANING OF THE CANON

The arrangement of the New Testament writings into their present order was itself a drawn-out affair, by no means agreed to by all. Some lists begin with Luke, others put John before Luke, allowing Luke and Acts to come together as they were certainly meant to do. Even the great Easter letter of Athanasius, the first to list the precise twenty-seven books we have in the canon, does not give them in the present order. He put the General Letters before Paul and inserted Hebrews into the middle of the Pauline Letters. What is the logic of the present order?

THE ORDER

That Revelation should come last in the canon was perhaps inevitable: both its widely disputed status and its contemplation of last things dictate that it be placed at the end. So too, the general priority of Gospel over apostle is logically necessary and is reflected in every list we possess. But in what kind of order are the Gospels themselves listed?

We cannot be certain, for no early writer discusses the reasons. Possibly Matthew was placed first because it made the best transition from the Hebrew Scriptures to the new writings. Both in style and content Matthew is the most Hebraic, continually quoting the Hebrew prophets to validate the story of Jesus. Mark and Luke seem to be grouped next because they are most like Matthew; John is put last because it deviates most from the common pattern of the others—and perhaps because it was the most disputed.

That this order obscured the connection between Luke and Acts was compensated for by the natural transition that Acts provided to the next major section, the writings of Paul. For Paul is the hero of the last half of Acts. His writings are arranged variously in different lists: Marcion began with Galatians, the letter in which Paul is most antithetical to Jewish tradition. The Muratorian Canon, quoted earlier, follows a curious order, attempting perhaps to be chronological or to counter Marcion's emphasis on Galatians and Romans.

The present order begins with Paul's most extensive argument (Romans), which seems like a systematic statement of his ideas; the rest are arranged in order of decreasing length (though first and second letters are always put together). Length seems to us a strange criterion, but the whole of the Qur'an is arranged according to length, beginning in Surah Two with the longest of Muhammad's recitations. Following the short note to Philemon, the General Letters appear, again in basic order of length from Hebrews to Jude.

THE STORY

The New Testament does not tell a story, but it does imply one. It is a very optimistic story, an account that begins with Abraham (Matt. 1:1) and culminates in the coming of the new Jerusalem (Revelation 22). Put another way, it is the story of the emergence of God's rule in the world. Abraham is the father of the faithful, the one called by God to forsake home and native Gods for a new land. In this new story, that "new" land now comes down out of heaven as a gift from God because Jesus the servant and son of God has lived, died, and been raised to new life. There are various ways to understand his life and death, reflected in the various Gospels, but the witness to him has spread throughout the world (Acts). The canon suggests that that witness is most fully presented in the teachings of Paul, but all the apostles bear witness to it. The final work shows that even now the risen Christ appears to his churches in these letters and he comes to them in the sacraments of baptism and Eucharist. As they worship God through him, the powers of evil are overthrown, and the kingdom of God arrives on earth.

This story has had profound influence on the history of Western civilization: it is the promise of the future, the new tomorrow, progress. From Augustine's *City of God* and the Christian culture of the Middle Ages to the secularized versions of the story in the modern notions of progressive liberalism and Marxism, it has shaped the vision of untold millions of people.

At the center of the Christian story stands the story of Jesus, or, more accurately, the stories of Jesus. We have seen that each Gospel writer told that story in a unique way. They differed in countless details. Of course, if one is determined enough and clever enough all the differences between the Gospels can be explained away. Since Augustine began this task nearly fifteen hundred years ago, in a work called *The Harmony of the Gospels*, more effort has been put into harmonizing them than in understanding them on their own terms. A literary approach, such as we have undertaken here, avoids such harmonization in order to avoid obscuring the meaning of each work. But these are important works with stories of more than passing interest, and few of us will be content not to probe behind the level of story to ask what actually happened. When we do, we raise the question of history.

CANON, STORY, AND HISTORY

> *Measureless pours forth*
> *The creative wantonness of bards,*
> *Nor trammels its utterance*
> *With history's truth.*
> (*Ovid* Amores 3.12.41)

Thus did the great poet of love, Ovid, recognize that the truth of poetry was not always the truth of history. Not only must a little poetic license be taken from time to time, the very art of poetry and narrative requires the writer to deceive us. We must believe that these words, sparse and planned, represent real life. We are to think that the narrative writer is telling us what happened when in fact we are being told far more. As the English satirist Jonathan Swift quipped: "Poets [are] liars by profession" ("Letter of Advice to a Young Poet" in Eliot, 1909 and several sites online).

Poets do lie, or, as we prefer to say, they create fictions. Just as the visual artists deceive us by portraying a three-dimensional object in two-dimensional space, so the verbal artists deceive us by making a highly selective and artfully arranged series of incidents seem real and natural. An essential feature of all art is to be artful, imaginative, fictional. We do not ask of a story whether it really happened; we ask what it means and how it achieves that meaning.

To apply this logic to the Gospels, we may say that to the extent they are stories artfully told we have no right to demand that they tell us just what happened. This is readily recognizable in regard to the parables Jesus told: thus, we do not ask whether a man actually went down from Jerusalem to Jericho, and the story of the good Samaritan is unaffected by such historical considerations. It is a true story whether or not it happened (Luke 10:29–37).

Yet the Gospels are not simply parables; they concern a real flesh-and-blood person, Jesus of Nazareth. All four Gospels insist on locating Jesus in space and time;

this is one trait that distinguishes them from many of the Gnostic gospels. Neverthe-less, we have seen that they disagree on scores of incidents from his genealogy to the stories of the empty tomb. These disagreements are all the more significant if we conclude, as do most scholars, that some of these writers had access to the works of the others. They felt free to change, rearrange, omit, and add. Apparently the gospel form did not restrict an author to simply the bare facts.

We do the Gospels an injustice if we read them as simple reports about Jesus. The Gospels present Jesus neither as his contemporaries might have understood him (they claim to have a new, fuller understanding) nor as historians might understand him (the Gospel writers see him as a living presence, not a dead figure from the past). Neither simple parables nor simple history, the Gospels contain historical information without being historical documents. (See the discussion and chart on pages 269–75.)

So one aspect of the problem of discovering the historical Jesus is that the sources from which we work are literary sources, intent on telling a story. They seek a char-acterization of Jesus for their own time, not a reconstruction of Jesus from an earlier time. But the problem is more complex, for the Gospel writers understood their sources of information about Jesus very differently than would a modern historian. Put most simply, whereas a modern historian considers only evidence from the life-time of Jesus, the Gospel writers had two additional sources that they regarded as equally revealing of Jesus.

Because they believed that Jesus had been raised from the dead, they believed he continued to communicate with his followers. Within their worldview there would be no sense in distinguishing historical words of Jesus from prophetic words of Jesus. The *Gospel of Thomas* claims that all its sayings are "the words of the living Jesus"; and the Gospel of John claims the power of the spirit to mediate the word of Jesus (John 16:14; see the discussion on pages 408–10). We see a clear example of this ongoing process in Rev. 1:12–3:22, where a prophet claims to hear the words of the living Jesus and to record them. Clearly many prophets heard many such words in the decades after Jesus' death, and it is likely that some of them found their way into the Gospels. This complicates the historian's task.

Another complication stems from another conviction of Jesus' earliest follow-ers: they believed that they could learn things about Jesus by studying the ancient Scriptures, for the prophets all pointed to him. (For more discussion of this idea that ancient scriptures really pointed to their own times, see pages 319–22.) Luke tells a story that shows this process at work, when two disciples encounter the risen Jesus, who reveals himself to them:

> *Beginning with Moses and all the prophets, he interpreted to them the things about himself in all the scriptures. (24:27)*

Thus, the Gospel writers had three sources that they thought provided information about Jesus: the memory of his followers, the words of his prophets who continued to encounter him after his death, and the words of the ancient prophets.

The problem of the historicity of the New Testament is one of the most challeng-ing issues raised by the modern study of the Bible. It is too complex to be resolved in a few pages. We can, however, clarify the true nature of the problem and show how some current scholars approach a solution, especially in regard to Jesus.

THE NATURE OF HISTORY

Just what do we mean when we use the expression the *historical Jesus*? In a general way, we all understand that we are trying to discover the things that Jesus actually said and did. Yet this expression is extremely ambiguous, rooted as it is in the ambiguity of the concept *history* in English usage. We may use the word *history* to mean what actually happened in the past. When we ask, was the resurrection of Jesus reported in the Gospels a historical event? we usually mean, did it actually happen? If we had been standing there that first Sunday morning, would we have seen it? Yet we also use the word *history* to mean an account of what happened in the past. History is what historians write. Now if we ask whether the resurrection is a historical event, we mean, would a historian writing about Jesus include such an event in the account?

Traditionally, historians encouraged us to view these two usages as meaning the same thing. For they were, they said, attempting to tell us just what happened. Modern historians have become more modest, recognizing the hypothetical nature of their enterprise, and a little reflection on the nature of writing history will further clarify the problem of a historical understanding of Jesus.

The most important limitation historians face is that they lack direct access to the subject they intend to study. The past is gone; only in comic strips and science fiction are people able to encounter the past directly. We have access only to certain evidence of the past. We assume that this evidence was caused by events, although we can never directly bring back these supposed events. The historian, then, gathers and evaluates this evidence, and infers what must have caused it.

Thus, the work of the historian is like that of the detective who gathers evidence to prove that someone did, or did not, commit some crime. The detective must, as Sherlock Holmes advised Watson, learn to think backward. Holmes's method, you will recall, was to gather all the evidence available. Once he had all of it, he could solve the crime. As he explained, his task was simply to deduce what event, and no other, would have left all this evidence. Holmes would certainly have made a first-class historian, for this deduction of events from evidence, as cause from effect, is the historian's main task.

We may carry our analogy one step further. Like the detective, the historian must follow certain rules in gathering and evaluating evidence. Some kinds of evidence are worth more than others. Firsthand accounts are far more valuable than hearsay. In a courtroom one may testify only to what one has personally seen or heard; rumors are not considered valid testimony. Yet even here, legal procedure calls for caution. If the defense can show that the person who claims to be an eyewitness to the crime is unreliable or a notorious liar, the testimony is questioned. Children and others with limited intelligence are allowed to testify only under very strict guidelines. If it can be shown that the witness has a vested interest in the outcome of the trial, the jury will have correspondingly less faith in the testimony. The historian exercises similar restraint with the sources.

Primary sources are preferable to secondary ones because the former come from the time and situation being investigated—rather like an eyewitness. Secondary sources, from a later time, may give information about the time and situation being investigated, but that information is filtered through later concerns. For the study of the Jesus movement between 50 and 60, Paul's Letters are primary sources; Acts is a secondary source. The Gospels are secondary sources for a history of Jesus but primary sources for the history of the last third of the first century. Like the attorney, the historian raises questions about the reliability of the witnesses, about how well informed they could have been, about the biases they show. Generally, modern historians are trained to be skeptical of their sources, to subject them to careful analysis, to prefer empirical and testable data, and to use only natural explanations. These factors raise problems for ancient history scholars, whose sources are few and distant, but the last point raises special problems in investigating religions.

Religions generally claim not to have natural causes; they are the work of God or the Gods. Although the historian cannot deny this possibility, it is outside the scope of historical investigation. The Athenians believed that Athens prospered because it was favored by the Goddess Athena; the modern historian must seek other causes. Christians believed they grew and prospered because the Holy Spirit empowered them; the historian must look for more natural causes. In neither case does the historian assert that the supernatural hypothesis is wrong; it is merely outside the scope of historical investigation. To take a modern example: children in the United States are commonly taught the three (or four or five) causes of the U.S. Civil War. The causes are all natural phenomena—regional competition, industrialization, invention of machinery, and so on. But President Lincoln believed that the Civil War was God's punishment on this country for failing to include the African slaves in the great Declaration of Independence that led to the Revolutionary War (in 1776). Thomas Jefferson had originally included freedom for the slaves as a natural right, blaming slavery on the British. But the paragraph had to be struck to get the southern colonies to sign the Declaration. Lincoln's theological explanation may be right, but it is not a historical explanation. It is well worth remembering that a historical explanation is only one kind of reckoning, one that plays according to the very strict rules of skepticism, criticism, empiricism, and naturalism. Other explanations play by other rules.

The historian seeks a natural explanation for the evidence left by the past— evidence best drawn from primary sources that stand up to rigorous and critical examination and provide data that can be tested. But history demands more than the assembling of facts.

The past becomes intelligible only when some historian makes sense out of the facts by producing a convincing interpretation of their significance. If we had an eyewitness account of the crucifixion of Jesus, it would be of immense help to the historian but would not itself be history, because it would lack historical perspective. It would fail, most basically, to interpret the historic significance of this event. A historian must provide context, understand relationships, demonstrate significance. This is one reason why history will never be an exact science, however scientific it may become. It will always depend on the skill, the insight, and the imagination of the historian.

And, one must add, the biases and values of the historian play their part. Though it is not recorded in any written source, it is widely reported that after World War II Winston Churchill declared: "History will be kind to us here. I know, for I will write it." He did, and it was. A Nazi history of that war would read somewhat differently. This subjective element in history cannot be ignored. The nineteenth-century goal of knowing only the facts is an illusion. History always remains a tentative reconstruction of the past based on the available evidence, which must then be rigorously tested.

Such history will possess varying degrees of probability based on the quality of the evidence and the skill of the historian. Some reconstructions are only possible, others probable, still others highly certain or apparently established beyond all reasonable doubt. But the historian may never claim certainty: the past is gone and our reconstruction of it remains ever open to revision.

Given these conditions, we can readily understand why writing a history of early Christianity is so difficult. There are so few sources available, and those we do have are strongly biased. The very nature of history as a skeptical, empirical, and tentative investigation is at odds with the attitudes of many people toward the things told in these documents. Even more difficult is the problem of the historical Jesus, because there are no primary sources. And the late secondary sources, on critical examination, seem to differ in numerous chronological and factual details. Further, they are all pervaded by a supernatural event: the resurrection of Jesus from the dead. How to achieve a historical interpretation of Jesus is a complex and controversial question. What follows is an attempt to trace the main contours of that debate and to show how some contemporary historians interpret Jesus.

THE HISTORICAL JESUS

A literary analysis of the Gospels shows how Jesus was portrayed by four different authors in four different situations. They give us clear historical information about how Jesus was regarded in the last third of the first century. But can the historian also discover there the necessary evidence to reconstruct a historical portrait of Jesus? We must be clear that the goal of research into the historical Jesus is a modern reconstruction of Jesus, according to modern notions of evidence. We simply have no access to the tangible Jesus of Nazareth—at least not till the time machine moves out of science fiction.

Historical reconstruction should be attempted only after the kind of literary analysis we have already engaged in, for the historian must be aware of the nature and purpose of the sources. And our basic sources for a reconstruction of the historical Jesus are the four canonical Gospels. Neither the noncanonical gospels nor the non-Christian writings that mention Jesus are of any significant help in historical reconstruction. Yet because the Gospels are documents of faith, the question of the historical Jesus has been understood as, can we get *behind* the Gospels to Jesus?

There was a time when historians understood their goal to be to get back to the earliest and best sources, on the assumption that the earlier source was the better. This was one of the chief motivations of both source and form criticism, but it proved faulty; the earlier sources as well as the later ones were documents of faith and imagination. This discovery resulted in an eclipse of historical-Jesus research, many asserting that it was impossible to reconstruct the life of Jesus. More recently, a so-called **new quest** has emerged, or perhaps we should say several new quests, for so far there is no unanimity on the goals, methods, or results of such study. There is only the general agreement that each incident and each saying must be subjected to historical analysis to determine, on the basis of certain criteria, whether an incident or saying is more, or less, likely to be historical.

Scholars differ in their basic approach to this problem. Some assume that the Gospel incidents are basically historical unless one can prove otherwise. Others assume that, given the creativity of the early church, only incidents or sayings that can be proven to be historical are to be accepted. Most take a middle position: they begin with aspects that can be fairly conclusively established and proceed from this base to more or less probable material, trying to establish a coherent portrait of Jesus.

Conservative critics, who tend to regard the Gospel material as historical unless it can be shown to be unhistorical, have developed what we may call *negative criteria*. As a practical matter, these criteria relate to only a small portion of the Jesus material, because only a few scenes can be shown to be unhistorical. Three negative criteria are often cited.

First, material should be judged to be unhistorical if it assumes a situation that did not exist at the time of Jesus. Thus, the instructions for dealing with a wayward brother, including bringing him before "the church" (Matt. 18:15–20), would not seem to be historical, because there was no "church" in Jesus' time. Nor would the commissioning scene at the end of Matthew (28:18–20), since neither the trinitarian baptismal formula nor the universal mission seemed to be known in the earliest church (compare Acts 2:38; 10:28; Gal. 2:7–9).

Second, material should be judged to be unhistorical if it contradicts other established material. This has a limited applicability, but surely Jesus did not cleanse the Temple on both Palm Sunday (Matt. 21:10–11) and Holy Monday (Mark 11:12–19) as well as at the beginning of his career (John 2:13–17). Of course, the historian must consider that people sometimes say and do contradictory things. None of our sources presents Jesus as a writer or even as a systematic thinker (like Plato's Socrates).

Third, material should be judged historically suspect if it can be shown to be a development of material found in another Gospel or in another place in the same Gospel. Thus the allegorical explanations of the parables are suspect, and Luke's (21:20) more elaborate description of the destruction of Jerusalem is less likely to be historical than the very general Markan description (13:14). Of Mark's three passion predictions (8:31; 9:31; 10:33), the more detailed and specific references are more suspect than the brief and generalized reference (9:31), though this does not prove that 9:31 is historical.

These negative criteria eliminate the more obvious anachronisms but do little to clarify who Jesus was, unless one is prepared simply to accept the rest. Modern historians, with their premise of skepticism, are not so prepared. Anyone who seeks to assert something must offer proof. Thus, *positive criteria* must be used to try to establish what is most probably historical. Six criteria are widely used today.

Discontinuity

The first criterion, which may appear a little odd and is widely misunderstood, *is that material should be judged historical if it can be shown that it is distinctive from both earlier Jewish and later Christian thought*. The logic here is impeccable and should be obvious: if an item cannot be easily traced to a time before or after Jesus, it is most reasonable to assume it comes from Jesus. Of course this is strange reasoning, because Jesus surely gained much from his Jewish heritage and passed much on to his followers. Admittedly, this criterion will not isolate what is most important about Jesus, nor does it imply that material that does not pass this test is questionable. It can only be used as a positive criterion. For this purpose it is extremely powerful: whatever this criterion reveals has the highest probability of being historical.

One example is Jesus' baptism by John, because baptism of fellow Jews is uncharacteristic of Judaism and because the early church did not believe Jesus needed such a baptism "for repentance" (Matt. 3:11; see Mark 1:4 and Luke 3:3). Therefore it is quite unlikely that either a general Jewish tradition was attributed to Jesus or that his followers later invented such a scene. It is likely historical.

Aspects of Jesus' teaching also pass this test, for example, the exhortation not to resist evil (Matt. 5:39–48) was uncharacteristic of both the early church and of Judaism. Similarly, the parables attributed to Jesus are often so startling, both in their teaching and their form, that there can be little doubt that he told parables and that we possess versions of many of them.

There is, however, a major difficulty in applying this criterion, for we are certain of very little about actual affairs in early Judaism or early Christianity. We must remember that we have no literary remains for the first two decades of the Jesus movement and little from the Jewish side during this crucial period. A second criterion is a somewhat less rigorous variant of this criterion that is still helpful.

Embarrassment

Material should be judged likely to be historical if it contains elements that are awkward for, or contradictory to, early beliefs about Jesus. The logic here is that people do not readily invent problems for themselves. By this criterion, too, the baptism of Jesus by John appears to be historical. Jesus' coming to John for baptism is awkward because John's baptism is one of repentance and because the master usually baptized the disciple. This embarrassment is evident in the developing tradition. Matthew stops to explain it (3:14–15); Luke obscures the detail that John baptized Jesus (3:20–32); John omits the baptism entirely; and the apocryphal *Gospel of the Nazarenes* has Jesus explicitly disclaim, "wherein have I sinned that I should go and be baptized by him?" (Fragment 2; quoted in Hennecke and Schneemelcher, 1991:1:160).

It might be too much to claim that Jesus started his career as a disciple of John, but almost certainly he was baptized by him. Using a similar logic, the notion that Jesus was executed by the Romans on a charge of insurrection is almost certainly historical. It was a fact that early followers were at some pains to explain away.

And consider the saying:

> But to what will I compare this generation? It is like children sitting in the market places and calling to one another.
> "We played the flute for you, and you did not dance;
> we wailed, and you did not mourn."
> For John came neither eating nor drinking, and they say, "He has a demon;"
> the Son of man came eating and drinking, and they say, "Look a glutton and a drunkard, a friend of tax collectors and sinners!"
>
> (Matt. 11:16–19)

Again, notice the implicit equality between John and Jesus. We find nothing of the later tendency to subordinate John. But even more significantly, we see here an evaluation of Jesus that no follower would have made up. Not only did early believers practice fasting like John and unlike Jesus (for example, Matt. 6:16 and 9:14–17), it is impossible to think of them inventing a description of Jesus as a glutton and a drunkard. Surely, this is a real charge leveled by some of his enemies. Jesus was apparently not sufficiently ascetic to fit some people's idea of a servant of God.

Using this criterion of embarrassment, we would attribute more historical weight to the version of the story in which Jesus shrinks back from being called "good" (Mark 10:18) than to the one in which it occasions no problem (Matt. 19:17). The saying that the kingdom of God is not coming with signs (Luke 17:20–21) seems in some tension with the apocalyptic beliefs characteristic of many early communities, but quite in harmony with another saying that declares: "If it is by the finger of God that I cast out demons, then the kingdom of God has come to you" (Luke 11:20). Both are probably historical sayings of Jesus.

One difficulty with this criterion is our limited knowledge of the great variety of forms of the early Jesus movements. What one movement might have found embarrassing, another movement might have found central to its understanding of Jesus. This difficulty can be addressed by focusing more narrowly on individual sources.

Incongruity

A third criterion argues that *material should be judged to be probably historical if it contains elements that are awkward for, or contradictory to, the ideas of the Gospel writer in whose work it is found.* At the least, such material was firmly embedded in the tradition before the time of that writer. Again, the story of Jesus' baptism is instructive, for we see a progressive diminution of the role of John. Already in Mark, John is clearly labeled the inferior predecessor (1:7), yet Mark did not hesitate to say clearly that Jesus came and was baptized by John (1:9). He is the only Gospel writer to be so explicit. Matthew introduced an explanatory dialogue justifying the event (3:14–15); Luke reported John's imprisonment before the baptism scene and never says John baptized him (3:20–21); John's Gospel omits the baptism altogether (1:29–34). John even has the Baptizer renounce any claim to messianic titles, not only Christ, but even Elijah or the prophet (1:20–21). The Gospel writers have a tendency to report only information that advances their own stories and convictions. When we find conflicting data, we may assume it is probably historical—at least it was fixed in the traditions that came to them.

The logic of historical reasoning here goes something like this: when we find people giving out information that they would rather not tell us, we can be confident that the material is trustworthy. If a colleague tells me she has not yet read a certain book, or a student tells me he has not read an assignment, I have no reason to doubt the report.

Thus the elements of apocalyptic thinking found in John, Luke's locating Jesus' home in Nazareth, Matthew's saying about an exclusive mission to Israel (10:5) and his exemption of the Pharisees from an active role in Jesus' death all gain in their probable historicity by being found in sources that would prefer not to admit such points. In both this and the previous criterion we might say that the historical probability is directly proportionate to the embarrassment factor: the more embarrassing the information, the more probable its historical accuracy. Thus, Jesus' betrayal by one of his chosen followers and the denial by Peter have a high degree of historical probability, for they are highly embarrassing incidents.

Multiple Sources

Fourth, *material found in separate sources should be judged likely to be historical.* This is the equivalent of two witnesses giving similar testimony in a trial—of course, one must be sure they did not confer. Thus Mark, Matthew, and Luke are not separate sources; the witnesses have conferred. The likely sources, based on source criticism, are Mark, Q, M, L, John, and perhaps other works like the *Gospel of Thomas* or the *Gospel of Peter* if these do not depend on the canonical Gospels. (See the discussion of source criticism in Chapter 7.) Paul would also count as a separate source. Material found in separate literary forms (for example, parable, miracle story, controversy story, aphorism) also has a higher probability of being historical.

This criterion does not validate specific events or sayings so much as it does typical kinds of things. We may be fairly certain that Jesus did not keep the Sabbath well and that he associated with all the wrong sorts of people, because such behavior occurs in all the sources. Surely Jesus was centrally concerned with the coming rule of God, for that concern appears in most sources. Other items that appear widely in the sources include Jesus gathering disciples; speaking in parables; healing people; emphasizing love of God, neighbor, and self; and taking a radical ethical stance.

The application of these four criteria—dissimilarity, embarrassment, incongruity, and multiple sources—to the gospel materials results in a body of material that has a strong probability of being historical. But that material alone is still not enough to form a historical account of Jesus. Two other criteria of a different kind, more synthetic than analytic, are often appealed to in order to expand the scope of the evidence. We may call them *explanation* and *coherence*.

Explanation

A fifth criterion attempts to take a larger view of the subject. *Material should be judged as likely historical when it explains what we know about Jesus through the other criteria.* How is it that Jesus' life had the impact that it did? Whatever Jesus said and did, he wound up at odds with most of his contemporaries. His own disciples forsook him. The religious and political leaders of his community rejected him. The occupying powers killed him. This is hard to explain unless there was something about his teachings and actions that others regarded as dangerous.

A major problem with many popular treatments of Jesus (including films like *The Last Temptation of Christ*) is that the image of Jesus they create is so anemic that it is hard to see why anyone would follow him, let alone be threatened by him. The historian must construe the evidence to explain the overall outcome of Jesus' life. Whereas the other criteria emphasize analysis, this one and the next attempt synthesis, asking, how should we put the evidence together to understand Jesus?

Coherence

The final criterion builds on the results of the first five. Having established a reasonable core of material that is quite likely to be historical, *other material that is coherent with this core material should be used to form a broad portrait of Jesus.* Can we integrate the various data around the one man, Jesus? In this final stage the narrative aspect of history comes closest to the narrative aspect of literature. The results of this final stage are only *possible*, perhaps approaching *probable*, if they are sensitively handled. Table 14.1 presents a synopsis of these criteria.

TABLE 14.1 CRITERIA TO ASSERT PROBABLE HISTORICITY

Criterion	Test	Level of Probability
Discontinuity	Unlike earlier Jewish tradition and later Christian tradition	Very high probability
Embarrassment	Awkward for early Christianity	Very high probability
Incongruity	In tension with other material in the same work	High probability
Multiple sources	Found in independent sources or in multiple forms	High probability
Explanation	Accounts for Jesus' rejection and death	Possible to probable
Coherence	Provides a cogent portrait of a believable person	Possible to probable

NOTE: The highest probability results from the use of multiple criteria in concert with each other.

Although it is beyond our scope here to reconstruct a portrait of the historical Jesus, let us consider a few specific incidents and then briefly sketch the work of a few scholars.

READING AND REFLECTION
Read some of the following passages and decide what level of historical probability you would assign to them based on these criteria.

Matthew 1–2 with Luke 1–2
Matthew 5–7 with Luke 6:17–49
Matthew 21:10–17 with Mark 11:12–19 and John 2:13–22
Matthew 28:18–20 with Acts 2:38; 10:28
Galatians 2:7–9
Luke 21:20 and Mark 13:14
Mark 8:31; 9:31; 10:33
Matthew 11:16–19
John 17:1–5

HISTORY, MYTH, AND LITERATURE

One of the earliest attempts to come to terms with the historical ambiguity of the Gospels used a certain concept of myth. David Friedrich Strauss (1808–1874) argued that the Gospels are mythic documents that attempt to portray ideas as if they were historical events (1972 [1840]:52, 81–82). He understood myth as a story created to teach a truth, rather like a parable. The most influential commentator of the modern period, Rudolf Bultmann, picked up this concept and, in order to make the Gospels accessible for our time sought to "demythologize" them, that is, to translate them back into ideas (1963:1–44). Obviously, Bultmann did not think it possible to speak meaningfully about the historical Jesus.

Although there is much to be learned from this endeavor to find meaning behind the historical reports, to dissolve the historic material into timeless truths seems in some tension with the basic thrust of the gospel as a literary form. Even if we concede that ultimate meaning lies behind these stories, so that we may speak of them as myth, the gospel form seems to require not myth *as* history but myth *in* history, and this requires a more adequate definition of *myth* than that of Strauss. Such a definition might draw on Plato's concept of myth as a representation of a reality that cannot be known directly, that is, it can be known only as the myth itself (*Timaeus* 29). It cannot be translated because "the meaning of the myth is inseparably associated with its mythic form" (R. M. Frye, 1973:30). As noted earlier, this concept of myth is closely allied with the concept of mimesis, which is the basis of literature (page 178). Literature uses the particular to present the universal; literature re-presents (mimesis) reality in such a way that the reader learns and infers the meaning of the events.

To the extent that the Gospels are literature, imaginative presentations of reality, they do not seek to present the reader with the facts for a life of Jesus but to so present Jesus that his real significance becomes clear. They are mythic in the sense that they reveal a reality beyond the events themselves, but a reality that abides in the events. This understanding of myth does not solve the problem of myth and history in the Gospels because it does not prove that a given element is historical. Yet it does resolve some of the tension in the older formulation, which regarded history and myth as mutually exclusive categories. They are not necessarily, and the concept of mimesis presents a fruitful alternative to this dichotomy by transcending, yet incorporating, myth and history.

Aristotle observed: "Poetry . . . is more philosophical and more significant than history" (*Poetics* 1451b; see his complete discussion in Chapter 8, pages 266–68). He meant that it was more valuable to see the significance of actions than to know who did what and when. But we have seen that modern history insists on meaning as well as facts, and to that extent it is poetry—art. As one modern literary critic has cogently argued, it is not a question of history *or* literature: "We can only get back to the Jesus of history through the Jesus of literature" (R. M. Frye, in Walker, 1978:302). This is true in two senses: the Gospels are literally all we have. If we cannot get to the historical Jesus through literature, we cannot get to him at all. More importantly, the Gospels as literature seek to present *their* views of Jesus as a real person. Although each presents a unique view of Jesus, the reader recognizes the same person in all four works. Frye wishes not to delve behind the Gospels to reach Jesus but to go through the Gospels to Jesus.

THE JESUS OF STORY, CANON, AND HISTORY

Precisely this impression of some unanimity in the Gospels' presentations of Jesus has allowed Christian interpreters to construct a larger portrait of Jesus, based on the Gospels but elaborating them into a more abstract synthesis. This Christian image of Jesus has shifted over time, with different eras emphasizing different things. One scholar characterizes the popular understanding of Jesus today this way:

> *As the divinely begotten Son of God, he was sent into the world for the purpose of dying on the cross as a means of reconciliation between God and humankind, and his message consisted primarily of inviting his hearers to believe that what he said about himself and his role in salvation was true. (Borg, 1987:2)*

Although this image owes something to the Gospel of John, it rests primarily on centuries of Christian preaching and piety. It presents the Jesus of the Christian story, not the Jesus of the Gospels and certainly not the historical Jesus.

Here we will only begin to sketch a historical picture of Jesus, based on the kinds of evidence suggested by the scholars who have developed the criteria discussed above.

First, these criteria do not produce any evidence with historical probability about the birth, childhood, or development of Jesus. This is, of course, not unusual; for the same could be said of nearly every figure from antiquity. We do have birth traditions in two sources (M and L), but they disagree on nearly every point. They converge only on the names of Jesus' parents and the place of birth. However, the Bethlehem tradition is easily accounted for as coming from the Hebrew Scriptures and so cannot be said to be even probable. Overwhelmingly (and embarrassingly) Jesus is from Nazareth. We must be content to say we know nothing significant historically about Jesus' origins. (For an example of what Christian piety found in these stories, however, see the second-century work *Protoevangelium of James* 7–24; available in J. K. Elliott, 1993:48–67, and Hennecke and Schneemelcher, 1991:1:370–88.)

Second, these criteria produce a wealth of material concerning the beginning and ending of Jesus' public activity. It is highly probable that Jesus began within the orbit of John the Baptizer, a prophet strongly anticipating the coming of God's judgment and calling for purity (washing). We cannot be certain when or why Jesus left the Baptizer's movement, perhaps only with the death of John and the failure of judgment to appear.

Like John, Jesus' life was ended by government action. Rejected by the Jerusalem authorities, betrayed by his own disciple, forsaken by all (but the women), Jesus was crucified by Pontius Pilate, probably in the spring of 30 CE. He died accused of insurrection, probably after a disturbance in the Jerusalem Temple.

Third, these criteria also yield considerable material about Jesus' teachings and actions between these two points of his career, but it is impossible to arrange this material in any chronological order. It is impossible to write a life of Jesus based on anything other than imagination, for we do not know the sequence of that life. We cannot even be sure of the length of Jesus' career—whether it lasted one year as portrayed in the synoptics, three or so years as in John, or perhaps even longer.

Very likely Jesus moved freely about Galilee and Judea, probably going up to the great feasts in Jerusalem as (only) the Gospel of John indicates. As Jesus moved about Palestine he did two typical kinds of things: he healed people, and he taught people. Neither is as simple as it sounds. Neither sickness nor health was understood in anything like our modern practice. Sickness was understood as a form of oppression, caused by some enemy. One ultimate cause of illness was thought to be possession by demons, so healing also involved overcoming such demons. Although we get the impression of Jesus healing someone at every turn, there are really only a few accounts narrated: perhaps a half-dozen exorcisms and a dozen healings. We can be reasonably sure that Jesus' contemporaries understood him to be someone with a greater power than these evil forces. What makes this conclusion highly probable is not only that such actions are found throughout the sources, but that his enemies could explain them as sorcery—a charge that had to be dealt with (criterion of embarrassment; see Mark 3:22–30).

This greater power of Jesus was understood to be God's Spirit, and it was precisely the possession of that Spirit that signaled the presence of God's rule, the focus of Jesus' teaching. Thus, there is a strong continuity between the action and the teaching of Jesus (coherence). Among the teachings that scholars would generally attribute to Jesus are the following:

> Blessed are you poor for yours is the kingdom of heaven.
> It is easier for a camel to go through the eye of a needle than for the rich to enter the kingdom of God.
> Anyone who comes to me and does not hate father and mother cannot be my disciple.
> Do not resist evil, but if anyone strikes you on the right cheek turn to him the other also.
> Love your enemies.
> I saw Satan fall like lightning from heaven.
> If I cast out demons by Beelzebul, by whom do your sons cast them out? Therefore they shall be your judges. But if it is by the finger of God that I cast out demons, then the kingdom of God has come upon you.
> The kingdom of God will not come with signs that can be checked beforehand; nor will they say, "Here it is!" or "There!" because the kingdom of God is already among you.
> Behold I have given you power to tread on serpents and scorpions, and over all the power of the enemy; and nothing shall hurt you.
> The kingdom of heaven is like a merchant in search of fine pearls, who, on finding one pearl of great value, went and sold all that he had and bought it.

Much else could be added (see, for example, Crossan's listing, 1991:xiii–xxvi), but these are sufficient to give a taste for the radical understanding of life as participating already in the rule of God, a reign that requires a reorientation of life and values. Scholars are generally agreed that the historical Jesus did not speak about believing in him or his teaching but about experiencing and living the power of God's kingdom.

It is this perception of Jesus as a person of extraordinary power, swaying the people to his vision of life, teaching a radical immediacy of God's rule that makes sense of both the willingness of some to follow him and the hostility of the rulers, leading eventually to his death (criterion of explanation). No doubt this experience of power also led to belief in his resurrection, though it is not possible to trace this historically. Because history is concerned with natural cause and effect, it can never judge whether or not Jesus was raised from the dead.

This very brief synopsis of the results of historical-Jesus research is meant only to indicate something of the state of the question today. Much more could be said and has been said by able scholars (for which see the resource section). But this is enough to indicate how historians today begin to reconstruct the actual figure of Jesus.

It is, however, impossible at this juncture to speak of any scholarly consensus about the historical Jesus. Even when there is broad agreement about what constitutes our best evidence, scholars construe that evidence in different ways, focus on different aspects as central, and choose very different paradigms within which to interpret the evidence. Larry W. Hurtado has sketched a categorization of recent approaches, identifying eight different portraits of Jesus.

Jesus the prophet who would restore Israel	E. P. Sanders
Jesus the Jewish holy man	Geza Vermes
Jesus the Christian Messiah	Ben Witherington III
Jesus the critic of Jewish religion	John P. Meier
Jesus the social visionary	Marcus J. Borg
Jesus the social revolutionary	Richard A. Horsley
Jesus the Galilean sage	Seàn Freyne
Jesus the Jewish Cynic	John Dominic Crossan

(I have modified the names of the approaches to make the point more clearly; see Hurtado in Arnal and Desjardins, 1997: 272–95.)

Such a list shows how erroneous it is to imagine that we have answered the question of the historical Jesus. Whether this failure stems from the biases of the interpreters or from some methodological failure, or both, and whether such failure can be overcome remains to be seen.

It is not so much that scholars disagree on the basic evidence as that they evaluate that evidence differently, focusing on some while downplaying other aspects. In addition, they choose basically different aspects of Jesus' historical setting within which to place the evidence. Thus, the same item, such as Jesus practicing exorcisms, looks different when it is regarded as the work of a Jewish teacher, the symbolic act of a prophet, or the action of a social revolutionary. Even with the explosion of historical-Jesus research and the appearance of numerous new studies, we cannot speak of an emerging consensus. There are as yet only multiple and competing scholarly reconstructions of the historical figure of Jesus.

But if the historical Jesus remains yet beyond our grasp, the literary Jesus is readily available. The Jesus stories we find in the canon are rich and diverse. Matthew, Mark, and Luke were not content merely to pass on the traditions they received. They reshaped them, reordered them, even invented new material to interpret Jesus as they knew him. John went even further, transforming the whole of the Jesus tradition into a particular way of viewing Jesus. Paul did not use much of the Jesus tradition in his Letters, though he perhaps did in his oral proclamation. For Paul, however, it was clearly the death of Jesus, an act of human obedience, that reversed the human disobedience of Adam, that grants righteousness to all those who take part in Christ and in his community. For Hebrews, Jesus became the great high priest, and for Revelation he was the transcendent, heavenly Lord; James had little to say about him.

Yet all this rich variety has a certain unity, a unity enhanced by the centuries of canon making. Behind all the New Testament writings, there stands a real, recognizable Jesus, identifiably the same person. Writings in which the vision of Jesus wandered too far from this common representation were finally relegated to the sidelines in the long and arduous process of canon making. Extraordinary imagination is at play, but in each case this imagination is disciplined by historical recollection. If we were to imagine the situation had all the gospels and other writings about Jesus been accepted, we would understand this point. For we would then be confronted with such a fantastic array of possibilities that all hope of recognizing the historical person would vanish. If only one gospel had been preserved, however, we would feel we knew Jesus exactly, mistaking the literary representation for the man himself. Having four Gospels, and other accounts as well, allows us to avoid this error and to obtain a richer picture of the subject of these works.

A modern man of letters offers us an insightful observation in this regard. This Oxford medievalist observed that

> There are characters whom we know to be historical but of whom we do not feel that we have any personal knowledge—knowledge by acquaintance; such are Alexander, Atilla, or William of Orange. There are others who make no claim to historical reality but whom, nonetheless, we know as we know real people: Falstaff, Uncle Toby, Mr. Pickwick. But there are only three characters who, claiming the first sort of reality, also have the second. And surely everyone knows who they are: Plato's Socrates, the Jesus of the Gospels, and Boswell's Johnson. (C. S. Lewis, 1967:156)

For C. S. Lewis this was primarily a literary insight, but it is also a historical conclusion. Now no one would claim that Plato's Socrates is the historical Socrates pure and simple. Yet he is recognizably the same Socrates.

And so it is beneath, or rather within, all the creative diversity of the New Testament. Each writer presents a unique portrait and story of Jesus; but reading them together one senses an encounter with recognizably the same person. But proof of that can never be found in a book like this. Here we can only provide some hints on how to read these ancient works. It would be a great mistake to substitute the reading of this for the reading of them. If you wish to hear their stories, you must read them. Read and imagine.

LEARNING ON YOUR OWN

REVIEWING THE CHAPTER

Names and Terms

Athanasius	King James Version	orthodox
codex	Marcion	papyrus
Erasmus	Muratorian Fragment	textual criticism
Jerome	new quest	

Issues and Questions

1. When, how, and by whom was the New Testament canon established?
2. Of the books now included in the New Testament canon, which were the most controversial and why?
3. What is the logic of the order of the writings in the New Testament?
4. What is the effect of attempts to harmonize the four Gospel stories into a unified account?
5. Why does a historian prefer primary sources?
6. Why do scholars not take the Gospels as simple historical accounts of Jesus?
7. How are negative criteria used to determine whether Gospel material is historical in our modern sense? Why do most scholars prefer to use positive criteria?
8. Why would most modern scholars accept Jesus' baptism by John as historical?
9. By which positive criterion would one decide whether Jesus was observant of the Sabbath?
10. Prepare to argue either for or against the notion that the New Testament presents a coherent view of the historical Jesus.
11. Why do many scholars believe it is impossible to separate the myth of Jesus from the history of Jesus?

TAKING THE NEXT STEP

One of the best treatments of the unity behind the real diversity of the New Testament writings is Dunn, 2006.

Bock, 2002, and Stanton, 1997, provide very readable introductions to the issues in studying Jesus. Gowler, 2007, provides an up-to-date overview of Jesus studies; see also Dunn and McKnight, 2005.

Topics for Special Studies

The Origin of the Present Canon of New Testament Writings

One of the best discussions is Grant, 1993, who rightly characterizes the process as a search for authenticity; see also his 1965 study. Metzger, 1987, is also highly recommended. See also McDonald, 2007; Barton, 1998; Farmer and Farkasfalvy, 1983; Gamble, 1984; Wall, 1992; Von Campenhausen, 1977; and Bruce, 1993. P. R. Davies, 1998, traces the canonization of the Hebrew Scriptures. Elliott and Moir, 1995, provide a good introduction to the manuscripts and to textual criticism. Porter, 2004, assesses the development of the canon of Paul's Letters.

On the process and techniques of writing see Derrenbacker, 2005; Roberts, 1984; and Millard, 2000.

J. A. Sanders, 1984, introduces the new concern for canon criticism (the concern to interpret the Bible within the context of the believing community). See also McDonald and Sander, 2002, and Wall, 1992.

The Canonization of One Particular Work

In addition to the works under the previous topic, commentaries will discuss the issue; works that eventually became part of the canon only after being disputed include Revelation, James, Jude, 1 and 2 Peter, and 2 and 3 John. Among the works that were excluded after being included by some are the *Apocalypse of Peter*, the *Acts of Paul*, and the *Shepherd of Hermas*. See the fuller list and discussion in Metzger, 1987:165–90.

Trobisch, 1994, explores the canonization of Paul's Letters; see also Porter, 2004, and Nienhuis, 2007.

Comparison of Marcion's Canon and the Muratorian Fragment

The early dating of the Muratorian Fragment has been challenged by Sundberg, 1973, who dates it to the fourth century, but Ferguson, 1982, reconsiders the evidence. Hahneman, 1992, discusses its place in the evolution of the canon, supporting a late date. Hall, 1995, reviews the arguments and supports an early date.

On Marcion, see Knox, 1942; Grant, 1993; Williams, 1989; Kalin, 1990; and chapter 7 of Wilson, 1995.

The Problem with Historical Knowledge of Jesus

A fine, concise statement of the problem is given by Jeremias, 1964. The best introductions to the issues are Tatum, 1999; Powell, 1998; and the encyclopedic work of Theissen and Merz, 1998, any chapter of which could be the beginning point of a significant research project. For a very skeptical view, see Lüdemann, 1999; for a moderate approach see Dunn, 2005; for conservative approaches, see Witherington, 1997, and Bauckham, 2006; for a more critical view see Funk, 2000 and 2002. For a range of views, see the anthologies of Arnal and Desjardins, 1997, and Evans and Porter, 1995. On the political issues in interpreting Jesus see Schüssler Fiorenza, 2000.

Harvey, 1966, treats the issues of historical knowledge about religion in a clear and provocative fashion. See also McIntire, 1977; Harvey, 1982; and Hedrick, 1999. A provocative work addressing both the issues of canon and history is Barr, 1984b (and 1984a).

On the difficulty of writing ancient history in general, see Finley, 1986.

For a comparison of historical and gospel images of Jesus see Stanton, 2002, and Marsh and Moyise, 2005.

Criteria Appropriate for Identifying Historical Information in the Gospels

Porter, 2000, provides a careful historical survey and reviews the current state of the problem. Meier, 1991–2001, has a clear discussion of the issues (also see his article in Kingsbury, 1996). Thiessen and Winter, 2002, provide an extensive historical discussion of the criterion of dissimilarity. Other useful discussions of criteria include Powell, 1998; Boring, 1985; Meyer, 1979:23–110; Walker, 1969; and McArthur, 1971. Scott, 1986, considers the parable tradition. The approach of the Jesus Seminar is outlined in Funk, Hoover, and the Jesus Seminar, 1993, and evaluated in Crossan, Johnson, and Kelber, 1999.

Jesus in the First-Century Context

Culture: Start with the fine anthology by Levine, Allison, and Crossan, 2006. For a social science analysis of kingdom language by Jesus and his culture, see Malina, 2001. For a feminist perspective on Jesus and women, see Corley, 2002.

Archaeology: Start with Reed, 2000; Crossan and Reed, 2001; and Horsley, 1996; see the interesting work of Rousseau and Arav, 1994; each has good notes and a good bibliography. See also Horsley, 1996; Edwards and McCollough, 1997; Shanks et al., 1994; and Finegan, 1992. For a history of the archaeology of early Christianity, see Frend, 1998.

Jesus in Noncanonical Sources

Major noncanonical gospels are collected and discussed by Cameron, 1982; Crossan, 1985, presents four. For discussions, see Borg, 1997; Hedrick, 1988; Stroker, 1990; and Wenham, 1985. For a survey of the sources outside the New Testament, the best discussion is Van Voorst, 2000, but see also Wenham, 1985, and Bruce, 1974, who assesses the issue of the validity of extrabiblical information about Jesus negatively. Kloppenborg, 2000, explores a precanonical source.

The best collection of noncanonical gospels is J. K. Elliott, 1996; the standard remains Hennecke and Schneemelcher, 1991, vol. 1.

Issues Raised by Historical-Jesus Studies

Apocalyptic or nonapocalyptic? Start with Kloppenborg and Marshall, 2005; contrast Allison, 1985 and 2005; Downing, 1988; and Crossan, 1991.

Anti-Semitism: See Kloppenborg and Marshall, 2005, and Arnal, 2005. For a Jewish view of Jesus see Levine, 2006; Le Beau, Greenspoon, and Hamm, 2000; and Vermes, 1981, 2001; see also Sanders, 1985.

Analysis of the Work of One of the Pivotal Figures in Historical-Jesus Research

Among the most important are David Friedrich Strauss, Albert Schweitzer, and Ernst Käsemann.

The original writings of many of the prime scholars are now available in English in the Lives of Jesus series, edited by Leander E. Keck (Fortress Press). Schweitzer, 1906, reviewed earlier scholarship and forever changed the nature of the field. For an overview, see Duling, 1979. See also Robinson, 1959, and Aulen, 1976.

Kissinger, 1985, includes an overview of the major scholars and bibliography. For the past 150 years, see Heyer, 1997. On U.S. scholars, see Hollenbach, 1989, and Fuller, 1987.

Analysis of the Work of a Contemporary Scholar

Important figures include John Dominic Crossan, John P. Meier, E. P. Sanders, and Geza Vermes; also see the list above at page 494.

See the works of each in the bibliography. Check the reviews of their works by other scholars in the *Index to Book Reviews in Religion* and the *Book Review Index*. Also see Arnal and Desjardins, 1997.

Compare One Topic in Works by Several Contemporary Scholars

Much could be learned by comparing specific points in Meier, 1991 (Roman Catholic); E. P. Sanders, 1995 (Protestant); Vermes, 1981 and 1993 (Jewish); Crossan, 1991 (liberal Catholic); and Marshall, 1977b (conservative Protestant).

Scholars sensitive to newer developments in literary theory include Boers, 1989; Crossan, 1973; and Freyne, 1988.

There is great diversity in understanding what Jesus meant by **kingdom of God**; start with Perrin, 1976; Scott, 1981; Allison, 1985; and Beasley-Murray, 1986. Horsley, 2002, takes a political approach; Moxnes, 1988, and Malina, 2001, take a more social approach.

Two other debated topics:

Miracles: Achtemeier, 1975c; Kee, 1986; Theissen, 1983; Bokser, 1985 (on the Rabbinic tradition).

Resurrection: On the general issue of how resurrection and immortality were understood, see Nickelsburg, 1972, and Cullmann, 1958. For a comparison of the resurrection narratives, see Fuller, 1980, and Osborne, 1984. For a Catholic scholar's perspective, see Perkins, 1984; for a skeptic's, see Lüdemann, 1994. Other interesting studies include Marxsen, 1990; R. Collins, 1984; Funk, 1996; and Sawicki, 1994.

Additional Books and Articles

The methodology of Robinson and Koester, 1971, has had enormous influence on later studies.

The classic work of W. Bauer, 1971, is still considered controversial.

For bibliographies, see White, 1988; Evans, 1989; and Evans and Chilton, 1994. See also Hultgren, 1988, and Kissinger, 1985 and 1979 (on parables). Heyer, 1997, and Theissen and Merz, 1998, have extensive bibliographies.

APPENDIX A
DOING YOUR OWN RESEARCH

WRITING RESEARCH PAPERS ON THE NEW TESTAMENT

Probably the chief value of a research paper in an introductory course is to help you learn your way around the appropriate sections of the library and the Internet, discovering the specialized resources available and how to use them. This section will provide a brief overview of those resources and suggestions on how to get started on research. An electronic version of this appendix is posted on my Web site, where all the links listed below are active: http://www.wright.edu/~david.barr/research.htm.

Getting Started

The first task is to find a suitable topic for research—that is, (1) a topic you are interested in, (2) one on which resources are available, and (3) one that is manageable in the time available before the due date. The resources sections at the ends of the chapters list a few potential topics; other topics will surely occur to you as you read the New Testament writings.

Once you have chosen a topic, the next step is to get an overview of it so that you will have a perspective from which you can pursue your own inquiry. Perhaps the discussion in class or in this text has already provided you sufficient perspective, but do not neglect the dictionaries and encyclopedias that are available. These reference works will usually identify what the issues are and provide a basic beginning bibliography.

The most comprehensive dictionary available is the six-volume *Anchor Bible Dictionary* (Freedman, 1992). However, the older *Interpreter's Dictionary of the Bible* (Buttrick, 1962 and 1976) is still useful. One-volume dictionaries are less valuable, but three of the best are the *Harper's Bible Dictionary* (Achtemeier, 1996), *Eerdmans Dictionary of the Bible* (Freedman, Myers, and Beck, 2000), and the *New Bible Dictionary* (Wood, 1996). The newer edition of *The International Standard Bible Encyclopedia* (Bromiley, 1988) is also useful.

Consulting a one-volume commentary can be helpful in getting an overview of a particular biblical writing or a thumbnail sketch of a particular passage. Four quite different works, each excellent in its own way, are available:

> *Harper's Bible Commentary* (Mays, 1998; produced in conjunction with the Society of Biblical Literature, the major professional association of biblical scholars)
>
> *The New Jerome Biblical Commentary* (Brown, Fitzmyer, and Murphy, 1990; the work of Roman Catholic scholars)
>
> *The International Bible Commentary* (Bruce, 1986; a conservative, evangelical work)
>
> *The Women's Bible Commentary* (Newsom and Ringe, 1992; focusing especially on issues of concern to women)

Two reference sets in related areas are the *Oxford Classical Dictionary* (Hornblower and Spawforth 1996), which contains fine introductions to Greek and Roman antiquity; and *Encyclopedia Judaica*, 22 volumes (Skolnick and Berenbaum, 2007); also available on CD-ROM, 1997.

Finding Resources

Your next task is to find the relevant scholarly literature on your subject. The small bibliographies in the dictionaries reference only the most important works, but each of these works will have its own bibliography of earlier works. The lists of topics at the end of each chapter in this book provide several suggestions, usually in the order they might be most useful. To find more recent work, you will need to use the scholarly indexes that are available in book form, on CD-ROM, and on the Internet.

The basic journal index for all aspects of religion studies is *Religion Index* (also known as the ATLA Religion Database). It is a comprehensive reference database, containing more than 1 million citations from over 1,400 international journal titles and 14,000 multiauthor works and book reviews related to religious studies from 1949 to the present. Available in book form, on CD-ROM, and online through subscription (possibly through your library), it is produced by the American Theological Library Association (see http://www.atla.com).

Two more-technical bibliographic guides also treat New Testament topics: the annual guide to the ancient world, *L'Année philologique*, especially in section 1 (Histoire littéraire, and its subdivision Littérature judéo-chrétienne) and section 5 (Histoire, and its subdivision, Histoire religieuse et mythologie). It covers works in English, French, and German. It is available in an online version (see http://www .annee-philologique.com/aph/). More comprehensive for biblical studies, but not as widely available, is *Elenchus Bibliographicus Biblicus*, a topical index to over 1,000 journals, published in Rome by the Biblical Institute Press.

Another strategy for finding recent work, especially for seminal works, is to find out who is citing these works in their footnotes. This can be done through the *Arts and Humanities Citation Index*. This work indexes articles and books according to the sources they cite. This too is available in electronic form; check with your librarian.

Another very valuable reference work is *New Testament Abstracts*, which provides short abstracts of articles from most of the important journals that deal with the New Testament. These abstracts can be very useful in deciding whether you need to get the article, should the article not be readily available in your library. This work also contains notices and abstracts of new books. The arrangement by biblical writing rather than by topic, makes it difficult to use, though there are periodic indexes. There are three issues per year, with the third issue containing an index by scripture passage and author. It is now available on CD-ROM and online (back to 1985), though with a limited search engine.

One other very useful work is available in both print and electronic form, *Religious and Theological Abstracts*. It too has the major benefit of including short abstracts of the articles indexed. The online version allows you to do a limited demonstration search (http://www.rtabst.org/).

The Internet

A wealth of information is available on the Internet, but also an ample supply of biased and erroneous information. For general guidelines for evaluating information from the Internet, see http://www.library.jhu.edu/researchhelp/general/evaluating/.

One way to find reliable information is to use the services of a New Testament scholar. The best such service is provided by Mark Goodacre at his site, http://ntgateway.com. As the name suggests, this is an index to other sites and resources, including a wealth of online articles and books. Also of great value is the site of Torrey Seland at http://www.torreys.org/bible/. Finally, the University of Pennsylvania maintains a rather full listing of sites for the study of Judaism and Christianity (http://ccat.sas.upenn.edu/rs/resources.html).

For information about the Greco-Roman world there are two very useful sites:

Diotima provides information for the study of women and gender in the ancient world (http://www.stoa.org/diotima/).

The Perseus project attempts to make a wide range of resource material available on the Web, including texts, art works, and archaeological information (http://www.perseus.tufts.edu).

Many general and Catholic resources are indexed at http://catholic-resources.org/.

You can find many ancient writings online; perhaps the best collection is http://www.earlychristianwritings.com/.

You can find a broad selection of early Jewish writings at http://www.earlyjewishwritings.com/.

The general format for citing material on the World Wide Web is similar to that for print citations, and the general principle is the same: give the reader enough information to find the original. If you know the author, list the item by author's name, last name first, followed by the full title of the item in quotation marks. If the item is part of a larger work, give the name of the larger work in italics, followed by any version or file number and the date of the document's creation or last revision. Next list the protocol (for example, http://) and the full URL, followed by the date of access in parentheses. For example:

Sanders, E. P. "The Question of Uniqueness in the Teaching of Jesus," 1990. http://www.biblicalstudies.org.uk/pdf/uniqueness_sanders.pdf (September 28, 2007).

"Ancient Olympic Events." *The Ancient Olympics*. February 21, 1997. http://www.perseus.tufts.edu/Olympics/sports.html (June 19, 2001).

More elaborate instructions for citing both print and Internet publications can be found at these sites:

http://www.columbia.edu/cu/cup/cgos/idx_basic.html
http://www2.h-net.msu.edu/~africa/citation.html
http://www.library.ualberta.ca/guides/citation/index.cfm

In addition to using your own library catalog, you can find the catalogs of most major research libraries now available online. These catalogs are very useful for discovering all that has been published on a specific topic; you can virtually browse the shelves by searching for a call number of a book on your topic. See the comprehensive listing at http://sunsite.berkeley.edu/Libweb/Academic_main.html.

There are a number of online discussion groups devoted to New Testament topics; most have archives of past discussion. You can find their addresses, rules for subscribing, and how to search their archives at http://ntgateway.com/E-Lists.htm. Among the more active and interesting groups are:

Synoptic-L is an e-mail conference for the discussion of the synoptic Gospels.

Corpus Paulinum is a moderated list for discussion of Paul.

CrossTalk (XTalk) focuses its discussion on the historical Jesus and early Christian origins.

Ioudaios-L is a moderated group for the discussion of Judaism in the Greco-Roman era.

GThomas E-group is devoted to the scholarly discussion of the *Gospel of Thomas*.

Blogs on biblical and related topics are multiplying (and disappearing); two bloggers attempt to keep an up-to-date list at http://www.biblioblogs.com/.

The Biblical Journals

The more important journals for the study of the New Testament include these:

The *Journal of Biblical Literature* is the professional journal of the Society of Biblical Literature and covers all aspects of biblical study. It is available both in print and online at http://www.sbl-site.org/Publications. [*JBL*]

New Testament Studies is the professional journal of the Studiorium Novi Testamentum Societas, based in England. [*NTS*]

The *Catholic Biblical Quarterly* is the professional journal of the Catholic Biblical Association. [*CBQ*]

Interpretation is published by Union Theological Seminary in Virginia and deals with all aspects of biblical literature. Issues often focus on a specific problem or kind of literature.

Novum Testamentum is a New Testament journal published by E. J. Brill, Leiden. [*NovT*]

Semeia was an experimental journal devoted to newer methods of study, especially literary and structuralist studies of biblical literature. Issues were devoted to specific themes or methods. It is now a book series, but the first 91 issues are available, some online at http://www.sbl-site.org/Publications/Publications_Journals_Semeia.aspx.

Journal for the Study of the Historical Jesus is published by Sage Publications and available electronically at http://jshj.sagepub.com. Check with your library for access.

Biblical Interpretation: A Journal of Contemporary Approaches is devoted to newer methods of study and published by Brill. It is available in both hard copy and electronically, at http://www.ingentaconnect.com/content/brill/bii. [*BibInt*]

Biblical Theology Bulletin is probably the best source today for articles on the social analysis of biblical writings and culture, many from an anthropological approach. [*BTB*]

Harvard Theological Review, despite its name, covers all aspects of the study of religion, including historical, archaeological, and literary approaches. [*HTR*]

Journal of the American Academy of Religion is the professional journal in general religion studies. [*JAAR*]

For an extensive list of relevant journals, see http://www.vanderbilt.edu/AnS/religious_studies/NTBib/annuals.html.

In addition, journals focusing on the study of Judaism and on classical antiquity often cover topics important for the study of the New Testament. Some of the more important ones are listed below.

Classical Antiquity

Transactions of the American Philological Association is a major journal for the study of classical Greece and Rome. [*TAPA*]

Aufstieg und Niedergang der römischen Welt is published in Germany but contains many articles in English. It specializes in major treatments of specific themes (indexed at http://www.uky.edu/As/classics/biblio/Anrw.html). [*ANRW*]

Other journals include *Antiquity; Classical Journal; Classical Quarterly; Classical World; Gnomon; Greece and Rome; Greek, Roman and Byzantine Studies; Hermes; Isis; Journal of Roman Studies;* and *Yale Classical Studies.*

Judaism

The *Hebrew Union Annual*, published by Hebrew Union College, deals with all aspects of the study of Judaism.

Jewish Quarterly Review; Journal for the Study of Judaism; Judaism: A Quarterly; and *Journal of Jewish Studies* are all useful references.

Jewish Literature

The sources for studying Rabbinic Judaism are vast, complex, and obscure. The most accessible English introduction is Neusner, 1995. Strack and Stemberger, 1996, is more advanced. Also see Safrai, 1987.

The earliest literature is the Mishnah, published from earlier oral tradition about 200 CE. It consists of sixty-three tractates, each on a separate topic. One of the most accessible is *Avot* (The Fathers). The standard English version of the Mishnah is that of Danby, 1933; there is a newer translation by Neusner, 1988.

The most important literature is the Talmud, which exists in two versions: the Jerusalem Talmud (published around 400 CE) and the Babylonian Talmud (published around 600 CE; the latter is the more authoritative and can be referred to simply as the Talmud). The Talmud is largely a vast commentary on the Mishnah, each discussion starting with a quotation from the Mishnah, then adding many comments and discussion by various rabbis. The standard English translation is published in thirty-six volumes (Epstein, 1935; see also Neusner, 1982–1993).

Other important literature includes the Tosefta (Additions); it contains further thoughts on the topics addressed in the Mishnah. The Midrashim (Investigations) are a series of commentaries on Scripture; there are many such commentaries from various periods of Jewish history. Finally, there are the Targumim, a series of Aramaic paraphrases of the Hebrew Scriptures.

One difficulty in citations is that many of the tractates, and even the whole works, can be called by different names. For example the tractate called "The Fathers" can be cited as *Avoth, Avot, Aboth, Pirke Aboth,* or *Mishnah Aboth.* The Mishnah is also spelled Mishna; the Jerusalem Talmud is also called the Palestinian Talmud, the Talmud of the Land of Israel, or simply Yerushalmi; the Babylonian Talmud is also called Bavli. Citations from the Mishnah will often just use the name of the tractate (for example, *Avot*), but may be cited as *Mishnah Avot* or *m. Avot.* Talmudic citations will include the name of the tractate and some indicator of which Talmud it is from, often just with an initial: TB or *b.* for the Babylonian Talmud; *y.* for the Jerusalem Talmud.

The literature known as the Dead Sea Scrolls is cited in a special format, consisting of a number, the letter Q, and a short abbreviation, for example 1QpHab. Interpreted this means the writing was found in cave 1 at Qumran and is titled Pesher Habakkuk. Thus 4QSD, is the Serek Damascus found in cave 4. Any book on the Scrolls, such as Wise, Abegg, and Cook, 1996, will contain a complete chart of the abbreviations and what they stand for.

General Guides

For academic journals, see Dawsey, 1988.

Reviews of important monographs may be located by using the *Index to Book Reviews in Religion* and the *Book Review Index.* Full reviews of most recent scholarly books can be found in the *Review of Biblical Literature (RBL),* published by the Society of Biblical Literature. A print edition is available annually by subscription; the online version can be accessed free at http://www.bookreviews.org.

Bibliographic guides are also available. Among the best are J. A. Fitzmyer, 1990b; Danker, 1993; and France, 1979. Each is annotated. Also useful is the minimally annotated listing of Scholer, 1973. Stuart, 1990, evaluates commentaries from a conservative perspective. For a guide to the classical world, see Bagnall, 1980. On Judaism, see Cutter and Oppenheim, 1982.

Many **specialized bibliographies** are also available. See the following bibliography for complete details:

New Testament—Harrington, 1985b; Hurd, 1966; Langevin, 1985; and Wagner, 1987; see also Minor, 1992, and Kiehl, 1988

Bible as literature—Gottcent, 1979; Minor, 1992; and Powell, Gray, and Curtis, 1992

Rhetoric and the Bible—Watson and Hauser, 1994

Jesus and the Gospels—Aune, 1980a; den Heyer, 1997; Evans, 1996; Garland, 1990; Hultgren, 1988; Kissinger, 1985; Longstaff and Thomas, 1988; McKnight and Williams, 2000; and White, 1988

Mark—Brooks, 1978; H. M. Humphrey, 1981; Kee, 1978; and Matera, 1987b

Matthew—Ziesler, 1985, and Harrington, 1975

Luke-Acts—Mattill, 1966; Mills, 1986; and Segbroeck, 1989

John—Belle, 1988; Bogart, 1978; and Koester, 1991

Sermon on the Mount and parables—Kissinger, 1975 and 1979

Paul—Nanos, 2000; Borchert, 1985; and Metzger, 1960

1 Peter—Casurella, 1996

Apocalypse—Muse, 1996

Roman religion—Beard, North, and Price, 1998

Judaism—Neusner, 1972b; Mor and Rappaport, 1982; Bourquin, 1990; and Kraft and Nickelsburg, 1985

Dead Sea Scrolls—Flint and VanderKam, 1998–1999; Fitzmyer, 1990a; and Murphy-O'Connor and Charlesworth, 1990

Josephus—Feldman, 1986

Philo—Runia, 2000, and Hilgert, 1977

Pseudepigrapha—Charlesworth, 1981 and 1987

Patronage—J. H. Elliott, 1987

Kinship—K. C. Hanson, 1994

Women—Pomeroy, 1991a

Prostitution—Ford, 1993

Slavery—Osiek, 1992a

City—Rohrbaugh, 1991

Ephesus—Oster, 1987

APPENDIX B
DETAILED CHRONOLOGY
OF THE NEW TESTAMENT ERA

Any chronology of ancient times can be only an approximation. The dates assigned to the various writings are quite uncertain. A question mark indicates extreme uncertainty. The dates of rulers and writers are more sure but still often involve guesswork. I have tried to place them near where they flourished (fl.) or when they published an important work. Most dates are drawn from the *Oxford Classical Dictionary*, the *Anchor Bible Dictionary*, and the *Interpreter's Dictionary of the Bible*.

Date	Major Events in Empire	Major Events in Palestine	Writers/Writings
BCE			
323	Death of Alexander	Beginning of Hellenistic Age	
			Beginning of translation of Torah into Greek (about 300?)
200		Seleucid rule	
	Beginnings of Roman expansion Temple of Cybele at Rome		Lysimachus (O/G) ?
170	Seleucid invasion of Egypt	Persecution of Antiochus Desecration of Temple Maccabean rebellion	Daniel
150	Jews Expelled from Rome Qumran founded (150 BCE–CE 70)	Pharisees and Sadducees begin to be mentioned	Septuagint Completed (300–150) Dead Sea Scrolls (150 BCE–70 CE) Polybius (H/G) (c. 200–118)
110			1 Maccabees 2 Maccabees Meleager (P/G) fl.
70			Posidonius (Ph/G) (135–50) Cicero (O/L) (106–43)
63		Pompey enters Jerusalem: Roman control	Lucretius (Ph/L) (94–55) Catullus (P/L) (84–54) Alexander Polyhistor (H/G)
54	Crassus loots Temple		
49	Civil war at Rome (–45)		
44	Assassination of Julius Caesar		Varro (H/L) (116–27)
37		Herod the Great, King of Judea	Diodorus of Sicily (H/G) fl.
31	Augustus defeats Antony at Actium		
27	Augustus rules (age 36)		Virgil (P/L) (70–19) Horace (P/L) (65–8)
4		Birth of Jesus ? Death of Herod Archelaus / Philip rule	Ovid (P/L) (43 BCE–CE 17) Livy (H/L) (59 BCE–CE 12) Nicholas of Damascus (H/G) (64 BCE–CE 6)

Date	Major Events in Empire	Major Events in Palestine	Writers/Writings
CE			Strabo (G/G) (64 BCE–CE 21)
6		Direct Roman rule of Palestine Hillel and Shammai	
14	Augustus dies; Tiberias rules (age 56) Jews expelled from Rome		Philo of Alexandria (30 BCE–CE 45)
26		Pilate rules (26–36)	
30		Death of Jesus	
	Paul at Damascus Temple to Augustus		
37	Tiberius dies; Caligula rules (age 25)		
41	Caligula assassinated; Claudius rules (age 51) Jews expelled from Rome	Herod Agrippa made king	
50		Felix rules (51–59)	Seneca (1–65) Paul (?–64) Thessalonians
54	Claudius dies; Nero rules (age 17)		Galatians / Corinthians / Philemon / Philippians
56			Romans
59		Festus rules (59–62)	
62		Death of James	Pliny the Elder (E/L) (23–79)
64	Fire at Rome—persecution Death of Paul, Peter ?		Colossians ?
66		First Judean War begins	
68	Suicide of Nero; civil chaos; Galba (age 71), Otho (age 36), and Vitellius (age 54) claim rule, die; Vespasian rules (age 60)		
70		Temple destroyed Yohanan ben Zakkai	Mark Josephus (H/G) (37–95), *Jewish War*
79	Eruption of Mount Vesuvius destroys Pompeii; death of Vespasian; Titus rules (age 40)		Longinus ?
81	Titus dies; Domitian rules (age 30)		Ephesians ?
			Matthew 1 Peter ? Luke-Acts; Quintilian (R/L) fl.
90		Gamaliel II Council of Yavneh ?	Josephus, *Jewish Antiquities* John Martial (P/L) (40–104) Apocalypse
96	Domitian dies; Nerva rules (age 66)		*1 Clement*
98	Death of Nerva; Trajan rules (age 45)		Dio Chrysostomos (Ph/G) (40–112?) Pastorals ?

Date	Major Events in Empire	Major Events in Palestine	Writers/Writings
			Apollonius of Tyana ?
			Tacitus (H/L) (56–115?)
			Plutarch (B/G) (50–120)
			Ignatius (G), *Letters*
			Pliny the Younger (L/L)
			(61–112),
			Letter to Trajan
117	Death of Trajan; Hadrian rules		Juvenal (P/L) (?60–130)
	(age 41)		*Gospel of Peter* ?
			Epictetus (Ph/G) (55–135)
			Papias
			Letter of Barnabas
			2 Peter ?
			Didache
		Rabbi Akiba (d. 132)	
135		Second Judean Revolt, by Bar	
		Kochba	Basilides
138	Hadrian dies; Antoninus Pius		Polycarp, *To the Philippians*
	rules (age 51)		
140		Jerusalem made a Gentile city:	*Apocalypse of Peter* ?
		Jupiter Capitolinus	
150	Martyrdom of Polycarp		Justin Martyr (G) (100–165)
			Marcion Valentinus
			Acts of Paul
160	Pius dies. Marcus Aurelius		
	rules (age 40)		
	Martyrdom of Justin at Rome		
			Tatian, *Diatessaron*
			Irenaeus (130–202)
			Hegesippus
170			Apuleius (P/L) (123–185),
			The Golden Ass
	Martyrdoms at Lyons		Lucian of Samosata (E/G)
	Martyrdoms at Scillium		(120–180?)
180	Aurelius dies; Commodus rules		Celsus (Ph/G) fl.
	(age 19)		Numenius (P/G) ?
			Dio Cassius
190	Commodus dies; Septimius		Galen (D/G) (129–199)
	Severus rules (48)		*Acts of Peter* ?
			Clement of Alexandria (E/G)
			(150–215)
			Tertullian (E/L) (160–240)
			Acts of the Pagan Martyrs ?
200			Mishnah (Hebrew)

Abbreviations: G = Greek author; L = Latin author

O = Orator; H = Historian; P = Poet; R = Rhetorician; Ph = Philosopher; G = Geographer; E = Essayist;

B = Biographer

BCE = Before Common Era (numbers same as BC); CE = Common Era (numbers same as AD)

BIBLIOGRAPHY

Abrahamsen, Valerie
1987 "Women at Philippi: The Pagan and Christian Evidence." *Journal for the Study of Religion* 2:17–30.

Abrams, M. H.
1953 *The Mirror and the Lamp: Romantic Theory and the Critical Tradition*. Oxford University Press.

Abrams, Philip
1982 *Historical Sociology*. Open Books.

Achtemeier, Elizabeth
1988 "The Impossible Possibility: Evaluating the Feminist Approach to the Bible and Theology." *Interpretation* 42:45–57.

Achtemeier, Paul J.
1970 "On the Historical-Critical Method in New Testament Studies." *Perspective* 11:289–304.

1972 "The Origin and Function of the Pre-Marcan Miracle Catenae." *Journal of Biblical Literature* 91:198–221.

1975a "The Lukan Perspective on the Miracles of Jesus: A Preliminary Sketch." *Journal of Biblical Literature* 95:547–62.

1975b *Mark*. Edited by G. Krodel. Fortress Press.

1975c "Miracles and the Historical Jesus: Mark 9:14–29." *Catholic Biblical Quarterly* 37:471–91.

1978 "Mark as Interpreter of the Jesus Tradition." *Interpretation* 32:339–52.

1985 *Romans*. John Knox Press.

1986 "Special Issue on Revelation." *Interpretation* 40, no. 3.

1987 *The Quest for Unity in the New Testament Church: A Study in Paul and Acts*. Fortress Press.

1990 "Omne Verbum Sonat: The New Testament and the Oral Environment of Late Western Antiquity." *Journal of Biblical Literature* 109:3–27.

1996 *First Peter*. Fortress Press.

Achtemeier, Paul J., et al., eds.
1996 *The HarperCollins Bible Dictionary*. Revised ed. HarperSanFrancisco.

Adam, A. K. M.
1995 *What Is Postmodern Biblical Criticism?* Fortress Press.

Adams, Edward, and David G. Horrell, eds.
2004 *Christianity at Corinth: The Quest for the Pauline Church*. Westminster John Knox Press.

Adams, R. M.
1973 *To Tell a Story: Narrative Theory and Practice*. Andrews Memorial Library, UCLA.

Akurgal, Ekrem, ed.
1985 *Ancient Civilizations and the Ruins of Turkey: From Prehistoric Times until the End of the Roman Empire*. Haset Kitabevi.

Aland, Barbara, and Kurt Aland
1987 *The Text of the New Testament: An Introduction to the Theory of Modern Textual Criticism*. Eerdmans.

Aland, Kurt
1961 "The Problem of Anonymity and Pseudonymity in Christian Literature of the First Two Centuries." *Journal of Theological Studies* n.s. 12:39–49.

1992 *Synopsis of the Four Gospels*. English ed. United Bible Societies.

Albright, William, and C. S. Mann
1971 *Matthew*. Anchor Bible. Doubleday.

Aldrete, Gregory S.
2004 *Daily Life in the Roman City: Rome, Pompeii and Ostia*. Greenwood Press.

Alexander, Loveday
1993 *The Preface to Luke's Gospel: Literary Convention and Social Context in Luke 1:1–4 and Acts 1:1*. Cambridge University Press.

Allison, Dale C.
1985 *The End of the Ages Has Come: An Early Interpretation of the Passion and Resurrection of Jesus*. Fortress Press.

1997 *The Jesus Tradition in Q*. Trinity Press International.

1998 *Jesus of Nazareth: Millenarian Prophet*. Fortress Press.

2005 *Studies in Matthew Interpretation Past and Present*. Baker Academic.

2005 *Resurrecting Jesus: The Earliest Christian Tradition and Its Interpreters*. T&T Clark.

Alston, Richard
1995 *Soldier and Society in Roman Egypt: A Social History*. Routledge.

Anderson, Bernhard W.
1975 *Understanding the Old Testament*. 3rd ed. Prentice Hall.

Anderson, H.
1964 *Jesus and Christian Origins*. Oxford University Press.

Anderson, Janice Capel
1983 "Matthew: Gender and Reading." *Semeia* 28:3–28.

1985   "Double and Triple Stories, the Implied Reader, and Redundancy in Matthew." *Semeia* 31:71–89.

1987   "Mary's Difference: Gender and Patriarchy in the Birth Narratives." *Journal of Religion* 67:183–202.

1991   "Mapping Feminist Biblical Criticism: The American Scene, 1983–1990." In *Critical Review of Books in Religion, 1991*, 21–44. Scholars Press.

1994   *Matthew's Narrative Web Over, and Over, and Over Again.* JSOT Press.

Anderson, Janice Capel, and Stephen D. Moore

1992   *Mark and Method: New Approaches to Biblical Studies.* Fortress Press.

Anderson, N. E.

1987   *Tools for Bibliographical and Backgrounds Research on the New Testament.* 2nd ed. Gordon-Conwell Theological Seminary.

Anderson, R. Dean, Jr.

1996   *Ancient Rhetorical Theory and Paul.* Kok Pharos.

Ante-Nicene Fathers

1981   *The Ante-Nicene Fathers: Translations of the Writings of the Fathers Down to* AD *325.* 10 vols. Edited by A. Roberts and J. Donaldson. Eerdmans.

Apostolic Fathers

        The Apostolic Fathers. Translated by K. Lake. Loeb. Harvard University Press, 1912.

Appian

        Appian's Roman History. Translated by H. White. Loeb. Harvard University Press, 1961.

Applebaum, Shim'on

1976   *Prolegomena to the Study of the Second Jewish Revolt.* British Archaeological Reports.

Appleby, Joyce, Lynn Hunt, and Margaret Jacob

1994   *Telling the Truth about History.* Norton.

Apuleius

        The Golden Ass. Translated by W. Addington. Loeb. Harvard University Press, 1915.
        The Golden Ass. Translated by J. Lindsay. Indiana University Press, 1962.

Aristophanes

        Aristophanes. Translated by B. J. Roberts. Loeb. Harvard University Press, 1924.

Aristotle

        The Art of Rhetoric. Translated by J. H. Freese. Loeb. Harvard University Press, 1967.
        On the Generation of Animals. Translated by A. L. Peck. Loeb. Harvard University Press, 1963.
        Poetics. Translated by W. H. Fyfe. Loeb. Harvard University Press, 1953.
        Poetics. Translated by L. Golden. Prentice Hall, 1968.

Armstrong, Paul B.

1990   *Conflicting Readings: Variety and Validity in Interpretation.* University of North Carolina Press.

Arnal, William E.

2005   *The Symbolic Jesus: Historical Scholarship, Judaism, and the Construction of Contemporary Identity.* Religion in Culture. Equinox Publishing.

Arnal, William E., and Michel Desjardins, eds.

1997   *Whose Historical Jesus?* Wilfrid Laurier University Press.

Arnold, Clinton E.

1989   *Ephesians: Power and Magic. The Concept of Power in Ephesians in Light of Its Historical Setting,* Society for New Testament Studies Monograph Series 63. Cambridge University Press.

1995   *The Colossian Syncretism: The Interface between Christianity and Folk Belief at Colossae.* J. C. B. Mohr.

Ascough, Richard S.

1998   *What Are They Saying about the Formation of Pauline Churches?* Paulist Press.

Ashbeck, D.

1971   "The Literary Genre of Matthew 1–2." *Bible Today* 57:572–78.

Ashton, John

1972   *Why Were the Gospels Written?* Fides Publishers.

1991   *Understanding the Fourth Gospel.* Oxford University Press.

1997   (ed.) *The Interpretation of John.* 2nd ed. Fortress Press.

2000   *The Religion of Paul the Apostle.* Yale University Press.

Attridge, Harold W.

1989   *The Epistle to the Hebrews.* Fortress Press.

2006   (ed.) *HarperCollins Study Bible: New Revised Standard Version, including the Apocryphal/Deuterocanonical Books.* Fully revised and updated ed. HarperSanFrancisco.

Attridge, Harold W., and Robert A. Oden

1984   *The Syrian Goddess [De Dea Syria].* Scholars Press.

Auerbach, Eric

1953   *Mimesis: The Representation of Reality in Western Literature.* Princeton University Press.

Augustine

        Harmony of the Gospels. The Works of Aurelius Augustine. Translated by M. Dods. T&T Clark, 1873.

Aulen, Gustaf Emmanuel H.
1976   *Jesus in Contemporary Historical Research.*
       Fortress Press.
Aune, David E.
1972   *The Cultic Setting of Realized Eschatology in
       Early Christianity.* Brill.
1975   "Christian Prophecy and Sayings of Jesus:
       An Index to Synoptic Pericopae Ostensibly
       Influenced by Early Christian Prophets." In
       Society of Biblical Literature Seminar Papers,
       2:131–42. Society of Biblical Literature.
1980a *Jesus and the Synoptic Gospels: A Biblio-
       graphical Study Guide.* InterVarsity Press.
1980b "Magic." *Aufstieg und Niedergang der römi-
       chen Welt* II, 23.2:1,507–57.
1981   "The Social Matrix of the Apocalypse of
       John." *Biblical Research* 26:16–32.
1983a "The Influence of Roman Imperial Court Cer-
       emonial on the Apocalypse of John." *Biblical
       Research* 28:5–26.
1983b *Prophecy in Early Christianity and the An-
       cient Mediterranean World.* Eerdmans.
1986   "The Apocalypse of John and the Problem
       of Genre." *Early Christian Apocalypticism:
       Genre and Social Setting,* edited by A. Y. Col-
       lins. *Semeia* 36:65–96. Scholars Press.
1987a "The Apocalypse of John and Graeco-
       Roman Revelatory Magic." *New Testament
       Studies* 33:481–501.
1987b *The New Testament in Its Literary Environ-
       ment.* Edited by W. Meeks. Westminster Press.
1988a *Greco-Roman Literature and the New Testa-
       ment.* Scholars Press.
1988b "Revelation." In *HarperCollins Bible Com-
       mentary.* Edited by J. L. Mays, 1300–1319.
       HarperSanFrancisco.
1990   "The Form and Function of the Proclamations
       to the Seven Churches (Revelation 2–3)." *New
       Testament Studies* 36:182–204.
1991   "On the Origins of the 'Council of Javneh'
       Myth." *Journal of Biblical Literature*
       110:491–93.
1997   *Revelation.* 3 vols. Thomas Nelson.
Austin, M. M.
1981   *The Hellenistic World from Alexander to
       the Roman Conquest: A Selection of Ancient
       Sources in Translation.* Cambridge University
       Press.
Avery-Peck, Alan J., and Jacob Neusner, eds.
2000   *Judaism in Late Antiquity: Part 4, Death,
       Life-after-Death, Resurrection and the
       World-to-Come in the Judaisms of Antiquity.*
       Brill.

Avi-Yonah, Michael
1976   *Gazetteer of Roman Palestine.* Hebrew Uni-
       versity of Jerusalem Press.
Babcock, Barbara A.
1978   *The Reversible World: Symbolic Inversion in
       Art and Society.* Cornell University Press.
Babcock, William S.
1990   *Paul and the Legacies of Paul.* Southern Meth-
       odist University Press.
Baby, Parambi
2003   *The Discipleship of the Women in the Gospel
       According to Matthew: An Exegetical Theo-
       logical Study of Matt. 27: 51b–56, 57–61 and
       28:1–10.* Pontificia Università Gregoriana.
Bacon, B. W.
1930   *Studies in Matthew.* Henry Holt.
1933   *The Gospel of the Hellenists.* Henry Holt.
Baer, R. A.
1970   *Philo's Use of the Categories Male and
       Female.* Brill.
Bagnall, Roger S.
1980   *Research Tools for the Classics.* Scholars
       Press.
Bagnall, Roger S., and Peter S. Derow
1981   *Greek Historical Documents: The Hellenistic
       Period.* Scholars Press.
Bailey, John A.
1978   "Who Wrote II Thessalonians?" *New
       Testament Studies* 25:131–45.
Bailey, Kenneth
1980   *Through Peasant Eyes: More Lucan Parables,
       Their Culture and Style.* Eerdmans.
Bailey, Martin J.
1990   "The Long Road to the NRSV." *Religion
       and Public Education (National Council on
       Religion in Public Education)* 17:45–50.
Baird, J. Arthur
1992   *A Comparative Analysis of the Gospel Genre:
       The Synoptic Mode and Its Uniqueness.* Ed-
       win Mellen Press.
Baird, William
2003   *History of New Testament Research.* 3 vols.
       Fortress Press.
Bakirtzix, Charalambos, and Helmut Koester, eds.
1998   *Philippi at the Time of Paul and after His
       Death.* Trinity Press International.
Bakker, Jan Theo
1994   *Living and Working with the Gods. Stud-
       ies of Evidence for Private Religion and Its
       Material Environment in the City of Ostia
       (100–500 AD).* J. C. Gieben.
Bal, Mieke
1988   *Murder and Difference: Gender, Genre, and
       Scholarship on Sisera's Death.* Indiana Uni-
       versity Press.

Balch, David L.
1981   *Let Wives Be Submissive: Domestic Code in 1 Peter.* Scholars Press.
1991   *Social History of the Matthean Community: Cross-Disciplinary Approaches.* Fortress Press.

Balch, David L., Wayne A. Meeks, and Everett Ferguson
1990   *Greeks, Romans, and Christians: Essays in Honor of Abraham J. Malherbe.* Fortress Press.

Balsdon, J. P. V. D.
1962   *Roman Women: Their History and Habits.* Bodley Head.
1969   *Life and Leisure in Ancient Rome.* McGraw-Hill.

Banks, Robert
1975   *Jesus and the Law in the Synoptic Tradition.* Cambridge University Press.
1994   *Paul's Idea of Community: The Early House Churches in Their Cultural Setting.* Revised ed. Hendrickson Publishers.

Barbour, Ian G.
1974   *Myths, Models, and Paradigms.* Harper & Row.

Barclay, John
1988   *Obeying the Truth: A Study of Paul's Ethics in Galatians.* T&T Clark.
1996   *Jews in the Mediterranean Diaspora: From Alexander to Trajan (323 BCE–117 CE).* T&T Clark.

Barclay, William
1955   *The Gospel of John.* 2 vols. Westminster Press.
1959   *The Revelation of John.* Daily Study Bible. Westminster Press.

Barker, Glenn W., William Lane, and J. Ramsey Michaels
1969   *The New Testament Speaks.* Harper & Row.

Barnett, Paul
1997   *The Second Epistle to the Corinthians.* Eerdmans.

Baron, Salo W.
1952   *A Social and Religious History of the Jews.* 2 vols. Columbia University Press.

Baron, Salo W., and Joseph L. Blau
1954   *Judaism: Postbiblical and Talmudic Period.* Bobbs-Merrill.

Barr, David L.
1976   "The Drama of Matthew's Gospel: A Reconsideration of Its Structure and Purpose." *Theology Digest* 24:349–59.
1984   "The Apocalypse as a Symbolic Transformation of the World: A Literary Analysis." *Interpretation* 38:39–50.
1986   "The Apocalypse of John as Oral Enactment." *Interpretation* 40:243–56.
1990   "The Reader of/in the Apocalypse: Exploring a Method." *Proceedings of the Eastern Great Lakes and Midwest Societies of Biblical Literature* 10:79–91.
1995   "Using Plot to Discern Structure in John's Apocalypse." *Proceedings of the Eastern Great Lakes and Midwest Societies of Biblical Literature* 15:23–33.
1996   "Blessed Are Those Who Hear: John's Apocalypse as Present Experience." In *Biblical and Humane: A Festschrift for John Priest,* edited by L. B. Elder, D. L. Barr, and E. S. Malbon, 87–103. Scholars Press.
1998   *Tales of the End: A Narrative Commentary on the Book of Revelation.* Vol. 1, *The Storytellers Bible.* Polebridge Press.
2001   "Waiting for the End That Never Comes: The Narrative Logic of Johns Story." In *Studies in the Book of Revelation,* edited by S. Moyise, 101–12. T&T Clark.
2003   (ed.) *Reading the Book of Revelation: A Resource for Students.* Society of Biblical Literature.
2006   (ed.) *The Reality of Apocalypse: Rhetoric and Politics in the Book of Revelation.* Society of Biblical Literature.

Barr, David L., and Judith L. Wentling
1984   "The Conventions of Classical Biography and the Genre of Luke-Acts." In *Luke-Acts: New Perspectives from the Society of Biblical Literature Seminar,* edited by C. H. Talbert, 63–88. Crossroad.

Barr, James
1976   "Story and History in Biblical Theology." *Journal of Religion* 56:1–17.
1984a   *Beyond Fundamentalism.* Westminster Press.
1984b   *Holy Scripture: Canon, Authority, Criticism.* Westminster Press.

Barrett, C. K.
1957   *A Commentary on the Epistle to the Romans.* Harper & Row.
1961   *Luke the Historian in Recent Study.* Epworth.
1963   *The Pastoral Epistles.* Oxford University Press.
1971   "Paul's Opponents in II Corinthians." *New Testament Studies* 17:233–54.
1974   *The First Epistle to the Corinthians.* Harper & Row.
1975a   *The Gospel of John and Judaism.* Fortress Press.
1975b   *Jesus and the Gospel Tradition.* SPCK Press.
1975c   *The Second Epistle to the Corinthians.* Harper & Row.

1977   *Reading through Romans.* Fortress Press.

1978   *The Gospel According to St. John.* Westminster Press.

1982   *Essays on Paul.* Westminster Press.

1985   *Freedom and Obligation: A Study of the Epistle of Galatians.* Westminster Press.

1987   *The New Testament Background: Selected Documents.* Harper & Row.

Barta, Karen A.

1988   *The Gospel of Mark.* Michael Glazier.

Bartchy, S. Scott

1973   *First-Century Slavery and 1 Corinthians 7:21.* Society of Biblical Literature Dissertation Series 11. Society of Biblical Literature.

1978   "Power, Submission and Sexual Identity among Early Christians Essays on New Testament Christianity." In *Essays on New Testament Christianity: Festschrift in Honor of Dean Walker,* edited by R. Wetzel, 225–46. Standard Publications.

Barth, Karl

1956   *Christ and Adam: Man and Humanity in Romans 5.* Translated by T. A. Small. Macmillan.

Barth, Markus

1974   *Ephesians.* 2 vols. Anchor Bible. Doubleday.

1979   "St. Paul—a Good Jew." *Horizons in Biblical Theology* 1:7–45.

Barth, Markus, and Helmut Blanke

2000   *The Letter to Philemon.* Eerdmans.

Bartlett, John R.

1997   *Archaeology and Biblical Interpretation.* Routledge.

Barton, John

1998   *Holy Writings, Sacred Text the Canon in Early Christianity.* Westminster John Knox Press.

Barton, Stephen C.

1994   *Discipleship and Family Ties in Mark and Matthew.* Cambridge University Press.

Barton, Tamsyn

1994a *Ancient Astrology.* Routledge.

1994b *Power and Knowledge: Astrology, Physiognomics, and Medicine under the Roman Empire.* University of Michigan Press.

Bassler, Jouette M.

1984   "The Widow's Tale: A Fresh Look at Tim. 3–16." *Journal of Biblical Literature* 103:23–41.

Bauckham, Richard J.

1983   *Jude, 2 Peter.* Word Books.

1988a "The Book of Revelation as a Christian War Scroll." *Neotestamentica* 22:17–40.

1988b "Pseudo-Apostolic Letters." *Journal of Biblical Literature* 107:469–94.

1993   *The Climax of Prophecy: Studies on the Book of Revelation.* T&T Clark.

1995   (ed.) *The Book of Acts in Its Palestinian Setting.* Eerdmans.

1998   (ed.) *The Gospels for All Christians: Rethinking the Gospel Audiences.* Eerdmans.

1999   *James: Wisdom of James, Disciple of Jesus the Sage.* Routledge.

2004   *Jude and the Relatives of Jesus in the Early Church.* T&T Clark.

2006   (ed.) *Jesus and the Eyewitnesses: The Gospels as Eyewitness Testimony.* Eerdmans.

Bauer, David R.

1988   *The Structure of Matthew's Gospel: A Study in Literary Design.* Almond Press.

1992   "The Major Characters of Matthew's Story: Their Function and Significance." *Interpretation* 46:357–67.

Bauer, Walter

1971   *Orthodoxy and Heresy in Earliest Christianity.* Edited by R. Kraft and G. Krodel. Fortress Press.

Bauman, Richard

1984   *Verbal Art as Performance.* Waveland Press.

Bauman, R. A.

1996   *Crime and Punishment in Ancient Rome.* Routledge.

Baumgarten, A. I.

1997   *The Flourishing of Jewish Sects in the Maccabaean Era: An Interpretation.* Brill.

Beale, Gregory K.

1984   *The Use of Daniel in Jewish Apocalyptic Literature and in the Revelation of St. John.* University Press of America.

1999   *The Book of Revelation: A Commentary on the Greek Text.* Eerdmans.

Bean, George

1966   *Aegean Turkey: An Archeological Guide.* Praeger.

Beard, Mary

1980   "Sexual Status of Vestal Virgins." *Journal of Roman Studies* 70:12–27.

1989   *Pagan Priests: Religion and Power in the Ancient World.* Cambridge University Press.

Beard, Mary, et al.

1991   *Literacy in the Roman World.* Journal of Roman Archaeology.

Beard, Mary, John North, and Simon Price

1998   *Religions of Rome.* 2 vols. Cambridge University Press.

Beardslee, William A.

1970   *Literary Criticism of the New Testament.* Fortress Press.

1991   *Margins of Belonging: Essays on the New Testament and Theology.* Scholars Press.

1994 "What Is It All About? Reference in New Testament Literary Criticism." In *The New Literary Criticism and the New Testament*, edited by E. V. McKnght and E. S. Malbon, 367–86. Trinity Press International.

Beare, F. W.
1958 *The First Epistle of Peter*. Blackwell.
1962a *The Earliest Records of Jesus: A Companion to the Synopsis of the First Three Gospels*. Abingdon Press.
1962b *St. Paul and His Letters*. Abingdon Press.
1982 *The Gospel According to Matthew*. Harper & Row.
1987 *Commentary on the Epistle to the Philippians*. Harper & Row.

Beasley-Murray, George R.
1986 *Jesus and the Kingdom of God*. Eerdmans.
1987 *John*. Word Books.

Beavis, Mary Ann
1987 "The Trial before the Sanhedrin (Mark 14:53–65): Reader Response and Greco-Roman Readers." *Catholic Biblical Quarterly* 49:581–96.
1988 "Women as Models of Faith in Mark." *Biblical Theology Bulletin* 18:3–9.
1989 *Mark's Audience: The Literary and Social Setting of Mark 4:11–12*. Journal for the Study of the New Testament Sup Series 33. Sheffield Academic Press.
1992 "Ancient Slavery as an Interpretive Context for the New Testament Servant Parables with Special Reference to the Unjust Steward (Luke 16:1–8)." *Journal of Biblical Literature* 111:37–54.

Beckwith, I. T.
1919 *The Apocalypse of John: Studies in Introduction*. Macmillan.

Beker, J. Christiaan
1980 *Paul the Apostle: The Triumph of God in Life and Thought*. Fortress Press.
1982 *Paul's Apocalyptic Gospel: The Coming Triumph of God*. Fortress Press.
1990 *The Triumph of God: The Essence of Paul's Thought*. Fortress Press.
1996 *Heirs of Paul: Paul's Legacy in the New Testament and in the Church Today*. Eerdmans.

Bell, Albert A.
1978 "Date of John's Apocalypse: The Evidence of Some Roman Historians Reconsidered." *New Testament Studies* 25:93–102.
2000 *Exploring the New Testament World*. Thomas Nelson.

Belle, G. van
1988 *Johannine Bibliography 1966–1986: A Cumulative Bibliography on the Fourth Gospel*. Leuven University Press.

Bellinger, William H., and William R. Farmer
1998 *Jesus and the Suffering Servant: Isaiah 53 and Christian Origins*. Trinity Press International.

Bellinzoni, A. J., Jr.
1985 *The Two-Source Hypothesis: A Critical Appraisal*. Mercer University Press.

Belo, Fernando
1981 *A Materialist Reading of the Gospel of Mark*. Orbis Books.

Benko, Stephen
1982 "Early Christian Magical Practices." In *Society of Biblical Literature 1982 Seminar Papers*. Scholars Press.
1993 *The Virgin Goddess: Studies in the Pagan and Christian Roots of Mariology*. Brill.

Bennett, W. J., Jr.
1975 "The Excavations at Antioch." In *Society of Biblical Literature 1975 Seminar Papers*. Scholars Press.

Berger, Peter L., and Thomas Luckmann
1966 *The Social Construction of Reality: A Treatise in the Sociology of Knowledge*. Anchor/Doubleday.

Bergman, Paul
1980 "Story Shapes That Tell a World: King David and Cinema's Patton." *Christian Scholars Review* 9:291–316.

Berlin, Adele
1983 *Poetics and Interpretation of Biblical Narrative*. Almond Press.

Bernard, L. W.
1967 *Justin Martyr: His Life and Thought*. Cambridge University Press.

Bernstein, Alan E.
1993 *The Formation of Hell: Death and Retribution in the Ancient and Early Christian Worlds*. Cornell University Press.

Best, Ernest
1965 *The Temptation and the Passion: The Markan Soteriology*. Edited by M. Black. Society for New Testament Studies Monograph Series 2. Cambridge University Press.
1967 *The Letter of Paul to the Romans*. Cambridge University Press.
1971 *I Peter*. Oliphants.
1972a *A Commentary on the First and Second Epistles to the Thessalonians*. Harper & Row.
1972b *The First and Second Epistles to the Thessalonians*. Black.
1977 "The Role of the Disciples in Mark." *New Testament Studies* 23:377–401.

1978a "The Miracles in Mark." *Review and Expositor* 75:539–54.

1978b "Peter in the Gospel According to Mark." *Catholic Biblical Quarterly* 40:547–58.

1986 *Disciples and Discipleship: Studies in the Gospel According to Mark.* T&T Clark.

1988a *Mark: The Gospel as Story.* T&T Clark.

1988b *Paul and His Converts.* T&T Clark.

Bettenson, Henry

1977 *Documents of the Christian Church.* 2nd ed. Oxford University Press.

Betz, Hans Dieter

1970 *Paul's Apology: II Corinthians 10–13 and the Socratic Tradition.* Center for Hermeneutical Studies.

1979 *Galatians: A Commentary on Paul's Letters to the Churches in Galatia.* Fortress Press.

1985 *2 Corinthians 8 and 9: A Commentary on Two Administrative Letters of the Apostle Paul.* Fortress Press.

Bickerman, Elias J.

1962 *From Ezra to the Last of the Maccabees: Foundations of Postbiblical Judaism.* Schocken Books.

1980 *Chronology of the Ancient World.* Cornell University Press.

Bilezikian, Gilbert

1977 *The Liberated Gospel: A Comparison of the Gospel of Mark and Greek Tragedy.* Baker Biblical Monograph Series. Baker Book House.

Birley, E.

1978 "The Religion of the Roman Army: 1895–1977." *Aufstieg und Niedergang der römischen Welt* II, 16.2:1,506–41.

Black, C. Clifton

1984 "Pauline Perspectives on Death in Romans 5–8." *Journal of Biblical Literature* 103:413–33.

1989 *The Disciples According to Mark: Markan Redaction in Current Debate.* Journal for the Study of the New Testament Supplement Series 27. JSOT/Sheffield Academic Press.

2001 *Mark Images of an Apostolic Interpreter.* Fortress Press.

Black, Matthew

1967 "From Schweitzer to Bultmann: The Modern Quest of the Historical Jesus." *McCormick Quarterly* 20:271–83.

1989 *Romans.* Eerdmans.

Blasi, Anthony J.

1988 *Early Christianity as a Social Movement.* Toronto Studies in Religion 5. Peter Lang.

1996 *A Sociology of Johannine Christianity.* Edwin Mellen Press.

Blevins, James L.

1984 *Revelation as Drama.* Broadman.

1988 *Revelation.* John Knox Press.

Bloch, Marc

1967 *The Historian's Craft.* Manchester University Press.

Blok, Josine, and Peter Mason

1987 *Sexual Asymmetry: Studies in Ancient Society.* J. C. Gieben.

Blomberg, Craig L.

1991 "The Liberation of Illegitimacy: Women and Rulers in Matthew 1–2." *Biblical Theology Bulletin* 21:145–50.

Bloom, Harold

1988 *Revelation of St. John the Divine.* Chelsea House.

Blount, Brian K.

2005 *Can I Get a Witness? Reading Revelation through African American Culture.* Westminster John Knox Press.

Blue, Brad

1994 "Acts and the House Church." In *The Book of Acts in Its Graeco-Roman Setting*, edited by D. W. J. Gill and C. H. Gempf, 116–22. Eerdmans.

Boatwright, Mary T.

1991 "Plancia Magna of Perge: Women's Roles and Status in Roman Asia Minor." In *Women's History and Ancient History*, edited by S. B. Pomeroy, 249–72. University of North Carolina Press.

Boccaccini, Gabriele

1998 *Beyond the Essene Hypothesis: The Parting of the Ways between Qumran and Enochic Judaism.* Eerdmans.

Bock, Darrell L.

2002 *Studying the Historical Jesus: A Guide to Sources and Methods.* Baker Academic.

Bockmuehl, Markus

1997 *Revelation and Mystery in Ancient Judaism and Pauline Christianity.* Eerdmans.

Boers, Hendrikus

1975 "The Form Critical Study of Paul's Letters: I Thessalonians as a Case Study." *New Testament Studies* 22:140–58.

1989 *Who Was Jesus? The Historical Jesus and the Synoptic Gospels.* Harper & Row.

1992 " 'We Who Are by Inheritance Jews; Not from the Gentile Sinners'." *Journal of Biblical Literature* 111:273–81.

1994 *The Justification of the Gentiles: Paul's Letters to the Galatians and Romans.* Hendrickson Publishers.

Boesak, Allan A.

1987a *Comfort and Protest: Reflections on the Apocalypse of John of Patmos.* Westminster Press.

1987b "The Woman and the Dragon: Struggle and Victory in Revelation 12." *Sojourners* 16:27–31.

Bogart, John

1977 *Orthodox and Heretical Perfectionism in the Johannine Community as Evident in the First Epistle of John.* Scholars Press.

1978 "Recent Johannine Studies." *Anglican Theological Review* 60:80–87.

Boissevain, Jeremy

1974 *Friends of Friends: Networks, Manipulators, and Coalitions.* St. Martin's Press.

Bolt, Peter G.

2003 *Jesus' Defeat of Death: Persuading Mark's Early Readers.* Cambridge University Press.

Bolter, J. David

1991 *Writing Space: The Computer, Hypertext, and the History of Writing.* L. Erlbaum Associates.

Bond, Helen K.

1998 *Pontius Pilate in History and Interpretation.* Cambridge University Press.

Bonsirven, Joseph

1964 *Palestinian Judaism in the Time of Jesus Christ.* Holt, Rinehart & Winston.

Bonz, Marianne Palmer

2000 *The Past as Legacy: Luke-Acts and Ancient Epic.* Fortress Press.

Boomershine, Thomas E.

1974 *Mark, the Story Teller: A Rhetorical-Critical Investigation of Mark's Passion and Resurrection Narrative.* Ph.D. diss., Union Theological Seminary, New York.

1987 "Peter's Denial as Polemic or Confession: The Implications of Media Criticism for Biblical Hermeneutics." *Semeia* 39:47–68.

1988 *Story Journey: An Invitation to the Gospel as Storytelling.* Abingdon Press.

Boorstin, Daniel J.

1983 *The Discoverers: A History of Man's Search to Know His World and Himself.* Random House.

Booth, Wayne C.

1974 *A Rhetoric of Irony.* University of Chicago Press.

1983 *The Rhetoric of Fiction.* 2nd ed. University of Chicago Press.

Borchert, Gerald L.

1985 *Paul and His Interpreters: An Annotated Bibliography.* Theological Students Fellowship.

Boren, H. C.

1977 *Roman Society: A Social, Economic and Cultural History.* D. C. Heath.

Borg, Marcus J.

1984 *Conflict, Holiness, and Politics in the Teachings of Jesus: Studies in the Bible and Early Christianity.* Edwin Mellen Press.

1986 "A Temperate Case for a Non-Eschatological Jesus." *Forum* 2:81–102.

1991 *Jesus: A New Vision: Spirit, Culture, and the Life of Discipleship.* HarperSanFrancisco.

1994 *Jesus in Contemporary Scholarship.* Trinity Press International.

1995 *Meeting Jesus Again for the First Time: The Historical Jesus and the Heart of Contemporary Faith.* HarperSanFrancisco.

1997 (ed.) *Jesus at 2000.* Westview Press.

Borgen, Peder

1963 "Observations on the Midrashic Character of John 6." *Zeitschrift fur die neutestamentliche Wissenschaft* 54:232–40.

1972 "Logos Was the True Light." *Novum Testamentum* 14:115–30.

1981 *Bread from Heaven: An Exegetical Study of the Concept of Manna in the Gospel of John and the Writing of Philo.* Brill.

1983 *Paul Preaches Circumcision and Pleases Men and Other Essays on Christian Origins.* Tapir/University of Trondheim.

1987 *Philo, John and Paul: New Perspectives on Judaism and Early Christianity.* Brown Judaic Studies 131. Scholars Press.

Borgman, Paul

2006 *The Way According to Luke Hearing the Whole Story of Luke-Acts.* Eerdmans.

Boring, M. Eugene

1982 *Sayings of the Risen Jesus: Christian Prophecy in the Synoptic Tradition.* Cambridge University Press.

1985 "Criteria of Authenticity: The Lucan Beatitudes as a Test Case." *Forum* 1:3–38.

1986 "The Theology of Revelation: 'The Lord Our God Almighty Reigns'." *Interpretation* 40:257–69.

1989 *Revelation.* Interpretation. John Knox Press.

1992 "The Voice of Jesus in the Apocalypse of John." *Novum Testamentum* 34:334–59.

1994 "Revelation 19–21: End without Closure." Princeton Seminary Bulletin Supplement Series 3:57–84.

Bornkamm, Günther

1960 *Jesus of Nazareth.* Harper & Row.

1970 "Authority to 'Bind' and 'Loose' in the Church in Matthew's Gospel: The Problem of Sources in Matthew's Gospel." In *Jesus and Man's Hope*, edited by D. G. Miller and D. Y. Hadidian, 1:37–50 Pittsburg: Pittsburg Theological Seminary.

1971 *Paul, Paulus*. Harper & Row.

Bornkamm, Günther, Gerhard Barth, and Heinz Joachim Held

1963 *Tradition and Interpretation in Matthew*. Westminster Press.

Bossman, David M.

1996 "Paul's Fictive Kinship Movement." *Biblical Theology Bulletin* 26:163–71.

Botha, Jan

1994 *Subject to Whose Authority? Multiple Readings of Romans 13*. Scholars Press.

Botha, J. Eugene

1991 *Jesus and the Samaritan Woman: A Speech Act Reading of John 4:1–42*. Brill.

Botha, Pieter J. J.

1988 "God, Emperor Worship and Society: Contemporary Experiences and the Book of Revelation." *Neotestamentica* 22:87–102.

1991 "Mark's Story as Oral Traditional Literature: Rethinking the Transmission of Some Traditions about Jesus." *Hervormde teologiese studies* 47:304–31.

Boucher, Madeleine

1969 "Some Unexplored Parallels to 1 Corinthians 11:11–12 and Galatians 3: 28: The New Testament and the Role of Women." *Catholic Biblical Quarterly* 31:50–58.

Bouquet, A. C.

1953 *Everyday Life in New Testament Times*. Charles Scribner's Sons.

Bourquin, D. R.

1990 *First-Century Palestinian Judaism: A Bibliography of Works in English*. Studies in Judaica and the Holocaust 6. Borgo.

Bovon, François

1987 *Luke the Theologian: Thirty-Three Years of Research (1950–1983)*. Pickwick Publications.

Bowersock, G. W.

1969 *Greek Sophists in the Roman Empire*. Clarendon Press.

Bowker, John

1973 *Jesus and the Pharisees*. Cambridge University Press.

Bowman, John W.

1955 "The Revelation to John: Its Dramatic Structure and Message." *Interpretation* 9:436–53.

Boxall, Ian

2006 *The Revelation of Saint John*. Hendrickson Publishers.

Boyarin, Daniel

2004 *Border Lines: The Partition of Judaeo-Christianity, Divinations*. University of Pennsylvania Press.

Boyer, Paul

1992 *When Time Shall Be No More: Prophecy Belief in Modern American Culture*. Belknap Press of Harvard University Press.

Bradley, Keith R.

1987 *Slaves and Masters in the Roman Empire: A Study in Social Control*. Oxford University Press.

1994 *Slavery and Society at Rome*. Cambridge University Press.

Brandon, S. G. F.

1967 *Jesus and the Zealots: A Study of the Political Factor in Primitive Christianity*. Manchester University Press.

Branick, Vincent P.

1985 "Apocalyptic Paul?" *Catholic Biblical Quarterly* 47:664–75.

1989 *The House Church in the Writings of Paul*. Zachaeus Studies. Michael Glazier.

Bratcher, Robert

1984 *A Translator's Guide to the Revelation to John*. United Bible Society.

Brawley, Robert L

1987 *Luke-Acts and the Jews: Conflict, Apology, and Conciliation*. Society of Biblical Literature Monograph Series 33. Scholars Press.

1990 *Centering on God: Method and Message in Luke-Acts*. Westminster John Knox Press.

Braxton, Brad Ronnell

2002 *No Longer Slaves: Galatians and African American Experience*. The Liturgical Press.

Bredlin, Mark R. J.

1999 "The Synagogue of Satan Accusation in Revelation 2:9." *Biblical Theology Bulletin* 28:160–64.

Breech, James

1983 *Silence of Jesus: The Authentic Voice of the Historical Man*. Fortress Press.

Bremen, Riet van

1983 "Women and Wealth." In *Images of Women in Antiquity*, edited by A. Cameron and A. Kuhrt, 223–42. Wayne State University Press.

Bremmer, Jan N., ed.

1996 *The Apocryphal Acts of Paul and Thecla*. Kok Pharos.

Bright, John

1953 *The Kingdom of God*. Abingdon Press.

1959 *A History of Israel*. Westminster Press.

Brilliant, Richard
1979   *Pompeii, AD 79: The Treasure of Rediscovery.*
        Crown.
Brinsmead, Bernard Hungerford
1982   *Galatians, Dialogical Response to
        Opponents.* Scholars Press.
Bristow, John Temple
1988   *What Paul Really Said about Women.* Harper
        & Row.
Bromiley, Geoffrey W.
1988   *The International Standard Bible
        Encyclopedia.* 4 vols. Eerdmans.
Broneer, O.
1971   "Paul and the Pagan Cults at Isthmia." *Harvard Theological Review* 64:169–87.
Brooks, J. A.
1978   "An Annotated Bibliography on Mark."
        Southwestern Journal of Theology 21:75–82.
Brooks, S. H.
1987   *Matthew's Community: The Evidence of His
        Special Sayings Material.* Sheffield Academic
        Press.
Brooten, Bernadette J.
1982   *Women Leaders in the Ancient Synagogue:
        Inscriptional Evidence and Background Issues.* Brown Judaic Studies 36. Scholars Press.
1996   *Love between Women: Early Christian
        Responses to Female Homoeroticism.*
        University of Chicago Press.
Brown, Colin
1976   *History, Criticism, and Faith.* InterVarsity
        Press.
Brown, Peter
1971   "The Rise and Function of the Holy Man in
        Late Antiquity." *Journal of Roman Studies*
        61:80–101.
1987   *The Body and Society: Men, Women, and
        Sexual Renunciation in Early Christianity.*
        Columbia University Press.
Brown, Raymond E.
1966   *The Gospel According to John.* Doubleday.
1971   "Jesus and Elisha." *Perspective* 12:85–104.
1975   "The Meaning of the Magi, the Significance of
        the Star." *Worship* 49:574–82.
1977   *The Birth of the Messiah: A Commentary on
        the Infancy Narratives in Matthew and Luke.*
        Doubleday.
1979   *The Community of the Beloved Disciple:
        The Life, Loves, and Hates of an Individual
        Church in the New Testament.* Paulist Press.
1981   *The Critical Meaning of the Bible.* Paulist
        Press.
1982   *The Epistles of John.* Doubleday.
1984   *The Churches the Apostles Left Behind.* Paulist Press.

Brown, Raymond E., et al.
1990   *John and the Dead Sea Scrolls.* Edited by
        J. Charlesworth. Christian Origins Library.
        Crossroad.
Brown, Raymond E., Karl Donfried, and John
        Reumann, eds.
1973   *Peter in the New Testament.* Augsburg Publishing House.
Brown, Raymond E., Joseph A. Fitzmyer, and
        Roland E. Murphy
1990   *The New Jerome Biblical Commentary.* Prentice Hall.
1992   *The New Jerome Bible Handbook.* The Liturgical Press.
Brown, Raymond E., and John Meier
1983   *Antioch and Rome. New Testament Cradles of
        Catholic Christianity.* Paulist Press.
Brown, Schuyler
1978   "Mission to Israel in Matthew's Central Section (Mt. 9:35–11:1)." *Zeitschrift fur
        die neutestamentliche Wissenschaft* 69:73–90.
1984   *The Origins of Christianity: A Historical
        Introduction to the New Testament.* Oxford
        University Press.
Bruce, F. F.
1954   *Commentary on the Acts of the Apostles.*
        Eerdmans.
1963a   *The Epistle of Paul to the Romans.* Eerdmans.
1963b   "To the Hebrews or the Essenes?" *New Testament Studies* 9:217–32.
1963c   "When Is Gospel Not a Gospel?" *Bulletin of
        the John Rylands Library* 45:319–39.
1969   *New Testament History.* Nelson.
1974   *Jesus and Christian Origins Outside the New
        Testament.* Eerdmans.
1977   *Paul: Apostle of the Heart Set Free.*
        Eerdmans.
1979   *Peter, Stephen, James and John: Studies in
        Early Non-Pauline Christianity.* Eerdmans.
1982   *1 and 2 Thessalonians.* Word Books.
1983   *Philippians.* Harper & Row.
1984a   *Epistles to the Colossians, to Philemon, and
        to the Ephesians.* Eerdmans.
1984b   *The Gospel of John.* Eerdmans.
1985   *The Pauline Circle.* Eerdmans.
1986   (ed.) *The International Bible Commentary:
        With the New International Version.* Revised
        ed. Zondervan.
1988   *The Book of the Acts.* Revised ed. Eerdmans.
1990   *Epistle to the Hebrews.* Eerdmans.
1993   "Some Thoughts on the Beginning of the New
        Testament Canon." In *The Bible in the Early
        Church,* edited by E. Ferguson, 85–108. Garland Publishing.

Bruner, Frederick Dale
1987   *Matthew: A Commentary.* 2 vols. Word Books.
Bryan, Christopher
1993   *A Preface to Mark: Notes on the Gospel in Its Literary and Cultural Settings.* Oxford University Press.
2000   *Preface to Romans: Notes on the Epistle in Its Literary and Cultural Setting.* Oxford University Press.
Buchanan, George Wesley
1972   *To the Hebrews.* Anchor Bible. Doubleday.
1978   *Revelation and Redemption: Jewish Documents of Deliverance from the Fall of Jerusalem to the Death of Nahmanides.* Western North Carolina Press.
Buechner, Frederick
1977   *Telling the Truth: The Gospel as Tragedy, Comedy, and Fairy Tale.* Harper & Row.
Bultmann, Rudolf
1910   *Der Stil der paulinischen Predigt und die kynischstoische Diatribe.* Vandenhoeck & Ruprecht.
1951   *The Theology of the New Testament.* Translated by Kendrick Grobel. Scribner.
1953   *Kerygma and Myth: A Theological Debate.* Harper & Row.
1971   *The Gospel of John: A Commentary.* Translated by G. R. Beasley-Murray. Edited by R. W. N. Hoare, and J. K. Riches. Westminster Press.
1972   *The History of the Synoptic Tradition.* Translated by J. Marsh. Blackwell.
1973   *The Johannine Epistles.* Fortress Press.
Burkill, T. A.
1959   "Anti-Semitism in St. Mark's Gospel." *Novum Testamentum* 3:34–53.
1963   *Mysterious Revelation: An Examination of the Philosophy of St. Mark's Gospel.* Cornell University Press.
Burnett, Fred W.
1981   *The Testament of Jesus—Sophia: A Redaction-Critical Study of the Eschatological Discourse in Matthew.* University Press of America.
Burridge, Richard A.
2004   *What Are the Gospels? A Comparison with Graeco-Roman Biography.* 2nd ed. Eerdmans.
2005   *Four Gospels, One Jesus?* 2nd ed. Eerdmans.
Burrus, Virginia
1987   *Chastity as Autonomy: Women in the Stories of the Apocryphal Acts.* Studies in Women and Religion 23. Edwin Mellen Press.

Burtchaell, James Tunstead
1992   *From Synagogue to Church: Public Services and Offices of the Earliest Christian Communities.* Cambridge University Press.
Butcher, S. H.
1951   *Aristotle's Theory of Poetry and Fine Art.* Dover.
Butler, B. C.
1951   *The Originality of St. Matthew.* Cambridge University Press.
Buttrick, George
1962   *The Interpreter's Dictionary of the Bible: An Illustrated Encyclopedia.* 5 vols. Abingdon Press.
Byrne, Brendan
1979   *Sons of God, Seed of Abraham: A Study of the Idea of Sonship of God of All Christians in Paul against the Jewish Background.* Biblical Institute Press.
1996   *Romans.* The Liturgical Press.
Byrskog, Samuel
2000   *Story as History—History as Story: The Gospel Tradition in the Context of Ancient Oral History.* Mohr Siebeck.
Cabannis, Allen
1970   *Liturgy and Literature.* University of Alabama Press.
Cadbury, Henry Joel
1920   *The Style and Literary Method of Luke.* Harvard University Press.
1955   *The Book of Acts in History.* Harper & Row.
1958   *The Making of Luke-Acts.* 2nd ed. Alec R. Allenson.
1962   *The Peril of Modernizing Jesus.* Macmillan.
Caird, G. B.
1963   *The Gospel of St. Luke.* Penguin Press.
1966   *A Commentary on the Revelation of St. John the Divine.* Harper & Row.
Callahan, Allen Dwight, Richard A. Horsley, and Abraham Smith, eds.
1998   *Slavery in Text and Interpretation. Semeia* 83/84. Society of Biblical Literature.
Callan, Terrance
1985   "The Preface of Luke-Acts and Historiography." *New Testament Studies* 31:576–81.
1990   *Psychological Perspectives on the Life of Paul: An Application of the Methodology of Gerd Theissen.* Edwin Mellen Press.
Calloud, Jean
1976   *Structural Analysis of Narrative.* Translated by Daniel Patte. *Semeia Supplements.* Fortress Press.
Cambridge Ancient History
1970   *Cambridge Ancient History.* 3rd ed. 12 vols. Cambridge University Press.

Cameron, Averil
  1990a *History as Text: The Writing of Ancient History.* University of North Carolina Press.
  1990b "Virginity as Metaphor: Women and the Rhetoric of Early Christianity." In *History as Text,* edited by A. Cameron, 181–205. University of North Carolina Press.

Cameron, Averil, and Amélie Kuhrt
  1983 *Images of Women in Antiquity.* Wayne State University Press.

Cameron, Ron
  1982 *The Other Gospels: Non-Canonical Gospel Texts.* Westminster Press.
  1984 *Sayings Traditions in the Apocryphon of James.* Fortress Press.

Camery-Hoggatt, Jerry
  1992 *Irony in Mark's Gospel: Text and Subtext.* Cambridge University Press.

Campbell, J. K.
  1964 *Honour, Family and Patronage: A Study of Institutions and Moral Values in a Greek Mountain Community.* Clarendon Press.

Campion, Nicholas
  1994 *The Great Year: Astrology, Millenarianism, and History in the Western Tradition.* Arkana.

Cannon, George E.
  1983 *Use of Traditional Materials in Colossians.* Mercer University Press.

Cantarella, Eva
  1987 *Pandora's Daughters: The Role and Status of Women in Greek and Roman Antiquity.* Johns Hopkins University Press.

Cantor, Norman, and Peter Klein
  1969 *Ancient Thought: Plato and Aristotle, Monuments of Western Thought.* Blaisdell.

Carcopino, J.
  1940 *Daily Life in Ancient Rome.* Yale University Press.

Carey, Greg
  1999 *Elusive Apocalypse: Reading Authority in the Revelation to John.* Mercer University Press.

Cargal, Timothy B.
  1991 "'His Blood Be upon Us and upon Our Children': A Matthean Double Entendre?" *New Testament Studies* 37:101–12.

Carlson, Stephen C.
  2005 *The Gospel Hoax: Morton Smith's Invention of Secret Mark.* Baylor University Press.

Carney, T. F.
  1975 *The Shape of the Past: Models and Antiquity.* Coronado Press.

Carpenter, Ronald H.
  1995 *History as Rhetoric: Style, Narrative, and Persuasion.* Columbia: University of South Carolina Press.

Carr, E. H.
  1973 *What Is History?* Penguin Books.

Carrington, Philip
  1957 *The Early Christian Church.* Vol. 2, *The Second Christian Century.* Cambridge University Press.

Carrol, Kenneth L.
  1981 "The Place of James in the Early Church." *Bulletin of the John Rylands Library* 44:49–67.

Carson, D. A., Douglas T. Moo, and Leon Morris
  1992 *Introduction to the New Testament.* Zondervan.

Carter, Warren
  1992 "Kernels and Narrative Blocks: The Structure of Matthew's Gospel." *Catholic Biblical Quarterly* 54:463–81.
  1996 *Matthew: Storyteller, Interpreter, Evangelist.* Hendrickson Publishers.
  2000 *Matthew and the Margins a Sociopolitical and Religious Reading.* Sheffield Academic Press.
  2001 *Matthew and Empire Initial Explorations.* Trinity Press International.

Cartlidge, David R., and David L. Dungan
  1993 *Documents for the Study of the Gospels.* Revised and enlarged ed. Fortress Press.

Case, Shirley Jackson
  1923 *The Social Origins of Christianity.* University of Chicago Press.

Casey, Juliana
  1980 *Hebrews.* Michael Glazier.

Casson, Lionel
  1974 *Travel in the Ancient World.* Allen and Unwin.
  1986 *Ships and Seamanship in the Ancient World.* Princeton University Press.
  1998 *Everyday Life in Ancient Rome.* Revised and expanded ed. Johns Hopkins University Press.

Castelli, Elizabeth A.
  1991 *Imitating Paul: A Discourse of Power.* Westminster John Knox Press.

Castelli, Elizabeth A., Stephen D. Moore, and Gary A. Phillips, eds.
  1995 *The Postmodern Bible: The Bible and Culture Collective.* Yale University Press.

Casurella, Anthony
  1996 *Bibliography of Literature on First Peter.* Brill.

Catchpole, David
  1993 *The Quest for Q.* T&T Clark.

Centers for Disease Control and Prevention
2001   *National Vital Statistic Report 1999.* Available from http://www.cdc.gov/nchs/fastats/lifexpec.htm.

Charles, J. Daryl
1991   "Jude's Use of Pseuepigraphical Source Material as Part of a Literary Strategy." *New Testament Studies* 37:130–45.
1993   *Literary Strategy in the Epistle of Jude.* University of Scranton Press.

Charles, R. H.
1920   *A Critical and Exegetical Commentary on the Revelation of St. John.* T&T Clark.
1963   *The Apocrypha and Pseudepigrapha of the Old Testament.* 2 vols. Oxford University Press.

Charlesworth, James H.
1972   *John and Qumran.* Geoffrey Chapman.
1981   *The Pseudepigrapha and Modern Research.* Scholars Press.
1983   (ed.) *The Old Testament Pseudepigrapha.* 2 vols. Doubleday.
1987   *New Testament Apocrypha and Pseudepigrapha: A Guide to Publications with Excurses on Apocalypses.* American Theological Library Association Bibliography Series 17. Scarecrow Press.
1992   (ed.) *The Messiah: Developments in Earliest Judaism and Christianity.* Fortress Press.

Chatman, Seymour
1978   *Story and Discourse: Narrative Structure in Fiction and Film.* Cornell University Press.

Cheney, Emily
1996   *She Can Read: Feminist Reading Strategies for Biblical Narrative.* Trinity Press International.

Chesnut, Glenn F.
1977   *The First Christian Histories: Eusebius, Socrates, Sozomen, Theodoret and Evagrius.* Editions Beauchesne.

Chevalier, Jacques M.
1997   *Postmodern Revelation: Signs of Astrology and the Apocalypse.* University of Toronto Press.

Chilstrom, Herbert W.
1983   *Hebrews: A New and Better Way.* Fortress Press.

Chilton, Bruce D.
1983   *A Galilean Rabbi and His Bible: Jesus' Use of the Interpreted Scripture of His Time.* Michael Glazier.
1989   *Profiles of a Rabbi: Synoptic Opportunies in Reading about Jesus.* Brown Judaic Studies 177. Scholars Press.

Chilton, Bruce D., and Craig A. Evans
1999   *James the Just and Christian Origins.* Brill.

Church, Forrester F.
1978   "Rhetorical Structure and Design in Paul's Letter to Philemon." *Harvard Theological Review* 7:17–33.

Cicero
        The Basic Works of Cicero. Translated by M. Hadas. Modern Library, 1951.
        The Education of the Orator. Translated by H. M. Hubbel. Loeb. Harvard University Press, 1971.
        Letters. Translated by E. O. Winstedt, W. G. Williams, and M. Cary. Loeb. Harvard University Press, 1962.
        Orator. Translated by H. M. Hubbel. Loeb. Harvard University Press, 1939.

Clark, Elizabeth
1983   *Women in the Early Church.* Michael Glazier.

Clark, Elizabeth, and Herbert Richardson
1977   *Women and Religion: A Feminist Sourcebook of Christian Thought.* Harper & Row.

Clark, Gregory
1990   *Dialogue, Dialectic, and Conversation: A Social Perspective on the Function of Writing.* Southern Illinois University Press.

Clark, Kenneth W.
1947   "The Gentile Bias in Matthew." *Journal of Biblical Literature* 66:165–72.
1960   "Worship in the Jerusalem Temple after AD 70." *New Testament Studies* 6:269–80.

Clarke, Howard W.
2003   *The Gospel of Matthew and Its Readers: A Historical Introduction to the First Gospel.* Indiana University Press.

Clarke, John R.
1991   *The Houses of Roman Italy, 100 BC–AD 250: Ritual, Space, and Decoration.* University of California Press.
1998   *Looking at Lovemaking: Constructions of Sexuality in Roman Art 100 BC–AD 250.* University of California Press.

Clarke, M. L.
1953   *Rhetoric at A Historical Survey.* Cohen & West.
1963   *Higher Education in the Ancient World.* Barnes & Noble.

Clay, Diskin
1984   *Lucretius and Epicurus.* Cornell University Press.

Cocceianus, Cassius Dio.
        Dio's Roman History. 9 vols. Translated by E. Cary and H. B. Foster. Loeb. Harvard University Press, 1914.

Cohen, Shaye J. D.

1983 "Conversion to Judaism in Historical Perspective: From Biblical Israel to Postbiblical Judaism." *Conservative Judaism* 36:31–45.

1984 "The Significance of Yavneh: Pharisees, Rabbis and the End of Jewish Sectarianism." *Hebrew Union College Annual* 55:27–53.

1987 *From the Maccabees to the Mishnah.* Westminster Press.

1993 (ed.) *The Jewish Family in Antiquity.* Scholars Press.

Cohen, Shaye J. D., and Ernest S. Frerichs, eds.

1993 *Diasporas in Antiquity.* Scholars Press.

Cohn-Sherbok, Dan, and John M. Court, eds.

2001 *Religious Diversity in the Graeco-Roman World. A Survey of Recent Scholarship.* Sheffield Academic Press.

Coleman-Norton, Paul R.

1966 *Roman State and Christian Church: A Collection of Legal Documents.* 2 vols. Allenson.

Collingwood, R. G.

1969 "The Limits of Historical Knowledge." In *The Historian as Detective: Essays on Evidence,* edited by R. W. Winks, 513–22. Harper & Row.

Collins, Adela Yarbro

1976 *The Combat Myth in the Book of Revelation.* Scholars Press.

1979 *The Apocalypse.* Michael Glazier.

1981 "Dating the Apocalypse of John." *Biblical Research* 26:33–45.

1984 *Crisis and Catharsis: The Power of the Apocalypse.* Westminster Press.

1985 *Feminist Perspectives on Biblical Scholarship.* Vol. 10, *Biblical Scholarship in North America.* Scholars Press.

1986 (ed.) *Early Christian Apocalypticism: Genre and Social Setting. Semeia* 36. Scholars Press.

1987 "Women's History and the Book of Revelation." In *Society of Biblical Literature 1987 Seminar Papers,* edited by K. H. Richard, 80–91. Scholars Press.

1990 *Is Mark's Gospel a Life of Jesus? The Question of Genre, Pere Marquette Theology Lecture, 1990.* Marquette University Press.

1992 *The Beginning of the Gospel: Probings of Mark in Context.* Fortress Press.

1993 "Feminine Symbolism in the Book of Revelation." *Biblical Interpretation* 1:20–33.

Collins, John J.

1979 *Apocalypse: The Morphology of a Genre. Semeia* 14. Scholars Press.

1984 *Daniel: With an Introduction to Apocalyptic Literature.* Eerdmans.

1995 *The Scepter and the Star: The Messiahs of the Dead Sea Scrolls and Other Ancient Literature.* Doubleday.

1997 *Seers, Sibyls and Sages in Hellenistic-Roman Judaism.* Brill.

1998 *The Apocalyptic Imagination: An Introduction to the Jewish Matrix of Christianity.* 2nd ed. Eerdmans.

1999 *Between Athens and Jewish Identity in the Hellenistic Diaspora.* 2nd ed. Eerdmans.

Collins, John J., and James H. Charlesworth

1991 *Mysteries and Revelations: Apocalyptic Studies since the Uppsala Colloquium.* Sheffield Academic Press.

Collins, John J., and Robert A. Kugler, eds.

2000 *Religion in the Dead Sea Scrolls.* Eerdmans.

Collins, Raymond F.

1984 *Studies on the First Letter to the Thessalonians.* Bibliotheca ephemeridum theologicarum lovaniensium 66: Peeters and Leuven University Press.

1988 *Letters That Paul Did Not Write: The Epistle to the Hebrews and the Pauline Psuedepigrapha.* Good News Series 28. Michael Glazier.

Colwell, Ernest Cadman

1970 *The Gospel of the Spirit.* Harper & Row.

Conner, W. R.

1984 *Thucydides.* Princeton University Press.

Conrad, Edgar

1985 "The Annunciation of Birth and the Birth of the Messiah." *Catholic Biblical Quarterly* 47:656–63.

Conway, Collene M.

1999 *Men and Women in the Fourth Gospel: Gender and Johannine Characterization.* Society of Biblical Literature.

Conzelmann, Hans

1961 *The Theology of St. Luke.* Harper & Row.

1973 *Jesus.* 2 vols. Fortress Press.

1975 *1 Corinthians.* Fortress Press.

1979 *Galatians.* Fortress Press.

1987 *Acts of the Apostles: A Commentary.* Translated by J. Limburg. Fortress Press.

Coogan, Michael D., ed.

2007 *The New Oxford Annotated Bible with the Apocrypha.* Augumented 3rd ed. Oxford University Press.

Cook, Edward M.

1994 *Solving the Mysteries of the Dead Sea Scrolls: New Light on the Bible.* Zondervan.

Cook, John G.

1995 *The Structure and Persuasive Power of Mark: A Linguistic Approach.* Scholars Press.

Cook, Michael J.

1978 *Mark's Treatment of the Jewish Leaders.* Brill.

Cope, Oliver Lamar
1976a "The Death of John the Baptist in the Gospel of Matthew; or, the Case of the Confusing Conjunction." *Catholic Biblical Quarterly* 38:515–19.
1976b *Matthew: A Scribe Trained for the Kingdom of Heaven*. Catholic Biblical Quarterly Monograph Series 5. Catholic Biblical Association.
1985 "On Rethinking the Philemon–Colossians Connection." *Biblical Research* 30:45–50.

Corley, Bruce C.
1983 *Colloquy on New Testament Studies: A Time for Reappraisal and Fresh Approaches*. Mercer University Press.

Corley, Kathleen E.
2002 *Women and the Historical Jesus: Feminist Myths of Christian Origins*. Polebridge Press.

Corrigan, Gregory
1986 "Paul's Shame for the Gospel." *Biblical Theology Bulletin* 16:23–27.

Corsini, Eugenio
1983 *The Apocalypse: The Perennial Revelation of Jesus Christ*. Edited by F. Moloney. Michael Glazier.

Cosby, Michael R.
1988 "The Rhetorical Composition of Hebrews 11." *Journal of Biblical Literature* 107:257–73.

Cotter, Wendy
1994 "Women's Authority Roles in Paul's Churches: Countercultural or Conventional?" *Novum Testamentum* 36:350–72.
1999 *Miracles in Greco-Roman Antiquity: A Sourcebook*. Routledge.

Countryman, L. William
1980 *The Rich Christian in the Church of the Early Empire: Contradictions and Accommodations*. Edwin Mellen Press.
1985a "How Many Baskets Full? Mark 8:14–21 and the Value of Miracles in Mark." *Catholic Biblical Quarterly* 47:643–55.
1985b *The Mystical Way in the Fourth Gospel: Crossing over into God*. Fortress Press.
1988 *Dirt, Greed, and Sex: Sexual Ethics in the New Testament and Their Implications for Today*. Fortress Press.

Court, John M.
1979 *Myth and History in the Book of Revelation*. John Knox Press.

Cousar, Charles B.
1990 *A Theology of the Cross: The Death of Jesus in the Pauline Letters*. Fortress Press.

Craddock, Fred B.
1981 *The Gospels*. Abingdon Press.
1990 *Luke*. John Knox Press.

Crafton, Jeffrey A.
1991 *The Agency of the Apostle: A Dramatistic Analysis of Paul's Responses to Conflict in 2 Corinthians*. Journal for the Study of the New Testament Supplement Series 51. Sheffield Academic Press.

Creed, J. M.
1930 *The Gospel According to St. Luke*. Macmillan.

Crites, Stephen
1971 "The Narrative Quality of Experience." *Journal of the American Academy of Religion* 39:291–311.

Crook, Zeba A.
2004 *Reconceptualising Conversion: Patronage, Loyalty, and Conversion in the Religions of the Ancient Mediterranean*. De Gruyter.

Crosby, Michael H.
1988 *House of Disciples: Church, Economics, and Justice in Matthew*. Orbis Books.

Crossan, John Dominic
1973 *In Parables: The Challenge of the Historical Jesus*. Harper & Row.
1979 *Finding Is the First Act: Trove Folktales and Jesus' Treasure Parable*. Fortress Press.
1985 *Four Other Gospels: Shadows on the Contours of the Canon*. Winston Press.
1985 *In Fragments: The Aphorisms of Jesus*. Harper & Row.
1986a *Sayings Parallels: A Workbook for the Jesus Tradition*. Fortress Press.
1986b "From Moses to Jesus: Parallel Themes." *Bible Review* 2:18–27.
1987 "The Cross That Spoke: The Earliest Narrative of the Passion and Resurrection." *Forum* 3:3–22.
1988 *The Cross That Spoke: The Origins of the Passion Narrative*. Harper & Row.
1991 *The Historical Jesus: The Life of a Mediterranean Jewish Peasant*. Fortress Press.
1998 *The Birth of Christianity: Discovering What Happened in the Years Immediately after the Execution of Jesus*. HarperSanFrancisco.

Crossan, John Dominic, Luke Timothy Johnson, and Werner H. Kelber
1999 *The Jesus Controversy Perspectives in Conflict*. Trinity Press International.

Crossan, John Dominic, and Jonathan L. Reed
2001 *Excavating Jesus: Beneath the Stones, Behind the Texts*. HarperSanFrancisco.

Crouch, James E.
1973 *The Origin and Intention of the Colossians Haustafel*. Vandenhoeck & Ruprecht.

Crowe, Jerome
1979   *Acts*. New Testament Message 8. Michael Glazier.
Cullmann, Oscar
1950   " 'Kyrios' as Designation for the Oral Tradition Concerning Jesus (1 Corinthians 7:1, 25; 9:14; 11:23; 15:3)." *Scottish Journal of Theology* 3:180–97.
1956   *The Early Church: Studies in Early Christian History and Theology*. Edited by A. J. B. Higgins. Westminster Press.
1958   *Immortality of the Soul or Resurrection of the Dead? The Witness of the New Testament*. Epworth.
1962   *Peter: Disciple, Apostle, Martyr*. Westminster Press.
1963   *The Christology of the New Testament*. Westminster Press.
1976   *The Johannine Circle*. Westminster Press.
Culpepper, R. Alan
1975   *The Johannine School: An Evaluation of the Johannine-School Hypothesis Based on an Investigation of the Nature of Ancient Schools*. Scholars Press.
1983   *Anatomy of the Fourth Gospel: A Study in Literary Design*. Fortress Press.
1984   "Story and History in the Gospels." *Review and Expositor* 81:467–78.
1994   *John, the Son of Zebedee: The Life of a Legend*. Fortress Press.
1997   "The Plot of John's Story." In *Gospel Interpretation: Narrative-Critical and Social-Scientific Approaches*, edited by Jack Dean Kingsbury, 188–99. Trinity Press International.
Culpepper, R. Alan, and C. Clifton Black, eds.
1996   *Exploring the Gospel of John: In Honor of D. Moody Smith*. Westminster John Knox Press.
Culpepper, R. Alan, and Fernando F. Segovia, eds.
1991   *The Fourth Gospel from a Literary Perspective*. Semeia 53. Scholars Press.
Cumont, Franz
1960   *Astrology and Religion among the Greeks and Romans*. Dover Publications.
Cutter, Charles, and M. F. Oppenheim
1982   *Jewish Reference Sources: A Selective, Annotated Bibliographic Guide*. Garland Publishing.
D'Angelo, Mary Rose
1984   *Moses in the Letter to the Hebrews*. Scholars Press.
1990   "Women in Luke-Acts: A Redactional View." *Journal of Biblical Literature* 109:441–61.

1992   "Abba and "Father": Imperial Theology and the Jesus Traditions." *Journal of Biblical Literature* 111:611–30.
Dahl, Nils Alstrup
1976   *Jesus in the Memory of the Early Church*. Augsburg Publishing House.
1991   *Jesus the Christ: The Historical Origins of Christological Doctrine*. Edited by D. H. Juel. Fortress Press.
Danby, Herbert
1933   *The Mishnah*. Oxford University Press.
Danker, Frederick W.
1976   *Luke*. Edited by G. Krodel. Fortress Press.
1982   *Benefactor: Epigraphic Study of a Greco-Roman and New Testament Semantic Field*. Clayton Publishing House.
1993   *Multipurpose Tools for Bible Study*. Revised and expanded ed. Fortress Press.
Danove, Paul L.
1993   *The End of Mark's Story: A Methodological Study*. Brill.
Darr, John A.
1992   *On Character Building: The Reader and the Rhetoric of Characterization in Luke-Acts*. Westminster John Knox Press.
1998   *Herod the Fox: Audience Criticism and Lukan Characterization*. Sheffield Academic Press.
Dart, John
1976   *Laughing Savior: The Discovery and Significance of the Nag Hammadi Gnostic Library*. Harper & Row.
Daube, David
1949   "Rabbinic Methods of Interpretation and Hellenistic Rhetoric." *Hebrew Union College Annual* 22:239–64.
Davids, Peter H.
1982   *The Epistle of James: A Commentary on the Greek Text*. Eerdmans.
1983   *James*. Harper & Row.
1990   *First Epistle of Peter*. Eerdmans.
Davies, Margaret
1993   *Matthew*. Sheffield Academic Press.
Davies, P. E.
1945   "Jesus and the Role of the Prophet." *Journal of Biblical Literature* 64:214–54.
Davies, Philip R.
1998   *Scribes and Schools: The Canonization of the Hebrew Scriptures*. John Knox Press.
Davies, Stevan L.
1980   *The Revolt of the Widows. The Social World of the Apocryphal Acts*. Southern Illinois Universtiy Press.
1995   *Jesus the Healer: Possession, Trance, and the Origins of Christianity*. Continuum.

Davies, W. D.

1964 *The Setting of the Sermon on the Mount.* Cambridge University Press.

1966 *The Sermon on the Mount.* Cambridge University Press.

1967 *Introduction to Pharisaism.* Fortress Press.

1977 "Paul and the People of Israel." *New Testament Studies* 24:4–39.

1980 *Paul and Rabbinic Judaism: Some Rabbinic Elements in Pauline Theology.* Fortress Press.

1983a *Jewish and Pauline Studies.* Fortress Press.

1983b "Reflections about the Use of the Old Testament in the New in Its Historical Context." *Jewish Quarerly Review* 74:105–36.

Davies, W. D., and D. C. Allison

1988 *A Critical and Exegetical Commentary on the Gospel According to Saint Matthew.* 3 vols. T&T Clark.

Davis, Charles Thomas

1973 "The Fulfillment of Creation: A Study of Matthew's Genealogy." *Journal of the American Academy of Religion* 41:520–35.

Davis, John

1977 *People of the Mediterranean: An Essay in Comparative Social Anthropology.* Routledge.

Dawsey, James M.

1986 *Lukan Voice: Confusion and Irony in the Gospel of Luke.* Mercer University Press.

1988 *A Scholar's Guide to Academic Journals in Religion.* Scarecrow Press.

Day, John

1985 *God's Conflict with the Dragon and the Sea in the Old Testament.* Cambridge University Press.

De Boer, Martinus C.

1988 *The Defeat of Death: Apocalyptic Eschatology in 1 Corinthians 15 and Romans 5.* Journal for the Study of the New Testament Supplement Series 22. JSOT/Sheffield Academic Press.

de Jonge, Marinus

1972 "Jewish Expectations about the Messiah According to the Fourth Gospel." *New Testament Studies* 19:246–70.

1977 (ed.) *Jesus: Stranger from Heaven and Son of God: Jesus Christ and the Christians in Johannine Perspective.* Edited by J. E. Steely. Society of Biblical Literature Sources for Biblical Study 11. Scholars Press.

1988 *Christology in Context: The Earliest Christian Response to Jesus.* Westminster Press.

1991 *Jesus, the Servant-Messiah.* Yale University Press.

1993 "The Conflict between Jesus and the Jews and the Radical Christology of the Fouth Gospel." *Perspectives in Religious Studies* 20:341–55.

De Villiers, P. G. R

1988 "The Lord Was Crucified in Sodom and Egypt: Symbols in the Apocalypse of John." *Neotestamentica* 22:125–38.

De Vos, Craig Steven

1999 *Church and Community Conflicts: The Relationships of the Thessalonian, Corinthian, and Philippian Churches with Their Wider Civic Communities.* Scholars Press.

Deissmann, Gustav A.

1957 *Paul.* Harper Torchbooks.

DeLaine, J., and D. E. Johnston, eds.

1999 "Roman Baths and Bathing: Part 1, Bathing and Society." In *Proceedings of the First International Conference on Roman Baths Held at Bath, England, 30 March–4 April 1992.* Journal of Roman Archaeology.

DeMaris, Richard E.

1995 "Corinthian Religion and Baptism for the Dead (I Cor 15:29): Insights from Archaeology and Anthropology." *Journal of Biblical Literature* 114:661–82.

Deming, Will

1995 *Paul on Marriage and Celibacy: The Hellenistic Background of 1 Corinthians 7.* Cambridge University Press.

den Heyer, C. J.

1997 *Jesus Matters: 150 Years of Research.* Trinity Press International.

DeRidder, Richard R.

1971 *The Dispersion of the People of God: The Covenantal Basis of Matthew 28:18–20 against the Background of Jewish Proselytism.* J. H. Kok.

Derrenbacker, Robert A., Jr.

2005 *Ancient Compositional Practices and the Synoptic Problem.* Peeters.

Derrett, J. Duncan M.

1971 "Law in the New Testament the Palm Sunday Colt." *Novum Testament* 13:241–58.

1973a "Figtrees in the Testament." *Heythrop Journal* 14:249–65.

1973b "The Good Shepherd: St. John's Use of Jewish Halakah and Haggadah." *Studia Theologica* 27:25–50.

1973c "The Manager at Bethlehem: Light on St. Luke's Technique from the Contemporary Jewish Religious Law." *Studia Evangelica* 6:86–94.

1974 "Allegory and the Wicked Vinedressers." *Journal of Theological Studies* 25:426–32.

1975a "Cursing Jesus: The Jews as 'Religious Perse-
cutors'." *New Testament Studies* 21:544–54.
1975b "Midrash in Matthew." *Heythrop Journal*
16:51–56.
1983 "Binding and Loosing (Matthew 16:19; 18:18;
John 10:23)." *Journal of Biblical Literature*
102:112–17.

Derwacter, Frederick Milton
1930 *Preparing the Way for Paul: The Proselyte
Movement in Later Judaism.* Macmillan.

deSilva, David Arthur
1995 *Despising Shame: Honor Discourse and Community Maintenance in the Epistle to the
Hebrews.* Scholars Press.
1998a "'Let the One Who Claims Honor Establish
That Claim in the Lord': Honor Discourse
in the Corinthian Correspondence." *Biblical
Theology Bulletin* 28:61–74.
1998b "The Persuasive Strategy of the Apocalypse: A
Socio-Rhetorical Investigation of Revelation
14:6–13." In *Society of Biblical Literature
Seminar Papers,* 785–806. Scholars Press.
2000 *Perseverance in Gratitude: A Socio-
Rhetorical Commentary on the Epistle
"To the Hebrews."* Eerdmans.

Detweiler, Robert
1977 *Story, Sign and Self: Phenomenology and
Structuralism as Literary-Critical Method.*
Fortress Press.

Dewey, Joanna,
1980 *Markan Public Debate: Literary Technique,
Concentric Structure, and Theology in Mark
2:1–3:6.* Edited by H. C. Kee. Society of Biblical Literature Dissertation Series 48. Scholars
Press.
1982 "Point of View and the Disciples in Mark." In
*Society of Biblical Literature 1982 Seminar
Papers,* 97–106. Scholars Press.
1989 "Oral Methods of Structuring Narrative in
Mark." *Interpretation* 43:32–44.
1991 "Mark as Interwoven Tapestry: Forecasts and
Echoes for a Listening Audience." *Catholic
Biblical Quarterly* 53:221–36.
1992 "Feminist Readings, Gospel Narrative, and
Critical Theory." *Biblical Theology Bulletin*
22:167–73.
1995 (ed.) *Orality and Textuality in Early Christian Literature. Semeia* 65. Scholars Press.
1996 "From Storytelling to Written Text: The Loss
of Early Christian Women's Voices." *Biblical
Theology Bulletin* 26:71–78.

Dewitt, Norman
1954 *St. Paul and Epicurus.* University of Minne-
sota Press.

Dey, L.
1981 *The Intermediary World and Patterns of Perfection in Philo and Hebrews.* Society of Biblical Literature Dissertation Series 25. Scholars
Press.

Dibelius, Martin
1935 *From Tradition to Gospel.* Charles Scribner.
1949 *Jesus.* Westminster Press.
1953 *Paul.* Westminster Press.
1956 *Studies in the Acts of the Apostles.* Edited by
H. Greeven. SCM Press.
1976 *James.* Edited by H. Greeven. Fortress Press.

Dibelius, Martin, and Hans Conzelmann
1972 *The Pastoral Epistles.* Translated by P. C. A.
Y. Buttolph. Fortress Press.

Dillistone, F. W.
1986 *The Power of Symbols in Religion and Culture.* Crossroad.

Dio, Chrysostom.
Discourses. Translated by J. W. Cahoon and
H. L. Crosby. Harvard University Press, 1932.

Diogenes, Laertius.
Lives of Eminent Philosophers. Translated by
R. D. Hicks. Harvard University Press, 1942.

Dixon, Suzanne
1988 *The Roman Mother.* Oklahoma University
Press.
1992 *The Roman Family.* Johns Hopkins University
Press.

Dodd, C. H.
1946 *The Johannine Epistles.* Harper & Row.
1951 *The Apostolic Preaching and Its Development.* Harper & Row.
1953 *The Interpretation of the Fourth Gospel.*
Cambridge University Press.
1963 *Historical Tradition in the Fourth Gospel.*
Cambridge University Press.

Donahue, John R.
1973 *Are You the Christ?* Society of Biblical Literature Dissertation Series 10. Scholars Press.
1978 "Jesus as the Parable of God in the Gospel of
Mark." *Interpretation* 32:369–86.
1988 *The Gospel in Parable: Metaphor, Narrative, and Theology in the Synoptic Gospels.*
Fortress Press.
1995 "Windows and Mirrors: The Setting of
Mark's Gospel." *Catholic Biblical Quarterly*
57:1–26.

Donaldson, Terence L.
1985 *Jesus on the Mountain: A Study of Matthean
Theology.* JSOT/Sheffield Academic Press.
1997 *Paul and the Gentiles: Remapping the
Apostle's Convictional World.* Fortress Press.

Donelson, Lewis R.
1986 *Pseudepigraphy and Ethical Argument in the Pastoral Epistles.* J. C. B. Mohr.

Donfried, Karl P.
1974 "The Allegory of the Ten Virgins (Mt. 25: 1–13) as a Summary of Matthean Theology." *Journal of Biblical Literature* 93:415–28.
1985 "The Cults of Thessalonica and the Thessalonian Correspondence." *New Testament Studies* 31:336–56.
1991 *The Romans Debate: Essays on the Origin and Purpose of the Epistle.* Revised and expanded ed. Hendrickson Publishers.

Donfried, Karl P., and Johannes Beutler
2000 *The Thessalonians Debate: Methodological Discord or Methodological Synthesis?* Eerdmans.

Dormeyer, Detlev
1998 *The New Testament among the Writings of Antiquity.* Sheffield Academic Press.

Dorsey, D.
1991 *The Roads and Highways of Ancient Israel.* Johns Hopkins University Press.

Doty, William G.
1973 *Letters in Primitive Christianity.* Fortress Press.

Doughty, D. J.
1979 "Women and Liberation in the Churches of Pauline Tradition." *Drew Gateway* 2:1–21.

Dover, K. J.
1989 *Greek Homosexuality.* Harvard University Press.

Downey, Glanville
1961 *A History of Antioch in Syria from Seleucus to the Arab Conquest.* Princeton University Press.

Downing, Francis Gerald
1964 "Toward the Rehabilitation of Q." *New Testament Studies* 11:169–81.
1988a *Christ and the Cynics: Jesus and Other Radical Preachers in First-Century Tradition.* Journal for the Study of the Old Testament Annual 4. JSOT/Sheffield Academic Press.
1988b "Compositional Conventions and the Synoptic Problem." *Journal of Biblical Literature* 107:69–85.
1992 "The Ambiguity of 'the Pharisee and the Toll-Collector' (Luke 18:9–14) in the Greco-Roman World of Late Antiquity." *Catholic Biblical Quarterly* 54:80–89.
2000 *Making Sense in (and of) the First Christian Century.* Sheffield Academic Press.

Draisma, Sipke, ed.
1989 *Intertextuality in Biblical Writings: Essays in Honor of Bas Van Iersel.* J. H. Kok.

Drake, H. A.
1976 *In Praise of Constantine: A Historical Study and New Translation of Eusebius Tricennial Orations.* University of California Press.

Droge, Arthur J.
1990 "The Status of Peter in the Fourth Gospel: John 18:10–11." *Journal of Biblical Literature* 109:307–11.

Drower, E. S.
1962 *The Mandaeans of Iraq and Iran: Their Cults, Customs, Magic, Legends and Folklore.* Brill.

Drury, John
1976 *Tradition and Design in Luke's Gospel: A Study in Early Christian Historiography.* John Knox Press.

Duff, Paul Brooks
2001 *Who Rides the Beast? Prophetic Rivalry and the Rhetoric of Crisis in the Churches of the Apocalypse.* Oxford University Press.

Duke, Paul D.
1985 *Irony in the Fourth Gospel.* John Knox Press.

Duling, Dennis C.
1979 *Jesus Christ through History.* Harcourt Brace Jovanovich.
1987 "Binding and Loosing: Matthew 16:19; Matthew 18:18; John 20:23." *Forum* 3:3–32.
2003 *The New Testament: History, Literature, and Social Context.* 4th ed. Wadsworth.

Dundees, Alan
1999 *Holy Writ as Oral Lit.* Rowman & Littlefield Publishers.

Dunderberg, Ismo
2006 *The Beloved Disciple in Conflict? Revisiting the Gospels of John and Thomas.* Oxford University Press.

Dungan, David
1971 *The Sayings of Jesus in the Churches of Paul: The Use of the Synoptic Tradition in the Regulation of Early Church Life.* Fortress Press.

Dunn, James D. G.
1980 *Christology in the Making: A New Testament Inquiry into the Origins of the Doctrine of the Incarnation.* Westminster Press.
1985 *The Evidence for Jesus.* Westminster Press.
1988 *Romans 1–8.* Word Books.
1990 *Jesus, Paul and the Law: Studies in Mark and Galations.* SPCK Press.
1993a *The Epistle to the Galatians.* Hendrickson Publishers.
1993b *The Theology of Paul's Letter to the Galatians.* Cambridge University Press.

2000   "Jesus in Oral Memory: The Initial Stages of the Jesus Tradition." In *Society of Biblical Literature 2000 Seminar Papers*, 287–326. Society of Biblical Literature.

2003a   *The Cambridge Companion to St. Paul*. Cambridge University Press.

2003b   *Christianity in the Making*. Vol. 1, *Jesus Remembered*. Eerdmans.

2005   *A New Perspective on Jesus: What the Quest for the Historical Jesus Missed*. Baker Academic.

2006   *Unity and Diversity in the New Testament: An Inquiry into the Character of Earliest Christianity*. 3rd ed. SCM Press.

Dunn, James D. G., and Scot McKnight, eds.

2005   *The Historical Jesus in Recent Research*. Eisenbrauns.

Dupont-Sommer, Andre

1961   *The Essene Writings from Qumran*. Peter Smith.

Ebeling, Gerhard

1985   *The Truth of the Gospel: An Exposition of Galatians*. Fortress Press.

Edelstein, Ludwig

1966   *Plato's Seventh Letter*. Brill.

Edson, Charles

1948   "Cults of Thessalonica." *Harvard Theological Review* 41:153–204.

Edwards, Douglas R., and C. Thomas McCollough

1997   *Archaeology and the Galilee: Texts and Contexts in the Graeco-Roman and Byzantine Periods*. Scholars Press.

Edwards, Otis Carl

1981   *Luke's Story of Jesus*. Fortress Press.

1989   *How Holy Writ Was Written: The Story of the New Testament*. Abingdon Press.

Edwards, Richard A.

1985   *Matthew's Story of Jesus*. Fortress Press.

1990   "Narrative Implications of Gar in Matthew." *Catholic Biblical Quarterly* 52:636–55.

Efird, James M.

1978   *Daniel and Revelation: A Study of Two Extraordinary Visions*. Judson Press.

1989   *Revelation for Today: An Apocalyptic Approach*. Abingdon Press.

Ehrman, Bart D.

1993   *The Orthodox Corruption of Scripture: The Effect of Early Christological Controversies on the Text of the New Testament*. Oxford University Press.

1998   *The New Testament and Other Early Christian Writings: A Reader*. Oxford University Press.

2005   *Misquoting Jesus: The Story Behind Who Changed the Bible and Why*. HarperSanFrancisco.

2006   *Studies in the Textual Criticism of the New Testament*. Brill.

Ehrman, Bart D., and Michael W. Holmes, eds.

1995   *The Text of the New Testament in Contemporary Research: Essays on the Status Quaestionis: A Volume in Honor of Bruce M. Metzger*. Eerdmans.

Eisenman, Robert

1986   *James the Just in the Habakkuk Pesher*. Brill.

Eisenstadt, S. N., and Louis Roniger

1980   "Patron-Client Relations as a Model of Structuring Social Exchange." *Comparative Studies in Society and History* 22:40–60.

1984   *Patrons, Clients and Friends: Interpersonal Relations and the Structure of Trust in Society*. Cambridge University Press.

Elder, Linda Bennett

1994   "The Woman Question and Female Ascetics among Essenes." *Biblical Archaeologist* 57:220–34.

Elenchus of Biblica.

        Elenchus of Biblica. Published annually. Pontifical Bible Institute Press.

Eliade, Mircea

1959   *Cosmos and History: The Myth of the Eternal Return*. Harper & Row.

Eliot, Charles W., ed.

1909   *English Essays from Sir Philip Sidney to Macaulay*. The Harvard Classics 27. P. F. Collier & Son.

Ellingworth, Paul, and Eugene A. Nida

1976   *A Translator's Handbook on Paul's Letters to the Thessalonians*. United Bible Societies.

Elliott, John H.

1984   "Philemon and House Churches." *The Bible Today* 22:145–50.

1986   (ed.) *Social-Scientific Criticism of the New Testament and Its Social World. Semeia* 45. Scholars Press.

1987   "Patronage and Clientism in Early Christian Society: A Reading Guide." *Forum* 3:39–48.

1990   *A Home for the Homeless: A Sociological Exegesis of First Peter, Its Situation and Strategy*. Fortress Press.

1991   "Household and Meals vs. Temple Purity: Replication Patterns in Luke-Acts." *Biblical Theology Bulletin* 21:102–8.

1993   *What Is Social-Scientific Criticism?* Fortress Press.

2000   *1 Peter a New Translation with Introduction and Commentary*. Doubleday.

Elliott, J. K.

1993a *The Apocryphal New Testament: A Collection of Apocryphal Christian Literature in an English Translation.* Oxford University Press.

1993b *The Language and Style of the Gospel of Mark.* Brill.

1996 *The Apocryphal Jesus: Legends of the Early Church.* Oxford University Press.

Elliott, Keith, and Ian Moir

1995 *Manuscripts and the Text of the New Testament: An Introduction of English Readers.* T&T Clark.

Elliott, Neil

1990 *The Rhetoric of Romans: Argumentative Constraint and Strategy and Paul's Dialogue with Judaism.* Journal for the Study of the New Testament 45. JSOT/Sheffield Academic Press.

1994 *Liberating Paul: The Justice of God and the Politics of the Apostle.* Orbis Books.

Elliott, Susan

1999 "Choose Your Mother, Choose Your Master: Galatians 4:21–5:1 in the Shadow of the Anatolian Mountain Mother of the Gods." *Journal of Biblical Literature* 118:661–83.

2003 *Cutting Too Close for Comfort: Paul's Letter to the Galatians in Its Anatolian Cultic Context.* T&T Clark.

Ellis, E. Earle

1961 *Paul and His Recent Interpreters.* Eerdmans.

1967 *The Gospel of Luke.* The Attic Press.

1972 *Eschatology in Luke.* Edited by J. Reumann. Fortress Press.

1984 *The World of St. John: The Gospel and the Epistles.* Eerdmans.

Ellis, E. Earle, and Max Wilcox

1969 *Noetestamentica et Semitica: Studies in Honour of Matthew Black.* T&T Clark.

Ellis, Peter F.

1974 *Matthew: His Mind and His Message.* The Liturgical Press.

1982 *Seven Pauline Letters.* The Liturgical Press.

Else, G. F.

1957 *Aristotle's Poetics: The Argument.* Harvard University Press.

1967 *Aristotle: Poetics.* University of Michigan Press.

Engberg-Pedersen, Troels

1994 *Paul in His Hellenistic Context.* Fortress Press.

Engels, Donald W.

1990 *Roman Corinth: An Alternative Model for the Classical City.* University of Chicago Press.

Enslin, Morton Scott

1927 "Paul and Gamaliel." *Journal of Religion* 7:360–75.

1957 *The Ethics of Paul.* Abingdon Press.

Epictetus. *Discourses.* Translated by W. Heinemann. Loeb. Harvard University Press, 1925.

Epp, Eldon Jay

2005 *Junia: The First Woman Apostle.* Fortress Press.

Epstein, Isadore

1935 *The Babylonian Talmud in English.* 36 vols. Soncino.

Erickson, Richard J.

1996 "Divine Injustice? Matthew's Narrative Strategy and the Slaughter of the Innocents (Matthew 2:13–23)." *Journal for the Study of the New Testament* 64:5–27.

Erim, Kenan T.

1986 *Aphrodisias: City of Venus Aphrodite.* Facts on File.

Esler, Philip F.

2003 *Conflict and Identity in Romans: The Social Setting of Paul's Letter.* Fortress Press.

Esler, Philip F., and Ronald A. Piper

2006 *Lazarus, Mary and Martha: A Social-Scientific and Theological Reading of John.* SCM Press.

Espy, John E.

1985 "Paul's Robust Conscience Re-Examined." *New Testament Studies* 31:161–88.

Eusebius

Ecclesiastical History. Translated by K. Lake. Loeb. Harvard University Press, 1959.

The History of the Church from Christ to Constantine. Translated by G. A. Williamson. Augsburg Publishing House, 1965.

Evans, Craig A.

1981 "On the Prologue of John and the Trimorphic Protennoia." *New Testament Studies* 27:395–401.

1996 *Life of Jesus Research: An Annotated Bibliography.* Revised ed. Brill.

Evans, Craig A., and Bruce D. Chilton, eds.

1994 *Studying the Historical Jesus: Evaluations of the State of Current Research.* Brill.

Evanson, Edward

1792 *The Dissonance of the Four Generally Received Evangelists.* Printed by G. Jermym.

Ewherido, Anthony O.

2006 *Matthew's Gospel and Judaism in the Late First Century CE: The Evidence from Matthew's Chapter on Parables (Matthew 13:1–52).* Peter Lang.

Exum, J. Cheryl, ed.
1987   *Tragedy and Comedy in the Bible. Semeia 32.*
Scholars Press.

Faas, Patrick
2003   *Around the Roman Table: Food and Feasting in Ancient Rome.* Palgrave Macmillan.

Faraone, Christopher, and Dirk Obbink, eds.
1991   *Magika Hiera: Ancient Greek Magic and Religion.* Oxford University Press.

Farmer, Ron
1997   *Beyond the Impasse: The Promise of a Process Hermeneutic.* Mercer University Press.
2005   *The Revelation to John: A Commentary for Today.* Chalice Press.

Farmer, William R.
1964   *The Synoptic Problem.* Macmillan.
1974   *The Last Twelve Verses of Mark.* Brill.
1976a   "The Post-Sectarian Character of Matthew and Its Post-War Setting in Antioch of Syria." *Perspectives in Religion Studies* 3:235–47.
1976b   *The Synoptic Problem: A Critical Analysis.* Western North Carolina Press.
1982   *Jesus and the Gospel: Tradition, Scripture, and Canon.* Fortress Press.

Farmer, William R., and D. M. Farkasfalvy
1983   *The Formation of the New Testament Canon.* Paulist Press.

Farrer, Austin
1955   "On Dispensing with Q." In *Studies in the Gospels,* edited by D. E. Nineham, 55–88. Blackwell.
1964   *The Revelation of St. John the Divine.* Oxford University Press.
1970   *A Rebirth of Images: The Making of St. John's Apocalypse.* Peter Smith.

Fee, Gordon D.
1984   *First and Second Timothy, Titus.* Harper & Row.

Fehribach, Adeline
1998   *The Women in the Life of the Bridegroom: A Feminist Historical-Literary Analysis of the Gospel of John.* The Liturgical Press.

Felder, Cain Hope, ed.
1991   *Stony the Road We Trod: African American Biblical Interpretation.* Fortress Press.
2002   *Race, Racism, and the Biblical Narratives.* Fortress Press.

Feldman, Louis H.
1950   "Jewish 'Sympathizers' in Classical Literature and Inscription." *Transactions of the American Philological Association* 81:200–208.
1986   *Josephus: A Supplementary Bibliography.* Cambridge University Press.
1993   *Jews and Gentile in the Ancient World: Attitudes and Interactions from Alexander to Justinian.* Princeton University Press.

Feldman, Louis H., and Gohei Hata
1989   *Josephus, Judaism, and Christianity.* Wayne State University Press.

Fenn, Richard K.
1997   *The End of Time: Religion, Ritual, and the Forging of the Soul.* The Pilgrim Press.

Fenton, John C.
1963   *The Gospel of St. Matthew.* Pelican Gospel Commentaries. Penguin Books.
1970   *The Gospel According to St. John.* Clarendon Press.

Ferguson, Everett
1982   "Canon Muratori: Date and Provenance." *Studia Patristica* 18:677–83.

Ferguson, John
1970   *The Religions of the Roman Empire: Aspects of Greek and Roman Life.* Cornell University Press.
1980   *Greek and Roman Religion: A Source Book.* Noyes Press.

Fiensy, David
1991   *The Social History of Palestine in the Herodian Period.* Edwin Mellen Press.

Filson, Floyd V.
1956   "Broken Patterns in the Gospel of Matthew." *Journal of Biblical Literature* 75:227–31.
1960   *The Gospel According to St. Matthew.* Harper & Row.

Finegan, Jack
1981   *The Archeology of the New Testament: The Mediterranean World of the Early Christian Apostles.* Westview Press.
1989   *Myth and Mystery: An Introduction to the Pagan Religions of the Biblical World.* Baker Book House.
1992   *The Archaeology of the New Testament: The Life of Jesus and the Beginning of the Early Church.* Revised ed. Princeton University Press.
1998   *Handbook of Biblical Chronology: Principles of Time Reckoning in the Ancient World and Problems of Chronology in the Bible.* Revised ed. Hendrickson Publishers.

Finley, M. I.
1973   *The Ancient Economy.* Sather Classical Lectures 43. University of California Press.
1986   *Ancient History: Evidence and Models.* Viking.

Finnegan, Ruth
1974   "How Oral Is Oral Literature?" *Bulletin of the School of Oriental and African Studies* 37:52–64.

Fiore, Benjamin
  1986   *The Function of Personal Example in the So-*
          cratic and Pastoral Epistles. Biblical Institute
          Press.
  1990   "Invective in Romans and Philippians."
          Proceedings of the Eastern Great Lakes
          and Midwest Societies of Biblical Literature
          10:181–89.
Fitzmyer, Joseph A.
  1971   "The Priority of Mark and the "Q" Source
          in Luke." In *Jesus and Man's Hope*, edited
          by D. G. Miller and Y. Hadidian, 1:131–70.
          Pittsburgh Theological Seminary.
  1978   "Crucifixion in Ancient Palestine, Qumran
          Literature, and the New Testament." *Catholic*
          Biblical Quarterly 10:493–513.
  1981   *The Gospel According to Luke.* 2 vols.
          Doubleday.
  1988   "The Aramaic Background of Philippians
          2:6–11." *Catholic Biblical Quarterly*
          50:470–83.
  1989a   *Luke the Theologian: Aspects of His Teach-*
          ing. Paulist Press.
  1989b   *Paul and His Theology: A Brief Sketch.* Pren-
          tice Hall.
  1990a   *The Dead Sea Scrolls: Major Publications and*
          Tools for Study. Scholars Press.
  1990b   *An Introductory Bibliography for the Study of*
          Scripture. Revised ed. Biblical Institute Press.
  1992   *Responses to 101 Questions on the Dead Sea*
          Scrolls. Paulist Press.
  1993   *Romans: A New Translation with Introduc-*
          tion and Commentary. Doubleday.
  1998   *The Acts of the Apostles: A New Transla-*
          tion with Introduction and Commentary.
          Doubleday.
  2000   *The Letter to Philemon: A New Transla-*
          tion with Introduction and Commentary.
          Doubleday.
Flint, Peter W., and James C. VanderKam, eds.
  1998   *The Dead Sea Scrolls after Fifty Years: A*
          Comprehensive Assessment. Brill.
Flusser, David
  1958   "The Dead Sea Sect and Pre-Pauline Christi-
          anity." *Scripta Hierosolymitana* 4:215–66.
  1975   "Two Anti-Jewish Montages in Matthew."
          Immanuel 5:37–45.
Foakes-Jackson, F. J.
  1931   *The Acts of the Apostles.* R. R. Smith.
Foerster, Werner
  1972   *Gnosis: A Selection of Gnostic Texts.* 2 vols.
          Oxford University Press.
Foley, Helene P.
  1982   *Reflections of Women in Antiquity.*
          Gordon & Breach.

  1986   *Ascetic Piety and Women's Faith: Essays in*
          Late Ancient Christianity. Edwin Mellen
          Press.
Forbes, Christopher
  1986   "Paul's Boasting and Hellenistic Rhetoric."
          New Testament Studies 32:1–30.
  1997   *Prophecy and Inspired Speech in Early*
          Christianity and Its Hellenistic Environment.
          Hendrickson Publishers.
Ford, J. Massynbaerde
  1993   "BTB Readers' Guide: Prostitution in the
          Ancient Mediterranean World." *Biblical The-*
          ology Bulletin 23:128–34.
Forestell, J. T.
  1979   *Targumic Traditions and the New Testament:*
          An Annotated Bibliography with a New Tes-
          tament Index. Scholars Press.
Forster, E. M.
  1962   *Aspects of the Novel.* Penguin Books.
Fortna, Robert T.
  1970   *The Gospel of Signs: A Reconstruction of*
          the Narrative Source Underlying the Fourth
          Gospel. Cambridge University Press.
  1988   *The Fourth Gospel and Its Predecessor: From*
          Narrative Source to Present Gospel. Fortress
          Press.
Fowl, Stephen
  1990   *The Story of Christ in the Ethics of Paul: An*
          Analysis of the Function of Hymnic Material
          in the Pauline Corpus. Journal for the Study
          of the New Testament Supplement Series 36.
          Sheffield Academic Press.
Fowler, Robert M.
  1981a   "Irony and the Messianic Secret in the Gospel
          of Mark." *Proceedings of the Eastern Great*
          Lakes Biblical Society 1:26–36.
  1981b   *Loaves and Fishes: The Function of the Feed-*
          ing Stories in the Gospel of Mark. Society
          of Biblical Literature Dissertation Series 54.
          Scholars Press.
  1985   "The Rhetoric of Indirection in the Gospel
          of Mark." *Proceedings of the Eastern Great*
          Lakes Society of Biblical Literature 5:47–56.
  1991   *Let the Reader Understand: Reader-*
          Response Criticism and the Gospel of Mark.
          Fortress Press.
France, R. T.
  1979   *A Bibliographical Guide to New Testament*
          Research. 3rd ed. JSOT/Sheffield Academic
          Press.
Francis, Fred O.
  1975   *Conflicts at Colossae: A Problem in the*
          Interpretation of Early Christianity. Scholars
          Press.

Francis, Fred O., and J. P. Sampley
1984   *Pauline Parallels.* 2nd ed. Fortress Press.
Frankfurter, David
1998   *Religion in Roman Egypt: Assimilation and Resistance.* Princeton University Press.
Franklin, Eric
1975   *Christ the Lord: A Study in the Purpose and Theology of Luke-Acts.* Westminster Press.
Fredriksen, Paula
1988   *From Jesus to Christ: The Origins of the New Testament Images of Jesus.* Yale University Press.
Freedman, David Noel
1992   *Anchor Bible Dictionary.* 6 vols. Doubleday.
Freedman, David Noel, Allen C. Myers, and Astrid B. Beck, eds.
2000   *Eerdmans Dictionary of the Bible.* Eerdmans.
Frei, Hans W.
1966   "Theological Reflections on the Gospel Accounts of Jesus' Death and Resurrection." *The Christian Scholar* 49:263–306.
1974   *The Eclipse of Biblical Narrative: A Study in Eighteenth and Nineteenth Century Hermeneutics.* Yale University Press.
Frend, W. H. C.
1967   *Martyrdom and Persecution in the Early Church.* Oxford University Press.
1982   *The Early Church.* Fortress Press.
1996   *The Archaeology of Early Christianity: A History.* Fortress Press.
Frey, Jean-Baptiste
1975   *Corpus Inscriptionum Judaicarum: Jewish Inscriptions from the Third Century* BC *to the Seventh Century* AD. Ktav.
Freyne, Seán
1980a   *Galilee from Alexander the Great to Hadrian: 323* BCE *to 135* CE: *A Study of Second Temple Judaism.* Michael Glazier.
1980b   *The World of the New Testament.* New Testament Message 2. Michael Glazier.
1988   *Galilee, Jesus, and the Gospels: Literary Approaches and Historical Investigations.* Fortress Press.
Friedman, Richard Elliott
1983   *The Poet and the Historian: Essays in Literary and Historical Biblical Criticism.* Scholars Press.
Friedman, Richard Elliott, and H. G. M. Williamson
1987   *The Future of Biblical Studies the Hebrew Scriptures.* Scholars Press.
Friesen, Steven J.
1993a   "Ephesus: Key to a Vision in Revelation." *Biblical Archaeology Review* 19:24–37.

1993b   *Twice Neokoros: Ephesus, Asia and the Cult of the Flavian Emperors.* Brill.
1995a   "Cult of the Roman Emperors in Ephesos: Temple Wardens, City Titles, and the Interpretation of the Revelation of John." In *Ephesos: Metropolis of Asia,* edited by H. Koester, 229–50. Trinity Press International.
1995b   "Revelation, Realia, and Religion: Archaeology in the Interpretation of the Apocalypse." *Harvard Theological Review* 88:291–314.
2001   *Imperial Cults and the Apocalypse of John: Reading Revelation in the Ruins.* Oxford Press University.
Frilingos, Christopher A.
2004   *Spectacles of Empire Monsters, Martyrs, and the Book of Revelation.* University of Pennsylvania Press.
Frye, Northrop
1957   *Anatomy of Criticism: Four Essays.* Atheneum.
Frye, Roland Mushat
1973   "On the Historical-Critical Method in New Testament Studies: A Reply to Professor Achtemeier." *Perspective* 14:28–33.
Fuller, Reginald H.
1962   *The New Testament in Current Study.* Scribner.
1977   "The 'Jews' in the Fourth Gospel." *Dialog* 16:31–37.
1980   *The Formation of the Resurrection Narratives.* Fortress Press.
1987   "Searching for the Historical Jesus: A Review of *Jesus and Judaism* by E. P. Sanders, Fortress Press, 1985." *Interpretation* 41:30.
Funk, Robert W.
1982   *Parables and Presence: Forms of the New Testament Tradition.* Fortress Press.
1990   *New Gospel Parallels: Mark.* Revised ed. Polebridge Press.
1995   *New Gospel Parallels.* 2 vols. 3rd ed. Polebridge Press.
1996   *Honest to Jesus: Jesus for a New Millennium.* HarperSanFrancisco.
2000   *The Once and Future Jesus.* Polebridge Press.
2002   *A Credible Jesus: Fragments of a Vision.* Polebridge Press.
Funk, Robert W., et al.
1988   *The Parables of Jesus: Red Letter Edition: A Report of the Jesus Seminar.* Polebridge Press.
Funk, Robert W., Roy W. Hoover, and the Jesus Seminar, eds.
1993   *The Five Gospels: The Search for the Authentic Words of Jesus.* Macmillan.

Furnish, Victor Paul
1968 *Theology and Ethics in Paul*. Abingdon Press.
1979 *The Moral Teaching of Paul: Selected Issues*. Abingdon Press.
1984 *Second Corinthians*. Anchor Bible. Doubleday.

Gaechter, Paul
n.d. *Die literarische Kunst im Matthaus-Evangelium*. Springer Verlag.

Gager, John G.
1974 "Gospels and Jesus: Some Doubts about Method." *Journal of Religion* 54:244–72.
1975 *Kingdom and Community: The Social World of Early Christianity*. Prentice Hall.
1982 "Shall We Marry Our Enemies? Sociology and the New Testament." *Interpretation* 36:256–65.
1983 *The Origins of Anti-Semitism: Attitudes toward Judaism in Pagan and Christian Antiquity*. Oxford University Press.
2000 *Reinventing Paul*. Oxford University Press.

Gamble, Harry
1975 "The Redaction of the Pauline Letters and the Formation of the Pauline Corpus." *Journal of Biblical Literature* 94:403–18.
1984 *The New Testament Canon: Its Making and Meaning*. Fortress Press.
1995 *Books and Readers in the Early Church: A History of Early Christian Texts*. Yale University Press.

Gardner, Jane F.
1986 *Women in Roman Law and Society*. Indiana University Press.
1993 *Being a Roman Citizen*. Routledge.

Garland, David E.
1979 *The Intention of Matthew 23*. Brill.
1990 *One Hundred Years of Study on the Passion Narratives*. Mercer University Press.
1993 *Reading Matthew: A Literary and Theological Commentary on the First Gospel*. Crossroad.

Garland, Robert
1989 *The Greek Way of Life: From Conception to Old Age*. Cambridge University Press.

Garnsey, Peter
1991 "Child Rearing in Ancient Italy." In *The Family in Italy from Antiquity to the Present*, edited by D. I. Kretzer and R. P. Saller, 48–65. Yale University Press.
1996 *Ideas of Slavery from Aristotle to Augustine*. Cambridge University Press.

Garrett, Susan R.
1987 *Magic and Miracle in Luke-Acts*. Ph.D. diss., Yale University, New Haven, Conn.

1989 *The Demise of the Devil: Magic and the Demonic in Luke's Writings*. Fortress Press.

Garrow, A. J. P.
2004 *The Gospel of Matthew's Dependence on the Didache*. T&T Clark.

Gartner, Bertil
1954 "The Habakkuk Commentary (DSH) and the Gospel of Matthew." *Studia Theologica* 8:1–24.

Gasque, W. Ward
1989 *A History of the Interpretation of the Acts of the Apostles*. Hendrickson Publishers.

Gaster, Theodor, 1976 *The Dead Sea Scriptures*. 3rd ed. Anchor Press.

Gaston, Lloyd
1970 *No Stone on Another: Studies in the Significance of the Fall of Jerusalem in the Synoptic Gospels*. Brill.
1987 *Paul and the Torah*. University of British Columbia Press.

Gaventa, Beverly Roberts
1986 *From Darkness to Light: Aspects of Conversion in the New Testament*. Fortress Press.

Gealy, Fred D.
1951 "The First and Second Epistles to Timothy and the Epistle to Titus." In *The Interpreter's Bible*, edited by George A. Buttrick et al., 11:341–551. Abingdon-Cokesbury Press.

Gellner, Ernest, and John Waterbury, eds.
1977 *Patrons and Clients in Mediterranean Societies*. Duckworth.

Genette, Gerard
1980 *Narrative Discourse: An Essay in Method*. Cornell University Press.

Gentili, Bruno
1979 *Theatrical Performances in the Ancient World: Hellenistic and Early Roman Theatre*. J. C. Gieben.

Georgi, Dieter
1986 *The Opponents of Paul in Second Corinthians: A Study of Religious Propaganda in Late Antiquity*. Fortress Press.
1992 *Remembering the Poor: The History of Paul's Collection for Jerusalem*. Abingdon Press.

Gerhardsson, Birger
1979 *Origins of the Gospel Tradition*. Translated by G. Lund. Fortress Press.
1998 *Memory and Manuscript: Oral Tradition and Written Transmission in Rabbinic Judaism and Early Christianity*. Eerdmans.

Getty, Mary Ann
1980 *Philippians and Philemon*. New Testament Message 14. Michael Glazier.

1988   "Paul and the Salvation of Israel: A Perspective on Romans 9–11." *Catholic Biblical Quarterly* 50:456–69.

Giblin, Charles Homer
1976   "Structural and Thematic Correlations in the Matthean Burial-Resurrection Narrative (Mt. 27:57–28:20)." *New Testament Studies* 21:406–20.

Gibson, Leigh, and Shelly Matthews, eds.
2005   *Violence in the New Testament.* T&T Clark.

Gieschen, Charles A.
1998   *Angelomorphic Christology: Antecedents and Early Evidence.* Brill.

Gilbert, Allan H.
1962   *Literary Criticism: Plato to Dryden.* American Book Co.

Gill, David W. J., and Conrad H. Gempf
1994   *The Book of Acts in Its Graeco-Roman Setting.* Eerdmans.

Gillman, Florence M.
1990   "Early Christian Women at Philippi." *Journal of Gender in World Religions* 1:59–79.
1992   *Women Who Knew Paul.* The Liturgical Press.

Gilmore, David D.
1987   *Honor and Shame and the Unity of the Mediterranean.* American Anthropological Association.

Glasson, T. Francis
1960   "Anti-Pharisaism in St. Matthew." *The Jewish Quarterly Review* 51:316–20.

Glatzer, Nahum N.
1959   *Hillel the Elder: The Emergence of Classical Judaism.* B'nai B'rith Hillel Foundations.
1969   *The Judaic Tradition.* Beacon Press.

Gnuse, R.
1985   *The Authority of the Bible: Theories of Inspiration, Revelation and the Canon of Scripture.* Paulist Press.

Goehring, James E., et al.
1990   *Gnosticism and the Early Christian World: In Honor of James M. Robinson.* Polebridge Press.

Golden, Leon
1962   "Catharsis." *Transactions of the American Philological Association* 93:51–60.
1965   "Is Tragedy the Imitation of a Serious Action?" *Greek, Roman, and Byzantine Studies* 6:283–89.
1969   "Mimesis and Katharsis." *Classical Philology* 66:147–52.
1976   "The Clarification Theory of Katharsis." *Hermes* 104 (band 4):437–52.

Golden, Leon, and O. B. Hardison
1968   *Aristotle's Poetics: A Translation and Commentary for Students of Literature.* Prentice Hall.

Goldmann, Lucien
1980   *Essays on Method in the Sociology of Literature.* Telos Press.

Goldstein, H. D
1966   "Mimesis and Catharsis Reexamined." *Journal of Aesthetics and Art Criticism* 24:567–77.

Goldsworthy, G.
1985   *The Lamb and the Lion: The Gospel in Revelation.* Thomas Nelson.

Good, E. M.
1984   "Apocalyptic as Comedy: The Book of Daniel." *Semeia* 32:41–70.

Goodacre, Mark S.
2002   *The Case against Q: Studies in Markan Priority and the Synoptic Problem.* Trinity Press International.

Goodenough, Erwin R.
1952   *Jewish Symbols in the Greco-Roman World.* 13 vols. Princeton University Press.

Goodman, Martin
1994   *Mission and Conversion: Proselytizing in the Religious History of the Roman Empire.* Clarendon Press.

Goodspeed, Edgar J.
1937   "Pseudonumity and Pseudepigraphy in Early Christian Literature." In *New Chapters in New Testament Study*, 169–88. Macmillan.
1950   *The Apostolic Fathers, an American Translation.* Harper.
1959   *Matthew, Apostle and Evangelist.* Winston Press.

Goodspeed, Edgar J., and Robert M. Grant
1966   *A History of Early Christian Literature.* University of Chicago Press.

Goodwater, L.
1975   *Women in Antiquity: An Annotated Bibliography.* Scarecrow.

Goranson, Stephen
1998   "Others and Intra-Jewish Polemic as Reflected in Qumran Texts." In *The Dead Sea Scrolls after Fifty Years: A Comprehensive Assessment*, edited by P. W. Flint and J. C. VanderKam, 2:534–51. Brill.

Gorman, Peter
1979   *Pythagoras: A Life.* Routledge.

Gottcent, J. H.
1979   *The Bible as Literature: A Selective Bibliography.* G. K. Hall & Co.

Gottwald, Norman K.
1985   *The Hebrew Bible: A Socio-Literary Intro-duction.* Fortress Press.

Goulder, M. D.
1974   *Midrash and Lection in Matthew.* SPCK Press.
1978   "Mark XVI:1–8 and Parallels." *New Testament Studies* 24:235–39.
1987   "The Pauline Epistles." In *The Literary Guide to the Bible*, edited by R. Alter and F. Kermode, 479–502. Harvard University Press.
1996   "Is Q a Juggernaut?" *Journal of Biblical Literature* 115:667–81.

Gowler, David B.
1989   "Characterization in Luke: A Socio-Narratological Approach." *Biblical Theology Bulletin* 1:54–62.
1991   *Host, Guest, Enemy, and Friend: Portraits of the Pharisees in Luke and Acts.* Peter Lang.
2007   *What Are They Saying about the Historical Jesus?* Paulist Press.

Grabbe, Lester L.
1992   *Judaism from Cyrus to Hadrian.* Volume 2, *The Roman Period.* Fortress Press.

Graf, Fritz
1997   *Magic in the Ancient World.* Harvard University Press.

Grant, Frederick C.
1926   *The Economic Background of the Gospels.* Russell & Russell.
1953   *Hellenistic Religions: The Age of Syncretism.* Liberal Arts Press, Bobbs-Merrill.
1957   *The Gospels: Their Origins and Their Growth.* Harper & Row.
1962a *Form Criticism.* Harper & Row.
1962b *Roman Hellenism and the New Testament.* Oliveroyd.

Grant, Michael
1977   *Jesus: An Historian's Review of the Gospels.* Charles Scribner's Sons.

Grant, Robert M.
1952   *Miracle and Natural Law in Greco-Roman and Early Christian Thought.* North Holland.
1961   *Gnosticism.* Harper & Row.
1963   *Historical Introduction to the New Testament.* Harper & Row.
1965   *The Formation of the New Testament Canon.* Harper & Row.
1966   *Gnosticism and Early Christianity.* Columbia University Press.
1967   *After the New Testament: Studies in Early Christian Literature and Theology.* Fortress Press.
1976   *Perspectives on Scripture and Tradition.* Notre Dame: Fides Publishers.

1977   *Early Christianity and Society: Seven Studies.* Harper & Row.
1980   *Eusebius as Church Historian.* Clarendon Press.
1986   *Gods and the One God.* Library of Early Christianity. Westminster Press.
1990   *Jesus after the Gospels: The Christ of the Second Century.* Westminster John Knox Press.
1993   *Heresy and Criticism: The Search of Authenticity in Early Christian Literature.* Westminster John Knox Press.

Grant, Robert M., and David Tracey
1984   *A Short History of the Interpretation of the Bible.* Fortress Press.

Grayston, Kenneth
1990   *The Gospel of John, Narrative Commentaries.* Trinity Press International.

Green, H. Benedict
1975   *The Gospel According to Matthew.* Oxford University Press.

Green, Joel B.
1987   *How to Read the Gospels and Acts.* InterVarsity Press.
1995   *Hearing the New Testament: Strategies for Interpretation.* Eerdmans.

Green, William Scott
1980   *Approaches to Ancient Judaism, 2.* Brown Judaic Studies 9. Scholars Press.

Grene, David, and Richmond Lattimore
1954   *The Complete Greek Tragedies: Sophocles I: Oedipus the King, Oedipus at Colonus, Antigone.* Washington Square Press.

Grenholm, Cristina, and Daniel Patte
2000   *Reading Israel in Romans: Legitimacy and Plausibility of Divergent Interpretations.* Trinity Press International.

Grieb, A. Katherine
2002   *The Story of Romans: A Narrative Defense of God's Righteousness.* Westminster John Knox Press.

Grimal, Pierre
1983   *Roman Cities.* Edited and translated by G. Michael Woloch. University of Wisconsin Press.

Gros Louis, Kenneth R. R., James S. Ackerman, and Thayer Warshaw
1974   *Literary Interpretations of Biblical Narratives: The Bible in Literature Courses.* Abingdon Press.

Grubb, Nancy
1997   *Revelations: Art of the Apocalypse.* Abbeville Press.

Grube, G. M. A.
1965   *The Greek and Roman Critics.* University of Toronto Press.

Gruenler, Royce Gordon
1982 *New Approaches to Jesus and the Gospels: A Phenomenological and Exegetical Study of Synoptic Christology.* Baker Book House.
Guelich, Robert A.
1976 "The Antithesis of Matthew 5:21–48: Traditional and/or Redactional?" *New Testament Studies* 22:444–57.
1982 *The Sermon on the Mount: A Foundation for Understanding.* Word Book.
Guijarro, Santiago
2000 "Healing Stories and Medical Anthropology: A Reading of Mark 10:46–52." *Biblical Theology Bulletin* 30:102–12.
Gundry, Robert H.
1967 *The Use of the Old Testament in St. Matthew's Gospel.* Novum Testamentum Supplements 18. Brill.
1982 *Matthew: A Commentary on His Literary and Theological Art.* Eerdmans.
1993 *Mark: A Commentary on His Apology for the Cross.* Eerdmans.
Gunther, John J.
1973 *St. Paul's Opponents and Their Background. A Study of Apocalyptic and Jewish Sectarian Teachings.* Brill.
Guthrie, Donald
1975 *New Testament Introduction.* InterVarsity Press.
1981 *Galatians.* New Century Bible Commentary. Eerdmans.
1987 *The Relevance of John's Apocalypse.* Eerdmans.
1990 *The Pastoral Epistles: An Introduction and Commentary.* Revised ed. Eerdmans.
Guthrie, Donald, and J. A. Moyer
1987 *The Eerdman's Bible Commentary.* 3rd ed. Eerdmans.
Gutt, Ernst-August
1986 "Matthew 9:4–17 in the Light of Relevance Theory." *Notes on Translation* 113:13–20.
Guttgemanns, Erhardt
1979 *Candid Questions Concerning Gospel Form Criticism: A Methodological Sketch of the Fundamental Problematics.* Pickwick Press.
Guy, H. A.
1972 "Did Luke Use Matthew?" *Expository Times* 28:245–47.
Hadas, Moses
1950 *History of Greek Literature.* Columbia University Press.
Hadas, Moses, and Morton Smith
1965 *Heroes and Gods.* Harper & Row.

Haddad, George M.
1949 *Aspects of Social Life in Antioch in the Hellenistic-Roman Period.* Ph.D. diss., University of Chicago.
Haenchen, Ernst
1970 "History and Interpretation in Johannine Passion Narrative." *Interpretation* 24:198–219.
1971 *The Acts of the Apostles: A Commentary.* Westminster Press.
1984 *John: A Commentary.* 2 vols. Fortress Press.
Hagner, Donald
1983 *Hebrews.* Good News Commentary Series. Harper & Row.
Hahneman, Geoffrey Mark
1992 *The Muratorian Fragment and the Development of the Canon.* Oxford University Press.
Hall, C. E.
1995 "The Debate over the Muratorian Fragment and the Development of the Canon." *Westminster Press Theological Journal* 57:437–52.
Hall, Robert G.
1990 "The Ascension of Isaiah: Community, Situation, Date and Place in Early Christianity." *Journal of Biblical Literature* 109:289–306.
Hallett, Judith P.
1984 *Fathers and Daughters in Roman Society: Women and the Elite Family.* Princeton University Press.
Hamerton-Kelly, Robert G.
1973 *Pre-Existence, Wisdom, and the Son of Man: A Study of the Idea of Pre-Existence in the New Testament.* Cambridge University Press.
1994 *The Gospel and the Sacred: Poetics of Violence in Mark.* Fortress Press.
Hamerton-Kelly, Robert G., and Robin Scroggs
1976 *Jews, Greeks and Christians: Religious Cultures in Late Antiquity. Essays in Honor of William Davies.* Brill.
Hamilton, Edith, and Huntington Cairns
1961 *Plato: The Collected Dialogues Including the Letters.* 71 vols. Bollingen Series. Princeton University Press.
Handlin, Oscar
1979 *Truth in History.* Harvard University Press.
Hanson, Ann E.
1991 "Ancient Illiteracy." In *Literacy in the Roman World,* edited by M. Beard et al., 159–98. Journal of Roman Archaeology.
Hanson, A. T.
1982 *The Pastoral Epistles: Pastoral Bible Commentary.* Eerdmans.
1987 *The Paradox of the Cross in the Thought of St. Paul.* JSOT/Sheffield Academic Press.

Hanson, J. A.
1959   *Roman Theater-Temples*. Greenwood Press.
Hanson, K. C.
1989   "The Herodians and Mediterranean Kinship: Part I, Genealogy and Descent." *Biblical Theology Bulletin* 19:75–84.
1994   "BTB Readers Guide: Kinship." *Biblical Theology Bulletin* 24:183–94.
1997   "The Galilean Fishing Economy and the Jesus Tradition." *Biblical Theology Bulletin* 27:99–111.
Hanson, K. C., and Douglas E. Oakman
1998   *Palestine in the Time of Jesus: Social Structures and Social Conflicts*. Fortress Press.
Hanson, Paul D.
1979   *The Dawn of Apocalyptic: The Historical and Sociological Roots of Jewish Apocalyptic Eschatology*. Revised ed. Fortress Press.
1983   *Visionaries and Their Apocalypses*. Fortress Press.
Hanson, R. P. C.
1967   *The Acts*. Oxford University Press.
Harding, Mark
1998   *Tradition and Rhetoric in the Pastoral Epistles*. Peter Lang.
2003   *Early Christian Life and Thought in Social Context a Reader*. T&T Clark.
Hare, Douglas R. A.
1967   *The Theme of the Jewish Persecution of Christians in the Gospel of St. Matthew*. New Testament Studies Monograph Series 6. Cambridge University Press.
Hare, Douglas R. A., and Daniel J. Harrington
1975   "Make Disciples of All the Gentiles (Mt. 28:19)." *Catholic Biblical Quarterly* 37:359–69.
Harnack, Adolf von
1901   *What Is Christianity?* Putnam.
1908   *Luke the Physician*. Williams and Norgate.
Harrington, Daniel J.
1975   "Matthean Studies since Joachim Rohde." *Heythrop Journal* 16:375–88.
1985a   *Interpreting the New Testament: A Practical Guide*. New Testament Message 1. Michael Glazier.
1985b   *The New Testament: A Bibliography*. Theological and Biblical Resources 2. Michael Glazer.
1988   *Maccabean Revolt: Anatomy of a Biblical Revolution*. Michael Glazer.
1993   "Paul and Judaism: Five Puzzles." *Bible Review* 9:18–25, 52.

Harrington, Wilfrid J.
1979   *Mark*. Michael Glazier.
1993   *Revelation*. The Liturgical Press.
Harris, H. A.
1985   *Sport in Greece and Rome*. Cornell University Press.
Harris, Michael A.
1989   *The Literary Function of the Hymns in the Apocalypse*. Ph.D. diss., Southern Baptist Theological Seminary, Louisville.
Harris, William V.
1989   *Ancient Literacy*. Harvard University Press.
Harrison, J.
1922   *Prolegomena to the Study of Greek Religion*. Cambridge University Press.
Harrison, R. K.
1985   *Major Cities of the Biblical World*. Thomas Nelson.
Harrison, R. K., B. K. Waltke, D. Guthrie, and G. Fee
1978   *Biblical Criticism: Historical, Literary, and Textual*. Zondervan.
Harstine, Stan
2002   *Moses as a Character in the Fourth Gospel: A Study of Ancient Reading Techniques*. Sheffield Academic Press.
Hartin, Patrick J.
1998   "Disciples as Authorities within Matthew's Christian-Jewish Community." *Neotestamentica* 32:389–404.
Harvey, A. E.
1982   *Jesus and the Constraints of History*. Westminster Press.
1985   *Alternative Approaches to New Testament Study*. SPCK Press.
Harvey, Van A.
1966   *The Historian and the Believer: The Morality of Historical Knowledge and Christian Belief*. Macmillan.
Hauerwas, Stanley, and L. Gregory Jones
1990   *Why Narrative? Readings in Narrative Theology*. Eerdmans.
Havelock, Eric A.
1963   *Preface to Plato*. Harvard University Press.
1982   *The Literate Revolution in Greece and Its Cultural Consequences*. Princeton University Press.
1986   *The Muse Learns to Write: Reflections on Orality and Literacy from Antiquity to the Present*. Yale University Press.
Havelock, Eric A., and Jackson P. Hershbell
1978   *Communication Arts in the Ancient World*. Hastings House.

Hawkin, J. D.
1972 "Incomprehension of the Disciples in Markan Redaction." *Journal of Biblical Literature* 91:491–500.

Hawkins, John Caesar
1909 *Horae Synopticae: Contributions to the Study of the Synoptic Problem.* Oxford University Press.

Hays, Richard B.
1983 *The Faith of Jesus Christ: An Investigation of the Narrative Substructure of Galatians 3:1–4:11.* Society of Biblical Literature Dissertation Series 56. Scholars Press.
1987 "Christology and Ethics in Galatians: The Law of Christ." *Catholic Biblical Quarterly* 49:268–90.
1989 *Echoes of Scripture in the Letters of Paul.* Yale University Press.

Hazlitt, Frances, and Henry Hazlitt
1984 *The Wisdom of the Stoics: Selections from Seneca, Epictetus, and Marcus Aurelius.* University Press of America.

Hedrick, Charles W.
1986 "The Treasure Parable in Matthew and Thomas." *Forum* 2:41–56.
1987 "Narrator and Story in the Gospel of Mark: Hermeneia and Paradosis." *Perspectives in Religious Studies* 14:238–58.
1988 (ed.) *The Historical Jesus and the Rejected Gospels. Semeia* 44. Scholars Press.
1994 *Parables as Poetic Fictions: The Creative Voice of Jesus.* Hendrickson Publishers.
1999 *When History and Faith Collide: Studying Jesus.* Hendrickson Publishers.

Hedrick, Charles W., and Robert Rodgson Jr.
1986 *Nag Hammadi, Gnosticism and Early Christianity.* Hendrickson Publishers.

Heil, John Paul
1987 *Paul's Letter to the Romans: A Reader-Response Commentary.* Paulist Press.
1989 "Reader-Response and the Irony of Jesus before the Sanhedrin in Luke 22:66–71." *Catholic Biblical Quarterly* 51:271–84.
1991a *The Death and Ressurection of Jesus: A Narrative-Critical Reading of Matthew 26–28.* Fortress Press.
1991b "The Narrative Structure of Matthew 27:55–28:20." *Journal of Biblical Literature* 110:419–38.
1992 *The Gospel of Mark as a Model for Action: A Reader-Response Commentary.* Paulist Press.

Heirs, Richard H.
1985 "'Binding' and 'Loosing': The Matthean Authorizations." *Journal of Biblical Literature* 104:233–50.

Helgeland, John
1978 "Roman Army Religion." *Aufstieg und Niedergang der römischen Welt* II, 16:1470–1500.
1986 "Their World and Ours: Ancient and Modern." *Helios* 13 n.s.:3–16.
1989 "Civil Religion, Military Religion: Roman and American." *Forum* 5:22–44.

Hellholm, David
1989 *Apocalypticism in the Mediterranean World and Near East: Proceedings of the International Colloquium on Apocalypticism, Uppsala, August 12–17, 1979.* 2nd ed. Mohr-Siebeck.

Helmer, Christine, and Christof Landmesser, eds.
2004 *One Scripture or Many? Canon from Biblical, Theological, and Philosophical Perspectives.* Oxford University Press.

Helms, Randel
1989 *Gospel Fictions.* Prometheus Books.

Hemer, Colin J.
1977 "Luke the Historian." *Bulletin of the John Rylands University Library* 60:28–51.
1986 *Letters to the Seven Churches of Asia in Their Local Setting.* JSOT/Sheffield Academic Press.

Hendrickx, Herman
1984 *Infancy Narratives: Studies in the Synoptic Gospels.* Geoffrey Chapman.

Hendrix, Holland L.
1984 *Thessalonians Honor Reclaimed,* Th.D. diss., Harvard University, Cambridge, Mass.

Hengel, Martin
1974a *Judaism and Hellenism: Studies in Their Encounter in Palestine During the Early Hellenistic Period.* 2 vols. Fortress Press.
1974b *Property and Riches in the Early Church: Aspects of a Social History of Early Christianity.* Fortress Press.
1976 *The Son of God: The Origin of Christology and the History of Jewish-Hellenistic Religion.* Translated by J. Bowden. Fortress Press.
1977 *Crucifixion in the Ancient World and the Folly of the Message of the Cross.* Translated by J. Bowden. Fortress Press.
1980a *Acts and the History of Earliest Christianity.* Translated by J. Bowden. Fortress Press.
1980b *Jews, Greeks, Andarbarians: Aspects of the Hellenization of Judaism in the Pre-Christian Period.* Translated by J. Bowden. Fortress Press.
1983 *Between Jesus and Paul: Studies in the History of Earliest Christianity.* Translated by J. Bowden. Fortress Press.
1991 *The Pre-Christian Paul.* In collaboration with Roland Deines. Trinity Press International.

Hennecke, Edgar, and Wilhelm Schneemelcher, eds.
1991–1992   *New Testament Apocrypha*. 2 vols. English edition edited by R. McL. Wilson. Revised ed. Westminster John Knox Press.

Henry, Patrick
1979   *New Directions in New Testament Study*. Westminster Press.

Herford, Robert T.
1952   *The Pharisees*. Beacon Press.
1962   *Pirke Aboth. The Ethics of the Talmud: Saying of the Fathers*. Schocken Books.
1971   *Talmud and Apocrypha: A Comparative Study of the Jewish Ethical Teaching in the Rabbinical Canon and Non-Rabbinical Sources in the Early Centuries*. Ktav.
1975   *Christianity in Talmud and Midrash*. Ktav.

Heschel, Abraham J.
1962   *The Prophets*. Harper & Row.

Hesiod
Works. Translated by H. G. Evelyn-White. Loeb. Harvard University Press, 1914.

Heyer, C. J. den
1999   *Paul: A Man of Two World*. Trinity Press International.

Heyob, Sharon Kelly
1973   *The Cult of Isis among Women in the Greco-Roman World*. Brill.

Higgins, A. J. B.
1953   "Priest and Messiah." *Vetus Testamentum* 3:321–36.
1967   "The Priestly Messiah." *New Testament Studies* 13:211–39.

Hilgert, E.
1977   "A Bibliography of Philo Studies, 1974–1975." *Studia Philonica* 4:1–6.

Hill, Craig C.
1992   *Hellenists and Hebrews: Reappraising Division within the Earliest Church*. Fortress Press.

Hill, David
1972   *The Gospel of Matthew*. Eerdmans.
1976   "On Suffering and Baptism in I Peter." *Novum Testamentum* 18:181–89.
1979   *New Testament Prophecy*. John Knox Press.

Hill, James Hamlyn, ed.
2006 [1894]   *The Earliest Life of Christ Ever Compiled from the Four Gospels Being the Diatessaron of Tatian*. Gorgias Press.

Hill, Robert Allan
1997   *An Examination and Critique of the Understanding of the Relationship between Apocalypticism and Gnosticism in Johannine Studies*. Edwin Mellen Press.

Himmelfarb, Martha
1983   *Tours of Hell: An Apocalyptic Form in Jewish and Christian Literature*. University of Pennsylvania Press.
1993   *Ascent to Heaven in Jewish and Christian Apocalypses*. Oxford University Press.

Hirsch, E. D.
1967   *Validity in Interpretation*. Yale University Press.
1976   *The Aims of Interpretation*. University Chicago Press.

Hobbs, Edward C.
1980   "A Quarter Century without Q." *Perkins Journal* 33:10–19.

Hock, Ronald F.
1978   "Paul's Tentmaking and the Problem of His Social Class." *Journal of Biblical Literature* 97:555–64.
1980   *The Social Context of Paul's Ministry: Tentmaking and Apostleship*. Fortress Press.

Hodges, Zane C.
1966   "The Women and the Empty Tomb." *Bibliotheca Sacra* 123:301–9.

Hoffmann, R. Joseph
1984   *Marcion, on the Restitution of Christianity: An Essay on Radical Paulinist Theology in the Second Century*. Scholars Press.

Holland, Glenn S.
1988   *The Tradition That You Received from Us: 2 Thessalonians in the Pauline Tradition*. Mohr–Siebeck.

Hollenbach, Paul
1989   "The Historical Jesus Question in North America Today." *Biblical Theology Bulletin* 19:11–22.

Holmberg, Bengt
1980   *Paul and Power: The Structure of Authority in the Primitive Church as Reflected in the Pauline Epistles*. Fortress Press.
1990   *Sociology and the New Testament: An Appraisal*. Fortress Press.

Homer
The Odyssey of Homer: A Modern Translation. Translated by R. Lattimore. Harper Torchbooks, 1967.

Hooke, S. H.
1935   "The Myth and Ritual Pattern in Jewish and Christian Apocalyptic." In *The Labyrinth: Further Studies on the Relationship between Myth and Ritual in the Ancient World*, edited by S. H. Hooke, 213–33. Macmillan.

Hooker, Morna
1959   *Jesus and the Servant: The Influence of the Servant Concept of Deutero-Isaiah in the New Testament*. SPCK Press

1972　"On Using the Wrong Tool." *Theology* 75:570–81.

1979　*Pauline Pieces.* Epworth.

1980　*A Preface to Paul.* Oxford University Press.

1990　*From Adam to Christ: Essays on Paul.* Cambridge University Press.

1997　*Beginnings: Keys That Open the Gospels.* Trinity Press International.

Horace

　　　On the Art of Poetry. Translated by H. R. Fairclough. Loeb. Harvard University Press, 1966.

Horbury, William

1998　*Jews and Christians in Contact and Controversy.* T&T Clark.

Horbury, William, and Brian McNeil, eds.

1981　*Suffering and Martyrdom in the New Testament.* Cambridge University Press.

Hornblower, Simon, and Antony Spawforth, eds.

1996　*Oxford Classical Dictionary.* 3rd ed. Oxford University Press.

Horrell, David G.

1999　(ed.) *Social-Scientific Approaches to New Testament Interpretation.* T&T Clark.

2000　*An Introduction to the Study of Paul.* Continuum.

Horsley, G. H. R.

1981　*New Documents Illustrating Early Christianity: A Review of the Greek Inscriptions and Papyri Published in 1976.* Macquarie University Press.

Horsley, Richard A.

1978　"How Can Some of You Say That There Is No Resurrection of the Dead? Spiritual Elitism in Corinth." (I Cor. 15:12)." *Novum Testamentum* 20:203–31.

1985　"Like One of the Prophets of Old: Two Types of Popular Prophets at the Time of Jesus." *Catholic Biblical Quarterly* 47:435–63.

1987　*Jesus and the Spiral of Violence: Popular Jewish Resistance in Roman Palestine.* Fortress Press.

1989　*The Liberation of Christmas: The Infancy Narratives in Social Context.* Crossroad.

1994　"Innovation in Search of Reorientation: New Testament Studies Rediscovering Its Subject Matter." *Journal of the American Academy of Religion* 62:1,127–66.

1995　*Galilee: History, Politics, People.* Trinity Press International.

1996　*Archaeology, History, and Society in Galilee: The Social Context of Jesus and the Rabbis.* Trinity Press International.

1997　(ed.) *Paul and Empire: Religion and Power in Roman Imperial Society.* Trinity Press International.

Horsley, Richard A., and Jonathan A. Draper

1999　*Whoever Hears You Hears Me: Prophets, Performance, and Tradition in Q.* Trinity Press International.

Horsley, Richard A., and John Hanson

1999　*Bandits, Prophets and Messiahs: Popular Movements at the Time of Jesus.* Trinity Press International.

Horst, P. W. Vander

1972　"Can a Book End with Gar? A Note on Mark XVI 8." *Journal of Theological Studies* 23:121–24.

Hoskyns, Sir Edwin

1947　*The Fourth Gospel.* Faber.

Houlden, J. L.

1970　*Paul's Letters from Prison.* Westminster Press.

1973　*The Johannine Epistles.* Harper & Row.

1989　*The Pastoral Epistles: I and II Timothy, Titus.* Trinity Press International.

Howard, George

1979　*Paul: Crisis in Galatia: A Study in Early Christian Theology.* Cambridge University Press.

Howard, Virgil

1977　"Did Jesus Speak about His Own Death?" *Catholic Biblical Quarterly* 39:515–27.

Howe, E. Margaret

1980　"Interpretations of Paul in the Acts of Paul and Thecla." In *Pauline Studies: Essays Presented to Professor F. F. Bruce on His Seventieth Birthday*, edited by D. A. Hagnar, 33–49. Eerdmans.

Howell, David B.

1990　*Matthew's Inclusive Story: A Study in the Narrative Rhetoric of the First Gospel.* Sheffield Academic Press.

Hubbard, Benjamin Jerome

1974　*The Matthean Redaction of a Primitive Apostolic Commissioning: An Exegesis of Matthew 28: 16–20.* Scholars Press.

Hubbard, David A., and Gerald F. Hawthorne

1983　*Philippians.* Word Books.

Hughes, Frank W.

1989　*Early Christian Rhetoric and 2 Thessalonians.* Sheffield Academic Press.

Hughes, Graham

1979　*Hebrews and Hermeneutics: The Epistle to the Hebrews as a New Testament Example of Biblical Interpretation.* Cambridge University Press.

Hultgren, Arland J.

1976   "Paul's Pre-Christian Persecutions of the Church: Their Purpose, Locale and Nature." *Journal of Biblical Literature* 95:97–111.

1979   *Jesus and His Adversaries: The Form and Function of the Conflict Stories in the Synoptic Tradition.* Augsburg Publishing House.

1985   *Paul's Gospel and Mission: The Outlook from His Letter to the Romans.* Fortress Press.

1988   *New Testament Christology: A Critical Assessment and Annotated Bibliography.* Greenwood Press.

Humphrey, Edith M.

1995   *The Ladies and the Cities: Transformation and Apocalyptic Identity in Joseph and Aseneth, 4 Ezra, the Apocalypse, and the Shepherd of Hermas.* Sheffield England: Sheffield Academic Press.

Humphrey, Hugh M.

1981   *A Bibliography for the Gospel of Mark 1954–1980.* Edwin Mellen Press.

Hunt, A. S., and C. C. Edgar, eds.

1932   *Select Papyri: I, Nonliterary Papyri, Private Affairs.* Loeb. Harvard University Press.

Hunter, Archibald M.

1961   *Paul and His Predecessors.* Westminster Press.

1966   *The Gospel According to St. Paul.* Revised ed. Westminster Press.

Hurd, John C.

1966   *Bibliography of New Testament Bibliographies.* Seabury Press.

1983   *The Origin of 1 Corinthians.* Mercer University Press.

1984   " 'The Jesus Whom Paul Preaches' (Acts 19:13)." In *From Jesus to Paul: Studies in Honour of Francis Wright Beare,* edited by P. Richardson and J. C. Hurd, 73–89. Wilfrid Laurier University Press.

Hurtado, Larry W.

1985   "Revelation 4–5 in the Light of Jewish Apocalyptic Analogies: A Distinctively Christian View of Heaven." *Journal for the Study of the New Testament* 25:105–24.

1986   *Mark: The Good News Commentary Series.* Edited by W. Gasque. Harper & Row.

1989   *Mark.* New International Biblical Commentary. Hendrickson Publishers.

1993   "Convert, Apostate or Apostle to the Nations: The 'Conversion' of Paul in Recent Scholarship." *Studies in Religion/Sciences Religieuses* 22:273–84.

Irenaeus

     Against Heresies, in Early Christian Fathers. Translated by C. C. Richardson. Westminster Press, 1970.

Isaac, B.

1984   "Judea after AD 70." *Journal for Jewish Studies* 35:44–50.

Isenberg, Sheldon

1974   "Millenarism in Greco-Roman Palestine." *Religion* 4:26–46.

Iser, Wolfgang

1974   *The Implied Reader: Patterns of Communication in Prose Fiction from Bunyan to Beckett.* Johns Hopkins University Press.

1978   *The Act of Reading: A Theory of Aesthetic Response.* Johns Hopkins University Press.

1989   *Prospecting: From Reader Response to Literary Anthropology.* Johns Hopkins University Press.

Jaffee, Martin S.

1997   *Early Judaism: Religious Worlds of the First Judaic Millennium.* Prentice Hall.

James, Montague Rhodes

1924   *The Apocryphal New Testament: Being the Apocryphal Gospels, Acts, Epistles, and Apocalypses.* Clarendon Press.

Jasper, David

1987   *The New Testament and the Literary Imagination.* Humanities Press.

Jeffers, James S.

1991   *Conflict at Social Order and Hierarchy in Early Christianity.* Fortress Press.

Jenkins, Ian

1986   *Greek and Roman Life.* Harvard University Press.

Jeremias, Joachim

1963   *The Parables of Jesus.* Translated by S. H. Hooke. Scribner.

1964   *Problem of the Historical Jesus.* Fortress Press.

1966   *The Eucharistic Words of Jesus.* Translated by N. Perrin. Scribner.

1969   *Jerusalem in the Time of Jesus: An Investigation into Economic and Social Conditions During the New Testament.* Translated by F. H. Cave and C. H. Cave. Fortress Press.

Jervell, Jacob

1972   *Luke and the People of God: A New Look at Luke-Acts.* Augsburg Publishing House.

1984   *The Unknown Paul: Essays on Luke-Acts and Early Christian History.* Augsburg Publishing House.

Jervell, Jacob, and Wayne A. Meeks
1977 *God's Christ and His People: Studies in Honor of Nils Alstrup Dahl.* Columbia University Press.

Jervis, L. Ann
1991 *The Purpose of Romans: A Comparative Letter Structure Investigation.* Journal for the Study of the New Testament Supplement Series 55. Sheffield Academic Press.

Jeske, Richard
1983 *Revelation for Today: Images of Hope.* Fortress Press.

Jewett, Robert
1979 *Chronology of Paul's Life.* Fortress Press.
1981 *Letter to Pilgrims: A Commentary on the Epistles to the Hebrews.* The Pilgrim Press.
1982a *Christian Tolerance. Paul's Message to the Modern Church.* Westminster Press.
1982b "Romans as an Ambassadorial Letter." *Interpretation* 36:5–20.
1986 *The Thessalonian Correspondence: Pauline Rhetoric and Millenarian Piety.* Fortress Press.
1993 *Saint Paul at the Movies: The Apostle's Dialogue with American Culture.* Westminster John Knox Press.

Johanson, Bruce C.
1987 *To All the Bretheren: A Text-Linguistic and Rhetorical Approach to I Thessalonians.* Vol. 16, *Coniectanea Biblica.* Almqvist & Wiksell International.

Johns, Loren L.
2003 *The Lamb Christology of the Apocalypse of John: An Investigation into Its Origins and Rhetorical Force.* Mohr Siebeck.

Johnson, Alfred M., Jr., ed.
1976 *New Testament and Structuralism: A Collection of Essays.* Pittsburgh: Pickwick Press.

Johnson, Elizabeth
1990 *Consider Jesus: Waves of Renewal in Christology.* Crossroad.

Johnson, Luke Timothy
1977 *The Literary Function of Possesions in Luke-Acts.* Society of Biblical Literature Dissertation Series 39. Scholars Press.
1996 *Letters to Paul's Delegates: 1 Timothy, 2 Timothy, Titus.* Trinity Press International.

Johnson, M.
1969 *The Purpose of the Biblical Genealogies.* Cambridge University Press.

Johnson, Marshall D.
1974 "Reflections on a Wisdom Approach to Matthew's Christology." *Catholic Biblical Quarterly* 36:44–64.

Johnson, Sherman
1987 *Paul the Apostle and His Cities.* Good News Studies 21. Michael Glazier.

Johnson, William G.
1978 "The Pilgrimage Motif in the Book of Hebrews." *Journal of Biblical Literature* 97:239–51.

Jonas, Hans
1992 *The Gnostic Religion: The Message of the Alien God and the Beginnings of Christianity.* 2nd ed. Routledge.

Jones, A. H. M.
1971 *The Cities of the Eastern Roman Provinces.* Clarendon Press.

Jones, Brian W.
1984 *The Emperor Titus.* Croom Helm.

Jordan, James N.
1987 *Western Philosophy: From Antiquity to the Middle Ages.* Macmillan.

Josephus, Flavius
 Antiquities of the Jews. Translated by H. S. J. Thackeray, R. Marcus, A. P. Wikgren, and L. H. Feldman. Loeb. Harvard University Press, 1926.
 Jewish War. Translated by H. Thackeray. Loeb. Harvard University Press, 1997.
 Works. Translated by H. Thackeray. Loeb. Harvard University Press, 1961.
 The Works of Josephus: Complete and Unabridged. New updated ed. Translated by W. Whiston. Hendrickson Publishers, 1987 [1777].

Judge, E. A.
1968 "Paul's Boasting in Relation to Contemporary Professional Practice." *Australian Biblical Review* 16:37–50.
1972 "St. Paul and Classical Society." *Jahrbuch für Antike und Christentum* 15:19–36.
1980 "The Social Identity of the First Christians: A Question of Method in Religious History." *Journal of Religious Histort* 11:201–17.
1982 *Rank and Status in the World of the Caesars and St. Paul.* University of Canterbury Press.
1991 "The Mark of the Beast, Revelation 13:16." *Tyndale Bulletin* 42:158–60.

Judge, E. A., and G. S. R. Thomas
1966 "The Origin of the Church at A New Solution?" *Reformed Theological Review* 25:81–94.

Juel, Donald H.
1977 *Messiah and Temple: The Trial of Jesus in the Gospel of Mark.* Society of Biblical Literature Dissertation Series 31. Scholars Press.
1983 *Luke-Acts: The Promise of History.* John Knox Press.

1994   *A Master of Surprise: Mark Interpreted.* Fortress Press.

Justin, Martyr
    Complete Writings. Translated by T. Falls. Catholic University Press, 1965.

Juvenal
    Satirae. Translated by G. G. Ramsay. Loeb. Harvard University Press, 1990.

Kahle, Paul
1947   *The Cairo Genizah.* Oxford University Press.

Kahler, Martin
1988   *The So-Called Historical Jesus and the Historic Biblical Christ.* Fortress Press.

Kalin, Everett R.
1975   "Early Traditions about Mark's Gospel: Canonical Status Emerges, the Story Grows." *Current Trends in Mission* 2:332–41.
1990   "Re-Examining New Testament Canon History: 1 The Canon of Origen." *Currents in Theology and Mission* 17:274–82.

Kampen, John
1988   *Hasideans and the Origin of Pharisaism: A Study in 1 and 2 Maccabees.* Edited by C. Cox. Society of Biblical Literature Septuagint and Cognate Studies Series 24. Scholars Press.

Kampen, Natalie Boymel, and Bettina Bergmann
1996   *Sexuality in Ancient Art: Near East, Egypt, Greece, and Italy.* Cambridge University Press.

Kang, Sa-Moon
1989   *Divine War in the Old Testament and in the Ancient Near East.* De Gruyter.

Karris, Robert J.
2006   *Eating Your Way through Luke's Gospel.* The Liturgical Press.

Käsemann, Ernst
1964   *Essays on New Testament Themes.* Allenson.
1968   *The Testament of Jesus: A Study of the Gospel of John in the Light of Chapter 17.* Translated by G. Krodel. Fortress Press.
1971   *Perspectives on Paul.* Fortress Press.
1980   *Commentary on Romans.* Eerdmans.
1984   *Wandering People of God: An Investigation of the Letter to the Hebrews.* Augsburg Publishing House.

Kaylor, R. David
1988   *Paul's Covenant Community: Jew and Gentile in Romans.* Westminster John Knox Press.

Kealy, Sean P.
1987   *Apocalypse of John.* Michael Glazier.
1990   *Jesus and Politics.* The Liturgical Press.
1997   *Matthew's Gospel and the History of Biblical Interpretation.* Mellen Biblical Press.
2005   *The Interpretation of the Gospel of Luke.* Edwin Mellen Press.

Keck, Leander E.
1966   "Introduction to Mark's Gospel." *New Testament Studies* 12:352–70.
1970   Lives of Jesus Series. Fortress Press.
1971   *A Future for the Historical Jesus: The Place of Jesus in Preaching and Theology.* Abingdon Press.

Keck, Leander E., and Victor Paul Furnish
1984   *The Pauline Letters.* Abingdon Press.

Keck, Leander E., and J. Louis Martyn
1980   *Studies in Luke-Acts.* Fortress Press.

Kee, Howard Clark
1973a   "Aretalogy and Gospel." *Journal of Biblical Literature* 92:402–22.
1973b   *The Origins of Christianity: Sources and Documents.* Prentice Hall.
1977a   *Community of the New Age: Studies in Mark's Gospel.* Westminster Press.
1977b   *Jesus in History: An Approach to the Study of the Gospels.* Harcourt Brace Jovanovich.
1978   "Mark's Gospel in Recent Research." *Interpretation* 32:353–68.
1980   *Christian Origins in Sociological Perspectives: Methods and Resources.* Westminster Press.
1983   *Miracle in the Early Christian World: A Study in Sociohistorical Method.* Yale University Press.
1984   *The New Testament in Context: Sources and Documents.* Prentice Hall.
1986   *Medicine, Miracle, and Magic in New Testament Times.* Cambridge University Press.
1989   *Knowing the Truth: A Sociological Approach to New Testament Interpretation.* Fortress Press.

Kee, Howard Clark, and Irvin J. Borowsky, eds.
1998   *Removing the Anti-Judaism from the New Testament.* American Interfaith Institute/ World Alliance.

Kee, Howard Clark, and Lynn H. Cohick, eds.
1999   *Evolution of the Synagogue: Problems and Progress.* Trinity Press International.

Keesmaat, Sylvia C.
1999   *Paul and His Story: (Re)Interpreting the Exodus Tradition.* Sheffield Academic Press.

Kelber, Werner H.
1974   *The Kingdom in Mark: A New Place and a New Time.* Fortress Press.
1976   *The Passion in Mark: Studies on Mark 14–16.* Fortress Press.
1979   *Mark's Story of Jesus.* Fortress Press.
1983   *The Oral and the Written Gospel: The Hermeneutics of Speaking and Writing in the Synoptic Tradition, Mark, Paul, and Q.* Fortress Press.

1987   "Biblical Hermeneutics and the Ancient Art of Communication." *Semeia* 39:97–105.

Keller, Catherine
1996   *Apocalypse Now and Then: A Feminist Guide to the End of the World.* Beacon Press.

Kelly, J. N. D.
1969   *The Epistles of Peter and Jude.* Harper & Row.
1987   *Commentary on the Pastoral Epistles.* Harper & Row.

Kennedy, George A.
1972   *The Art of Rhetoric in the Roman World (300 BC–AD 300).* Vol. 2 of *A History of Rhetoric.* Princeton University Press.
1984   *New Testament Interpretation through Rhetorical Criticism.* Studies in Religion. University of North Carolina Press.

Kent, J. P. C.
1978   *Roman Coins.* Photos by Max and Albert Hirmer. Harry N. Abrams.

Kenyon, Fredric G.
1932   *Books and Readers in Ancient Greece and Rome.* Clarendon Press.

Kermode, Frank
1967   *The Sense of an Ending: Studies in the Theory of Fiction.* Oxford University Press.
1979   *The Genesis of Secrecy: On the Interpretation of Narrative.* Harvard University Press.

Kerr, A. J.
1991   "'No Room in the Kataluma'." *Expository Times* 103:15–16.

Kidd, Reggie
1990   *Wealth and Beneficence in the Pastoral Epistles: A "Bourgeois" Form of Early Christianity?* Society of Biblical Literature Dissertation Series 122. Scholars Press.

Kiehl, Erich H.
1988   *Building Your Biblical Studies Library: A Survey of Current Resources.* Concordia Publishing House.

Kierspel, Lars
2006   *The Jews and the World in the Fourth Gospel: Parallelism, Function, and Context.* Mohr Siebeck.

Kiley, Mark
1986   *Colossians as Pseudepigraphy.* Vol. 4 of *The Biblical Seminar.* JSOT/Sheffield Academic Press.

Kilpatrick, G. D.
1946   *The Origins of the Gospel According to St. Matthew.* Clarendon Press.

Kim, Chan-Hie
1975   "The Papyrus Invitation." *Journal of Biblical Literature* 94:391–402.

Kim, Jean K.
1999   "'Uncovering Her Wickedness': An Inter(Con)Textual Reading of Revelation 17 from a Postcolonial Feminist Perspective." *Journal for the Study of the New Testament* 73:61–81.

Kimelman, R.
1981   "Birkat Ha-Minim and the Lack of Evidence for an Anti-Christian Jewish Prayer in Antiquity." In *Jewish and Christian Self-Definition,* edited by E. P. Sanders, 2:226–44. Fortress Press.

King, Karen, ed.
1988   *Images of the Feminine in Gnosticism.* Fortress Press.

Kingsbury, Jack Dean
1969   *The Parables of Jesus in Matthew 13: A Study in Redaction-Criticism.* John Knox Press.
1973   "Structure of Matthew's Gospel and His Concept of Salvation." *Catholic Biblical Quarterly* 35:451–74.
1975   *Matthew: Structure, Christology, Kingdom.* Fortress Press.
1977   *Matthew.* Fortress Press.
1979   "The Figure of Peter in Matthew's Gospel as a Theological Problem." *Journal of Biblical Literature* 98:67–83.
1981   *Jesus Christ in Matthew, Mark, and Luke.* Fortress Press.
1983   *The Christology of Mark's Gospel.* Fortress Press.
1985   "The Figure of Jesus in Matthew's Story. A Rejoinder to David Hill." *Journal for the Study of the New Testament* 25:61–81.
1988   *Matthew as Story.* 2nd ed. Fortress Press.
1989   *Conflict in Mark: Jesus, Authorities, Disciples.* Fortress Press.
1992a   "The Plot of Matthew's Story." *Interpretation* 46:347–56.
1992b   (ed.) "Special Issue on the Gospel of Matthew." *Interpretation* 46, no. 4.
1996   "Special Issue on the Historical Jesus." *Interpretation* 50, no. 4.
1997   (ed.) *Gospel Interpretation: Narrative-Critical and Social-Scientific Approaches.* Trinity Press International.

Kinukawa, Hisako
1994   *Women and Jesus in Mark: A Japanese Feminist Perspective.* Orbis Books.

Kirby, John
1988   "The Rhetorical Situations of Revelation 1–3." *New Testament Studies* 34:197–207.

Kissinger, Warren S.

1975 *The Sermon on the Mount: A History of Interpretation and Bibliography.* Scarecrow Press.

1979 *The Parables of Jesus: A History of Interpretation and Bibliography.* Scarecrow Press.

1985 *The Lives of Jesus: A History and Bibliography.* Garland Publishing.

Kittel, Gerhard, ed.

1964 *Theological Dictionary of the New Testament.* 10 vols. Translated and edited by G. W. Bromiley. Eerdmans.

Klauck, Hans-Josef

2006 *Ancient Letters and the New Testament: A Guide to Context and Exegesis.* Baylor University Press.

Klausner, Joseph

1955 *The Messianic Idea in Israel from the Beginning to the Completion of the Mishnah.* Macmillan.

1961 *From Jesus to Paul.* Beacon Press.

Klijn, A. F. J.

1980 *An Introduction to the New Testament.* Brill.

Klijn, A. F. J., and G. J. Reinink

1973 *Patristic Evidence for Jewish-Christian Sects.* Brill.

Klink, Edward W.

2007 *The Sheep of the Fold: The Audience and Origin of the Gospel of John.* Cambridge University Press.

Kloppenborg, John S.

1986 "The Formation of Q and Antique Instructional Genres." *Journal of Biblical Literature* 105:443–62.

1987 *The Formation of Q: Trajectories in Ancient Wisdom Collections.* Fortress Press.

2000 *Excavating Q: The History and Setting of the Sayings Gospel.* Fortress Press.

Kloppenborg, John S., and John W. Marshall

2005 *Apocalypticism, Anti-Semitism and the Historical Jesus Subtexts in Criticism.* T&T Clark.

Kloppenborg, John S., and Stephen G. Wilson, eds.

1996 *Voluntary Associations in the Greco-Roman World.* Routledge.

Knight, Douglas A.

1985 *Hebrew Bible and Its Modern Interpreters.* Fortress Press.

Knight, Jonathan

1988 *Luke's Gospel.* Routledge.

1999 *Revelation.* Sheffed Academic Press.

Knox, Bernard

1980 *Word and Action: Essays on the Ancient Theater.* Johns Hopkins University Press.

Knox, John

1935 *Philemon among the Letters of Paul.* University of Chicago Press.

1942 *Marcion and the New Testament: An Essay on the Early History of the Canon.* University of Chicago Press.

1987 *Chapters in a Life of Paul.* Revised ed. Mercer University Press.

Koch, Klaus

1969 *The Growth of the Biblical Tradition: The Form-Critical Method.* Scribner.

Koenig, John

1984 *New Testament Hospitality: Partnership with Strangers as Promise and Mission.* Fortress Press.

Koester, Craig R

1991 "R. E. Brown and J. L. Martyn: Johannine Studies in Perspective." *Biblical Theology Bulletin* 21:51–55.

2003 *Symbolism in the Fourth Gospel: Meaning, Mystery, Community.* 2nd ed. Fortress Press.

Koester, Helmut

1971 "Gnomai Diaphoroi: The Origin and Nature of Diversification in the History of Early Christianity." In *Trajectories through Early Christianity*, edited by J. M. Robinson and H. Koester, 114–57 Fortress Press.

1982 *History, Culture, and Religion of the Hellenistic Age: Introduction to the New Testament.* 2 vols. Fortress Press.

1990 *Ancient Christian Gospels: Their History and Development.* Trinity Press International.

1995 (ed.) *Epheros: Metropolis of Asia.* Trinity Press International.

1998 (ed.) *Pergamom—Citadel of the Gods: Archaeological Record, Literary Description, and Religious Development.* Trinity Press International.

2000 *Introduction to the New Testament.* 2 vols. 2nd ed. De Gruyter.

Koester, Helmut, and Holland L. Hendrix

1987 *Archaeological Resources for New Testament Studies: A Collection of Slides on Culture and Religion in Antiquity.* Vol. 1. Trinity Press International.

Kohler, Kaufmann

1970 "The Origin and Composition of the Eighteen Benedictions." In *Contributions to the Scientific Study of the Jewish Liturgy*, edited by J. Petuchowski, 52–90. Ktav.

1973 *Origins of the Synagogue and the Church.* Arno Press.

Koloskie-Ostrow, Ann Olga, and Claire L. Lyons, eds.
1997 *Naked Truths: Women, Sexuality, and Gender in Classical Art and Archaeology.* Routledge.

Kovacs, Judith L., Christopher Rowland, and Rebekah Callow
2004 *Revelation: The Apocalypse of Jesus Christ.* Blackwell.

Kraabel, Alf Thomas
1978 "Paganism and Judaism: The Sardis Evidence." In *Paganisme, Judaisme, Christianisme: Influences et affrontements dans le monde antique,* edited by A. Benoit, M. Philonenko, and C. Vogel, 13–33. Boccard.

Kraeling, C. H.
1951 *John the Baptist.* Scribner.

Kraeling, Emil G.
1962 *Rand McNally Bible Atlas.* Rand McNally.

Kraemer, Ross S.
1988 *Maenads, Martyrs, Matrons, and Monastics: A Sourcebook on Women's Religion in the Greco-Roman World.* Fortress Press.
1992 *Her Share of the Blessings: Women's Religions among Pagans, Jews, and Christian in the Greco-Roman World.* Oxford University Press.

Kraft, Robert, and George W. E. Nickelsburg, eds.
1985 *Early Judaism and Its Modern Interpreters.* Scholars Press.

Krause, Martin
1981 *Gnosis and Gnosticism: Papers Read at the Eighth International Conference on Patristic Studies.* Brill.

Kraybill, J. Nelson
1996 *Imperial Cult and Commerce in John's Apocalypse.* Sheffield Academic Press.

Kreitzer, Larry J.
1987 *Jesus and God in Paul's Eschatology.* Journal for the Study of the New Testament Supplement Series 19. JSOT/Sheffield Academic Press.
1996 *Striking New Images: Studies on Roman Imperial Coinage and the New Testament World.* Sheffield Academic Press.

Krentz, Edgar
1975 *The Historical-Critical Method.* Fortress Press.
1977 "The Egalitarian Church of Matthew." *Currents in Theology and Mission* 4:333–41.

Krentz, Edgar, John Koenig, and Donald H. Juel
1986 *Galatians, Philippians, Philemon, 1 Thessalonians.* Augsburg Publishing House.

Kretzer, David I., and Richard P. Saller
1991 *The Family in Italy from Antiquity to the Present.* Yale University Press.

Krieger, Murray
1964 *A Window to Criticism: Shakespeare's Sonnets and Modern Poetics.* Princeton University Press.

Krodel, Gerhard A.
1989 *Revelation.* Augsburg Publishing House.
1993 *The Deutero-Pauline Letters: Ephesians, Colossians, II Thessalonians, I & II Timothy, Titus.* Revised ed. Fortress Press.

Kuck, David W.
1991 *Judgement and Community Conflict: Paul's Use of Apocalyptic Judgement Language in 1 Corinthians 3:5–4:5.* Brill.

Kugelman, Richard
1980 *James and Jude.* Vol. 19 of *New Testament Message a Biblical-Theological Commentary.* Michael Glazier.

Kümmel, Werner Georg
1966 *Introduction to the New Testament.* Revised ed. Abingdon Press.
1972 *The New Testament: The History of the Investigation of Its Problems.* Abingdon Press.

Kurz, William S.
1989 "The Beloved Disciple and Implied Readers: A Socio-Narratological Approach." *Biblical Theology Bulletin* 19:100–107.
1990 *Farewell Addresses in the New Testament.* Michael Glazier.
1993 *Reading Luke-Acts: Dynamics of Biblical Narrative.* Westminster John Knox Press.

Kustas, George
1976 *Diatribe in Ancient Rhetorical Theory.* University of California Press.

Kyle, Donald G.
1987 *Athletics in Ancient Athens.* Brill.

Kysar, Robert
1975 *The Fourth Evangelist and His Gospel: An Examination of Contemporary Scholarship.* Augsburg Publishing House.
1984 *John's Story of Jesus.* Fortress Press.
1986a *1, 2, 3 John.* Augsburg Publishing House.
1986b *John.* Augsburg Publishing House.
1991 "Johannine Metaphor—Meaning and Function: A Literary Case Study of John 10:1–18." *Semeia* 53:81–111.
2007 *John: The Maverick Gospel.* 3rd ed. John Knox Press.

Labahn, Michael, and L. J. Lietaert Peerbolte
2006 *Wonders Never Cease: The Purpose of Narrating Miracle Stories in the New Testament and Its Religious Environment.* European Studies on Christian Origins. T&T Clark.

Lachs, Samuel Tobias
  1987 *Rabbinic Commentary on the New Testament: The Gospels of Matthew, Mark, and Luke.* Ktav.

Laistner, Max Ludwig Wolfram
  1963 *Greater Roman Historians.* Berkley: University of California Press.

Lambrecht, Jan
  1981 *Once More Astonished: The Parables of Jesus.* Crossroad.

Lampe, Peter
  1999 *From Paul to Valentinus: Christians at Rome in the First Two Centuries.* Fortress Press.

Landels, J. G.
  1981 *Engineering in the Ancient World.* Berkley: University of California Press.

Lane, Michael, ed.
  1970 *Introduction to Structuralism.* Basic Books.

Lane, Thomas J.
  1996 *Luke and the Gentile Mission: Gospel Anticipates Acts.* Peter Lang.

Lane, William
  1974 *The Gospel According to Mark.* Eerdmans.

Langevin, Paul-Emile
  1985 *Bibliographie Biblique, 1930–1983.* 3 vols. Les Presses de l'Université.

Lapide, Pinchas, and Peter Stuhlmacher, eds.
  1984 *Paul: Rabbi and Apostle.* Augsburg Publishing House.

Laqueur, Thomas
  1990 *Making Sex: Body and Gender from the Greeks to Freud.* Harvard University Press.

LaSor, W. S.
  1956 "The Messiahs of Aaron and Israel." *Vetus Testamentum* 6:425–29.

Lategan, Bernard C., and William S. Vorster
  1985 *Text and Reality: Aspects of Reference in Biblical Texts.* Fortress Press.

Lausberg, Heinrich
  1998 *Handbook of Literary Rhetoric: A Foundation for Literary Study.* Brill.

LaVerdiere, E. A., and W. G. Thompson
  1976 "New Testament Communities in Transition: A Study of Matthew and Luke." *Theological Studies* 34:567–97.

Lawrence, Louise Joy
  2003 *An Ethnography of the Gospel of Matthew: A Critical Assessment of the Use of the Honour and Shame Model in New Testament Studies.* Mohr Siebeck.

Laws, Sophie
  1981 *The Epistle of James.* Harper & Row.

  1989 *In the Light of the Lamb: Imagery, Parody, and Theology in the Apocalypse of John.* Michael Glazier.

Layton, Bentley, ed.
  1980 *The Rediscovery of Gnosticism: Proceedings of the Conference at Yale March 1979.* Brill.

  1995 *The Gnostic Scriptures: A New Translation with Annotations and Introductions.* Doubleday.

Leaney, Alfred Robert Clare
  1958 *A Commentary on the Gospel According to St. Luke.* Black.

  1984 *The Jewish and Christian World, 200 BC to AD 200.* Vol. 7 of *Cambridge Commentaries on Writings of the Jewish and Christian World.* Cambridge University Press.

Lefkowitz, Mary R.
  1986 *Women in Greek Myth.* Johns Hopkins University Press.

Lefkowitz, Mary R., and Maureen B. Fant
  1977 *Women in Greece and Rome.* Samuel-Stevens.

  1992 *Women's Life in Greece and A Source Book in Translation.* 2nd ed. Johns Hopkins University Press.

Lehne, Susanne
  1990 *The New Covenant in Hebrews.* Journal for the Study of the New Testament Supplement Series 44. Sheffield Academic Press.

Leivestad, Ragnar
  1987 *Jesus in His Own Perspective: An Examination of His Sayings, Actions, and Eschatological Titles.* Translated by D. E. Aune. Augsburg Publishing House.

Lentz, Tony M.
  1989 *Orality and Literacy in Hellenic Greece.* Southern Illinois University Press.

Leon, Harry J.
  1960 *The Jews of Ancient Rome.* Jewish Publication Society of America.

Lesses, Rebecca Macy
  1998 *Ritual Practices to Gain Power: Angels, Incantations, and Revelation in Early Jewish Mysticism.* Trinity Press International.

Levi-Strauss, Claude
  1967 "The Effectiveness of Symbols." In *Structural Anthropology*, 181–202. Anchor/Doubleday.

Levine, Amy-Jill
  1988 *The Social and Ethnic Dimensions of Matthean Social History: "Go Nowhere among the Gentiles . . ." Matt. 10:5b.* Edwin Mellen Press.

  1991 *"Women Like This" New Perspectives on Jewish Women in the Greco-Roman World.* Society of Biblical Literature Early Judaism and Its Literature 1. Scholars Press.

2006 *The Misunderstood Jew: The Church and the Scandal of the Jewish Jesus.* HarperSanFrancisco.

Levine, Amy-Jill, Dale C. Allison, and John Dominic Crossan, eds.

2006 *The Historical Jesus in Context.* Princeton University Press.

Levine, Amy-Jill, and Marianne Blickenstaff

2003 *A Feminist Companion to John.* 2 vols. Sheffield Academic Press.

2004 *A Feminist Companion to Matthew.* The Pilgrim Press.

Levine, Lee I.

1989 *The Rabbinic Class of Roman Palestine.* Jewish Theological Seminary.

1996 "The Nature and Origin of the Palestinian Synagogue Reconsidered." *Journal of Biblical Literature* 115:425–48.

Levinskaya, Irina

1996 *The Book of Acts in Its Diaspora Setting.* Edited by B. W. Winter. Vol. 5 of *Book of Acts in Its First Century Setting.* Eerdmans.

Lewis, C. S.

1958 *Reflections on the Psalms.* Harcourt Brace and World.

1967 "Modern Theology and Biblical Criticism." In *Christian Reflections*, edited by Walter Hooper. Eerdmans.

Lewis, Jack

1991 *The English Bible from KJV to NIV: A History and Evaluation.* 2nd ed. Baker Book House.

Lewis, J. P.

1964 "What Do We Mean by Jabneh?" *Journal of the Bible and Religion* 32:124–32.

Lewis, L. A.

1991 "An African American Appraisal of the Philemon-Paul-Onesimus Triangle." In *Stony the Road We Trod*, edited by C. H. Felder, 232–46. Fortress Press.

Lewis, Naphtali

1989 *The Documents of the Bar Kochba Period in the Cave of Letters: Greek Papyri.* Israel Exploration Society.

1994 *Life in Egypt under Roman Rule:* Clarendon Press.

Licht, J.

1978 *Storytelling in the Bible.* Magnes Press.

Liebeschutetz, John H. W. G.

1973 *Antioch: City and Imperial Administration in the Late Roman Empire.* Clarendon Press.

Lierman, John

2006 *Challenging Perspectives on the Gospel of John.* Mohr Siebeck.

Lieu, Judith

1985 "'Grace to You and Peace': The Apostolic Greeting." *Bulletin of the John Rylands University Library* 66:172–73.

1986 *The Second and Third Epistles of John: History and Background.* T&T Clark.

1991 *The Theology of the Johannine Epistles.* Cambridge University Press.

Lieu, Judith M., John North, and Tessa Rajak, eds.

1992 *The Jews among Pagans and Christians in the Roman Empire.* Routledge.

Lightfoot, J. B.

1959 *Saint Paul's Epistles to the Colossians and to Philemon.* Zondervan.

Lightfoot, Robert Henry

1939 *Locality and Doctrine in the Gospels.* Harper & Row.

1950 *The Gospel Message of St. Mark.* Oxford University Press.

1956 *St. John's Gospel: A Commentary.* Oxford University Press.

Lightstone, Jack N.

1984 *The Commerce of the Sacred: Mediation of the Divine among Jews in the Greco-Roman Diaspora.* Brown Judaic Studies 59. Scholars Press.

Lincoln, Andrew T.

1990 *Ephesians.* Word Books.

Lindars, Barnabas

1961 *New Testament Apologetic: The Doctrinal Significance of the Old Testament Quotations.* SCM Press.

1981 "John and the Synoptics: A Test Case." *New Testament Studies* 27:287–94.

1984 *Jesus Son of Man: A Fresh Examination of the Son of Man Sayings in the Gospels.* Eerdmans.

1985 "The Sound of the Trumpet: Paul and Eschatology." *Bulletin of the John Rylands University Library* 67:766–82.

1990 *John.* JSOT/Sheffield Academic Press.

1991 *The Theology of the Letter to the Hebrews.* Cambridge University Press.

Lindblom, Johannes

1972 *Prophecy in Ancient Israel.* Fortress Press.

Lindsell, Harold

1976 *The Battle for the Bible.* Zondervan.

Linton, Gregory

1991 "Reading the Apocalypse as Apocalypse." In *Society of Biblical Literature 1991 Seminar Papers*, 161–86. Scholars Press.

Lipman, Eugene J.

1970 *The Mishnah: Oral Teachings of Judaism.* Schocken Books.

Lischer, Richard
1984 "The Limits of Story." *Interpretation* 38:26–38.

Little, Joyce A.
1984 "Paul's Use of Analogy: A Structural Analysis of Romans." *Catholic Biblical Quarterly* 46:82–90.

Lofland, John
1966 *Doomsday Cult: A Study of Conversion, Proselytization, and Maintenance of Faith.* Prentice Hall.

Logan, A. H. B.
2006 *The Gnostics: Identifying an Early Christian Cult.* T&T Clark.

Logan, A. H. B., and A. J. M. Wedderburn
1983 *The New Testament and Gnosis: Essays in Honour of Robert McL. Wilson.* T&T Clark.

Lohfink, Gerhard
1979 *The Bible: Now I Get It! A Form-Criticism Handbook.* Translated by Daniel Coogan. Doubleday.

Lohr, Charles
1961 "Oral Techniques in the Gospel of Matthew." *Catholic Biblical Quarterly* 23:403–35.

Lohse, Eduard
1971 *Colossians and Philemon: A Commentary on the Epistles to the Colossians and to Philemon.* Edited by H. Koester and translated by W. R. Poehlmann and R. J. Karris. Fortress Press.
1976 *The New Testament Environment.* Abingdon Press.
1981 *The Formation of the New Testament.* Abingdon Press.

Long, A. A.
1974 *Hellenistic Philosophy: Stoics, Epicureans, Skeptics.* Scribner.

Longenecker, Richard N.
1981 *The Christology of Early Jewish Christianity.* Baker Book House.

Longman, Tremper
1987 *Literary Approaches to Biblical Interpretation.* Zondervan.

Longstaff, Thomas R. W.
1980 "Crisis and Christology: The Theology of the Gospel of Mark." *Perkins Journal* 33:28–40.
1981 "The Women at the Tomb: Matthew 28:1 Re-examined." *New Testament Studies* 27:277–82.

Longstaff, Thomas R. W., and Page A. Thomas
1988 *The Synoptic Problem: A Bibliography 1716–1988.* Mercer University Press.

Love, Stuart L.
1993 "The Household: A Major Social Component for Gender Analysis in the Gospel of Matthew." *Biblical Theology Bulletin* 23:21–31.

Lucian
Works. Translated by A. M. Harmon. Loeb. Harvard University Press, 1969.

Luck, George
1985 *Arcana Mundi: Magic and the Occult in the Greek and Roman Worlds: A Collection of Ancient Texts.* Johns Hopkins University Press.

Lucretius
On the Nature of Things. Translated by W. H. D. Rouse and M. F. Smith. Loeb. Harvard University Press, 1992.

Lüdemann, Gerd
1984 *Paul, Apostle to the Gentiles: Studies in Chronology.* Fortress Press.
1989 *Opposition to Paul in Jewish Christianity.* Fortress Press.
1994 *The Resurrection of Jesus: History, Experience, Theology.* Fortress Press.
1996 *Heretics: The Other Side of Early Christianity.* Westminster John Knox Press.
2001 *Jesus after Two Thousand Years: What He Really Said and Did.* Prometheus Books.

Lull, David J.
1980 *The Spirit in Galatia: Paul's Interpretation of Pneuma as Divine Power.* Scholars Press.
1986 "The Law Was Our Pedagogue: A Study in Galatians 3:19–25." *Journal of Biblical Literature* 105:481–98.

Lund, Nils
1931 "The Influence of Chiasmus upon the Structure of the Gospels." *Australian Theological Review* 13:27–48.

Luther, Martin
1961 *Lectures on Romans.* Westminster Press.

Luz, Ulrich
2007 *Matthew 1–7: A Commentary.* Revised ed. Augsburg Publishing House.

Lyall, Francis
1984 *Slaves, Citizens, Sons: Legal Metaphors in the Epistles.* Zondervan.

Lyons, George
1985 *Pauline Autobiography: Toward a New Understanding.* Society of Biblical Literature Dissertation Series 73. Scholars Press.

MacDonald, Dennis Ronald, ed.
1982 *The Apocryphal Acts of Apostles. Semeia* 38. Scholars Press.
1983 *The Legend and the Apostle: The Battle for Paul in Story and Canon.* Westminster Press.

1986 "From Audita to Legenda: Oral and Written Miracle Stories." *Forum* 2:15–26.

1987 *There Is No Male and Female: The Fate of a Dominical Saying in Paul and Gnosticism.* Harvard Dissertations in Religion 20 Fortress Press.

MacDonald, J. J.
1969 "Was Romans XVI a Separate Letter?" *New Testament Studies* 16:369–72.

MacDonald, Margaret Y.
1988 *The Pauline Churches: A Socio-Historical Study of Institutionalization in the Pauline and Deutero-Pauline Writings.* Society for New Testament Studies Monograph Series 60. Cambridge University Press.

1996 *Early Christian Women and Pagan Opinion: The Power of the Hysterical Woman.* Cambridge University Press.

MacIver, Robert M.
1971 "The Family as Government in Minature." In *The Imprint of Roman Institutions: Western Man: An Interdisciplinary Introduction to the History of Western Civilization*, edited by D. W. Savage. Holt, Rinehart & Winston.

Mack, Burton L.
1987 *A Myth of Innocence: Mark and Christian Origins.* Fortress Press.

1990 *Rhetoric and the New Testament.* Fortress Press.

Mack, Burton L., and Vernon K. Robbins
1990 *Patterns of Persuasion in the Gospels.* Polebridge Press.

Mackay, Ian D.
2004 *John's Relationship with Mark: An Analysis of John 6 in the Light of Mark 6–8.* Mohr Siebeck.

MacKenzie, Robert K.
1997 *The Author of the Apocalypse: A Review of the Prevailing Hypothesis of Jewish-Christian Authorship.* Edwin Mellen Press.

MacMullen, Ramsay
1966 *Enemies of the Roman Order: Treason, Unrest, and Alienation in the Empire.* Harvard University Press.

1971 "Social History in Astrology." *Ancient Society* 2:105–16.

1974 *Roman Social Relations, 50 BC to AD 284.* Yale University Press.

1980 "Women in Public in the Roman Empire." *Historia* 29:208–18.

1981 *Paganism in the Roman Empire.* Yale University Press.

1985 "Conversion: A Historian's View." *The Second Century* 5:67–81.

1986 "Judicial Savagery in the Roman Empire." *Chiron* 16:147–66.

MacMullen, Ramsay, and Eugene N. Lane
1992 *Paganism and Christianity, 100–425 CE: A Sourcebook.* Fortress Press.

MacRae, George W., and Eldon Jay Epp
1987 *The New Testament and Its Modern Interpreters: SBL the Bible and Its Modern Interpreters.* Fortress Press.

Magness, J. Lee
1986 *Sense and Absence: Structure and Suspension in the Ending of Mark's Gospel. Semeia Studies.* Scholars Press.

Maier, Harry O.
1991 *The Social Setting of the Ministry as Reflected in the Writings of Hermas, Clement and Ignatius.* Wilfrid Laurier University Press.

2002 *Apocalypse Recalled: The Book of Revelation after Christendom.* Fortress Press.

Malbon, Elizabeth Struthers
1980 "Mythic Structure and Meaning in Mark: Elements of a Levi-Straussian Analysis." *Semeia* 16:97–132.

1983 "Fallible Followers: Women and Men in the Gospel of Mark." *Semeia* 28:29–48.

1984 "The Jesus of Mark and the Sea of Galilee." *Journal of Biblical Literature* 103:363–77.

1986 "Disciples/Crowds/Whoever: Markan Characters and Readers." *Novum Testamentum* 28:104–30.

1989 "The Jewish Leaders in the Gospel of Mark: A Literary Study of Characterization." *Journal of Biblical Literature* 108:259–81.

1991a *Narrative Space and Mythic Meaning in Mark.* Sheffield Academic Press.

1991b "The Poor Widow in Mark and Her Poor Rich Readers." *Catholic Biblical Quarterly* 53:589–604.

1993 "Text and Contexts: Interpreting the Disciples in Mark." *Semeia* 62:81–102.

2000 *In the Company of Jesus Characters in Mark's Gospel.* Westminster John Knox Press.

2002 *Hearing Mark a Listener's Guide.* Trinity Press International.

Malbon, Elizabeth Struthers, and Adela Berlin, eds.
1993 *Characterization in Biblical Literature. Semeia 63.* Scholars Press.

Malbon, Elizabeth Struthers, and Sharyn Dowd
2006 "The Significance of Jesus' Death in Mark: Narrative Context and Authorial Audience." In *The Trial and Death of Jesus: Essays on the Passion Narrative in Mark*, edited by G. v. Oyen and T. Shepherd, 1–32. Peeters.

Malherbe, Abraham J.

1968   "The Beasts at Ephesus." *Journal of Biblical Literature* 87:71–80.

1970   "Gentle as a Nurse': The Cynic Background of I Thess II." *Novum Testamentum* 12:203–17.

1977   "Ancient Epistolary Theorists." *Ohio Journal of Religion Studies* 5:3–73.

1983a "Exhortation in the First Thessalonians." *Novum Testamentum* 25:238–56.

1983b *Social Aspects of Early Christianity.* 2nd ed. Fortress Press.

1984   *The Cynic Epistles: A Study Edition.* Scholars Press.

1986   *Moral Exhortation, a Greco-Roman Sourcebook.* Edited by W. Meeks. Library of Early Christianity 4. Westminster Press.

1987   *Paul and the Thessalonians: The Philosophic Tradition of Pastoral Care.* Fortress Press.

1989   *Paul and the Popular Philosophers.* Fortress Press.

Malina, Bruce J.

1973   "Jewish Christianity: A Select Bibliography." *Australian Jouurnal of Biblial Archaeology* 5:60–65.

1981   *The New Testament World: Insights from Cultural Anthropology.* John Knox Press.

1982   "Social Sciences and Biblical Interpretation." *Interpretation* 37:229–42.

1984   "Jesus as Charismatic Leader?" *Biblical Theology Bulletin* 14:55–62.

1986a *Christian Origins and Cultural Anthropology: Practical Models for Biblical Interpretation.* John Knox Press.

1986b "Religion in the World of Paul: A Preliminary Sketch." *Biblical Theology Bulletin* 16:92–101.

1987   "Wealth and Poverty in the New Testament and Its World." *Interpretation* 41:354–67.

1988   "Patron and Client: The Analogy Behind Synoptic Theology." *Forum* 4:2–32.

1989a "Christ and Time: Swiss or Mediterranean?" *Catholic Biblical Quarterly* 51:1–31.

1989b "Dealing with Biblical (Mediterranean) Characters: A Guide for U.S. Consumers." *Biblical Theology Bulletin* 19:127–41.

1992   "Is There a Circum-Mediterranean Person? Looking for Stereotypes." *Biblical Theology Bulletin* 22:66–87.

1993   *Windows on the World of Jesus: Time Travel to Ancient Judea.* Westminster John Knox Press.

1995   *On the Genre and Message of Revelation: Star Visions and Sky Journeys.* Hendrickson Publishers.

1996   "Rhetorical Criticism and Social-Scientific Criticism: Why Won't Romanticism Leave Us Alone?" In *Rhetoric, Scripture and Theology: Essays from the 1994 Pretoria Conference*, edited by S. E. Porter and T. H. Olbricht, 72–101. Sheffield Academic Press.

Malina, Bruce J., and Jerome H. Neyrey

1988   *Calling Jesus Names: The Social Value of Labels in Matthew.* Polebridge Press.

Malina, Bruce J., and Richard L. Rohrbaugh

1992   *Social Science Commentary on the Synoptic Gospels.* Fortress Press.

1998   *Social Science Commentary on the Gospel of John.* Fortress Press.

Maly, Eugene H.

1979   *Romans.* Michael Glazier.

Manson, T. W.

1966   *The Servant Messiah.* Cambridge University Press.

Manson, William

1930   *The Gospel of Luke.* Harper.

Maranda, Pierre, and E. K. Maranda

1971   *Structural Analysis of Oral Tradition.* University of Pennsylvania Press.

Marcus, Joel

1988   "The Gates of Hades and the Keys of the Kingdom." *Catholic Biblical Quarterly* 50:443–55.

1992   "The Jewish War and the Sitz im Leben of Mark." *Journal of Biblical Literature* 111:441–62.

2000   *Mark 1–8: A New Translation with Introduction and Commentary.* Doubleday.

Marguerat, Daniel

1999   "The Enigma of the Silent Closing of Acts (28:16–31)." In *Jesus and the Heritage of Israel*, 284–304. Trinity Press International.

Marsh, Clive, and Steve Moyise

2005   *Jesus and the Gospels.* T&T Clark.

Marshall, I. Howard

1977a *I Believe in the Historical Jesus.* Eerdmans.

1977b *New Testament Interpretation: Essays on Principles and Methods.* Eerdmans.

1978a *Acts and the History of Earliest Christianity.* Fortress Press.

1978b *The Epistles of John.* Edited by F. F. Bruce. Eerdmans.

1978c *The Gospel of Luke.* Eerdmans.

1982   *The Acts of the Apostles: An Introduction and Commentary.* Eerdmans.

1983   *1 and 2 Thessalonians: Based on the Revised Standard Version.* Eerdmans.

Marshall, John W.

2001   *Parables of War: Reading John's Jewish Apocalypse.* Wilfrid Laurier University Press.

Marshall, Peter
1987   *Enmity in Corinth: Social Conventions in Paul's Relations with the Corinthians*. J. C. B. Mohr.

Martin, Dale B.
1990   *Slavery as Salvation: The Metaphor of Slavery in Pauline Christianity*. Yale University Press.
1995   *The Corinthian Body*. Yale University Press.

Martin, Francis
1988   *Narrative Parallels to the New Testament*. Resources for Biblical Stdies 22. Scholars Press.
1991   "Feminist Hermeneutics: An Overview. Part One." *Communio: International Catholic Review* 18:144–63.

Martin, Luther H.
1983   "Why Cecropian Minerva? Hellenistic Religious Syncretism as System." *Numen* 30:131–45.
1987   *Hellenistic Religions: An Introduction*. Oxford University Press.

Martin, R. A., and J. H. Elliott
1982   *James, 1–2 Peter/Jude*. Augsburg Publishing House.

Martin, Ralph P.
1973a   *Colossians: The Church's Lord and the Christian Liberty: An Expository Commentary with Present-Day Application*. Zondervan.
1973b   *Mark: Evangelist and Theologian*. Zondervan.
1975   *The Four Gospels*. Eerdmans.
1986   *Second Corinthians*. Word Books.
1987   *The Epistle of Paul to the Philippians: An Introduction and Commentary*. InterVarsity Press.
1991   *Ephesians, Colossians, and Philemon*. John Knox Press.

Martin, Troy
1992   *Metaphor and Composition in 1 Peter*. Scholars Press.

Martyn, J. Louis
1985   "Apocalyptic Antinomies in Paul's Letter to the Galatians." *New Testament Studies* 31:410–24.
1998   *Galatians a New Translation with Introduction and Commentary*. Doubleday.
2003   *History and Theology in the Fourth Gospel*. 3rd ed. Westminster John Knox Press.

Marwick, Lawrence
1979   *Biblical and Judaic Acronyms*. Ktav.

Marxsen, Willi
1969   *Mark the Evangelist: Studies on the Redaction History of the Gospel*. Abingdon Press.

Mason, Steven Neil
1991   *Flavius Josephus on the Pharisees: A Composition-Critical Study*. Brill.

Matera, Frank J.
1987a   "The Plot of Matthew's Gospel." *Catholic Biblical Quarterly* 49:233–53.
1987b   *What Are They Saying about Mark? The Latest Research on the First Gospel*. Paulist Press.
1992   *Galatians*. The Liturgical Press.
1993   "'He Saved Others; He Cannot Save Himself': A Literary-Critical Perspective on the Markan Miracles." *Interpretation* 47:15–26.

Matthews, Victor H., Don C. Benjamin, and Claudia Camp, eds.
1996   *Honor and Shame in the World of the Bible*. Scholars Press.

Mattill, A. J., and Mary Bedford Mattill
1966   *A Classified Bibliography of Literature on the Acts of the Apostles*. Brill.

Maynard-Reid, Pedrito U.
1985   *Poverty and Wealth in James*. Orbis Books.

Mayo, Philip L.
2006   *"Those Who Call Themselves Jews": The Church and Judaism in the Apocalypse of John*. Pickwick Publications.

Mays, James L.
1974   "Special Issue on Structuralism." *Interpretation* 28, no. 2.
1978   "Special Issue on Mark." *Interpretation* 32, no. 4.
1981   *Interpreting the Gospels*. Fortress Press.

Mays, James L., et al.
1988   *Harper's Bible Commentary*. Harper & Row.

McArthur, Harvey K.
1964   "Basic Issues: A Survey of Recent Gospel Research." *Interpretation* 18:39–55.
1971   "Burden of Proof in Historical Jesus Research." *Expository Times* 82:116–19.

McCane, Byron R.
1990   "Let the Dead Bury Their Dead: Secondary Burial and Matthew 8:21–22." *Harvard Theological Review* 83:31–43.

McCasland, Vernon S.
1962   "Travel and Communications in the NT." *The Interpreter's Dictionary of the Bible: An Illustrated Encyclopedia*, edited by G. Buttrick, 4:690–93. Abingdon Press.

McDonald, Hugh D.
1980   *Commentary on Colossians and Philemon*. Word Books.

McDonald, Lee Martin
2007   *The Biblical Canon: Its Origin, Transmission, and Authority*. 3rd ed. Hendrickson Publishers.

McDonald, Lee Martin, and James A. Sanders
2002   *The Canon Debate*. Hendrickson Publishers.

McEleney, Neil J.
1973   "Conversion, Circumcision and the Law."
       New Testament Studies 20:319–41.
1990   "Peter's Denials—How Many? To Whom?"
       Catholic Biblical Quarterly 52:467–72.

McIntire, C. T.
1977   *God, History, and Historians. An Anthol-
       ogy of Modern Christian Views of History.*
       Oxford University Press.

McKay, A. G.
1975   *Houses, Villas and Palaces in the Roman
       World Aspects of Greek and Roman Life.*
       Cornell University Press.

McKenzie, John L.
1968   *Second Isaiah.* Doubleday.
1976   *Light on the Gospels: A Reader's Guide.*
       Thomas More Press.

McKenzie, Steven L., and Stephen R. Haynes
1993   *To Each Its Own Meaning: An Introduction
       to Biblical Criticisms and Their Application.*
       Westminster John Knox Press.

McKim, Donald K., ed.
1998   *Historical Handbook of Major Biblical Inter-
       preters.* InterVarsity Press.

McKnight, Edgar V.
1969   *What Is Form Criticism?* Fortress Press.
1985   *The Bible and the Reader: An Introduction to
       Literary Criticism.* Fortress Press.

McKnight, Scot
1991   *A Light to the Nations: Jewish Missionary
       Activity in the Second Temple Period.* For-
       tress Press.

McKnight, Scot, and Matthew C. Williams
2000   *The Synoptic Gospels: An Annotated Bibliog-
       raphy.* Baker Books.

McNamara, Martin
1983   *Palestinian Judaism and the New Testament.*
       Michael Glazier.

McNeile, Alan Hugh
1961   *The Gospel According to St. Matthew.*
       Macmillan.

McVann, Mark
1991   "Baptism, Miracles, and Boundary Jumping in
       Mark." *Biblical Theology Bulletin* 21:151–57.

McWhirter, Jocelyn
2006   *Bridegroom Messiah and the People of God.*
       Cambridge University Press.

Meade, David G.
1986   *Pseudonymity and Canon: An Investiga-
       tion into the Relationship of Authorship
       and Authority in Jewish and Early Christian
       Tradition.* Eerdmans.

Mealand, David L.
1980   *Poverty and Expectation in the Gospels.*
       SPCK Press.

Meeks, Wayne A.
1972a "The Man from Heaven in Johannine Sec-
       tarianism." *Journal of Biblical Literature*
       91:44–72.
1972b *The Writings of St. Paul.* Norton.
1983   *The First Urban Christians: The Social World
       of the Apostle Paul.* Yale University Press.
1986   *The Moral World of the First Christians.*
       Westminster Press.

Meeks, Wayne A., and Robert Wilken
1978   *Jews and Christians in Antioch in the First
       Four Centuries of the Common Era.* Society
       of Biblical Literature Sources for Biblical
       Study 13. Scholars Press.

Meier, John P.
1976   *Law and History in Matthew's Gospel: A Re-
       dactional Study of Matthew 5:17–48.* Biblical
       Institute Press.
1977   "Nations or Gentiles in Matthew 28:19?"
       Catholic Biblical Quarterly 39:94–102.
1979   *The Vision of Matthew: Christ, Church, and
       Morality in the First Gospel.* Paulist Press.
1990   "Jesus in Josephus: A Modest Proposal."
       Catholic Biblical Quarterly 52:76–103.
1991–2001 *A Marginal Jew: Rethinking the Histori-
       cal Jesus.* 3 vols. Doubleday.

Menken, M. J. J.
2004   *Matthew's Bible: The Old Testament Text of
       the Evangelist.* Peeters.

Mercer, Calvin
1990   "Contemporary Language and New Transla-
       tions of the Bible: The Impact of Feminism."
       *Religion and Public Education (National
       Council on Religion in Public Education)*
       17:89–98.

Merenlahti, Petri
2002   *Poetics for the Gospels? Rethinking Narrtive
       Criticism.* Continuum.

Merkley, P.
1970   "New Quests for Old: One Historian's Obser-
       vation on a Bad Bargain." *Canadian Journal
       of Theology* 16:203–18.

Metzger, Bruce M.
1952   "On the Translation of John 1:1." *Expository
       Times* 63:125–26.
1960   *Index to Periodical Literature on the Apostle
       Paul.* Eerdmans.
1971   *A Textual Commentary on the Greek New
       Testament.* United Bible Society.
1972   "Literary Forgeries and Canonical Pseude-
       pigrapha." *Journal of Biblical Literature*
       91:3–24.
1987   *The Canon of the New Testament: Its Origin,
       Development, and Significance.* Clarendon
       Press.

1992a "Recent Translations: A Survey and Evaluation." *Southwestern Journal of Theology* 34:5–12.

1992b *The Text of the New Testament: Its Transmission, Corruption and Restoration*. 3rd ed. Oxford University Press.

1993 *Breaking the Code: Understanding the Book of Revelation*. Abingdon Press.

2001 *The Bible in Translation Ancient and English Versions*. Baker Academic.

Meye, R. P.

1969 "Mark 16:8: The Ending of Mark's Gospel." *Biblical Research* 14:33–43.

Meyer, Ben F.

1979 *The Aims of Jesus*. SCM Press.

Meyer, Marvin W.

1986 "The Light and Voice on the Damascus Road." *Forum* 2:27–35.

1987 *The Ancient Mysteries: A Sourcebook*. Harper & Row.

Meyer, Marvin W., and Paul Allan Mirecki, eds.

1995 *Ancient Magic and Ritual Power*. Brill.

Michaels, J. Ramsey

1986 *John*. Hagerstown: Harper & Row.

1989 *I Peter*. Word Biblical Themes. Word Books.

1991 "Revelation 1:19 and the Narrative Voices of the Apocalypse." *New Testament Studies* 37:604–20.

1992 *Interpreting the Book of Revelation*. Baker Book House.

Millard, Alan R.

2000 *Reading and Writing in the Time of Jesus*. New York University Press.

Miller, Donald G., and Y. Hadidian

1971 *Jesus and Man's Hope*. 2 vols. Pittsburgh Theological Seminary.

Miller, E. L.

1983 "The Logic of the Logos Hymns: A New View." *New Testament Studies* 29:552–61.

Miller, James D.

1997 *The Pastoral Letters as Composite Documents*. Cambridge University Press.

Miller, Patricia Cox

1998 *Dreams in Late Antiquity: Studies in the Imagination of a Culture*. Princeton University Press.

Miller, Robert J., ed.

1994 *The Complete Gospels: Annotated Scholars Version*. Revised ed. HarperSanFrancisco.

Miller, Stephen G.

1991 *Arete: Greek Sports from Ancient Sources*. University of California Press.

Mills, Watson A.

1986 *A Bibliography of Periodical Literature on the Acts of the Apostles 1962–1984*. Brill.

1988 *The Holy Spirit: A Bibliography*. Hendrickson Publishers.

Minear, Paul S.

1974 "The Disciples and the Crowds in the Gospel of Matthew." In *Gospel Studies in Honor of Sherman Elbridge Johnson*, edited by M. H. Sheperd Jr. and E. C. Hobbs, 28–44. Anglican Theological Review.

1981 *New Testament Apocalyptic*. Abingdon Press.

1982 *Matthew: The Teacher's Gospel*. The Pilgrim Press.

1983 "The Original Function of John 21." *Journal of Biblical Literature* 102:85–98.

Mink, L. O.

1969 "History and Fiction as Modes of Comprehension." *New Literary History* 1:541–58.

Minor, Mark

1992 *Literary-Critical Approaches to the Bible: An Annotated Bibliography*. Locust Hill Press.

Mitchell, Margaret M.

1991 *Paul and the Rhetoric of Reconciliation: An Exegetical Investigation of the Language and Composition of I Corinthians*. J. C. B. Mohr.

Mitton, C. L.

1976 *Ephesians*. Oliphants.

Moessner, David P.

1982 "Jesus and the Wilderness Generation: The Death of the Prophet Like Moses According to Luke." In *Society of Biblical Literature 1982 Seminar Papers*, 319–40. Scholars Press.

1983a "Luke 9:1–50: Luke's Preview of the Journey of the Prophet Like Moses of Deuteronomy." *Journal of Biblical Literature* 102:575–605.

1983b "Paul and the Pattern of the Prophet Like Moses in Acts." In *Society of Biblical Literature 1983 Seminar Papers*, 203–12. Scholars Press.

1989 *Lord of the Banquet: The Literary and Theological Significance of the Lukan Travel Narrative*. Fortress Press.

1999 (ed.) *Jesus and the Heritage of Israel: Luke's Narrative Claim upon Israel's Legacy*. Trinity Press International.

Mohrlang, Roger

1984 *Matthew and Paul: A Comparison of Ethical Perspectives*. Cambridge University Press.

Moltmann-Wendell, Elizabeth

1982 *The Women around Jesus*. Translated by J. Bowden. Crossroad.

Momigliano, Arnaldo

1971 *The Development of Greek Biography: Four Lectures*. Harvard University Press.

1977 *Essays in Ancient and Modern Historiography*. Wesleyan University Press.

Montague, George T.
1989   *Companion God: A Cross–Cultural Commentary on the Gospel of Matthew.* Paulist Press.

Montefiore, Claude G.
1927   *The Synoptic Gospels.* 2 vols. 2nd ed. Ktav.

Montefiore, Claude G., and H. Loewe
1974   *A Rabbinic Anthology: Selected and Arranged with Comments and Introductions.* Schocken Books.

Moore, G. F.
1927   *Judaism in the First Centuries of the Christian Era: The Age of the Tannaim.* 3 vols. Harvard University Press.

Moore, M. S.
1982   "Jesus Christ, Superstar (Rev. 22:16b)." *Novum Testamentum* 24:82–91.

Moore, Stephen D.
1989   *Literary Criticism and the Gospels: The Theoretical Challenge.* Yale University Press.
1992   *Mark and Luke in Poststructuralist Perspectives: Jesus Begins to Write.* Yale University Press.

Mor, M., and U. Rappaport
1982   *Bibliography of Works on Jewish History in the Hellenistic and Roman Periods, 1976–1980.* Historical Society of Israel.

Morgan, Robert
1974   "New Testament in Religious Studies." *Religious Studies* 10:385–406.

Morgan, Robert, and John Barton
1988   *Biblical Interpretation.* Oxford University Press.

Morris, Leon
1959   *The First and Second Epistles to the Thessalonians; the English Text with Introduction, Exposition, and Notes.* Eerdmans.
1989   *1, 2 Thessalonians.* Word Publishing.

Mounce, Robert H.
1977   *The Book of Revelation.* Eerdmans.
1986   *Matthew.* Harper & Row.

Mowinckel, Sigmund, ed.
1956   *He That Cometh.* Blackwell.

Moxnes, Halvor
1988   *The Economy of the Kingdom: Social Conflict and Economic Relations in Luke's Gospel.* Fortress Press.
1997a   (ed.) *Constructing Early Christian Families: Family as Social Reality and Metaphor.* Routledge.
1997b   "The Social Context of Luke's Community." In *Gospel Interpretation*, edited by J. D. Kingsbury, 166–80. Trinity Press International.

1999   "The Historical Jesus: From Master Narrative to Cultural Context." *Biblical Theology Bulletin* 28:135–49.

Moyise, Steve
1995   *The Old Testament in the Book of Revelation.* Sheffield Academic Press.
2001   (ed.) *Studies in the Book of Revelation.* T&T Clark.

Muilenburg, James
1969   "Form Criticism and Beyond." *Journal of Biblical Literature* 88:1–18.

Mullins, Terence Y.
1980   "Topos as a NT Form." *Journal of Biblical Literature* 99:541–57.

Munck, Johannes
1959   *Paul and the Salvation of Mankind.* John Knox Press.
1967   *The Acts of the Apostles.* Anchor Bible. Doubleday.

Munro, Winsome
1982   "Women Disciples in Mark." *Catholic Biblical Quarterly* 44:225–41.
1983   *Authority in Paul and Peter: The Identification of a Pastoral Stratum in the Pauline Corpus.* Cambridge University Press.

Murphy, Frederick J.
1998   *Fallen Is Babylon: The Revelation of John.* Trinity Press International.

Murphy-O'Connor, Jerome
1975   "The Structure of Matthew XIV–XVII." *Revue Biblique* 82:360–84.
1978   "Corinthian Slogans in 1 Cor 6:12–20." *Catholic Biblical Quarterly* 40:391–96.
1983   *St. Paul's Corinth: Texts and Archaeology.* Good News Studies 6. Michael Glazier.
1988   "I Corinthians 11:2–16 Once Again." *Catholic Biblical Quarterly* 50:265–74.
1991   *The Theology of the Second Letter to the Corinthians.* Cambridge University Press.
1995   *Paul the Letter-Writer: His World, His Options, His Skills.* The Liturgical Press.
1996   *Paul: A Critical Life.* Clerendon Press.

Murphy-O'Connor, Jerome, and James H. Charlesworth, eds.
1990   *Paul and the Dead Sea Scrolls.* Crossroad.

Murray, Gilbert
1955   *Five Stages of Greek Religion.* Doubleday.

Muse, Robert L.
1996   *The Book of Revelation: An Annotated Bibliography.* Garland Publishing.

Myers, Ched
1988   *Binding the Strong Man: A Political Reading of Mark's Story of Jesus.* Orbis Books.

Nanos, Mark D.

1996   *The Mystery of Romans: The Jewish Context of Paul's Letter.* Fortress Press.

2002   *The Galatians Debate: Contemporary Issues in Rhetorical and Historical Interpretation.* Hendrickson Publishers.

Neill, Stephen Charles, and Tom Wright

1988   *Interpretation of the New Testament: 1861–1986.* Oxford University Press.

Neusner, Jacob

1962   *A Life of Rabban Yohanan Ben Zakkai, ca. 1–80 CE.* Brill.

1971   *The Rabbinic Traditions about the Pharisees before 70.* 3 vols. Brill.

1972a   *The Study of Judaism: Bibliographic Essays.* Ktav.

1972b   *There We Sat Down: Talmudic Judaism in the Making.* Abingdon Press.

1975a   *Christianity, Judaism and Other Greco-Roman Cults: Studies for Morton Smith at Sixty.* Brill.

1975b   *First Century Judaism in Crisis: Yohananen Zakkai and the Renaissance of Torah.* Abingdon Press.

1977   "History and Structure: The Case of Mishnah." *Journal of the American Academy of Religion* 45:161–92.

1978   "From Scripture to Mishnah. The Origins of Tractate Niddah." *Journal of Jewish Studies* 29:135–48.

1979   *From Politics to Piety: The Emergence of Pharisaic Judaism.* 2nd ed. Ktav.

1981   *Judaism: The Evidence of the Mishnah.* University of Chicago Press.

1982   *The Talmud of the Land of Israel.* 35 vols. University of Chicago Press.

1984a   *Formative Judaism: Religious, Historical, and Literary Studies: Torah, Pharisees, and Rabbis.* Scholars Press.

1984b   *Major Trends in Formative Judaism, First Series: Society and Symbol in Political Crisis.* Scholars Press.

1984c   *Messiah in Context: Israel's History and Destiny in Formative Judaism.* Fortress Press.

1984d   "Messianic Themes in Formative Judaism." *Journal of the American Academy of Religion* 52:357–74.

1986   *The Fathers According to Rabbi Nathan: An Analytical Translation and Explanation.* Scholars Press.

1988   *The Mishnah: A New Translation.* Yale University Press.

1995   *The Classics of Judaism: A Textbook and Reader.* Westminster John Knox Press.

Neusner, Jacob, Peder Borgen, and Ernest S. Frerichs, eds.

1988   *The Social World of Formative Christianity and Judaism: Essays in Tribute to Howard Clark Kee.* Fortress Press.

Neusner, Jacob, William S. Green, and Jonathan Smith

1987   *Judaisms and Their Messiahs at the Turn of the Christian Era.* Cambridge University Press.

Newman, Barclay, and Philip C. Stine

1988   *A Translator's Handbook on the Gospel of Matthew: Helps for Translators.* United Bible Societies.

Newport, Kenneth G. C.

1990   "A Note on the 'Seat of Moses' (Matthew 23:2)." *Andrews University Seminary Studies* 28:53–58.

Newsom, Carol A., and Sharon H. Ringe

1992   *The Women's Bible Commentary.* Westminster John Knox Press.

Newsome, James D.

1992   *Greeks, Romans, Jews: Currents of Culture and Belief in the New Testament World.* Trinity Press International.

Newton, Michael

1985   *The Concept of Purity at Qumran and the Letters of Paul.* Society for New Testament Studies Monograph Series 53. Cambridge University Press.

Neyrey, Jerome H.

1981   "Decision Making in the Early Church: The Case of the Canaanite Woman." *Science et espirit* 33:373–78.

1988   *An Ideology of Revolt: John's Christology in Social Science Perspective.* Fortress Press.

1990   *Paul, in Other Words: A Cultural Reading of His Letters.* Westminster John Knox Press.

1991a   *The Social World of Luke-Acts: Models for Interpretation.* Hendrickson Publishers.

1991b   "'Without Beginning of Days or End of Life' (Hebrews 7:3): Topos for a True Diety." *Catholic Biblical Quarterly* 53:439–55.

1993   *2 Peter, Jude.* Anchor Bible. Doubleday.

1998a   *Honor and Shame in the Gospel of Matthew.* Westminster John Knox Press.

1998b   "Questions, Chreiai, and Challenges to Honor: The Interface of Rhetoric and Culture in Mark's Gospel." *Catholic Biblical Quarterly* 60:657–81.

2007   *The Gospel of John.* Cambridge University Press.

Neyrey, Jerome H., and Bruce J. Malina

1996   *Portraits of Paul: An Archaeology of Ancient Personality.* Westminster John Knox Press.

Nicholl, Colin R.
2003   *From Hope to Despair in Thessalonica: Situating 1 and 2 Thessalonians.* Cambridge University Press.

Nicholson, Godfrey
1983   *Death as Departure: The Johannine Descent-Ascent Schema.* Scholars Press.

Nickelsburg, George W. E.
1972   *Resurrection, Immortality, and Eternal Life in Intertestamental Judaism.* Harvard University Press.
1977   "Good News/Bad News: The Messiah and God's Fractured Community." *Current Trends in Mission* 4:324–32.
1981   *Jewish Literature between the Bible and the Mishnah: A Historical and Literary Introduction.* Fortress Press.

Nickelsburg, George W. E., and John Collins
1980   *Ideal Figures in Ancient Judaism: Profiles and Paradigms.* Septuagint and Cognate Studies 12. Scholars Press.

Nickelsburg, George W. E., and George W. MacRae
1986   *Christians among Jews and Gentiles: Essays in Honor of Krister Stendahl.* Fortress Press.

Nickle, Keith F.
1966   *The Collection: A Study of Paul's Strategy.* Studies in Biblical Theology 48. SCM Press.
1980   *The Synoptic Gospels: Conflict and Consensus.* John Knox Press.

Nida, Eugene A.
1964   *Toward a Science of Translating: With Special Reference to Principles and Procedures Involved in Bible.* Brill.

Niederwimmer, Kurt
1998   *The Didache.* Translated by L. M. Maloney. Edited by H. W. Attridge. Fortress Press.

Niedner, Frederick A., Jr.
1989   "Rereading Matthew on Jerusalem and Judaism." *Biblical Theology Bulletin* 19:43–47.

Nilsson, Martin P.
1925   *A History of Greek Religion.* Clarendon Press.

Nineham, D. E.
1963   *The Gospel of St. Mark.* Pelican Gospel Commentaries. Penguin Books.
1965   *Historicity and Chronology in the New Testament.* SPCK Press.

Nkhoma, Jonathan Samuel
2005   *The Use of Fulfilment Quotations in the Gospel According to Matthew.* Zomba, Malawi: Kachere Series.

Nock, Arthur Darby
1937   "The Genius of Mithraism." *Journal of Roman Studies* 27:108–13.

1961   *Conversion: The Old and the New in Religion from Alexander the Great to Augustine of Hippo.* Oxford University Press.
1963   *St. Paul.* Harper Torchbooks.
1964   *Early Gentile Christianity and Its Hellenistic Background.* Harper & Row.

Nolland, John
1990   *Luke 1–9:20.* Word Biblical Commentary 35A. Word Books.
1998   "The Sources for Matthew 2:1–12." *Catholic Biblical Quarterly* 60:283–300.

Norton, David
2004   *A History of the Bible as Literature.* Cambridge University Press.

Novak, Ralph Martin
2001   *Christianity and the Roman Empire: Background Texts.* Trinity Press International.

O'Brien, Peter Thomas
1977   *Introductory Thanksgivings in the Letters of Paul.* Brill.

O'Day, Gail R.
1986   *Revelation in the Fourth Gospel: Narrative Mode and Theological Claim.* Fortress Press.

O'Day, Gail R., and Susan Hylen
2006   *John.* Westminster John Knox Press.

O'Day, Gail R., and David Peterson, eds.
1999   *The Access Bible: New Revised Standard Version with the Apocryphal/ Deuterocanonical Books.* Oxford University Press.

O'Leary, Stephen D.
1994   *Arguing the Apocalypse: A Theory of Millennial Rhetoric.* Oxford University Press.

O'Neil, Edward
1977   *Teles (the Cynic Teacher).* Society of Biblical Literature Texts and Translations, Graeco-Roman Religion Series 11. Scholars Press.

O'Toole, Robert F.
1984   *Unity of Luke's Theology: An Analysis of Luke-Acts.* Good News Studies 9. Michael Glazier.

Oakman, Douglas E.
1986   *Jesus and the Economic Question of His Day.* Edwin Mellen Press.
1987   "The Buying Power of Two Denarii: A Comment on Luke 10:35." *Forum* 3:33–38.

Oliver, H.
1963   "The Lucan Birth Stories and the Purpose of Luke-Acts." *New Testament Studies* 10:202–26.

Oliver, R. P.
1951   "The First Medicean Manuscript of Tacitus and the Titulature of Ancient Books." *Transactions of the American Philological Association* 82:232–61.

Olivovba, Viera
1985   *Sports and Games in the Ancient World*. St. Martin's Press.

Onasander
       Strategikos. Translated by Illinios Greek Club. Loeb. Harvard University Press, 1923.

Ong, Walter J.
1967   *The Presence of the Word: Some Prolegomena for Cultural and Religious History*. Yale University Press.
1977   *Interfaces of the Word: Studies in the Evolution of Consciousness and Culture*. Cornell University Press.
1982   *Orality and Literacy: The Technologizing of the Word*. Methuen.

Ortner, Sherry, and Harriet Whitehead
1981   *Sexual Meanings: The Cultural Construction of Gender and Sexuality*. Cambridge University Press.

Orton, D. E.
1989   *The Understanding Scribe: Matthew and the Apocalyptic Ideal*. Journal for the Study of the Old Testament Supplement Series 25. Sheffield Academic Press.

Osborne, Grant R.
1984   *The Resurrection Narratives: A Redactional Study*. Baker Book House.
2002   *Revelation*. Baker Academic.

Osborne, Robin
1987   *Classical Landscape with Figures*. Sheridan House.

Osiek, Carolyn
1980   *Galatians*. Vol. 12 of *New Testament Message: A Biblical-Theological Commentary*. Michael Glazier.
1984   *What Are They Saying about the Social Setting of the New Testament?* Paulist Press.
1992a "BTB Readers Guide: Slavery in the Second Testament World." *Biblical Theology Bulletin* 22:174–79.
1992b "The Social Sciences and the Second Testament: Problems and Challenges." *Biblical Theology Bulletin* 22:88–95.

Osiek, Carolyn, and David L. Balch
1997   *Families in the New Testament World: Households and House Churches*. Westminster John Knox Press.

Osiek, Carolyn, Margaret Y. MacDonald, and Janet H. Tulloch
2006   *A Woman's Place: House Churches in Earliest Christianity*. Fortress Press.

Oster, Richard E.
1976   "The Ephesian Artemis as an Opponent of Early Christianity." *Jahrbuch für Antike und Christentum* 19:24–44.
1987   *A Bibliography of Ancient Ephesus*. Scarecrow Press.
1988   "When Men Wore Veils to Worship: The Historical Context of 1 Corinthians 11:4." *New Testament Studies* 34:481–505.

Overman, J. Andrew
1990   *Matthew's Gospel and Formative Judaism: The Social World of the Matthean Community*. Fortress Press.
1996   *Church and Community in Crisis*. Trinity Press International.

Owens, E. J.
1991   *The City in the Greek and Roman World*. Routledge.

Page, S. H.
1985   "The Suffering Servant between the Testaments." *New Testament Studies* 31:481–97.

Pagels, Elaine H.
1973   *The Johannine Gospel in Gnostic Exegesis: Heracleon's Commentary on John*. Society of Biblical Literature Monograph Series 17. Abingdon Press.
1974   "Paul and Women: A Response to Recent Discussion." *Journal of the American Academy of Religion* 42:538–49.
1975   *The Gnostic Paul: Gnostic Exegesis of the Pauline Letters*. Fortress Press.
2004   *Beyond Belief: The Secret Gospel of Thomas*. Vintage Books.
2006   "The Social History of Satan: Part 3, John of Patmos and Ignatius of Antioch: Conrasting Visions of 'God's People'." *Harvard Theological Review* 99:487–505.

Painter, John
1981   "The Farewell Discourses and the History of the Johannine Community." *New Testament Studies* 27:525–43.
1993   *The Quest for the Messiah: The History, Literature and Theology of the Johannine Community*. Abingdon Press.
1997   *Mark's Gospel*. Routledge.
1999   *Just James: The Brother of Jesus in History and Tradition*. Personalities of the New Testament. Fortress Press.

Parsenios, George L.
2005   *Departure and Consolation the Johannine Farewell Discourses in Light of Greco-Roman Literature*. Brill.

Parsons, Mikeal C.
2007   *Luke: Storyteller, Interpreter, Evangelist*. Hendrickson Publishers.

Parsons, Mikeal C., and Richard I. Pervo
1993   *Rethinking the Unity of Luke and Acts*. Fortress Press.

Parsons, Mikeal C., and Joseph B. Tyson
1992   *Cadbury, Knox and Talbert: American Contributions to the Study of Acts.* Scholars Press.

Patte, Daniel
1976   *What Is Structural Exegesis?* Fortress Press.
1983a   *Narrative Discourse in Structural Exegesis: John 6 and I Thessalonians. Semeia 26.* Scholars Press.
1983b   *Paul's Faith and the Power of the Gospel: A Structural Introduction to the Pauline Letters.* Fortress Press.
1985a   *The Gospel According to Matthew: A Structural Commentary on Matthew's Faith.* Fortress Press.
1985b   "Reading Paul So as to Hear His Gospel Anew." *Chicago Studies* 24:339–56.

Pattemore, Stephen
2004   *The People of God in the Apocalypse: Discourse, Structure, and Exegesis.* Cambridge University Press.

Patten, Priscilla, and Rebecca Patten
1991   *The World of the Early Church: A Companion to the New Testament.* Edwin Mellen Press.

Patzia, Arthur G.
1984   *Colossians, Philemon, Ephesians,* Harper & Row.

Payne, Michael
1989   "Voice, Metaphor, and Narrative in the Book of Revelation." *Bucknell Review* 33:364–72.

Pearson, Birger A.
1971   "I Thessalonians 1:13–16: A Deutero-Pauline Interpolation." *Harvard Theological Review* 64:79–94.
1990   "Gnosticism as Platonism." In *Gnosticism, Judaism and Egyptian Christianity,* 148–64. Fortress Press.

Penner, Todd C., and Caroline Vander Stichele, eds.
2003   *Contextualizing Acts: Lukan Narrative and Greco-Roman Discourse.* Society of Biblical Literature Symposium Series 20. Society of Biblical Literature.

Peradotto, John, and J. P. Sullivan
1984   *Women in the Ancient World: The Arethusa Papers.* State University of New York Press.

Peristiany, John G.
1965   *Honour and Shame: The Values of Mediterranean Society.* Weidenfeld and Nicolson.

Perkins, Pheme
1980   *The Gnostic Dialogue: The Early Church and the Crisis of Gnosticism.* Paulist Press.
1981   *Hearing the Parables of Jesus.* Paulist Press.
1984   *Resurrection: New Testament Witness and Contemporary Reflection.* Doubleday.
1993   *Gnosticism and the New Testament.* Fortress Press.
1997   *Ephesians.* Abingdon Press.
2000   *Peter: Apostle for the Whole Church.* Personalities of the New Testament. Fortress Press.

Perrin, Norman
1967   *Rediscovering the Teachings of Jesus.* Harper & Row.
1969   *What Is Redaction Criticism?* Fortress Press.
1971   "Christology of Mark: A Study in Methodology." *Journal of Religion* 51:173–87.
1972a   "The Evangelist as Author: Reflection on Method in the Study and Interpretation of the Synoptic Gospels and Acts." *Biblical Research* 17:5–18.
1972b   "Historical Criticism, Literary Criticism, and Hermeneutics: The Interpretation of the Parables of Jesus and the Gospel of Mark Today." *Journal of Religion* 52:361–75.
1976   *Jesus and the Language of the Kingdom: Symbol and Metaphor in New Testament Interpretation.* Fortress Press.
1977   *The Resurrection According to Matthew, Luke and John.* Fortress Press.

Perry, Ben Edwin
1964   *Secundus the Silent Philosopher.* Cornell University Press.

Pervo, Richard I.
1987   *Profit with Delight: The Literary Genre of the Acts of the Apostles.* Fortress Press.
1990   *Luke's Story of Paul.* Fortress Press.
1999   "Israel's Heritage and Claims upon the Genre(s) of Luke and Acts: The Problems of a History." In *Jesus and the Heritage of Israel: Luke's Narrative Claim upon Israel's Legacy,* edited by D. P. Moessner, 127–43. Trinity Press International.

Peters, T.
1973   "Jesus' Resurrection: An Historical Event without Analogy." *Dialog* 12:112–16.

Petersen, Norman R.
1974   "On the Notion of Genre in Via's 'Parable and Example Story': A Literary-Structuralist Approach." *Semeia* 1:134–81.
1978a   *Literary Criticism for New Testament Critics.* Fortress Press.
1978b   "'Point of View' in Mark's Narrative." *Semeia* 12:97–121.
1980   (ed.) *Perspectives on Mark's Gospel. Semeia* 16. Scholars Press.
1985   *Rediscovering Paul: Philemon and the Sociology of Paul's Narrative World.* Fortress Press.
1993   *The Gospel of John and the Sociology of Light: Language and Characterization in the Forth Gospel.* Trinity Press International.

Petersen, Paul D.
  1984   *Paul the Apostle and the Pauline Literature: A Bibliography Selected from the ATLA Religion Database.* 4th ed. American Theological Library Association.

Peterson, Eugene H.
  1988   *Reversed Thunder: The Revelation of John and the Praying Imagination.* Harper & Row.

Pfitzer, V. C.
  1967   *Paul and the Agon Motif: Traditional Athletic Imagery in Pauline Literature.* Brill.

Phillips, J. B.
  1972   *The New Testament in Modern English.* 2nd ed. Macmillan.

Phillips, Peter M.
  2006   *The Prologue of the Fourth Gospel a Sequential Reading.* T&T Clark.

Philo
          Philo of Alexandria. Translated by F. H. Colson and G. Whitaker. Loeb. Harvard University Press, 1924.
          The Works of Philo: Complete and Unabridged. New updated version. Translated by C. D. Yonge. Hendrickson Publishers, 1993 [1854].

Philostratus, Flavius
          Life of Apollonius of Tyana. Translated by F. C. Conybeare. Loeb. Harvard University Press, 1912.

Piaget, Jean
  1970   *Structuralism.* Translated and edited by Chaninah Maschler. Basic Books.

Pines, S.
  1966   *The Jewish Christians of the Early Centuries According to a New Source.* Brill.

Pippin, Tina
  1992   *Death and Desire: The Rhetoric of Gender in the Apocalypse of John.* Westminster John Knox Press.
  1999   *Apocalyptic Bodies: The Biblical End of the World in Text and Image.* Routledge.

Pitt-Rivers, Julian Alfred
  1963   *Mediterranean Countrymen: Essays in the Social Anthropology of the Mediterranean.* Mouton.

Plato
          Collected Dialogues of Plato. Translated by E. Hamilton. Princeton University Press, 1961.
          Dialogues. Translated by H. N. Fowler. Loeb. Harvard University Press, 1938.
          Euthyphro, Apology, Crito, Phaedo. Translated by H. N. Fowler. Loeb. Harvard University Press, 1990.

Pleket, H. W.
  1961   "Domitian, the Senate and the Provinces." *Mnemosyne* 14:296–315.

Plescia, Joseph
  1971   "On the Persecution of the Christians in the Roman Empire." *Latomus* 30:120–32.

Pliny
          Letters. Translated by W. Melmoth and W. Hutchinson. Loeb. Harvard University Press, 1915.

Pliny the Elder
          Natural History. Translated by H. Rackham, W. Jones, and D. Eichhol. Loeb. Harvard University Press, 1938.

Plutarch
          Lives: Demosthenes and Cicero, Alexander and Caesar. Vol. 7. Translated by B. Perrin. Loeb. Harvard University Press, 1962.

Polaikoff, Michael B.
  1987   *Combat Sports in the Ancient World: Competition, Violence, and Culture.* Yale University Press.

Polycarp
          Letter to the Philippians. Translated by K. Lake. Loeb. Harvard University Press, 1912.

Polzin, Robert M.
  1977   *Biblical Structuralism: Method and Subjectivity in the Study of Ancient Texts. Semeia Supplements* 5. Fortress Press.

Pomeroy, Sarah B.
  1975   *Goddesses, Whores, Wives and Slaves: Women in Classical Antiquity.* Schocken Books.
  1991a   "The Study of Women in Antiquity: Past, Present, and Future." *American Journal of Philology* 112:263–68.
  1991b   *Women's History and Ancient History.* University of North Carolina Press.

Pomeroy, Sarah B., and Stanley M. Burstein
  1984   *Ancient History.* 2nd ed. M. Wiener.

Portefaix, Lilian
  1988   *Sisters Rejoice. Paul's Letter to the Philippians and Luke-Acts as Received by First Century Phillipian Women.* Vol. 20, *Coniectanea Biblica New Testament Series.* Stockholm: Almqvist and Wiksell International.

Porter, Stanley E.
  1997   (ed.) *Handbook of Classical Rhetoric in the Hellenistic Period 330 BC–AD 400.* Brill.
  2000   *The Criteria for Authenticity in Historical-Jesus Research: Previous Discussion and New Proposals.* Sheffield Academic Press.
  2004   *The Pauline Canon.* Brill.

Porton, Gary G.
  1979   "Midrash: Palestinian Jews and the Hebrew Bible in the Greco-Roman Period." In *Aufstieg*

und Niedergang der römischen Welt, edited
by H. Temporini and W. Hasse, II, 19.2:
103–38. De Gruyter.

Powell, Mark Allan
1990 "The Religious Leaders in Luke: A Literary-Critical Study." *Journal of Biblical Literature*
109:93–110.
1991 *What Is Narrative Criticism?* Fortress Press.
1992a "The Plot and Subplots of Matthew's Gospel."
New Testament Studies 38:187–204.
1992b "Toward a Narrative-Critical Understanding
of Matthew." *Interpretation* 46:341–46.
1992c *What Are They Saying about Acts?* Paulist
Press.
1997 *Fortress Press Introduction to the Gospels.*
Fortress Press.
1998a *Jesus as a Figure in History: How Modern
Historians View the Man from Galilee.* Westminster John Knox Press.
1998b (ed.) *The New Testament Today.* Westminster
John Knox Press.

Powell, Mark Allan, Cecile G. Gray, and
Melissa C. Curtis
1992 *The Bible and Modern Literary Criticism: A
Critical Assessment and Annotated Bibliography.* Vol. 22 of *Bibliographies and Indexes in
Religious Studies.* Greenwood Press.

Praeder, Susan Marie
1981 "Luke-Acts and the Ancient Novel." In
*Society of Biblical Literature 1981 Seminar
Papers*, 269–92. Scholars Press.

Pregeant, Russell
1978 *Christology Beyond Dogma: Matthew's
Christ in Process Hermeneutic.* Fortress Press.

Prevost, Jean-Pierre
1993 *How to Read the Apocalypse.* Crossroad.

Price, Jonathan J.
1992 *Jerusalem under Siege: The Collapse of the
Jewish State 66–70 CE.* Brill.

Price, Reynolds
1978 *A Palpable God: Thirty Stories Translated
from the Bible with an Essay on the Origins
and Life of Narrative.* Atheneum.

Price, S. R. F.
1984a "Gods and Emperors: The Greek Language
of the Roman Imperial Cult." *Journal of Hellenic Studies* 104:79–95.
1984b *Rituals and Power: The Roman Imperial Cult
in Asia Minor.* Cambridge University Press.

Priest, John F.
1963 "The Messiah and the Meal in 1QSa." *Journal
of Biblical Literature* 82:95–100.

Prior, Michael
1989 *Paul the Letter-Writer and the Second Letter
to Timothy.* Sheffield Academic Press.

Pritchard, James
1955 *Ancient Near Eastern Texts Relating to the
Old Testament.* Princeton University Press.

Pritchard, John Paul
1972 *A Literary Approach to the New Testament.*
University of Oklahoma Press.

Provan, Iain
1996 "Foul Spirits, Fornication and Finance: Revelation 18 from an Old Testament Perspective."
Journal for the Study of the New Testament
64:81–100.

Przybylski, Benno
1980 *Righteousness in Matthew and His World of
Thought.* Cambridge University Press.

Puskas, Charles B.
1993 *The Letters of Paul: An Introduction.* The
Liturgical Press.

Quast, Kevin
1989 *Peter and the Beloved Disciple: Figures for a
Community in Crisis.* Journal for the Study
of the New Testament Supplement Series 32.
Sheffield Academic Press.

Quinn, Jerome D., and William C. Wacker
1999 *The First and Second Letters to Timothy.*
Eerdmans.

Quintilian
*Institutio Oratoria [On the Training of an
Orator].* Translated by H. E. Butler. Loeb.
Harvard University Press, 1920.

Rabinowitz, Peter J.
1987 *Before Reading: Narrative Conventions and
the Politics of Interpretation.* Cornell University Press.

Rad, Gerhard von
1965 *The Message of the Prophets.* Harper & Row.

Rader, Rosemary
1983 *Breaking Boundaries: Male/Female Friendship in the Early Christian Communities.*
Paulist Press.

Räisänen, Heikki
1987 *Paul and the Law.* Fortress Press.
1990 *Beyond New Testament Theology: A Story
and a Programme.* SCM Press.

Ramsay, William M.
1906 *The Letters to the Seven Churches of Asia
and Their Place in the Plan of the Apocalypse.*
Hodder and Stoughton.
1960 *The Cities of St. Paul, Their Influence on His
Life and Thought. The Cities of Eastern Asia
Minor.* Baker Book House.
1962 *St. Paul: The Traveller and the Roman Citizen.* Baker Book House.

Rapske, Brian
1994 *The Book of Acts and Paul in Roman Custody.* Eerdmans.

Rawson, Beryl
1986   *The Family in Ancient New Perspectives.*
        Cornell University Press.
1991   *Marriage, Divorce, and Children in Ancient
        Rome.* Oxford University Press.
Rawson, Beryl, and Paul Weaver
1997   *The Roman Family in Italy: Status, Senti-
        ment, Space.* Oxford University Press.
Reddish, Mitchell
1995   *Apocalyptic Literature: A Reader.* Hendrick-
        son Publishers.
Reece, James M.
1979   *1 and 2 Thessalonians.* Michael Glazier.
Reed, Jonathan L.
2000   *Archaeology and the Galilean Jesus: A Re-
        examination of the Evidence.* Trinity Press
        International.
Reeder, Ellen D.
1995   *Pandora's Box: The Roles of Women in
        Ancient Greece.* Institute for Mediterranean
        Studies. Video recording.
Reedy, C. J.
1972   "Mark 8:31–11:10 and the Gospel Ending: A
        Redaction Study." *Catholic Biblical Quarterly*
        34:187–97.
Reicke, Bo
1964   *The Epistles of James, Peter, and Jude.* An-
        chor Bible. Doubleday.
1968   *The New Testament Era: The World of the
        Bible from 500 BC to AD 100.* Fortress Press.
Reid, Barbara E.
1996   *Choosing the Better Part? Women in the Gos-
        pel of Luke.* The Liturgical Press.
        Reimer, Ivoni Richter, 1995 *Women in the
        Acts of the Apostles: A Feminist Liberation
        Perspective.* Fortress Press.
Reinhartz, Adele
1997   "A Nice Jewish Girl Reads the Gospel of
        John." In *Bible and Ethics of Reading*, edited
        by D. N. Fewell and G. Phillips, *Semeia*
        77:177–93. Scholars Press.
2002   *Befriending the Beloved Disciple: A Jewish
        Reading of the Gospel of John.* Continuum.
Renan, Ernest
1955 [1863]   *The Life of Jesus*, with introduction by
        J. H. Holmes. Modern Library.
Renault, Mary
1966   *The Mask of Apollo.* Pantheon Books.
Resseguie, James L.
2001   *The Strange Gospel: Narrative Design and
        Point of View in John.* Brill.
Reumann, John
1968   *Jesus in the Church's Gospels: Modern
        Scholarship and the Earliest Sources.* Fortress
        Press.

1977   "A History of Lectionaries: From the Syna-
        gogue at Nazareth to Post Vatican II." *Inter-
        pretation* 31:116–30.
Reumann, John, and Walter F. Taylor, Jr.
1985   *Ephesians, Colossians.* Augsburg Publishing
        House.
Reynolds, Joyce Marie
1987   *Jews and Godfearers at Aphrodisias: Greek
        Inscriptions with Commentary.* Cambridge
        Philological Society.
Reynolds, Leighton Durham
1974   *Scribes and Scholars: A Guide to the Trans-
        mission of Greek and Latin Literature.* Clar-
        endon Press.
Rhoads, David M.
1976   *Israel in Revolution 6–74 CE: A Political His-
        tory Based on Josephus.* Fortress Press.
1984   *Dramatic Performance of the Gospel of
        Mark.* Select. Video recording.
2005   (ed.) *From Every People and Nation: The
        Book of Revelation in Intercultural Perspec-
        tive.* Fortress Press.
Rhoads, David M., Joanna Dewey, and Donald Michie
1999   *Mark as Story: An Introduction to the Narra-
        tive of a Gospel.* 2nd ed. Fortress Press.
Rhoads, David M., and Kari Syreeni
1999   *Characterization in the Gospels Reconceiving
        Narrative Criticism.* Sheffield Academic Press.
Rice, D. G., and J. E. Stambaugh, eds.
1979   *Sources for the Study of Greek Religion.* So-
        ciety of Biblical Literature Sources for Biblical
        Study 14. Scholars Press.
Richard, Earl
1990   "Contemporary Research on 1 (& 2) Thes-
        salonians." *Biblical Theology Bulletin*
        20:107–15.
Richard, Pablo
1995   *Apocalypse: A People's Commentary on the
        Book of Revelation.* Orbis Books.
Richards, Randolph
1991   *The Secretary in the Letters of Paul.* Wis-
        senschaftliche Untersuchungen zum Neuen
        Testament 42. Mohr-Siebeck.
Richards, William A.
2002   *Difference and Distance in Post-Pauline
        Christianity: An Epistolary Analysis of the
        Pastorals.* Peter Lang.
Richardson, Cyril
1967   *The Christianity of Ignatius of Antioch.* Co-
        lumbia University Press.
1970   (ed.) *Early Christian Fathers: Newly Trans-
        lated and Edited.* Westminster Press.
Richardson, Peter
1996   *Herod, King of the Jews and Friend of the
        Romans.* University of South Carolina Press.

Richardson, Peter, and David Granskou
  1986   *Paul and the Gospels*. Vol. 1 of *Anti-Judaism in Early Christianity*. Wilfrid Laurier University Press.
Richardson, Peter, and Stephen Westerholm
  1991   *Law in Religious Communities in the Roman Period: The Debate over Torah and Nomos in Post-Biblical Judaism*. Wilfrid Laurier University Press.
Riches, John
  1980   *Jesus and the Transformation of Judaism*. Seabury Press.
  1983   "The Sociology of Matthew: Some Basic Questions Concerning Its Relationship to the Theology of the New Testament." In *Society of Biblical Literature 1983 Seminar Papers*, 259–71. Scholars Press.
  1993   *A Century of New Testament Study*. Trinity Press International.
Riches, John Kenneth, and David C. Sim
  2005   *The Gospel of Matthew in Its Roman Imperial Context*. T&T Clark.
Risenfeld, H.
  1970   *The Gospel Tradition*. Fortress Press.
Rist, John M.
  1978a   *On the Independence of Matthew and Mark*. Cambridge University Press.
  1978b   *Stoics*. Vol. 1 of *Major Thinkers*. University of California Press.
Rivkin, Ellis
  1978   *A Hidden Revolution: The Pharisees' Search for the Kingdom Within*. Abingdon Press.
Robbins, Vernon K.
  1973   "The Healing of Blind Bartimaeus in the Markan Theology." *Journal of Biblical Literature* 92:224–43.
  1978   "By Land and by Sea: The We-Passages and Ancient Sea Voyages." In *Perspectives on Luke-Acts*, edited by C. Talbert, 215–42. Association of Baptist Professors of Religion.
  1979   "Prefaces in Graeco-Roman Biography and in Luke Acts." *Perspectives in Religious Studies* 6:94–108.
  1984   *Jesus the Teacher: A Socio-Rhetorical Interpretation of Mark*. Fortress Press.
  1989   *Ancient Quotes and Anecdotes: From Crib to Crypt, Foundations and Facets*. Polebridge Press.
Roberts, Colin H., and T. C. Skeat
  1984   *The Birth of the Codex*. Oxford University Press.
Roberts, T. A.
  1966   "Gospel Historicity: Some Philosophical Observation." *Religious Studies* 1:185–202.

Robinson, James M.
  1959   *A New Quest of the Historical Jesus*. A. R. Allenson.
  1971   "Dismantling and Reassembling of the Categories of New Testament Scholarship." *Interpretation* 25:63–77.
  1982   *The Problem of History in Mark and Other Marcan Studies*. Fortress Press.
  1988   (ed.) *The Nag Hammadi Library in English*. 3rd ed. Harper & Row.
Robinson, James M., and Helmut Koester
  1971   *Trajectories through Early Christianity*. Fortress Press.
Robinson, John A. T.
  1962   *Twelve New Testament Studies*. SCM Press.
  1976   *Redating the New Testament*. Westminster Press.
Robinson, Thomas A.
  1993   *The Early Church: An Annotated Bibliography of Literature in English*. Scarecrow Press.
Roetzel, Calvin J.
  1985   *The World That Shaped the New Testament*. John Knox Press.
  1998   *The Letters of Paul: Conversations in Context*. 4th ed. John Knox Press.
Rohrbaugh, Richard L.
  1991   "BTB Readers Guide: The City in the Second Testament." *Biblical Theology Bulletin* 21:67–75.
  1993   "The Social Location of the Marcan Audience." *Biblical Theology Bulletin* 23:114–27.
Rolland, P.
  1972   "From Genesis to the End of the World: The Plan of Matthew's Gospel." *Biblical Theology Bulletin* 2:155–76.
Rollins, Wayne G.
  1963   *The Gospels: Portraits of Christ*. Westminster Press.
Roloff, Jürgen
  1981   "Luke's Presentation of Paul." *Evangelische Theologie* 39:510–31.
  1993   *The Revelation of John: A Continental Commentary*. Fortress Press.
Rosche, T. R.
  1960   "The Words of Jesus and the Future of the Q Hypothesis." *Journal of Biblical Literature* 79:210–20.
Rose, H. R.
  1951   *A Handbook of Greek Literature*. E. P. Dutton.
  1959   *Religion in Greece and Rome*. Harper & Row.
Rossing, Barbara R.
  1999   *The Choice between Two Cities: A Wisdom Topos in the Apocalypse*. Trinity Press International.

2004 *The Rapture Exposed: The Message of Hope in the Book of Revelation.* Westview Press.

Rost, L.
1976 *Judaism Outside the Hebrew Canon: An Introduction to the Documents.* Abingdon Press.

Rostovtzeff, Mihail
1930 *A History of the Ancient World.* Clarendon Press.
1957 *The Social and Economic History of the Roman Empire.* 2 vols. Clarendon Press.
1986 *The Social and Economic History of the Hellenistic World.* Clarendon Press.

Roth, Robert P.
1973 *Story and Reality: An Essay on Truth.* Eerdmans.

Roth, Wolfgang
1988 *Hebrew Gospel: Cracking the Code of Mark.* Meyer Stone.

Roukema, Riemer
1999 *Gnosis and Faith in Early Christianity: An Introduction to Gnosticism.* Trinity Press International.

Rousseau, John J., and Rami Arav
1994 *Jesus and His World: An Archaeological and Cultural Dictionary.* Fortress Press.

Rousselle, Aline
1988 *Porneia: On Desire and the Body in Antiquity.* Blackwell.

Rowe, Christopher Kavin
2006 *Early Narrative Christology: The Lord in the Gospel of Luke.* De Gruyter.

Rowland, Christopher
1982 *The Open Heaven: A Study of Apocalyptic in Judaism and Early Christianity.* Crossroad.
2002 *Christian Origins: An Account of the Setting and Character of the Most Important Messianic Sect of Judaism.* 2nd ed. SPCK Press.

Rowley, H. H.
1963 *The Relevance of Apocalyptic: A Study of Jewish and Christian Apocalypses from Daniel to the Revelation.* 3rd ed. Association Press.

Royalty, Robert M.
1998 *The Streets of Heaven: The Ideology of Wealth in the Apocalypse of John.* Mercer University Press.
2002 "Dwelling on Visions: On the Nature of the So-Called 'Colossians Heresy'." *Biblica* 83:329–57.

Rubenstein, Richard
1972 *My Brother Paul.* Harper & Row.

Rudolph, Kurt
1983 *Gnosis: The Nature and History of Gnosticism.* Harper & Row.

Ruiz, Jean-Pierre
1989 *Ezekiel in the Apocalypse: The Transformation of Prophetic Language in Revelation 16:17–19:10.* Peter Lang.
1992 "Betwixt and Between on the Lord's Day: Liturgy and the Apocalypse." In *Society of Biblical Literature 1992 Seminar Papers,* 654–72. Scholars Press.

Runia, David T.
2000 *Philo of Alexandria: An Annotated Bibliography, 1987–1996: With Addenda for 1937–1986.* Brill.

Russell, D. A.
1981 *Criticism in Antiquity.* University of California Press.

Russell, D. A., and M. Winterbottem
1972 *Ancient Literary Criticism: The Principal Texts in New Translations.* Clarendon Press.

Russell, D. S.
1964 *The Method and Message of Jewish Apocalyptic: 200 BC–AD 100.* Old Testament Library. Westminster Press.

Russell, Jeffrey Burton
1997 *A History of Heaven: The Singing Silence.* Princeton University Press.

Russell, Letty M., ed.
1985 *Feminist Interpretation of the Bible.* Westminster Press.

Safrai, S.
1987 *The Literature of the Sages: Part 1, Oral Tora, Halakha, Mishna, Tosefta, Talmud, External Tractates.* Fortress Press.

Safrai, S., and M. Stern
1974 *The Jewish People in the First Century: Historical Geography, Political History, Social, Cultural and Religious Life and Institutions.* 2 vols. Fortress Press.

Sakenfeld, Katharine Doob
1988 "Feminist Perspectives on Bible and Theology." *Interpretation* 42:5–18.

Saldarini, Anthony J.
1974 "The End of the Rabbinic Chain of Tradition." *Journal of Biblical Literature* 93:97–106.
1989 *Pharisees, Scribes and Sadducees in Palestinian Society: A Sociological Approach.* Michael Glazier.
1994 *Matthew's Christian Jewish Community.* University of Chicago Press.

Saller, Richard P.
1994 *Patriarchy, Property and Death in the Roman Family.* Cambridge University Press.

Sampley, Paul J.

1980   *Pauline Partnership in Christ: Christian Community and Commitment in Light of Roman Law.* Fortress Press.

Samply, Paul J., et al.

1978   *Ephesians, Colossians, II Thessalonians, the Pastoral Epistles.* Fortress Press.

Sandelin, Karl-Gustav

1986   *Wisdom as Nourisher: A Study of an Old Testament Theme, Its Development within Early Judaism, and Its Impact on Early Christianity.* Åbo Akademi.

Sanders, E. P.

1977   *Paul and Palestinian Judaism: A Comparison of Patterns of Religion.* Fortress Press.

1980   *The Shaping of Christianity in the Second and Third Centuries.* Fortress Press.

1983   *Paul, the Law and the Jewish People.* Fortress Press.

1985   *Jesus and Judaism.* Fortress Press.

1991a *Judaism: Practice and Belief 63 BCE–63 CE.* Trinity Press International.

1991b *Paul.* Oxford University Press.

1995   *The Historical Figure of Jesus.* Penguin Books.

Sanders, E. P., A. I. Baumgarten, Alan Mendelson, and Ben Meyer

1981–1982 *Jewish and Christian Self-Definition.* 3 vols. Fortress Press.

Sanders, E. P., and Margaret Davies

1989   *Studying the Synoptic Gospels.* Trinity Press International.

Sanders, Jack T.

1971   *The New Testament Christological Hymns: Their Historical Religious Background.* Society for New Testament Studies Monograph Series 15. Cambridge University Press.

1975   *Ethics in the New Testament.* Fortress Press.

1987   *The Jews in Luke-Acts.* Fortress Press.

1993   *Schismatics, Sectarians, Dissidents, Deviants: The First 100 Years of Jewish Christian Relations.* Trinity Press International.

Sanders, James A.

1984   *Canon and Community: A Guide to Canonical Criticism.* Fortress Press.

1987   *From Sacred Story to Sacred Text: Canon as Paradigm.* Fortress Press.

Sandmel, Samuel

1961   "Parallelomania." *Journal of Biblical Literature* 81:1–13.

1965   *We Jews and Jesus.* Oxford University Press.

1969   *The First Century in Judaism and Christianity: Certainties and Uncertainties.* Oxford University Press.

1970   "Prolegomena to a Commentary on Mark." In *New Testament Issues*, edited by R. Batey, 45–56. Harper & Row.

1974   *A Jewish Understanding of the New Testament.* Ktav.

1978a *Anti-Semitism in the New Testament?* Fortress Press.

1978b *Judaism and Christian Beginnings.* Oxford University Press.

1979a *The Genius of Paul: A Study in History.* Fortress Press.

1979b *Philo of Alexandria: An Introduction.* Oxford University Press.

Sandt, Huub van de, ed.

2005   *Matthew and the Didache: Two Documents from the Same Jewish-Christian Milieu?* Fortress Press.

Sappington, Thomas J.

1991   *Revelation and Redemption at Colossae.* Journal for the Study of the New Testament Supplement Series 53. Sheffield Academic Press.

Sawicki, Marianne

1994   *Seeing the Lord: Resurrection and Early Christian Practices.* Fortress Press.

2000   *Crossing Galilee: Architectures of Contact in the Occupied Land of Jesus.* Trinity Press International.

Sawyer, Deborah F.

1996   *Women and Religion in the First Christian Centuries.* Routledge.

Scaer, Peter J., and Stanley E. Porter

2005   *The Lukan Passion and the Praiseworthy Death.* New Testament Monographs 10. Sheffield Phoenix Press.

Schaberg, Jane

2002   *The Resurrection of Mary Magdalene: Legends, Apocrypha, and the Christian Testament.* Continuum.

2006   *The Illegitimacy of Jesus: A Feminist Theological Interpretation of the Infancy Narratives.* Expanded twentieth anniversary ed. Sheffield Phoenix Press.

Schäfer, Peter

1997   *Judeophobia: Attitudes toward the Jews in the Ancient World.* Harvard University Press.

Schick, Edwin A.

1977   *Revelation: The Last Book of the Bible.* Fortress Press.

Schiffman, Lawrence H.

1991   *From Text to Tradition: A History of Second Temple and Rabbinic Judaism.* Ktav.

Schildgen, Brenda Deen

1998   *Crisis and Continuity: Time in the Gospel of Mark.* Sheffield Academic Press.

Schillebeeckx, Edward C. F.

1979   *Jesus: An Experiment in Christology.* Seabury
        Press.

1980   *Christ: The Experience of Jesus as Lord.*
        Translated by J. Bowden. Seabury Press.

Schmidt, Daryl

1983   "I Thessalonians 2:13–16: Linguistic Evidence
        for an Interpolation." *Journal of Biblical
        Literature* 102:269–79.

Schmidt, Karl Ludwig

1919   *Der Rahmen der Geschichte Jesus [The
        Framework of the Story of Jesus].* Trowitsch
        & Sons.

Schmithals, Walter

1965   *Paul and James.* Translated by D. M. Barton.
        Studies in Biblical Theology 46. SCM Press.

1972   *Paul and the Gnostics.* Abingdon Press.

Schnackenburg, Rudolf

1980   *The Gospel According to St. John.* Translated
        by K. Smith. 3 vols. Seabury Press.

Schneemelcher, Wilhelm, and R. McL. Wilson

2003   *New Testament Apocrypha.* 2 vols. Revised
        ed. Westminster John Knox Press.

Schneider, Jane

1971   "Of Vigilance and Virgins: Honor, Shame and
        Access to Resources in Mediterranean Societ-
        ies." *Ethnology* 10:1–24.

Schneidermeyer, W.

1971   "Galatians as Literature." *Journal of Reli-
        gious Thought* 28:132–38.

Schneiders, Sandra M.

1982   "Women in the Fourth Gospel and the Role of
        Women in the Contemporary Church." *Bibli-
        cal Theology Bulletin* 12:35–45.

1989a   "Does the Bible Have a Postmodern
        Message?" In *Postmodern Theology:
        Christian Faith in a Pluralist World,*
        edited by F. B. Burnham, 56–73. Harper
        & Row.

1989b   "Feminist Ideology, Criticism, and Biblical
        Hermeneutics." *Biblical Theology Bulletin*
        19:3–10.

1991   *The Revelatory Text: Interpreting the New
        Testament as Sacred Scripture.* Fortress Press.

Schoedel, William R.

1984   *Ignatius of Antioch: A Commentary on the
        Seven Letters of Ignatius.* Fortress Press.

Schoeps, Hans Joachim

1961   *Paul: The Theology of the Apostle in the Light
        of Jewish Religious History.* Westminster
        Press.

Scholder, Klaus

1990   *The Birth of Modern Critical Theology:
        Origins and Problems of Biblical Criticism*
        in the Seventeenth Century. Trinity Press
        International.

Scholem, Gershom G.

1995   *Major Trends in Jewish Mysticism.* Schocken
        Books.

Scholer, David M.

1973   *A Basic Bibliographic Guide for New Testa-
        ment Exegesis.* Eerdmans.

Scholes, Robert, and Robert Kellogg

1966   *The Nature of Narrative.* Oxford University
        Press.

Schottroff, Luise

1995   *Lydia's Impatient Sisters: A Feminist Social
        History of Early Christianity.* Westminster
        John Knox Press.

Schowalter, Daniel N.

1993   *The Emperor and the Gods: Images from the
        Time of Trajan.* Fortress Press.

Schuller, Ellen M.

1986   *Non-Canonical Psalms from Qumran:
        A Pseudepigraphic Collection.* Scholars Press.

Schürer, Emil

1973   *The History of the Jewish People in the Age
        of Jesus Christ (175 BC–AD 135).* Edited by G.
        Vermes, F. Miller, and M. Goodman. 3 vols.
        T&T Clark.

Schüssler Fiorenza, Elisabeth

1973   "Apocalyptic and Gnosis in the Book of
        Revelation and Paul." *Journal of Biblical
        Literature* 92:565–81.

1977   "Composition and Structure of the Book
        of Revelation." *Catholic Biblical Quarterly*
        39:344–66.

1981   *Invitation to the Book of Revelation.* Image
        Books.

1983   *In Memory of Her: A Feminist Theologi-
        cal Reconstruction of Christian Origins.*
        Crossroad.

1985   *Bread Not Stone: The Challenge of Feminist
        Biblical Interpretation.* Beacon Press.

1988   "The Ethics of Interpretation: De-centering
        Biblical Scholarship." *Journal of Biblical
        Literature* 107:3–17.

1991   *Revelation: Vision of a Just World.* Fortress
        Press.

1992   *But She Said: Feminist Practices of Biblical
        Interpretation.* Beacon Press.

1993   (ed.) *Searching the Scriptures: A Feminist
        Introduction.* Crossroad.

1994   *Jesus, Miriam's Child, Sophia's Prophet:
        Critical Issues in Feminist Christology.*
        Continuum.

1996   "Challenging the Rhetorical Half-Turn:
        Feminist and Rhetorical Biblical Criticism."
        In *Rhetoric, Scripture and Theology: Essays*

from the 1994 Pretoria Conference, edited by S. E. Porter and T. H. Olbricht, 28–53. Sheffield Academic Press.

1998   *The Book of Revelation: Justice and Judgment.* 2nd ed. Fortress Press.

1999   *Rhetoric and Ethic: The Politics of Biblical Studies.* Fortress Press.

2000   *Jesus and the Politics of Interpretation.* Continuum.

2001   *Wisdom Ways: Introducing Feminist Bbilical Interpretation.* Orbis Books.

Schutter, William L.

1989   *Hermeneutic and Composition in I Peter.* J. C. B. Mohr.

Schwartz, Seth

1990   *Josephus and Judean Politics.* Brill.

Schweitzer, Albert

1964a   *Paul and His Interpreters: A Critical History.* Schocken Books.

1964b   *The Quest of the Historical Jesus: A Critical Study of Its Progress from Reimarus to Wrede.* Macmillan.

Schweizer, Eduard

1961   *Church Order in the New Testament.* Allenson.

1965   *The Church as the Body of Christ.* SPCK Press.

1970   *The Good News According to Mark.* John Knox Press.

1975   *The Good News According to Matthew.* John Knox Press.

1977   "Towards a Christology of Mark?" In *God's Christ and His People: Studies in Honor of Nils Alstrup Dahl*, edited by J. Jervell and W. Meeks, 29–42. Columbia University Press.

Scott, Bernard Brandon

1981   *Jesus, Symbol-Maker for the Kingdom.* Fortress Press.

1986   "Essaying the Rock: The Authenticity of the Jesus Parable Tradition." *Forum* 2:3–53.

1989   *Hear Then the Parable: A Commentary on the Parables of Jesus.* Fortress Press.

Scroggs, Robin

1972   "Paul and the Eschatological Woman." *Journal of the American Academy of Religion* 40:283–303.

1977   *Paul for a New Day.* Fortress Press.

1983   *The New Testament and Homosexuality.* Fortress Press.

Sebesta, Judith Lynn, and Larissa Bonfante

1993   *The World of Roman Costume.* University of Wisconsin Press.

Seeley, D.

1990   *The Noble Death: Graeco-Roman Martyrology and Paul's Concept of Salvation.* Journal

for the Study of the Old Testament Supplement Series 28. JSOT/Sheffield Academic Press.

Segal, Alan F.

1990   *Paul the Convert: The Apostolate and Apostasy of Saul the Pharisee.* Yale University Press.

1991   "Matthew's Jewish Voice." In *Social History of the Matthean Community: Cross-Disciplinary Approaches*, edited by D. L. Balch, 3–37. Fortress Press.

2004   *Life after Death a History of the Afterlife in the Religions of the West.* Doubleday.

Segbroeck, F. van

1989   *The Gospel of Luke: A Cumulative Bibliography, 1973–88.* Leuven University Press.

Segovia, Fernando F.

1991   *The Farewell of the Word: The Johannine Call to Abide.* Fortress Press.

Segovia, Fernando F., and Mary Ann Tolbert

1994–1995   *Readings from This Place.* 2 vols. Fortress Press.

Seim, Turid Karlsen

1994   *The Double Message: Patterns of Gender in Luke and Acts.* Abingdon Press.

Seland, Torrey

1995   *Establishment Violence in Philo and Luke: A Study of Non-Conformity to the Torah and Jewish Vigilante Reactions.* Brill.

Sellew, Phillip

1992   "Interior Monologue as a Narrative Device in the Parables of Luke." *Journal of Biblical Literature* 111:239–53.

Seltzer, Robert M.

1989   *Religions of Antiquity: Selections from the Encyclopedia of Religion.* Macmillan.

Senior, Donald

1975   *Jesus: A Gospel Portrait.* Pflaum-Standard.

1980   *1 & 2 Peter.* New Testament Message 20. Michael Glazier.

1987   "'With Swords and Clubs . . .': The Setting of Mark's Community and His Critique of Abusive Power." *Biblical Theology Bulletin* 17:10–20.

Setzer, Claudia

1994   *Jewish Responses to Early Christians: History and Polemics, 30–150 CE.* Fortress Press.

Sevenster, J. N.

1975   *The Roots of Pagan Anti-Semitism in the Ancient World.* Supplements to Novum Testament 41. Brill.

Shanks, Hershel, ed.

1992   *Christianity and Rabbinic Judaism: A Parallel History of Their Origins and Early Development.* Biblical Archaeological Society.

Shanks, Hershel, Stephen J. Patterson, Marcus J. Borg, and John Dominic Crossan
1994   *The Search for Jesus: Modern Scholarship Looks at the Gospels: Symposium at the Smithsonian Institution, September 11, 1993.* Biblical Archaeology Society.

Shelton, Jo-Ann R.
1987   *As the Romans Did: A Sourcebook in Roman Social History.* Oxford University Press.

Shepherd, Massey H., Jr.
1960   *The Paschal Liturgy and the Apocalypse.* John Knox Press.

Sherk, Robert K.
1988   *The Roman Empire: Augustus to Hadrian.* Translated Documents of Greece and Rome 6. Cambridge University Press.

Sherwin-White, A. N.
1966   *The Letters of Pliny: A Historical and Social Commentary.* Clarendon Press.

Shochat, Y.
1985   "The Change in the Roman Religion at the Time of the Emperor Trajan." *Latomus* 44:317–36.

Shubert, Paul
1939   *The Form and Function of the Pauline Thanksgiving.* Alfred Topelmann.

Shuler, Philip L.
1982   *A Genre for the Gospels: The Biographical Character of Matthew.* Fortress Press.

Sidebottom, E. M.
1967   *James, Jude, and 2 Peter.* Thomas Nelson.

Silberman, Lou H., ed.
1987   *Orality, Aurality and Biblical Narrative. Semeia 39.* Scholars Press.

Sim, David C.
1998   "Are the Least Included in the Kingdom of Heaven? The Meaning of Matthew 5:19." *Hervormde teologiese studies* 54:573–87.

Simon, Marcel
1967   *Jewish Sects at the Time of Jesus.* Translated by J. H. Farley. Fortress Press.

Sissa, Giulia
1990   *Greek Virginity.* Translated by A. Goldhammer. Harvard University Press.

Skinner, Marilyn B.
1986   *Rescuing Creusa: New Methodological Approaches to Women in Antiquity. Helios 13.* Texas Tech.

Skolnick, Fred, and Michael Berenbaum, eds.
2007   *Encyclopedia Judaica.* 22 vols. 2nd ed. Macmillan.

Slingerland, Dixon
1991   "Acts 18:1–18, the Gallio Inscription, and Absolute Pauline Chronology." *Journal of Biblical Literature* 110:439–49.

Sloyan, Gerard S.
1983   *Jesus in Focus: A Life in Its Setting.* Twenty-Third Publications.
1988   *John.* John Knox Press.
1996   "The Gnostic Adoption of John's Gospel and Its Canonization by the Church Catholic." *Biblical Theology Bulletin* 26:125–32.
2006   *What Are They Saying about John?* Revised ed. Paulist Press.

Slusser, Dorothy M., and Gerald H. Slusser
1967   *The Jesus of Mark's Gospel.* Westminster Press.

Sly, Dorothy
1990   *Philo's Perception of Women.* Scholars Press.

Smalley, Stephen S.
1984   *1, 2, and 3, John.* Word Books.
1987   "John's Revelation and John's Community." *Bulletin of the John Rylands Library* 69:549–71.

Smallwood, E. Mary
1976   *The Jews under Roman Rule: From Pompey to Diocletian: A Study in Political Relations.* Brill.

Smart, James D.
1975   *Doorway to a New Age: A Study of Paul's Letter to the Romans.* Westminster Press.

Smiga, G.
1991   "Romans 12:1–2 and 15:30–32 and the Occasion of the Letter to the Romans." *Catholic Biblical Quarterly* 53:257–73.

Smit, Dirk J.
1996   "Theology as Rhetoric? Or: Guess Who's Coming to Dinner?." In *Rhetoric, Scripture and Theology: Essays from the 1994 Pretoria Conference*, edited by S. E. Porter and T. H. Olbricht, 393–422. Sheffield Academic Press.

Smith, Abraham
1995   *Comfort One Another: Reconstructing the Rhetoric and Audience of I Thessalonians.* Westminster John Knox Press.

Smith, Dennis E.
1981   "Meals and Morality in Paul and His World." In *1981 Society of Biblical Literature Seminar Papers*, 319–40. Scholars Press.
1990   (ed.) *How Gospels Begin. Semeia 52.* Scholars Press.

Smith, D. Moody
1974   "Johannine Christianity: Some Reflections on Its Character and Delineation." *New Testament Studies* 21:222–48.
1976   *John.* Fortress Press.
1980   "John and the Synoptics: Some Dimensions of the Problem." *New Testament Studies* 26:445–73.

1989   *Johannine Christianity: Essays on Its Setting, Sources and Theology.* University of South Carolina Press.

1991   *First, Second, and Third John.* Westminster John Knox Press.

1992   *John among the Gospels: The Relationship in Twentieth Century Research.* Fortress Press.

Smith, James Henry
1951   *The Great Critics.* Norton.

Smith, J. Z.
1975   "Good News Is No News: Aretalogy and Gospel." In *Christianity, Judaism and Other Greco-Roman Cults,* edited by J. Neusner, 21–38. Brill.

Smith, Morton
1971   "Prolegomena to a Discussion of Aretalogies, Divine Men, the Gospels, and Jesus." *Journal of Biblical Literature* 90:174–99.

1973   *The Secret Gospel: The Discovery and Interpretation of the Secret Gospel According to Mark.* Harper & Row.

Smith, Robert H.
1984   *Hebrews.* Augsburg Publishing House.

1995   "Why John Wrote the Apocalypse (Rev 1:9)." *Currents in Theology and Mission* 22:356–61.

Smith, Stephen H.
1996   *A Lion with Wings: A Narrative-Critical Approach to Mark's Gospel.* Shefield Academic Press.

Smith, Terence V.
1985   *Petrine Controversies in Early Christianity: Attitudes Towards Peter in Christian Writings of the First Two Centuries.* J. C. B. Mohr.

Snodgrass, Klyne R.
1992   "Matthew's Understanding of the Law." *Interpretation* 46:368–378.

Snowden, Frank M., Jr.
1991   *Before Color Prejudice: The Ancient View of Blacks.* Harvard University Press.

Snyder, Graydon F.
1985   *Ante Pacem: Archeological Evidence of Church Life before Constantine.* Mercer University Press.

Snyder, Jane McIntosh
1989   *The Woman and the Lyre: Women Writers in Classical Greece and Rome.* Southern Illinois University Press.

Soards, Marion L.
1987a   *The Apostle Paul: An Introduction to His Writings and Teachings.* Paulist Press.

1987b   "Käsemann's 'Righteousness' Reexamined." *Catholic Biblical Quarterly* 49:264–67.

Solmsen, Friedrich
1985   *Isis among the Greeks and Romans.* Harvard University Press.

Sophocles
     Sophocles (Including Oedipus the King). Translated by W. Heinemann. Loeb. Harvard University Press, 1962.

Soukup, Paul A., and Robert Hodgson
1997   *From One Medium to Another: Basic Issues in Communicating the Scriptures in New Media.* Sheed & Ward and American Bible Society.

Soulen, Richard N.
1976   *Handbook of Biblical Criticism.* John Knox Press.

Southern, Pat
1997   *Domitian: Tragic Tyrant.* Indiana University Press.

Sparks, Jack N.
1978   *The Apostolic Fathers: Contemporary Translations of These Early Christian Writings.* Thomas Nelson.

Spector, Sheila A.
1984   *Jewish Mysticism: An Annotated Bibliography on the Kabbalah in English.* Garland Publishing.

Speidel, Michael P.
1982   "The Career of a Legionary." *Transactions of the American Philological Association* 112:209–14.

Spencer, Patrick E.
2007   *Rhetorical Texture and Narrative Trajectories of the Lukan Galilean Ministry Speeches Hermeneutical Appropriation by Authorial Readers of Luke-Acts.* T&T Clark.

Spencer, Robert F.
1969   *Forms of Symbolic Action.* Seattle: University of Washington Press.

Spivey, Robert A., and D. Moody Smith
1995   *Anatomy of the New Testament: A Guide to It's Structure and Meaning.* 5th ed. Prentice Hall.

Stacey, David
1977   *Interpreting the Bible.* Hawthorn Books.

Stagg, Evelyn, and Frank Stagg
1978   *Women in the World of Jesus.* Westminster Press.

Staley, Jeffrey L.
1988   *The Print's First Kiss: A Rhetorical Investigation of the Implied Reader in the Fourth Gospel.* Society of Biblical Literature Dissertation Series 82. Scholars Press.

1991   "Stumbling in the Dark, Reaching for the Light: Reading Character in John 5 and 9." *Semeia* 53:55–80.

Stambaugh, John E., and David L. Balch
1986   *The New Testament in Its Social Environment.* Westminster Press.
Stanley, D. M.
1961   "Paul's Figurative Language Influenced by Oral Tradition of Jesus' Parables." *Catholic Biblical Quarterly* 23:26–39.
Stanton, Graham N.
1974   *Jesus of Nazareth in New Testament Preaching.* Cambridge University Press.
1989   *The Gospels and Jesus.* Oxford University Press.
1992a   "The Communities of Matthew." *Interpretation* 46:379–91.
1992b   *A Gospel for a New People: Studies in Matthew.* T&T Clark.
1994   (ed.) *The Interpretation of Matthew.* T&T Clark.
1997   *Gospel Truth? New Light on Jesus and the Gospels.* Trinity Press International.
2002   *The Gospels and Jesus.* 2nd ed. Oxford University Press.
Stark, Rodney
1996   *The Rise of Christianity: A Sociologist Reconsiders History.* Princeton University Press.
Starr, J.
1932   "The Unjewish Character of the Markan Account of John the Baptist." *Journal of Biblical Literature* 51:227–37.
Starr, Raymond J.
1987   "The Circulation of Literary Texts in the Roman World." *Classical Quarterly* 37:213–33.
Stegemann, Ekkehard W., and Wolfgang Stegemann
1999   *The Jesus Movement: A Social History of Its First Century.* Fortress Press.
Stegner, William Richard
1967   "Wilderness and Testing in the Scrolls and in Matthew 4:1–11." *Biblical Research* 12:18–27.
1989   *Narrative Theology in Early Jewish Christianity.* John Knox Press.
Stein, Robert H.
1981   *An Introduction to the Parables of Jesus.* Westminster Press.
2001a   *Studying the Synoptic Gospels: Origin and Interpretation.* 2nd ed. Baker Academic.
2001b   *Synoptic Problem: An Introduction.* 2nd ed. Baker Book House.
Stendahl, Krister
1964   "Quis et Unde: An Analysis of Matthew 1–2." In *Judentum, Urchristentum, Kirche: Festschrift für Joachim Jeremias,* edited by W. Eltester, 94–105. Alfred Topelmann.
1965   *Immortality and Resurrection: Death in the Western World; Two Conflicting Currents of Thought.* Macmillan.

1966   *The Bible and the Role of Women: A Case Study in Hermeneutics.* Fortress Press.
1968   *The School of St. Matthew and Its Use of the Old Testament.* Fortress Press.
1976   *Paul among the Jews and Gentiles, and Other Essays.* Fortress Press.
1995   *Final Account: Paul's Letter to the Romans.* Fortress Press.
Sterling, G. E.
1992   *Historiography and Self-Definition: Josephus, Luke-Acts, and Apologetic Historiography.* Brill.
Stern, Ephraim, Ayelet Lewinson-Gilboa, and Joseph Aviram
1993   *The New Encyclopedia of Archaeological Excavations in the Holy Land.* 4 vols. Simon and Schuster.
Stern, Menahem
1974   *Greek and Latin Authors on Jews and Judaism.* 2 vols. Brill.
Stewart, A. F.
1977   "To Entertain an Emperor: Sperlonga, Laokoon, and Tiberius at the Dinner Table." *Journal of Roman Studies* 67:76–90.
Stibbe, Mark W. G.
1992   *John as Storyteller.* Cambridge University Press.
1993   *The Gospel of John as Literature.* Brill.
Stock, Augustine
1984   *Call to Discipline: A Literary Study of Mark's Gospel.* Michael Glazier.
Stock, Brian
1983   *The Implications of Literacy: Written Language and Models of Interpretation in the Eleventh and Twelfth Centuries.* Princeton University Press.
Stockhausen, Carol L.
1989   *Letters in the Pauline Tradition: Ephesians, Colossians, and I Timothy, II Timothy, and Titus.* Messages of Biblical Spirituality 13. Michael Glazier.
Stone, Michael E.
1980   *Scriptures, Sects and Visions: A Profile of Judaism from Ezra to the Jewish Revolts.* Fortress Press.
1984   *Jewish Writings of the Second Temple: Apocrypha, Pseudepigrapha, Qumran Sectarian Writings, Philo, Josephus.* Fortress Press.
Stowers, Stanley K.
1981   *The Diatribe and Paul's Letter to the Romans.* Scholars Press.
1984   "Social Status, Public Speaking and Private Teaching: The Circumstances of Paul's Preaching Activity." *Novum Testamentum* 26:59–82.

1986   *Letter Writing in Greco-Roman Antiquity.* Library of Early Christianity 5. Westminster Press.

1994   *A Rereading of Romans: Justice, Jews, and Gentiles.* Yale University Press.

Strabo
        Geography. Translated by H. L. Jones. Loeb. Harvard University Press, 1931.

Strack, Hermann Leberecht, and Günter Stemberger, eds.
1996   *Introduction to the Talmud and Midrash.* 2nd ed. Fortress Press.

Strauss, David Friedrich
1972 [1840]   *Das Leben Jesu: The Life of Jesus Critically Examined.* Translated by G. Eliot and edited by P. Hodgson. Fortress Press.

1976   *The Christ of Faith and the Jesus of History.* Translated by L. E. Keck. Fortress Press.

Strayer, Joseph R.
1958   "The State and Religion: An Exploratory Comparison in Different Cultures: Greece and Rome, the West, Islam." *Comparative Studies in Society and History* 1:38–43.

Streeter, Burnett H.
1924   *The Four Gospels: A Study in Origins.* Macmillan.

Strelan, Rick
1996   *Paul, Artemis, and the Jews in Ephesus.* De Gruyter.

Stroker, William D.
1990   *Extracanonical Sayings of Jesus.* Society of Biblical Literature Resources for Biblical Study 18. Scholars Press.

Stuart, Douglas K
1990   *A Guide to Selecting and Using Bible Commentaries.* Word Publishing.

Stube, John Carlson
2006   *A Graeco-Roman Rhetorical Reading of the Farewell Discourse.* T&T Clark.

Stuckenbruck, Loren T.
1995   *Angel Veneration and Christology: A Study in Early Judaism and in the Christology of the Apocalypse of John.* J. C. B. Mohr.

Suetonius, Tranquillus
        The Lives of the Twelve Caesars. Translated by J. C. Rolfe. Loeb. Harvard University Press, 1914.

Suggs, M. Jack
1970   *Wisdom, Christology, and Law in Matthew's Gospel.* Harvard University Press.

Sumney, Jerry L.
1990   *Identifying Paul's Opponents: The Question of Method in 2 Corinthians.* Journal for the Study of the Old Testament Supplement Series 40. Sheffield Academic Press.

Sundberg, A. C., Jr.
1973   "Canon Muratori: A Fourth-Century List." *Harvard Theological Review* 66:1–41.

Swain, Lionel
1980   *Ephesians.* New Testament Message: A Biblical Theological Commentary 13. Michael Glazier.

Swartley, Willard M.
1997   "The Role of Women in Mark's Gospel: A Narrative Analysis." *Biblical Theology Bulletin* 27:16–22.

Sweet, J. P. M.
1990   *Revelation.* Trinity Press International.

Sweet, Waldo E.
1987   *Sport and Recreation in Ancient Greece.* Oxford University Press.

Swetnam, James
1981   *Jesus and Isaac: A Study of the Epistle to the Hebrews in the Light of the Aqedah.* Biblical Institute Press.

Sykes, S. W.
1983   "Story and Eucharist." *Interpretation* 37:365–76.

Tabor, James D., and Michael O. Wise
1992   "The Messiah at Qumran." *Biblical Archaeology Review* 18:60–63, 65.

Tacitus
        The Annals. Translated by J. Jackson. Loeb. Harvard University Press, 1937.
        De vita agricolae. Translated by H. Furneaux. Loeb. Harvard University Press, 1922.
        The Histories. Translated by J. Jackson. Loeb. Harvard University Press, 1963.

Talbert, Charles H.
1974   *Literary Patterns, Theological Themes, and the Genre of Luke-Acts.* Scholars Press.

1975   "The Concept of Immortals in Mediterranean Antiquity." *Journal of Biblical Literature* 94:419–36.

1977   *What Is a Gospel? The Genre of the Canonical Gospels.* Fortress Press.

1978   *Perspectives on Luke-Acts.* Perspectives in Religious Studies, Special Series 5. Association of Baptist Professors of Religion.

1982   *Reading Luke: A Literary and Theological Commentary on the Third Gospel.* Crossroad.

1984a   *Acts.* John Knox Press.

1984b   *Luke-Acts. New Perspectives from the Society of Biblical Literature Seminar.* Crossroad.

1986   *Perspectives on First Peter.* Mercer University Press.

1994　*The Apocalypse: A Reading of the Revelation of John.* Westminster John Knox Press.

2005　*Reading John: A Literary and Theological Commentary on the Fourth Gospel and the Johannine Epistles.* Revised ed. Smyth & Helwys.

Talbert, Charles H., and Edgar V. McKnight

1972　"Can the Griesbach Hypothesis Be Falsified?" *Journal of Biblical Literature* 91:338–68.

Tannehill, Robert C.

1975　*The Sword of His Mouth.* Fortress Press.

1977　"The Disciples in Mark: The Function of a Narrative Role." *The Journal of Religion* 57:386–405.

1985　"Israel in Luke-Acts: A Tragic Story." *Journal of Biblical Literature* 104:69–85.

1990　*Narrative Unity of Luke-Acts: A Literary Interpretation.* 2 vols. Fortress Press.

1996　*Luke.* Abingdon Press.

2005　*The Shape of Luke's Story Essays on Luke-Acts.* Cascade Books.

Tarn, W. W.

1961　*Hellenistic Civilisation.* 3rd ed. World Publishing.

Tatian

　　　Diatessaron. Translated by J. H. Hill. Gorgias Press, 2006 [1894].

Tatum, W. Barnes

1994　*John the Baptist and Jesus: A Report of the Jesus Seminar.* Polebridge Press.

1999　*In Quest of Jesus: A Guidebook.* Revised and enlarged ed. John Knox Press.

Taylor, Joan E.

1997　*The Immerser: John the Baptist within Second Temple Judaism.* Eerdmanss.

Taylor, N. H.

1991　"The Composition and Chronology of Second Corinthians." *Journal for the Study of the New Testament* 44:67–87.

Taylor, Vincent

1926　*Behind the Third Gospel.* Oxford University Press.

1935　*The Formation of the Gospel Tradition.* Macmillan.

1959　"The Original Order of Q." In *New Testament Essays: Studies in Memory of Thomas Walter Manson, 1893–1958,* edited by A. J. B. Higgins, 246–69. University of Manchester Press.

1966　*The Gospel According to St. Mark.* Macmillan.

Teixidor, Javier

1977　*Pagan God: Popular Religion in the Greco-Roman Near East.* Princeton University Press.

Telford, William R., ed.

1997　*The Interpretation of Mark.* 2nd ed. T&T Clark.

Theissen, Gerd

1978　*Sociology of Early Palestinian Christianity.* Translated by J. Bowden. Fortress Press.

1982　*The Social Setting of Pauline Christianity: Essays on Corinth.* Translated by J. H. Schutz. Fortress Press.

1983　*The Miracle Stories in the Early Christian Tradition.* Translated by F. McDonagh. T&T Clark.

1986　*Psychological Aspects of Pauline Theology.* Translated by J. P. Galvin. Fortress Press.

1987　*The Shadow of the Galilean: The Quest of the Historical Jesus in Narrative Form.* Translated by J. Bowden. Fortress Press.

1991　*The Gospels in Context: Social and Political History in the Synoptic Tradition.* Translated by L. M. Maloney. Fortress Press.

Theissen, Gerd, and Annette Merz

1998　*The Historical Jesus: A Comprehensive Guide.* Translated by J. Bowden. Fortress Press.

Theissen, Gerd, and Dagmar Winter

2002　*The Quest for the Plausible Jesus: The Question of Criteria.* Westminster John Knox Press.

Thesleff, H.

1965　*The Pythagorean Texts of the Hellenistic Period.* Åbo Akademi.

Thessaloniki Ephorate of Byzantine Antiquities

1985　*Thessaloniki and Its Monuments.* Ephorate of Byzantine Antiquities.

Thomas, K. J.

1977　"Torah Citations in the Synoptics." *New Testament Studies* 24:85–96.

Thomas, Robert L., and Stanley N. Gundry

1978　*A Harmony of the Gospels with Explanations and Essays.* Moody Press.

Thompson, Cynthia

1988　"Hairstyles, Head-Coverings, and St. Paul." *Biblical Archaeologist* 51:99–115.

Thompson, G. H. P.

1972　*The Gospel According to Luke.* Oxford University Press.

Thompson, James W.

1982　*The Beginnings of Christian Philosophy: The Epistle to the Hebrews.* Catholic Biblical Association.

Thompson, Leonard L.

1969　"Cult and Eschatology in the Apocalypse of John." *Journal of Religion* 49:330–50.

1986　"A Sociological Analysis of Tribulation in the Apocalypse of John." *Semeia* 36:147–74.

1989   "The Literary Unity of the Book of Revelation." *Bucknell Review* 33:347–63.

1990   *The Book of Revelation: Apocalypse and Empire.* Oxford University Press.

1998   *Revelation.* Abingdon Press.

Thompson, Lloyd A.
1989   *Romans and Blacks.* 2 vols. University of Oklahoma Press.

Thompson, Marianne Meye
1988   *The Humanity of Jesus in the Fourth Gospel.* Fortress Press.

Thompson, William
1970   *Matthew's Advice to a Divided Community.* Biblical Institute Press.

Thorpe, James
1970   *The Aims and Methods of Scholarship in Modern Languages and Literature.* 2nd ed. Modern Language Association.

Throckmorton, Burton H., Jr.
1961   *Romans for the Layman.* Westminster Press.

1967   *Gospel Parallels: A Synopsis of the First Three Gospels, RSV.* 3rd ed. Nelson.

1992   *Gospel Parallels: A Synopsis of the Synoptic Gospels (NRSV).* Thomas Nelson.

Thrupp, Sylvia
1962   *Millennial Dreams in Action: Essays in Comparative Studies.* Mouton.

Thurén, Lauri
1990   *The Rhetorical Strategy of 1 Peter with Special Regard to Ambiguous Expressions.* Åbo Akademi.

Thurston, Bonnie Bowman
1989   *The Widows: A Women's Ministry in the Early Church.* Fortress Press.

Tidball, Derek
1984   *The Social Context of the New Testament: A Sociological Analysis.* Zondervan.

Tiede, David L.
1972   *The Charismatic Figure as Miracle Worker.* Society of Biblical Literature.

1980   *Prophecy and History in Luke-Acts.* Fortress Press.

1988   *Luke.* Augsburg Publishing House.

Tigchelaar, Eibert J. C.
1987   "More on Apocalyptic and Apocalypses." *Journal for the Study of Judaism* 18:137–44.

Tilborg, S. van
1972   *Jewish Leaders in Matthew's Gospel.* Brill.

Toesing, Holly Joan
1995   "Politics of Insertion: The Pericope of the Adulterous Woman and Its Rhetorical Context at John 7:52." *Proceedings of the Eastern Great Lakes and Midwest Societies of Biblical Literature* 15:1–14.

Tolbert, Mary Ann
1978   *Perspectives on the Parables: An Approach to Multiple Interpretations.* Fortress Press.

1983   (ed.) *The Bible and Feminist Hermeneutics. Semeia* 28. Scholars Press.

1989   *Sowing the Gospel: Mark's World in Literary-Historical Perspective.* Fortress Press.

Towner, P. H.
1989   *The Goal of Our Instruction: The Structure of Theology and Ethics in the Pastoral Epistles.* Sheffield Academic Press.

Trafton, Joseph L.
2005   *Reading Revelation: A Literary and Theological Commentary.* Revised ed. Smyth & Helwys.

Trenchard, Warren C.
1982   *Ben Sira's View of Women: A Literary Analysis.* Scholars Press.

Trepp, Leo
1982   *Judaism: Development and Life.* 3rd ed. Wadsworth.

Trevett, Christine
1989   "The Other Letters to the Churches of Asia: Apocalypse and Ignatius of Antioch." *Journal for the Study of the Old Testament* 37:117–35.

Trexler, Richard C.
1997   *The Journey of the Magi: Meanings in History of a Christian Story.* Princeton University Press.

Trites, Allison A., William J. Larkin, and Philip Wesley Comfort
2006   *The Gospel of Luke.* Tyndale House Publishers.

Trobisch, David
1994   *Paul's Letter Collection: Tracing the Origins.* Fortress Press.

Trocme, Etienne
1975   *The Formation of the Gospel According to Mark.* Westminster Press.

Trompf, G. W., ed.
1990   *Cargo Cults and Millenarian Movements: Transoceanic Comparisons of New Religious Movements.* Religion and Society 29. Mouton de Gruyter.

Trotter, F. Thomas
1968   *Jesus and the Historian.* Westminster Press.

Tuckett, Christopher
1983a   "I Corinthians and Q." *Journal of Biblical Literature* 102:607–19.

1983b   *The Messianic Secret.* Issues in Religion and Theology 1. Fortress Press.

1984   *Synoptic Studies: The Ampleforth Conferences of 1982 and 1983.* JSOT Press.

1987   *Reading the New Testament: Methods of Interpretation.* Fortress Press.

Tyson, Joseph B.
1976   "Sequential Parallelism in the Synoptic Gospels." *New Testament Studies* 22:276–308.
1986   *The Death of Jesus in Luke-Acts*. University of South Carolina Press.
1988   *Luke-Acts and the Jewish People: Eight Critical Perspectives*. Augsburg Publishing House.
1992   *Images of Judaism in Luke-Acts*. University of South Carolina Press.
2006   *Marcion and Luke-Acts a Defining Struggle*. University of South Carolina Press.

Tzventan, Todorov
1975   *The Fantastic: A Structural Approach to a Literary Genre*. Cornell University Press.

Ulansey, David
1989   *The Origins of the Mithraic Mysteries: Cosmology and Salvation in the Ancient World*. Oxford University Press.
1991   "The Heavenly Veil Torn: Mark's Cosmic Inclusio." *Journal of Biblical Literature* 110:123–25.

Ulfgard, Haken
1989   *Feast and Future: Revelation 7:9–17 and the Feast of Tabernacles*. Almqvist & Wiksell.

Urbach, E. E.
1975   *The Sages: Their Concepts and Beliefs*. Magnes Press.

Uro, Risto
1998   *Thomas at the Crossroads: Essays on the Gospel of Thomas*. T&T Clark.

Vallee, Gerard
1981   *A Study in Anti-Gnostic Polemics: Irenaeus, Hippolytus, and Epiphanius*. Edited by J. Ouellette. Wilfrid Laurier University Press.

van der Horst, Pieter Willem
1990   *Essays on the Jewish World of Early Christianity*. Vanderhoeck & Ruprecht.

van der Horst, Pieter Willem, and Gerard Mussies
1990   *Studies on the Hellenistic Background of the New Testament*. Utrechtse theologische reeks 10. University of Utrecht Press.

van Iersel, Bas
1980   "The Gospel According to St. Mark—Written for a Persecuted Community?" *Nederlands Theologisch Tijdschrift* 34:15–37.

van Staden, P., and A. G. van Aarde
1991   "Social Description or Social-Scientific Interpretation? A Survey of Modern Scholarship." *Hervormde teologiese studies* 47:55–87.

Van Voorst, Robert E.
1989   *Ascents of James*. Scholars Press.
2000   *Jesus Outside the New Testament: An Introduction to the Ancient Evidence*. Eerdmans.

VanderKam, James C.
1994   *The Dead Sea Scrolls Today*. Eerdmans.

Vermès, Géza
1981a *The Gospel of Jesus the Jew: Riddel Memorial Lectures, 48th Series*. University of Newcastle.
1981b *Jesus the Jew: An Historian's Reading of the Gospels*. Fortress Press.
1984   *Jesus and the World of Judaism*. Fortress Press.
1987   *The Dead Sea Scrolls in English*. 3rd ed. Penguin Books.
1993   *The Religion of Jesus the Jew*. Fortress Press.
2001   *The Changing Faces of Jesus*. Viking Compass.

Vermès, Géza, and Martin Goodman
1989   *The Essenes: According to the Classical Sources*. JSOT/Sheffield Academic Press.

Vermès, Géza, and Pamela Vermès
1977   *The Dead Sea Scrolls: Qumran in Perspective*. Collins.

Verner, David C.
1983   *The Household of God: The Social World of the Pastoral Epistles*. Scholars Press.

Veyne, Paul
1987   *A History of Private Life: From Pagan Rome to Byzantium*. Edited by P. Aries and G. Duby. Belknap Press of Harvard University Press.

Via, Dan O., Jr
1967   *The Parables: Their Literary and Existential Dimension*. Fortress Press.
1973   "Parable and Example Story: A Literary-Structuralist Approach." *Linguistica Biblica* 25:21–30.
1975   *Kerygma and Comedy in the New Testament: A Structuralist Approach to Hermeneutic*. Fortress Press.

Via, E. Jane
1985   "Women, the Discipleship of Service and the Early Christian Ritual Meal in the Gospel of Luke." *St. Luke's Journal of Theology* 29:37–60.
1987   "Women in the Gospel of Luke." In *Women in the World's Religions: Past and Present*, edited by U. King, 38–55. Paragon House.

Vielhauer, Phillipp
1950   "On the 'Paulinism' of Acts." In *The Writings of St. Paul*, edited by W. Meeks, 166–75. Norton.

Virgil
       Works. 2 vols. Translated by H. R. Fairclough and revised by G. P. Goold. Loeb. Harvard University Press, 1999.

Viviano, Benedict T.

1993 "Eight Beatitudes at Qumran and in Matthew? A New Publication from Cave Four." *Svensk Exegetisk Arsbok* 58:71–84.

2007 *Matthew and His World: The Gospel of the Open Jewish Christians: Studies in Biblical Theology. Novum Testamentum et orbis antiquus, Studien zur Umwelt des Neuen Testaments.* Vandenhoeck & Ruprecht.

Vogt, Joseph

1975 *Ancient Slavery and the Ideal of Man.* Harvard University Press.

Von Campenhausen, Hans

1977 *The Formation of the Christian Bible.* Translated by J. A. Baker. Fortress Press.

Von Wahlde, Urban C.

1989 *The Earliest Version of John's Gospel: Recovering the Gospel of Signs.* Michael Glazier.

1990 *Johannine Commandments: I John and the Struggle for the Johannine Tradition, Theological Inquiries.* Paulist Press.

1993 "The Gospel of John and the Presentation of Jews and Judaism." In *Within Context: Essays on Jews and Judaism in the New Testament,* edited by D. P. Efroymson, E. J. Fisher, and L. Klenicki, 67–84. The Liturgical Press.

Vorster, W. S.

1988 "'Genre' and the Revelation of John: A Study in Text, Context and Intertext." *Neotestamentica* 22:103–23.

Votaw, Clyde Weber

1970 *The Gospels and Contemporary Biographies in the Greco-Roman World.* Facet Books 27. Fortress Press.

Waetjen, Herman C.

1976 *The Origin and Destiny of Humanness: An Interpretation of the Gospel According to Matthew.* Omega Books.

1989 *A Reordering of Power: A Socio-Political Reading of Mark's Gospel.* Fortress Press.

Wagner, Gunter

1987 *An Exegetical Bibliography of the New Testament.* 3 vols. Mercer University Press.

Wainwright, Arthur

1993 *Mysterious Apocalypse: Interpreting the Book of Revelation.* Abingdon Press.

Wainwright, Elaine M.

1991 *Towards a Feminist Critical Reading of the Gospel According to Matthew.* De Gruyter.

Walaskay, Paul W.

1984 *"And So We Came to Rome": The Political Perspective of Saint Luke.* Cambridge University Press.

Walker, Susan

1993 "Women and Housing in Classical Greece: The Archaeological Evidence." In *Images of Women in Antiquity,* edited by A. Cameron and A. Kuhrt, 81–91. Routledge.

Walker, William O.

1969 "Quest for the Historical Jesus: A Discussion of Methodology." *Anglican Theological Review* 51:38–56.

1975 "1 Corinthians 11:2–16 and Paul's Views Regarding Women." *Journal of Biblical Literature* 94:94–110.

1978 *Relationships among the Gospels: An Interdisciplinary Dialogue.* Trinity University Monograph Series 5. Trinity University Press.

1988 "Text-Critical Evidence for Interpolations in the Letters of Paul." *Catholic Biblical Quarterly* 50:622–31.

1989 *Harper's Bible Pronunciation Guide.* Harper & Row.

Wall, Robert W.

1991 *Revelation.* Hendrickson Publishers.

1992 *The New Testament as Canon.* Sheffield Academic Press.

1997 *Community of the Wise: The Letter of James.* Trinity Press International.

Wallace, Richard, and Wynne Williams

1998 *The Three Worlds of Paul of Tarsus.* Routledge.

Wallace-Hadrill, Andrew

1988 "The Social Structure of the Roman House." *Papers of the British School at Rome* 56:55–56.

1989 *Patronage in Ancient Society.* Routledge.

Wallace-Hadrill, D. S.

1982 *Christian Antioch: A Study of Early Christian Thought in the East.* Cambridge University Press.

Wallis, R. T.

1972 *Neoplatonism.* Duckworth.

Walsh, Richard

1989 "Tragic Dimensions in Mark." *Biblical Theology Bulletin* 19:94–99.

Walters, James C.

1993 *Ethical Issues in Paul's Letter to the Romans: Changing Self Definitions in Earliest Roman Christianity.* Trinity Press International.

Wanamaker, Charles A.

1990 *The Epistles to the Thessalonians: A Commentary on the Greek Text.* Eerdmans.

Wansbrough, Henry

1991 *Jesus and the Oral Gospel Tradition.* JSOT/Sheffield Academic Press.

Ward, Ronald Arthur
1973   *Commentary on 1 & 2 Thessalonians.* Word Books.

Warner, Martin, ed.
1990   *The Bible as Rhetoric: Studies in Biblical Persuasion and Credibility.* Routledge.

Warner, Rex
1958   *The Greek Philosophers.* New American Library.

Watson, Duane F.
1988   *Invention, Arrangement, and Style: Rhetorical Criticism of Jude and 2 Peter.* Scholars Press.

1991   *Persuasive Artistry: Studies in New Testament Rhetoric: In Honor of George A. Kennedy.* Journal for the Study of the New Testament Supplement Series 50. Sheffield Academic Press.

Watson, Duane F., and Alan J. Hauser
1994   *Rhetorical Criticism of the Bible: A Comprehensive Bibliography with Notes on History and Method.* Brill.

Watson, F.
1985   "The Social Function of Mark's Secrecy Theme." *Journal for the Study of the New Testament* 24:49–69.

Watson, Francis
1986   *Paul, Judaism, and the Gentiles: A Sociological Approach.* Society for New Testament Studies Monograph Series 56. Cambridge University Press.

Watson, G. R.
1985   *The Roman Soldier.* Cornell University Press.

Watson, Karen Ann
1973   "A Rhetorical and Sociolinguistic Model for Analysis of Narrative." *American Anthropologist* 75:243–64.

Weaver, Dorothy Jean
1990   *Matthew's Missionary Discourse: A Literary Critical Analysis.* Sheffield Academic Press.

Webb, Robert L.
1991   *John the Baptizer and Prophet: A Socio-Historical Study.* Sheffield Academic Press.

Webster, Jane S.
2003   *Ingesting Jesus: Eating and Drinking in the Gospel of John.* Society of Biblical Literature.

Wedderburn, A. J. M.
1987   *Baptism and Resurrection: Studies in Pauline Theology against Its Graeco-Roman Background.* J. C. B. Mohr.

1989a   *Paul and Jesus: Collected Essays.* Journal for the Study of the New Testament Supplement Series 37. Sheffield Academic Press.

1989b   "Paul and Jesus: Similarity and Continuity." In *Paul and Jesus: Collected Essays,* 117–43. Sheffield Academic Press.

1991   *The Reasons for Romans.* Fortress Press.

Weeden, Theodore J.
1971   *Mark: Traditions in Conflict.* Fortress Press.

Wegner, Judith
1988   *Chattel or Person: The Status of Women in the Mishnah.* Oxford University Press.

Weima, Jeffrey A. D.
1994   *Neglected Endings: The Signficance of the Pauline Letter Closings.* Sheffield Academic Press.

Weinrich, William C.
2005   *Revelation.* InterVarsity Press.

Welborn, L. L.
1987   "On the Discord in Corinth: I Corinthians 1–4 and Ancient Politics." *Journal of Biblical Literature* 106:85–111.

Welch, John W.
1981   *Chiasmus in Antiquity: Structures, Analysis, Exegesis.* Gerstenberg.

Wellek, Rene, and Austin Warren
1956   *Theory of Literature.* 3rd ed. Harcourt Brace and World.

Wells, George Albert
1976   *Did Jesus Exist?* Prometheus Books.

Wengst, Klaus
1987   *Pax Romana and the Peace of Jesus Christ.* Fortress Press.

Wenham, David
1985   *The Jesus Tradition Outside the Gospels.* JSOT/Sheffield Academic Press.

1995   *Paul: Follower of Jesus or Founder of Christianity?* Eerdmans.

Westcott, Brooke Foss
1958   *The Gospel According to St. John.* James Clark.

Westerholm, Stephen
1984   "'Letter' and 'Spirit': Foundation of Pauline Ethics." *New Testament Studies* 30:229–48.

1988   *Israel's Law and the Church's Faith: Paul and His Recent Interpreters.* Eerdmans.

1999   *Preface to the Study of Paul.* Eerdmans.

White, Hayden
1972   "The Structure of Historical Narrative." *Clio* 1:5–20.

1973   *Metahistory: The Historical Imagination of Nineteenth-Century Europe.* Johns Hopkins University Press.

White, John L.
1982   "The Greek Documentary Letter Tradition: Third Century BCE to Third Century CE." *Semeia* 22:89–106.

1983   "Saint Paul and the Apostolic Letter Tradition." *Catholic Biblical Quarterly* 45: 433–44.

1984   (ed.) *Studies in Ancient Letter Writing. Semeia* 22. Scholars Press.

1986   *Light from Ancient Letters.* Fortress Press.

1987   "The Way of the Cross: Was There a Pre-Markan Passion Narrative?" *Forum* 3:35–50.

White, Leland J.
1988   *Jesus the Christ: A Bibliography.* Michael Glazier.

White, L. Michael
1990   *Building God's House in the Roman World: Architectural Adaptation among Pagans, Jews, and Christians.* Johns Hopkins University Press.

1991a   "Crisis Management and Boundary Maintenance: The Social Location of the Matthean Community." In *Social History of the Matthean Community,* edited by D. Balch, 211–47. Fortress Press.

1991b   "Finding the Ties That Bind: Issues from Social Description." *Semeia* 56:3–22.

White, L. Michael, and O. Larry Yarbrough, eds.
1995   *The Social World of the First Christians: Essays in Honor of Wayne A. Meeks.* Fortress Press.

White, N.
1983   *The Handbook of Epictetus.* Hackett Publishing.

Whittaker, Molly
1984   *Jews and Christians: Graeco-Roman Views.* Cambridge University Press.

Wiedemann, Thomas
1981   *Greek and Roman Slavery: A Source Book.* John Hopkins University Press.

Wild, Robert A.
1985   "The Image of Paul in the Pastoral Letters." *Bible Today* 23:239–45.

Wilder, Amos N.
1971   *Early Christian Rhetoric: The Language of the Gospel.* Harvard University Press.

1976   *Theopoetic: Theology and Religious Imagination.* Fortress Press.

1982   *Jesus' Parables and the War of Myths: Essays on Imagination in the Scriptures.* Fortress Press.

1983   "Story and Story-World." *Interpretation* 37:353–64.

1990   *The Bible and the Literary Critic.* Fortress Press.

Wiley, Tatha
2005   *Paul and the Gentile Women: Reframing Galatians.* Continuum.

Wilken, Robert L.
1984   *The Christians as the Romans Saw Them.* Yale University Press.

Wilkes, John
1972   *The Roman Army.* Cambridge University Press.

Williams, C. S. C.
1964   *A Commentary on the Acts of the Apostles.* Edited by H. Chadwick. A. & C. Black.

Williams, David John
1999   *Paul's Metaphors: Their Context and Character.* Hendrickson Publishers.

Williams, David Salter
1989   "Reconsidering Marcion's Gospel." *Journal of Biblical Literature* 108:477–96.

Williams, Michael A.
1996   *Rethinking "Gnosticism": An Argument for Dismantling a Dubious Category.* Princeton University Press.

Williams, R. Rhys
1987   *Let Each Gospel Speak for Itself.* Twenty-Third Publications.

Williams, Sam K.
1997   *Galatians.* Abingdon Press.

Williamson, Ronald
1970   *Philo and the Epistle to the Hebrews.* Brill.

Willis, Wendell Lee
1985   *Idol Meat in Corinth: The Pauline Argument in I Corinthians 8 and 10.* Scholars Press.

Wills, Lawrence
1984   "The Form of the Sermon in Hellenistic Judaism and Early Christianity." *Harvard Theological Review* 77:277–99.

1991   "The Depiction of the Jews in Acts." *Journal of Biblical Literature* 110:631–54.

Wilson, Ian
1985   *Jesus: The Evidence.* Harper & Row.

Wilson, J. Christian
1993   "The Problem of the Domitianic Date of Revelation." *New Testament Studies* 39:586–605.

Wilson, R. McL.
1968   *Gnosis and the New Testament.* Blackwell.

1973   "How Gnostic Were the Corinthians?" *New Testament Studies* 19:65–74.

Wilson, R. S.
1933   *Marcion: A Study of a Second Century Heretic.* J. Clarke.

Wilson, Stephen G.
1973   *The Gentiles and the Gentile Mission in Luke-Acts.* Cambridge University Press.

1986   *Anti-Judaism in Early Christianity: Separation and Polemic.* Studies in Christianity and Judaism 2. Wilfrid Laurier University Press.

1995   *Related Strangers: Jews and Christians, 70–135 CE.* Fortress Press.

Wimbush, Vincent L.
1987   *Paul, the Worldy Ascetic: Response to the World and Self-Understanding According to 1 Corinthians 7.* Mercer University Press.
2003   *The Bible and African Americans: A Brief History.* Fortress Press.

Wink, Walter
1980   *Transforming Bible Study: A Leader's Guide.* Abingdon Press.
1993   *Cracking the Gnostic Code: The Powers in Gnosticism.* Scholars Press.
1998   *The Powers That Be: Theology for a New Millennium.* Doubleday.
1999   (ed.) *Homosexuality and Christian Faith: Questions of Conscience for the Churches.* Fortress Press.

Winkler, John J.
1990   *The Constraints of Desire: The Anthropology of Sex and Gender.* Routledge.

Winter, Bruce W., and Andrew D. Clarke
1993   *The Book of Acts in Its Ancient Literary Setting.* Eerdmans.

Wire, Antoinette
1990   *The Corinthian Women Prophets: A Reconstruction through Paul's Rhetoric.* Fortress Press.
1991   "Gender Roles in a Scribal Community." In *Social History of the Matthean Community,* edited by D. L. Balch, 87–121. Fortress Press.

Wise, Michael, Martin Abegg, Jr., and Edward Cook
1996   *The Dead Sea Scrolls: A New Translation.* HarperSanFrancisco.

Witherington, Ben III
1988   *Women in the Earliest Churches.* Society for New Testament Studies Monograph Series 59. Cambridge University Press.
1992   *Jesus, Paul, and the End of the World: A Comparative Study in New Testament Eschatology.* InterVarsity Press.
1994   *Paul's Narrative Thought World: The Tapestry of Tragedy and Triumph.* Westminster John Knox Press.
1995   *Conflict and Community in Corinth: A Socio-Rhetorical Commentary on 1 and 2 Corinthians.* Eerdmans.
1997   *The Jesus Quest: The Third Search for the Jew of Nazareth.* 2nd ed. InterVarsity Press.
2006   *Matthew.* Smyth & Helwys.

Witt, R. E.
1997   *Isis in the Ancient World.* Johns Hopkins University Press.

Wojcik, Jan
1989   *The Road to Emmaus: Reading Luke's Gospel.* Purdue University Press.

Wolfson, Harry Austryn
1947   *Philo: Foundations of Religious Philosophy in Judaism, Christianity, and Islam.* Harvard University Press.

Woll, D. Bruce
1981   *Johannine Christianity in Conflict: Authority, Rank and Succession in the First Farewell Discourse.* Society of Biblical Literature Dissertation Series 60. Scholars Press.

Wood, D. R. W., ed.
1996   *New Bible Dictionary.* 3rd ed. InterVarsity Press.

Worsley, Peter
1968   *The Trumpet Shall Sound: A Study of "Cargo" Cults in Melanesia.* 2nd ed. Schocken Books.

Worth, Roland H., Jr.
1992   *Bible Translations: A History through Source Documents.* McFarland.

Wrede, William
1971 [1901]   *The Messianic Secret.* Translated by J. C. G. Greig. J. Clarke.

Wright, N. T.
1992   *The New Testament and the People of God.* SPCK Press.
1996   *Jesus and the Victory of God.* Fortress Press.
1999   *The Millennium Myth.* Westminster John Knox Press.
2002   *The Contemporary Quest for Jesus.* Fortress Press.

Wuellner, Wilhelm
1976   "Paul's Rhetoric of Argumentation in Romans." *Catholic Biblical Quarterly* 38:330–51.
1979   "Greek Rhetoric and Pauline Argumentation." In *Early Christian Literature and the Classical Intellectual Tradition: In Honorem Robern M. Grant,* edited by W. R. Schoedel and R. L. Wilken, 177–88. Éditions Beauchesne.

Xenophon
        Memorabilia and Oeconomicus. Translated by E. C. Marshant. Harvard University Press, 1968.

Yadin, Yigael
1958   "The Dead Sea Scrolls and the Epistle to the Hebrews." In *Aspects of the Dead Sea Scrolls,* edited by C. Rabin and Y. Yadin, 36–55. Magnes Press.
1966   *Masada: Herod's Fortress Press and the Zealots' Last Stand.* Random House.
1971   *Bar Kokhba: The Rediscovery of the Legendary Hero of the Last Jewish Revolt against Imperial Rome.* Random House.

Yamada, Kota
1996 "A Rhetorical History: The Literary Genre of the Acts of the Apostles." In *Rhetoric, Scripture and Theology: Essays from the 1994 Pretoria Conference*, edited by S. E. Porter and T. H. Olbricht, 230–50. Sheffield Academic Press.

Yamauchi, Edwin M.
1983 *Pre-Christian Gnosticism: A Survey of the Proposed Evidence*. Baker Book House.
1987 *New Testament Cities in Western Asia Minor*. Baker Book House.

Yavetz, Zvi
1988 *Slaves and Slavery in Ancient Rome*. Transaction Publishers.

Young, Allan
1982 "The Anthropologies of Illness and Sickness." *Annual Review of Anthropogy* 11:315–48.

Young, Brad H.
1989 *Jesus and His Jewish Parables: Rediscovering the Roots of Jesus' Teaching*. Paulist Press.

Zanker, Paul
1990 *The Power of Images in the Age of Augustus*. Translated by A. Shapiro. University of Michigan Press.

1998 *Pompeii: Public and Private Life*. Translated by D. L. Schneider. Harvard University Press.

Zeitlin, Irving M.
1988 *Jesus and the Judaism of His Time*. Blackwell.

Zeitlin, Solomon
1940 "The Crucifixion of Jesus Re-examined." *Jewish Quarerly Review* 31:327–69.

Ziesler, J. A.
1979 "Luke and the Pharisees." *New Testament Studies* 25:146–57.
1983 *Pauline Christianity*. Oxford University Press.
1985 "Which Is the Best Commentary? I. The Gospel According to St. Matthew." *Expository Times* 97:67–71.
1989 *Paul's Letter to the Romans*. SCM Press.

Zimmerli, Walther
1965 *The Servant of God*. SCM Press.

Zinserling, Verena
1972 *Women in Greece and Rome*. Translated by L. A. Jones. Abner Schram.

CREDITS

Introduction. 4: Top, Used by permission from Hirmer Fotoarchiv Munchen/Hirmer Verlag, Munich.

Chapter 1. 28: Top, © David L. Barr. **33:** Top, Copyright Alinari/Art Resource, NY. **41:** Bottom, © David L. Barr. **43–45:** Indiana University Press: Excerpts from Apuleius' *The Golden Ass*, translated by Jack Lindsay, 1960. **44:** Top, Copyright Alinari/Art Resource, NY. **49:** Based on an idea from an unpublished paper by Jerome H. Neyrey, "Deception, Ambiguity, and Revelation: Matthew's Judgmental Scenes in Social-Science Perspective," draft, 1990.

Chapter 3. 80–82: Reprinted by permission of the publishers and the trustees of the Loeb Classical Library. Cambridge, Mass.: Harvard University Press, by the President and Fellows of Harvard College. The Loeb Classical Library® is a registered trademark of the President and Fellows of Harvard College. **81:** Top, © David L. Barr. **87:** Bottom, Copyright Alinari/Art Resource, NY. **89:** Top, Used by permission from Hirmer Fotoarchiv Munchen/Hirmer Verlag, Munich. **93:** Reprinted by permission of the publishers and the trustees of the Loeb Classical Library. Cambridge, Mass.: Harvard University Press, by the President and Fellows of Harvard College. The Loeb Classical Library® is a registered trademark of the President and Fellows of Harvard College.

Chapter 4. 106: Top, Copyright Alinari/Art Resource, NY. **114:** Top, © David L. Barr. **117:** Reprinted by permission of the publishers and the trustees of the Loeb Classical Library. Cambridge, Mass.: Harvard University Press, by the President and Fellows of Harvard College. The Loeb Classical Library® is a registered trademark of the President and Fellows of Harvard College. **117:** Reprinted by permission of the publishers and the trustees of the Loeb Classical Library. Cambridge, Mass.: Harvard University Press, by the President and Fellows of Harvard College. The Loeb Classical Library® is a registered trademark of the President and Fellows of Harvard College. **128:** Reprinted by permission of the publishers and the trustees of the Loeb Classical Library. Cambridge, Mass.: Harvard University Press, by the President and Fellows of Harvard College. The Loeb Classical Library® is a registered trademark of the President and Fellows of Harvard College. **129:** From *St. Paul's Corinth*, by Jerome Murphy-O'Connor, OP (Michael Glazier, 1983:163). Used by permission from Jerome Murphy-O'Connor. **135–136:** Reprinted by permission of the publishers and the trustees of the Loeb Classical Library. Cambridge, Mass.: Harvard Univer-

sity Press, by the President and Fellows of Harvard College. The Loeb Classical Library® is a registered trademark of the President and Fellows of Harvard College.

Chapter 5. 155: Reprinted by permission of the publishers and the trustees of the Loeb Classical Library. Cambridge, Mass.: Harvard University Press, by the President and Fellows of Harvard College. The Loeb Classical Library® is a registered trademark of the President and Fellows of Harvard College. **157:** Top, Copyright Alinari/Art Resource, NY. **158:** From *St. Paul's Corinth*, by Jerome Murphy-O'Connor, OP (Michael Grazier, 1983:154). Used by permission from Jerome Murphy-O'Connor. **170:** Top, Courtesy of the Israel Antiquities Authority. **170–172:** Penguin Books Ltd. Excerpts from *The Dead Sea Scrolls in English*, by G. Vermes, pp. 82–83, 92–93, copyright © G. Vermes, 1962, 1965, 1968, 1975. Reprinted by permission of Penguin Books Ltd. **176–177:** Reprinted by permission of the publishers and the trustees of the Loeb Classical Library. Cambridge, Mass.: Harvard University Press, by the President and Fellows of Harvard College. The Loeb Classical Library® is a registered trademark of the President and Fellows of Harvard College.

Chapter 6. 189: Top, © David L. Barr. **197:** Top, Copyright Alinari/Art Resource, NY. **199:** Reprinted by permission of the publishers and the trustees of the Loeb Classical Library. Cambridge, Mass.: Harvard University Press, by the President and Fellows of Harvard College. The Loeb Classical Library® is a registered trademark of the President and Fellows of Harvard College. **205–206:** Westminster Press: Excerpts from *New Testament Apocrypha*: Volume One, by Edgar Hennecke, edited by Wilhelm Schneemelcher; English translation edited by R. McL. Wilson. Copyright © 1959 J. C. B. Mohr (Paul Siebeck), Tubingen; English translation © 1963 Lutterworth Press. Excerpts from *New Testament Apocrypha*: Volume Two, edited by Wilhelm Schneemelcher and Edgar Hennecke; English translation edited by R. McL. Wilson. Published in the USA by The Westminster Press, 1966. Copyright © 1964 J. C. B. Mohr (Paul Siebeck), Tubingen; English translation © 1965 Lutterworth Press. Used by permission of the Westminster Press, Philadelphia, PA. **206:** Westminster Press: Excerpts from *New Testament Apocrypha*: Volume One, by Edgar Hennecke, edited by Wilhelm Schneemelcher; English translation edited by R. McL. Wilson. Copyright © 1959 J. C. B. Mohr (Paul Siebeck), Tubingen; English translation © 1963 Lutterworth Press. Excerpts from

INDEX

Body
  bibliography, 147
  congregation as, 192
  views of, 135
Book of Revelation. *See* Apocalypse
Books, 195
  production of, 478
  publication of, 13
Bultmann, Rudolf, and form
    criticism, 265

Caesar, Julius, 30
Canaanite woman, 324
Canon, 242
  defined, 19
  Eusebius' reports, 477
  order of, 480
  process of formation, 472–78
  story of, 479, 480
Catholic, defined, 473
Causality, personal versus
    mechanical, 281
Census, in Luke, 5
Chain of being, 114
  and patriarchy, 140
Character, and ethos, 13
Characterization, 271, 291, 330
Charts
  apocalyptic view of history, 91
  apocalyptic views, 59
  authorship, 95
  continuum of Jews and Gentiles, 337
  cultural values, 7
  gospel sources, 263
  gospels and events, 272
  Matthew's thematic
      correlations, 315
  Matthew's verbal repetitions, 314
  oral traditions and gospels, 264
  rhetoric types, 15
  shared gospel traditions, 260
  structure of rhetoric, 16
  survival rates, 40
Chiasmus, 285, 323
Children
  abandonment of, 40, 41, 202, 335
  education of, 43
  role of, 39
Christ
  and Adam, 114, 178
  body of, 176
  in Ephesians, 189
  as second Adam, 164
Christos, defined, 156
Chrysostom, John, 378
Church
  as hierarchy, 193
  organization in Pastorals, 198
  as universal, 189

Cicero, 10, 352
Circumcision, 112, 116, 139, 211
City
  in the Apocalypse, 455
  bibliography, 62, 102
  decline in importance, 118
  Jews in, 335
  nature of, 89
  role of, 118
  typical development, 111, 128
Classes, 33
Claudius, 56
Clement of Alexandria, 187, 391
Clement of Rome, 188
Cleopatra, 202
Clients, role of, 42
Closure, 297
Codex, defined, 478
Coin
  Augustus deified, 89
  Judea, 4
Collection, 159, 161
Colossians
  historical situation, 190
  reading guide, 192
Communion. *See* Eucharist
Community, as temple, 231
Confessions of Augustine, 13
Conversions, Jewish, 116
Conzelmann, Hans, view of Luke-
    Acts, 358
Corinth, 79, 128, 159
  Asclepius temple, 130
Corinthians, 103, 128,
    129–44, 148
  bibliography, 146
  First, as rhetoric of concord, 141
  letters to, 128
  problems of, 132
  Second, as rhetoric of
      controversy, 141
Courts, and the nature of juries, 13
Covenant, new, 234
Criticism, defined, 258
Crucifixion, in Mark, 296
Cultural values
  bibliography, 62
  comparison chart, 7
Culture
  bias of, 5
  holistic, 376
  integrated, 459
  Mediterranean, 7
Cynicism, 56
Cynics, and morality, 133

David, 61, 67, 69, 72
Day of the Lord, 98
  ethical implications, 86

Dead Sea Scrolls, 170, 320, 330, 338
  bibliography, 182, 345
  importance of, 169
  rules for living, 170
Death, 136
  facing, 59
  and immortality, 136
  of Jesus, in Apocalypse, 446
  and resurrection, 136
Deliberative rhetoric, 14
  in Hebrews, 227
Demosthenes, 133
Devil. *See* Satan
Dialogue, defined, 152
Dialogue with Trypho, 210
Diaspora, 117
  and synagogue, 372
Diatessaron, 256, 276
Diatribe, defined, 152
Didache, 66
  compared to James, 224
Dio Cassius, 202
Dio Chrysostomus, 129
Diogenes the Cynic, 58
Disciples
  in John, 413
  in Luke-Acts, 360
  in Mark, 293
  in Matthew, 332
Docetism, defined, 423
Domitian, 458
Double tradition, defined, 262
Dualism, 396, 421
  body/spirit, 137

Economy, and religion, 462
Education, 43
Egnatian Way, and trade, 89
Elijah, 74, 287
  as final prophet, 74
Emperor
  divine status, 49
  worship of, 88, 444, 455, 462, 470
Empty tomb stories
  compared, 253
  and geography, 265
Encomium, 14
End of the age, 84
  and age to come, 91
  defined, 90
Enoch, 74, 226, 232, 247
Enoch, Second, 435
Ephesians
  historical context, 190
  reading guide, 192
  view of Christ, 189
Ephesus, 189, 376
Epictetus, 177, 402
Epicureanism, 58

Judicial rhetoric, 13
Junia, apostle, 159
Juries, nature of, 13
Justin Martyr, 210
Juvenal, 117, 202

Kee, Howard Clark, 294
King James Version, 479
Kingdom of God, 91
  in the Apocalypse, 466
  beginning of, 311
  in Luke-Acts, 363
  in Mark, 284
  in Matthew, 326
  at Qumran, 169
  as rule of God, 284
  as service, 296
Kochba, Simon bar, 70

Language
  Greek versus English, 17
  in Palestine, 64
Last Supper, and form criticism, 264
Latrine, 27
Law, 194
  expanded at Qumran, 170
  in Pastorals, 198
  validity of, 154
Lazarus, sign of Jesus, 406
Legalism, defined, 221
Leisure activities, 45
Letters
  bibliography, 101
  Catholic, 217
  form of, 80
  Jewish, 218
  as literature, 10
  samples, 80
  stories implicit in, 10
  structure of, 10
Letters of John, reading guide, 419
Letters of Paul, innovation, 82
Lewis, C. S., 495
Life cycle, idealized, 43
Life expectancy, 40
Literacy
  bibliography, 82
  rates, 55
Literary criticism, 9
  review of method, 266
Literary reading, 274
Literary theory, bibliography on, 24
Literature, 3
  and history, 267
Loeb Classical Library, 25
Logos, 13, 206
  defined, 400
  and God, 177
  in Hebrew Scriptures, 401

meanings of, 400–404
  in Philo, 231
  in Stoicism, 401
Longinus, 268
Lucian, 353
Luke
  birth story, 3
  reading and reflection, 364
  See also Luke-Acts
Luke-Acts
  adventure story, 377
  apocalyptic muted, 367, 370
  apostles in, 360
  ascension, 370
  authorship, 383
  baptism of Jesus, 350
  bibliography, 387
  boundaries, 373
  characterization, 379
  characterization of disciples, 360
  characterization of Jesus, 368
  characterization of minor charac-
    ters, 379
  compared with Mark, 350, 351,
    354, 355, 358, 361, 364
  compared with Matthew, 349, 358,
    364, 378
  date of, 378
  death of Jesus, 368
  as defense of the Jesus movement,
    367, 381, 383
  disciples, 360
  ending, 378, 380
  future, 364
  Gentiles, 360, 374
  geography, 354
  history, view of, 355
  Jews in, 360, 368, 375, 381
  John the Baptizer, view of, 358
  journey to Jerusalem, 362
  kingdom of God, 363
  language of, 351
  medical language in, 384
  omission of Mark's duplication, 361
  opening, 355, 370
  parallels, bibliography, 388
  parallels between Gospel and, 354
  Paul, bibliography, 387
  Paul presented differently, 375
  Peter, 352, 373
  Pharisees, 380
  plot, 355
  point of view, 377
  preface, 348, 350
  purpose, 384
  reading guide, 354
  as romance, 369
  as second volume, 349
  setting, 381

speeches in, 352
structure of, 353
symbolic use of space, 362
temple, 355, 356, 359, 365
tragedy or comedy, 380
we-passages, 377
women in, 379
Luther, Martin, 167

Maccabees, 231, 337
Magic, 118, 376
  bibliography, 149
Malachi, 286
Malbon, Elizabeth Struthers, 298
Malina, Bruce, 7
Manicheans, 204
Maps
  Alexander's empire, 29
  Asia Minor, 191
  Greece, 80
  Greece and Asia Minor, 121
Marcion, 188, 204, 335, 383, 476,
    477, 480
  bibliography, 497
  canon of, 186
  and Pastorals, 196
  rejected Hebrew Scriptures, 475
Marduk, 437
Mark
  authorship, 280
  crucifixion scene, 296
  disciples, 293
  dual feeding stories, 293
  ending of, 297
  first written Gospel, 260
  geography, 298
  John Mark, 280
  miracles, 289
  opening of, 285
  and Peter, 280
  plot, 281
  priority of, 260
  reading guide, 283
  secrecy theme, 288
  setting, 300, 301
  way as metaphor, 299
  women in, 295
Marriage, 39, 41, 202
  bibliography, 214
  laws, 203
Mary Magdalene, 254, 295
Matthew
  authorship, 334, 342
  birth story, 317
  Canaanite woman, 324
  characterization of Jesus, 331
  characterization of leaders, 333
  compared with Mark, 310
  compared with Mark and Luke, 322